00149

Introduction to the

New Testament

ROBERT W. CRAPPS
EDGAR V. McKNIGHT
DAVID A. SMITH

All of Furman University

John Wiley & Sons, New York • Chichester • Brisbane • Toronto

ISBN 471-07010-6

Library of Congress Catalog Card Number: 72–75637

PRINTED IN THE UNITED STATES OF AMERICA

10 9 8 7 6 5

To the late Winston Chandler Babb

Preface

The New Testament has carved its own respected place in human history. Widely read, often quoted, and sometimes studied, it has become the base for the religious faith of many and a fascinating subject for inquiry by both Christians and non-Christians. This textbook is designed for a beginning course in the study of this important body of literature. The approach is historical and interpretive, attempting to understand the New Testament from within the temporal and ideational context which gave it birth. The writings are understood properly only within the framework of the early Christian Church, and the primitive Church, particularly its motivating ideas, is discovered only through the writings which came out of its earliest life and thought. This mutual relationship of New Testament and Church is presupposed in this work. The New Testament, other early literature, and non-literary resources are used to give a clear overall picture of the development of the primitive Church and early Christian literature. Likewise, the religious faith which molded the writings is considered in interpreting them. Throughout, the study is placed in its larger Jewish and Hellenistic setting, but faithfulness to the nature of the Church and its literature demands careful attention to the distinctive religious milieu and emphases of the early Christian community.

Three objectives have guided the authors in their writing: (1) the provision of a foundation of understanding with which the serious student can reliably begin biblical study, (2) the stimulation of an intense interest in the subject which will spur him far beyond these beginnings, and (3) the intensification of the student's regard for the scriptures—their nature, message, origin, and relevance to human existence. If these objectives have been realized to any meaningful degree, our efforts have been justified.

Little previous preparation by the student has been assumed. Indeed, the student who has had no previous acquaintance with the Hebrew and Christian scriptures will find the textbook readily understandable. For maximum benefit, both to students whose heritage emphasizes the scriptures and to those unacquainted with these writings, primary biblical material must be used in conjunction with the textbook. Particularly this is important in Part I, "Foundation of the Church: Life and Teachings of Jesus," a study of the Synoptic tradition with special attention to the sayings and narratives of the earthly Jesus. An edition of the first three Gospels which arranges the materials in parallel columns will be extremely valuable for comparing the Gospel traditions about Jesus. We therefore have included in this section paragraph references to *Gospel Parallels: A Synopsis of the First Three Gospels,* edited by Burton H. Throckmorton, Jr., one of the better arrangements of the Gospel materials. However, direct references to the scripture passages under consideration are also included, so that any edition or arrangement of the Gospels may be used. Other parts of the New Testament may be studied in a variety of translations and versions. Throughout, therefore, the use of primary materials is indispensable.

This text is designed as a companion volume to *People of the Covenant: An Introduction to the Old Testament* by Henry Jackson Flanders, Jr., Robert W. Crapps, and David A. Smith, published by The Ronald Press Company. These two volumes complement each other as texts for courses or course sequences covering the full sweep of Old and New Testament history and literature.

Since no one can divorce himself completely from his religious orientation when he writes about religion, the particular bias of the writers ought to be acknowledged. We are Christians and churchmen. We confess that for us, God speaks supremely in the person of Jesus Christ; that the Church is the people of God, the new Israel, the continuation of the work of God in Christ; and that the New Testament is an authentic and faithful witness of the Church to the meaning and significance of God's activities in her midst. We have, however, made the conscious effort to deal with the data dispassionately without the aim of religious persuasion. We hope therefore that the textbook will be found useful by students from a variety of religious backgrounds and with different presuppositions.

As aids to the student, maps and illustrations have been included. Additional readings are suggested at the end of each chapter and include books of various levels of difficulty and technicality. The chronology chart in the Appendix will serve as a guide to the period of New Testament history. Since recent biblical study has become increasingly replete with technical terms, a glossary is provided to clarify items not ordinarily found in a standard dictionary or of particular meaning in the context of New Testament study.

To express our indebtedness to all who have contributed to this work is impossible. The footnotes and bibliography indicate only a portion of scholars, known and unknown, from whom we have received help. Our families were a major source of comfort and strength, and with deep gratitude we acknowledge the love and forbearance of our wives and children. Our colleagues in the department of religion at Furman University have given indispensable support and wise counsel. We are especially indebted to Professor T. C. Smith, who has read the manuscript and offered valuable suggestions.

The administration of Furman University has not only supported, but also encouraged, the writing. The library staff has provided assistance in research. Mr. Fon Scofield, Jr., made available an extensive photograph collection from which illustrations could be selected. Misses Mimi Raper and Genene Hensley patiently typed early drafts from our handwritten copy, and Mrs. Clara Smith made an immeasurable contribution by typing the final draft of the manuscript.

The scripture quotations in this publication are from the Revised Standard Version of the Bible, copyright 1946 and 1952 by the Division of Christian Education, National Council of Churches, and are used by permission.

Robert W. Crapps
Edgar V. McKnight
David A. Smith

Greenville, South Carolina,
March, 1969

Contents

Abbreviations

Antiquities—Josephus, *Antiquities of the Jews.*

EH—Eusebius, *Ecclesiastical History*

FBK—Feine-Behm-Kümmel, *Introduction to the New Testament*

IB—*Interpreter's Bible*

IDB—*Interpreter's Dictionary of the Bible*

JBL—*Journal of Biblical Literature*

JBR—*Journal of Bible and Religion*

JTS—*Journal of Theological Studies*

KJV—King James Version

NTS—*New Testament Studies*

RSV—Revised Standard Version

Wars—Josephus, *Wars of the Jews*

Introduction to the
New Testament

1

Background for
New Testament Study

THE NEW TESTAMENT AND THE EARLY CHRISTIAN MOVEMENT

The New Testament tells of the life and activities of Jesus Christ and the growth of the early Christian community. The rediscovery of Jesus or the early Church is, however, a far more complex process than a mere reading of the New Testament to recover its facts. The New Testament is basically a book of religious faith and its interpretation must consider not only the facts that are reported but also the time and culture out of which it came, as well as the faith perspective which caused it to be written in the way that it was written. The New Testament's story about Jesus is witness to how the Church interpreted him, and its reflection of early Christian developments is molded by how the Church understood itself in relationship to Jesus. Therefore, any serious study of the New Testament must honestly attempt to recapture the life and times which produced the literature in order that New Testament data may be placed in their real context. This method is sometimes called the historical-critical approach.[1] It recognizes that the New Testament is human literature produced by men and that the same basic procedure used to understand any other writing must be used to understand New Testament literature. Thus, the geographical and political setting of the writer and original readers, the religious and philosophical ideas of the time,

[1] "Critical" comes from a Greek root meaning "to judge" or "to decide" in the light of evidence.

3

and all other human historical factors must be considered in interpretation.

Because of the distinctive character of New Testament literature, the study of early Christian history and the interpretation of the New Testament are two facets of the same issue. Sections of the New Testament provide insight into the first century world and in turn this knowledge may be applied to the interpretation of New Testament literature. The biblical writings must be placed in their historical context to be properly understood, but major sources for understanding the New Testament period are the documents themselves. Basically, however, the literature is not about the first century, but about Jesus and the Church. The concerted effort to clarify the reciprocal relationship between the early Christian community and the literary expression of its faith in Jesus and its self understanding lies close to the heart of serious New Testament study and is the task to which we address ourselves.

A Survey of the New Testament Period

The scope of New Testament study is at least vaguely defined in the New Testament. The events described in the New Testament took place during the period of the Roman Empire. In 63 B.C. the Romans established authority over Palestine through Pompey's entry into Jerusalem and exaction of an annual tribute to Rome, and the Roman control over the eastern region continued until well past the period of New Testament history. Although specific details in Christian developments through about A.D. 150 remain obscure, the broad outline of this history is fairly clear. The Four Gospels, and particularly Mark, Luke, and Matthew, describe the general pattern of Jesus' ministry and permit Jesus to be put in historical context. Luke gives information that Jesus was born sometime before the death of Herod the Great in 4 B.C. Little is known of his life until he was baptized by John the Baptist in the fifteenth year of Tiberius Caesar (the second emperor of the Roman Empire, who ruled A.D. 14–37) and began a private and public mission as a religious teacher. For some time Jesus ministered in Palestine, primarily in the northern province of Galilee. About the year A.D. 30 he was crucified in Jerusalem,[2] an event considered by his followers to epitomize the meaning of his life and mission.

---

[2] For a discussion of the dates for these and other events in the New Testament period and for a presentation of the basis of arriving at the dates, see G. B. Caird, "Chronology of the New Testament," *IDB,* I, pp. 599–607.

The book of Acts, Paul's letters, and the rest of the New Testament documents center essentially upon the life of the Church from the time of Jesus' crucifixion until toward the end of the first century. Disciples of Jesus, soon after his death, began to proclaim in Jerusalem that he was Israel's Messiah, the Christ in whom a new age had dawned. Peter, James the brother of Jesus, and other Jewish followers of Christ were leaders in this early movement. Rapidly the community grew in Jerusalem as an intimate part of Judaism, but shortly expanded into non-Jewish territory, Samaria, Syria, Asia Minor, Greece and remote parts of the Mediterranean world. Increasingly, the movement separated from the Jewish establishment and larger numbers of Gentiles were included as adherents of the faith.

One of the most effective of the early missionaries was Saul of Tarsus, converted about A.D. 33 and bearer of the gospel to Asia Minor, Macedonia, Greece, and possibly even Spain before his death in the sixties. The major portion of Acts is devoted to the missionary accomplishments of Saul, better known as Paul, but the New Testament does not contain a narrative of developments after the sixties. The writings coming from the last third of the first century and the early decades of the second do, however, indicate that the Church established itself throughout the empire, that her relations with entrenched political power grew strained and that the Church began to develop both her theology and basic patterns of internal organization.

The Church and the New Testament

The New Testament arose out of the history of the Church as it sought to formulate its own convictions and evangelize those outside its fold. Followers of Christ, understanding themselves as the new Israel, the people of God, the Church, carried the "good news" (gospel) throughout the Roman Empire. In numerous ways this activity called forth writings expressing faith in Jesus and a sense of mission in his behalf. The communication of the gospel, carried out at first by oral means, eventually involved the writing of narratives and sayings of Jesus and later the production of the Gospels themselves.

Even before the Four Gospels were written, however, churches established by Christ's followers needed guidance on doctrinal and ethical matters and turned to revered spiritual leaders for help. Letters to individuals and to congregations met these needs and consequently were preserved and circulated among the churches. As the

Church began to struggle with its need for order and organization and as persecutions faced by the Church demanded comfort and instruction, writings were directed to these problems. Thus, the first Christian writings were products of an assortment of situations and issues in the Church. Consequently the New Testament, composed of these varied documents, is not a single unified work, but is quite obviously and naturally a collection of diverse writings, arising from different purposes and written from scattered parts of the empire over a long period of time.

However, a basic unity underlies the wide diversity of the New Testament writings. In simplest terms the unity is Jesus Christ. Whether early or late, whoever the author or whatever the destination, regardless of the immediate purpose, every writing has Jesus Christ as the central figure. An early confession of faith found in I Corinthians 15:3–8 declares the primacy of Christ in the Church's unified testimony:

> For I delivered to you as of first importance what I also received, that Christ died for our sins in accordance with the scriptures, that he was buried, that he was raised on the third day in accordance with the scriptures, and that he appeared to Cephas, then to the twelve. Then he appeared to more than five hundred brethren at one time, most of whom are still alive, though some have fallen asleep. Then he appeared to James, then to all the apostles. Last of all, as to one untimely born, he appeared also to me.

In this passage, written about twenty years after the resurrection, Paul is concerned to preserve a tradition "of first importance" which had been passed on to him. The essence of that tradition is Jesus Christ, dead, buried, and raised "in accordance with the scriptures," of whom all bear witness. This affirmation was focal for all that the early Church did or said. Paul himself and his letters illustrate the comprehensive character of the Christ-centered confession. First Corinthians, and the remainder of Paul's letters do not contain primarily preaching about Jesus Christ; rather they deal largely with specific doctrinal and practical problems. Nonetheless, the Apostle's criterion for resolving the problems is the centrality of Christ. Even the most practical Corinthian letter reminds recalcitrants to resolve their difficulties because ". . . you are Christ's; and Christ is God's" (3:23) and to remember that Christ Jesus is "our wisdom, our righteousness and sanctification and redemption" (1:30).

The Four Gospels certainly present Christ as the central figure in the Christian movement. The statement in John 20:30–31 may indeed be taken as a general statement of purpose for all of the Gospels.

> Now Jesus did many other signs in the presence of the disciples, which are

not written in this book; but these are written that you may believe that Jesus is the Christ, the Son of God, and that believing you may have life in his name.

The later New Testament writings continue to present Jesus Christ as the central figure. Important variations in the emphasis and means of describing the significance of Jesus Christ appear in the various books, but from the earliest traditions to the latest compositions Jesus Christ is the central figure and faith in him permeates whatever form the writing takes.

DEVELOPMENT OF NEW TESTAMENT LITERATURE

Origins

A long process separates the early teaching and preaching concerning Jesus Christ from the volume of twenty-seven writings which, with the Hebrew scriptures, are considered authoritative by the Church and which have been transmitted to the peoples of the world in their own language. The process entailed the Church's cherished memory of Jesus, a longitudinal development by which that memory took normative form, specific situations calling forth specific writings, and the tedious growth of a collection of writings accepted by the Church as religiously authentic.

Initially the "Bible" of the early Church was the Hebrew scriptures, generally in Greek translation.[3] The first Christians saw no need to cast aside their scriptures; indeed they interpreted Jesus as the fulfillment of all that God had begun to do "in the law and the prophets." Eventually, however, the growing Church found it both practical and necessary to formalize and preserve their statement of the "good news" of Jesus Christ and out of this process developed a corpus of uniquely Christian writings,[4] which, alongside the Hebrew scriptures, became the Bible of the Christian community.

Letters of Paul. The earliest of the writings which have come down to us from the early Church are the letters of Paul. These are real letters written for specific purposes to individuals, churches, and groups of churches. They deal with almost every conceivable problem and situation arising in the churches of the Roman Empire in the

[3] See below, pp. 15, 17.
[4] Christians came to refer to the Hebrew scriptures as the "old" testament and to the Christian scriptures as the "new" testament. ("Testament" comes from the Latin *testamentum*, which was a translation of the Greek *diatheke*, "covenant.")

decade A.D. 50–60. Although the Pauline letters are in the form and language of other letters of the period, they originate from an *apostle* of Jesus Christ, that is, they claim an authority derived from Jesus himself. Paul declares himself on equal footing with the earlier Jerusalem apostles, a position affirmed by the Church, which permits him to write, as well as to speak, with authority.

Thirteen letters in our New Testament are traditionally traced to Paul and appear in the following order: Romans, I Corinthians, II Corinthians, Galatians, Ephesians, Philippians, Colossians, I Thessalonians, II Thessalonians, I Timothy, II Timothy, Titus, and Philemon. It is generally acknowledged that some of these letters do not come directly from Paul and that the form of some which can be traced to him may have been altered.[5] Certainly the letters were not written in the order in which they appear. The arrangement was probably determined simply by the length of the letter, with the longest one first and the shortest last.

Gospels. A second type of material grew out of the concern of the early Church to preserve its understanding of Jesus. The material was rooted in the earthly Jesus, but quite naturally its preservation was colored by the faith of the early Church that Jesus was centrally important to God's action in history. Thus, the Christian community aimed to do more than preserve data about Jesus; rather it purposed to spread the "good news," that is, the gospel, of Jesus Christ.[6] Originally the story of Jesus, the gospel, was preserved orally. This method of transmitting the gospel was a more formal and reliable procedure than may be thought, for in the Jewish tradition disciples of a teacher remembered the teachings and transmitted them to his own disciples in the same form as he received them. A high level of authority was given to materials that could be traced to those closest to the teacher and those who had seen and heard were considered the most authentic. Out of such an informal, but surprisingly reliable, circumstance the gospel story began to emerge in the early Church. From the earliest days the gospel began to take normative form so that by the time the Gospels were written resources were already available.

The prologue to the Gospel of Luke gives evidence of the way in

[5] The question of Pauline authorship of each of the writings bearing his name will be dealt with in later chapters.

[6] The English word "gospel" is from the Anglo-Saxon word "god-spell," a story of a god. The meaning of the term in the New Testament, however, comes from the Greek word it translates, *euangelion*, which means "good news." For a more detailed etymology and discussion of the use of "gospel," see *IDB*, II, pp. 442–443.

which the tradition concerning Jesus Christ was transmitted. The writer speaks of the events of Jesus "just as they were delivered to us by those who from the beginning were eyewitnesses and ministers of the word." [7] He is also aware that "many have undertaken to compile a narrative of the things which have been accomplished among us." [8] Obviously some of the oral material was written down at an early date and the Gospels, especially the first three, utilized both oral tradition and early written materials as sources. A careful comparison of the Gospels has led most scholars to conclude that Mark is the oldest, and that Matthew and Luke used Mark in the preparation of their Gospels. Since Matthew and Luke also contain a body of material common to each other but absent from Mark, it is assumed that they used another source, usually called Q (from the German *Quelle*, or "source"), which contained mainly the sayings of Jesus. These three Gospels came into existence between 65 and 90. Although each one of them is addressed to a specific situation and has a distinctive character of its own, they share a common general approach to the life of Jesus and together are called the Synoptic Gospels.[9]

The Gospel of John was written later and has no demonstrable literary relationship with the Synoptics. However, the gospel tradition seems to be known to the writer of the Fourth Gospel and is used by him in a unique way to demonstrate that "Jesus is the Christ, the Son of God." [10] These four books, John and the Synoptics, represent a distinctive kind of literary vehicle found in the New Testament. They aim not so much to state a propositional truth that is being taught as to proclaim a deed that is announced by God.[11] The form itself grows out of the Church's concern to witness to its conviction that Jesus brings salvation to all men.

Other New Testament Writings. In addition to the letters bearing Paul's name and the Four Gospels, ten other writings are a part of the New Testament canon. The Book of Acts, the second volume in a set in which Luke is the first volume, describes the expansion of the early Church from the time of Jesus' resurrection to the imprisonment of Paul in Rome. It is the only canonical narrative of events during the middle third of the first century. Six of the remaining nine writings

[7] Luke 1:2.

[8] Luke 1:1.

[9] A full discussion of the distinctive character and specific situation (*Sitz im Leben*) of each Gospel may be found below, Chapter 13.

[10] John 20:31.

[11] O. A. Piper, "Gospel," *IDB,* II, p. 444.

are in letter form (James, I Peter, II Peter, II John, III John, and Jude); two are theological treatises (Hebrews and I John). All of these writings treat specific questions which arose in the early Christian community.

One apocalyptic book appears in the New Testament. "Apocalyptic" comes from a Greek word which means "uncover, reveal," and refers to a type of Jewish and early Christian literature which purports to show how God will act in the future on behalf of his people. The picture of the future is frequently couched in the form of dreams, and elaborate symbols and imagery are used. The book of Revelation falls in this literary category and was written in the last of the first century to Christians who were facing persecution at the hands of the Roman emperor. The work is sometimes referred to as "The Apocalypse" and shares the characteristics of the numerous non-canonical apocalypses written in the period between 200 B.C. and A.D. 200.

Canonization

The twenty-seven books which are now included in the New Testament were not the only early Christian writings, but they are those which came to be considered religiously authoritative in a long and complex process of canonization. The words *canon* and *canonization* are to be traced to an ancient Babylonian word meaning "reed," an instrument used early as a measuring device. Hence canonization refers to the process whereby materials were "measured" by certain standards and demonstrated to contain the voice of authentic religious authority. Books relating to the life of Jesus and the vitality of the early Church were slowly collected and preserved. Through the years of Church development following the time of the earthly Jesus a specific and fixed collection of works gradually emerged. Through this process of canonization, a New Testament collection of twenty-seven books, no more and no less, came to be considered as scripture, that is as authoritative for the faith and life of the Church. By the fourth century A.D. the shape of our present New Testament had become definitely established.[12]

Collecting the Books. The intriguing story of canonization begins with a period of collection. Writings produced by early Christians were found valuable for expressing their faith and commitment and so were preserved and used by congregations throughout the Roman Empire. The writings continued to exist because of their religious

[12] See FBK, pp. 334–358, for a full treatment of the origin of the canon.

value and gradually some writings came to be associated with each other because of such things as common origin or subject matter. Even before the authoritative canon assumed its present form, smaller collections were made for use by the Church. Probably the earliest of such collections were letters of Paul. Because the Apostle was respected so highly, churches began to exchange copies of his letters, especially those that dealt with issues or situations which were shared by the congregations. Some of the apostles' letters were written with the intention that they be passed around. In Colossians he advises that "when this letter has been read among you, have it read also in the church of the Laodiceans; and see that you read also the letter from Laodicea." [13] The circulation of Paul's writings undoubtedly hastened their collection. Evidence of this is seen in II Peter: "So also our beloved Paul wrote to you according to the wisdom given him, speaking of this as he does in all his letters." [14]

How the letters of Paul came to be formed into a collection is uncertain. Possibly the practice alluded to in Colossians was followed throughout the Pauline churches; that is, individual churches formed their own collections through exchanging letters. Or possibly the collection was made by an individual Christian who was concerned with fuller use of Paul's writings. Edgar J. Goodspeed suggests that this man was Onesimus, the fugitive slave won to Christ by Paul and sent home with a letter to his owner, Philemon. Beginning with the letter he knew best, the letter to Philemon, Onesimus visited the churches of Paul, collected the writings from the churches, and published them.[15] Goodspeed's idea is attractive, but actually has little evidence to support it. But whether the Pauline collection was initially made by an individual or came about through the informal exchange of letters, the writings were gathered and gained a wide circulation before they achieved canonical stature. Soon, perhaps as early as the writing of II Peter around A.D. 150, the Pauline collection was considered religiously authoritative. Speaking of the letters of Paul, the writer declares, "There are some things in them hard to understand, which the ignorant and unstable twist to their own destruction, as they do the other scriptures." [16] Here Paul's letters were clearly equated with "other scriptures."

---

[13] Col. 4:16.
[14] II Peter 3:15b–16a.
[15] See Edgar J. Goodspeed, *An Introduction to the New Testament*, pp. 121–124, 210–221, for a presentation of this idea.
[16] II Peter 3:16b.

The achievement of high religious esteem was not nearly so complicated a process for the Gospels as for Paul's letters. The subject matter of the Gospel and its distinctive literary character as a proclamation about Jesus assured its authoritative status in the early Church. It is still difficult, however, to determine with precision how four Gospels instead of one came to be acknowledged in the Church or, for that matter, how only four from the many Gospels which were composed in the early Christian generations were selected. Seemingly the present canonical collection occurred in a relatively short time. Each Gospel immediately after it was written must have been accepted and used primarily by the community in which it was produced. Rapidly, even before all the canonical Gospels were written (as shown in Luke's prologue), the works began to circulate more widely and naturally came to be associated with each other. The passing of eyewitnesses to Jesus' life and teachings made the preservation of these books all the more important. Some scholars have contended that the collection of Four Gospels existed by the beginning of the second century, but this cannot be demonstrated. Shortly after the middle of the second century, however, the canon of Four Gospels was definitely known and used. Justin Martyr, an early apologist who made his home in Rome in the mid-second century, spoke of the "memoirs of the Apostles" [17] which were used by the Christians in Sunday worship. His reference is clearly to "gospels" as seen by earlier references in the same work.[18]

The Idea of A Canon. In a sense the values which caused the New Testament writings to be circulated and preserved were those which caused them to be considered scripture, but a distinction must be made between "collection" and "canon." The Church did not immediately consider the collections to be of the same religious stature as the Hebrew scriptures, but it is logical to believe that there was a tendency in this direction. The precipitating cause for the development of a New Testament canon may have been the crisis occasioned by Marcion, a second century Christian. Marcion was reared in orthodox circles, but came under the influence of pessimistic Gnostic ideas that the material, historical world was basically evil. The evil world was created by the God of the Old Testament, who had been somewhat contaminated by contact with the material world. In this tradition Marcion became persuaded that an impassable gulf existed between the Old Testament God and the God of love revealed in Jesus Christ.

[17] *Apology,* 67:3.
[18] *Ibid.,* 66:3.

Accordingly, he rejected the Hebrew scriptures entirely and made a specific group of Christian books his "canon." Since in his opinion Paul alone had remained faithful to the gospel of Jesus, Marcion made the ten letters of Paul known to him the core of his canon. To these books he joined Luke's Gospel, the work of an associate of Paul. He apparently removed from all of these works references to the God of Israel, which he found offensive.

Although Marcion was excommunicated by the Church, he was successful in organizing followers and spreading his teachings. Since the churches tracing their origin to Marcion discarded the Hebrew scriptures, they were obliged to form a canon of Christian writings. Whether or not orthodox churches began to make lists of authoritative books to counteract the influence of Marcion and his churches, the behavior of the rebel Christian certainly encouraged the formation of a less reactionary canon.

The process of canonization was probably further accelerated by the necessity for the Church to respond to the Montanus threat. Montanus was a pagan priest who was converted to Christianity in the mid-second century. He declared that he and his followers were the instruments of a new revelation. The Church was forced to react to Montanus' claim to divine revelation by emphasizing its own claims as the instrument through whom God was at work. A part of the assertion was the emphasis upon the canon. To point up the futility of Montanus' claim of a new revelation, the Church pointed to its scripture as if to say, "God has spoken!" Thus the *basic* Christian documents were considered completed.

The Fixing of The Canon. Although the canon of twenty-seven books was not established until the fourth century, lists containing most of them existed much earlier. The earliest list is in a document now called the Muratorian Canon. This canon takes its name from L. A. Muratori, who discovered it and published it in 1740. The document was written by an unknown author toward the end of the second century in Rome, and offers a list of books "received" in the Roman Church. Although the canon is damaged at the beginning, its list of books has been ascertained as follows:

Matthew	I, II Corinthians	I, II Timothy
Mark	Galatians	Titus
Luke	Ephesians	I, II John
John	Philippians	Jude
Acts	Colossians	Wisdom of Solomon
Romans	I, II Thessalonians	

The document mentions the Apocalypse of John and the Apocalypse of Peter "which some of our friends will not have read in the churches." The Shepherd of Hermas is mentioned as a recently written book which ought to be read, but not among the prophets or apostles.

That this list reflects the general situation in the Church at the end of the second century is evidenced by the writing of the three great theologians of the period, Irenaeus of Lyon, Tertullian of Carthage, and Clement of Alexandria. The works of each of these three indicate a familiarity with the concept of a canon; but that there were some variations in the books accepted by them as canonical is evident in the comparison below: [19]

Irenaeus	*Tertullian*	*Clement*
Gospels (4)	Gospels (4)	Gospels (4)
Paul's Letters (13)	Paul's Letters (13)	Paul's Letters (14) including Hebrews
Acts	Acts	Acts
I Peter	I Peter	
I John	I John	
II John		
	Jude	
The Apocalypse	The Apocalypse	The Apocalypse

Irenaeus knows Hebrews, James, II Peter, III John, and Jude, but is still undecided about their status. He quotes the Shepherd of Hermas as scripture and also prizes I Clement, but probably does not regard the latter as scripture. Tertullian, reflecting what occurs in the African church, does not mention James, II Peter, II John, or III John. He cites Hebrews as written by Barnabas and not quite canonical. In addition to the above books which came to be included in the final Christian canon, Clement of Alexandria accepted some additional writings as inspired: The Apocalypse of Peter, the Preaching of Peter, the Epistle of Barnabas, I Clement, the Didache, and the Shepherd of Hermas. Obviously by the end of the second century the Church was well on the way to the present canon of the New Testament scripture. Some of the writings, however, were not yet established and other works not in our New Testament were being used as canonical.

The relatively fluid character of the New Testament canon continued into the fourth century. Before then all Christian writers express some uncertainty in their references to a set collection, but slowly the churches came to an agreement reflected in the thirty-ninth Festal letter of Athanasius, bishop of Alexandria. In this Easter letter of A.D.

[19] FBK, pp. 344–345.

367 he named a fixed canon of both the Old and New Testaments. His listing designated the twenty-seven books of our New Testament as alone canonical. In the letter Athanasius not only named the books which the Church had accepted, but also those rejected and some books for use in the Church although they were not canonical.

Transmission of the New Testament

The early Christians were not content merely to enjoy the benefits of the New Testament writings by themselves. They were convinced that these works contained vital messages for all men. Therefore, as the Church expanded in the non-Greek speaking world, the writings were reproduced and passed along to others in their own language.

Transmission in the Early Period. Jesus and the early disciples spoke the Aramaic language, and possibly early Christian documents, no longer extant, existed in Aramaic. Greek was the language of the Roman Empire, however, and very early the Christian message began to circulate in the Greek language. Indeed, insofar as we can ascertain, all the New Testament books were written initially in Greek. This Greek is quite different from the language of the classical writers. A comparison of the Greek New Testament with first century papyri and other literary remains of the Roman Empire indicate that the New Testament was written basically in a non-literary Greek, usually called the *Koine. Koine* is a Greek adjective meaning "common"; hence reference is to the common, ordinary language of everyday life.[20]

A variety of writing materials was available in the period when the New Testament was produced (these include clay tablets, stone, bone, wood, leather, various metals, potsherds, papyrus, and parchment), but almost surely the earliest writings of the New Testament were transmitted on papyrus rolls. The material for the rolls came from the papyrus plant which grew plentifully in the marshes of the ancient East. The plant stem was cut into sections about a foot long, and each section was then cut into thin strips. A layer of these strips was placed on a flat surface with another layer placed on top with fibers at right angles to the lower layer. The layers were pressed together to form one sheet, and a number of sheets were then glued together and wound around a stick to produce a roll.

Very early Christians began to use another form which had some

---

[20] See E. C. Colwell, "The Greek Language," *IDB,* II, pp. 479–487, for a concise treatment of the Greek language of the New Testament period.

advantage over the roll. This was the codex or leaf-book form. Instead of the papyrus sheets being glued together to form a roll, they were folded in the middle and sewed together. It has even been suggested that the Gentile Christians adopted the codex form for their scriptures to differentiate the usage of the Church from that of the synagogue, since the synagogue transmitted the Old Testament by means of rolls. Parchment, a writing material made from animal skins, was also used to reproduce copies of the scriptures. The hair was removed and the skins were washed, smoothed, and dressed with chalk. Parchment was used for both the roll and the codex and, because of its durability, gradually supplanted papyrus as writing material.

The preservation of accurate copies of the New Testament manuscripts was the responsibility of Christian scribes. In light of the crude materials available and the looseness of writing style (from the modern viewpoint), this was no easy task. Sentences and even words were written without division and punctuation was used only sparingly. If the word division were uncertain or the punctuation unclear, the meaning of the sentence might be ambiguous. Thus the scribe carried the responsibility for preserving the clear meaning of the text, as well as for accuracy of reproduction. Their ability to do this with accuracy is attested through a careful study of the manuscripts.

No contemporary narrative account of the early transmission of the New Testament in Greek exists. However, approximately five thousand Greek manuscripts containing all or part of the New Testament are available for scholarly study. Many of these are late manuscripts, but all of them are helpful in a study of the history of the transmission of the Greek New Testament. From them educated conjectures can be made about the history of the transmission in the very early period of the Church. B. F. Westcott and F. J. A. Hort, British scholars of the late nineteenth century, are perhaps the best known of the scholars who have attempted to use the existing manuscripts to discover the process by which the New Testament writings were transmitted.[21] Since each manuscript differs in some ways from other manuscripts, they may be compared and organized into groups based on similarities and differences. The classic definition of the method is given by these eminent scholars: "the proper method of Genealogy consists . . . in the more or less complete recovery of the texts of successive ancestors by analysis and comparison of the varying texts of their respective descendants, each ancestoral text so recovered being in its

---

[21] This procedure is usually referred to as "textual criticism."

turn used, in conjunction with other similar texts, for the recovery of the text of a yet earlier common ancestor." [22] By this method of comparison the relationships may be traced further and further back in the hopes of getting close to the original form. Westcott and Hort traced the manuscript ancestry to three basic types of texts which they designated the Neutral Text, the Alexandrian Text, and the Western Text. Hort felt that the manuscripts containing the Neutral Text reflected early uncontaminated copying of the original New Testament. The other major groups contained either considerable contaminations (Western Texts) or revision and "improvements" (Alexandrian Texts). Westcott and Hort concluded that from these basic sources, editors in successive revisions produced still other texts.

The work of Westcott and Hort clarifies the process of New Testament transmission in the early period, but it certainly is not final and normative. Usually modern textual critics find this work the standard with which they must begin. However, they believe that position must be modified, feeling that it is more correct to see a very early period during which there was a multiplication of variations in the copies, intentional and unintentional. Ernest Colwell says that "out of the chaos and confusion of the first few centuries . . . one finds a tangle such as the mangrove creates with its jungle of roots on the shore of shallow bayous in Florida." [23] He agrees with Westcott and Hort, however, that by the fourth century "certain large trees appear, easily distinguishable from one another." [24]

Early Translations. As the Christian message spread among non-Greek-speaking peoples, the scriptures were translated into a host of other languages. Before the end of the first century Christianity had spread into Mesopotamia. The city of Edessa soon became the chief center of this Christianity and from here the gospel spread eastward. The language of this area was Syriac, a Semitic language related to Aramaic. We are told by Eusebius [25] that Hegesippus, a Jewish Christian writer of the second century, used the scriptures in Syriac form, so translations existed by the mid-second century. Although no Syriac manuscripts dating from this early period now exist, two old Syriac versions of the Gospels which evolved from the early period and date

[22] Brooke Foss Westcott and Fenton John Anthony Hort, *The New Testament in the Original Greek: Introduction and Appendix*, p. 57, as quoted in Ernest C. Colwell, *What Is the Best New Testament?*, pp. 35–36.
[23] Colwell, *What Is the Best New Testament?*, pp. 62–63.
[24] *Ibid.*
[25] *EH*, II, xxii.

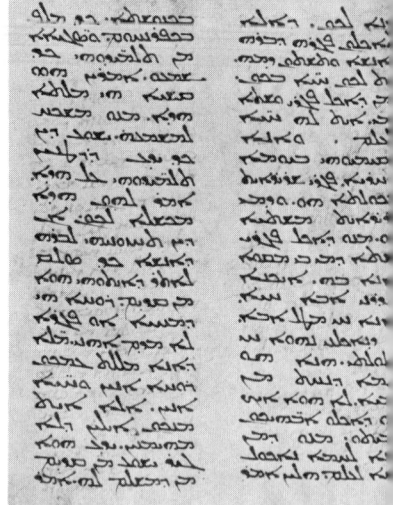

(a)

(b)

(c)

(d)

to the fourth or fifth century are available. Also, there is evidence that the Gospels existed in a different form shortly after the mid-second century. Tatian, an Assyrian Christian, meshed the Four Gospels into one continuous narrative, and this "Diatessaron" became very popular.[26] Whether the Diatessaron of Tatian was earlier than the Old Syriac version of the Gospels is still disputed.

The Christians in the Syriac church eventually became concerned for a standard Syriac Bible to replace the variety of versions. The standard edition of the Syriac New Testament is the revision of Rabbula, bishop of Edessa from A.D. 411 to 435. This revision of the New Testament, along with the Syriac Old Testament, constitutes the Peshitta, which has remained the "authorized version" of the Bible in the Syriac-speaking churches.

Latin translations of the New Testament were also demanded by the spread of the Church. When the gospel came to North Africa, it came into a part of the Roman Empire where Latin, and not Greek, was the leading, official, and civilized language. Further, the planting of Christianity in Rome itself made Latin translation necessary. Although Greek was used by the educated in Rome, the lower strata of society, among whom the gospel also spread, used only Latin. The Bible needed to be made available for them.

Latin translations of the New Testament existed in North Africa by the close of the second century. Toward the end of the century persecution of Christians erupted in parts of Africa, and the record of their trial tells that believers claimed to have "books, and letters of Paul, a just man" in their chest. Likely these writings were in Latin. Further, Tertullian of Carthage, who wrote in the late second and early third

---

[26] The Diatessaron was later condemned by the main body of the Church.

Figure 1–1. An assortment of biblical manuscripts: (a) Codex Sinaiticus opened at the end of Luke (left page) and the beginning of John (right page). The codex dates to the fourth century A.D. and contains a good deal of the Old Testament, the entire New Testament, and the apocryphal *Epistle of Barnabas* and *Shepherd of Hermas*. (Source: British Museum.) (b) Leaf from the Chester Beatty papyri, a number of papyrus leaves purchased about 1930 by Beatty from a dealer in Egypt, illustrating Romans 11:3–12. (Source: Chester Beatty Library, Dublin.) (c) Three fragments from one leaf of a copy of Matthew's Gospel in codex form; the codex probably dates from the late second century A.D. (Source: Oxford University Press.) (d) Portion of a Syriac manuscript dating from the fifth century A.D. (Source: British Museum.)

centuries, shows traces of a Latin translation of the scriptures. Also, Cyprian of Carthage, martyred in A.D. 258, quotes from a Latin Bible. Several manuscript copies of the New Testament in the Old Latin version from Africa and Europe dating from the fourth century are extant.

By the close of the fourth century the limitations of the early Latin translations became evident to Christians in the Roman Church. The complaint that there were almost as many readings as copies of the Old Latin version seems no more than a slight exaggeration. Augustine declared that "in the early days of the faith every man who happened to get his hands upon a Greek manuscript, and who thought he had any knowledge, were it ever so little, of the two languages, ventured upon the work of translation." [27] The roughness and disunity among these copies of the Old Latin versions led Pope Damasus in A.D. 382 to request Jerome, considered the most capable biblical scholar then living, to revise the Latin Bible. Although the exact text of Jerome's work cannot be ascertained because of corruption in its transmission, his translation, called the *Vulgate*, became the standard Latin version and remains the official version of the Bible in the Roman Catholic Church.

Translations into the Egyptian dialects and Gothic followed the earlier Syriac and Latin versions. When the Christian faith first spread to Egypt, no translation was needed because the reading public used Greek with facility. But Christianity eventually worked down to levels of society in which translations into native Egyptian dialects became necessary. Portions of the New Testament were translated into the Sahidic dialect by the beginning of the third century. The Gothic version was produced by Bishop Ulfilas during the mid-fourth century when some of the Goths on the northern frontier of the Roman Empire became converts to the Christian faith.

English Translations of the New Testament. Translation of the New Testament into English was a relatively late development. The beginnings of the English language can be traced to the arrival of the Angles, Saxons, and Jutes in Britain in the fifth century. In the sixth and seventh centuries they were evangelized and eventually desired the gospel in their own language—Anglo-Saxon or Old English. In this Old English period some paraphrases of biblical narratives were put into verse form by Caedmon, herdsman for the abbey at Whitby; and some actual translations of sections of both the Old and the New

[27] Augustine, *On Christian Doctrine*, II, 11.

Testaments were made. Bede, an early English historian and theologian, is reported to have translated the Gospel of John, completing it with his dying breath on Ascension Day, 735; and King Alfred is reported to have translated a section of Acts. Four complete manuscripts and five fragmentary manuscripts of Anglo-Saxon Gospels are extant.

Soon after the Norman conquest of 1066, the language of Britain underwent a change due to the influence of the invading French. The New Testament was soon translated into this modified language. To this Middle English period belong the work of John Wycliffe and the Ormulum, a metrical paraphrase of the Gospels. Two English versions of the entire Bible are associated with Wycliffe. These versions were translated from the Latin Vulgate between 1380 and 1397.

In the fifteenth and sixteenth centuries several movements combined to make English translations of the New Testament more numerous. The revival of learning made the knowledge of Greek more accessible to scholars, and printing, introduced about the middle of the fifteenth century, made the publication of the New Testament easier. Also in this period Luther precipitated the Reformation, thereby giving a tremendous impetus to the translation and circulation of the Bible in the language of the common man.

William Tyndale ranks high in the list of Bible translators. He translated the New Testament from the Greek and published this work in 1526. The work of Tyndale influenced the many English versions of the Bible which appeared in rapid succession over the next several decades. In 1534 and 1535 Tyndale himself issued revisions of his New Testament. In 1535 an English translation by Miles Coverdale appeared. This translation was based on two Latin versions, as well as on the Tyndale English version and German translations of Luther and Zwingli. John Rogers, a friend of Tyndale and pseudonymously known as "Thomas Matthew," published in 1537 some Tyndale and Coverdale materials, including Tyndale's New Testament. This Bible is commonly referred to as "Matthew's Bible."

The work of lawyer Richard Taverner is important. Taverner was an accomplished Greek scholar who made some changes in New Testament translation which were preserved in later translations. The work of Taverner appeared in 1539. In the same year there also appeared the Great Bible, a revision of Matthew's Bible made by Miles Coverdale. Since Coverdale was commissioned by Sir Thomas Cromwell, the Great Bible was the first authorized English version.

The Geneva version of the New Testament appeared in 1557 and the entire Bible appeared in 1560 as a result of political and religious changes in England. When Queen Mary prohibited the printing and use of the English Bible in churches, many English citizens sought refuge at Geneva and there revised the English Bible. In spite of the inclusion of chapter summaries and marginal notes which brought about reaction later, the Geneva Bible became the most popular Bible of the period. It was *the* Bible for the people and held this position for three-quarters of a century, being replaced only by the King James Version.

The Bishop's Bible was published in 1568 when Queen Elizabeth proclaimed that "the whole Bible of the largest volume in English" be placed in every church. Since copies of the Great Bible were not available in large enough quantity, Archbishop Parker suggested that the bishops themselves revise the English Bible and publish it for the purpose of placing it in the churches.

The King James Version grew out of a conference of King James and some Puritans on February 10, 1604. King James ordained that "a translation be made of the whole Bible, as consonant as can be to the original Hebrew and Greek; and this to be set out and printed without any marginal notes, and openly to be used in all churches of England in time of divine service." [28] The result was the King James Bible, published in 1611:

> Containing the Old and New Testaments
> Translated Out of the Original Tongues
> And With the Former Translations Dili-
> gently Compared and Revised, By His
> Majesty's Special Command

For two and a half centuries the King James Version remained the authorized version for English-speaking peoples, but in the middle of the nineteenth century increased knowledge of the original text, especially of the New Testament, additional early manuscripts of the New Testament, and better knowledge of the Old Testament Hebrew made further revision necessary. The Church of England took the lead in the revision, and with the cooperation of scholars from nearly all Christian bodies, the English Revised Version of the New Testament was published in 1881 and of the Old Testament in 1885. American biblical scholars had a limited part in the work and the American Standard Version is a variant edition of the English Revised Version. The American edition, containing the renderings preferred by the

---

[28] Quoted in F. F. Bruce, *The English Bible: A History of Translations*, p. 96.

American scholars cooperating in the English work, was published in 1901.

A great mass of new discoveries made necessary still other translations of the Bible in the twentieth century. Much progress in the historical and comparative study of the original biblical languages and the recent discovery of a "vast quantity of writings in related Semitic . . . has greatly enlarged our knowledge of the vocabulary and grammar of Biblical Hebrew and Aramaic." [29] The Revised Standard Version is the authorized American version resulting from these discoveries. The International Council of Religious Education [30] led in the activities resulting in the Revised Standard Version. The New Testament volume of this work was published in 1946 and the Old Testament in 1952.

The New Testament volume of a New English Bible appeared in 1961. It is the work of British scholars and constitutes a fresh translation instead of a revision of the old authorized English Revised Version. The translators of the New Testament declare, "We have conceived our task to be that of understanding the original as precisely as we could (using all available aids), and then saying again in our own native idiom what we believe the author to be saying in his." [31] Thus the translation process goes on and will continue as additional information and manuscripts clarify the meaning of the original languages and as current language forms change.

THE GEOGRAPHY OF THE NEW TESTAMENT

The New Testament world was basically the Roman Empire. Even Palestine, the land bridge between the ancient civilizations of Egypt and Mesopotamia, must be viewed not only as a part of the East, but also more importantly as a part of the Roman Empire. At its zenith the Roman Empire included the whole Mediterranean world. The limits were Britain to the northwest, Morocco to the southwest, Egypt and Arabia to the southeast, and Turkey and Rumania to the northeast. This huge empire came into existence through a long process of expansion from the little city-state of Rome. In 275 B.C. Rome gained control of Italy and was able to enter the struggle for world power with the successors of Alexander the Great. The expan-

---

[29] "Preface," *The Holy Bible: Revised Standard Version*, p. vi.

[30] Through merger and reorganization the ICRE became a part of the Division of Christian Education of the National Council of Churches of Christ in the United States of America.

[31] "Introduction," *The New English Bible: New Testament*.

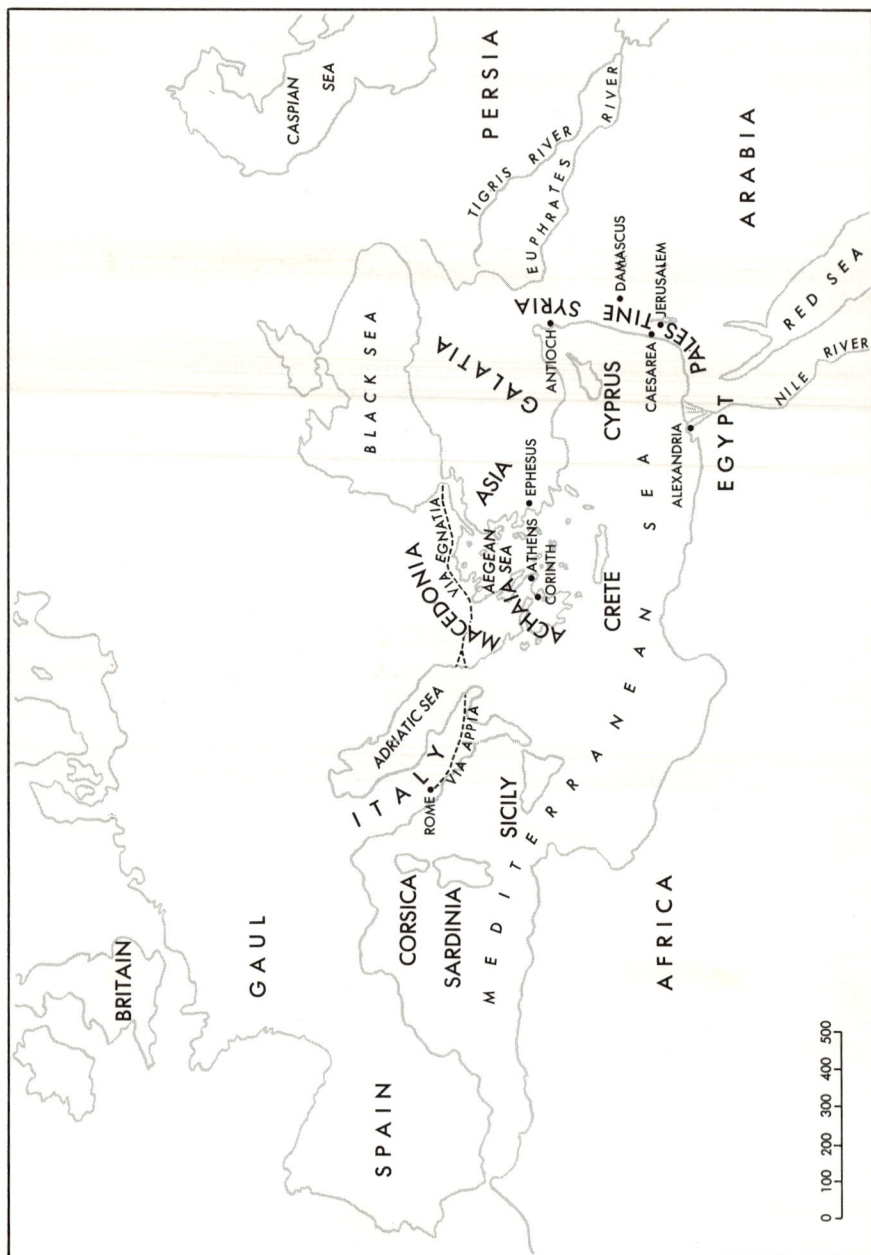

Figure 1-2. The Roman World.

sion of Roman power continued until Augustus became the supreme force and the real founder of the Roman Empire. Even after Augustus' rise to power, additional areas were made provinces of Rome.

Palestine

The life and ministry of Jesus is set completely in the land of Palestine. Therefore, a thorough knowledge of the tiny country is important for understanding the Gospels and the life and ministry of Jesus Christ. Palestine is very small. Its length is described in the Bible as "from Dan to Beersheba" (I Kings 4:25), a distance of only one hundred and fifty miles. The distances from east to west are even less. From Accho on the northern coast to the Sea of Galilee is only twenty-eight miles; and from Gaza on the southern coast to the Dead Sea is only fifty-four miles. Although the area is small, it is amazingly varied. Mount Hermon, just north of Dan, is nine thousand feet above sea level, while much of the Jordan valley is below sea level. The surface of the Dead Sea is lower than any other part of the earth's surface.

Geographically Palestine is divided into four major parts: the coastal plain, the hill country, the Jordan valley, and the Transjordan. The Mediterranean Sea borders Palestine on the west and forms a long coastal plain running the entire length of the country. Since the coast is not marked by any bays or inlets which could supply good ports, it was not particularly important to the life of Palestine.

The hill country was of primary importance and interest because the well-known areas of Galilee, Samaria, and Judea were here. Jesus' home was in Galilee. There he grew up and conducted the major part of his public ministry. Part of upper Galilee reached a height of three thousand feet, but lower Galilee was not so high and enjoyed a milder climate and very productive soil. Nazareth and the towns around the Sea of Galilee were located in lower Galilee. Here among fertile basins growing grain, olives, and grapes, Jesus spent his early life.

Samaria was separated from Galilee by the famous Valley of Jezreel and extended south to a line from Jericho to the Valley of Aijalon. Two notable mountains are in Samaria: Mount Ebal (3100 feet) and Mount Gerizim (2910 feet). These mountains were held sacred by the Samaritans and a temple of the Samaritans was built on Mount Gerizim. Samaria was isolated from Jewish life by a centuries old rift between its inhabitants and those of Judea.

The hill country of Judea is south of Samaria and north of the

Figure 1–3. The wilderness of Judea, the barren mountainous wasteland south and east of Jerusalem. (Source: Paul Popper Ltd.)

Nabatean-Arabian Negeb. Judea contained the city of Jerusalem, by far the most important city of Palestine, and thereby became the most important of the three areas of the hill country for the Jews in the time of Jesus.

Running almost parallel to and east of the hills of Palestine is a great valley which is part of a giant geological fault extending southward from Syria through the Red Sea. Three bodies of water connected by the Jordan River were located in this valley. The Huleh Basin was in the north, a little farther south was the Sea of Galilee, and still farther south was the Dead Sea.

Immediately to the east of the Jordan were inhabited lands in the Transjordan. Of some significance in the New Testament period was the Decapolis (Matthew 4:25; Mark 5:20; 7:31), a federation of Greek cities established by successors of Alexander the Great in the area forming the Gilead of the Old Testament. The region in which these

Figure 1–4. The wilderness in the valley of Jericho, showing the Jordan River just before it reaches the Dead Sea. (Source: Philip Gendreau.)

cities were created forms roughly a triangle with the western angle at Scythopolis, the northern at Damascus and the southern at Philadelphia. Beyond the Decapolis and the other inhabited lands immediately east of the Jordan was the Arabian desert with dry sands and hot sun making regular habitation impossible.

Asia Minor

Asia Minor is the land bridge connecting southwest Asia with southeast Europe. Mountain ranges run along the northern and southern edges with an elevated plateau between. Toward the west the mountain ranges draw near to one another and slope gradually to the coast, opening into plains and river valleys which contain many towns mentioned in the New Testament. During the New Testament period, Asia Minor was divided into numerous provinces, several mentioned in the Book of Acts and the letters of Paul.

Macedonia and Greece

Macedonia provided the major land route between Asia and the West, including Rome. It is introduced in the New Testament story when Paul journeyed from Troas across the Aegean to Philippi on the second missionary journey. Macedonia had provided the initial stage for the activities of Philip of Macedon and his son Alexander the Great, who united the Greek lands and spread the Greek empire as far as Egypt and Babylon. In 148 B.C. Macedonia became a Roman province, and Thessalonica was named as the seat of its administration.

Greece is known in the New Testament as Achaia. For a time (A.D. 15–44) Achaia and Macedonia were united into one province by the Romans, but just before Paul's activities in the Greek lands Achaia became a separate province with its administration center at Corinth.

The origin and early spread of the Christian faith took place primarily within these geographical areas—Palestine, Asia Minor, Macedonia and Greece, and Rome itself. To study the New Testament and the history of the early Christian Church with understanding is to move freely in this world marked by topographical and cultural diversity, but unified under the Roman standard.

THE JEWISH WORLD IN THE TIME OF JESUS

The Historical Background

Influences from Israelite religion, Greek culture and philosophy, and Roman power and law shaped the world in which Jesus lived. An understanding of Jesus and his teaching must attempt to place him in the real institutional and ideational environment which had been molded over a period of at least two thousand years.

Israel's History: The Old Testament Period.[32]   The history of Israel begins with the patriarchal ancestors who moved from northwestern Mesopotamia to Canaan sometime after 2000 B.C. They belonged to a mass of Amorite peoples whose migrations flooded the Near East for about four centuries. In Canaan they lived as nomads in the central hill country. When famine struck Canaan, many moved to Egypt. Some settled there and were eventually enslaved by the Egyptian pharaohs. Early in the thirteenth century B.C. they escaped from Egypt under the leadership of Moses. This event was the most crucial in their history, for they viewed their escape as an act of Yahweh their God. In fact, they believed that Yahweh had chosen them as his particular people. A generation was spent in the wilderness. Most important among the events of this period was a revelatory experience at Sinai, a holy mountain, where they claimed to have received their law from God.

In the second half of the thirteenth century the Israelites moved into Canaan, conquering some Canaanites and settling among others. Kindred peoples who had never moved to Egypt joined the returning Israelites and together they formed a loosely-organized religious confederacy. The unifying factor was the worship of Yahweh at a central sanctuary. The confederacy lasted for two hundred years during which Israel secured her hold on Canaan. At the end of this period fear of the Philistines, strong enemies who settled on the Palestinian coast while Israel settled in the hills, led Israel to establish a monarchy with Saul as king. Under David, Saul's successor, the monarchy blossomed into an empire which was short-lived due to the unwise policies of Solomon, David's son. When Solomon died (922 B.C.), the people separated into two kingdoms, Israel in the north and Judah in the south. These states became the pawns of Assyria, Babylon, and Egypt. Israel fell to Assyria in 722/721 B.C. and its people were relocated throughout the Assyrian empire. At about the same time Judah became a virtual vassal of Assyria and remained so until Babylon overthrew Assyria in 612 B.C. Judah's fortunes, however, did not really change, only the place of her vassalage, now Babylon. In 587 B.C. Babylon overran Judah and carried her important citizens into exile. When Babylon lost supremacy to Persia in 539 B.C., some of these exiles returned and re-established a Judean state under Persian sovereignty.

---

[32] For further information the reader is referred to Flanders, Crapps, and Smith, *People of the Covenant: An Introduction to the Old Testament,* or a similar work.

The faith and religious traditions of Israel were born and shaped in the context of these fortunes of the Israelite people.

The Period of Greek Sovereignty and the Maccabean Revolt. The Jewishness of Jesus' world, however, had been profoundly affected by the conquest of the East by Alexander the Great and the Hellenization of the Semitic states under subsequent Greek rulers. Alexander's father Philip of Macedon, had prepared the way for Alexander's phenomenal success by enticing or compelling all the small Greek city-states into an Hellenic league. When he died before leading them in wars of conquest, his son carried out his ambitions on an even grander scale. After two years during which he became supreme in Greece, Alexander crossed the Hellespont into Asia in 334 B.C. and soon routed a Persian army of twenty thousand and thus gained control of west and south Asia Minor. During the next year, he moved into Syria where he again defeated the Persians. Alexander moved south, taking Tyre and Gaza by siege. When the young Macedonian entered Egypt, he was received as savior and deliverer. In 331 he again met the Persians, this time near the site of old Nineveh and moved virtually unopposed to capture the heartland of Persia. He went on then to India and finally died of fever in Babylon in 323 B.C. The military exploits of Alexander unified the East under a Greek banner, but more important his conquests fostered the spread of Greek ideas and culture to an extent which cannot be overestimated.

At Alexander's death his kingdom was divided among his generals. The new kingdoms remained Greek in culture and outlook. Palestine lay between the two most powerful of them, the Ptolemaic kingdom of Egypt and the Seleucid kingdom of Syria.[33] Palestine was the object of each's desire. The Jewish community was divided in its loyalties. The high priesthood, supported by most of the populace, sided with the Seleucids, but some with business interests in Egypt supported the Ptolemies. For several decades neither Syria nor Egypt could remain the superior power, and Judea often suffered in the conflict between the two. When finally in 198 B.C. a Syrian ruler, Antiochus III, secured Judea for the Seleucid kingdom, conditions appeared bright for the Jews. Antiochus cancelled their taxes for three years, promised compensation for the cities destroyed in the wars, exempted priests and other cultic personnel from poll and crown taxes, and aided in the reconstruction of Jerusalem and the temple.

[33] Named for Alexander's generals, Ptolemy and Seleucus, who established dynasties in the respective kingdoms.

A storm broke over Judea, however, in 175 when assassination and infanticide brought Antiochus IV Epiphanes to the throne. In an attempt to solidify the East against Rome he tried to Hellenize the heterogeneous populations of the area. His aggressive and leveling policies of Hellenization were the immediate cause of a Jewish revolt. The ruling class of Judea favored the Hellenization policies; some even wished to turn Jerusalem into a Hellenistic city. Merchants and the priesthood alike were caught up in insidious intrigues to win the favor of their Greek overlords and power for themselves. The common people, on the other hand, saw no reason to give up the religious traditions of their fathers for alien paganism. They had nothing to gain from collaboration with Syria. Therefore, when Antiochus' policies became intolerable, they rebelled.

Antiochus began an all-out campaign to conquer Egypt but was thwarted by Rome, which ordered him out of Egypt at once. Rumor spread in Judea that Antiochus had died and attempts were made to oust his appointees in Jerusalem. Antiochus took sweeping revenge. Jerusalem was treated as an enemy city. The city was looted and many inhabitants were slaughtered without cause. The temple was defiled and the cult suspended. An altar to Zeus was erected at the place of the Jewish altar and swine were sacrificed on it. Sacrifices to Greek deities were made compulsory for the Jews and the practice of Judaism was outlawed under penalty of death.

Prominent among the common people who reacted violently was the priestly family of Mattathias. When the king's officers came to their village of Modein to enforce Greek sacrifice, Mattathias killed both the king's representatives and the first Jew who stepped forward to obey the aliens. He then proclaimed, "Let every one who is zealous for the law and supports the covenant come out with me!"[34] Mattathias was joined by many other Jews and a revolt was on. When elderly Mattathias died, leadership of the movement passed to his son Judas, who was called Maccabeus.[35] Aided by his brothers and with considerable military skill and courage, Judas so successfully harassed the Greeks that the proscriptions against Jewish worship were withdrawn. Just three years after it had been profaned, the temple was purified and the Jews renewed their cult. 164 B.C. became a signal date in Judaism commemorated annually in the feast of Hanukkah (Rededication).

[34] I Maccabees 2:27.
[35] Judas was nicknamed Maccabee, which means "mallet-headed" or "hammerer."

Many Jews were satisfied with this achievement. Most, however, continued the struggle in pursuit of independence and, when Antiochus Epiphanes died, the resistance movement became a full-scaled war for political liberty. When Judas was killed in battle, his brothers continued to lead the fight until Simon broke the Seleucid hold on Judea in 142 B.C. and became secular and religious head of an independent Jewish state.

Independence unfortunately was fairly short-lived. Maccabean rule was not as effective as Maccabean revolt. Ruling as the Hasmonean dynasty (named for a family ancestor), the Maccabees eventually combined political and religious leadership, serving as both king and high priest. The Hasmoneans were at times as incompetent and ruthless as the Greeks they had replaced; nevertheless they successfully created a Jewish state with which even Rome had to reckon. They also fostered a study of Jewish traditions which gave impetus to scribal activity in copying, studying, and teaching the literature which later became canonized as Jewish scripture. Jewish nationalism and religious zeal were quickened by their successes, which were not, however, of a kind to endure.

The Hasmonean dynasty ended with Roman intervention in the complicated political affairs of the Jews. Two Hasmonean claimants to the throne created a political morass that threatened to engulf the nation. The Jews themselves appealed to Rome for help. Roman sovereignty had already been extended to Syria and was reaching toward the Euphrates and was certainly willing to intervene in Judea. In 63 B.C. Pompey, the Roman leader in the East, seized Jerusalem from the contending Jewish factions and a new era dawned for Judaism.

The Period of Roman Control. Roman policy in the East was essentially *laissez faire*. She made no attempt to Romanize, continuing instead the policies begun by the Greeks. Local governments were left to manage their own affairs and native courts settled difficulties by local law. Roman administrators saw that law and order prevailed, that travel and communication were safe, and that taxes were paid. Nevertheless the average Jew saw Rome as an enemy. Her control in Palestine was initially administered through Hyrcanus, a Hasmonean, who was high priest, and by Antipater, whose background and position is uncertain. Antipater, an Idumean who was motivated by personal ambition, was without question, however, a capable public servant who won the respect of various Roman governors, Pompey, and even Julius Caesar. Josephus described him as "a man that had distinguished himself for piety and justice, and love to his country." [36] Antipater's son Herod was made governor of Galilee in 47 B.C. and, when he proved his loyalty to Rome in the hectic times before and after the murder of Julius Caesar in 44, was appointed king of Judea. He seized Jerusalem from the Hasmonean authorities there, quieted all of Palestine, and married Mariamne, a Hasmonean. This union won him some acceptance in Jewish circles and by 37 B.C. Herod had gained full control of his kingdom.

Herod was a good ruler, but not a popular one. He was hated as a tool of Rome and as the one who brought an end to Hasmonean rule. However, for nearly forty years he governed the land with loyalty to Rome and with the good of the realm in mind. Appearances of prosperity and culture filled the Jewish state. Cities were built and renovated. Among these were Samaria and Caesarea. The latter was built to provide a port on a harborless coast and soon became the leading city of Palestine. The temple in Jerusalem was rebuilt with a splendor not known before. Palestine was at peace and was safe. Personally Herod was ambitious and vain. He dealt harshly and quickly with any threats to his personal position. Relatives and political opponents alike were victims of his suspicions. Opposition to Herod centered in Judea, where his death in 4 B.C. was eagerly hailed. Elsewhere he seems to have been accepted and perhaps was even popular. Everywhere "his subjects, both Jews and Gentiles, found that his hand, though heavy, was just." [37]

When Herod died, he willed his kingdom to his three sons, Archelaus, Antipas, and Philip. Archelaus was to be given the title king to rule over Judea, Samaria, and Idumea, the most significant areas ruled by his father. This had to be confirmed by Rome. The brothers went to Rome to plead their case. Archelaus and Antipas both claimed the kingship, with Philip supporting Archelaus. There was also a representation of Jews who wanted to be rid of all the Herods.[38] The resolution was in accord with Herod's will, except Archelaus was named ethnarch with the promise of kingship if he proved worthy. Archelaus was ethnarch of Judea, Samaria, and Idumea; Antipas was tetrarch of Galilee, Perea, and Jewish territory east of the Jordan; Philip was tetrarch of the area east and north of the Sea of Galilee. Philip was well liked by his subjects and ruled until his death in A.D.

[36] *Antiquities,* XIV, xi, 4.
[37] Morton S. Enslin, "New Testament Times," *IB*, VII, p. 104.
[38] This may lie behind Jesus' parable in Luke 19:12ff.

34. Antipas remained five years longer in Galilee; then he was deposed and banished by a new emperor. Archelaus fared even less well. Judea became the scene of insurrection and riots against Archelaus and in A.D. 6 the emperor Augustus banished him on a charge of gross mismanagement. His province was brought under the direct rule of Rome, governed by a procurator. Procurators were directly responsible to the emperor and remained in office as long as their administration was approved.

Contrary to popular opinion, the procurators were not bad rulers. They allowed their people as much freedom as possible. In fact, most of the actual control of Judea was in the hands of the Sanhedrin and much of the revenue collected was spent bettering the province. The first four procurators are of no real interest to us. The fifth was Pontius Pilate, who was involved in the crucifixion of Jesus. Overall Pilate was a good governor and was kept in office ten years by the emperor. He did, however, have several clashes with the Jews of which the tragic one involving Jesus was the most infamous.

The Judaism of Jesus' Day

The Cultus. Post-exilic Judaism was dominated by cultus and Torah, both originally under the administration of the priesthood. Cultic changes, however, had accompanied the rise of the synagogue and the rabbinical interpretation of the law.

1. TEMPLE. The temple was the center of Jewish cultic life. On its altar a daily public sacrifice was offered to God on behalf of all the people. On feast days and the Sabbath there were additional sacrifices and elaborate ceremonies. As a sacred place the temple was held in particular reverence in all Jewish hearts. For them it was the holiest of all holy places, particularly sanctified by God's presence. Its inner courts were sacrosanct and closed to secular activities; the outer courts were used for public gatherings of all kinds.

The organization of the temple was complicated and involved the cooperation of many persons. Its personnel included temple singers and other musicians, porters to open and attend the gates, special servants who prepared for the daily public services, and treasurers and administrators. The temple, however, was the special province of the priesthood who both preserved and administered the cult. Some twenty thousand priests served the temple in twenty four courses. The High Priest, who was the head of the priesthood, enjoyed considerable power in both religious and secular matters. Inevitably these leaders were chosen from the same small group and so the High Priesthood represented an exclusive aristocracy. The entire priesthood, in fact, was a closed society, maintained by offerings brought to the temple, and lived a life set apart from the rest of Judaism. Control of the cultus gave them unusual power in Judea.[39]

2. SYNAGOGUE. The other great institution in post-exilic Judaism was the synagogue. The synagogue probably originated during the exile in Babylon and became an established institution in the period of the Dispersion (the scattering of the Jews during and after the exile) when large numbers of Jews were separated from the temple. The synagogue provided a local center of worship and study independent of the temple. Nothing in this innovation was hostile to the temple; it was intended as complementary.

The synagogue was a "meeting place for the pious." [40] Singing of Psalms and congregational prayers were important parts of its ritual, but reading from the scripture (the Torah and Prophets) constituted the focal point of its assembly. The Torah was read in Hebrew and in Palestinian synagogues the reading was followed by an explanation in Aramaic. This was followed, if a competent person was present, by a discourse on the text.[41] The recognized leader was the rabbi who read and interpreted the scripture, but others also had the privilege of teaching in the synagogue. Any Jew who chose to do so might expound the scriptures. The exposition of Torah made teaching an important function of the synagogue and eventually this institution became a place of schooling for anyone desiring to be an expert in the law. The synagogue was also the place where children received their basic education.

3. FAMILY PIETY. For centuries the home life of simple Jewish people had been oriented to religion so that the family was a strategic institution for preserving Judaism. Torah made parents responsible for teaching their children the traditions of their people and instilling an unsophisticated faith in God. Israelites took this responsibility seriously and thus passed on the hope of redemption from generation to generation. The home was also where Passover was ordinarily observed, celebrating the greatest event in Israel's history and their fondest assurance of the future.

---

[39] See below on Sadducees and Torah.
[40] C. Guignebert, *The Jewish World in the Time of Jesus*, p. 75.
[41] George F. Moore, *Judaism*, I, p. 291.

The Sects of Judaism. Most Jews in Jesus' day lived simple lives with religion and piety occupying varying proportions of their concerns and energies. Personal and family necessities prevented their participation in any public attempts to structure religious or political life. Some, however, were involved with others of similar persuasion in various communities or associations which out of balance to their size significantly affected all of Jewish life. Five sects emerged in post-exilic Judaism.

1. SADDUCEES. The Sadducees were the priestly aristocratic party of Jerusalem, whose interest centered in the temple. They apparently emerged as a party during Maccabean times among the Hasmonean priesthood. They were defenders of their priestly prerogatives and were consequently concerned about the temple cultus and the interpretation of Torah. Since Israel was viewed as a theocratic state in which the law of God was administered by the priesthood, the Sadducees also had extensive political interests. They controlled the Sanhedrin of Jerusalem, a court that had legislative, executive, and judical functions. The Sanhedrin's freedom to exercise these responsibilities depended upon the political regime in power. It was somewhat restricted under Roman procuratorship but in most matters wielded considerable authority. To maintain their prerogatives the Sadducees cooperated with the secular authority to the degree necessary to protect cultic and priestly integrity.

For the Sadducees the Torah was the authoritative law of God. All else was commentary or interpretation. Oral and written tradition, subject to change and interpretation, belonged to the Pharisees and the synagogue but played no part in the life of the Sadducees. The will of God was known through the Sadducees' immediate interpretation of Torah. The Sadducees denied the doctrine of the resurrection, ideas of all future punishments and rewards, and the existence of angels and spirits. All of these ideas were apparently rejected because they were not found in the Torah.

When Roman armies destroyed Jerusalem and the temple in A.D. 70, the Sadducees suffered heavily and, since the temple was not rebuilt, never returned to their influential role in Judaism. The continuity of Jewish life was left to the Pharisees, who had long been the Sadducees' rivals.

2. PHARISEES. The most influential party in Judaism was the Pharisees. They were never numerous; Josephus says they numbered about six thousand, but their hold upon the minds of the people was strong.

They originated among lay interpreters of the law in the post-exilic period, probably under the Hasmoneans.

The chief characteristic of the Pharisees was their legalism. They were noted for their strict accuracy in interpretation of the Torah, building around it a "wall" of tradition. The basis of their interpretation, however, was not confined to the Torah. The Pharisees admitted a broader canon of scripture, including both the Old Testament Prophets and Writings. Their legalistic rigorism in interpreting scripture led to an affected concern for ritual purification. They tried zealously to obey the Levitical laws as interpreted by Pharisaic traditional observances and ordinances, even shunning the non-Pharisee as ceremonially unclean. Because of the rigorous concern for ritual and religious purity, the Pharisees created a narrow society "where contact between members of the exclusive sect and the rest of the population was avoided or regulated by a system of elaborate legal precautions designed to minimize or remove ritual uncleanness contracted in the unavoidable intercourse of daily life." [42]

The Pharisees accepted the doctrines of resurrection and future rewards and punishments. Acts 23:8 states that ". . . the Sadducees say that there is no resurrection, nor angel, nor spirit; but the Pharisees acknowledge them all." Apparently Pharisaic acceptance of traditions other than the Torah led them to accept ideas categorically rejected by Sadducees. A prolonged and bitter ideological struggle developed between the two groups. On one side was priestly authority and temple tradition; on the other lay interpretation of Torah and religious exclusiveness.

Pharisees controlled the synagogues and consequently had more influence on the life and faith of Judaism than any other group. Both Greek and Roman authorities were jealous of Pharisaic power over the average Jew but were wise enough not to take action against them. When Judaism was forced to abandon temple cult in the events following Roman destruction of Jerusalem in A.D. 70, Pharisaic leadership was able to conserve and restructure Jewish faith and life.

3. ESSENES. The Essenes were a withdrawal community of particular importance in the time of Jesus. They are best known through recent discoveries in the Judean desert. Since 1947 a large portion of Essene literature, including scriptures of ancient Israel, and their community establishment at Qumran have been found and studied. These new data essentially confirm what was known from other ancient

[42] Matthew Black, "Pharisees," *IDB,* III, p. 776.

Figure 1–5. Cave IV, located west of the Dead Sea near the Wadi Qumran, where manuscript fragments which once had constituted over 300 separate books were discovered. (Source: Foreign Mission Board, Southern Baptist Convention.)

sources. Like the Sadducees and Pharisees, the Essenes apparently originated during the Maccabean times. They believed themselves to be the people of the new covenant; *i.e.*, the people of God's future. They were concerned with the eschaton, the end of history, and hoped to share in its glory.

About four thousand Essenes were scattered in the villages and towns of Judea. They tended to avoid the larger cities because of the danger there of ritual defilement. Some lived at Qumran, something of a wilderness retreat serving as a type of headquarters for the movement. Here they practiced a community life, sharing property and goods and responsibility and labor. Admission to the community was by strict initiation, and, once a candidate was accepted, he was subject to the authority of his superiors and to rigid discipline. Within their communities the Essenes participated in ritual meals and ceremonies of cleansing. They also offered sacrifices, believing themselves to be the true priests of God. Study of the scriptures was particularly important to the Essenes, who interpreted them in light of their eschatological expectations. They believed that the promises of God foretold by the prophets were to be fulfilled in their communities and therefore searched the scripture as clue to their present and future.

Certain ideas were common to the Essenes and the early Church and some scholars associate John the Baptist and Jesus with an Essene community, perhaps Qumran. Evidence, however, is not adequate to allow us to make much of such associations. Common ideas and similar practices seem best accounted for by common concerns and circumstances.

4. ZEALOTS. The Zealot gave himself to God "to be an agent of God's righteous wrath and judgment against idolatry, apostasy, and any transgression of the law which excited God's jealousy." [43] The more extreme were warlike Jewish rebels who opposed foreign rule, especially Roman. They were doubtless the moving spirit behind some of the revolts against Roman authority which kept Palestine in recurring turmoil. It would be incorrect to assume that they represented a community or sect in the way that Sadducees, Pharisees, and Essenes did.

5. HERODIANS. Still another group existed in first century Palestine, Jews who supported Rome. These may be the Herodians who are mentioned in Mark (3:6; 12:13) and Matthew (22:16) as opponents of Jesus. Apparently they had supported Herod or the Herodian dynasty. These men represent the continuity of acceptance of the Hellenizing policies begun by the Greeks. Since few of the common people had ever actively supported foreign rule, the Herodians must have been persons of means and influence. Tax collectors and other Roman civil servants may loosely be termed Herodians, but like "Zealots" this term does not seem to define a particular organized group.

Religious Tradition: Scripture. The Jews had no official canon of scripture in the time of Jesus. Certain of their religious writings, how-

---

[43] W. R. Farmer, "Zealot," *IDB*, IV, p. 936.

ever, had long been held in particular esteem. Word of priest and prophet were especially thought to be expressive of the will of God and by post-exilic times the Torah (the first five books of the Old Testament) was unquestionably accepted as the authoritative law of God. The Prophetic collection also was widely accepted and respected and most of the books in the Writings, the third section of the Hebrew scriptures, had already been accorded a special place in Jewish minds and hearts.

Torah, however, was supreme as the rule of Jewish life and basis of their religious hope. The word *torah* is usually translated "law," but "law" does not capture all the nuances of the Hebrew term. Torah means "instruction" or "teaching," but is also used to refer to the whole of divine revelation. The Torah had gradually been accorded an increasing place of importance. Separated from the historical context from which it had sprung, it came to be viewed as unchanging, unalterable, and eternal. It was portrayed as existing before Israel.[44]

Judaism also developed an oral tradition or interpretation of the law. Since the written law did not cover all the contingencies of life, some adjustments were necessary if Torah was to be applicable to changing conditions. Therefore, custom became as established as Torah and much law which did not survive the exile in written form was remembered and applied. The Pharisaic community was primarily responsible for the elaboration of such oral traditions. The oral law interpreted "the ordinances of the written law, explaining their contents and defining their scope."[45] Interpretations which were legal in character were called Halachah; those of ethical or devotional nature were Haggadah. Sometimes the oral tradition took the form of running commentary on the text (Midrash), but increasingly it was passed on without reference to a scriptural passage. The method used was repetition (Mishna).

Sadducees and Pharisees differed over the validity of the oral traditions. For the Pharisees, and consequently for most Jews, tradition was as weighty as Torah. In fact, written and canonical law and tradition interpretation were both often referred to as Torah. Sadducees, on the other hand, rejected all tradition, accepting only the Mosaic Torah. First century Judaism cannot be understood apart from the controversy over tradition's validity and the resultant centrality of both Torah and its interpretation.

[44] Cf. The Wisdom of ben Sirach 16:26–17:24; Jubilees 2:15–33; 3:8–14; 6:17f.; 16:20–31.

[45] I. Epstein, "Talmud," *IDB*, IV, p. 511.

Besides the Torah, Prophets, and Writings, and the traditional interpretations thereof (especially of Torah), Judaism accorded particular significance to additional bodies of religious literature which were later rejected when the Palestinian Jewish canon was closed around A.D. 100. Included were some apocalyptic writings rife with eschatological speculation, historical or semi-historical productions like I and II Maccabees, and Wisdom writings like The Wisdom of Jesus ben Sirach. Such works, however, were of lesser consequence for Palestinian Jewish life than the works which later were canonized. Of the latter, Torah (especially Genesis and Deuteronomy), Isaiah, Jeremiah, and Psalms seem to have been particularly influential.

Jewish Eschatological Hope. Beyond the repeated failures and tragedies of her history Judaism looked for the future and final redemptive activity of God. When Israel had truly repented of her sins and when testing and trials were over, the ideal age would dawn. All Judaism believed this. They were not, however, agreed about how it would come to pass.

Some hoped for a restoration of the monarchy and the glory of David's reign, which Judaism increasingly tended to idealize. The ideal king anticipated by the prophets would be anointed and enthroned. He would lead Israel to new greatness and to a place of respect among the nations. The messianic prince would arise in the ordinary course of events, but God would be present with him to vindicate his righteousness and establish the ideal age. The exact identity of this messiah was not agreed upon and some even expected him to embody priestly as well as royal functions.

For some Jews, though, hope for the future could never rest upon a kingly figure. Kings had failed too many times. Instead of an ideal monarchy they dreamed of a theocracy with God himself directly in control. God would establish his kingdom, a perfectly righteous rule which would replace the imperfect and often evil rule of men.

Traditions like these are typical of prophetic eschatology and characterized Jewish thought down to the exile. After the exile, however, continued contact with Persian thought introduced cataclysmic change into eschatological expectation. The idea of direct divine intervention in continuing history was paralleled by a theory of a divine judgment which would end history. History would not move gradually toward the realization of the divine purpose and the ideal age. It would end in the cataclysmic clash between forces of good and evil. The world would be destroyed and unrighteous men would be judged and punished. The righteous would then inherit a new earth. The descriptions of the end of the present age and birth of a new world are dominated by the figure of a divine judge who would inaugurate the age to come. He is both judge of the present evil age and lord over the new age which his judgmental action makes possible. Apocalyptic literature abounds with this kind of eschatology.

Even though their styles are different, prophetic and apocalyptic eschatology have common expectation of an age of bliss in which righteous Jews would share central place. Christians found both traditions appropriate forms for expressing the fulfillment of the hope experienced in Jesus. Jesus Christ became for the Church both Messiah and judge of history.

SUGGESTED READINGS

General Introductions to the New Testament

DAVIES, W. D., *Invitation to the New Testament* (Doubleday, 1966). A non-technical book written for laymen by a noted New Testament scholar.

FEINE, PAUL, JOHANNES BEHM, and WERNER G. KÜMMEL, *Introduction to the New Testament* (Abingdon, 1966). A complete revision and translation of a time-tested German introduction to the New Testament. Best for reference purposes.

FULLER, REGINALD H., *A Critical Introduction to the New Testament* (Duckworth, 1966). Good, modern, concise introduction to individual New Testament books.

GOODSPEED, EDGAR J., *An Introduction to the New Testament* (University of Chicago Press, 1937). Standard work by well-known American New Testament scholar.

GRANT, ROBERT M., *A Historical Introduction to the New Testament* (Harper, 1963). Particularly helpful for understanding the development of the New Testament Canon and the major problems of New Testament interpretation.

HUNTER, A. M., *Introducing the New Testament* (Westminster, 2nd ed. rev., 1958). Simple, reliable introduction by a conservative but critical British scholar.

MCNEILE, A. H., *An Introduction to the Study of the New Testament* (Clarendon Press, 1953). One of the best New Testament introductions.

PRICE, J. L., *Interpreting The New Testament* (Holt, Rinehart and Winston, 1961). A popular introduction.

SANDMEL, SAMUEL, *A Jewish Understanding of the New Testament* (Hebrew Union College Press, 1956).

WIKENHAUSER, ALFRED, *New Testament Introduction* (Herder & Herder, 1963). An excellent Roman Catholic introduction.

New Testament Text, Version, and Canon

BARCLAY, WILLIAM, *The Making of the Bible* (Abingdon, 1961). Includes both New and Old Testament. Brief, but helpful.

BEARE, FRANCIS W., "Canon of the N. T.," *IDB*, Vol. I. Concise but comprehensive.

BRUCE, F. F., *The English Bible* (Oxford, 1961). A history of translations from the earliest English versions to the New English Bible.

COLWELL, ERNEST CADMAN, *What is the Best New Testament?* (University of Chicago Press, 1952). Written for laymen by an American New Testament textual critic.

FILSON, FLOYD V., *Which Books Belong in the Bible?* (Westminster, 1957). Brief and helpful on the Canon.

KENYON, FREDERIC, *Our Bible and the Ancient Manuscripts* (Harper, 5th ed. rev., 1958).

METZGER, BRUCE M., *The Text of the New Testament* (Oxford, 1964). One of the best books on the New Testament text in print.

PARVIS, M. M., "N. T. Text," *IDB*, Vol. IV. Concise and comprehensive.

SCHNEEMELCHER, W., "The History of the New Testament Canon," in Hennecke-Schneemelcher, *New Testament Apocrypha*, Vol. I.

SOUTER, ALEXANDER, *The Text and Canon of the New Testament* (Allenson, 2nd ed. revised by C. S. C. Williams, 1954).

Geography

BALY, DENIS, *The Geography of the Bible* (Harper, 1957). Up-to-date, illustrated study.

MAY, HERBERT G., *Oxford Bible Atlas* (Oxford, 1962).

SMITH, GEORGE ADAM, *The Historical Geography of the Holy Land* (Doran, 1902). Dated, but still classic.

WRIGHT, G. ERNEST, and FLOYD V. FILSON, *The Westminster Historical Atlas to the Bible* (Westminster, rev. ed., 1956).

Jewish Background

BOX, G. H., *Judaism in the Greek Period* (Oxford, 1936).

GRANT, FREDERICK C., *Ancient Judaism and the New Testament* (Macmillan, 1959).

MOORE, GEORGE FOOT, *Judaism in the First Centuries of the Christian Era*, 3 vols. (Harvard University Press, 1927–30). A classic study on Judaism.

OESTERLEY, W. O. E., *The Jews and Judaism in the Greek Period* (S.P.C.K., 1941).

PFEIFFER, ROBERT H., *History of New Testament Times with an Introduction to the Apocrypha* (Harper, 1949).

PART I

Foundation of the Church:
Life and Teachings
of Jesus

2

Sources for a Study
of Jesus

Jesus was an actual person who lived in Palestine during the first third of the first century A.D. Facts concerning the historical Jesus, as facts concerning any other person in ancient history, must be gleaned from the ancient sources which deal directly and indirectly with him. The Four Gospels of the New Testament are the most complete sources for a study of Jesus. They are not the only sources, however; Jesus is so central to the Christian movement that attention must be given to all of the possible sources of information.

SOURCES APART FROM THE GOSPELS

The sources other than the Gospels give only snatches of information. Jesus is mentioned merely in passing by some early Jewish and Roman writers. Early Christian writers whose works did not gain a place in the New Testament treat Jesus and his teachings more frequently and directly. Most important, however, among the sources apart from the Gospels are other New Testament writings which give some information about Jesus.

Early Non-Christian Writers

During the early Christian centuries, Jewish and Roman writings were flourishing. Of course, none of these writings deal primarily with Jesus. The writers were interested in interpreting the Jewish traditions, recording Jewish and Roman history, and composing "lives" of leading Roman officials. But Jesus *is* mentioned in passing by several of these authors.

The Jewish Writers. The major part of Jesus' ministry was spent in Galilee, which was not a center of Jewish literary activity, and there is no evidence of Jesus' contact with contemporary Jewish writers, such as Philo, the Jewish writer in Alexandria, Egypt. It is not surprising, therefore, that Jesus is mentioned only infrequently in contemporary Jewish literature. References do occur in the Jewish materials which came into fixed form in the Talmud and in the writings of the Jewish historian Josephus.

1. THE TALMUD. The Talmud is the repository of Jewish interpretation of the Law from the time of Ezra to the middle of the sixth century of the Christian era. It contains legal materials, moral reflections, homilies, apologies, maxims of wordly wisdom, metaphysical speculations, traditions of Israel's past, visions of its future, and other materials. Just as Christian literature of this period of conflict between Jews and Christians contains references to the Jews, so the Jewish literature mentions Jesus Christ and his followers. References on both sides are often polemical or defensive, however, and their historical value is questionable. One of the passages which refer to Jesus in the Babylonian Talmud [1] is declared by the Jewish scholar Joseph Klausner to have "greater historical value" than the others.[2]

On the eve of the passover Yeshu was hanged. For forty days before the execution took place, a herald went forth and cried, "He is going forth to be stoned because he has practiced sorcery and enticed Israel to apostasy. Anyone who can say anything in his favour, let him come forward and plead on his behalf." But since nothing was brought forward in his favour, he was hanged on the eve of the passover.

This statement, and the other references in the Talmud, oppose the claims of Christian tradition, and it is difficult to assign independent historical value to the Talmudic traditions. They are probably dependent upon the various Christian traditions which they attempt to discredit. Note, for example, that in the passage quoted above, Jesus is sentenced to be stoned. According to Jewish tradition, this is the correct punishment; [3] but according to the passage quoted, Jesus is hung instead of stoned. It seems that the passage attempts to justify Jesus'

[1] Sanhedrin, 43a.
[2] Joseph Klausner, *Jesus of Nazareth: His Life, Times, and Teaching*, p. 27.
[3] The Mishnah, Sanhedrin, 7, 4.

condemnation from the Jewish point of view; the tradition that Jesus was crucified was so firmly fixed, however, that the writers could not go so far as to say that the sentence of stoning was carried out.[4]

In spite of its polemical bias the witness of the most ancient rabbis as given in the Talmud has some value. They attempt to destroy the validity of Christian truth by altering and interpreting the Christian tradition. They do not, in fact they cannot, deny its basis. The Talmudic evidence is sufficient to make clear that there is no reason at all to doubt the existence of Jesus. Moreover Klausner regards the early statements in the Talmud to substantiate some facts about Jesus.

There are reliable statements to the effect that his name was Yeshu'a (Yeshu) of Nazareth; that he "practiced sorcery"—(*i.e.*, performed miracles, as was usual in those days) and beguiled and led Israel astray; that he mocked at the words of the Wise; that he expounded Scripture in the same manner as the Pharisees; that he had five disciples; that he said that he was not come to take aught away from the Law or to add to it; that he was hanged (crucified) as a false teacher and beguiler on the eve of the Passover which happened on a Sabbath; and that his disciples healed the sick in his name.[5]

2. JOSEPHUS. Additional information about Jesus comes from Flavius Josephus, a Jewish historian born in Jerusalem in the late 30's A.D. He was a member of a priestly family, received a good education, and became a member of the party of the Pharisees. During the Jewish war with Rome (A.D. 66–70), Josephus first fought as an officer with the Jewish forces and later was captured by the Romans. Gaining their favor, however, he was set free and lived thereafter in Rome, devoting himself to historical and literary work. Four works of Josephus have been preserved [6] and, although these works treat the period when early Christianity was active, no allusion to the Christian movement appears in any of them. Josephus' silence on the Christian movement, along with the scarcity of allusion to the general messianism of the first century, is probably due to his over-all apologetic purpose. He is writing to present Judaism to his Roman readers in the best possible light, and references to Christianity and other Jewish messianic move-

---

[4] See Maurice Goguel, *The Life of Jesus*, p. 72.

[5] Klausner, *Jesus of Nazareth*, p. 46.

[6] *The Jewish War*, a history of Jewish nationalism from around 175 B.C. to the Jewish War of A.D. 66–70; *The Antiquities of the Jews*, a history of the Jews from creation to the revolt of A.D. 66; *A Life*, a sequel to the *Antiquities*, defending his career and earlier writings; and *Against Apion*, a reply to criticisms of himself and the Jewish people.

ments, might have detracted from that purpose. In his *Antiquities,* however, two passages do mention Jesus:

> About the same time came Jesus, a wise man, if indeed we should call him a man. For he was a doer of miracles and the master of men who received the truth with joy. And he attracted to himself many of the Jews and many Greeks. He was the Christ, and, when after his denunciation by our leading citizens, Pilate condemned him to be crucified, those who had cared for him previously did not cease to do so, for he appeared three days afterwards, risen from the dead, just as the prophets of the Lord had announced this and many other marvels concerning him. And the group which is called that of the Christians has not yet disappeared.[7]

> Ananus called a Sanhedrin together, brought before it James, the brother of Jesus, who was called the Christ, and certain others . . . and he caused them to be stoned.[8]

The authenticity of the first passage is open to rather serious question. It does exist in the earliest Greek manuscripts of Josephus' works, but none of the manuscripts goes back earlier than the eleventh century. The real question of origin arises out of an internal study of the passage. Could Josephus actually say such things about Jesus? It seems that only a Christian could have made these statements and Josephus was not a Christian. It seems best to conclude that Josephus originally made some passing reference to Jesus which was expanded by later Christian writers to make the passage more of a confessional statement about Jesus. This modification must have taken place fairly early, for Eusebius, a Christian leader of the early fourth century, knew the passage.[9]

The second passage more probably comes directly from Josephus. Early Christian writers attributed the statement to the Jewish historian and no real reason precludes assigning its authorship to him. Both passages together, however, add no essential data to the canonical story of Jesus. They do affirm that he really lived.

The Roman Historians. Information concerning Jesus and the early Christian movement in Roman writers is scanty. That this is so may at first be a surprise because the dominance assumed by Christianity in later centuries leads easily to a belief that it always had this importance. For Roman society, however, first century Christianity was simply another superstition from the East. It was important only as

[7] *Antiquities,* XVIII, 3, 3.
[8] *Antiquities,* XX, 9, 1.
[9] Hennecke and Schneemelcher, eds., *New Testament Apocrypha,* I, pp. 436–437, for a brief treatment of the authenticity of the quotations and for a bibliography.

the cause of political and social disturbances; hence the Roman writers Pliny the Younger, Tacitus, and Suetonius speak of Christ and his disciples in the context of political and social ferment.

1. PLINY. One of the more important Roman references to early Christianity occurs in a letter written by Pliny the Younger to the Roman emperor Trajan. In the first of the second century Pliny had been sent by Trajan to be the governor of Bithynia. The senate usually appointed the provincial governor, but Bithynia had fallen into such a poor state of affairs that the emperor himself sent the "upright and conscientious, but irresolute [and] pedantic" [10] Pliny to reorganize affairs in the province. Among other difficulties, he faced an unusual set of problems with the Christians, and in a letter dated about A.D. 110 he asked the emperor for instructions. Pliny was convinced that Christianity was merely a "perverse and extravagant superstition." The Christians themselves, he stated in the letter,

. . . maintained . . . that the amount of their fault or error had been this, that it was their habit on a fixed day to assemble before daylight and recite by turns a form of words to Christ as a God; and that they bound themselves with an oath, not for any crime, but not to commit theft or robbery or adultery, not to break their word, and not to deny a deposit when demanded.[11]

Pliny's letter affirms the presence of Christianity in Bithynia and illustrates the conflict with the authorities which sometimes occurred. The specific descriptions of Christian beliefs and practices, however, arise from an examination of Christians about their faith and cannot be taken to represent an independent non-Christian source for information concerning Jesus.

2. TACITUS. The *Annals* of Tacitus provides another important reference to Christianity. Tacitus was a Roman historian who had earlier held political office, serving as a provincial governor from A.D. 112 to 116. He wrote two important historical works: *Histories*, which covers the period of Roman history from A.D. 68 to 96, and *Annals*, which covers the period from 14 to 68. Tacitus intended to paint a vivid picture of Roman life under the Caesars of the first century. The bitterness which the historian felt toward the tyrannical rulers of the period is not hidden.

In his *Annals*, Tacitus gives information concerning the great fire of

[10] J. Stevenson, ed., *A New Eusebius: Documents Illustrative of the Church to A.D. 337*, p. 13.
[11] *Ibid.*, p. 14.

Rome and tells of the people's suspicions that Nero was responsible. In the context of the report he mentions Christians and Christ.

But all human effort, all the lavish gifts of the emperor, and the propitiations of the gods, did not banish the sinister belief that the conflagration was the result of an order. Consequently, to get rid of the report, Nero fastened the guilt and inflicted the most exquisite tortures on a class hated for their abominations, called Christians by the populace. Christus, from whom the name had its origin, suffered the extreme penalty during the reign of Tiberius at the hands of one of our procurators, Pontius Pilate, and a deadly superstition, thus checked for the moment, again broke out not only in Judaea, the first source of the evil, but also in the City, where all things hideous and shameful from every part of the world meet and become popular.[12]

Tacitus is obviously drawing upon information procured from some source. The generally negative attitude toward the "deadly superstition" and the view that the Christian movement did not reawaken until the time of Nero show clearly that Tacitus was not drawing upon a Christian source. A Christian would not have been so derogatory toward his own faith. Nor does Tacitus seem to be dependent upon a Jewish source. The statement refers to Jesus as "the Christ" and seemingly suggests that Christianity is tied to the Jewish nationalistic movement, which affirmations a Jew would not make. Apparently Tacitus knew a secular source which connected Christianity with the Christ, who was crucified under Pontius Pilate.

The evidence from Tacitus is important, not because it gives information which the Christian sources do not give, but because it confirms some of the information we have in the Christian sources.

3. SUETONIUS. Two important references appear in the work of Suetonius, a young friend of Pliny. In about the year A.D. 120 while he was secretary to the emperor Hadrian, Suetonius published *The Lives of the Twelve Caesars*. The work is not history in any scientific sense. "It is a mere assemblage of superficial facts, spiced with gossip or even scandal," [13] but at two places in the work mention is made of Christianity. In his *Life of Nero*, Suetonius mentions the persecution of the Christians, "Punishment was inflicted on the Christians, a class of men given to a new and wicked superstition." [14] Nothing is said, however, about Jesus Christ. In his *Life of Claudius*, he tells of the expulsion of the Jews from Rome. "Since the Jews constantly made disturbances at the instigation of Chrestus, he expelled them from

[12] *Ibid.* p. 2.
[13] D. P. Lockwood, *A Survey of Classical Roman Literature*, II, p. 242.
[14] *New Eusebius*, p. 3.

Rome . . ." [15] The interest in this passage centers around the name "Chrestus," whose similarity to "Christus" is obvious. Is he simply an unknown Jewish agitator who stirred up trouble among the Jews at Rome? Or is this a reference to Jesus Christ? Possibly Suetonius, viewing the Christian message as an outsider, was referring to Jesus Christ and thought that this "Chrestus" about whom the people were speaking was actually in Rome at the time.

Obviously the Roman historians do not give us a great deal of information concerning Jesus Christ. The evidence from Tacitus is solid evidence against any theory of the non-historicity of Jesus, but neither Tacitus nor the other writers have preserved information to supplement the knowledge of the life of Jesus which we have in the Christian sources.

Early Noncanonical Christian Sources

In addition to the New Testament a great deal of early Christian literature has been transmitted which contains information about Jesus and teachings purported to come from Jesus. Collections of this early Christian literature have been made and can be consulted with ease.[16]

Agrapha. A variety of documents contain words ascribed to Jesus which are not in the best manuscripts of the four canonical Gospels. These sayings, or "agrapha" (literally, "unwritten things"), were perhaps remembered by his disciples, transmitted in oral form, and eventually written down. Some of these sayings of Jesus are found in New Testament writings outside the Gospels. First Corinthians 11:23–25 and Acts 20:35 contain sayings which are clearly attributed to Jesus:

For I received from the Lord what I also delivered to you, that the Lord Jesus on the night when he was betrayed took bread, and when he had given thanks, he broke it, and said, "This is my body which is for you. Do this in remembrance of me." In the same way also the cup, after supper, saying, "This cup is the new covenant in my blood. Do this, as often as you drink it, in remembrance of me." [17]

In all things I have shown you that by so toiling one must help the weak, remembering the words of the Lord Jesus, how he said, "It is more blessed to give than to receive." [18]

[15] *New Eusebius,* p. 1.

[16] An introductory guide is M. R. James, *The Apocryphal New Testament.* A more recent work is Hennecke and Schneemelcher, eds., *New Testament Apocrypha,* I.

[17] I Cor. 11:23–25.

[18] Acts 20:35.

Some of the inferior manuscripts of the canonical Gospels also contain sayings attributed to Jesus which are not contained in the oldest and best manuscripts. A frequently noted saying is found in Codex Bezae at Luke 6:4, addressed by Jesus to the man found working on the sabbath: "Man! if thou knowest what thou doest, blessed art thou! But if thou knowest not, thou art cursed and a transgressor of the law." The fact that a reading does not belong to the genuine text of the Gospel does not preclude the possibility that it does go back to Jesus himself. Statements like the one just quoted could well be genuine teachings from Jesus which for some reason or another were not incorporated in the Gospels.

Early Christian, and some non-Christian, writings outside the New Testament also contain some quotations attributed to Jesus. Some of these may go back directly or indirectly to the Synoptic tradition, others are from extant apocryphal gospels, but some derive from sources with which we are not familiar. Among papyri discovered at the turn of the twentieth century in Egypt were copies of short sayings ascribed to Jesus. The sayings, copied from apocryphal sources, are contained in fragments of codices, papyrus rolls, and even on the back of a property writ.

A few of the important agrapha from various sources are listed below: [19]

There will be dissentions and squabbles. (Justin Martyr, *Dialogue with Trypho*, XXXV, 3.)

No one can attain the kingdom of heaven who has not gone through temptation. (Tertullian, *On Baptism*, XX, 2.)

Ask for the great things, and God will add to you what is small. (Clement of Alexandria, *Stromaties*, 1, XXIV, 158.)

He who is near me is near the fire; he who is far from me is far from the kingdom. (Origen, *On Jeremiah*, Homily 20,3; Gospel of Thomas, Logion 82.)

(He who today) stands far-off will tomorrow be (near) (to you). (Papyrus Oxyrhynchus, 1224.)

While it is probable that some of the agrapha may represent an authentic tradition which may in some way be traced back to Jesus, they offer no significant supplement for knowledge of the historical Jesus.[20]

---

[19] These and other agrapha are quoted in Hennecke and Schneemelcher, eds., *New Testament Apocrypha*, I, pp. 85–116. Some of the most important of the sayings which parallel sayings in the first three Gospels are noted in *Gospel Parallels: A Synopsis of the First Three Gospels*.

[20] J. Jeremias judges that the agrapha may be seen as consisting: "(a) of tendentious coinings of sayings of the Lord; (b) of barefaced legendary inventions or legendary transferences to Jesus . . . ; (c) of Biblical and extra-Biblical cita-

Apocryphal Gospels. Still another possible source of information about Jesus is noncanonical or apocryphal "gospels," a number of which are known today.[21] Some are known only through quotations or references in early writers; the names of others are known only through lists of noncanonical books issued by early ecclesiastical groups. But some noncanonical gospels have survived from the date of origin, being copied and transmitted through the centuries, and some of these which had been lost for centuries have been rediscovered in modern times. The most valuable discovery of "lost" gospels was made at Nag Hammadi, in upper Egypt, in 1946. Thirteen Coptic codices (manuscripts in book form) with nearly eight hundred pages were uncovered. They have been dated as early as the third century and are thought to be based upon Greek originals. The codices contain about fifty different works, some previously unknown and some known only by title, quotations in early writers, or translation in other languages. Once work began on the manuscripts, nearly a decade after the discovery, it was learned that the writings once belonged to a church or monastery, the ruins of which were near the site of discovery. It is obvious that the documents were preserved by Gnostics, for some of the writings are plainly Gnostic writings and others show Gnostic tendencies.[22]

Even a cursory reading of the noncanonical gospels shows that they do not compare with the canonical Gospels. Some of them are similar to modern biblical novels in that they attempt to write fuller lives of Jesus and the disciples than the canonical Gospels give by supplying incidents and information some of which is plausible, some of which

---

tations which, because of slips of memory, have inadvertently been transferred to Jesus; (d) of sayings of Jesus given in the Gospels, which have been remodelled and worked up; (e) of sayings the attestation of which occasions doubt . . . ; (f) a very small residue of sayings in the case of which content, form, and attestation justify the opinion that they stand on a level with the sayings of our Lord (themselves historically of very differing value) contained in our four Gospels." J. Jeremias, "Isolated Sayings of the Lord," Hennecke and Schneemelcher, eds., *New Testament Apocrypha*, I, pp. 86–87. Jeremias quotes eleven sayings which may belong in the last category. But he gives some reasons for doubting a few of these, and he also lists five other sayings which may belong in that category.

[21] See Hennecke and Schneemelcher, eds., *New Testament Apocrypha*, I, pp. 71–84, 117–531.

[22] An account of the discovery and contents is given by W. Van Unnik in *Newly Discovered Gnostic Writings*. Another, and fuller, description of the discovery with a translation of the Gospel of Thomas is J. Doresse, *The Secret Books of the Egyptian Gnostics*. K. Grobel edited and translated *The Gospel of Truth* in 1960, and *The Gospel of Thomas* was published with text and translation by Harper and Row in 1959.

is not. Other apocryphal gospels support a particular religious view-point or interpret Jesus in the light of a particular heresy. The Proto-evangelium of James, for example, provides an imaginary account of the birth of the Virgin Mary, her upbringing, and the birth of Jesus. The Infancy Story of Thomas gives a group of miracles purportedly wrought by Jesus as a small boy. The Coptic Gospel of Thomas (to be differentiated from the Infancy Story of Thomas), one of the volumes of the Coptic Gnostic library found in Egypt, is a collection of purported sayings of the exalted Lord which are to be considered revelatory discourses and which are to mediate "gnosis" (knowledge) and bring "life." Some of the materials in these apocryphal gospels may come from the early tradition. In them traditions about Jesus and his disciples not recorded in the canonical Gospels may be preserved, but their significance is small indeed.

New Testament Writings Apart from the Gospels

The earliest data in the New Testament about Jesus come from the Pauline epistles, and there is additional material about Jesus in some of the later writings. Although information about Jesus in non-gospel New Testament material is not plentiful, it is valuable, for it confirms the viewpoint of the Gospels that Jesus was an actual historical figure. The way that notices of Jesus are given shows that the early Christians presupposed both the historicity of Jesus and some knowledge of his life and teaching.

Letters of Paul. Paul's major letters, the undisputed ones, tell that Jesus was a man born of a woman and subject to the law (Galatians 4:4). He was an Israelite, a descendant of David (Romans 1:3; 9:5). Jesus' brothers are mentioned (I Corinthians 9:5) and one is named as James (Galatians 1:19). Jesus carried on a ministry among Jews (Romans 15:8) with a circle of disciples known as "the Twelve" (I Corinthians 11:23–26). He was betrayed. He was crucified, buried, and on the third day he was raised from the dead (II Corinthians 13:4; I Thessalonians 2:14–15; I Corinthians 15:4).

In addition to references to the life of Jesus, Paul gives teachings of Jesus, some of which are clearly related to the Synoptic tradition. A most important saying of Jesus in Paul has been quoted above (I Corinthians 11:23–25). It tells of the institution of the Lord's Supper, citing Jesus' words as a part of the ritual. In I Corinthians 7:10–11 Paul writes, "To the married I give charge, not I but the Lord, that the wife should not separate from her husband (but if she does, let her remain single or else be reconciled to her husband)—and that the husband should not divorce his wife." [23] That Paul is confident of giving an actual quotation from Jesus is seen as Paul later, in the case of the unmarried, admits that he has "no command of the Lord" (I Corinthians 7:25). And the instruction he gives to Christians married to pagans is clearly his own instruction, "To the rest I say, not the Lord . . ." (I Corinthians 7:12). In I Corinthians 9:14, "In the same way, the Lord commanded that those who proclaim the gospel should get their living by the gospel," Paul establishes the right of those who proclaim the gospel to be supported by the churches through an appeal to a command from Jesus. Paul also gives evidence that his readers are aware of other facts from the life of Jesus. These facts are not reported by Paul, but knowledge of them is necessary to make sense of Paul's writings.[24]

Later New Testament Writings. The later New Testament writings report some facts from the life of Jesus, and, perhaps more important, presuppose the historicity of Jesus and knowledge of his life. The Epistle to the Hebrews not only contains details concerning Jesus, but also rests its teachings upon the foundation of Jesus and his death. It is obvious in Hebrews that the manifestation of Christ had taken place recently (1:2), and that his message had been passed on by those who had received his teachings (2:3). The sufferings and temptations of Jesus are used to encourage Christians who are enduring persecution (2:18; 4:15; 5:8), and the epistle treats the fate of Jesus as comparable to the fate which every man faces (9:27–28). Beyond Hebrews, the books of II Peter and Revelation are helpful. Second Peter alludes to the transfiguration (1:16–18). The book of Revelation is aware of the Gospel tradition and alludes to some specific facts in the life of Christ. Jesus Christ had a human history (1:5; 5:9; 11:8); he was slain, and, because of this, is worthy to open the seals (5:6); he is the one who was dead and is alive again (1:18; 2:8). The book of Revelation also reflects the belief in Jesus' Davidic descent (5:5; 22:16).

Clearly the materials in the New Testament apart from the Gospels provide no great amount of information which is not contained in the canonical Gospels. Yet the writers of the New Testament presuppose information about the historical Jesus and build their writings upon this knowledge, and what information is contained in their writings

[23] Compare Mark 10:11–12 and Matt. 5:32.
[24] See Romans 15:8; I Cor. 13; Gal. 3:1; Philippians 2:5–11.

confirms the information of the Gospels. One historian of the life of Jesus asserts that in the light of extremely skeptical judgments of the validity of the Gospels' witness to Jesus "it is important for the historian to be able to state that the testimony of Paul confirms that of the Gospels, and confirms its reliability." [25] Thus the non-gospel material in the New Testament, like noncanonical references to Jesus, add little to the over-all picture of Jesus, but it does confirm the historicity of Jesus and some of the events recorded in the Synoptic Gospels.

THE CANONICAL GOSPELS

The scanty data available outside the Gospels make it clear that no serious study of Jesus can proceed on the basis of such limited information. An historical figure emerges, but no real story of Jesus can be reconstructed. Any large scale presentation of the life and teachings of Jesus then depends upon the four canonical Gospels. However, as with sources for any other historical person or event, the nature of the Gospels must be determined and appropriate means devised for their use in a study of Jesus.[26]

The Nature of the Gospels

Religious Literature. The Gospels are plainly not objective presentations of Jesus' life and teachings. The writers were Christians who had accepted Jesus as Christ and Lord and who were writing because of this very fact! The Christians believed that what God had promised in the Hebrew Scriptures had begun to be accomplished in Jesus of Nazareth. The new age had been inaugurated in his coming, a beginning adequately attested by his resurrection. The report in the Book of Acts on Peter's sermon in Jerusalem sounds this note:

Men of Israel, hear these words: Jesus of Nazareth, a man attested by God with mighty works and wonders and signs which God did through him in your midst, as you yourselves know—this Jesus, delivered up according to the definite plan and foreknowledge of God, you crucified and killed by the hands of lawless men. But God raised him up, having loosed the pangs of death, because it was not possible for him to be held by it.[27]

The Gospels are written from this Christian perspective for quite definite religious purposes. The writer of the Gospel of John frankly

---

[25] Goguel, *The Life of Jesus*, p. 119.
[26] See Stephen Neill, *The Interpretation of the New Testament, 1861–1961*, pp. 104–136, for a survey of developments in the study of the life of Jesus by means of the Gospels.
[27] Acts 2:22–24.

gives his evangelistic aim in telling about Jesus: "These are written that you may believe that Jesus is the Christ, the Son of God, and that believing you may have life in his name." [28] He was not primarily interested in discussing the questions about what Jesus did and what Jesus said. Rather, he is concerned with who Jesus was, that is, the meaning of the entire Christ event. In some sense Jesus' words and deeds are presupposed and questions of theological import are asked, "Who was the One who did these things? Who was the man who taught these things?" John's testimony is that he is the "only Son from the Father" (1:14), "the Lamb of God" (1:29), "Rabbi" (1:38), "the Messiah" (1:41), and consequently attention must be given to his deeds and words. Although the Synoptic Gospels do not state their purpose in such a direct way, that they are controlled by a theological purpose is seen from their general content, organization, and specific treatment of Jesus Christ.

Written by Later Disciples. As written documents the Gospels date from a period sometime after Jesus' life and ministry. The Synoptic Gospels, acknowledged by scholars to stand closest to traditions going back to Jesus, were written not by original disciples of Jesus but by later Christians. The earliest was written sometime around A.D. 65. The names of Mark and Luke are connected with the Second and Third Gospels [29] although these men were not among the earliest disciples. Matthew's name is connected with the First Gospel, but there is good reason to believe that the apostle Matthew did not write the Gospel in its present form.[30] None of the Gospels, therefore, were written by eye witnesses or companions of Jesus.

Dependent Upon Oral Sources. Since the Gospels are not the stenographic reports of those who had seen and heard Jesus, they are necessarily dependent upon earlier sources—originally oral sources. This lack of direct relationship of the Gospels to the historical events in the life of Jesus is both advantageous and disadvantageous. From the point of a scientific history, the Gospels suffer severe limitations. The traditions contained in them have been selected and modified by the Christians who were passing them on. The faith of the Christian community could not have failed to affect the selection of the tradition and the formation of each unit of the tradition. When the Gospels

[28] John 20:31.
[29] See below, pp. 460–462, 463.
[30] See below, pp. 474–475.

are studied, account must be taken not only of the events reported but also of the faith which molded the Gospel tradition.

However, the process of oral transmission did preserve narratives and sayings of Jesus which would otherwise have been lost! If there had been no oral transmission, no information would be available. Further, the process of oral transmission was a relatively dependable method of preservation in the first century. The orally transmitted word was more highly valued among the Jews of the first century than it is today, actually being regarded as important as the written word, perhaps more highly valued by some. One rabbi paid the tribute to a disciple that "he was like a well-plastered cistern that loses not a drop." [31]

Paul gives evidence of the transmission of the Jesus tradition among early Christians. In a letter to the church at Corinth Paul declared that his message was that which he had received from those Christians before him.

For *I delivered to you* as of first importance *what I also received*, that Christ died for our sins in accordance with the scripture, that he was buried, that he was raised on the third day in accordance with the scriptures, and that he appeared to Cephas, then to the twelve.[32]

The verb Paul uses means "to pass on what one has received." It is equivalent to the Latin word *traditio,* from which derives the English word "tradition." [33]

The process of oral transmission continued even during and after the tradition in the Gospels was written down. The author of the Gospel of Luke acknowledged dependence upon oral tradition:

Inasmuch as many have undertaken to compile a narrative of the things which have been accomplished among us, just as they were delivered to us by those who from the beginning were eyewitnesses and ministers of the word, it seemed good to me also, having followed all things closely from some time past, to write an orderly account for you, most excellent Theophilus, that you may know the truth concerning the things of which you have been informed.[34]

A comparison of different treatments of the same sayings of Jesus suggests that, although these were transmitted in a manner analogous to the transmission of the teachings of other rabbis, the words of Jesus were presented and transmitted with the freedom gained from the

---

[31] Quoted in Francis Beare, *The Earliest Records of Jesus,* p. 54.
[32] I Cor. 15:3–5. Italics added.
[33] See also I Cor. 11:23ff.
[34] Luke 1:1–4.

awareness that their meaning, not their form, was the important thing. A great English New Testament scholar, B. F. Westcott, declared concerning this fact, "Thank God, we are not called to rehearse a stereotyped tradition, but to unfold a growing message." [35]

Dependent Upon Written Sources. Written materials as well as oral materials are mentioned in Luke's prologue, indicating that the Gospels utilized written sources as well as oral traditions. The Synoptic Gospels' dependence upon written sources is confirmed by a comparison of the Gospels with one another. When the three are studied side by side, it becomes clear that (1) their content and arrangement of materials are closely related, (2) the basic course of Jesus' activities is the same in each, (3) the narratives portraying Jesus' ministry are used in a similar way, and (4) the discourses of Jesus share the same characteristics in the Synoptics. The close relationship extends to matters of style, language, and even specific wording. Such marked similarity in subject matter, arrangement, and external form leads to the inevitable conclusion that the Synoptics are somehow literarily related to one another. But the literary relationship cannot be a simple one, for at places the three Gospels differ significantly from one another in form and content.

They are certainly far from being carbon copies of each other. For example, each Gospel has its own way of beginning its story. Mark opens with the ministry of John and the baptism of Jesus; Matthew and Luke both have rather extensive birth narratives, but these birth stories differ from one another in essential features. Even such a routine item as Jesus' genealogy is molded differently in terms of each Gospel's purpose. Matthew and Luke have great amounts of discourse material which is missing in Mark, but in turn they vary considerably in their presentation of the discourse material. Matthew presents the material in five long discourses, while Luke collects it along with narrative materials in the sections 6:2–8:3 and 9:51–18:14. Each Gospel also has unique material, Matthew and Luke containing much more than Mark. Clearly the Synoptics use their sources, both oral and written, to develop distinctive theological interpretation of Jesus, considered by all these to be pivotal to the Church's life and faith.

The Use of the Gospels in a Study of Jesus

The nature of the Gospels demands that any use of the Gospels in a study of the historical Jesus take into account the transmission of

[35] Quoted in Beare, *The Earliest Records of Jesus,* p. 54 n.

the narratives and sayings of Jesus during the oral period, the literary relationships of the Synoptic Gospels, and the theological viewpoints and literary activity of the individual Gospel writers. Intensive scholarly studies have been carried on in each of these areas. The earliest study, "source criticism," concentrated on the literary relations of the Synoptic Gospels. Later, emphasis centered on the oral period; this study is called "form criticism." Next came studies of each Gospel as a literary unit or "redaction criticism." [36]

Source Criticism. The scientific study of the literary relationships of the Synoptic Gospels has been carried on since the eighteenth century and some positive results have assisted in a study of the historical Jesus.[37] The solution of the Synoptic problem (that is, the possible literary relationships between Mark, Matthew, and Luke) has led to three basic affirmations: (1) Mark is the earliest written Gospel and was used as a source by both Matthew and Luke. (2) Matthew and Luke share a large body of material not present in Mark, called Q (from the German *Quelle*, "source"). (3) Matthew and Luke each had sources peculiar to themselves. M is used to designate Matthew's peculiar material, L for Luke's.

1. THE PRIORITY OF MARK. A number of facts combine to make the priority of Mark a logical conclusion. The material of Mark is almost completely contained in Matthew and Luke—only six short sections of Mark are found in neither Matthew nor Luke. Within the material common to Mark, Matthew, and Luke there is extensive agreement in vocabulary. The most logical explanation is that Mark was written first and later Matthew and Luke used Mark, incorporating large blocks of his material and often utilizing his vocabulary. The following sections from the Synoptic Gospels illustrate the literary relationship between the three. A careful comparison clearly shows that the three accounts are essentially the same with some minor editorial additions by Matthew and Luke.

[36] Since the findings of redaction criticism relate more specifically to each Gospel, these are dealt with in connection with the study of the individual Gospels. See below, pp. 451–498.

[37] The ancients, of course, noted the similarities and differences between the Synoptic Gospels, but they assumed that these were due to the *different* eyewitnesses of the *same* events. The Fathers, especially Augustine, held Matthew as the original Gospel with Mark as a condensed version of Matthew and Luke depending upon both Mark and Matthew. See Burnett H. Streeter, *The Four Gospels: A Study of Origins,* for a full treatment of evidence concerning the relationships of the Gospels. See FBK, pp. 33–60, for a concise treatment of the "Synoptic Problem."

Matthew 22:15–22	*Mark 12:13–17*	*Luke 20:20–26*
Then the Pharisees went and took counsel how to entangle him in his talk. And they sent their disciples to him, along with the Herodians,	And they sent to him some of the Pharisees and some of the Herodians, to entrap him in his talk. And they came and	So they watched him, and sent spies, who pretended to be sincere, that they might take hold of what he said, so as to deliver him up to the authority and jurisdiction of the governor. They asked him, "Teacher, we know that you speak and teach rightly, and show no partiality,
saying, "Teacher, we know that you are true, and teach the way of God truthfully, and care for no man; for you do not regard the position of men.	said to him, "Teacher, we know that you are true, and care for no man; for you do not regard the position of men, but truly teach the way of God.	but truly teach the way of God.
Tell us, then, what you think. Is it lawful to pay taxes to Caesar, or not?"	Is it lawful to pay taxes to Caesar, or not? Should we pay them, or should we not?"	Is it lawful for us to give tribute to Caesar, or not?"
But Jesus, aware of their malice, said "Why put me to the test, you hypocrites? Show me the money for the tax." And they brought him a coin.	But knowing their hypocrisy, he said to them, "Why put me to the test? Bring me a coin, and let me look at it." And they brought one.	But he perceived their craftiness, and said to them, "Show me a coin.
And Jesus said to them, "Whose likeness and inscription is this?" They said, "Caesar's." Then he said to them, "Render therefore to Caesar the things that are Caesar's, and to God the things that are God's." When they heard it,	And he said to them, "Whose likeness and inscription is this?" They said to him, "Caesar's." Jesus said to them, "Render to Caesar the things that are Caesar's, and to God the things that are God's." And they	Whose likeness and inscription has it?" They said, "Caesar's." He said to them, "Then render to Caesar the things that are Caesar's, and to God the things that are God's."
		And they were not able in the presence of the people to catch him by what he said; but marveling at his answer they were silent.
they marveled; and they left him and went away.	were amazed at him.	

The sequence of the narratives in the Gospels also points to the priority of Mark. In the material parallel to Mark, Matthew and Luke generally agree with the Marcan sequence. When the Marcan sequence is not followed, Matthew and Luke rarely agree with each other.

Changes in the language and subject matter in the materials common to Matthew, Mark, and Luke is a third argument for the priority of Mark. Matthew and Luke often modify the Semitically-colored Greek of Mark and other awkward Greek constructions to a better form of Greek. Changes in the subject matter also constitute important evidence. In Matthew 3:16, for example, the word "immediately" is not understandable in the context, but it is easily explained when Mark's use by Matthew is assumed, for Mark 1:10, "and when he came up out of the water, immediately he saw the heavens open and the spirit descending upon him like a dove," provides the word. Again, in Matthew 9:2 there is no indication of a cause for Jesus observing the faith of the men who brought the paralytic; but Mark 2:4 tells about the unusual task of bringing the sick through the dug-up roof, which is evidence of their faith. Matthew and Luke are clearly dependent upon Mark.

2. THE EXISTENCE OF Q. Matthew and Luke have an extensive amount of common material which is not taken from Mark. This body of material is usually referred to as Q and may be illustrated from numerous places in Matthew and Luke. Compare Jesus' saying on the watchful householder in Matthew and Luke.

Matthew 24:43–44	*Luke 12:39–40*
But know this, that if the householder had known in what part of the night the thief was coming, he would have watched and would not have let his house be broken into. Therefore you also must be ready; for the Son of man is coming at an hour you do not expect.	But know this, that if the householder had known at what hour the thief was coming, he would have been awake and would not have left his house to be broken into. You also must be ready; for the Son of man is coming at an hour you do not expect.

The passages above and many other passages in Matthew and Luke are almost identical to each other, but have no parallel in Mark. Obviously these bear some literary relationship to each other. The most simple possibilities are (1) that Matthew used Luke, (2) that Luke used Matthew, or (3) that both Matthew and Luke used a common source. Explanations (1) and (2) are generally rejected for several reasons. The different arrangement of the material in each Gospel points away from this solution. In Luke this common material is mainly in two sections inserted into the Marcan narrative; [38] in Matthew the material is contained mainly in five major discourses of Jesus.[39] If Matthew used Luke or Luke used Matthew, it is difficult to explain why either rearranged the material. Perhaps as important is the internal evidence. At times the material appears in a more original form in Matthew and at times it is more original in Luke. This certainly argues against either one being used by the other.

Hence the most likely resolution of their literary relationship is the third possibility. Matthew and Luke not only used Mark, but also a non-Marcan source. This non-Marcan material common to Matthew and Luke is called Q. It is, of course, impossible to reconstruct the original source from the materials in Matthew and Luke (just as Mark could not be reproduced precisely from the Marcan content of Matthew and Luke). Yet the basic character of Q is evident. It is mainly a collection of the sayings of Jesus to which are added also some material about John the Baptist, a narrative of the temptations of Jesus, several controversy stories, and miracles.

Why the Q collection was created and whether it was written or oral are matters of continuing speculation and debate. The frequent verbal agreements of Matthew and Luke suggest, but do not prove, that the source was written, and generally Q must have come into existence to meet needs of the Christian community. The sayings of Jesus, now the risen Lord, would have given continuing direction to the life of the Christian community. Nonetheless more is unknown than known about this illusive document.

3. MATERIAL PECULIAR TO MATTHEW AND LUKE. There is additional material in Matthew and Luke the origin of which is unexplained from the assumption of the sources Mark and Q. That is to say, both Matthew and Luke contain material peculiar to themselves. Some of the material peculiar to either Gospel could have come from Q, and some is perhaps the direct composition of the authors of the Gospels; but all of the material peculiar to Matthew and Luke cannot be explained on these bases. Likely some other sources were used.

A number of years ago the assumption was that there were two written documents roughly equal to the unique material of each Gospel. Matthew's special source was called "M," and Luke's was designated "L." Today there is great hesitation in crediting the special material

---

[38] Luke 6:20–8:3 and 9:51–18:14.
[39] Matt. 5–7; 10; 13; 18; and 23–25.

of Matthew and Luke to *written* sources. It is still possible that one or both Gospel writers drew heavily from one important written collection, each selecting materials distinctive to himself, but more probably the symbols M and L should be used to designate simply the special material of Matthew and Luke without pronouncing a judgment about either the existence or the nature of these sources.

This analysis of the sources of the Synoptic Gospels does give some help in a treatment of the life and teachings of Jesus. It shows that the framework of the life as presented by the Synoptics was not in-

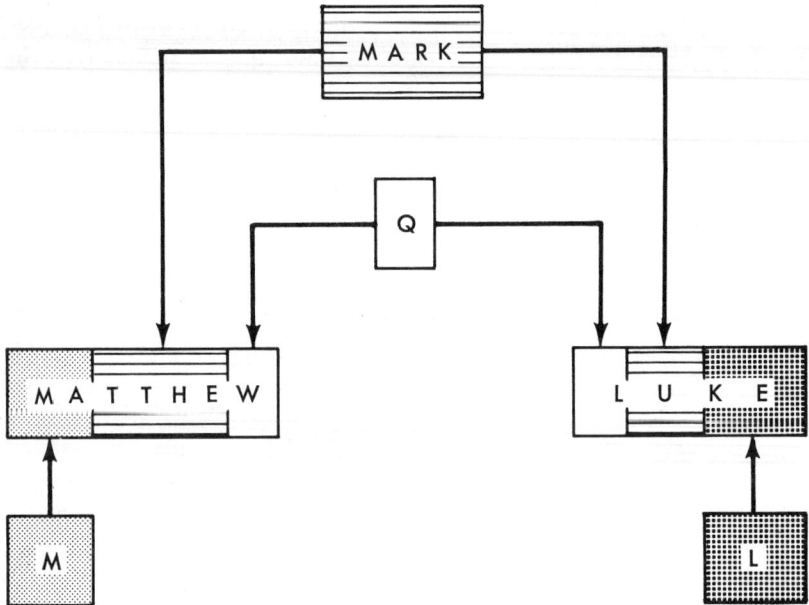

Figure 2–1. Diagram showing the literary relationships of the Synoptic Gospels. The size of the rectangles corresponds roughly to the number of verses in the sources.

dependently designed by three writers, but came from Mark. The analysis also demonstrates that the teachings of Jesus were not originally placed in an unalterable chronological or topical order but that Matthew and Luke arranged them freely as best fitted their confessional portrait of Jesus. Source criticism is a valuable tool to study specific sayings and narratives, but even its most scientific use fails to take account of all aspects of the nature of the Gospels.

Form Criticism. An analysis of the sources of the Synoptic Gospels obviously does not carry us back to Jesus himself. Not only do Matthew and Luke use earlier written and oral traditions produced for religious purposes, but Mark itself developed out of earlier materials. The literary analysis of the Gospels, then, forces us back to the oral period, and this is exactly the history of Gospel criticism. At the beginning of the twentieth century a school of study known as "form criticism" developed as a tool to study the traditions of the Gospel in the oral period.[40]

1. ORIGIN OF FORM CRITICISM. Form criticism of the Gospels developed out of the scholarly concern to get beyond study of the literary relationships of the Gospels to each other. Vincent Taylor characterized it as "the child of disappointment" of source criticism. But it was also influenced by developments of studies in Greek literature and in Old Testament literature which dealt with recurring literary forms which were altered in the process of transmission. By careful study of the forms scholars were able to trace the traditional forms to earlier stages. H. Gunkel, an Old Testament scholar, applied the method of form criticism to the narratives of Genesis, and when two of his students applied his principles to the study of the Gospels, New Testament form criticism was born. These men were Martin Dibelius and Rudolf Bultmann.[41]

The term "form" is used because it was held that the traditions in the Gospels could be analyzed in terms of the forms in which they circulated in the oral period. It was also supposed that the process of transmission effected changes and developments in the forms. The challenge was to determine the history of the tradition so that the earliest forms of the narratives and sayings of Jesus could be determined.

2. PRESUPPOSITIONS OF FORM CRITICISM. The method of form criticism becomes logical only when two basic presuppositions are accepted. First, the sayings of Jesus and narratives about Jesus circu-

[40] See E. Basil Redlich, *Form Criticism: Its Value and Limitations,* and Rudolf Bultmann and Karl Kundsin, *Form Criticism: A New Method of New Testament Research,* for an introduction to the discipline of form criticism. See also Martin Dibelius, *From Tradition to Gospel,* and Rudolf Bultmann, *The History of the Synoptic Tradition.*

[41] See Dibelius, *From Tradition to Gospel,* and Bultmann, *History of the Synoptic Tradition.* The original German editions of both works appeared after World War I (1919 and 1921, respectively). Both works have passed through several editions and have now been translated into English.

lated orally as independent units. For numerous reasons it is generally thought that the chronological and topographical framework of Mark does not go back to Jesus himself but is at least partly the creation of the author. Attention is called especially to the vague notices of time and place in the Gospel of Mark. Orally transmitted units lie behind the organization in Mark. Very early, even before the writing of Mark, oral units may have been joined into connected narratives. One of the earliest of these was the passion narrative with the basic scheme of Last Supper, arrest, trial, crucifixion, and resurrection appearances. The second basic presupposition is that the needs of the early Christian community played an important role in the selection, formation, and transmission of the sayings and narratives. Both of these presuppositions are accepted by all who use form criticism.

Within this context of agreement, however, scholarly opinion varies widely about the original form of the sayings and narratives and their history in the life of the early Church. Some see the Church as the formulator of the tradition with little concern for historical events; others believe that the Christian community only molded historical reality in the form of its own faith. Some emphasize preaching as the most important factor in transmitting the material; others stress worship. Other factors would certainly include teaching or instruction, conflict and debate with the Jews, and church administration. There is general agreement about some of the forms which the materials took, but there is also some disagreement, especially about the terms to be used and the specific form to be attributed to certain passages.[42]

3. METHOD OF FORM CRITICISM. Vincent Taylor provides a useful, although not necessarily unique, vocabulary for the study of form criticism. Taylor is a cautious form critic who evaluated the method in 1933, over a decade after it was introduced.[43] He classifies the forms of the units of tradition as pronouncement stories, sayings, parables, miracle stories, and stories about Jesus.[44]

[42] The form critics also vary in their estimate of the historical value of the individual sections of the Synoptic tradition. Bultmann in particular is noted for his "skeptical" position regarding the historicity of much of the material of the Synoptic tradition.

[43] Vincent Taylor, *The Formation of the Gospel Tradition.*

[44] Bultmann divides the sayings of the Gospel tradition into (1) logia, or wisdom sayings; (2) prophetic and apocalyptic sayings; (3) legal sayings and church rules; (4) I-sayings in which Jesus speaks of himself; (5) parables; (6) apothegms, a decisive saying or pronouncement as the climax of a brief narrative. He also gives narrative materials as: (1) miracle stories, and (2) historical narratives and legends. Martin Dibelius divides the narrative material into five forms: (1) paradigms; (2) *Novellen* or wonder stories; (3) legends, edifying stories of a

(a) *Pronouncement stories* are brief narratives of an encounter of Jesus with one or more persons which culminate in a statement or pronouncement of Jesus. The stories contain words of Jesus useful in preaching, teaching, and controversy with outside opponents. It is possible that some of the narratives are "typical" scenes created out of the Church's memory of Jesus to act as a carrier for the saying. Mark 12:13–17 illustrates the pronouncement story at its best. The attached pronouncement is italicized.

And they sent to him some of the Pharisees and some of the Herodians, to entrap him in his talk. And they came and said to him, "Teacher, we know that you are true, and care for no man; for you do not regard the position of men, but truly teach the way of God. Is it lawful to pay taxes to Caesar, or not? Should we pay them, or should we not?" But knowing their hypocrisy, he said to them, "Why put me to the test? Bring me a coin, and let me look at it." And they brought one. And he said to them, "Whose likeness and inscription is this?" They said to him, "Caesar's." Jesus said to them, *"Render to Caesar the things that are Caesar's, and to God the things that are God's."* And they were amazed at him.

(b) *Sayings.* Many sayings of Jesus circulated independently of the narrative framework of the pronouncement story. The Gospels contain collections of such sayings. Some of these seem to be collections of sayings which were grouped somewhat artificially during the oral period. Mark 4:21–25 is such a collection.

And he said to them, "Is a lamp brought in to be put under a bushel, or under a bed, and not on a stand? For there is nothing hid, except to be made manifest; nor is anything secret, except to come to light. If any man has ears to hear, let him hear." And he said to them, "Take heed what you hear; the measure you give will be the measure you get, and still more will be given you. For to him who has will more be given; and from him who has not, even what he has will be taken away."

But in certain instances the collections in our Gospels may go back to a sequence of sayings given in that form by Jesus and transmitted as a group until they were written down. This form is illustrated by Luke 6:27–38.

"But I say to you that hear, Love your enemies, do good to those who hate you, bless those who curse you, pray for those who abuse you. To him who strikes you on the cheek, offer the other also; and from him who takes

---

holy person; (4) the passion story; and (5) myths which tell of the invasion of human life by supernatural power. Sayings are organized by Dibelius into: (1) wisdom sayings; (2) comparisons or similitudes; (3) narratives parables; (4) prophetic utterances; (5) concise commands; (6) more elaborate demands; and (7) sayings concerning the nature of the speaker.

away your cloak do not withhold your coat as well. Give to every one who begs from you; and of him who takes away your goods do not ask them again. And as you wish that men would do to you, do so to them.

"If you love those who love you, what credit is that to you? For even sinners love those who love them. And if you do good to those who do good to you, what credit is that to you? For even sinners do the same. And if you lend to those from whom you hope to receive, what credit is that to you? Even sinners lend to sinners, to receive as much again. But love your enemies, and do good, and lend, expecting nothing in return; and your reward will be great, and you will be sons of the Most High; for he is kind to the ungrateful and the selfish. Be merciful, even as your Father is merciful.

"Judge not, and you will not be judged; condemn not, and you will not be condemned; forgive, and you will be forgiven; give, and it will be given to you; good measure, pressed down, shaken together, running over, will be put into your lap. For the measure you give will be the measure you get back."

(c) *Parables.* A rich element in the early Christian tradition is the parables. A parable is a narrative of a commonplace experience which suggests an analogy to a spiritual truth. The Gospels, of course, contain numerous parables; a well-known one appears in Mark 4:3–8.

"Listen! A sower went out to sow. And as he sowed, some seed fell along the path, and the birds came and devoured it. Other seed fell on rocky ground, where it had not much soil, and immediately it sprang up, since it had no depth of soil; and when the sun rose it was scorched, and since it had no root it withered away. Other seed fell among thorns and the thorns grew up and choked it, and it yielded no grain. And other seeds fell into good soil and brought forth grain, growing up and increasing and yielding thirtyfold and sixtyfold and a hundredfold."

The parable is used to express a single truth independent of the parable itself, but in transmission the parable sometimes tended to be allegorized. Mark 4:13–20 is an allegory based on the parable in Mark 4:3–8.

And he said to them, "Do you not understand this parable? How then will you understand all the parables? The sower sows the word. And these are the ones along the path, where the word is sown; when they hear, Satan immediately comes and takes away the word which is sown in them. And these in like manner are the ones sown upon rocky ground, who, when they hear the word, immediately receive it with joy; and they have no root in themselves, but endure for a while; then, when tribulation or persecution arises on account of the word, immediately they fall away. And others are the ones sown among thorns; they are those who hear the word, but the cares of the world, and the delight in riches, and the desire for other things, enter in and choke the word, and it proves unfruitful. But those that were sown upon the good soil are the ones who hear the word and accept it and bear fruit, thirtyfold and sixtyfold and a hundredfold."

(d) *Miracle Stories.* Numerous miracle stories narrate miraculous acts of Jesus. The form of the Synoptic miracle stories is the same as the form of Jewish and Hellenistic miracle stories. The general pattern includes three elements: a description of the circumstances, a statement of the miraculous act, and a description of the consequences. Mark 1:40–45 shows the pattern of the miracle story.

And a leper came to him beseeching him, and kneeling said to him, "If you will, you can make me clean." Moved with pity, he stretched out his hand and touched him, and said to him, "I will; be clean." And immediately the leprosy left him, and he was made clean. And he sternly charged him, and sent him away at once, and said to him, "See that you say nothing to any one; but go, show yourself to the priest, and offer for your cleansing what Moses commanded, for a proof to the people." But he went out and began to talk freely about it, and to spread the news, so that Jesus could no longer openly enter a town, but was out in the country; and people came to him from every quarter.

Certain narratives of a miraculous act are included among the pronouncement stories [45] and in at least one instance two miracle stories are combined in the same narrative.[46]

(e) *Stories about Jesus.* Taylor classifies as "stories about Jesus" all the narrative material which does not fit into the categories above. He admits that the stories in the category "stories about Jesus" have no common structural form, but almost all of them center upon Jesus.[47] Taylor suggests that practical aims and not narrative interests were responsible for the formation of these stories. As the stories were transmitted the figure of Jesus came into stronger focus and secondary features faded out.

Form criticism is clearly very subjective and not a method which supersedes all other methods of study. However, it can be used as an important tool for clarifying the early forms of the gospel tradition and elaborating the meaning of Jesus for early believers. Taylor declares:

Form-Criticism is not an instrument by which we can solve the problems of Gospel Origins, but it can play its part in that task. It will break in our hands if we use it for ends for which it was never intended; for other purposes it cannot be bettered. It has certainly succeeded in pointing out definite narrative-forms which meet us in popular tradition, and has made important suggestions regarding the life-story of these and the causes which

[45] See Mark 2:3–12.
[46] Mark 5:21–43.
[47] Some of them are about other persons, such as the story of the birth of John the Baptist.

gave them shape. But its most valuable service is that it helps us to penetrate the hinterland of the decades from 30 to 50 A.D. and place ourselves in imagination among the young Palestinian communities, so that we can enter the 'twilight-period' and, in the words of A. Myer, 'are permitted still to be earwitnesses, to hear the disciples of Jesus and through them Jesus Himself.' [48]

The Current Quest.   Gospel criticism has moved from source criticism to form criticism to a study of each Gospel as a theological creation, a creation which uses previous oral and written material to be sure, but a work which places the materials in the context of a particular religious interpretation. The specific interests of each writer must be kept in mind when the Gospels are used in the effort to discover the life and teachings of Jesus.

It has become increasingly clear that the Gospel writers were not concerned to present a comprehensive biography of Jesus and that a scientific biography of Jesus cannot be written by using their work. The initial result of this insight, perhaps particularly the result of the work of Rudolf Bultmann and his followers, was a profound skepticism concerning any knowledge of the historical Jesus. In a work written in 1926 Bultmann said, "I do indeed think that we can now know almost nothing concerning the life and personality of Jesus, since the early Christian sources show no interest in either, are moreover fragmentary and often legendary; and other sources about Jesus do not exist." [49]   Bultmann judged that the study of the life and personality of the earthly Jesus was impossible because of the nature of the sources, but he also saw such study as unnecessary and illegitimate since the basis of Christian faith is not the earthly Jesus but the Christ of faith proclaimed by the Church. In light of such radical skepticism some scholars refused to take the form critical method seriously. Generally, however, the method has been accepted but some initial extreme conclusions of form critics have been challenged and modified. Many of these revisions have given more serious consideration to the impact of the activities and sayings of Jesus on followers who formed the core of the early Christian community and to the importance of the presence of eye witnesses in the early Christian community during the very period when the traditions about Jesus were remembered, interpreted, and transmitted.

Contemporary scholarship is positive in its attitude toward the possibilities of the use of source and form criticism to arrive at genuine

---

[48] Taylor, *The Formation of the Gospel Tradition*, pp. 20–21.
[49] *Jesus and the Word*, p. 8.

understanding of the traditions of the historical Jesus. In fact, it is common to speak of a "new quest" for the historical Jesus. This quest is not the same as the pre-source and form criticism quest. It recognizes the impossibility of writing a biography of Jesus, but does feel that serious work can be done in a treatment of the person and teachings of Jesus Christ.

Ernst Käsemann, a student of Bultmann, gave a major impetus for the new quest in an address on "The Problem of the Historical Jesus" in October, 1953. He plainly disagreed with Bultmann's view that it is not legitimate to go beyond the proclamation of the Church to treat the historic Jesus. He pointed out that the earliest Christians were concerned not only with the Christ of faith but also with the earthly Jesus.[50] In 1956, shortly after Käsemann's address, another student of Bultmann, Günther Bornkamm, published a pioneering work in the new quest entitled *Jesus of Nazareth*. Bornkamm took up the question of the historical Jesus raised by Käsemann: ". . . it cannot be seriously maintained that the Gospels and their tradition do not allow enquiry after the historical Jesus. Not only do they allow, they demand this effort." [51] Many specialized studies are now being written on the words and deeds of Jesus.[52]

The modern quest utilizes insights of several disciplines. It recognizes that the Synoptic tradition was transmitted in the oral period in independent units (with the exception of the passion narrative) and that the tradition was used by the Church in different environments: the Palestinian Jewish-Christian church which preached to Jews in Palestine; the Hellenistic Jewish church which confronted the Judaism outside of Palestine; and the Hellenistic Gentile church which confronted a completely Hellenistic world. Our Gospels were written in the context of the Gentile mission and the authentic tradition in them must have passed through the various stages of development of the Church.

Students agree that the results of source criticism must be applied

[50] The address by Käsemann is in English translation in *Essays on New Testament Themes*. J. M. Robinson, *A New Quest of the Historical Jesus*, treats the origins of the new quest. He also shows that some scholars have been studying and writing on the historical Jesus apart from a thoroughgoing form critical approach.

[51] Bornkamm, *Jesus of Nazareth*, p. 22.

[52] Representative of these studies in the English-speaking world are Reginald H. Fuller, *Interpreting the Miracles* and *The Foundations of New Testament Christology;* Harvey K. McArthur, *Understanding the Sermon on the Mount;* W. D. Davies, *The Setting of the Sermon on the Mount;* and Norman Perrin, *Rediscovering the Teaching of Jesus.*

to the tradition in a study of the earthly Jesus. When a unit of the tradition occurs in all three Synoptic Gospels, Mark is to be taken as the earliest written form of that unit. When a unit of the tradition occurs in Mark and Q, the unit may be carried back even further. It is incorrect, however, to assume that a unit in Mark and/or Q is necessarily more primitive than a unit in the material unique to Matthew or to Luke since the materials all passed successively through Palestinian and Hellenistic stages. Also, since the sources Mark, Q, M, and L may be regarded as relatively independent, the possibility of the historicity of a unit which is repeated in two or more sources may be regarded as being increased.

Form criticism in its strictest sense is then applied to the unit of tradition, when possible, to trace the history of the tradition and discover its earliest form. The principle of multiple attestation found helpful in a study of the sources helps here also. When a teaching of Jesus or an historical fact concerning Jesus occurs in more than one form the possibility of the authenticity of that teaching or fact is increased. If, for example, a piece of factual information occurs in a pronouncement story, a miracle story, and a parable, it may be assumed that the fact was not created for the forms, but existed before the forms were created.

What next? It cannot be assumed that the unit of tradition which has been studied with the methods of source and form criticism goes back to Jesus even in the earliest form which can be discovered. How may we distinguish between authentic and inauthentic material? Since Jesus spoke Aramaic and ministered in Palestine, two additional clues are afforded. If a saying attributed to Jesus has Aramaic traits or if it reflects the Palestinian world, it may be considered authentic.[53] Genuine sayings of Jesus would have been spoken in Aramaic and would reflect the Palestinian conditions, but of course so would sayings of the Palestinian church after Jesus. So the linguistic and environmental criteria must be applied with some care and used in conjunction with other tests.

Rudolf Bultmann, in his treatment of the parables, gave criteria which enables scholars to judge that a *saying* is authentic. He indicated that a parable is to be considered authentic where its content cannot be attributed to the Judaism of Jesus' day or to the later church, that is, where the content is opposed to contemporary Jewish

[53] These principles are applied by Joachim Jeremias in his works *The Parables of Jesus* and *The Eucharistic Words of Jesus*. See also, his *The Problem of the Historical Jesus*.

morality and piety, and where the parable contains no traits which could be attributed to later Christianity.[54] This may be stated positively in a form which is found useful by students of the earthly Jesus: we may be sure that sayings attributed to Jesus are authentic when they differ from contemporary Judaism or from the post-Easter proclamation of the Church. This criterion of dissimilarity or distinctiveness is, of course, a criterion which leads to minimal rather than maximal results. Jesus may have used a teaching of Judaism, and the early church's proclamation could have come from Jesus. But the following of the criterion of distinctiveness is judged by students of the quest to be much safer than following the principle of accepting everything in doubt.

The criterion of consistency or coherence has been suggested to supplement the criterion of dissimilarity or distinctiveness.[55] This standard may be applied after the central message of Jesus has been established by other tests. The criterion may be stated thus: material may be considered authentic if it is consistent with or coheres with the material established as authentic by the test of distinctiveness.[56]

The new quest utilizes the results of the critical studies of source, form, and redaction criticism and admits that a complete scientific biography of Jesus will not be written because the sources are not available. Nevertheless, the major sources, the Gospels, present an historical Jesus who spoke and acted, and the remainder of the New Testament, indeed the entire Christian movement, derives from Jesus Christ. A study of Jesus by means of an informed study of the Gospels is necessary and possible. All the answers may not become self-evident, but the work and words of Jesus do lie behind the Synoptic tradition. The tradition bears witness to the early Church and to the convictions of the specific Gospels writers, but it also highlights insight into the life of Jesus of Nazareth.

SUGGESTED READINGS

Noncanonical Sources

HENNECKE, EDGAR, *New Testament Apocrypha*, Vol. I, ed. Wilhelm Schneemelcher, tr. R. Mcl. Wilson (Westminster, 1963).

[54] See Bultmann, *History of the Synoptic Tradition*, p. 205.
[55] C. E. Carlston, "A Positive Criterion of Authenticity?" *Biblical Research*, VII (1962), 33–34.
[56] See Reginald H. Fuller, *A Critical Introduction to the New Testament*, pp. 94–103, for a summary of the method used in the current quest for the historical Jesus and for a summary of the "authentic Jesus tradition."

General Introductions to the Gospels

GRANT, FREDERICK C., *The Gospels: Their Origin and Their Growth* (Harper, 1957).

Commentaries on the Synoptic Gospels

FILSON, FLOYD V., *The Gospel According to St. Matthew* (Harper, 1960).
JOHNSON, SHERMAN E., *The Gospel According to St. Mark* (Harper, 1960).
LEANEY, A. R. C., *A Commentary on the Gospel According to St. Luke* (Harper, 1958).
TAYLOR, VINCENT, *The Gospel According to St. Mark: The Greek Text with Introduction, Notes, and Indices* (St. Martin's Press, 1952).

Source and Form Criticism

BULTMANN, RUDOLF, *The History of the Synoptic Tradition* (Harper, 1963). Application of form criticism to the Synoptic tradition by a "radical" form critic. First published in German in 1921.
BULTMANN, RUDOLF, and KARL KUNDSIN, *Form Criticism* (Harper, 1962). A re-issue of classic essays on the form-critical method.
DIBELIUS, MARTIN, *From Tradition to Gospel* (Scribner's, 1935). Form-critical treatment of the tradition by a conservative critic. First published in German in 1919.
McKNIGHT, EDGAR V., *What Is Form Criticism* (Fortress Press, 1969).
STREETER, BURNETT H., *The Four Gospels* (Macmillan, revised, 1951). This book marks the high point in the source analysis of the Synoptic Gospels.
TAYLOR, VINCENT, *The Formation of the Gospel Tradition* (St. Martin's, 1953). A conservative evaluation of form criticism, first published in 1933.

Lives of Jesus

BORNKAMM, GÜNTHER, *Jesus of Nazareth* (Harper, 1960). One of the few recent "lives" of Jesus using modern critical presuppositions and methods.
DIBELIUS, MARTIN, *Jesus* (Westminster, 1949). A "life" of Jesus using Dibelius' conservative form-critical approach. First published in German in 1939.
GOGUEL, MAURICE, *Jesus and the Origins of Christianity*, 2 vols. (Harper, 1960). First published in French in 1932. One of the best modern "lives" of Jesus.
SCHWEITZER, ALBERT, *The Quest of the Historical Jesus: A Critical Study of its Progress from Reimarus to Wrede* (Macmillan, 1955). First published in German in 1906. Traces the critical study of Jesus to the beginning of the twentieth century. An important book.
TAYLOR, VINCENT, *The Life and Ministry of Jesus* (Abingdon, 1955). A helpful, brief introduction to the life and ministry of Jesus.

3

Jesus' Galilean Ministry

A broad framework which each of the Synoptics uses for reporting their life of Jesus may be discovered from scanning the Gospels. First Jesus appears in connection with John by whom he is baptized. Then, Jesus goes to Galilee, which serves as the center for an early ministry of public and private teaching. After this early ministry Jesus goes to Jerusalem where the final teachings, arrest, crucifixion, burial, and resurrection occur. This skeleton framework comes, of course, from the Gospel of Mark. Matthew and Luke follow the outline in a general way, but place additional material (Q, M, and L) within the framework and make some alterations in the Marcan sequence.

The precise *sequence* of sayings and narratives in Mark does not go back to the time of Jesus and cannot be used uncritically, but the choice of the Marcan framework by Matthew and Luke indicates that they attached some value to the general Marcan outline. The prologue to Luke indeed points to the existence of narratives of "the things which have been accomplished among us," from which both Luke and Matthew selected Mark's framework. The deliberate choice of the Marcan narrative as the basic framework for the presentation of the ministry of Jesus by Matthew and Luke is evidence of their evaluation of the Marcan framework.

C. H. Dodd, building upon a suggestion of Martin Dibelius, attempted to show that a broad general outline of Jesus' ministry was preserved in the Church's teaching. "We can trace in the Gospel according to Mark a connecting thread running through much of the narrative, which has some similarity to the brief summary of the story of Jesus in Acts x and xiii, and may be regarded as an expanded

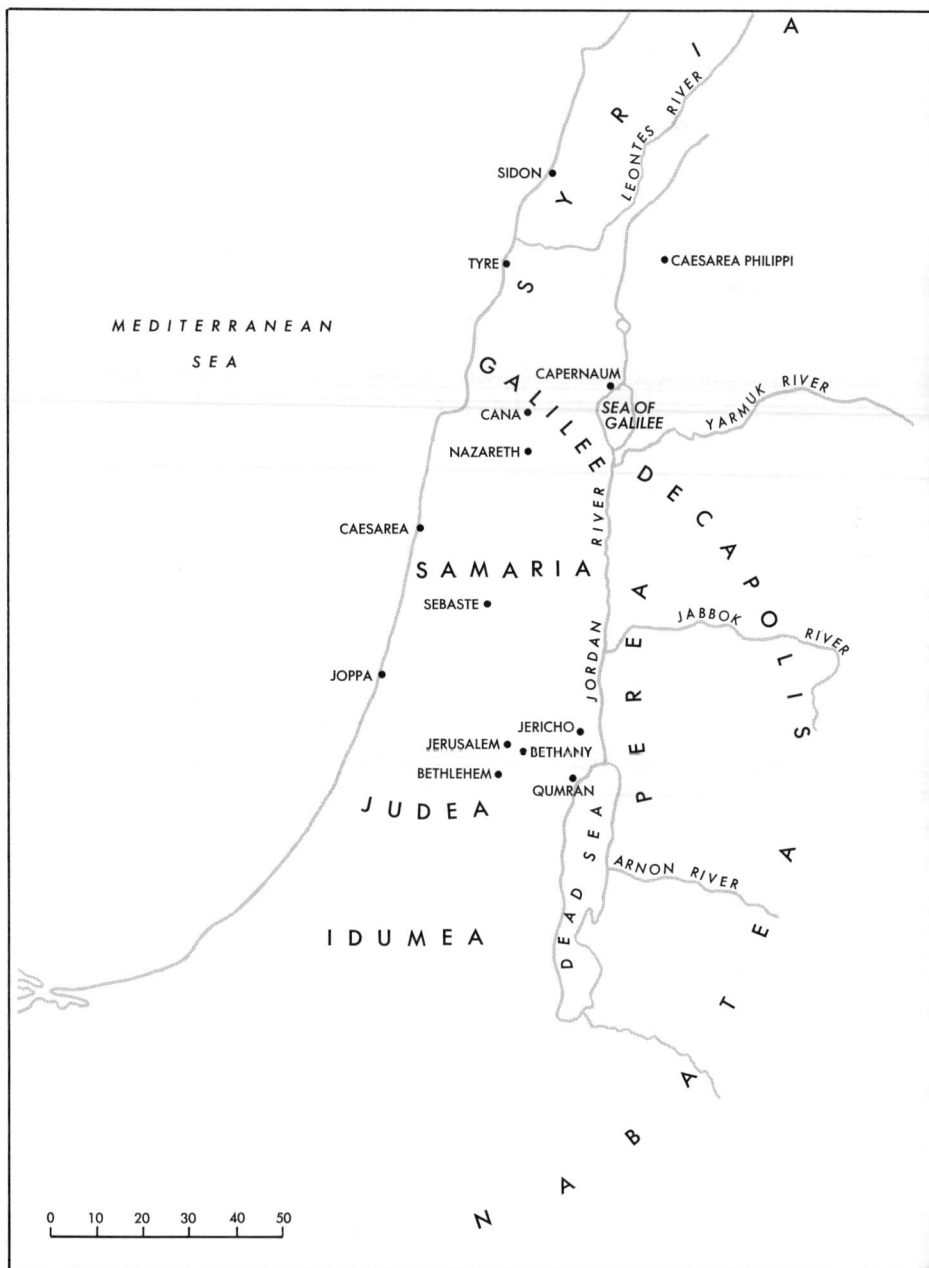

Figure 3–1. Palestine in Jesus' time.

form of what we may call the historical section of the kerygma." [1]
Such a view cannot be established with any degree of certainty; and,
even if the view is accepted, it does not establish the historicity of
the precise sequence in Mark. The conclusion that the Gospels should
be read as straightforward history ought not be drawn. Neither Matthew nor Luke felt obligated to follow the Marcan outline in detail;
they alter the sequence at several places. Their modifications, however, are relatively mild and the basic pattern of Mark is preserved.

To be sure, sheer logic dictates the placing of some narratives and
sayings at specific places within the framework of Jesus' life. For example, the Galilean location of many incidents is confirmed by information in the units themselves.[2] The shift of scene from Galilee to
Jerusalem is indicated by Luke 13:31–33, which is judged on form
critical principles to be authentic.[3] The Jerusalem location of scenes
reported after the triumphal entry is also evidence of a shift of scene
and testifies to a ministry in Jerusalem. But beyond this kind of logic
and the limited witness of the Synoptic Gospels the precise arrangement of events and sayings remains quite illusive.

PREPARATION FOR THE MINISTRY

Each of the Synoptics has some preparatory activities before Jesus'
actual ministry begins. Mark, followed by Matthew and Luke, contains an account of the ministry of John the Baptist, Jesus' baptism by
John, and Jesus' temptations. Matthew and Luke also include infancy narratives which serve as theological prologues to their story of
Jesus' ministry.

The Infancy and Childhood Narratives

The earliest canonical sources, indeed the overwhelming majority
of the New Testament writings, do not emphasize the ancestry, birth,

---

[1] C. H. Dodd, *The Apostolic Preaching and Its Developments*, p. 46. See 'The
Framework of the Gospel Narrative," *Expository Times*, XLIII (June, 1932),
396–400, for the development of this thesis. A refutation appears in D. E. Nineham, "The Order of Events in St. Mark's Gospel," *Studies in the Gospels: Essays
in Memory of R. H. Lightfoot*, D. E. Nineham, ed., pp. 223–239.

[2] See, for example, Mark 1:14–39 in which the incidents clearly have a Galilean
setting.

[3] See Bultmann, *The History of the Synoptic Tradition*, pp. 35, 36.

and infancy of Jesus.[4] Matthew and Luke alone have materials which tell of Jesus' parentage, birth, and early years; and even in these Gospels the narratives are introductory and secondary. Only in a chronological treatment of Jesus are the birth narratives first. They are theological reflections upon the meaning of Jesus from a post-resurrection perspective. For the early Christians the passion narrative was most important. Because of his death and resurrection the disciples saw in Jesus the "Word" of God and used the most exalted terms to speak of him, "Messiah," "Son of God," "Son of Man." From this perspective they became concerned about the nature of his life and teachings and then finally about his birth and infancy. Thus the infancy narratives were important to the Church only because they clarified the meaning and significance of Jesus the Christ.

The accounts in Matthew and Luke are totally independent (not Q material) of one another, but there is agreement on several points. Jesus was born in Bethlehem during the reign of Herod the Great and brought up in Nazareth in Galilee. The mother of Jesus was Mary, who was a virgin at the time of Jesus' birth. Mary's husband was Joseph, who was of the lineage of David. In both Gospels the name "Jesus" is given by the angel of the annunciation. In both also the conception is seen as a creative act of the Holy Spirit.

The two accounts have been so harmonized by Christian piety in Christmas stories and plays that differences between them have been overlooked. In Matthew, Joseph is a significant figure: the annunciation is made to Joseph in a dream; Joseph discovers that Mary is pregnant and is persuaded to divorce her until he is told by an angel in a dream that the conception is of the Holy Spirit. In Luke, the annunciation is to Mary in a waking state, and Joseph's reaction to Mary's pregnancy is not mentioned. Indeed, in Luke Joseph appears only incidentally. Matthew alone contains the story of the magi, while Luke alone tells of the shepherds. Matthew assumes that Bethlehem is the home of Mary and Joseph and says that after the flight into Egypt they would have returned to Bethlehem except for their fear of Archelaus. Using an exodus motif, he takes the holy family to Egypt and subsequently returns them to Nazareth. Luke considers Nazareth to be the home of Joseph and Mary. They go to Bethlehem because of a census, present Jesus in the temple in Jerusalem after

---

[4] The question of the virgin birth especially has been debated to a degree far out of proportion to its place in the Synoptic tradition. For discussions of the question see: Vincent Taylor, *The Historical Evidence for the Virgin Birth;* J. Gresham Machen, *The Virgin Birth of Christ;* and Thomas Boslooper, *The Virgin Birth.*

his birth, and return to Nazareth, not thinking of a trip to Egypt. Luke alone tells of the birth of John the Baptist. The genealogy in Matthew traces Jesus' lineage to David and Abraham, emphasizing his relation to Israel. Luke carries Jesus' ancestry back to Adam, emphasizing Jesus' relationship to all mankind.

The differences in the infancy stories illustrate a considerable freedom in the development of this tradition not found elsewhere in the Synoptics and, therefore, an evaluation of the historical information contained in the accounts is exceedingly difficult. Do any of the stories rest upon actual historical occurrences? If so, which ones? Are the stories primarily the products of an intense concern to see Jesus in the light of the Old Testament? Are the stories entirely theological, giving in narrative form the total impression made by Jesus Christ upon his followers? "Some persons may consider that these questions pose clearcut options, but perhaps one should reckon with a combination of these three factors. There are kernels of fact in most legends; figurative speech and song are the most adequate means of expressing the real meaning of certain events . . . If, as seems likely, the nativity stories of the Gospels had their original setting in the worship of early Palestinian churches, many different influences might have conspired to give them their distinctive forms." [5] Each unit must be studied independently to discover its witness to Jesus Christ. Even if and when historicity is established, the interpretation of the individual units must incorporate the faith conviction which undergirded their production and preservation in the early Christian community.

The Matthean Infancy Narrative (Matthew 1-2). Matthew begins with a genealogy which contains forty-six names of individuals from Abraham to Jesus. Most significant are Abraham and David. To Abraham was made the promise that in him all the families of the earth would be blessed, and the Messiah of Jewish expectation was to be the "son of David," the greatest king of Israel. So in the beginning Matthew presents the idea that the promises of God to Israel have been fulfilled in Jesus.[6]

The stories of the annunciation to Joseph and the birth of Jesus (Matthew 1:18-25) give an important role to dreams, a vehicle which does not impress modern man as much as the ancients. Revelation

---

[5] James L. Price, *Interpreting the New Testament*, p. 304.
[6] The distinctive purposes of each Gospel dramatically affect the choice and use of individual units of tradition. See below, Chapter 13.

by dreams is common in the Old Testament and in Greek and Roman literature. No ancient reader would question the authority of the dream experience by which Joseph was informed of the divine nature of Mary's son Jesus.[7]

The statement of 1:22 that "all this took place to fulfill what the Lord had spoken by the prophet" is a characteristic feature of Matthew and indicates the eagerness of the writer to relate Jesus to the expectations of God's deliverance. The early Christians experienced in Jesus all that they had anticipated and tended to read the Hebrew scriptures in the light of their experiences. Specific passages of the Hebrew Bible which dealt with other matters in the original literary and historical contexts were given "messianic" significance.[8] Matthew's revision of Isaiah 7:14 illustrates this point:

> Behold, a virgin shall conceive and
>   bear a son,
> and his name shall be called
>   Emmanuel. (Matthew 1:23)

In Isaiah in its original context the passage was not a specific messianic prophecy of the virgin birth. However, Matthew uses the verse in a messianic context and stressed the idea of virginity not necessarily included in the original Isaiah passage. The Greek version of Isaiah 7:14 did include the idea of a virgin birth and Matthew 1:23 agrees with the Greek translation from the Hebrew.

The visit of the magi (2:1–12) is an episode full of theological significance in Matthew. It places the birth of Jesus in Bethlehem in fulfillment of Micah's prophecy (Micah 5:2), dates the birth in the days of Herod the king, and introduces Jesus as "king of the Jews." To Matthew the Micah connection further shows that Jesus completes Jewish messianic hopes. Herod's concern testifies to the child's significance. Even magi, eastern astrologers who supposedly ascertain earthly events of import from heavenly signs, saw Jesus' star and acclaim him "king of the Jews." The dream-guided refusal of the wise men to return to Herod shows God's purposes prevailing over Herod's evil designs.

The accounts of the flight to Egypt, the sojourn there, and the return from Egypt (2:13–23) parallel the story of Moses and are evidence that Matthew saw Jesus as a second and greater Moses. Again, Matthew presents "evidence" from the prophets to demonstrate the

---

[7] The name *Jesus* is the Greek rendering of the Hebrew *Joshua*, "Yahweh saves" or "Yahweh is salvation."

[8] A full discussion of the fulfillment of scripture in Matthew is given in Krister Stendahl, *The School of St. Matthew and Its Use of the Old Testament.*

correctness of his interpretation. A passage from Hosea which referred originally to Israel's exodus from Egypt in the past [9] illustrates
that, "Out of Egypt have I called my son." Rabbinic Judaism taught
that the exodus under Moses would be the pattern for the greater
eschatological deliverance of God's people. Matthew tells these stories,
therefore, to depict Jesus as the eschatological king of Israel.

The Lucan Infancy Narrative (Luke 1–2). The Lucan infancy narrative skillfully weaves together stories of the annunciation, birth, and
childhood of both Jesus and John the Baptist. This material is unique
to Luke and distinguished from the rest of the special Lucan material
by its unity and Semitic style. Indeed, some hold that Luke 1–2 is
based upon a translation from an original Hebrew or Aramaic document. The Lucan infancy narrative may well depend upon a pre-
canonical written source, but likewise it may be a composition of the
Gospel writer based upon several traditions. But whatever their
source, Luke has edited his materials in light of his larger interests.[10]

The promise of the Baptist's birth made to the aged priest Zechariah
(1:5–25) sets the stage for the narrative. Parallels to the story of the
birth of Samuel (I Samuel 1) can be seen here. The picture is one of
a godly couple who have no children, but bear their state with faith
and hope in God. The divine messenger brings assurance of God's
providence and promises them a son who will "turn many of the sons
of Israel to the Lord their God" and who will carry out this mission
"in the spirit and power of Elijah" as depicted in Malachi.

The annunciation to Mary (1:26–38) parallels the announcement
to Zechariah, and the message of the angel recalls the sentiment of
II Samuel 7:13–16 and Isaiah 9:6–7:

And the angel said to her, "Do not be afraid, Mary, for you have found favor
with God. And behold, you will conceive in your womb and bear a son, and
you shall call his name Jesus. He will be great, and will be called the Son of
the Most High; and the Lord God will give to him the throne of his father
David, and he will reign over the house of Jacob forever; and of his kingdom
there will be no end." (1:30–33)

Mary's questioning of this announcement is met with the assertion of
supernatural conception. Further, what is happening to Elizabeth,
the mother of John the Baptist, is a sign that God is able to perform
his promise to Mary. Elizabeth "in her old age has also conceived a
son; and this is the sixth month with her who was called barren. For
with God nothing will be impossible." (1:36–37)

[9] Cf. Matt. 2:15 with Hosea 11:1.
[10] See below, pp. 463–464, 467–473.

Mary's visit to Elizabeth (1:39–56) shows Elizabeth extolling Mary's unborn babe and Mary herself. "Blessed are you among women, and blessed is the fruit of your womb! And why is this granted me, that the mother of my Lord should come to me?" The superior position of Mary and her son may be stressed as a polemic against a Baptist movement active in Luke's day. The movement venerated John over Jesus, claiming that John was actually born first and ministered before Jesus began his ministry. Luke acknowledges John's greatness as the messenger, but also emphasizes his subordination to Jesus, acknowledged even in the womb. Twice it is stated that the babe in Elizabeth's womb leaped when Mary met Elizabeth (1:41, 44).

Mary's response is the first of four Lucan poems known in the Western world (from the first words of the Latin translation) as the Magnificat (1:46–55), Benedictus (1:67–79), Gloria in Excelsis (2:14), and Nunc Dimittis (2:29–32). The Magnificat expresses first the joy and gratitude of Mary and then blesses God for his action on behalf of Israel.[11]

And Mary said,

> My soul magnifies the Lord,
> and my spirit rejoices in God my
>   Savior,
> for he has regarded the low estate
>   of his handmaiden.
> For behold, henceforth all
>   generations will call me blessed;
> for he who is mighty has done great
>   things for me,
> and holy is his name.
> And his mercy is on those who fear
>   him
> from generation to generation.
> He has shown strength with his arm,
> he has scattered the proud in the
>   imagination of their hearts,
> he has put down the mighty from
>   their thrones,
> and exalted those of low degree;
> he has filled the hungry with good
>   things,
> and the rich he has sent empty away.
> He has helped his servant Israel,
> in remembrance of his mercy,
> as he spoke to our fathers,
> to Abraham and to his posterity for
>   ever. (Luke 1:46–55)

[11] There is some textual evidence which credits Elizabeth, rather than Mary, with the Magnificat.

This has been modeled on the song of Hannah in I Samuel 2:1–10; almost every phrase is from this song or another section of the Old Testament. The Jewish tone of the Magnificat indicates that it may have been used in Jewish circles before its use in Christian worship and Luke's Gospel. The theme of the exultation of the lowly and the fall of the mighty, however, is one which fits well with Luke's interests.

Luke recounts the birth of John the Baptist (1:57–80) in a very simple style. After circumcision, the child is named John, and Zechariah, released from his dumbness, gives a statement known to us as the Benedictus. In the hymn used by Luke there is the repetition of the Davidic theme and the expectation of a new Elijah.[12] The Benedictus blesses God for raising up "a horn of salvation for us in the house of his servant David," and declares that John "will be called the prophet of the Most High." The Benedictus, as the Magnificat, may have come into Christian use from Jewish circles.

Luke's story of Jesus' birth (2:1–20) carefully locates the event, underscores the Gospel's interest in the poor and lowly, and introduces significant titles to be applied to the new baby. According to Luke, the birth occurs during the reign of Caesar Augustus when Quirinius was governor of Syria.[13] An inn in Bethlehem, to which Mary and Joseph had come for a census, provides the place. An angel announces the event to ordinary shepherds in the field. The announcement indicates the meaning of what is happening: "to you is born this day in the city of David a Savior, who is Christ the Lord." The babe is not only in David's line, but also Savior, Christ, and Lord.

The account of the circumcision and presentation (2:21–40) shows that all of the requirements of the law in connection with the birth of a son were met in the case of Jesus.[14] Jesus was circumcised on the eighth day, but Luke subordinated this to the naming of Jesus. Even as the requirements of the law are met, the deeper significance of Jesus is stressed. The law declared that the first born belonged to God; hence, Jesus was presented to God and then redeemed by a gift of money. Also, sacrifice was made to remove Mary's ritual unclean-

---

[12] Cf. Luke 1:69 with Psalm 18:2; 132:17; also Luke 1:76 with Malachi 3:1.

[13] Augustus ruled from 31 B.C. to A.D. 14, and Quirinius was governor of Syria A.D. 6–9. But Matt. 2:1 indicates that Jesus was born "in the days of Herod the King," who died in 4 B.C., and it is usually reckoned that Jesus' birth was about 8–4 B.C. It is difficult to harmonize the information about Quirinius in Luke with other information. Luke's accuracy in dating has been defended by a suggestion (based on an inscription) that Quirinius held a position of military authority in Syria before he actually became governor. Luke then would be referring to an earlier "rule" of Quirinius.

[14] See Lev. 12:6–8; Ex. 13:11–16.

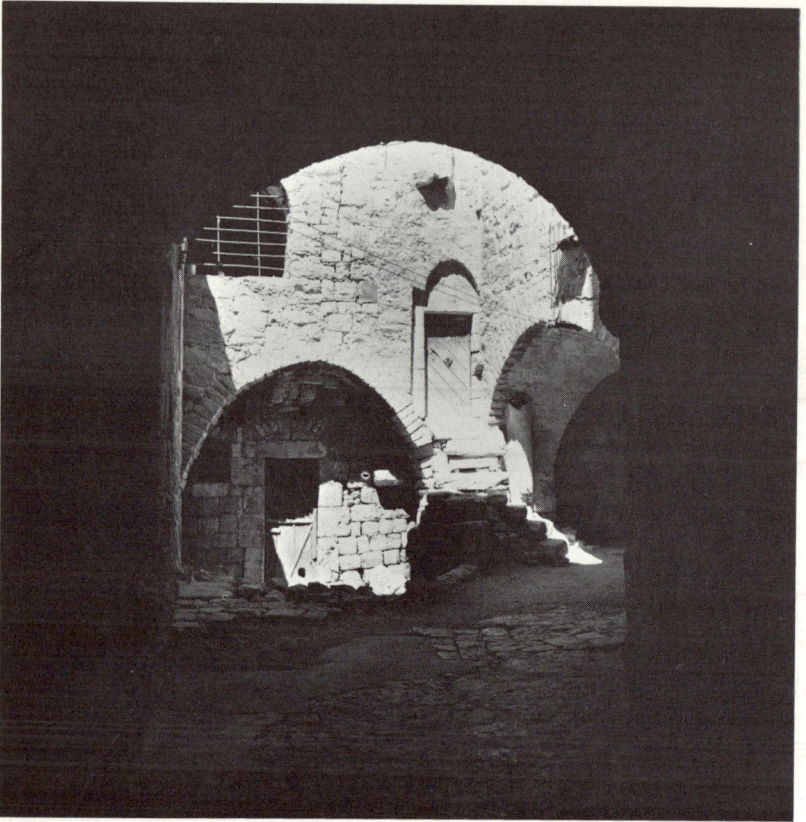

Figure 3–2. An inn with a stable below, dating from the first century and located in Bethlehem. (Source: Foreign Mission Board, SBC.)

ness due to childbirth. During the ceremonies of presentation at the temple forty days after the birth, Simeon, an aged devout man who had anticipated the coming of Messiah to redeem Israel, recognized Jesus and declared his significance in what is known as the Nunc Dimittis. To Mary he spoke words of warning that "this child is set for the fall and rising of many in Israel" and "a sword will pierce through your own soul also." The prophetess Anna also was there, gave thanks to God, and spoke of Jesus "to all who were looking for the redemption of Jerusalem."

Luke's genealogy of Jesus (3:23–24) cannot be harmonized with that in Matthew. He connects the genealogy to the baptism and beginning of Jesus' ministry, not to his birth. Luke uses fifty-six names from Jesus to Abraham compared with Matthew's forty-two and identifies "Heli" instead of "Jacob" as Jesus' grandfather. Luke traces the ancestry of Jesus back to Adam instead of simply to Abraham as does Matthew. Although some similarities do appear in the two genealogies (some names are in common and both agree that Jesus was a son of Abraham and David), Luke's genealogy, like Matthew's, is used for his own distinctive purpose: to stress Jesus' relation to the whole human race and to God himself.

Luke alone of the Gospels inserts an episode between the infancy and the beginning of Jesus' ministry (2:41–52). It is the story of Jesus' visit to the Jerusalem temple at Passover when he was twelve years old. The episode is true to Jewish life in Palestine in the first century, depicting a typical Galilean pilgrimage to Jerusalem for the great festival of the Jewish year. According to Luke, Jesus accompanied his parents to the holy city and remained in Jerusalem when the caravan, after the week of Passover observance, began the return journey. Since they travelled with a large group, Mary and Joseph did not miss Jesus until nightfall and finally found him in the temple "sitting among the teachers." When questioned about his activities the boy responded, "How is it that you sought me? Did you not know that I must be in my Father's house?" Luke uses this story to illustrate Jesus' intellectual and spiritual growth and to relate his infancy stories to the stories of Jesus' baptism and ministry.

The infancy narratives are most valuable as *theological* prologues to the ministry of Jesus. They do not aim to be simple historical narratives, but to show from a post-resurrection perspective who spoke the words and performed the deeds of Jesus. But some historical information is incorporated. Jesus was a Galilean, whose hometown was Nazareth. His family was Jewish; they observed the practices of Judaism. Mary was the mother of Jesus and her husband was Joseph. F. C. Grant says that Luke has with historic imagination

. . . recreated . . . the long-vanished figures of the family of Jesus and of John, the atmosphere of simple but noble Jewish piety which dominated Jesus' home in Nazareth and influenced his whole development. The deep religious feeling which still throbs in the Lukan canticles . . . , the glowing hope of the coming national liberation and the restoration of the ancient Davidic kingdom, the profound motives of humility and loyalty and obedience to the divine will—all this is indispensable for understanding Jesus, his life and times, his teaching, and his personal character.[15]

---

[15] F. C. Grant, "Jesus Christ," *IDB*, II, pp. 879–880.

John the Baptist

In all Four Gospels and Acts and the sources behind the Gospels the activities of John the Baptist are presented as a part of the story of Jesus.[16]

John's Activities (1.[17] Mark 1:1–6; Matthew 3:1–6; Luke 3:1–6). In the Synoptic Gospels John is a prophet proclaiming the day of the Lord. He is in the wilderness in answer to the prophecy of Isaiah proclaiming, "Prepare the way of the Lord, make his paths straight." [18] Mark adds a quotation from Malachi which speaks of the messenger which the Lord will send to prepare for the coming of the day of judgment, "Behold, I send my messenger before thy face, who shall prepare thy way."

The date of John's ministry is very carefully given by Luke:

In the fifteenth year of the reign of Tiberius Caesar, Pontius Pilate being governor of Judea, and Herod being tetrarch of Galilee, and his brother Philip tetrarch of the region of Iturea and Trachonitis, and Lysanias tetrarch of Abilene, in the high-priesthood of Annas and Caiaphas . . . (3:1–2).

The most specific chronological note is the "fifteenth year of the reign of Tiberius Caesar." The problem arises, however, that Tiberius actually reigned jointly with Augustus from A.D. 12 to the death of Augustus in A.D. 14. Is the fifteenth year to be calculated from the beginning of the reign of Tiberius with Augustus in A.D. 12, or from the year in which he actually took office alone? In the first case the fifteenth year would have to be taken as A.D. 27–28, and in the latter case it would be 28–29.

Mark and Matthew describe the dress and diet of John as very austere, a skin held together with a leather girdle for clothing and

---

[16] For a critical study of John the Baptist, see Carl H. Kraeling, *John the Baptist*.

[17] This number and the numbers preceding scripture passages throughout the chapters on the Synoptic tradition refer to the paragraphs in *Gospel Parallels: A Synopsis of the First-Three Gospels* in which the Synoptic material commented on is arranged in a convenient form for study. Both the paragraph number and the scripture references are given, for the chapters can be studied with the Gospels alone as well as with *Gospel Parallels*.

[18] In the prophecy from Isaiah the phrase "in the wilderness" is attached to the following verb to read, "In the wilderness prepare the way of the Lord." The cry of the prophet is not raised in the wilderness; however, the Greek version allows "in the wilderness" to be attached to the prophet and enables one to find in the statement a prophet preaching in the wilderness.

what was at hand in the wilderness—locusts and wild honey—for his food. This suggests the figure of Elijah, the great solitary prophet of early Israel, and reinforces the emphasis on John as the one preparing for the coming Messiah. The Synoptic accounts stress John's preaching, but the titles given him, "John the Baptist" and "John the baptizer," emphasize his activity. The accounts clearly state that John baptized those who came to him. This baptism was neither merely a Jewish ceremonial cleansing, a Jewish proselyte baptism, nor, of course, Christian baptism. Although John's baptism was akin to earlier practices of Judaism, it was a new act marked by "repentance for the forgiveness of sins."

John's Preaching (2–5. Mark 1:7–8; Matthew 3:7–12; Luke 3:7–20). John's baptism is tied to his call to repentance. The meaning of the act is found only in John's message. Both Matthew (3:7–10) and Luke (3:7–9) illustrate his preaching with almost no variation—the order is identical and only two insignificant changes occur in the wording. In Matthew the discourse is delivered to "many of the Pharisees and Sadducees," but in Luke the audience is simply "the multitudes." The message concerned the final events of history, the devastating judgment of the end:

"You brood of vipers! Who warned you to flee from the wrath to come? Bear fruit that befits repentance, and do not presume to say to yourselves, 'We have Abraham as our father'; for I tell you, God is able from these stones to raise up children to Abraham. Even now the axe is laid to the root of the trees; every tree therefore that does not bear good fruit is cut down and thrown into the fire." (Matthew 3:7b–10)

John's preaching is eschatological. He speaks of "the wrath to come" and declares that "even now the axe is laid to the root . . ." Preparation for the devastating judgment can be made only by repentance and personal righteousness; being descended from Abraham is not enough. Thus John stands in the best of Israel's prophetic tradition against the perverted legalistic emphasis of priestly religion. Luke (3:10–14) adds some concrete examples of John's ethical precepts. The multitude is exhorted to share clothing and food with the needy; tax collectors are to be fair in their collections; soldiers are to act decently, not robbing the citizens or expressing dissatisfaction with their wages. John's eschatological teaching includes a prophecy of one "who is mightier than I" who "will baptize you with the Holy Spirit." Matthew and Luke add details about the activities of the

Coming One. He will not only baptize with the Holy Spirit but also "with fire." The figure of the farmer separating wheat from the chaff is used to describe the thoroughness of his judgment. No wonder that John was later disillusioned by the more gentle activities of Jesus and sent from prison to ask, "Are you he who is to come, or shall we look for another?" (64. Matthew 11:3; Luke 7:19.) Luke concludes his account of John the Baptist with his imprisonment by Herod the tetrarch. (5. Luke 3:19–20.) Mark and Matthew bring John's story to conclusion by describing his arrest and execution by Herod (110–111. Mark 6:14–29; Matthew 14:1–12), but place it later in their account.

The Baptism and Temptation of Jesus

The beginning of Jesus' ministry is definitely related to the activities of John the Baptist. Jesus' baptism by John is declared by even the most cautious historians of Jesus and John the Baptist to be "one of the most certainly verified occurrences" of the life of Jesus.[19] No follower of Jesus would have introduced a story which seemed to make Jesus subordinate to John unless it were solid historical fact!

The Baptism (6. Mark 1:9–11; Matthew 3:13–17; Luke 3:21–22). The Synoptics, however, are concerned about more than the historical fact of Jesus' baptism; they show the greater import of the baptism for the ministry of Jesus. The heavens open, the Spirit descends, and a voice from heaven reveals Jesus as Son of God. In Mark the experience is given to Jesus alone. In Matthew Jesus alone experiences the Spirit of God descending like a dove, but the other events are seen and heard by others present. Luke emphasizes even more the objectivity of the events; he makes the Holy Spirit come down "in bodily form, as a dove." The quotations from Psalms 2 and Isaiah 42 are significant, for Psalm 2 is a messianic psalm which tells of the ideal king of Israel's future to whom universal dominion is given by God.[20] Isaiah 42 and other servant poems in Deutero-Isaiah speak of the servant of Yahweh, the suffering servant who brings God's teaching and restores justice to the nations.[21] Too much of Jesus' later life and ministry should not be read back into the baptismal experience, but un-

---

[19] Günther Bornkamm, *Jesus of Nazareth*, p. 54. See also Rudolf Bultmann, *History of the Synoptic Tradition*, tr. John Marsh, pp. 247, 424; Carl H. Kraeling, *John the Baptist*, p. 131.

[20] See Acts 4:25–29 for early Christian use of Psalm 2.

[21] Cf. Isaiah 42:1–4; 49:1–6; 50:4–11; 52:13–53:12.

Figure 3–3. The Jordan River at a traditional site of the baptism of Jesus. (Source: Foreign Mission Board, SBC.)

doubtedly it was a decisive event in Jesus' growing consciousness of the Father and his own mission.[22]

The Temptation (8. Mark 1:12–13; Matthew 4:1–11; Luke 4:1–13). The temptation narratives are given by Mark and Matthew as a sequel to the experience of Jesus at his baptism. Luke inserts his genealogy between the two episodes to break somewhat the relationship of the two stories. The temptation narratives (given in detail only by Matthew and Luke) contain elements which forbid a literal reading of the materials. They clearly aim to reveal the inner experience of Jesus

[22] See Gerhard Kittel, "Abba," *Theological Dictionary of the New Testament,* pp. 5–6, and Joachim Jeremias, *The Central Message of the New Testament,* pp. 9–30.

—the working of the mind of Jesus as he struggles with the character of his ministry. There is temptation to ask for external signs and assurances of sonship and, perhaps more important, there is temptation to fulfill his ministry by means not appointed by God. If the baptism represents a rudimentary commitment of Jesus to his mission, as yet not fully understood, the temptations depict Jesus' struggle with the basic nature of messiahship.

"Command these stones to become loaves of bread." Jesus is tempted to concern himself primarily with physical needs of men.

Figure 3—4. The traditional Mount of Temptation located opposite the site of ancient Jericho. Half-way up the mountain (left) stands a monastery. (Source: Jordan Tourist Department.)

"Throw yourself down" from the temple expressed another temptation. At least one Jewish idea of Messiah is that he would appear suddenly on the roof of the temple,[23] and the sign Jesus is tempted to perform

[23] Babylonian Talmud, Pesikta Rabba, 162a, reads, "When King Messiah is revealed, he comes and stands upon the roof of the *holy place:* then will he announce to the Israelites and say, 'Ye poor, the time of your redemption is come.'" This tradition, however, says nothing of the Messiah casting himself down from the temple.

would certainly impress people. Should messiahship aim to win a following through the spectacular miracle? The third temptation was to obtain "all the kingdoms of the world," perhaps crusade for freedom from the power of Rome. This was a live option for the Messiah. Many Jews in the first century thought the Messiah would come to lead a military campaign to rid Palestine of Roman oppression. Should Jesus identify with this sentiment and captivate an immediate following? The specific responses given by Jesus are quotations from Deuteronomy.[24] In the original context in Deuteronomy the sentences are addressed to Israel to make the Israelites know the promises and demands of the covenant with God. Israel fails to hear and obey, but Jesus is the new Israel manifesting the obedience which the old Israel failed to manifest. Although the specific nature of messiahship is not made clear in the temptations narrative, Jesus affirms his obedience and loyalty to God. This faith pervades his subsequent mission.

THE MINISTRY

The Synoptic Gospels indicate that Jesus began his ministry after John the Baptist was arrested and that his ministry was centered in Galilee, a small insignificant region in northern Palestine.[25] Galilee had never been a center of Jewish life and thought; in the Old Testament period few Israelites lived there and the region was called "Galilee of the nations" (or Gentiles).[26] Official Judaism was centered in Jerusalem in Judea, not in Galilee, but Jesus did not choose to begin his ministry in Judea by enlisting Judaism's leaders. Rather, he went to Galilee and, like John the Baptist, assumed a ministry independent of official Judaism. But quite unlike John, Jesus' ministry was more informal and itinerant. Whereas John had dwelt in the Jordan valley, calling for repentance, telling of the coming kingdom, and baptizing those *who came to him;* Jesus carried out his ministry by *visiting* the towns and villages of Galilee. He moved among the people in his own region and ministered by his deeds and the spoken word.

[24] Cf. Deut. 8:3; 6:13; 6:16.

[25] The Gospel of John says that Jesus opened his ministry while John the Baptist was still carrying on his active ministry (John 3:23; 4:1) and that before John's imprisonment Jesus ministered in Galilee (2:1–12), Jerusalem (2:13–3:21), Judea, (3:22), and Samaria (4:1–42). The historical information in John is strongly colored by his theological purposes, and the actual historical development is probably more accurately reflected in the Synoptic Gospels.

[26] Cf. Isaiah 9:1 and Matt. 4:15 where the Isaiah passage is quoted from the Septuagint.

Early Preaching and the Call of the First Disciples

The First Preaching in Galilee (9. Mark 1:14–15; Matthew 4:12–17; Luke 4:14–15). Mark and Matthew agree upon the basic message of Jesus in his early Galilean preaching. Mark gives a simple, summary statement: "The time is fulfilled, and the kingdom of God is at hand; repent, and believe in the gospel." Matthew states the thrust of Jesus' message as: "Repent, for the kingdom of heaven is at hand," changing "kingdom of God" to "kingdom of heaven" because of his customary hesitation to use the divine name. Although Matthew omits "the time is fulfilled," he has just emphasized the idea of fulfillment in 4:14.[27] Luke also underscores the fulfillment theme in the episode of the rejection at Nazareth (4:21). So the Synoptics agree that the coming of Jesus is the time of the fulfillment of God's promises of salvation.[28]

"The Kingdom of God is at hand," Jesus declared. The verb translated "is at hand" may mean "has come near" or "is here." The exact meaning of the phrase must be determined by the total context of Jesus' teaching and the early Church's beliefs about the kingdom of God.[29] The kingdom is not defined by Jesus. Nevertheless, it is a term which would have called forth certain definite ideas to Jesus' hearers. The basic meaning of the term *kingdom* is "reign" or "rule" not "realm" or "domain." The rule or reign of God was a familiar idea to the Israelites. The Old Testament describes God as king (Isaiah 43:15; Psalm 103:19). Israel acknowledged God as king in the covenant, and when an individual accepted the Torah, he became a part of the kingdom. During the two or three centuries before Christ, the "kingdom of God" came to have added meaning.

The Hebrew prophets had anticipated a glorious future in which God would establish his rule and grant his people complete fellowship with himself. The Jewish people, however, had experienced domination and oppression at the hands of one power after another. The present for them was an evil age. In their historical situation they saw no hope for the restoration of an independent Israel and the fulfill-

---

[27] Jesus' ministry is seen by Matthew as the fulfillment of a prophecy from Isaiah (9:1–2) which originally spoke of God's deliverance of the people of Galilee under Assyrian domination eight centuries before Christ.

[28] See also Galatians 4:4 and II Cor. 1:20.

[29] See the articles on *basileia* and related words by K. L. Schmidt, H. Kleinknecht, K. G. Kuhn, and Gerhard von Rad in *Theological Dictionary of the New Testament*, I, pp. 564- 593, and Norman Perrin, *The Kingdom of God in the Teaching of Jesus*.

ment of the prophecy concerning the glorious future. Their faith in God, however, enabled them to see that his purposes would yet be accomplished. Although the kingdom had not come through the process of historical events, it would come through God's intervention. The two eschatological possibilities of historical fulfillment and divine intervention represent respectively prophetic and apocalyptic views. Jesus' proclamation that "the kingdom is at hand" would have been interpreted against the background of apocalyptic eschatology [30] and would mean that the end of history was here, the approach of "the age to come." In Jesus himself God had intervened to bring his purposes to completion. In the light of this inbreaking of God's rule, the people are to "repent and believe in the gospel."

The Rejection at Nazareth (10. Luke 4:16–30). Luke's presentation of Jesus' early preaching varies from that of Mark and Matthew. Although he acknowledges that Jesus earlier "taught in their synagogues, being glorified by all" (4:15), the first account he gives of Jesus' preaching is that in the synagogue at Nazareth. It is obvious from Luke itself that the experience in Nazareth was not chronologically first. Jesus had already worked at Capernaum, and reference is made to this in the account of his preaching in Nazareth. Since Matthew and Mark place the experience at Nazareth later in Jesus' ministry, Luke must have had special reason for giving prominence to the Nazareth event. It is for him, key both to the nature of Jesus' ministry in continuing history, and to the dimensions of Jesus' messiahship.[31] This experience at Nazareth shows Jesus' reading a section from the book of Isaiah which he relates to himself and his ministry.

> The Spirit of the Lord is upon me,
> because he has anointed me to preach good news to the poor.
> He has sent me to proclaim release to the captives
> and recovering of sight to the blind,
> to set at liberty those who are oppressed,
> to proclaim the acceptable year of the Lord.   (4:18–19)

The people refused to accept such implications, however, and Jesus acknowledged that "no prophet is acceptable in his own country," giving examples of earlier servants of God who ministered

---

[30] For a treatment of the strong eschatological note in Jesus' teachings, an emphasis upon the "imminent future" of the Kingdom, see Werner Georg Kümmel, *Promise and Fulfillment: The Eschatological Message of Jesus*, tr. Dorothea M. Barton, 3rd rev. ed.

[31] See below, p. 469, and Hans Conzelmann, *The Theology of St. Luke*, pp. 31–38.

to Gentiles from whom came a favorable response. Luke places this episode early to serve as a theological introduction to Jesus' ministry.

The Call of the First Disciples (11. Mark 1:16–20; Matthew 4:18–22). Mark and Matthew follow the account of Jesus' early preaching with the call of the first disciples.[32] The call is abrupt with no hint of prior contact between Jesus and the disciples. Perhaps the men had heard Jesus preach before this invitation was given and accepted.[33] Their response, whatever the case, was immediate; they left business and family to follow Jesus. These early disciples were Peter, Andrew, James and John, the most frequently mentioned disciples, whose names head the lists of disciples given in the Gospels.

Although the story of the call of the initial followers is strangely succinct, it must have been profitable for early Church use as an example to win followers to Jesus Christ. Some would say the event was manufactured by the Church for this purpose. However, its historicity is supported by the lifelike details. "This strange figure— 'fishers of men'—to which there is no real parallel in earlier literature and which was never taken up into general Christian usage, could not have survived except as a fragment of genuine reminiscence and could hardly have been transmitted except in the context of the scene to which it belongs—a scene of fishermen at their daily tasks." [34]

Exorcisms and Healings (12–16; 45. Mark 1:21–45; Matthew 4:23–25; 7:28–8:4; 8:14–17; Luke 4:31–5:16)

The Synoptic story of Jesus gives a significant place to exorcisms and healings as items which made Jesus popular with the crowds. Mark records a number of such events in 1:21–45. Luke follows closely the Marcan account, adding only a miraculous catch of fish in 5:1–11. Matthew, on the other hand, arranges some of the Marcan materials to serve as an introduction to the Sermon on the Mount, omits some, and transfers some to the later ministry of Jesus. In Mark the stories are closely connected and compose the actions of a single day in Capernaum. This caused Jesus' fame to "spread everywhere throughout all the surrounding region of Galilee" and led to a preaching tour of Galilee. Most of this section (1:21–39) "stands apart from others in that it is based on the earliest personal testimony" and forms a relatively self-contained unit which is best explained by the view that

---

[32] For a knowledgeable treatment of discipleship, see Bornkamm, *Jesus of Nazareth*, pp. 144–152.

[33] John 1:35–42.

[34] Beare, *The Earliest Records of Jesus*, p. 47.

Figure 3–5. A view of the southern end of the Sea of Galilee. Across the Sea of Galilee may be seen the Transjordan Plateau with the Yarmuk Valley to the right. (Source: Foreign Mission Board, SBC.)

Peter himself so related the events of the day when Jesus came to his native town for the first time.[35]

This series of stories represents Jesus as very popular because he performed miracles of healing. The idea of miracle often creates difficulty for modern man because his world-view and presuppositions differ from those of the first century. Modern man may define miracle as that which is contrary to nature, and he may view the universe as so controlled by unalterable universal laws that nothing supernatural can occur. Such a clear division of life into natural and supernatural categories may be typical for the modern mind, but it was not for the ancients. For first century man both the natural and supernatural were areas of God's action. God sent sun and rain; he also performed acts contrary to "nature." Thus, those to whom Jesus spoke would have defined miracle as "an event, whether natural or supernatural, in which

[35] Taylor, *The Gospel according to St. Mark,* pp. 170–171. Taylor says that this complex of stories is comparable with 4:35–5:43; 6:30–56; 7:24–37; and the passion narrative.

one sees an act or revelation of God." [36]   For them the primary question was God, not natural law.

If one believes in God, that God creates the universe, sustains it, and controls it, most of the difficulties of miracles have thereby been dealt with. One who believes in God will believe in the possibility of miracles. On the other hand, he will admit that his belief in miracles results from his belief in God and in God's continuing control of the world.[37]

The Christian belief in Jesus as the incarnate Son of God, then, makes the miracle stories credible. This does not mean that belief in Jesus demands uncritical belief in the miracle stories. Various tools of historical research must be employed with both caution and honesty. Their use in relation to the narratives and teachings of Jesus produces strong evidence that Jesus effected a number of healings. Jesus' opponents admitted his powers, but explained them differently from Jesus and his disciples. Clearly the disciples of Jesus, who transmitted the stories and put them in the present form in our Gospels, knew Jesus as a miracle worker and honestly reported stories they were convinced were true.[38] Sayings of Jesus, the authenticity of which is established by the severest tests of form critics, attest to his healings. In Matthew 12:28 (paralleled by Luke 11:20) Jesus says, "But if it is by the spirit of God that I cast out demons, then the kingdom of God has come upon you." This passage cannot be attributed to the Church or to contemporary Judaism for it makes no explicit assertion of Jesus' messiahship and the eschatology is different from contemporary Judaism. Bultmann says that this passage can "claim the highest degree of authenticity which we can make for any sayings of Jesus: it is full of that feeling of eschatological power which must have characterized the activity of Jesus." [39]   It should be noted, however, that miracle stories were not limited to the Bible in ancient times; Jewish and Hellenistic literature contain accounts of miracles. Hence, the miracles of Jesus *per se* could not *prove* the uniqueness of Jesus to a first century man.[40]

Jesus in the Synagogue at Capernaum (12. Mark 1:21–28; Luke 4:31–37). The exorcism of the unclean spirit in the synagogue at

[36] S. V. McCasland, "Miracle," *IDB*, III, p. 392.

[37] *Ibid.*, pp. 394–395.

[38] For a form-critical treatment of the miracles of Jesus, see Reginald H. Fuller, *Interpreting the Miracles*. Although Fuller, p. 39, concludes that certainty cannot be established by a critical study, "the tradition that Jesus did perform exorcisms and healings (which may also have been exorcisms originally) is very strong . . ."

[39] Bultmann, *The History of the Synoptic Tradition*, p. 162.

[40] Bultmann, pp. 231–238, gives a convenient collection of miracle stories from Jewish and Hellenistic literature.

Figure 3–6. The ruins of an ancient synagogue on a site probably occupied by Capernaum in Jesus' time. The synagogue dates to the second or third century, but probably stands on the same ground as a synagogue of Jesus' day. (Source: Israel Office of Information.)

Capernaum takes place after teachings which astonished the people, "For he taught them as one who had authority, and not as the scribes." [41] The story presupposes the belief that illness, particularly mental illness, was caused by demons. This belief was generally held, even by the formally educated men of Jesus' day. It is instructive to read such accounts as contemporary reports of real experiences which have rational explanations in the light of modern psychological studies.

One writer has diagnosed epilepsy in the case of the child in Mark 9:17–27, a manic-depressive psychosis in the case of the Gerasene demoniac, and hysteria in the case of the man in the synagogue (Mark

[41] Matthew places this statement of Mark at the conclusion of the Sermon on the Mount, which for him illustrated the verse.

1:23–26).[42] A psychiatrist evaluated the diagnoses and agreed that "the record of the boy with convulsions in Mark 9:17–27 is quite clear, so that the diagnosis cannot be questioned . . . The case record of the Gerasene, Mark 5:1–20, also is full enough to allow conclusions to be drawn . . ." He questions whether the man in the synagogue of Capernaum is a case of hysteria. He says that he "might well have been a case of a paranoidal form of schizophrenia." [43] But adequate information is not available to determine the nature of the affliction in all cases, and this certainly was not the interest of the Church or Gospel writers. The emphasis in Mark and Luke is on Jesus—his person, his teachings, his "authority" and "power," his reaction to the need of the demoniac. He casts out the unclean spirit with a word—not by some current magical practice!

The Healing of Peter's Mother-in-Law (13. Mark 1:29–31; Matthew 8:14–15; Luke 4:38–39). The healing of Peter's mother-in-law parallels the earlier expulsion of the demon. Indeed the statement of Luke that Jesus "rebuked the fever, and it left her" indicates that the fever was caused by a demon. (Mark himself says that "the fever left her.") The healing was complete and the woman immediately took up her tasks of entertaining the group. It has been pointed out that "we have here a healing story of the very simple type, in a very precise historical setting, to which indeed there is no exact similar parallel elsewhere in Mark." The details in the story "do not normally belong to the elaboration of a healing story" and the story itself "would lose greatly in impressiveness, if the identity of the patient were not mentioned." From the beginning the story was about Peter's mother-in-law.[44]

The Sick Healed at Evening (14. Mark 1:32–34; Matthew 8:16–17; Luke 4:40–41). At sundown that evening, Mark declares, a mass of sick people came to where Jesus was and he "healed many" and "cast out many demons." Luke heightens this by stating that "every one of them" was healed. He also makes the recognition of Jesus by the

---

[42] S. Vernon McCasland, *By the Finger of God: Demon Possession and Exorcism in Early Christianity in the Light of Modern Views of Mental Illness*, pp. 32–44.

[43] David C. Wilson, in the introduction to McCasland's volume, p. x.

[44] R. H. Lightfoot, *The Gospel Message of St. Mark*, p. 22. Fuller, pp. 34, 49, says bluntly that the story is "undoubtedly a personal reminiscence of Peter himself." He indicates that it is an exception to the rule in the case of miracle stories because "it contains no sayings to give it a theological point, it is simply related because Peter remembered it . . ."

demons more specific. They cry, "You are the Son of God!" "They knew that he was the Christ," that is, even the dreaded demons who were hostile to God's cause in the world were forced to confess that Jesus, who thwarted their control over their diseased victims, was God's Messiah.

Departure from Capernaum (15. Mark 1:35–38; Luke 4:42–43). Mark and Luke conclude their description of this part of Jesus' ministry with reference to a general ministry beyond Capernaum. Accordingly Jesus retires from healing the masses and the disciples follow, reporting that "every one is searching for you." Jesus tells them of his plans for a ministry to other towns in the area. Since Luke has not yet introduced the disciples in the Gospel story, he here makes some changes in the Marcan narrative. Reference to the disciples is omitted. The ministry beyond Capernaum, doubtless lasting for some time, is summarized by Mark, "And he went throughout all Galilee, preaching in their synagogues and casting out demons."

The Healing of a Leper (45. Mark 1:40–45; Matthew 8:1–4; Luke 5:12–16). Mark appends to this series of stories an episode of the healing of a leper. There is no indication of place or time in Mark, but Luke does give the vague setting "in one of the cities," and Matthew places it after the Sermon on the Mount. The form of this story suggests that it, like many stories about Jesus, circulated as an independent unit instead of as an incident in a continuous narrative.

The term translated "leprosy" in the incident probably does not literally mean leprosy.[45] The Greek translators of the Hebrew Bible and the New Testament writers use the same term to designate both true leprosy and other curable skin diseases which could be declared to be cured by priests under the Mosaic law.[46] The sufferer in the story has a distressing skin disease which has affected him emotionally and socially, as well as physically. The act of Jesus is presented to emphasize the emotional response of Jesus to the needs of the sufferer.

The Sermon on the Mount

The Gospels emphasize that Jesus was a teacher and each of them contains many of his teachings. Matthew's decision to parallel Jesus

---

[45] R. K. Harrison, "Leprosy," *IDB*, III, pp. 111–113. See also K. P. C. A. Gramberg, "Leprosy and the Bible," *The Bible Translator,* XI (January, 1960), 10–23.

[46] See Lev. 13 and 14.

with Moses influences his presentation of Jesus' teachings in a unique way. He arranges his Gospel into five parts (corresponding with the Torah or five books of Moses) each of which contains a discourse or groups of sayings. The Sermon on the Mount is the first of the five discourses so arranged by Matthew. It is a compilation of sayings from Q, Matthew's special material, and Mark. Luke has many of the same sayings in two sections of his Gospel: The Sermon on the Plain which begins and ends like the Sermon on the Mount, and the "travel narrative" (Luke 9:51–18:14). The Sermon on the Mount illustrates the way Matthew typically deals with Jesus' teachings. Throughout his Gospel, Matthew chooses and arranges teaching material, not according to the time and place of delivery or the audience and circumstances of the particular teachings, but according to subject matter. In the Sermon on the Mount Matthew has brought together the ethical teachings of Jesus from a variety of circumstances and placed them into a comprehensive account.[47] First comes a declaration of blessedness, of God's favor, upon those who aspire to live under God's rule and a statement of the influence of those who live under his rule (5:3–16). Next are teachings on the relation of Jesus' message to the Jewish law and illustrations of the relationship (5:17–48). Closely related to this section is a group of sayings on almsgiving, prayer, and fasting (6:1–18). The final section contains teachings and illustrations of practical ethical behavior (6:19–7:12) and a concluding challenge (7:13–27).

Introduction (18. Matthew 5:1–2; Luke 6:12; 20). In the introduction to the sermon Matthew (and Luke in the Sermon on the Plain) emphasizes that the disciples are those to whom the sermon is primarily addressed. The ethical teachings of Jesus are designed for those who have responded to the proclamation of the reign of God, to those who have committed themselves as disciples of Jesus Christ. Jesus' ethical teaching presupposes and indeed forms a part of his teaching on the Kingdom. God's kingdom, his saving rule, has been manifested; those who experience this rule are to live in a new way—the kingdom way. Of course, some elements of the sermon may make some sense in other contexts, but the sermon as a whole is misunderstood if it is taken as an ethical system independent of religion. Rather the Sermon on the Mount is the description of life in the kingdom of God, *i.e.* life over which God rules.

---

[47] Two books which treat the content and meaning of the ethical teaching of Jesus in the historical setting of his ministry are: Harvey K. McArthur, *Understanding the Sermon on the Mount,* and W. D. Davies, *The Setting of the Sermon on the Mount.*

The Beatitudes and Parables of Salt and Light (19, 20. Matthew 5:3–16; Luke 6:20–23; 11:33; 14:34–35). The first major section of the sermon gathers a group of pointed ethical statements commonly called beatitudes, from the Latin translation of the word with which each begins. The beatitudes cannot be understood as a practical political or social program; they are completely contrary to the realities of any existing social order. They are *eschatological*, describing the character and blessedness of those who have a part in God's kingdom. The beatitudes describe the citizens of the kingdom as those who trust in God with a single-minded love and who, though oppressed by the world, are merciful to others and the bearers of peace. The promises of blessedness are at the same time descriptions of the kingdom; to be in the kingdom means to be comforted, to inherit the earth, to be satisfied, to obtain mercy, to see God, and to be called sons of God. The *eschaton* then reverses the fortunes of those who have known only poverty and persecution but have been sincerely devoted to God's reign. The similitudes of salt and light in Matthew show the influence of such citizens of the kingdom. Kingdom citizens, like salt and light, are to be useful. Disciples have a role to play *in the world*.

Jesus' Teachings and the Jewish Law (21–27. Matthew 5:17–48; Luke 6:27–36; 12:57–59; 16:18). Matthew 5:17–48 compares and contrasts the old and the new law. There is no doubt that there was controversy between Jesus and traditional Judaism over the law. But early Christians, particularly those from a Jewish background, were concerned about the relationships of Jesus' teaching to the Torah. Matthew faces the problem from their perspective and attempts to demonstrate that the teachings of Jesus are not contrary to the basic religious teachings of Israel. They are indeed the Torah's true interpretation. Mark and Luke, however, wrote primarily for Gentile readers who were not essentially interested in the Jewish law.

The introductory section dealing with the law (5:17–20) might seem to make Jesus more legalistic than the most legalistic Pharisee.[48] Jesus' statement strongly supports the law:

[48] The rabbis themselves spoke of seven types of Pharisees: (1) the *Shikmi* Pharisee "who performs the action of shechem," and is circumcised from an unworthy motive; (2) the *Nikri* Pharisee "who knocks his feet together," walking in exaggerated humility; (3) the *Kizai* Pharisee who is so anxious to avoid looking upon a woman that he dashes his face against the wall; (4) the "pestle" Pharisee whose head is bowed like a pestle in a mortar; (5) the Pharisee who constantly exclaims, "What further duty is for me that I may perform it," as though he had fulfilled every obligation; (6) the Pharisee from love; and (7) the Pharisee from fear. The Babylonian Talmud, Sotah, 22b.

Think not that I have come to abolish the law and the prophets . . . For truly, I say to you, till heaven and earth pass away, not an iota, not a dot, will pass from the law until all is accomplished. (5:17–18)

However, Jesus understood that the ethics of the kingdom must surpass merely keeping any legal code. Other teachings of Jesus criticize requirements held to be centrally important by the Jews, and Jesus' notorious disregard of contemporary sabbath laws make it clear that he did not simply approve contemporary Jewish standards of righteousness. Kingdom requirements demand more than keeping regulations:

. . . unless your righteousness exceeds that of the scribes and Pharisees, you will never enter the kingdom of heaven. (5:20)

A major section of the sermon proceeds to illustrate how the righteousness of the kingdom must get beyond the righteousness of the scribes and Pharisees. Illustrations about murder (5:21–26), adultery (5:27–30), divorce (5:31–32), swearing (5:33–37), retaliation (5:38–42), and love of enemies (5:43–48) shift particular teachings of Judaism from external observance to the more central matters of motive and action. The member of God's kingdom is not satisfied merely to keep the law, but evaluates his action on the deeper levels of intention. Jesus, of course, does not intend to set forth new laws to be applied in an existing social order. Consider the difficulty of carrying out the law on adultery in the case of every lustful look! Instead he describes essential traits of attitude and character of those whose lives have been, like that of Jesus, captured by God.

Almsgiving, Prayer, and Fasting (28–31. Matthew 6:1–18; Luke 11:2–4). The theme of the contrast between Jesus and Judaism, is continued in Matthew 6:1–18, a section which discusses three religious practices of Judaism—almsgiving, prayer, and fasting. In every case deeds done for the purpose of winning the approval of men are contrasted with deeds done "in secret" for the approval of God. The general teaching is the introductory sentence, "Beware of practicing your piety before men in order to be seen of them; for then you will have no reward from your Father who is in heaven" (6:11). It should not be thought that Judaism taught the publicizing of almsgiving, prayer, and fasting so as to gain public approval. Indeed, Judaism at its best would have agreed with Jesus' general interpretation of religious behaviour found in this section of the sermon. But in Jesus' day, as in the modern day, there were hypocrites who publicized their good deeds and worship for applause of society. To these Jesus says, "You have been paid in full." Their "religious" acts had sought and gained man's approval; they had achieved fully their desired ends.[49] Nothing remained for God to reward. Contrariwise, those acts directed toward God receive God's response. To emphasize the point Jesus uses the hyperbole:

But when you give alms, do not let your left hand know what your right hand is doing . . .
. . . But when you pray, go into your room and shut the door and pray to your Father who is in secret . . . (6:3, 6)

This kind of behavior, that is, religious acts which by motive purpose to please God, the "Father who sees in secret will reward."

The subject of prayer provides Matthew an appropriate place to include the "Lord's Prayer." It appears in the sermon as an example of the right kind of prayer in contrast to the prayer of the hypocrites. The model is indeed brief, but in its simple petitions deals with the fundamental needs of all men. The prayer consists basically of three petitions: for the coming of God's kingdom, for the provision of the needs for earthly existence, and for the forgiveness of sin. Those who have accepted God's reign are to pray for the kingdom's coming, daily bread, and deliverance from evil so that God's will may be accomplished "on earth as in heaven." The prayer can be paralleled in Jewish literature and life (the Kaddish and The Eighteen Benedictions) and Jesus doubtless used these older materials to form a model prayer for his followers.

Practical Ethical Behavior (32–44. Matthew 6:19–7:29; Luke 6:31, 37–38, 41–49; 11:9–13, 34–36; 12:22–31; 13:23–27; 16:13). The remainder of the sermon deals with a variety of matters. The sayings of 6:19–34 are loosely related to the theme of possession. The theme is epitomized in the statement, "Seek first his kingdom and his righteousness, and all these things shall be yours as well" (6:33). Food, clothes, and other physical needs are not ignored in the teaching, but physical needs are subordinated to the encompassing need for God to rule life. Again, overstatement is used to stress the importance of the principle. The kingdom and God's righteousness consume the concern of the believer. Such an appeal must have been particularly pointed for a people who in Jesus' day lived on a bare subsistence economy with economic worries heightening their nervous anxiety about daily life. Even to those whose bread came with great difficulty Jesus preached that citizens of the kingdom give first place to God and his rule!

[49] The Greek verb used in 6:2, 5, 16, occurs in the papyri as a formula of receipt, "Paid in full!"

Matthew 7:1–12 is an assorted group of sayings which fit loosely the theme of behavior to neighbors. Verse 12 stands as the meaning and conclusion of the section, "So whatever you wish that men do to you, do so to them; for this is the law and the prophets." This Golden Rule is found in a negative form in Judaism. Hillel, the great first century rabbi, is credited with telling a prospective proselyte to Judaism, "What is hateful to you, do not to your neighbor: that is the whole Torah, while the rest is the commentary thereof; go and learn it." [50] The principle that one should not do to others what one does not wish to have done to himself is also found in such places as Stoic philosophy and Confucian teachings. Many people have recognized that this principle is good for social relationships, but Jesus does not aim simply to give, in positive instead of negative form, a piece of prudential secular advice. Rather he places the old regulation in a new context. For him the experience of God's rule is the basis of the Golden Rule. Kingdom citizens share God's love and anxiously exhibit the same love toward others. The Sermon on the Mount concludes with a call to response, to "enter the narrow gate," to be "like a wise man who built his house upon the rock." Jesus uses the Old Testament figure of the two ways [51] to challenge men to decide in favor of God's rule and likens their life to a house constructed on a sure foundation.

Conflicts

The Gospel portrayal of Jesus includes a controversy motif which both serves the purposes of the individual Synoptics and reflects real historical data. In Mark 2:1–36, and its parallels in Matthew and Luke, a series of stories show conflict between Jesus and his opponents. They relate the healing of a paralytic, the call of Levi, the question about fasting, plucking ears of grain on the sabbath, and the healing of a man with a withered hand. Luke follows the same order as Mark without introducing other materials, but Matthew adds a good bit of material after the first three stories, including his second major discourse. The stories are obviously organized and presented from the perspective of the complete gospel story. Mark, for example, concludes the entire section with the statement that, "The Pharisees went out, and immediately held counsel with the Herodians against him, how to destroy him," introducing the suffering theme that is so significant to

---

[50] Babylonian Talmud, Shabbat, 31a. See also Tobit 4:15 and Ecclesiasticus 31:15.
[51] See Psalm 1; Jer. 17:5–8; 21:8.

Mark and pointing toward the death of Jesus. But conflict between Jesus and Judaism on such matters as those discussed in the stories in this section is admitted to be an historical fact by the severest form critics. Rudolf Bultmann cautiously concedes, ". . . We can say the following concerning Jesus' activity: characteristic for him are exorcisms, the breach of the sabbath commandment, the abandonment of ritual purifications, polemic against Jewish legalism, fellowship with outcastes, such as publicans and harlots, sympathy for women and children . . ."[52]

The controversies identify the opponents of Jesus as scribes and Pharisees. They criticized Jesus for forgiveness of sins associated with healing, eating with "sinners and tax-collectors," failure to fast, and failure to observe sabbath regulations. They essentially accuse Jesus of being out of line with Jewish religious custom. He defends himself by identifying his action with the best of prophetic tradition, and by stating his purpose of ministering to the sick and sinful. Here there is again an interpretation of Jesus' ministry in light of Isaiah 61, "to bring good tidings to the afflicted . . . to comfort those who mourn." In each controversy Jesus is victorious over his opponents, and, as already indicated, this results in the decision to destroy him.

The Healing of the Paralytic (52. Mark 2:1–12; Matthew 9:1–8; Luke 5: 17–26). The healing of the paralytic is a story with two related elements: a discussion between Jesus and his opponents over his authority to forgive sins and a miracle of healing by Jesus. The healing is given as evidence that Jesus does have authority to forgive sins. The saying of Jesus, "But that you may know that the Son of man has authority on earth to forgive sins . . . I say to you, rise, take up your pallet and go home," is important for an understanding of the earthly Jesus and of later Christology. According to the Synoptic Gospels, "Son of man" was Jesus' favorite self-characterization. The term is used by Jesus in sayings speaking of the present activity of the Son of man (Mark 2:10, 28; Matthew 8:20; 11:19), the future coming of the Son of man (Mark 8:38; 13:26; 14:62; Matthew 24:27, 37, 39, 44), and the imminent passion of the Son of man (Mark 8:31; 9:31; 10:33–34). Some of the passages clearly identify Jesus with the Son of man and others distinguish the two from each other. The term is used by Jesus in Mark, Q, M, and L. Moreover, outside of the sayings attributed to

---

[52] Rudolf Bultmann, "The Primitive Christian Kerygma and the Historical Jesus," *The Historical Jesus and the Kerygmatic Christ*, eds. Braaten and Harrisville, p. 22.

Jesus, there are only a few isolated passages where New Testament writers use Son of man as a title for Jesus (Acts 7:56; Hebrews 2:5–7; and Revelation 1:13). Son of man was not used by the later Church as the decisive title for Jesus. That Jesus used the term seems to be the only conclusion possible using our critical principles; although the Church did preserve and interpret the Son of man sayings in light of their beliefs about Jesus, it did not use the name as the decisive title for Jesus. Since, therefore, the Son of man concept was not that meaningful to the Church, these sayings were not invented and put on the lips of Jesus by the believing community. Rather they must have originated with Jesus himself.

What was meant by the term Son of man? The term is used several ways in the Old Testament. It sometimes means simply "man." [53] Frequently in Ezekiel it is used as God's address to the prophet and here means "O man." More importantly, the term at certain places indicates one who is involved in the work of judgment and salvation. In Daniel 7 the Son of man is mentioned as one who "came to the ancient of days and was presented before him. And to him was given dominion and glory and kingdom, that all peoples, nations, and languages should serve him; his dominion is an everlasting dominion, which will not pass away, and his kingdom one that shall not be destroyed." In a section of the Book of Enoch [54] a Son of man comes to establish God's kingdom. Although the Similitudes of Enoch may date from a later period, they seem to give evidence of an idea in pre-Christian Judaism. It seems clear that there was in the pre-Christian Jewish apocalyptic tradition a figure of the Son of man who was involved in the work of judgment and salvation.

In some passages of the Synoptic Gospels the Son of man may best be translated as "man" or "I," but other references are clearly apocalyptic. Most scholars agree that sooner or later Jesus identified himself with the apocalyptic Son of man and applied the title to himself. Accordingly, the earthly Jesus is not yet the glorified Son of man, but he regards himself as already possessing the authority and performing the functions of the coming Son of man.

In Mark 2:10 Son of man may be translated "I" or even "man," and in the original saying, Jesus may have made no reference to the apocalyptic Son of man; but it seems that as it is used by the Gospel writers

[53] Num. 23:19; Job 35:8; Psalm 80:17; Jer. 49:18.
[54] Chapters 37–71, "the Similitudes of Enoch."

there is a claim of sovereignty for Jesus in the term Son of man as well as in the act of healing.[55]

The Call of Levi (53. Mark 2:13–17; Matthew 9:9–13; Luke 5:27–32). The episode in Mark 2:13–17 is made up of the call of Levi followed by a meal at which tax-collectors and sinners are present. Jesus' opponents protest his eating with such people, and Jesus defends his action with a pronouncement, "Those who are well have no need of a physician, but those who are sick; I came not to call the righteous, but sinners." Form critics emphasize that the Church's interest in the story is the pronouncement of verse 17. The Church, like Jesus, had a mission to all sorts of people. The episode is used in the Synoptics, however, to illustrate further the conflict between Jesus and his opponents.

The Question about Fasting (54. Mark 2:18–22; Matthew 9:14–17; Luke 5:33–39). The question about fasting arises because Jesus' disciples do not follow the practice of John's disciples and the Pharisees. The law called for fasting on the day of atonement; but the Pharisees also fasted each week, and special fasts were observed at other times. The answer of Jesus is given in three word-pictures: a wedding, a garment, and wineskins. The figure of the wedding and the bridegroom is significant, for the kingdom of God was frequently pictured as a wedding feast. Jesus claims that the kingdom is in some sense at hand and that he himself is central in the kingdom. The sayings concerning the garment and the wineskins show the general relationship of Christianity to Judaism—Christianity cannot be contained in the old forms of Judaism. Thus both Jesus in giving these teachings and the Church in preserving them in the Gospels move away from Christianity's Jewish origins.

Plucking Ears of Grain on the Sabbath (69. Mark 2:23–28; Matthew 12:1–8; Luke 6:1–5). Two controversies revolve around Jesus' failure to observe the sabbath. That the issue was a real one for Jesus and the early Christians is shown by the fact that the issue is dealt with in two episodes in Mark, in two Lucan stories (13:10–17; 14:1–6),

---

[55] For a report on the discussion of "Son of man," see A. J. B. Higgins, "Son of Man *Forshung* since 'The Teaching of Jesus,'" *New Testament Essays; Studies in Memory of Thomas Walter Manson 1893–1958*, ed. A. J. B. Higgins, pp. 119–135; Reginald H. Fuller, *The New Testament in Current Study*, pp. 37–42; and Matthew Black, "The Son of Man Problem in Recent Research and Debate," *Bulletin of the John Rylands Library*, XLV (March, 1963), 305–318.

and in two Johannine stories (5:1–19; 9:1–41). The controversy over plucking ears of grain comes to a climax in a pronouncement of Jesus, "The sabbath was made for man, not man for the sabbath; so the Son of man is Lord even of the sabbath." Matthew and Luke change this to read simply, "The Son of man is Lord of the sabbath," and Matthew adds "I tell you, something greater than the temple is here." What is meant by Son of man here? The term may refer to Jesus himself or, since Son of man at times means simple "man," the idea may be that man as man is superior to the sabbath. A rabbinic comment on Exodus 31:14 taught that, "The Sabbath is delivered unto you, and ye are not delivered to the Sabbath." [56] But whether to man as man or Jesus Christ as Son of man, the Gospel writers clearly intend to subordinate sabbath law. Consistent with Jesus' typical ethical point of view, sabbath law is interpreted as a means toward a moral end, but not as the end itself.

The Man with the Withered Hand (70. Mark 3:1–6; Matthew 12:9–14; Luke 6:6–11). The healing of the man with the withered hand is the second episode showing in a concrete way the attitude Jesus had toward the sabbath. Jesus' answer to his own question, "Is it lawful on the sabbath to do good or to do harm, to save life or to kill?" is made plain when he said to the man with the withered hand, "Stretch out your hand." The story also demonstrates the hostility of the Pharisees to Jesus. They were watching so they could accuse Jesus of breaking the sabbath. When he healed the man, they "immediately held counsel with the Herodians against him, how to destroy him."

Discipleship

The disciples of Jesus play an important role in the entire gospel story. The call of the first disciples was noted earlier in Mark 1:16–20 and parallels. The Gospels also tell of the choice of a special group of twelve disciples from the larger group, instructions to the disciples, and the mission of the twelve in Galilee.

The Call of the Twelve (72. Mark 3:13–19; Matthew 10:1–4; Luke 6:12–16). Jesus is reported by the Gospels to have chosen twelve from among his followers "to be with him, and to be sent out to preach and have authority to cast out demons." The title "apostle" is not used

[56] R. Simeon B. Menasya quoted in Taylor, *The Gospel According to St. Mark,* p. 219.

in Mark, and probably the use of the term in the later Church caused Luke and Matthew to use it in their accounts of the call of the twelve.

The names of the twelve are given at this point in the Gospels and in Acts 1:13. The two pairs of brothers, Simon Peter and Andrew, James and John, are prominent. Then comes Philip, Bartholomew, Matthew, Thomas, James the son of Alphaeus, Thaddaeus,[57] Simon the Cananean,[58] and Judas Iscariot.[59] All except the first four names and Judas Iscariot are little more than names in the Gospels' presentation of Jesus. Only Peter, James, and John continue to be prominent after the death of Jesus, and Peter is far more important in the history of the early Church than the other two. Although some of the twelve disciples are little more than names, the historicity of the call of twelve is not to be doubted. The inclusion of Judas Iscariot in the group was a problem faced by the early Church and surely the Church would not have created a tradition which involved such a difficulty. Paul's mention of the twelve in I Corinthians 15 further supports the authenticity of the tradition.

The *group* of twelve, probably all Jewish laymen from Galilee, is important for the ministry of Jesus. The choice of *twelve* is an enacted parable showing the meaning of Jesus' ministry. There were twelve tribes of Israel; the disciples represent the twelve tribes. Here is the beginning of the new Israel which Jesus is forming!

The Sending Out of the Twelve (109. Mark 6:6–13; Matthew 9:35; 10:1, 9–11, 14; Luke 9:1–6). All three Synoptic Gospels give an account of the sending out of the twelve. Luke includes an additional account of a mission of seventy disciples (10:1–20).[60] The twelve were sent out two by two to preach the gospel and to heal, that is, to carry out the mission of Jesus as his commissioned representatives. The account of the charge emphasizes the necessary urgency and haste. Surprisingly, no detailed report of the work of the disciples is given. Mark simply states that "they went out and preached that men should repent. And they cast out many demons, and anointed with oil many that were sick and healed them." Luke says that "they departed and went through the villages, preaching the gospel and healing everywhere." Matthew gives no word about the execution of the mission.

[57] Luke and Acts say Judas, the son of James, instead of Thaddaeus.
[58] Or the Zealot according to Luke and Acts.
[59] Judas Iscariot is, of course, omitted from the Acts' roster.
[60] The number seventy or seventy-two according to Jewish reckoning stands for the nations of the world, and Luke may see in the mission of the seventy a foreshadowing of the Gentile mission.

Instruction of the Twelve (58–63. Matthew 9:35–11:1). The Church was particularly interested in the instructions given to the first disciples, for their mission was also the mission of the later Church. For example, Matthew, who is quite interested in the life and mission of the early Church, places more importance upon the discourse to the disciples than even the other writers, making it the subject of the second major discourse in his Gospel. The mission charge to the twelve in Matthew, like the Sermon on the Mount, is a compilation of sayings from the various sources and from various historical contexts. The saying in 10:18, for example, "You will be dragged before governors and kings for my sake, to bear testimony before them and the Gentiles," anticipates an historical context much later than that which it occupies in the Gospel. Obviously Matthew has moved material from the apocalyptic discourse in Mark 13 to this earlier discourse, disregarding the fact that some elements are quite incompatible with the context of an early mission in Galilee. The sayings in the mission charge reflect events not only in the life of Jesus, but also, more important for the early Christians and Gospel writers, in the activity and the life of the early Church.

Teaching in Parables

The teachings of Jesus abound in similes, metaphors, and other rather typical figures of speech which serve to make his message heard and understood by his followers. The figurative use of language was very common in the Old Testament and Jesus' use of these figures is in no way surprising or unique. However, another form of teaching related to the figurative use of language which appears less frequently in the Old Testament but regularly in the teachings of Jesus is the parable. Jesus' use of the parable is extensive, but has long been misunderstood. Until the last of the nineteenth century the parables were treated as allegories in which every detail had spiritual significance. An effort was made to discover the meaning of these figures through attention to the minutest parts of the parable with little concern for its overall motif. At the last of the nineteenth century, however, Adolph Jülicher demonstrated that the parables were not allegories whose details were to be applied specifically, but unified stories concerned more directly with a single idea.[61] Since the time of Jülicher, scholars have made progress in determining the specific teaching of the parables. Jülicher emphasized general moral teachings as the points of the

---

[61] A. Jülicher, *Die Gleichnisreden Jesu*, 2 vols.

parables, but later scholars [62] have given more attention to how the major point of each of the parables is related to an immediate situation of Jesus' ministry. An understanding of the central significance of Jesus and his ministry is necessary for an understanding of the meaning of the parables.[63]

Mark has a collection of parables in 4:1–32. Matthew used these parables and those from his other sources to compile his third major discourse. Luke does not follow Mark here as closely as at other points. He gives only the parable of the sower, the reason for speaking in parables, the interpretation of the parable of the sower, and the purpose of parables. He later gives the parable of the mustard seed, but other materials in Mark 4:1–32 and Matthew 13:1–42 are omitted by Luke altogether.

The Parable of the Sower (90, 93. Mark 4:1–9, 13–20; Matthew 13:1–9, 18–23; Luke 8:4–8, 11–15). The parable of the sower is a simple story of a farmer sowing seed on the variety of soils in a Palestinian field. Some soil does not permit growth, but some good soil does and it brings forth grain, "growing up and increasing and yielding thirtyfold and sixtyfold and a hundredfold." The emphasis is not on the seed wasted but on the abundance of the harvest. The parable is one of assurance and encouragement. Did it serve to assure Jesus' disciples that the proclamation of the kingdom would prosper although it seemed that some efforts were wasted? It may be directly related to the kingdom of God, illustrating that after the sowing of past ages and much apparent failure, the kingdom has now come. Although the general message of the parable is clear, the precise point is not. The interpretation of the parable of the sower (93. Mark 4:13–20; Matthew 13:18–23; Luke 8:11–15) gives specific significance to the details of the parable. It is the type of interpretation which would be valuable in the early Church and is probably the creation of Mark or the early Church to clarify the parable coming from Jesus. Although the parable stresses the abundance of the harvest, the interpretation

---

[62] C. H. Dodd, *The Parables of the Kingdom*, and Joachim Jeremias, *The Parables of Jesus.*

[63] C. H. Dodd emphasized that the parables concerned the Kingdom of God which had arrived in Jesus Christ. See his, *The Parables of the Kingdom.* Joachim Jeremias, *The Parables of Jesus*, tr. S. H. Hooke, followed Dodd's lead, pointing out the veiled kingliness and the necessity for decision implied in the parables. Dan O. Via, Jr., *The Parables: Their Literary and Existential Dimension*, has criticized the "severely historical" approach of parable study and suggests that some of the parables are literary works, genuine works of art, the message of which must be gained from a study of the parable itself, as an aesthetic object.

focuses upon the hearer as a vital part of the process. He is the soil upon which the seed falls.

The Reason for Speaking in Parables (91. Mark 4:10–12; Matthew 13:10–15; Luke 8:9–10). The statement of the reason for speaking in parables reveals more about the historical situation of the early Church than it does about Jesus. The Hellenistic world was more accustomed to allegories which veiled truth than to parables which illustrated and expounded truth more directly. The early Church knew that the *result* of the primitive preaching and teaching was not a faithful response by all of Israel. Rather, as is seen in Romans 9–11, Israel had not yet responded. So Mark, in light of this awareness of the early Church, gives the *purpose* of parables as the concealment of truth from the uninitiated and the revelation of truth to the initiated. Concealment, however, was certainly not Jesus' purpose in using parables.[64]

In the context of Jesus' ministry it is possible to understand Mark 4:10–11 to affirm that many were unable to understand Jesus and his teachings because they were unwilling to respond to the kingdom of God. The term "parable" in this case would have the meaning of "riddle," and the original reference would have been not to the parables *per se* but to Jesus' teaching in general.[65] It is also often pointed out that the Greek particle translated "so that" in Mark 4:12 may be a mistranslation of an Aramaic particle which either may express purpose or be used as a relative pronoun. It is supposed that here Jesus used the particle as a relative pronoun, but it was mistranslated into the Greek as an expression of purpose. Parables are for those *who* do not understand not *in order that* they may not understand.[66] It is also true that Mark 4:12 can be read as a Semitic statement in which no real distinction is made between cause and result. Thus the statement may reflect the consequences and not the motive for parables. The *result* of parabolic speech is misunderstanding but the *purpose* is understanding.

The Seed Growing Secretly (95. Mark 4:26–29). The short parable of the seed growing secretly is found only in Mark. It accurately reflects the work of the Palestinian farmer whose day began at sunrise and portrays the growth, ripening, and harvest of the grain planted by

---

[64] Matthew changes Mark's "so that" to "because"—". . . I speak to them in parables, because seeing they do not see . . ." Indeed, the Greek particle used by Mark may be causal, just as Matthew interpreted it.

[65] See Jeremias, *The Parables of Jesus*, pp. 13–17.

[66] See T. W. Manson, *The Teaching of Jesus*, pp. 77–80.

the farmer. But what meaning does it have for Jesus and the kingdom of God? Several possibilities are suggested: that Jesus' ministry has begun a process which must go on to completion without dependence upon human activity (emphasizing "of itself"), that the development of God's kingdom is gradual ("first the blade . . ."), that men are involved in the growth of the kingdom as they are involved in the growth of grain (a man "scatters seed," but the seed grows "he knows not how"), that the kingdom has come with the ministry of Jesus ("the harvest has come"). Although the first three interpretations are possible, the last one, accepted by C. H. Dodd and Joachim Jeremias in some form, fits very well in the context of Jesus' ministry as it has been conceived. Dodd says that "we must conceive Jesus not as sowing the seed, nor yet as watching the growth and predicting a harvest in the future, but as standing in the presence of the ripe crop, and taking active steps to 'put in the sickle.' " [67]

The Parable of the Weeds (96, 100. Matthew 13:24–30, 36–43). Matthew alone gives the parable of the weeds (13:24–30) and its interpretation (13:36–43). This parable is a vividly told story of agricultural life in Palestine. The weeds in the story are taken to be darnel, which grew in abundance and which so resembled wheat in the early stages of growth that they were difficult to distinguish from each other. The major emphasis in the story is the response of the farmer when he learns that weeds grow among the wheat. The farmer rejects a premature separation, but he does specify that separation will eventually take place. The parable is set in the context of the religion of Jesus' day with its divisions and separatists groups, and suggests Jesus' practice of welcoming tax collectors and sinners to the dismay of other more "religious" groups. The parable may be taken as a refusal to allow divisions based on human judgment and a promise that judgment will come, indeed has already begun, in the coming of the kingdom in Jesus. The interpretation of the parable (13:36–43) is more suggestive of the historical situation in the time of the early Church and is an application of the major point of the parable to the Church of Matthew's day by the evangelist himself. The stress in Matthew's interpretation is upon the future judgment. Although Jesus gave the parable in the midst of his eschatological ministry and proclamation of the coming of the kingdom, Matthew interprets the teaching as he stands between

---

[67] Dodd, *Parables of the Kingdom*, p. 179. This interpretation is necessary when the ministry of Jesus, including the proclamation of the Kingdom, is seen as the eschatological crisis in which God confronts men in Jesus Christ and demands immediate decision in light of the crisis. See Jeremias, *Parables of Jesus*, pp. 91–92.

the cross and the parousia. In the interval the Church is faced with the problem of unrighteous members and internal discipline. Matthew understands that the coming of the Son of man will rid the kingdom of all "causes of sin and all evil doers" and "the righteous will shine like the sun in the kingdom of their father."

The Mustard Seed and the Leaven (97–98. Mark 4:30–32; Matthew 13:31–33; Luke 13:18–21). The parable of the mustard seed and the parable of the leaven are twin parables which get across their point by contrast. The parable of the mustard seed compares the kingdom to "the smallest of all the seeds on earth which becomes the greatest of all shrubs." The fact that the mustard is not actually the smallest of seeds is quite beside the point that Jesus is making through hyperbolic contrast. From "the smallest" to "the greatest" emphasizes the great growth resulting from a small beginning.[68] The parable of the leaven compares the kingdom to a small bit of leaven which leavens a mass of dough. Jesus' audience understood these parables as "telling how, by the same miraculous power, from the most insignificant beginnings, from the poor little band of Jesus' disciples, out of a thing of nought, God was causing his Kingdom to grow." [69]

The Hidden Treasure, the Pearl, the Net, and the Householder (101–103. Matthew 13:44–52). Mark concluded his series of parables with the parable of the mustard seed and a concluding statement (4:33–34), but Matthew gives additional parables from his own peculiar sources to complete his third discourse. The parables of the hidden treasure and the pearl of great price point out the surpassing worth of the kingdom. Everything must be given up in order to gain it. The parable of the net in its present form resembles the parable of the tares and speaks of judgment.[70] Matthew concludes his compilation with a parable of the householder. The follower of Jesus has in his treasury both "what is new and what is old," that is, both the law and the gospel. Evidently Matthew's particular interests play a part

[68] Dodd declares that the reference to the birds of the air making nests in the shade of the tree "is a clear reference to Old Testament passages (Dan. iv. 12, Ezek. xxxi. 6, xvii. 23), where a tree sheltering the birds is a symbol for a great empire offering political protection to its subject states." Then the parable would be emphasizing that "the time has come when the blessings of the Reign of God are available for all men." *The Parables of the Kingdom*, pp. 190–191.

[69] Jeremias, *The Parables of Jesus*, p. 91.

[70] T. W. Manson, *The Sayings of Jesus*, p. 197, suggests that 13:47 formed a parable by itself and was a parable of missionary work which appealed to all sorts of men.

in his conclusion, i.e. he is concerned to show the continuity between Judaism and the Church. The Church possesses the law as reinterpreted and expanded by Jesus.[71]

Mighty Works

Following the parables of 4:1–34, Mark gives a series of Jesus' mighty works (4:35–5:43). Stories of the stilling of the storm on the lake, the exorcism of the Gadarene demoniac, the raising of Jairus' daughter, and the healing of the woman with the issue of blood are told in great detail to show Jesus as a miracle worker. Vincent Taylor [72] correctly points out the value of studying these stories as a definite form of oral tradition deeply imbedded in the life and faith of early Christians. The stories may be thought of as "miracle stories" whose significance is found, at least in part, in their *form*. Each episode is related in three essential parts. First, circumstances surrounding the miracle are told. Then, the miracle itself is recorded. Finally, the outcome is described. A careful analysis of this form of each story assists the reader in distinguishing between stories which have been greatly colored by the Church and those which stand nearer the primitive accounts. By comparing the miracle stories with Jewish and Hellenistic tradition the worth of the Gospel stories is revealed; there is no serious reason to think that the Gospel miracles have been formed merely by a process of borrowing.[73] A form-critical study of the miracles "supplies no basis for the inference that doctrinal interests were responsible for their formation, or indeed that they arose out of any other motive than the desire to illustrate the power and compassion of Jesus." [74] This does not mean that the miracle episodes may, therefore, be read as simple history. Form criticism does not supply a scientific explanation of the historical problem of miracles, but rather assists in clarifying the literary tradition out of which the materials were preserved. In this sense criticism may increase the historical value of the stories, but their acceptance or rejection as accurate and adequate portrayals of Jesus remains in the area of faith. The problem "does not admit of any solution which can be called scientific, for our decision includes a personal element which cannot be removed; it depends on our world view, our estimate of the person of Christ, and

---

[71] See below, pp. 480–481.
[72] See Taylor, *The Formation of the Gospel Tradition*, pp. 119–141.
[73] See Fuller, *Interpreting the Miracles*, pp. 33–35.
[74] Taylor, *The Formation of the Gospel Tradition*, p. 141.

our use of the principles of historical criticism." [75] The modern believer, like the early Church, must decide what, if any, authentic word comes from these stories.

The Miracle Stories and the Gospel Writers. The miracle stories must be viewed from the perspectives of the ministry of Jesus, the early Christians who transmitted the stories, and the Gospel writers. Obviously, the Gospel writers arranged the materials according to their individual purposes. Luke, for example, follows the order of Mark but alters the context. Mark shows Jesus in the same boat from which he had taught the parables, but Luke introduces the series of miracles with an abrupt general statement, "One day he got into a boat with his disciples . . ." (Luke 8:22). Matthew places the miracle stories in an earlier stage of the ministry and separates the first two miracles from the last two by the story of the healing of the paralytic and the call of Matthew (Matthew 9:1–17). Further Luke and Matthew present the stories from some different perspectives than Mark. In the stilling of the storm, for example, Mark shows Jesus sternly rebuking the disciples, "Why are you afraid? Have you no faith?" Luke and Matthew soften the rebuke. Luke asks simply, "Where is your faith?" and Matthew designates the disciples as men of "little" rather than "no" faith. This alteration may be due to the growing respect for the apostles in the history of the Church.

The Stilling of the Storm (105. Mark 4:35–41; Matthew 8:18, 23–27; Luke 8:22–25). The stilling of the storm shows Jesus' power to control the forces of nature. "Whatever view is taken of the miraculous element in the story, there can be little doubt that the story belongs to the best tradition, probably that of an eye-witness and presumably Peter." [76] What really happened? The Sea of Galilee, 650 feet below sea level with hills around, experienced the sudden rise and fall of storms; and it is possible to think of coincidence when reading the story. Nevertheless, the disciples did not so interpret it. They saw in Jesus a power superior to the wind and waves of nature.

The Gadarene (Gerasene) Demoniac (106. Mark 5:1–20; Matthew 8:28–34; Luke 8:26–39). The incident of the healing of the Gadarene demoniac is not quite so simple, although its basic meaning seems fairly clear. The location of the event, important to an understanding

---

[75] Taylor, *The Formation of the Gospel Tradition*, p. 134; Fuller, *Interpreting the Miracles*, pp. 8–17.

[76] Taylor, *The Gospel According to St. Mark*, p. 272.

of the story, cannot be certainly established. In Mark the best reading locates it in Gerasa, but this is thirty miles southeast of the Sea of Galilee and cannot fit the story. Perhaps Matthew's "Gadarene" was an attempt to correct the primitive error. In the fourth century Origen suggested that Gergesa on the Lake of Galilee fitted the Gospel description. The precise location is not centrally important, but its general location on the eastern shore of the Sea of Galilee, a Gentile region, is crucial for interpreting the episode. Swine, considered unclean animals by the Jews, would certainly have been herded only by Gentiles. Further, Jewish disciples of Jesus' day would have had less difficulty accepting Jesus' destruction of property because of the Jewish attitude toward swine. In fact, the story of the swine is humorous when read from a first century perpective. The difficulty of the details gives no reason for doubting that the story is a true story of Jesus' curing a maniac. The scene changes from the man to the swine to the town people and back to the man, but the central feature in all is the exorcism, with an emphasis on the complex and dangerous nature of the man's trouble.

Jairus' Daughter and the Woman with the Hemorrhage (107. Mark 5:21–43; Matthew 9:18–26; Luke 8:40–56). The miracles of the raising of Jairus' daughter and the woman with the hemorrhage ("issue of blood") are woven together in a unique way for the Synoptic Gospels. The connecting links in the stories in Mark make it "reasonable to infer that the connection is historical, and not merely literary."[77] Jesus had traveled westward across the Sea of Galilee where Jairus, the president of a synagogue, met him and asked help for his daughter. As Jesus accompanied Jairus with a great crowd, a woman who had suffered a hemorrhage for twelve years touched Jesus' clothing and the hemorrhage ceased. As Jesus talked with her, some from Jairus' house came with the news that Jairus' daughter was dead. Jesus, however, assured Jairus, "Do not fear, only believe," went on to the house and told the crowd, "The child is not dead but sleeping," and entered the house and raised her. The stories in Mark read like a "record based on personal testimony."[78] Luke follows Mark closely, but Matthew abbreviates the account of both miracles. Note that Mark and Luke first report that the girl is dying, but Matthew reports from the first, "My daughter has just died . . ." Matthew, therefore, has no place for the messengers coming later with word

[77] *Ibid.*, p. 289.
[78] *Ibid.*, p. 285.

about the death of the girl. Matthew also shortens the report of the healing of the woman with the hemorrhage. Speculation has been made about the exact condition of the daughter of Jairus and sometimes the assumption has been made that she was only in a coma. It is then assumed that the Gospel writers transformed her recovery into a miracle story. Mark does report initially that the girl is "at the point of death" and, even after the report comes that she is dead, Jesus says, "The child is not dead but sleeping." The people interpret this as a literal statement and laugh at him. The Gospel writers, reporting from their experience of the resurrection of Jesus, do not speculate. They aim to report that the girl was dead and Jesus restored her. Matthew makes the Marcan account even more explicit to emphasize the main issue at stake, namely, that even death itself must yield to Jesus' power.

This study of the Synoptic tradition concerning the Galilean ministry of Jesus reinforces the view that a detailed biography of Jesus cannot be written. Yet a clear picture of Jesus emerges. Jesus came out of the John the Baptist movement and began his independent ministry after John's death. Jesus' ministry centered in the proclamation of the kingdom of God, the rule or reign of God which was breaking through in the ministry of Jesus. Not only did Jesus proclaim the kingdom, primarily through parables, but he also actualized the rule of God in his deeds—in his exorcisms and in his relationship with the outcast. The following chapters continue and enlarge the basic picture gained through a study of this earlier material.

SUGGESTED READINGS

The Birth of Jesus

TAYLOR, VINCENT, *The Historical Evidence of the Virgin Birth* (Clarendon Press, 1920). A dispassionate treatment of the subject.

John the Baptist

KRAELING, C. H., *John the Baptist* (Scribner's, 1951). Excellent book on the Baptist.

Jesus' Preaching and Teaching

DODD, C. H., *The Parables of the Kingdom* (Scribner's, 1961). Made a decisive breakthrough in the modern study of the parables. First published in 1935.

HUNTER, A. M., *A Pattern for Life* (Westminster, 1953). Describes the making, manner, matter, and meaning of the Sermon on the Mount in popular language.

——, *Interpreting the Parables* (Westminster, 1960). A popular but knowledgeable treatment of Jesus' parables.

JEREMIAS, JOACHIM, *The Parables of Jesus* (Scribner's, 1962). First published in German in 1947. The best book on the parables. Available in abridged edition.

McARTHUR, HARVEY K., *Understanding the Sermon on the Mount* (Harper, 1960). Gives summary of ways Christians have regarded the Sermon.

WILDER, AMOS N., "The Sermon on the Mount," IB, Vol. VII. Good summary of nature and relevance of the Sermon.

Jesus' Healing

FULLER, REGINALD H., *Interpreting the Miracles* (Westminster, 1963). A form-critical approach to the miracle stories.

McCASLAND, S. VERNON, *By the Finger of God* (Macmillan, 1951). A good account of the understanding modern psychotherapy gives to Jesus' healings.

RICHARDSON, ALAN, *The Miracle Stories of the Gospels* (S.C.M., 1941). A helpful study of miracles.

4

Ministry Beyond Galilee;
Journey to Jerusalem

The Synoptic sources for studying Jesus end his Galilean ministry after the return of the twelve from their mission (Mark 6:30, Matthew 14:13, Luke 9:10). From Mark 6:30 on, Jesus is presented as withdrawing from Galilee, moving from place to place, and eventually making a journey to Jerusalem. No clear reason for this action is given by the Gospels. Their interpreters have made a number of suggestions. Some say that Jesus' movements during this period constitute a flight from Herod. The stories of Herod's fears about Jesus (Mark 16:14–16) and the murder of John the Baptist (Mark 6:17–29) are given immediately before the withdrawal and possibly Jesus himself was an object of suspicion at the court of Herod.[1] But others deny that he is fleeing from Herod. They cite the response of Jesus to certain Pharisees who told him to depart because Herod desired to kill him: "Behold, I cast out demons and perform cures today and tomorrow, and the third day I finish my course. Nevertheless, I must go on my way today and tomorrow and the day following, for it cannot be that a prophet should perish away from Jerusalem" (Luke 13:32–33). Accordingly Jesus' movement did not come from fear of Herod, but resulted from the conscious choice of Jesus in light of his understanding of his mission. Herod's hostility may have caused Jesus to envision the revolutionary excitement that might be provoked by Herod's hostil-

---

[1] See F. Crawford Burkitt, *The Gospel History and Its Transmission*, pp. 93–94; Maurice Goguel, *The Life of Jesus*, tr. Olive Wyon, pp. 359–364; and Hans Lietzmann, *The Beginnings of the Christian Church*, tr. Bertram Lee Woolf, pp. 70–71.

ity and so withdrew to restrain his followers from armed rebellion against Rome.[2]

Still others frequently suggest that the failure of the people of Galilee to understand the message of Jesus caused him to withdraw. T. W. Manson declared, "I regard this withdrawal as a flight, but far more a flight from the dangerous enthusiasm of his friends than from the suspicion, and fears of his enemies."[3] Thus, the withdrawal is understood as necessary to avoid further arousing invalid messianic expectations among his followers.

The sources, however, do not justify any convincing conclusion that Jesus' withdrawal and journey to Jerusalem were simply either a flight from Herod, an attempt to avoid armed rebellion, or an escape from a supposed failure of the Galilean mission. The Gospels, for example, do not show Jesus' movement to be directed against political rulers, either Rome or Herod; Jesus' ministry was not in the political centers. Nor do the Gospels report failure in Galilee extensive enough to cause Jesus to change the locale of his ministry. "The Gospels seem more likely to be historically correct when they report that success and failure, popularity and enmity, had been part and parcel of Jesus' life from the start . . ."[4] Although these may have been contributing factors in Jesus' decision, they certainly were not determinative. The dominant reason for the movement of Jesus from Galilee to Jerusalem must have been a desire to minister in Jerusalem. "The reason why Jesus sets out with his disciples on his journey to Jerusalem cannot be doubted. It was to deliver the message of the coming Kingdom of God in Jerusalem also, Jerusalem which Jesus himself calls the city of God, 'the city of the Great King' (Matthew 5:35)."[5]

Strategically in the Synoptics, an account of a ministry beyond Galilee is placed just after the ministry in Galilee and just before the journey to Jerusalem which results in Jesus' crucifixion. The rationale of the evangelists seems to be twofold: (1) to introduce a further mission of Jesus and (2) to begin the story of his death. Subsequent events suggest that this was a period of Jesus' contemplation upon his ministry and preparation for further work in the south. In retrospect,

[2] Vincent Taylor, *The Life and Ministry of Jesus*, pp. 126–127.

[3] T. W. Manson, *The Servant-Messiah: A Study of the Public Ministry of Jesus,* p. 71. See also C. H. Dodd, "The Life and Teaching of Jesus Christ," *A Companion to the Bible,* ed. T. W. Manson, p. 383; and Taylor, *The Life and Ministry of Jesus,* p. 127.

[4] Günther Bornkamm, *Jesus of Nazareth,* tr. Irene and Fraser McLuskey with James M. Robinson, p. 153.

[5] *Ibid.,* p. 154.

however, the Gospel writers understood that the most important item still to happen was the crucifixion.[6]

WITHDRAWAL FROM GALILEE

During the period of withdrawal and before the journey to Jerusalem, Jesus conducted a ministry beyond Galilee through a series of significant events leading to the climactic "confession" at Caesarea Philippi.

The Ministry Beyond Galilee

Mark 6:14–8:26 contains a series of stories in which Jesus ministers almost completely outside Galilee. The section is introduced by the story about Herod's opinion of Jesus and the account of the death of John the Baptist. The return of the twelve and the feeding of the five thousand with events immediately following and the feeding of the four thousand with events immediately following complete the section.

Luke follows Mark in giving the opinion of Herod concerning Jesus, the death of John, and the feeding of the five thousand; but afterwards he omits almost two chapters of the Marcan narrative, moving directly from the feeding of the five thousand to the experiences of Caesarea Philippi. Matthew, on the other hand, faithfully follows the Marcan sequence beginning at 6:1 and moving on through the end of the Gospel with few omissions or transpositions. Matthew, of course, does add new material to the Marcan outline.

Herod's Opinion of Jesus (110. Mark 6:14–16; Matthew 14:1–2; Luke 9:7–9). Mark introduces this phase of ministry by stating Herod's opinion of Jesus: "John, whom I beheaded, has been raised." Matthew follows Mark in making Herod agree with a popular idea that explained Jesus' power by identifying him with a resurrected John the Baptist. Luke, however, alters the idea by having Herod say, "John I beheaded; but who is this about whom I hear such things?" The deliberate alteration of the Marcan report rejects the idea that Jesus could be John *redivivus*. Mark includes at this point a rather detailed description of John's death at the hands of Herod, an account which is revised by Matthew and omitted by Luke. This Herod is Herod Antipas, the son of Herod the Great who had taken charge of Galilee and Peraea when his father died in 4 B.C. He continued as

---

[6] Note Matthew 16:21f.; Luke 9:2; Mark 8:3.

tetrarch of the area until A.D. 39. The entire episode serves as a sort of connecting link or introduction to Jesus' ministry beyond Galilee.

The Feeding of the Five Thousand (112. Mark 6:30–44; Matthew 14:13–21; Luke 9:10–17). The feeding of the five thousand occupies a major place in the Gospel description of the ministry beyond Galilee. It is the only miracle reported by all four Gospel writers.[7] After the disciples had returned to Jesus to report on their mission, Jesus and the disciples went away by boat "to a lonely place by themselves." A throng gathered, Jesus taught and the time grew late, the crowd became hungry but no food was available. Jesus discussed the problem with the disciples and they, at his request, found five loaves and two fish. Jesus then proceeded to feed the people.

And taking the five loaves and the two fish he looked up to heaven, and blessed, and broke the loaves, and gave them to the disciples to set before the people; and he divided the two fish among them all. And they all ate and were satisfied. And they took up twelve baskets full of broken pieces and of the fish. (Mark 6:41–43)

As the story is read, parallels can be seen to a regular meal and, perhaps more important, to the Last Supper and the repetition of the Supper in the early Church. These similarities have led some to question whether this episode should be read as a miracle in the sense of a supernatural act. Some elements of the story itself are taken to show that the incident was non-miraculous. For example, the disciples and the people were not surprised at the multiplication of the loaves and fish. Further, the act seems somewhat contrary to the total context of Jesus' ministry in which he consistently avoided spectacular deeds which would attract a crowd without an understanding of his real intention.

It is also possible to explain the story in such ways as to deemphasize the supernatural aspects contained in it. The story may be real as an allegory showing Jesus as the Bread of Life. Striking similarities with certain Old Testament episodes may be pointed out and made crucial for interpreting the Gospel event: God fed the Israelites with manna, and Elisha could cause twenty loaves to feed one hundred men. Thus it could be concluded that the story here aims to portray Jesus as greater than a Moses or an Elisha. A much less likely notion is that Jesus simply set an example and the crowd brought out their lunch and shared the food which they had earlier hidden. The miracle

---

[7] Cf. John 6:4–14 with the Synoptic passages.

would then be in the changed attitudes of the people.[8] All these ideas are interesting and suggestive, but they move from an interpretative bias and help little in either establishing or discounting historicity. What actually happened can no longer be recovered. "Since the feeding of the multitude occupies such a clearly defined place at a critical turn of the ministry, we may reasonably suppose that it grew out of a genuine memory," [9] but the telling of the story in the Gospels has certainly been shaped by later theology. Whether supernatural miracle or ordinary meal, the Church and the evangelists saw in the episode a dramatic demonstration of the character of Jesus and his ministry. Although the entire episode may be colored by the faith of the early Church and analogies drawn by believers between the feeding and their experience around the Lord's table, the writers recount more than an early ritual meal. To them the multiplication of loaves and fish reveals God's presence, so full and complete that even twelve baskets of fragments remain.

Walking on the Water and Healings at Gennesaret (113, 114. Mark 6:45–56; Matthew 14:22–36). The feeding of the five thousand is followed in Mark with the trip across the Sea of Galilee. The disciples leave for Bethsaida (6:45) but land at Gennesaret (6:53), to some an indication that Mark has combined two narratives originally independent of one another. Others, presupposing that the narratives were transmitted accurately together, attribute the change of destination to the "contrary wind" (6:48). During the stormy trip, Jesus appeared suddenly to the disciples while they were on the water. When he entered the boat, the wind ceased. Mark indicates that the disciples were "utterly astounded, for they did not understand about the loaves, but their hearts were hardened." This story would have meant much to the writer and early Christians who often faced peril. Here Jesus, known as resurrected Lord, is pictured as present in the midst of difficulty.[10] Even overwhelming danger subsides in his presence.

---

[8] Albert Schweitzer is the most noted exponent of the view that the meal was a ritual meal, a symbol of the messianic banquet. *The Quest of the Historical Jesus,* tr. W. Montgomery, pp. 377–379. For other interpretations and a bibliography, see Taylor, *The Gospel According to St. Mark,* pp. 321–322.

[9] Fuller, *Interpreting the Miracles,* p. 37.

[10] Fuller, *Interpreting the Miracles,* pp. 58–59, says that "here is revelation of the Old Testament God in the person of Jesus." In the Old Testament Yahweh walks on the water (Ps. 77:19; Job 9:8; 38:16) and the sea stands for the "power of chaos and death which threatens God's kingly rule. The theological point of this story is that in Jesus God is asserting his sovereignty over the uncanny realm of Satan."

Upon arrival at Gennesaret Jesus is confronted with the sick, who are healed merely by the touch of the fringe of Jesus' garment. The account of miracles in Mark 6:53–56 is a generalized summary of Jesus' activities composed from details in the actual miracle stories. The "touch of the fringe," for example, brings to mind the story of the healing of the woman with the hemorrhage (Mark 5:25–34). Such summaries really give little explicit direct evidence for the healing ministry of Jesus, but

. . . are valuable as supplementary testimony to the general tradition. They show that the separate stories which have been preserved are only a selection from a larger body of memories. They also have a negative value, for they contain no raisings from the dead and no nature miracles. This suggests that even if Jesus did perform miracles of that type, they were highly exceptional, not regular features of his ministry.[11]

What Defiles a Man (115. Mark 7:1–23; Matthew 15:1–20). The complex of Jesus' sayings on "what defiles a man" would have been exceptionally valuable to the early Church. The sayings begin with an overt pronouncement on the tradition of the elders (7:1–8) followed by four sayings on the same subject (9–13, 14–15, 17–19, 20–23). Moderns would treat the subject of defilement as inconsequential, but the first century Jews took it with deadly seriousness. Indeed, the Mishnah devotes a tractate to the subject of hand washing, a religious ritual to take away ceremonial defilement. In the Marcan and Matthean episode the conflict is over the oral law of the Pharisees. The struggle between Jews and Christians over the oral law continued into the life of the early Church and so gave these materials continuing relevance. The basic point of Jesus and of the Christians is stated as: "There is nothing outside a man which by going into him can defile him; but the things which come out of a man are what defile him." "When one considers the significance which was attached to the commandment for ritual cleanness . . . already in the Old Testament and not only in contemporary Jewish practice, one learns to appreciate the revolutionary meaning of the saying."[12] There is a real distinction between the teaching of Jesus and the rabbis of his day. The authority of the rabbis is *derived* from scripture and the authoritative exegesis of the "fathers." Jesus' teaching, on the other hand, "never consists merely in the interpretation of an authoritatively given sacred text, not even when words of scripture are quoted. The reality of God and the authority of his will are always directly present, and are fulfilled in him."

---

[11] Fuller, *Interpreting the Miracles*, pp. 35–36.
[12] Bornkamm, *Jesus of Nazareth*, p. 98.

Jesus "even dares to confront the literal text of the law with the immediately present will of God." [13]

The Syrophoenician Woman (116. Mark 7:24–30; Matthew 15:21–28). At first glance the story of the Syrophoenician woman looks like just another miracle story, but the circumstances suggest that the evangelists saw in the event far more than just another of Jesus' healings. The setting of the story is "the region of Tyre and Sidon" and the woman beseeching Jesus to heal her daughter was a Greek. [14] To her entreaty Jesus responded, "Let the children first be fed, for it is not right to take the children's bread and throw it to the dogs." The woman immediately saw the point. Jesus' ministry was first to the Jews ("the children"), not the Gentiles. But her response redirected the analogy to favor her request, "Yes, Lord; yet even the dogs under the table eat the children's crumbs." Although the Jews were the initial recipients of the gospel, the Gentiles too were ultimately included among its beneficiaries. Having made this point, possibly for the observing disciples, Jesus said to the woman, "For this saying you may go your way; the demon has left your daughter." In the context of Jesus' work, the story emphasizes that his ministry is to Israel, but it foreshadows a ministry of the Church beyond the limits of Israel. Such a story, showing the faith of a Gentile, would have appealed to early Gentile Christians and would have reminded Jewish Christians of the universal nature of the gospel and their responsibility to carry it beyond Palestinean borders.

Mark next has Jesus return from the north to the Sea of Galilee after which he heals a deaf man with a speech impediment. (117. Mark 7:31–37). Matthew simply gives a general statement of the healing of many sick persons (Matthew 15:29–31).

The Blind (118–121. Mark 8:1–26; Matthew 15:32–16:12). The stories in Mark 8:1–26 can be united under the general theme of "the blind." The series includes the miracle of the feeding of the four thousand, [15] the story of the Pharisees' demand for a sign from heaven which records Jesus as refusing to use signs to authenticate himself

---

[13] *Ibid.*, p. 57.

[14] Matthew calls her a Canaanite. This and other differences in Matthew's account suggests that Matthew had access to both Mark and another tradition and used both traditions to form his story.

[15] This story is strikingly similar to the feeding of the five thousand and may be another version of the same story. In this case, two different accounts of the same event would have grown up. Mark (and Matthew following him) would have known the two different versions and taken them to be separate incidents.

and his message, the discourse on leaven in which Jesus is apparently warning against the evil religious and political influence of Herod and the Pharisees, and the episode of the healing of the blind man at Bethsaida with its unique feature of stages in the development of the cure. The stories in this complex are impossible to understand simply as a narration of Jesus' ministry. No doubt they were originally based upon historical tradition, but were extracted from their historical context by the evangelist and arranged to declare a specific religious message to the Christians of Mark's day, Christians who had failed to understand. (Note the over-emphasis on the disciple's stupidity in Mark 8:14–21.)

The feeding of the four thousand is a sign of Jesus' person, of the glory of God (Mark 8:1–10). The unbelieving Pharisees were spiritually blind and could not see the sign even when they were demanding a sign (Mark 8:11–12). The disciples themselves were so blinded by preoccupation with the problem of bread that they failed to perceive its true source (Mark 8:14–21). Misunderstanding Christians of Mark's day are clearly in mind also! But to them Jesus brings light as he gave sight to the blind man of Bethsaida (Mark 8:22–26). ". . . as in the days of His flesh, Jesus was still the Giver of Light. Not once, but twice, had He laid His hands on a blind man near Bethsaida who at first saw men only as trees walking, but in the end was restored and saw all things clearly. So it had been with the disciples; so it would be again." [16]

Confession at Caesarea Philippi; Transfiguration

The Synoptic description of Jesus' ministry beyond Galilee is concluded with a group of narratives and sayings set around Caesarea Philippi, a village northeast of the Sea of Galilee at the foot of Mt. Hermon. These materials provide a fitting climax to the preceding ministry, but more decisively they prepare for the Jerusalem journey and the passion. Heretofore the kingdom of God had been the key theme of Jesus' teaching with hardly a mention of the cross. The experience at Caesarea Philippi, however, introduces the theme which will become the motif for all that follows. "From that time Jesus began to show his disciples that he must go to Jerusalem and suffer many things . . . and be killed" (Matthew 16:21). The cross of Jesus and the call for believers to bear their own crosses is the thread which unifies all else that the Synoptics have yet to say about their "Christ, the Son of the living God."

[16] Taylor, *The Gospel According to St. Mark,* p. 97.

The Confession at Caesarea Philippi (122. Mark 8:27–33; Matthew 16:13–23; Luke 9:18–22). The confession of Caesarea Philippi and the first prediction of the passion is reported in all three Synoptics, but with significant variations. A comparison of Matthew and Mark is particularly instructive. Mark has Jesus ask his disciples about the current opinions concerning himself. "Who do men say that the Son of man is?" The response indicates that the people think of Jesus as a leader and spokesman for God to be revered and heard, but Mark's real interest is not public opinion about Jesus. The real issue hinges upon Peter's declaration when pressed to state the disciples' opinion. He vigorously declared, "You are the Christ." According to Mark, Jesus neither commends Peter nor openly accepts the title. (Note also that Luke omits the rebuke of Peter, perhaps because of later respect for the apostle.) Rather, he begins to discuss the suffering of the Son of man. Matthew, however, follows Peter's confession with some non-Marcan material in which Jesus commends Peter, "Blessed are you, Simon Bar-Jona! For flesh and blood has not revealed this to you, but my Father who is in Heaven." Quite possibly Matthew here follows a practice seen elsewhere in the Gospel, namely, uniting materials from different literary and historical contexts. The early Church quite openly interpreted Jesus as God's Messiah, but the hesitation of Jesus in accepting the title (as shown by Mark) undoubtedly reflects historical reality more accurately. Since the term had political and military overtones quite at odds with Jesus' mission,[17] he in all probability would have avoided its use. Early Christians, however, could not fail to look back upon Caesarea Philippi from the perspective of their resurrection faith to understand the teacher of the disciples to be God's Messiah. Thus the story is not only an episode from the life of Jesus, but also a christological confession from the Church itself.

An important point in Mark is Jesus' prediction of his passion. Again, early Christians recorded the prediction after the actual events and their faith has influenced the recording. But there is no reason to challenge the essential historicity of the saying of Jesus.[18] Jesus sees

---

[17] See the form-critical treatment of the episode in Fuller, *The Foundations of New Testament Christology*, p. 109. Fuller sees the episode as a pronouncement story in which "Jesus rejects Messiahship as a merely human and even diabolical temptation."

[18] Francis W. Beare says that "unless we are to deny the very possibility of predictive prophecy, there seems to be no sufficient reason for challenging these sayings. It is surely not hard to suppose that Jesus was clear-sighted enough to foresee that the opponents of his ministry would sooner or later bring him to his death, and that his faith in God was so strong as to keep him calmly confident that his death would not be the end of the story." See his *The Earliest Records of Jesus*, p. 139.

that this ministry will bring him to death. But this is not the end. "After three days" (a short time) he will rise again. That suffering had no place in Peter's conception of Jesus' ministry is made plain by Peter's rebuke of Jesus. Matthew is more explicit than Mark, "God forbid, Lord! This shall never happen to you." For the Synoptics the idea is made all the more clear by the blindness of the Apostle. Jesus, who suffers, is the Christ!

The Conditions of Discipleship (123. Mark 8:34–9:1; Matthew 16:24–28; Luke 9:23–27). Jesus' prediction of his sufferings is followed by sayings which include his followers in the sufferings. "If any man would come after me, let him deny himself and take up his cross and follow me." For the disciples, and, perhaps more important for understanding the shaping of these words, for the early Church, sayings about the cross and death were not read from the comfortable context of figurative language. For countless numbers of early believers Jesus' words had the authentic ring of immediate and literal meaning. Consider Christians in Rome during and immediately after the persecution under Nero when death for one's faith was a real possibility. These sayings exhort such Christians to "deny himself and take up his cross," assures them that "whoever loses his life for my sake and the gospel's will save it," warning that "whoever is ashamed of me and of my words in this adulterous and sinful generation, of him will the Son of Man also be ashamed." The assurance of the near coming of God's kingdom with power served to bolster those who presently suffered for the sake of Jesus. A meaningful reading of the sayings for modern Christians ought to recapture the intense *Sitz im Leben* against which they were written.

The Transfiguration (124. Mark 9:2–8; Matthew 17:1–8; Luke 9:28–36). The transfiguration must be studied against the background of Jesus' prediction of his passion and of the sayings which involve his followers in his sufferings. Here an effort is made to express intimate, personal religious experiences in tangible words, a task relatively impossible in writing that purports to be scientific history, much less in works admittedly molded by religious faith. Thus, the reconstruction of what exactly happened upon the mountain is impossible. As an historical event the transfiguration may be interpreted as a visionary, mystical type of event related directly to the surrounding discussion of suffering and passion. Many factors must be considered in interpreting the event—the emotional state of the disciples after the prediction of the passion, the limited nature of language in communicating such religious experiences, the experiences and needs of later Christians. But whatever is concluded about the historicity of the story, the transfiguration must have deepened and confirmed the Petrine confession "in an incommunicable experience of prayer and religious insight." [19] Jesus is seen in celestial glory with Moses and Elijah, cryptic figures for the Law and the Prophets. What God has been doing in former days, he is now bringing to completion in his suffering son. The transfigured state is a forecast of the life of Jesus after the dire events have taken place.

The Coming of Elijah and an Epileptic Boy Healed (125, 126. Mark 9:9–29; Matthew 17:9–21; Luke 9:37–43). A conversation and an illustration provide the denouement for the transfiguration. As he came down from the mountain with the disciples, Jesus "charged them to tell no one what they had seen, until the Son of man should have risen from the dead." This charge meant little to the disciples, and they asked about the "Elijah" spoken of in the book of Malachi (4:5–6), who according to popular Jewish expectations was to precede the Messiah's arrival. Jesus explains then that an "Elijah" has already come in John the Baptist and his fate is a reflection of what will happen to the Son of man. "Elijah does come first to restore all things; and how is it written of the Son of man, that he should suffer many things and be treated with contempt? But I tell you that Elijah has come, and they did to him whatever they pleased, as it is written of him" (Mark 9:12). Jesus then relates what had happened to John to his imminent suffering and death. Mark then illustrates with the story of the healing of the epileptic boy the work of the suffering servant. The healing manifests the power of Jesus to help and to save.

THE JOURNEY FROM THE NORTH

All three Synoptics include Jesus' journey from the north to Jerusalem, although each handles the material in a slightly different way. Mark indicates the journey in 9:30 and in 10:1 [20] and emphasizes in it Jesus' private teachings to the disciples. Even when questions from outsiders are introduced, as in 10:2 and 10:17, Jesus' answers are mainly given to the disciples. Matthew places his fourth major discourse (Matthew 18:1–35) just before the departure from Galilee and

[19] Taylor, *The Gospel According to St. Mark*, p. 388. See pp. 386–388, for other interpretations which range from an objective historical experience to a purely symbolic interpretation.
[20] See also 10:17; 10:32; 10:46; and 11:1.

then follows Mark in a general way for the journey to Jerusalem. Luke not only gives the journey, but also makes it a significant turning point in his Gospel (9:51).[21] Indeed, Luke gives an expansive account of the journey in 9:51–18:14. This material, "Luke's Special Section," is independent of Mark and is composed of both Q and L material.

The Journey Through Galilee

Mark 9:30 records that "they went on from there and passed through Galilee," and Mark 10:1 says, "And he left there and went to the region of Judea and beyond the Jordan . . ." Between these two notices no detailed narrative covers the travel. Rather a series of somewhat disconnected teachings (the second prediction of the passion, the question about greatness, the strange exorcist, and teachings on temptations with a saying concerning salt) are inserted. Some of these materials are related to themes typical of the mission beyond Galilee, but others seem to be rather artificially inserted for reasons known only to the author.

The Second Prediction of the Passion (127. Mark 9:30–32; Matthew 17:22–23; Luke 9:43–45). The second prediction is the simplest of the three predictions of the passion.[22] It states the reason for the journey to Jerusalem. Jesus is going to Jerusalem to die. This is obvious to the evangelist who writes after the event. The fact that it "cannot be that a prophet should perish away from Jerusalem" (Luke 13:33) is known to Jesus himself, but the later experience of Jesus' teaching ministry in Jerusalem indicates that another purpose for the journey to Jerusalem was to proclaim the Kingdom there. Jesus wanted to teach there also, even if it precipitated reactions which would lead to suffering.

The Dispute about Greatness (129. Mark 9:33–37; Matthew 18:1–5; Luke 9: 46–48). The primary interest in this section is the saying, "If any one would be first, he must be last of all and servant of all." In fact, the saying seems to have been placed somewhat artificially in this context so that it would be remembered. Notice that in Mark 9:35 Jesus is pictured as sitting down and calling the twelve, but the immediately preceding verses indicate that the disciples were already in the house with Jesus. The phrase, "And he sat down and called the

---

[21] See also 13:22; 17:11; and 19:11.
[22] Cf. Mark 8:27–33 and 10:32–34.

twelve," betrays the independent setting of the saying about first and last.

This section also creates another context for the purpose of introducing a related saying. Jesus' recognition of a child is the context for the saying, "Whoever receives one such child in my name receives me; and whoever receives me, receives not me but him who sent me." In addition to connected narratives and sayings, fragmentary stories and sayings circulated in the early Church. Fragments like these could have been sufficiently important to insure their transmission. It is impossible to be certain about this, but "the genuineness of the traditions, and particularly that of the sayings, is not affected by this uncertainty." [23]

The Strange Exorcist and Sayings on Temptations and Salt (130–132. Mark 9:38–50; Matthew 18:6–9; Luke 9:49–50). The sayings in Mark 9:37–50 illustrate how some of the sayings of Jesus were memorized and transmitted by early Christians. "In my name" in 9:37 leads to the introduction of the story of the strange exorcist which includes the catch word "in my name" (9:38–41). The saying on receiving little children in 9:37 in a similar way leads to the saying in 9:42 about offending little ones. Then the word "fire" in 9:43 and 48 suggested the saying in 9:49, "For every one will be salted with fire," and the reference to salt leads to the three sayings on salt in Mark 9:50. Such structuring of the sayings occurred, according to Vincent Taylor, "to assist catechumens in committing the sayings to memory." A pre-Marcan compiler "appears to have taken his cue from the original parallelism in 43–7 and has selected for his purpose sayings which were of particular interest to the Roman community . . ." [24]

The catechetical methods of the pre-Gospel period which were at work in these verses may appear somewhat artificial, but by methods like these many of the sayings of Jesus were organized and transmitted before being written down. Moreover, "behind the catch words we see signs of poetical forms used by Jesus Himself which the compiler recognized and used." [25]

Matthew's Fourth Major Discourse (129, 131, 133–136. Matthew 18:1–35). Matthew utilizes some of the Marcan material and combines it with Q and M material to form his fourth major discourse. The discourse gives principles which govern the life of Jesus' followers

[23] Taylor, *The Gospel According to St. Mark*, p. 404.
[24] *Ibid.*, p. 409.
[25] *Ibid.*, p. 410.

Figure 4–1. An olive press located in Capernaum. Olives were placed in the round stone trough and the heavy millstone was rolled around inside the trough. This millstone was the type Jesus had in mind when he said, "Whoever causes one of these little ones who believe in me to sin, it would be better for him if a great millstone were hung round his neck and he were thrown into the sea" (Mark 9:42). (Source: Foreign Mission Board, SBC.)

in the Church. Believers are not to compete for greatness, but to model their attitude on the simple humility of a child. Kingdom members must be cautious not to cause others to sin (18:6–9). They must exercise care over those entrusted to them as the shepherd who leaves the ninety-nine sheep and goes in search of the "one who went astray" (18:10–14). Expulsion from the fellowship is to be made only after every possible effort is made to win the offender (18:15–20). Forgiveness must have no limits (18:21–22), an idea enforced with the parable of the forgiven debtor (18:23–25). By these guidelines followers of Christ turn away from selfish goals to organize their behavior around kingdom interests.

Luke's Special Section

Luke 9:51–18:14 is a lengthy section in which Mark is used at most in only a few phrases. This special section has the form of a journey through the northern part of Judea. The theme of a journey is reiterated by Luke (9:51, 53; 13:21, 33; 17:11; 18:31; 19:11, 28), but there are many indications that much more than an historical account of Jesus' travel is being given. The absence of detailed chronological and geographical accounts of the travels shows that more than geography is involved in the Jerusalem journey; "Jerusalem" is as much a theological as a geographical goal. In addition, all of the narratives and sayings which Luke places here did not fall originally in this time and place in Jesus' ministry. The needs of the Christian community in Luke's day and Luke's own theological purposes must account for the contents of the section.

Two themes recur throughout the narrative. First, Jesus is going to Jerusalem to suffer and die in accordance with the will of God. The first verse of the narrative states, "When the days drew near for him to be received up, he set his face to go to Jerusalem." Second, the disciples are to perform an apostolic witness for which they are being prepared.[26] However, the theological movement in the section is difficult to mark out precisely. The materials may be considered a very loosely organized collection dealing with these two themes. But Donald G. Miller has given a suggestive division with intelligible ordering of the teachings.[27] According to Miller the theme for the entire section is "Messiah Moves Toward Jerusalem: The Kingdom of the Servant" and it deals with "Jesus' teachings on the Kingdom in the light of the Suffering Servant who was its King." The entire body of material is then broken by Miller into six divisions: servants of the kingdom (9:51–10:24), characteristics of the kingdom (10:25–12:59), membership in the kingdom (13:1–14:35), the God of the kingdom (15:1–32), warnings to kingdom members (16:1–18:30), and the king moves toward his kingdom (18:31–19:27).

---

[26] See FBK, p. 99, for a summary of the treatment of various scholars on this travel narrative.

[27] Donald G. Miller, *The Gospel According to Luke*, in the *Layman's Bible Commentary*, ed. Balmer H. Kelley, pp. 101–134.

As important as the material is from a theological perspective, its organization by Luke gives little if any historical information about the earthly Jesus. Nevertheless, the independent units in the tradition are historically helpful. The material peculiar to Luke in this special section is particularly rich in authentic sayings and parables which help us to understand the message of Jesus. (The Marcan and Q material used by Luke is treated elsewhere.) Of course, before the parables and sayings can be interpreted in the context of Jesus' teaching ministry, they must be divorced from the artificial context into which they have been placed by Luke.

The Parable of the Good Samaritan (144. Luke 10:29–37). This parable is placed by Luke in the context of a Marcan account of a lawyer who asked Jesus about the primary commandment in the law. Mark and Matthew conclude the account with the command to love God and to "love your neighbor as yourself," but Luke, perhaps from the key word "neighbor," has the lawyer ask Jesus, "And who is my neighbor?" Although the context is obviously created by Luke, it is not necessarily strained. The question as to what Leviticus 19:18 meant by "neighbor" must have been typically debated among the rabbis and Jesus may often have been party to such discussions. What were the limits of the duty of loving? Did it extend beyond fellow countrymen? The Pharisees generally excluded even non-Pharisees of their own race.

Jesus' reply does not really aim to answer the question by defining neighbor, but rather rebukes any attempt to set limits to love. An extreme example is chosen by Jesus as a means to emphasize the truth. Two religious leaders failed to manifest love toward a fellow Jew, perhaps assuming that the injured man was dead and refusing to come close to the body for fear of breaking the defilement law.[28] By contrast a despised Samaritan, with no hope of return for the investment of his concern, tended the wounded man. The outcast Samaritan kept the law of love in a way that those who were openly committed to the law were unwilling to do. Such a dramatic contrast made Jesus' point inescapable. Love requires a radical obedience which excludes no human being from its genuine concern.

The Friend at Midnight (147. Luke 11:5–8). Luke has placed the parable of the friend at midnight in the midst of sayings on prayer. In this context, the parable encourages its hearers to persevere in

[28] See Leviticus, 21:1.

prayer in confidence that God will grant what is needed. When separated from this context, it is an analogy which stresses the confidence believers may have in God. This basic point of the parable comes clear when it is interpreted within the context of ordinary Palestinean life. The typical oriental wife, with no commercial shops to depend upon, made bread for the family before sunrise. Generally neighbors would have known who had bread left over and, when an emergency such as the parable depicts arose in the evening, a person in distress would have known where to seek help. The house to which the man in the parable went at midnight was a peasant's house consisting of a single room in which the family slept on a raised platform. The door was bolted and the whole family would be disturbed if the father arose, unbolted the door, and provided the bread needed. Yet to refuse assistance to a neighbor in need was inconceivable! Oriental hospitality made it unthinkable that the request would be refused. "If the friend, roused from his sleep in the middle of the night, without a moment's delay hastens to fulfil the request of a neighbor in distress, even though the whole family must be disturbed by the drawing of the bolt, how much more will God. He is a God who harkens to the cry of the needy and comes to their help." [29]

The Parable of the Rich Fool (156. Luke 12:13–21). An argument over the division of an inheritance is the context for both a saying and a parable of Jesus which emphasize the folly of a life committed merely to gaining material wealth. Jesus' teaching here contains nothing unique. This parable is similar in emphasis to Ecclesiasticus 11:18–19 and may be dependent upon the passage:

> There is a man who is rich through
>   his diligence and self-denial,
>   and this is the reward allotted to
>   him:
> When he says, "I have found rest,
>   and now I shall enjoy my goods!"
> He does not know how much time will
>   pass until he leaves them to others
>   and dies.

Of course, Jesus could well have used traditional materials to stress that possession of property is irrelevant to the age to come and subordinate to the present rule of God.

[29] Jeremias, *The Parables of Jesus,* pp. 118–119.

Repentance or Destruction (162. Luke 13:1–9). Twin sayings of Jesus (about slaughtered Galileans and people killed by the fall of the tower) with a pronouncement (". . . unless you repent you will all likewise perish") introduce the parable of the fig tree. The twin sayings stress the disaster coming upon Israel if it fails to repent; and the parable, with the fig tree as an ancient symbol of Israel,[30] in this context probably reinforces the threat of disaster unless Israel repents.[31] The parable viewed alone emphasizes the concern of the winedresser to save his fig tree—perhaps Israel will repent. Luke, writing long after the ministry of Jesus, knows that Israel has not repented, but shows Jesus ministering hopefully to Israel seeking to make her fruitful. The parable expresses a hope that deferment of the threatened destruction will allow time for repentance and make destruction unnecessary.

Two Pronouncement Stories (163, 168. Luke 13:10–17; 14:1–6). Two pronouncement stories with healings as the context depict the attitude of Jesus toward Jewish sabbath regulations. In each story the miracle of healing is clearly not the center of interest. The story of the healing of a woman with a "spirit of infirmity" (an exorcism) leads to Jesus' response to the ruler of the synagogue, "Does not each of you on the sabbath untie his ox or his ass from the manger, and lead it away to water it? And ought not this woman, a daughter of Abraham whom Satan bound for eighteen years, be loosed from this bond on the sabbath day?" If an inferior beast like an ox or an ass is loosed from a manger to be watered on the sabbath, should not a *daughter of Abraham* be loosed from a terrible infirmity on the sabbath! The answer to this argument from the less important to the more important is obvious.

Likewise the second story leads to a pronouncement on sabbath observance. The healing of a man with dropsy introduces Jesus' statement, "Which of you, having an ass or an ox that has fallen into a well, will not immediately pull him out on the sabbath day?" If an ass or an ox is aided on the sabbath, how much more should a man be healed on the sabbath! Thus, both episodes clarify that Jesus considers the needs of suffering human beings to take precedence over sabbath law.

Teaching on Humility (169. Luke 14:7–14). In 14:7–14 Luke has joined a series of sayings on the general subject of humility. Again,

[30] Cf. Hosea 9:10; Micah 7:1; Jeremiah 8:13; 24:1–2.

[31] "And if it bears fruit next year, well and good; but if not, *you can cut it down.*" Luke 13:9, italics added.

Luke has created the context, but here it is more strained than in previous sections. Jesus would neither have openly rebuked his fellow guests and hosts as depicted nor sanctioned such behavior. The materials aim primarily, however, to caricature the self-seeking behavior of those who desire reward in the judgment. Jesus' teaching comes through advice on table manners: take the lowest place voluntarily, an exhortation with an equivalent in Proverbs 25:6–7:

> Do not put yourself forward in the
> king's presence
> or stand in the place of the great;
> for it is better to be told, "Come up
> here,"
> than to be put lower in the presence
> of the prince.

The conclusion of the saying of Jesus, "For everyone who exalts himself will be humbled, and he who humbles himself will be exalted," however, is not to be understood simply as teaching the reward of a guest for modest behavior in a home. The verse speaks of God's eschatological activity; the proud will be humbled and the humble will be exalted by God. In fact, in the age to come relationships will not be defined according to the usual social amenities (14:12–14). The blessing of God comes not by paying social obligations but by generosity extended to "the poor, the maimed, the lame, the blind" who cannot repay in kind.

The God of the Kingdom (172, 173. Luke 15:1–32). A series of three parables (the lost sheep, the lost coin, and the prodigal son) is used by Luke to express the truth that the God of the kingdom is one who loves sinners. The Lucan context for these parables is typical of the situation in Jesus' ministry where tax collectors and sinners heard Jesus gladly and Jesus accepted and even had table fellowship with them, an association which religious leaders strenuously condemned. The parables speak vivid words of reassurance to sinners considered beyond the pale by religious leaders; they also reproach leaders who are offended at the good news of Jesus and appeal to them to share Jesus' attitude toward those who are religious outcasts.

A shepherd, his friends, and neighbors rejoice when a lost sheep is found; a woman, her friends, and neighbors rejoice when a lost coin is found. So God is overjoyed at the sinner who repents. Thus the parables of the lost sheep and the lost coin comfort sinners and reproach leaders who, unlike God, despise sinners.

The parable of the prodigal son even more clearly shows the boundless love of God and relates it to both the tax collectors and sinners and the Pharisees and scribes. The first half of the parable depicts God's goodness, his grace and boundless love. The teaching is drawn in a lifelike story of a Jewish boy who demanded from his father the portion of family property which fell to him (According to Deuteronomy 21:17 this was a third of all that the father owned.) so that he could leave the confining life in his home and go into the world to live independently. The boy ended up feeding unclean swine, an occupation which carried him beyond the pale of Judaism. No doubt Jesus' hearers would have agreed that in his father's eyes the son was the same as dead. A Jewish father could never accept back such a disgraced son! But the father not only restored the wayward boy *as son* but also treated him as a guest, honoring with robe, ring, shoes, and feast. The father is an image of God, who graciously accepts on a basis other than Jewish legalism those who were rejected by the laws of the religious leaders.

The parable is addressed to the critics of the good news, those who condemn the acceptance of sinners on a basis of grace rather than law; and the second part of the parable is addressed directly to the critics. They are like the elder brother who was offended at his father's generous action. The elder brother is justified fully according to the legal concept of justice. He, unlike his squandering brother, had served faithfully and *deserved* better treatment than the son who had wasted his portion of the family fortune in wayward living. Accordingly the father seems completely unfair in giving preferential treatment to the prodigal. But this is the very point of the parable. God accepts persons on the basis of grace, not justice. The return of the son was an extraordinary situation and old rules of justice must be surpassed. The scribes and Pharisees were unwilling to do this, as the elder brother refused to receive the prodigal. Here Jesus' proclamation of the eschatological forgiveness of sins

was a situation in which the reality of God and his love was being revealed in a new and decisive way, and in which, therefore, the joys of the salvation time were suddenly available to those who had longed for them so long and so earnestly. The tragedy was that the new situation demanded a willingness to sacrifice principles and attitudes previously regarded as essential to the life of the community and its relationship with God, and for this many were unprepared. The new wine was bursting the old wine skins.[32]

[32] Perrin, *Rediscovering the Teaching of Jesus*, p. 97.

The Unjust Steward (174. Luke 16:1–13). The steward in the parable in Luke 16:1–13 is incompetent and flagrantly dishonest, but Jesus used him as an example. What is there about the steward worthy to be emulated? An emergency arose when the steward's wastefulness was discovered and his master advised him that his stewardship was to be taken away. "What shall I do, since my master has taken the stewardship away from me? I am not strong enough to dig and I am ashamed to beg," the man said. Then he quickly summoned his master's debtors and had them falsify the accounts, inscribing smaller amounts on the bills. The master (either the master of the steward or Jesus) is quoted as commending the man for his prudence. Of course, what is commended is not his dishonest dealings but his astuteness in providing for his own welfare. Verse 9 adds another interpretation commending the prudent use of wealth. The parable itself, divorced from the secondary interpretations in verses 8 and 9, may be seen as a challenge to resolute action in light of the coming of God's kingdom.

You are in the same position as this steward who saw the imminent disaster threatening him with ruin, but the crisis which threatens you, in which, indeed, you are already involved, is incomparably more terrible. This man . . . did not let things take their course, he acted, unscrupulously no doubt, though we are not concerned with that here, but boldly, resolutely, and prudently, with the purpose of making a new life for himself. For you, too, the challenge of the hour demands prudence, everything is at stake! [33]

The Rich Man and Lazarus (177. Luke 16:19–31). The theme of the reversal of fortunes in the afterlife seen in the first part (19–26) of this parable is well known in the literature of the ancient world. Numerous illustrations occur in rabbinic literature and the following story of the tax collector and the pious student is a good example:

Two pious men lived together in Ashkelon, devoting themselves to the study of the Law. One of them died and no honour was paid to him at his funeral. Bar Ma'yon, a tax collector, died and the whole town honoured his funeral. The remaining pious man was deeply disturbed and cried out that the wicked in Israel did not get their deserts. But his dead companion appeared to him in a dream and told him not to despise the ways of God in Israel. He himself had committed one evil deed and hence had suffered dishonour at his funeral, whereas Bar Ma'yon had committed one good deed and for that had been honoured at his. What evil deed had the pious man committed? On one occasion he had put on his phylacteries in the wrong order. What good deed had the tax collector committed? Once he had given a breakfast for the leading men of the town and they had not come. So he

[33] Jeremias, *The Parables of Jesus*, pp. 127–128.

gave orders that the poor were to be invited to eat it, that it should not go to waste. After some days the pious man saw his dead companion walking in the garden of paradise beside fountains of water; and he saw Bar Ma'yon the tax collector lying on the bank of a river, he was striving to reach the water and he could not.[34]

The first part of Jesus' parable, then, is not to give information about the state of men after death. The parable uses the current popular notions of Jesus' day to express the idea that impiety and lawlessness are punished while devotion and humility are rewarded in the afterlife.

Jesus' hearers would have already been familiar with this reversal-of-fortunes theme, and so would not have considered the teaching of Jesus on this point particularly unusual or startling. The second part of the parable (27–31), however, deals with a more distinctive issue. In these verses disbelief in life after death is challenged. The parable, probably addressed to Sadducees who did not believe in the resurrection of the dead, asserts the reality of life after death even if it cannot be proven. The request for proof of resurrection cannot be granted and would be superfluous since Moses and the prophets already give evidence of the resurrection and the life to come. "If they do not hear Moses and the prophets, neither will they be convinced if someone should rise from the dead."

The Servant's Wages (181. Luke 17:7–10). In the parable of the farmer and his slave (not servant) Jesus uses a story from everyday life in Palestine to express a spiritual truth. The slave does not accumulate merit by carrying out his responsibilities because his time and labor belong to the master, who has the right to demand obedient service. So the citizen of God's kingdom has no claim on God's merit by service beyond the line of duty. The parable fits Jesus' preaching to Pharisees, who thought they achieved righteousness through their good deeds; it is a demand for the renunciation of Pharisaic self-righteousness. Of course, details of the story should not be pressed as if the parable were an allegory. For example, Jesus is not making the inconsiderate master's demands a figure to speak of the attitude of God. Rather the parable warns that even maximum services cannot force a claim upon God's graciousness.

The Parable of the Unjust Judge (185. Luke 18:1–8). The parable of the unjust judge is almost a doublet of the parable of the friend

---

[34] Jerusalem Talmud, Sanhedrin 6, 23c. The translation given here comes from Norman Perrin, *Rediscovering the Teaching of Jesus,* pp. 111–112.

at midnight.[35] Luke sets both stories in a context which stresses prayer. The unjust judge parable is introduced by a general statement, "And he told them a parable, to the effect that they ought always to pray and not lose heart." But, as in the case of the earlier parable, the story is told by Jesus to say more about the character of the God of the kingdom than about prayer. A widow brought her case, apparently a money matter, to the judge hoping for a hearing. She was too poor to bribe the officials to gain a hearing, so her only weapon was persistence. The judge tires of her nagging and hears her case. If "a judge who neither feared God nor regarded man" can be forced through continual pleading to respond to a poor widow, how much more can the God of the kingdom, who has graciously forgiven, be trusted! The confidence in God taught in the parable leads naturally to the practice of prayer, but it is incorrect to apply the parable first to the practice of prayer and conclude that one must cry to God insistently in order for him to hear. The parable teaches trust in God and, hence, confidence in prayer.

The Parable of the Pharisee and the Publican (186. Luke 18:9–14). "Some who trusted in themselves that they were righteous and despised others" (i.e., Pharisees) is the group to whom the parable of the Pharisee and the publican is addressed in the Lucan context. Scenes of such individuals entering the temple at the appointed hour of prayer must have been familiar and the teaching of the parable itself confirms that Pharisees are among the hearers.

The prayer of the Pharisee is taken from life. A very similar prayer from the first century has been handed down in the Talmud:

I thank thee, O Lord, my God, that thou hast given me my lot with those who sit in the seat of learning, and not with those who sit at the streetcorners; for I am early to work, and they are early to work; I am early to work on the words of the Torah, and they are early to work on things of no moment. I weary myself, and they weary themselves; I weary myself in profit, thereby, while they weary themselves to no profit. I run and they run; I run toward the life of the age to come, and they run toward the well of the pit.[36]

The Pharisee was *not* like other people. He *was* righteous. His fasting twice in the week went far beyond the law which called for only one annual fast on the Day of Atonement. He gave tithes on everything he had, even the grain and other products which would have already been tithed by the farmer.

---

[35] See above, pp. 137–138.

[36] Quoted by Jeremias, *The Parables of Jesus,* p. 113, from Babylonian Talmud, Ber., 28b.

The publican, on the other hand, had no claim to righteousness. People generally considered him on a level with robbers and shunned associations with him. This general attitude toward the publican was justified, for through his profession he had excluded himself from the ministry of Judaism.

He and his family are in a hopeless position, since for him repentance involves, not only the abandonment of his sinful way of life, i.e. of his calling, but also the restitution of his fraudulent gains plus an added fifth. How can he know everyone with whom he has had dealings? Not only is his situation hopeless, but even his cry for mercy.[37]

The forgiveness of the reprobate publican was beyond the imagination of Jesus' hearers, but that was precisely what happened. ". . . this man went down to his house justified . . ." God is the God of the despairing, the hopeless, the sinner. He rejects the self-righteous and welcomes even the outcast who recognizes his need for forgiveness.

The Journey to Jerusalem

The tenth chapter of Mark brings Jesus to Jerusalem, but, as in 9:30–50, it omits detailed information about the journey. Here the Gospel writer (or an earlier compiler) places a complex of teachings on such subjects as marriage and divorce, children, wealth, and rewards in the framework of a fairly sketchy travel narrative. Neither Matthew nor Luke add any definite information concerning the journey to Jerusalem. Matthew follows Mark closely, introducing his parable of the laborers in the vineyard (Matthew 20:1–16) into the Marcan material. Luke omits Jesus' teaching about marriage and the story of Jesus and the sons of Zebedee and adds the story of Zacchaeus and the parable of the pounds; otherwise Luke follows his Marcan source. The lack of chronological information in the primary sources at this stage in the journey is due to their lack of a biographical interest, and the temptation to go beyond the sources and imagine situations for the various sayings and parables must be resisted.[38]

Marriage and Divorce (187. Mark 10:1–12; Matthew 19:1–12). In Mark 10:1–12 the central emphasis is the pronouncement of Jesus climaxing in the declaration, "What therefore God has joined together, let not man put asunder." The question of the Pharisees, "Is it lawful

[37] Jeremias, *The Parables of Jesus*, p. 114.
[38] Taylor, *The Life and Ministry of Jesus*, pp. 156–160.

for a man to divorce his wife?" was a matter of interest often discussed by the rabbis, especially as framed by Matthew, "Is it lawful to divorce one's wife for any cause?" (Matthew 19:3) Divorce was permitted by the law in Deuteronomy 24:1 when a husband "has found some indecency in her . . ." The School of Shammai interpreted this to mean that divorce was permitted only for adultery. The School of Hillel, however, permitted divorce for less significant offences. Jesus states the ideal in his pronouncement: God in marriage establishes a permanent union in which two persons become as one. The statements in Mark 10:10–12 and Matthew 19:9 recognize that the principle must be applied to situations which do not always meet the ideal. The two evangelists differ in their interpretation of the practical application of the ideal. Matthew permits a husband to divorce his wife in the case of adultery, but makes no allowance for a woman divorcing her husband. Mark, however, has no "except" clause and the practice of women divorcing their husbands is reflected.

"Suffer Little Children" (188. Mark 10:13–16; Matthew 19:13–15; Luke 18:15–17). The saying about children is placed superficially after the teaching on marriage with which it has no inherent relationship and it seems clear that the topical arrangement was not original. The primary statement is 10:14b, "Let the children come to me, do not hinder them; for to such belongs the kingdom of God." Both Matthew and Luke remove reference to Jesus' human emotions, omitting his actions of displeasure and embracing the children.

The Rich Young Man (189. Mark 10:17–31; Matthew 19:16–30; Luke 18:18–30). The episode of the rich man (Matthew alone calls him "the young man," perhaps from the declaration in Mark 10:20 that he had observed the commandments "from my youth") is made up of three sections: discussion with the rich man (17–22); the comments of Jesus to his disciples and their reactions (23–27); and Peter's question and Jesus' answer (28–31). Again, there is a superficial relationship to the preceding unit regarding children. The theme of both is the condition for entrance into the kingdom of God. In the previous episode the condition is child-likeness; in this story it is renunciation and following the Lord. The theme is brought clearly into focus in the second part of the episode. After the rich man had gone away because he was unwilling to renounce his riches, Jesus said to the disciples, "Truly, I say to you, there is no one who has left house or brothers or sisters or mother or father or children or lands, for my sake and for the gospel, who will not receive a hundredfold now in this time, houses and brothers and sisters and mothers and children and lands, with persecutions, and in the age to come eternal life." The saying stresses the need for renunciation and paints the contrast between the rich man who refused to renounce his possessions and the disciples who had left everything to follow their Lord.

The Laborers in the Vineyard (190. Matthew 20:1–16). Matthew alone has the parable of the laborers in the vineyard, inserted just after the material about the rich man. The position of the parable here may be due to its verbal similarity to the last verse in the earlier account. Both stories conclude with the Marcan idea that ". . . many that are first will be last, and the last first." [39] Thus, for Matthew the laborers in the vineyard parable illustrate the same theme which has been discussed in the rich man episode. But additionally the latter parable is concerned with a householder who does not deal with his laborers on a strict basis of exact payment for services rendered. It is a message of comfort for sinners entering the kingdom at "the eleventh hour" and a message of rebuke for those earlier members of the kingdom who protest that such sinners are treated equally with those "who have borne the burden of the day and the scorching heat." Neither should make kingdom commitments simply anticipating the amount of rewards.

The Third Prediction of the Passion (191. Mark 10:32–34; Matthew 20:17–19; Luke 18:31–34). The Synoptics place a third prediction of the passion [40] as "they were on the road, going up to Jerusalem." Here are included more details than in the earlier predictions and clearly knowledge of the passion events in Jerusalem influenced the form of this prediction. Matthew is aware of the form of Jesus' death although Mark does not mention crucifixion. This modification in the written materials evidently reflects similar adaptations which took place during the oral stage.

Jesus and the Sons of Zebedee (192. Mark 10:35–45; Matthew 20:20–28; Luke 22:24–27). In Mark, James and John come forward to Jesus and ask for chief places in the coming time of Jesus' glory. Luke omits this incident and Matthew names the mother of James and John as the one requesting the chief places for her sons. Apparently, the later writers sought to relieve the apostles of such an unworthy scheme. Jesus' answer is not unexpected, "You do not know what you

---

[39] Mark 10:31. Cf. Matt. 19:30; 20:16.
[40] Cf. Mark 8:31; 9:31.

are asking. Are you able to drink the cup that I drink, or to be baptized with the baptism with which I am baptized?" After the apostles boldly declared, "We are able," Jesus acknowledged that, although they would drink the cup and experience the baptism, "to sit at my right hand or at my left is not mine to grant, but it is for those for whom it has been prepared." It is sometimes asserted that here a detailed statement of the future martyrdom of James and John was made after the actual event. However, there is no certain evidence that John died with James in A.D. 44; he may then have still been living when the Gospels were written. The tradition that the apostles contended for chief places seems to be authentic, and no serious reason precludes that Jesus here intends to refer generally to the difficulties which followers would face and not specifically to the fate of James and John. The authenticity of the tradition is supported by the improbability that the church would invent such a story to the discredit of early apostles.

The request of the sons of Zebedee provides the setting for sayings of Jesus about rank among Christians. They are introduced by a statement that the ten "began to be indignant at James and John" and conclude with an appeal to service based on the fact that "the Son of Man also came not to be served but to serve, and to give his life as a ransom for many." In the context of Jesus' ministry the term "ransom" is best interpreted metaphorically to stress that Jesus has given himself into the father's hands and lives a life devoted to God's will, not that God demands payment for his forgiveness. The rule of God is made available freely in the ministry of Jesus. In the teachings of early Christianity the death of Christ was sometimes interpreted as the payment for forgiveness, but such a literal application is not part of the Synoptic understanding of Jesus' teaching.

Bartimaeus and Zacchaeus (193, 194. Mark 10:46–52; Matthew 20: 29–34; Luke 18:35–19:10). Two stories set in Jericho, the healing of Bartimaeus and the story of Zacchaeus, are a part of the Synoptic tradition. The story of the cure of the blind beggar Bartimaeus is told by all three Synoptic writers with great detail and vividness. The location is precise, the man is named, the action of the beggar is recounted in detail, suggesting that the account may have originated with an eyewitness. In its present context, however, it is more than a report of another mighty work. The story, placed just before the entry into Jerusalem, prepares the reader for the entry. Bartimaeus called Jesus by the messianic title "Son of David" and Jesus responded by healing him, "Go your way; your faith has made you well." No rebuke is given, for soon the title "Son of David" will be proclaimed publicly during the entry into Jerusalem. The messianic character of the story makes it a proper prelude to the story of the entry.

The story of Zacchaeus, quite similar to the call of Levi in Mark (2:13–17), is found only in Luke. Zacchaeus, the chief tax collector in Jericho, an important customs center on the main route from Galilee to Judea and Egypt, was rich but hated by his countrymen and excluded from membership in the covenant community of God. Such a man would surely not share the blessings of Messiah's reign! But the story vividly shows that Jesus was not a Messiah who would exclude even an apostate Jew, a chief tax collector, but one who received Zacchaeus as a "Son of Abraham."

The Parable of the Pounds (195. Matthew 25:14–30; Luke 19:11–27). The parable of the pounds or talents as found in Matthew and Luke gives an interesting and instructive example of the use made of Jesus' teachings by the early Church and Gospel writers. A comparison of the two accounts illustrates two versions of the same parable. The basic design of the story is the same: a wealthy man going on a journey entrusts money to his servants who are to trade during his absence. When the master returns, he inspects the accounts and rewards those who have properly invested the money, but takes away even the original sum from those who concentrated on keeping their money intact and thereby failed to produce an increase. The emphasis is upon the ones who guarded the money and did not use it to proper ends. The original parable has been embellished in both Matthew and Luke. In Matthew the amounts of money are increased; in Luke the number of servants is multiplied (although only three are mentioned in the accounting). Possibly Luke's version has been affected by some actual Jewish history, the journey of the eldest son of Herod the Great to Rome to obtain permission to rule after the death of his father. At this time delegates of the Jewish people also went to Rome to oppose Archelaus' request.[41]

Viewed from the context of Jesus' ministry, the parable could easily be addressed to the representatives of official Judaism who were so careful to preserve their religion that they failed to fulfill its mission to the world. But the arrangement of the Gospel material indicates a wider application of the parable in the early Church. The parable is given in the midst of teaching which emphasized the eschatological

[41] Jeremias, *The Parables of Jesus,* p. 21.

kingdom of God. The Church in the time of Matthew and Luke stood between the cross and the parousia and the parable in both of these Gospels is applied to the parousia and the last judgment. A parable of Jesus condemning official Judaism in Jesus' proclamation of the rule of God is applied to the Church as it faces the parousia. The Church, like the wise servant and unlike constricted Judaism, must wisely trade with its stewardship to prepare for the parousia. Matthew's placement of the parable in the eschatological discourse of chapters 24–25 which speaks of the end of the age and the last judgment and his subsequent description of the great judgment confirm this analysis. Luke's rather artificial introduction to the parable, indicating that Jesus told the story because "they supposed that the kingdom of God was to appear immediately," reflects his concern to explain that the expectation of an early coming of the Lord was an error. It is used to indicate that Jesus himself taught that there would be a relatively long interval. Therefore the Church must be busy about its task.

The materials in the Synoptic tradition covering the ministry beyond Galilee and the journey to Jerusalem are similar to earlier materials in that they do not allow us to reconstruct a detailed chronological and geographical account of Jesus' life. Yet, a convincing *portrait* of Jesus is painted by the materials. The early preaching, teaching, and healing ministry of Jesus in Galilee leads to a decision to go to Jerusalem to present his eschatological challenge to the heart of Judaism. In this section, particularly in the material unique to Luke, are authentic parables and sayings which amplify the picture of Jesus' proclamation of the kingdom seen in earlier material. Although Jesus goes to Jerusalem to proclaim the kingdom of God in word and deed, he is aware of the dangers involved in such a journey. Jesus' own suffering and death will be the consequence of this challenge in Jerusalem.

SUGGESTED READINGS

See the appropriate chapters in the commentaries and "Lives of Jesus" suggested in Chapter 2 and the books on Jesus' preaching, teaching, and healing suggested in Chapter 3.

5

Jerusalem: Ministry, Crucifixion, Resurrection

The Synoptic Gospels conclude their story of Jesus with his ministry in Jerusalem, climaxed by his crucifixion and resurrection. Jesus' dramatic entry into Jerusalem, other activities preceding a ministry of teaching, and a body of teaching itself lead up to the story of the passion. For the early Christians, the passion of Jesus Christ was of primary importance. Indeed, the account of Jesus' passion was the first connected narrative to be composed. The account of Jesus' earlier activities in Jerusalem, as well as the earlier sections of the Gospels, were composed, therefore, after the passion narrative and on the basis of the theological meaning which the crucifixion and resurrection had for early believers.

THE MINISTRY

The events from the entry to the passion are presented by Mark in a chronological framework of three days. During the first day, Jesus entered the city and visited the temple before returning to Bethany, a small village on Jerusalem's outskirts, for the night. The events of the next day include the cursing of the fig tree and the cleansing of the temple. On the third day the fig tree is observed "withered away to its roots," Jesus entered the temple, engaged in a series of controversies with the Pharisees and Sadducees, and, after the episode of the widow's gift, went to the Mount of Olives where he delivered an apocalyptic discourse to some of his disciples. In Matthew only two

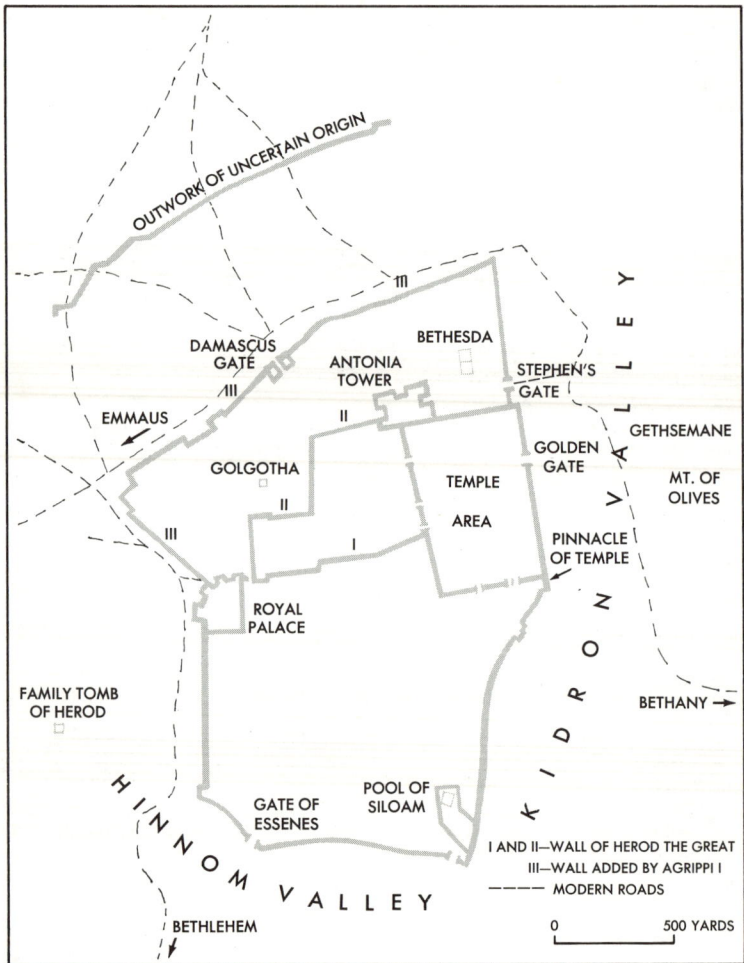

Figure 5–1. First Century Jerusalem.

days are mentioned, and in Luke the indications of time are omitted. It is clear that the chronological framework of Mark is arbitrary. There is not the full information about the preliminary Jerusalem ministry that there is about the passion of Jesus.

Events Preceding the Ministry

The Entry into Jerusalem and the Prediction of the Destruction of Jerusalem (196, 197. Mark 11:1–10; Matthew 21:1–9; Luke 19:28–44).

The entry into Jerusalem fits well into the purpose of the journey to Jerusalem. Dibelius says,

The Galilean prophet and holy man, well known among his nearer country-men, decides to seek out the capital of the country, the city whose character is determined by the priestly nobility, by Pharisaism, and by the Roman garrison. Here is the center of worship; here the Pharisees play a special role; from here, it is hoped, the Kingdom of God will take its start . . . In Jerusalem the new movement will present itself to the authorities of the country; in Jerusalem the ultimate verdict must be pronounced; in Jerusalem the hopes of the Kingdom of God will be realized.[1]

The entry, then, plays a significant role in Jesus' confrontation of the religious establishment and in his teachings about himself. The event

Figure 5–2. Bethany, a small village on the eastern slope of the Mount of Olives less than two miles from Jerusalem. Jesus often visited this village, the hometown of Lazarus. (Source: Paul Popper Ltd.)

is an object lesson of prophetic symbolism given by Jesus to show what kind of Messiah he is.[2] The teaching is clear in Mark; Jesus is

[1] Martin Dibelius, *Jesus,* p. 62.
[2] For Old Testament parallels, see Ezek. 4:1–5:17; Jer. 19:1–15.

no political Messiah, no man of war. He is lowly, riding upon an ass.
No doubt Mark has the prophecy of Zechariah 9:9 in mind:

> Rejoice greatly, O daughter of Zion!
> Shout aloud, O daughter of
> Jerusalem!
> Lo, your king comes to you;
> triumphant and victorious is he,
> humble and riding on an ass,
> on a colt the foal of an ass.

Figure 5–3. The Golden Gate, a post-New Testament structure, is almost
in the center of the eastern wall of the city of Jerusalem. A legend holds
that Jesus entered through this gate (now blocked up) on Palm Sunday.
(Source: Jordan Tourist Department.)

The messianic allusion in Mark, however, is restrained, for the Marcan
account could reflect an entry of Jesus in which the people hailed him
as their famous and respected teacher without making explicit messianic claims. Contrariwise, Matthew's account makes the entry more
explicitly messianic. The words of Zechariah are quoted and the people shout, "Hosanna to the Son of David."

Luke adds a prediction of the destruction of Jerusalem in his account of the entry (197. Luke 19:39–44). The entire section, Luke

19:37–44, including the prediction, may be an independent version of Jesus' approach to Jerusalem. Of course, the Gospel of Luke was composed after the actual siege of Jerusalem around A.D. 70 and the saying of Jesus here has no doubt been modified by knowledge of the actual events, "but there is every reason to hold that Jesus foresaw and predicted the fall of Jerusalem and the destruction of the Temple as clearly as Jeremiah had done more than six hundred years earlier." [3]

The Cleansing of the Temple (198–201. Mark 11:11–25; Matthew 21:10–22; Luke 19:45–48). Mark 11:11–25 consists of four episodes which relate to the cleansing of the temple: an inspection of the temple the day before the cleansing, the cursing of the fig tree the next morning on the way to the temple, the cleansing of the temple, and a statement on the meaning of the withered fig tree. The cleansing of the temple is central in all three Synoptic Gospels. Luke omits all episodes except the cleansing of the temple. Matthew, omitting the preliminary inspection of the temple, places the cleansing of the temple immediately after the entry and combines the cursing of the fig tree with words on the meaning of the withered fig tree. The inclusion of the fig tree episode is strange indeed. It is difficult to believe that Jesus cursed the tree simply because he was hungry and the tree had no fruit! Probably the event is intended as an acted parable whose symbolic meaning may be related to Judaism. Israel has failed to produce the fruits God intended, so she is condemned to perish.[4]

After his account of the cleansing of the temple, Mark reports some teachings of Jesus reportedly occasioned by witnessing the now-withered fig tree. The sayings, however, really do not relate directly to the occasion and here again must be teachings of Jesus introduced and arranged by Mark for teaching purposes.

Closely connected with the cursing of the fig tree is the cleansing of the temple. Jesus forcefully removed the traders and all their goods from the temple and justified his action, "Is it not written, 'My house shall be called a house of prayer for all the nations?' But you have made it a den of robbers." This action is presented as precipitating

---

[3] Francis W. Beare, *The Earliest Records of Jesus,* p. 206.

[4] Vincent Taylor, however, says, "Probably the best explanation of the narrative is that the parable of the Fig Tree in Lk. xiii. 6–9, or a similar parable, has been transformed into a story of fact, or that in primitive Christian tradition a popular legend came to be attached to a withered fig tree on the way to Jerusalem." See his, *The Gospel According to St. Mark,* p. 459.

the opponents of Jesus to plan to destroy him. "And the chief priests and the scribes heard it and sought a way to destroy him . . ."

Just as the entry of Jesus dramatically confronted Jerusalem with the messianic authority of Jesus, so the cleansing of the temple confronted the leaders with Jesus' authority. According to the Synoptics, the cleansing of the temple "is more than an act of reform intended simply to restore the temple service to its original purity. The scene that Jesus saw in the outer temple court was not particularly offensive to a Jew. It is in keeping with the activities which up to the present day attend all pilgrimages." [5] Jesus' act carries far deeper import related directly to his own mission. When he put an end to the activities of selling and exchanging money, he was cleansing "the sanctuary for the approaching kingdom of God . . . With good reason, then, all the Gospels connect the story of the cleansing of the temple with Jesus' dispute with the leaders of the nation about the 'authority' which entitles him to this action." [6]

Teachings to Opponents

At this point in the Jerusalem ministry, after the entry and preliminary activities and before the passion narrative, the Synoptic Gospels present a number of sayings Jesus directed at his opponents. There is no compelling reason to believe that all of the incidents occurred at this particular time. Perhaps some of them belong to earlier periods in Jesus' ministry. In Mark five conflict stories, each of which is built around a significant saying of Jesus, provide the basic structure of the presentation. Mark's account deals with questions about (1) authority, (2) tribute to Caesar, (3) the resurrection, (4) the great commandment, and (5) the Messiah as David's son. These stories are punctuated by the parable of the wicked tenants and conclude with a warning against the scribes. Although Luke transfers his version of the question about the great commandment into another context, he and Matthew follow Mark quite closely. Matthew precedes the parable of the wicked tenants with the parable of two sons and follows it with the parable of the marriage feast. He also gives a lament of Jesus over Jerusalem after the woes against the Pharisees.

---

[5] Günther Bornkamm, *Jesus of Nazareth*, p. 158.

[6] *Ibid.*, pp. 158–159. Reginald H. Fuller ·concludes, "If the combination of the triumphal entry with the temple cleansing is pre-Markan and rests on authentic memory, then we may take it that Jesus' intention was to go to the temple to lay down the final challenge of his eschatological message at the heart of Judaism." See Fuller, *The Foundations of New Testament Christology*, p. 114.

Luke includes both the marriage feast and the lament, but places them in different contexts.

The Question about Authority (202. Mark 11:27–33; Matthew 21: 23–27; Luke 20:1–8). Since the main authority in Jerusalem was the council or Sanhedrin, any discussion of authority raised by implication the question of the role of this religious body. The real issue raised by the scribes, elders, and chief priests was, "Has the council given you legal authority to do what you are doing?" Jesus transferred the question of authority to a higher realm by countering with the question, "Was the baptism of John from heaven or from men? Answer me." By this question Jesus not only put the religious leaders on the defense rather than himself, but also by implication made his point emphatically clear. Jesus' authority, as John's, was from God, not the Sanhedrin.

The Parable of the Two Sons (203. Matthew 21:28–32). The stories of conflict are interrupted by parables which are placed here because they appropriately rebuke Jesus' opponents. The parables of the two sons, the wicked tenants, and the marriage feast teach basically the same thing: the leaders of Israel have proved unworthy and the very ones whom the leaders despised will take their place in the kingdom. The point of the parable of the two sons (found only in Matthew) is evident. Although the leaders of Judaism give lip service to God, they, like the untrustworthy son, do not obey his will. Others, even tax collectors and harlots, begin with an open refusal to follow God, but later they repent at the preaching of John and believe. In the final analysis they are better than religious leaders whose verbal commitments are not matched by work in the vineyard.

The Parable of the Wicked Tenants (204. Mark 12:1–12; Matthew 21:33–46; Luke 20:9–19). Details in the parable of the wicked tenants so closely resemble what happened to Jesus that some have questioned whether the story originated with him, supposing that the Church may have designed the parable to pass judgment upon those who crucified Jesus. Recent studies of the parable, however, confirm its authenticity. C. H. Dodd and Joachim Jeremias point out that the parable is true to life. It "is a realistic description of the revolutionary attitude of the Galilean peasants toward the foreign landlords, an attitude which had been aroused by the Zealot movement which had its headquarters in Galilee." [7] Jeremias raises the question "whether the slaying of the

[7] Joachim Jeremias, *The Parables of Jesus*, p. 58.

son is not too crude a feature for a story taken from real life" and responds that the impression the story intended to produce made the intensification of the wickedness of the tenants necessary. "Their depravity must be as starkly emphasized as possible. The introduction of the figure of the only son is the result, not of theological considerations, but of the inherent logic of the story . . . Hence, we are left with the conclusion that Mk. xii, 1ff. is not an allegory, but a parable bearing directly on a definite situation." [8] Thus, the details of the parable must not be pressed into allegorical interpretations. The central point is that as a landlord punishes the wicked tenants, so God will punish those unfaithful leaders to whom his vineyard Israel had been entrusted. The vineyard will be given to others. The Church, however, could not fail to see the obvious relationship of some of the details to Jesus himself, an interest reflected in the preservation of the story.

The Parable of the Marriage Feast (205. Matthew 22:1–14; Luke 14:16–24). The parable of the marriage feast has the same main theme as the previous two parables. God's invitation to his great banquet, a striking symbol of the kingdom, is being rejected by respectable leaders whose places are being taken by the outcasts, "the poor and maimed and blind and lame." The Church had witnessed not only the inclusion of the outcasts of Israel, but also the Gentiles. This historical reality is reflected in Luke 14:22–24, where guests are invited from "the highways and hedges." Matthew's expansion shows additional details from the later history of the Church. He assumes both the Roman destruction of Jerusalem (Matthew 22:7) and the presence of sin among Church members (22:11–12).

Tribute to Caesar (206. Mark 12:13–17; Matthew 22:15–22; Luke 20:20–26). The second of the five conflict stories concerns tribute to the emperor. This was a burning question in Jesus' day and remained so in the years up to the fall of Jerusalem. Jesus' answer not only escaped the trap set for him by his opponents (either of the two positions proposed would have increased opposition to Jesus), but also served as a guide for the followers of Christ to determine their allegiance in later difficult days. "Render to Caesar the things that are Caesar's and to God the things that are God's." This pronouncement in its direct application to the situation in Palestine in Jesus' day declares that the duty to pay taxes to Caesar is not in conflict with the payment of God's claims. In fact, the obligation to pay taxes is paral-

---

[8] *Ibid.,* p. 60.

lel with the obligation to pay back to God what is due to him. This teaching cannot be taken to mean that God and "Caesar" are separate spheres, for Jesus taught that the claims of God are all embracing. But, within the divine order obligations are due and must be paid to the state. David Daube sees the question on tribute as the first in a series of questions which follows a four-fold form familiar to first century rabbis. Daube suggests that the four questions have been put together according to this rabbinic pattern by Mark or a previous narrator. In this pattern, questions concerning a point of law would come first (concerning tribute to Caesar). Next came questions not bearing on the law but concerning apparent contradictions between different scriptural texts (about David's son). Then came mocking questions, "designed to ridicule a belief of the Rabbi" (the question concerning the resurrection). And finally questions about principles which one could follow and become successful (the great commandment) completed the four-fold pattern. Daube believes that Mark rearranges the typical sequence in order that the question asked by Jesus himself (about David's son) might be placed last to serve as a climax of the series.[9]

The Resurrection (207. Mark 12:18–27; Matthew 22:23–33; Luke 20:27–40). The question concerning the resurrection belongs to the pattern discussed above. The mocking questions, according to Daube, are all directed against the same belief, namely, belief in resurrection. "For example, did the child brought back to life by Elisha convey uncleanness, as a corpse? Or on resurrection, will the dead need sprinkling, having been in contact with corpses?" [10] The Sadducees, who did not believe in resurrection, intended their question to ridicule the belief held by Jesus. Jesus' answer is twofold. First he deals with the manner of resurrection life: ". . . in the resurrection they neither marry nor are given in marriage." The second part of his answer is more straightforward, asserting the fact of resurrection: "He is not God of the dead, but of the living." The statement illustrates a type of exegesis which would have been more persuasive to hearers in Jesus' day than to a modern audience, but the key point is clear. Men whose faith is in God share a life which surpasses death. Vincent Taylor summarizes:

Yet, strangely enough, in a deeper sense the passage suggests the one consideration which above all others confirms the modern Christian in his be-

[9] David Daube, *The New Testament and Rabbinic Judaism*, pp. 158–169.
[10] *Ibid.*, p. 159.

lief in life after death; for to him his hope is based, not on Platonic arguments concerning the nature of the soul, but upon the experience of communion with God. It is this idea of fellowship with God that the Old Testament emphasizes in its nearest approaches to a doctrine of immortality.[11]

The Great Commandment (208. Mark 12:28–34; Matthew 22:34–40; Luke 10:25–28). In Mark the question, "Which commandment is the first of all?" is put to Jesus by a scribe who is not engaging in controversy, but simply raising a subject often discussed among the rabbis. The Lucan parallel, found earlier in an introduction to the parable of the good Samaritan, indicates, to the contrary, that the questioner is a lawyer who "stood up to put him to the test." Luke may have adapted the Marcan story to fit his purposes or he may have had a different version of the same incident. The question was important, for the reputable rabbi should have been able to distinguish priorities among the many commandments in the law of Moses. Jesus' answer (the answer is given by the lawyer in Luke) linked the commandment to love God with the one to love neighbor. These two commandments came from the Old Testament (Deuteronomy 6:5 and Leviticus 19:18) and the combination was made before Jesus' day in *The Testament of the Twelve Patriarchs.* The lawyer then could well have answered, as Luke indicates. Jesus' answer would thus have been in the Israel's best prophetic and religious tradition.

About David's Son (209. Mark 12:35–37; Matthew 22:41–46; Luke 20:41–44). Jesus turned on his questioners and asked the last question, "How can the scribes say that the Christ is the son of David?" Daube suggests that this change (and the form of the earlier three questions to some extent) had been influenced by the traditional Jewish service on the eve of Passover. In the service questions were answered as if from four types of sons: the "wise son" asked about all the various laws of Passover, the "wicked son" asked a scoffing question, the "son of plain piety" raised a simple question about the festival's meaning, and the son "who does not know how to ask, and whose father, therefore, must take the initiative in opening the instructions." [12]

Jesus' question seems to demand an answer which denies Messiah to be the son of David, but such is not the case. This conclusion is clearly contrary to other teachings in the Gospels and the Davidic descent of Jesus was not questioned in the Church. Daube suggests

[11] Taylor, *The Gospel According to St. Mark,* p. 484.
[12] Daube, *The New Testament and Rabbinic Judaism,* pp. 163–164.

that if the treatment of the question is analogous to the rabbinic treatment, "the answer implied is not that one notion is right and the other wrong, but that both are right in different contexts." [13] As Paul put it in Romans, Jesus was "descended from David according to the flesh" but more important, he was "designated Son of God in power according to the spirit of holiness by his resurrection from the dead" (1:3–4).

Woes against the Pharisees (210. Mark 12:37–40; Matthew 23:1–36; Luke 20:45–47). Mark's controversy section closes with the statement against the scribes. The "woes" are also found in Matthew and Luke. The teachings of the scribes had just been attacked; here their practices come under evaluation. No doubt the hostile relation of later Christianity with Judaism influenced the selection and statement of the sayings of Jesus against Jewish leaders, but obviously hostility also existed in Jesus' day. Although all relations with Jewish leaders were not hostile, what conflict there was would have been intensified during the Jerusalem ministry.

Luke includes woes against Jewish leaders in his earlier travel narrative, but in this section he follows Mark almost word for word. Matthew, however, expands Mark's statements with material from Q (used by Luke in his earlier woes) and from M, and uses this section of woes against the scribes and Pharisees as the beginning of his fifth major discourse (Matthew 23–25).

The Lament over Jerusalem and the Widow's Gift (211, 212. Mark 12:41–44; Matthew 23:37–39; Luke 13:34–35; 21:1–4). Matthew concludes his discourse against the Pharisees with Jesus' lament over Jerusalem. This is Q material which Luke utilizes earlier in the travel narrative (Luke 13:34–35). Mark, followed by Luke, places the story of a widow's gift between Jesus' teaching to his opponents and an apocalyptic discourse addressed to his disciples. It is an isolated fragment perhaps placed at this point in the Gospel because the setting is the temple and because the term "widow" in Mark 12:42 is verbally linked with the "widows'" houses in the conclusion of the woes against the scribes (Mark 12:40). The climax of the story is the saying on giving, "Truly, I say to you, this poor widow has put in more than all those who are contributing to the treasury. For they all contributed out of their abundance; but she out of her poverty has put in everything she had, her whole living" (Mark 12:43–44).

These sundry teachings seem to point up Jesus' confrontation with

[13] *Ibid.*, p. 163.

Figure 5–4. A panoramic view of the city of Jerusalem from the Mount of Olives across the Kidron Valley. The Golden Gate may be seen and the Dome of the Rock (a Moslem mosque) now stands on the site of the ancient Jewish temple. (Source: Foreign Mission Board, SBC.)

Jerusalem as the religious center of Judaism and in the Synoptic arrangement prepare for the passion story. "Jerusalem," accused in Matthew of "killing the prophets and stoning those who are sent," is left "forsaken and desolate" before Jesus, "who comes in the name of the Lord" (23:37–39). But before the Synoptics turn to the events by which Jesus comes into his glory, they report a major discourse which looks toward the future of God's cause.

The Apocalyptic Discourse

Mark has placed just before the passion narrative a lengthy discourse of Jesus (Mark 13:1–37) which is full of highly symbolic language. Both Matthew and Luke follow Mark closely, Luke making some minor changes and Matthew adding at the conclusion a great deal of M and Q material.[14] The discourse illustrates a distinctive type

[14] Luke uses this Q material in his travel narrative.

of literary form represented more extensively in the Old Testament book of Daniel and the New Testament Revelation (see below, pp. 438–440). This form of writing is referred to as apocalyptic and, because its imagery usually presupposes a key for its understanding, is difficult to analyze from the perspective of Jesus' ministry.

"Apocalypse," the Greek word for "unveiling" or "revelation," is the term given to a number of writings in the second century B.C. through the second century A.D. which purport to give a view of the future purposes of God. The writer's message is couched in exaggerated and sometimes bizarre figures of speech, so that it is meaningless to those who are not initiated in the images. For those who understand the language, however, the message becomes intelligible and forceful. Apocalypse, as in the case of Daniel and Revelation, grows out of a particular crisis and is written to encourage the people of God in that crisis. Since its language is very figurative, meaning must be determined with great care.

The content of Jesus' apocalyptic discourse presents its own distinctive problems. The discourse as it now stands seems quite disjointed and contains somewhat contradictory statements. The introductory words of Mark 13 discuss the destruction of the temple, but the remainder of the chapter deals with the end of the age and the parousia of the Son of man. Although verse 32 declares that, "Of that day or that hour no one knows, not even the angels in heaven, nor the Son, but only the Father," the earlier verses purport to give specific details as to the time of the end of the age. In verse 14 reference is made to "the reader," but the chapter is in the form of a discourse of Jesus to his disciples. Evidently the material has undergone revisions that have not been too concerned to keep details reconciled.

Mark 13 is clearly a composition giving insight into the situation of the later Church, as well as into the teachings of Jesus. Some scholars have isolated the obvious apocalyptic verses (5–8, 14–20, 24–27) and designed them as a "little apocalypse" addressed by a Palestinian Christian to Christians facing a crisis in Jerusalem sometime before A.D. 70. Subsequently these verses were used as the nucleus for the arrangement of the teachings of Jesus in Mark 13.[15] Others, however, while recognizing the composite nature of Mark 13, deny the theory of a "little

[15] The hypothesis that a small apocalypse forms the basis of Mark 13 has been held since the work of T. Colani (*Jesus-Christ et les croyances messianiques des son tempes,* 1864, pp. 201–202). This small Jewish or Jewish-Christian work is said to have been edited by Christians in anticipation of the siege of Jerusalem. For a careful analysis of the different sources of Mark 13 see Wilfred L. Knox, *The Sources of the Synoptic Gospels,* I, pp. 103–114.

apocalypse" as the basis for the chapter. G. R. Beasley-Murray, for example, suggests that "the discourse must either be an expansion of what Jesus spoke in explanation of Mark 13:2 or was spoken on one occasion and reproduced in a fragmentary condition through casual quotation (hence its disjointedness)." Although Mark 13 was not spoken precisely in its present form, "the contents of the discourse have high claim to authenticity." [16] But however Mark 13 came to its present form, its language must not be interpreted literally, but as apocalyptic literature bearing the marks of this particular literary device.[17] Further, later events certainly influenced the presentation of Jesus' apocalyptic teachings, as a comparison of Mark 13:14 with its parallels clearly shows. In Mark the saying is given in general form prior to the actual events of A.D. 70. Luke and Matthew, however, can only read Mark in light of the siege of Jerusalem.

Destruction of the Temple (213. Mark 13:1–4; Matthew 24:1–3; Luke 21:5–7). The stage for the discourse is set by Jesus' prediction of the destruction of the temple. His pronouncement, "Do you see these great buildings? There will not be left here one stone upon another that will not be thrown down," is reminiscent of the prophets of Israel (see Micah 3:12; Jer. 26:6, 18) and may show Jesus' insight into the smoldering religious and political circumstances of the first century. But, viewed in the context of Jesus' earlier teachings concerning the religious leaders and in light of prophetic tradition, the reference to destruction of the temple is to be understood as more than a political disaster. It is the judgment of God.

Four disciples questioned Jesus privately as he "sat on the Mount of Olives opposite the temple"; "Tell us, when will this be, and what will be the sign when these things are all to be accomplished." The question in its Marcan context may be limited to the destruction of the temple. This destruction, however, is an eschatological event itself, pointing to the coming age which the Church understood to be the nearby day when God's cause would be vindicated. The second part of the Marcan question seems to point to the wider symbolism which the Church saw in Jerusalem's destruction. Matthew spells this out

---

[16] G. R. Beasley-Murray, *A Commentary on Mark Thirteen*, p. 11, n.1. Beasley-Murray, *Jesus and the Future*, pp. 1–80, gives a comprehensive discussion of the presuppositions, formulation, and development of the little Apocalypse theory.

[17] See M. Rist, "Apocalypticism," *IDB*, I, 157–161, for a brief discussion of the features of apocalyptic literature. See also H. H. Rowley, *The Relevance of Apocalyptic*.

Figure 5–5. The wailing wall, a portion of the west wall of the temple of Herod left standing after the destruction in A.D. 70, shows the stones of the temple spoken of by Jesus. (Source: Foreign Mission Board, SBC.)

specifically, "Tell us, when will this be, and what will be the sign of your coming and of the close of the age?"

The Coming of the Parousia (214–217. Mark 13:5–23; Matthew 24: 4–25; Luke 21:8–24). Jesus' response begins with calls for watchfulness on the part of the disciples "that no one leads you astray." False messiahs will come (notice Matthew's interpretation of Mark 13:6) and wars and natural calamities will take place. Events are commonly described in this way in apocalyptic works. The important point is that there is no need for fear in the presence of either the destruction of Jerusalem or the coming end time. Disciples are not only encouraged to face the future with confidence, but also called to "take heed to yourselves" in light of various troubles. They will be faced with trial and tribulation, but may take heart in the presence of the Holy Spirit. Even when brother turns against brother, the believer may be assured that "he who endures to the end will be saved." The description of the troubles may have been influenced by actual difficulties faced by the persecuted Church, but there is no reason to doubt that the prediction could be substantially from Jesus himself. Followers of Christ would certainly be subject to persecution.

A new item is introduced into the discussion in "the desolating sacrilege," a thinly-veiled reference to the abomination wrought by the Seleucid Antiochus when he offered a heathen sacrifice in the temple.[18] The Synoptics here use a familiar symbol to refer to events which cannot be spoken of literally, but which are known to the reader (as seen in the admonition, "let the reader understand"). If the desolating sacrilege is the Roman power forcibly occupying Jerusalem and setting up its insignia in the temple, the caution can be understood. Beasley-Murray says, "That Jesus anticipated such a disaster for his nation is clear from other passages . . . It was an anticipation springing fundamentally from his spiritual insight. Its expression in the manner here inferred is not unworthy of him and is harmonious with his other teaching." [19] The sayings in Mark 13:15–20 depict war-time conditions so severe that the Synoptics repeat their warning against false messiahs and false prophets. Readers must take heed so that they, having been told beforehand, will not be led astray.

The Day of the Son of Man (218, 219. Mark 13:24–27; Matthew 24:26–31; Luke 17:23–24, 37; 21:25–28). The parousia of the Son of man is set in the context of these terrible woes. Celestial portents, drawn from an Old Testament background [20] and used regularly in apocalyptic writings, picture the intense drama of the end of the age. The climax is reached with the coming of the Son of man who gathers "his elect from the ends of the earth to the ends of heaven." This portrayal of the parousia of the Son of man set alongside sayings on the destruction of Jerusalem must have created some problem for the Church when the destruction of Jerusalem was already past and the coming of the Son of man a future event. This historical circumstance may at least partially explain why the Church expected an early arrival,

---

[18] See Dan. 9:27 and the *Oxford Annotated Bible* notation on the verse.
[19] Beasley-Murray, *A Commentary on Mark Thirteen*, p. 57.
[20] Cf. Isaiah 13:10; 34:4; Ezek. 32:7f.; Amos 8:9; Joel 2:10.

in their lifetime, of the Son of man. But for Jesus both events lie in the future, even if not too distant. For him, as understood by the Synoptics, the fall of the temple, bound up with the destruction of the city of Jerusalem, portends the eschatological action of God in history.

The destruction is related to the parousia, not merely because the two events must occur within a generation, but because the former is an integral part of the judgments of God that prepare for the latter . . . Mk. 13 is silent on what lies between the ruin of the city and the parousia of the Son of Man; it is enough for the connection between the two events to be established. "Jerusalem destroyed, the curtain falls." In this respect Mk. 13 truly represents the mind of Christ. It does not reveal all that mind; it does not even give all that Jesus spoke on the occasion described; but it is right in showing that Jesus did not know the ebb and flow of time and history. Its nature he knew; its End he knew; but not its extent. Behind the fallen curtain, many an act of the drama of humanity was to be played. The intermediate scenes were hidden from his eyes, the last unveiled. Beyond desolation he saw restoration.[21]

Conclusion of the Discourse (220–229. Mark 13:28–37; Matthew 24:32–25:46; Luke 12:39–46; 17:26–27; 34–35; 19:12–27; 21:29–36). Concluding the eschatological discourse is a series of sayings encouraging watchfulness: the parable of the fig tree, the time of the parousia, and Mark's ending to the discourse. Luke replaces Mark's ending with his own (223. Luke 21:34–36), emphasizing the dangers of Christians being overcome by the attractions of the world. Matthew also omits Mark's ending and gives additional materials from Q and M which have the general theme of watchfulness.[22] Like a wary householder protecting his property or wise bridesmaidens awaiting the groom's arrival, believers must be prepared for the Son of man, who comes unannounced. Indeed those who anticipate his arrival must, like a wise servant investing his master's funds, work toward that day when judgment comes. Matthew concludes with the forceful parable of the last judgment, whose meaning is plain: the Son of man who judges is Jesus himself, the judgment comes at his parousia, and its basis is deeds of mercy. Undoubtedly this passage was useful in the early Christian movement to encourage charity to all the afflicted and needy. Pre-Christian parallels to these teachings appear in Egyptian and rabbinic literature, which like the Marcan passage

. . . lay down the principle that works of mercy will be the decisive factor in the Judgment. But what a difference! Both in the Egyptian Book of the

---

21 Beasley-Murray, *Jesus and the Future*, p. 204.
22 224–229. Matt. 24:37–25:46.

Dead and in the Midrash the dead man boasts of his good deeds . . . How differently sounds the surprised question of the righteous in vv. 37–39 of our passage, to say nothing of the conception that in the persons of the poor and wretched, men are confronted by the hidden Messiah. But it is this very conception which is attested as belonging to the early tradition by such sayings as we find in Mk. ix, 37, 41. Our pericope, although it may not be authentic in every detail, contains, in fact, "features of such startling originality that is difficult to credit them to anyone but the Master himself." [23]

THE PASSION AND RESURRECTION NARRATIVE

The passion and resurrection narrative is found in Mark 14–16 and the parallels in Matthew 26–28 and Luke 22–24. In contrast to materials dealing with portions of Jesus' earlier life and mission, the Synoptic story of the passion forms a coherent whole, a continuous narrative of events beginning with a conspiracy of Jews to get rid of Jesus and concluding with the empty tomb. Mark's account is the most primitive, but Matthew and Luke are in basic agreement with Mark's presentation. Even the passion narrative of the Fourth Gospel parallels the Marcan account. Here, then, the writers seem to be holding closely to a tradition which is more weighty than the traditions of earlier events in Jesus' life and ministry. Moreover, the narrative, as read in its present form in the Gospels, suggests a connected historical account. ". . . the course of events is convincingly portrayed, and, while difficulties arise in several points, the narrative as a whole is marked by a realism and a sobriety of tone which leave on the mind a good impression of its historical value." [24]

The primitive Christian community early demanded a continuous narrative of the passion of Jesus, a narrative like that which is in our Gospels. Its preaching and worship rested primarily upon assertions about the central importance of the crucified and resurrected Christ, as illustrated in the Pauline declaration, "For Jews demand signs and Greeks seek wisdom, but we preach Christ crucified, a stumbling block to Jews and folly to Gentiles, but to those who are called, both Jews and Greeks, Christ, the power of God and the wisdom of God" (I Corinthians 1:22–24). On this ground alone, "we must presuppose the early existence of a Passion narrative complete in itself since preaching, whether for the purpose of the mission or of worship, required some such a text." [25] In this sense, the passion narrative was *the* essential part of the gospel story for early Christians. The re-

[23] Jeremias, *The Parables of Jesus*, p. 144.
[24] Vincent Taylor, *The Formation of the Gospel Tradition*, p. 45.
[25] Martin Dibelius, *From Tradition to Gospel*, tr. Bertram Lee Woolf, p. 23.

mainder served to introduce Jesus' passion. It is no surprise then that the passion narratives represent the earliest continuous narrative in the Gospels, materials which go back to the most primitive tradition. The nature of the passion narrative and the needs of the early Church confirm that "what we have in the primitive Passion Narrative is the stark recital of facts, with only a minimum of the current interpretation—the story of Jesus' death as it was recited in the early Christian communities for almost forty years before Mark took pen in hand to write out the full story of Jesus as he had heard it and as he understood it." [26] It is wrong, of course, to conclude that there is no religious interest and interpretation in the passion narrative. The enumeration of Old Testament passages to show that the passion is a "combination of divine decrees" [27] shows that the hand of the Church has been upon the materials, but the essential story has been unaltered.

Conspiracy, Betrayal, and Arrest

The Conspiracy of the Jews (231. Mark 14:1–2; Matthew 26:1–5; Luke 22:1–2). A plot of the chief priests and the scribes to arrest Jesus and kill him introduces the passion narrative. It was the time of Passover and the leaders decide to act "not during the feast, lest there be a tumult of the people." Mark does not clarify whether they intend to arrest Jesus before the feast or after the feast. In either case the plan of the religious leaders is inconsistent with the Marcan version of later action indicating that Jesus was arrested "during the feast." Taylor says, "The most probable hypothesis is that, while Mark may have thought the priests intended to execute Jesus before the Feast, they themselves purported to act subsequently, but were able to proceed almost at once 'with subtilty' owing to the treachery of Judas." [28]

The Anointing at Bethany (232. Mark 14:3–9; Matthew 26:6–13). Interrupting the story of the conspiracy is an account of the anointing at Bethany, an exception to the rule that the passion story is a unity which holds together from beginning to end, ". . . a woman came with an alabaster jar of ointment of pure nard, very costly, and she broke the jar and poured it over his head" (Mark 14:3). The story could be omitted without harm to the narrative. Since the story of Jesus' anointing can be separated without interrupting the sequence, it probably was not at first a part of the passion narrative. The event undoubtedly

---

[26] Frederick C. Grant, *The Earliest Gospel*, p. 186.
[27] See Bornkamm, *Jesus of Nazareth*, pp. 155–158.
[28] Taylor, *The Gospel According to St. Mark*, p. 529.

occurred at some other point in Jesus' life and later became connected with the passion narrative as an anointing of Jesus' body for burial. Jesus' interpretation makes it clear that "she has anointed my body beforehand for burying." The anointing is of a king who gives himself for others. Hence, Jesus refuses to condemn the woman for wastefulness, but accepts her act as "a beautiful thing" anticipating his passion.[29]

Judas Betrays Jesus (233. Mark 14:10–11; Matthew 26:14–16; Luke 22:3–6). The report of the conspiracy of the Jewish leaders continues with the account of Judas coming to them to betray Jesus. The act is described simply. Judas came to betray Jesus, the leaders were glad and promised Judas money, Judas then sought an opportunity to carry out the plot. The Gospels offer no explanation for the action of Judas, a silence which has caused all sorts of motives to be assigned to him. Some have seen him as a greedy traitor willing to sell his soul for so little a price; others interpret him as a zealot devotee simply seeking to force his master into an aggressive mission against Rome. The Synoptics, however, do not even hint at his motivation and too much interpretation should not proceed from conjecture.

Upper Room (234–237. Mark 14:12–25; 10:42–45; Matthew 26:17–29; 19:28; 20:25–28; Luke 22:7–38). The high point among the events which precede Jesus' arrest is a last meal shared with his apostles. Some parts of the account suggest that the meal was a Passover. Mark describes preparations for a Passover and the time references (14:12, 14, 16) in his account suggest that the last supper was such a meal. Other details, however, do not demand this time arrangement. Moreover, the Fourth Gospel stated explicitly that the meal was on the evening before the Passover. It may be best to leave open the question as to whether or not Jesus' last meal was the actual Passover meal, but the interpretation of the acts and words of Jesus must be made in light of the general circumstances of that festival. Even if the meal were not the Passover meal, it would have had some features of such a meal.[30]

At evening Jesus and the twelve participate in the supper. Mark

[29] Luke 7:36–50 tells of a similar anointing.
[30] See Joachim Jeremias, *The Eucharistic Words of Jesus*, pp. 15–88, for a detailed treatment of the question whether the last supper was a Passover meal. Jeremias, p. 88, concludes that, *"Jesus' avowal of abstinence, the words of interpretation and the command to repetition first became fully understandable when they are set within the context of the passover ritual.* It should also be emphasized, however, that the Last Supper would still be surrounded by the atmosphere

tells of Jesus' prediction of his betrayal and the institution of the Lord's Supper during the meal. Luke's story of the last supper includes additionally materials from Q and L and so is longer than that of either Mark or Matthew. Mark's prediction of the betrayal is impressive in its restraint and solemnity. Jesus states that one of the twelve, "one who is eating with me," "one who is dipping bread in the same dish with me," will betray him. Judas is not mentioned specifically nor is there any indication of who the traitor might be. Matthew's expansion of the story, however, clearly designates the traitor: "Judas, who betrayed him, said, 'Is it I, Master?' He said to him, 'You have said so.' " Matthew's account shows a later development in the treatment of Judas which is carried further in the Gospel of John.[31]

The prediction of betrayal is followed by the institution of the Lord's Supper, a ceremonial act designed to commemorate Jesus' death. The simplicity of the story is marked, both in its narration and the details of its symbolism. Jesus took the ordinary table bread, blessed and broke it, and gave it to the disciples saying, "Take; this is my body." Then he took a cup of the usual table wine, gave thanks, and gave it to them, saying, "This is my blood of the covenant, which is poured out for many." He concludes with a third saying, "Truly, I say to you, I shall not drink again of the fruit of the vine until that day when I drink it new in the kingdom of God." The words here build upon the Old Testament understanding that sinful man may depend upon the covenant God to deliver. As in the Exodus from Egypt Yahweh delivered Israel from their bondage, so now God in a new covenant mediates salvation in Jesus' death.

Matthew's account is basically the same as Mark's, but Luke gives an independent account which speaks of the cup and then the bread.[32] The earliest written form of the institution of the Lord's Supper is found, not in the Gospels, but in Paul's correspondence to the Corinthians. In I Corinthians 11:23–25 the Apostle says,

For I received from the Lord what I also delivered to you, that the Lord Jesus on the night when he was betrayed took bread, and when he had given

---

of the Passover even if it should have occurred on the evening before the feast." See J. C. Rylaarsdam, "Passover and Feast of Unleavened Bread," *IDB*, III, 663–668, for a brief discussion of the Passover as it was conducted in the New Testament period. See also the Tractate *Pesahim* ("Passover") in the Mishnah.

[31] Cf. John 13:23–30.

[32] Perhaps there is another mention of the cup in Luke. The readings of the manuscripts vary. The *RSV* omits the mention of the cup in Luke 22:20, following Codex Bezae which, in spite of its tendency to add rather than omit materials, leaves out 22:20.

thanks, he broke it, and said, "This is my body which is for you. Do this in remembrance of me." In the same way also the cup, after supper, saying, "This cup is the New Covenant in my blood. Do this, as often as you drink it, in remembrance of me."

The Pauline and Marcan versions are very similar although independent. Vincent Taylor compares the various accounts and concludes that "the Markan narrative commends itself as one of the oldest, if not the most ancient, of the accounts which reveal the singularly original manner in which Jesus conceived the nature of His redemptive death and related the Eucharist thereto." [33]

Luke places after the institution of the Supper a complex of sayings which are not found here in Matthew and Mark. The prophecy of betrayal (found in Mark before the institution) is placed here by Luke. He also gives here a version of the story of the request for prestigious places by sons of Zebedee, and brings forward the prophecy of Peter's denial, placed by Mark on the way to the Mount of Olives.

The saying on the two swords (Luke 22:35–38) has no parallel or alternate version in the other Gospels. The passage taken literally reads like a Zealot's statement and is difficult to understand on the lips of Jesus. It advocates violence, quite contrary to the attitude of Jesus' entire life and teachings. The suggestion that it is an ironical statement, however, makes it plausible as a statement of Jesus. When he says, "Let him who has no sword sell his mantle and buy one," he "looks back on the earlier days when He sent the disciples out on the Mission journey . . . Then they could expect hospitality and a friendly welcome. Now nobody will give them a crust or a copper, and he who kills them will think he does God a service." Jesus accepts this rejection with faith in God and the conviction that his own career has been lived in accord with God's will. But the disciples do not see this. They are aware of the growing hostility and see in the saying about a sword "a token that the Master is at last going to rouse Himself to action. If he is for fighting, they are with Him. And they have two swords. They are ready to die like men." [34]

---

[33] Taylor, *The Gospel According to St. Mark*, p. 543. See Jeremias, *The Eucharistic Words of Jesus*, pp. 138–203, for a treatment of the question of the oldest text of the Eucharistic words of Jesus. Jeremias, pp. 188–189, concludes that Mark "stands linguistically nearest to the original tradition" and that he preserves "a considerably older form of the tradition than Paul and also than Luke." See Werner G. Kümmel, *Promise and Fulfillment*, tr. Dorothea M. Barton, pp. 119–121, for a different opinion.

[34] T. W. Manson, *The Sayings of Jesus*, p. 341.

Figure 5–6. Spreading branches of ancient olive trees shade a pathway in the Garden of Gethsemane on the Mount of Olives. (Source: Arab Information Center.)

Gethsemane (238–240. Mark 14:26–52; Matthew 26:30–56; Luke 22:31–34, 39–53). The Synoptic portrayal of Jesus relates several important items to the period just after Jesus' last meal with his disciples in the upper room. Accordingly, the group, with the exception of

Judas Iscariot, went to Gethsemane, a garden outside Jerusalem across the Kidron Valley. Mark reports that on the way to Gethsemane Jesus (1) predicted that all the disciples would fall away, quoting from Zechariah 13:7, (2) promised that he would go before the disciples into Galilee, and (3), after Peter's strong protest, predicted that Peter would deny him three times "this very night, before the cock crows twice." The experiences of Peter would have been valuable reassurances to Christians in times of persecution, temptation, and faithlessness, and certainly the Church must have relished the preservation of these materials. Undoubtedly, however, they are rooted in genuine historical events. It is difficult to conceive that the Church would have passed on statements so derogatory except on the testimony of Peter himself.

At Gethsemane the deep distress of Jesus and the human frailty of even the closest disciples are vividly portrayed. Jesus "began to be greatly distressed and troubled." He told Peter, James, and John, "My soul is very sorrowful, even to death." In his prayer he addressed God as "Abba, Father." "Abba" was the term a child would use in addressing his father. "It was something new, something unique and unheard of, that Jesus dared to take this step and to speak with God as a child speaks with his father, simply, intimately, securely. There is no doubt then that the *Abba* which Jesus uses to address God reveals the very basis of his communion with God." [35] Jesus' prayer was that, if possible, "the hour might pass from him," that the "cup" might be removed from him. The "hour" and "cup" clearly refer to suffering and death. "Yet not what I will, but what thou wilt," is an integral part of the prayer, and the conclusion of the narrative is evidence of the victory won, strength for the experiences which are ahead.

Jesus' arrest takes place immediately after the prayer in Gethsemane. Those arresting Jesus, probably the temple police sent by the Jewish leaders, are led by Judas, who betrays Jesus with a kiss. A disciple attempts to defend his master with a sword and Jesus protests the method of arrest, "Have you come out as against a robber, with swords and clubs to capture me? Day after day I was with you in the temple teaching, and you did not seize me." Mark alone adds an interesting comment about a young man who followed Jesus after the other disciples fled, only to flee himself when the officers attempted to take him (Mark 14:51–52). It is often conjectured that the writer of the Gospel of Mark is speaking of himself in these verses, but this is quite uncertain.

[35] Joachim Jeremias, *The Central Message of the New Testament*, p. 21.

Trial, Crucifixion, and Resurrection

The passion narrative continues without a break through the trials before the religious and political leaders, the crucifixion, burial, and resurrection. At points the narrative is difficult to reconcile with contemporary practices known from other sources, but it must be remembered that these materials were important to the Church more because they preserved the real theological import of Jesus' life [36] than as narratives of detailed accuracy.

Jesus Before the Sanhedrin (241–242. Mark 14:53–15:1; Matthew 26:57–27:2; Luke 22:54–23:1). The Synoptics describe Jesus' trial before both Jewish and Roman authority; he appears before both the Sanhedrin and Pilate. Mark's account of Jesus' trial before the Sanhedrin, to which is added the story of Peter's denial, can be divided into three sections: (1) The setting in which Jesus is brought before an assembly of "all the chief priests and the elders and the scribes" and Peter is in "the courtyard of the high priest," (2) the night session of the council during which the leaders failed to find testimony against Jesus, the high priest questioned Jesus, and the council "condemned him as deserving death" and mistreated him, and (3) the account of Peter's denial. If the account of Jesus before the council is treated as a formal trial ending in a verdict of guilty, the Jewish regulations governing trials, as we know them from later sources, were clearly violated. It is entirely possible that an irregular trial without regard for the rules took place or that laws governing Jewish trials (as known from the tractate *Sanhedrin* of the Mishnah) were not enforced during Jesus' time. But also, any attempt to interpret these materials from a legal point of view must remember that the Synoptics were evangelists, not court stenographers. Further, from the Gospels themselves it is possible to infer a formal trial held, according to Jewish rules, in the morning. Mark may have mistaken an earlier informal hearing for the formal trial. Luke, it will be noted, gives this interpretation: "When day came, the assembly of the elders of the people gathered together, both chief priests and scribes; and they led him away to their council" (22:66). Mark also acknowledges that there was a consultation of the whole council in the morning before the delivery of Jesus to Pilate. It seems best then to conclude that, while there may have been an

---

[36] See below, pp. 457, 471–472, 495–497.

earlier informal meeting, a formal trial took place according to Luke's timetable.[37]

The Death of Judas (243. Matthew 27:3–10). Matthew alone of the Synoptic Gospels tells of the death of Judas, which he places before the trial of Jesus by Pilate. Matthew relates the event to a field, called the Field of Blood, which existed in his day and to an Old Testament scripture [38] speaking of thirty pieces of silver. Matthew's account must be compared with Acts 1:16–20, which says that Judas bought a field with his reward and that he fell and burst open, hence the field was called the Field of Blood. The two accounts are difficult to harmonize although they apparently arise from a similar tradition, both attempting to explain the unusual name of the field. At any rate, Matthew is attempting to show through the Old Testament scriptures that God was at work in the tragic events of the conclusion of Jesus' life.

Jesus Before Pilate (244–246. Mark 15:2–15; Matthew 27:11–26; Luke 23:2–25). Mark begins his account of the trial of Jesus before Pilate bluntly with a question of Pilate, "Are you the King of the Jews?" Jesus' answer, "You have said so," is not a denial, but neither is it an unconditional affirmation. Obviously the question could not be answered with a simple "yes" or "no." Jesus would affirm the statement, but in his own way.

When charges were brought by the chief priests, Jesus remained silent.[39] Pilate, perceiving "that it was out of envy" that the chief priests brought Jesus before him and hoping to accomplish his release without antagonizing the religious leaders, appealed to the supposed custom of releasing a prisoner for which the crowd asked.[40] Pilate offered a choice between a known criminal Barabbas and Jesus, evidently anticipating that Jesus would be chosen. However, the crowd, stirred up by the religious leaders, asked for Barabbas' release and for Jesus' crucifixion and Pilate "wishing to satisfy the crowd, released for them Barabbas; and having scourged Jesus, he delivered him to be crucified."

The accounts in Matthew and Luke show what sort of changes took place during the transformation of the traditions of Jesus' trial and condemnation. Both Jewish and Roman officials are involved. The

---

[37] For a full critical discussion of the Synoptic tradition of the trial of Jesus, see Paul Winter, *On the Trial of Jesus.*

[38] Zech. 11:12–13 with reminiscences of Jer. 18:1f. and 36:6–9ff.

[39] Cf. Isaiah 53:7 which may be in mind here.

[40] Evidence for such a custom is limited to this reference in the Gospels.

evidence of the Gospels here is supported by the historical situation in the time of Jesus. Matthew and Luke, however, emphasize the responsibility of the Jewish leaders. Luke alters Mark's suggestion that Pilate suspected the leaders of bringing charges against Jesus because of envy into three direct assertions that Pilate found Jesus not guilty (Luke 23:4, 14, 22) and before the people declared him to be innocent. The account of Jesus' examination before Herod, found only in Luke, fits his emphasis. Pilate knows Jesus to be innocent and tries to get Herod to take responsibility. Luke makes the point that even Herod fails to find Jesus guilty. Matthew follows Mark closely, but two small additions emphasize the Roman procurator's failure to view Jesus as a criminal. In 27:19 Matthew tells of a message sent by Pilate's wife to her husband, "Have nothing to do with that righteous man, for I have suffered much over him today in a dream," and in Matthew 27:24 Pilate "washed his hands before the crowd, saying, 'I am innocent of this man's blood, see to it yourselves.'" The response of the people, "His blood be on us and on our children!" is used to emphasize rather dramatically that Rome is not responsible. The Gospel account of the trial of Jesus certainly was colored by Jewish-Christian hostility and by the necessity for Christians to avoid Roman suspicion in the time of the early Church. But the account clearly shows what was the case: Jesus was seized by the leaders of the Jews who delivered him to the Roman procurator who had him crucified.

Mocking by the Soldiers (247. Mark 15:16–20; Matthew 27:27–31). Mark and Matthew tell of soldiers mocking Jesus after the sentence. Luke's unique account of Jesus before Herod contains a story of the mocking of Jesus, and he omits the account of mocking at this point. Such action by Roman soldiers against rebellious Jews is quite understandable. The soldiers had heard charges against Jesus as King of the Jews and go through a mock ritual of worship before leading him away for crucifixion.

The Crucifixion (248–250. Mark 15:21–41; Matthew 27:32–56; Luke 23:26–49). With the issue settled, the Synoptics begin the account of Jesus' death by crucifixion. Customarily the condemned man carried the crossbeam upon which he would die, but in the Gospels Simon of Cyrene, perhaps a Passover pilgrim, was compelled to carry the cross on the road to Golgotha. Mark alone says that Simon was the father of Alexander and Rufus, suggesting that the sons had personal significance for Mark and his readers. Luke alone tells of the

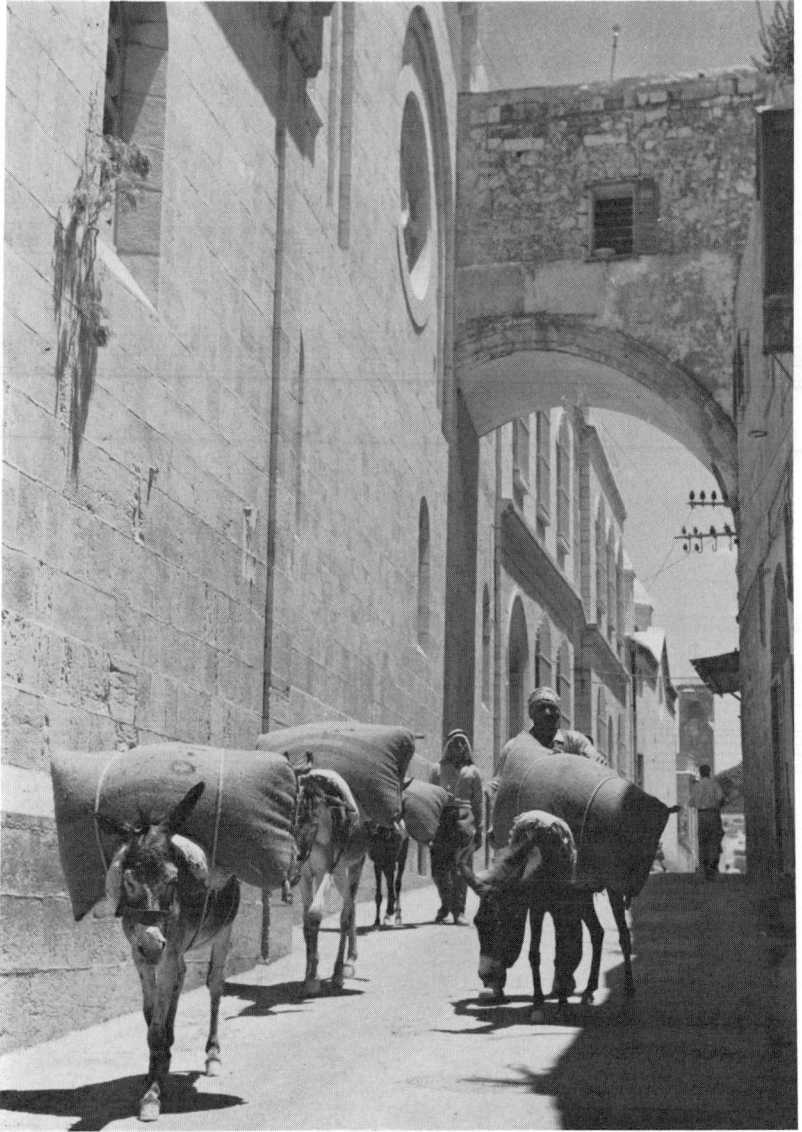

Figure 5–7. The Via Dolorosa, the route used by pious pilgrims to represent the way Jesus went from the governor's headquarters to Golgotha bearing his cross. The road is spanned by the "Ecce Homo" arch, so called because of the tradition that Pilate showed Christ crowned with thorns to the people from this arch. (Source: Paul Popper Ltd.)

Figure 5–8. Gordan's Calvary, regarded by some as the place of Jesus' crucifixion. (Source: Foreign Mission Board, SBC.)

crowd following on the road to Golgotha and of Jesus' warnings about the desperate days ahead.

The crucifixion took place at Golgotha, a site outside the walls of the city. The word Golgotha means "skull" [41] and may originate from either the common use of the site for executions or the cranial shape of rock or hillock. Before the actual act of crucifixion, Jesus, following ancient Jewish custom,[42] was offered wine with myrrh as a drug, but Jesus refused. The act of crucifixion itself is stated but not described in detail; it was well enough known in the ancient world not to need elaboration. The victim was fastened to the cross, a single stake or a stake with a crossbeam, by ropes or nails and exposed, naked and unable to move, until death came, perhaps after days of suffering.

Jesus' garments were divided among the soldiers, who cast lots to decide what each should take. This action, as others at the crucifixion, was seen and interpreted in light of Psalm 22, but the historical situation provided for the goods of the victim to be disposed of in this way.

[41] The commonly used *Calvary* comes from the Latin equivalent.
[42] See Prov. 31:6.

In accord with Roman custom an inscription containing the charge against Jesus was affixed to the cross. The contents, of course, reflect official contempt and scorn; authorities did not really accept him as "king of the Jews." Two thieves are mentioned by all three Synoptics as being crucified with Jesus. According to Mark and Matthew both participated in ridiculing Jesus. Luke alone says that one of the criminals defended Jesus against the taunting of the others asking, "Jesus, remember me when you come into your kingly power." According to Luke's report, he is rewarded with Jesus' words, "Truly, I say to you, today you will be with me in Paradise."

The death of Jesus is reported with an intensity fitting its importance for the evangelists. At the sixth hour "there was darkness over the whole land until the ninth hour." Reference here could be to a "black sirocco," [43] an east wind which darkened the atmosphere, but the occurrence at the time of Jesus' death would be seen as a miracle. Such natural occurrences frequently were associated with the death of great men, and the incident may be included to emphasize the greatness of Jesus and the sympathy of the heavens themselves with his sufferings.

At the ninth hour Jesus cried out in Hebrew (or Aramaic) the opening words of Psalm 22, "My God, my God, why hast thou forsaken me?" The words were misunderstood by some of the bystanders who said, "Behold, he is calling Elijah." What Jesus actually meant by these words is not certain. Is the cry an indication of Jesus' sense of desolation? If so, the statement of Glover is appropriate, "I have sometimes thought there never was an utterance that reveals more amazingly the distance between feeling and fact." [44] Is the cry to be understood in the total context of Psalm 22 as a cry of victory? Seemingly the Church searched the Old Testament for scriptures which could be applied to Christ and in using Psalm 22 to understand the crucifixion would have taken the cry in the light of the entire Psalm.

When Jesus "uttered a loud cry, and breathed his last," the Synoptics tell that "the curtain of the temple was torn in two from top to bottom." Of course, this is no mere statement of fact. Who would be interested in a piece of cloth far away from the place of the crucifixion?

---

[43] Although Maurice Goguel declares such an hypothesis unnecessary, he gives an account by one of his students of an experience of such an east wind which darkened the whole atmosphere in Jerusalem during a visit in April 15–16, 1927. Maurice Goguel, *The Life of Jesus*, tr. Olive Wyon, p. 242, n. 2.

[44] T. R. Glover, *The Jesus of History*, p. 192, quoted in Taylor, *The Gospel According to St. Mark*, p. 594.

The torn curtain separated the Holy of Holies, the inner sanctuary symbolizing God's dwelling, from the remainder of the temple. Only the high priest had access to the Holy of Holies. Thus here the theology of Mark is stated: the death of Jesus opens the way to the presence of God once and for all.[45]

Matthew adds a number of elements to the account of the tearing of the curtain. These additions, the earthquake, the splitting of the rocks, and the walking of the dead are not as symbolic as the rending of the veil of the temple. They are similar to stories of amazing events accompanying the death of other great men and serve to underline the significance of Jesus and his death. The centurion's witness may be taken as the recognition of greatness in the one crucified. Luke's quotation is simply, "Certainly, this man was innocent." But Mark's quotation, "Truly this man was a son of God!" may be read as a superstition on the part of the soldier or as a more weighty confession of Jesus in the Christian sense.

The Burial of Jesus (251–252. Mark 15:42–47; Matthew 27:57–66; Luke 23:50–56). The story of the burial of Jesus by Joseph of Arimathea, a respected and pious Jew, is recognized by the most careful critics of the tradition as a historical account.[46] The burial was late Friday afternoon. The sabbath began at sunset on Friday, and no time could be lost if ritual purity was to be maintained.[47] Joseph, therefore, received permission from Pilate and buried Jesus in a rock tomb.

Matthew alone tells of placing a guard at the tomb. This story was added because of an early controversy between Christians and their opponents regarding the death of Jesus. The report had spread among the Jews that Jesus' disciples came by night and stole him away (Matthew 28:15),[48] and the story of the guard at the tomb refuted this Jewish report.

The Empty Tomb (253. Mark 16:1–8; Matthew 28:1–10; Luke 24:1–11). The earliest written account of the resurrection is Paul's account in I Corinthians 15 (verses 3–8; 20–24). Paul makes no mention

---

[45] See Heb. 6:19ff.; 9:8ff.

[46] Rudolf Bultmann says that apart from sections of verses 44, 45, and 47, "This is an historical account which creates no impression of being a legend . . ." Bultmann, *The History of the Synoptic Tradition*, tr. John Marsh, p. 274.

[47] See Deut. 21:23.

[48] The report is evidence that the Jews as well as Christians were convinced that an empty grave was involved in the final event. Of course, a different explanation was given by each group.

of the empty tomb, but there is a strong statement on the resurrection of Jesus and the presence of the risen Christ among a wide variety of followers. Mark's Gospel as we have it concludes with an account of the resurrection and emphasizes the fact, logically lying behind the appearance of the risen Christ, of an empty tomb.[49]

Matthean and Lucan Appearances (Matthew 28:11–20; Luke 24:13–53)

Although Mark concludes with the story of the empty tomb and the fearful and astonished women, Matthew and Luke give additional stories of Jesus' appearances. Matthew tells of an appearance in Galilee where Jesus gives a final commission to his disciples (28:16–20). The commission is presented by Matthew at a time when the Christian Church had become in reality a world faith through the death and resurrection of Jesus Christ.

The words which he here attributes to Jesus give expression to fundamental convictions by which the Church continues to live: the faith that all power in heaven and on earth is given to the crucified and risen Lord, the knowledge that she bears an apostolic commission to carry his Gospel of salvation to all the nations, and the confidence that he is with her and will continue to be with her to the end of time.[50]

Luke's post-resurrection narrative is much more detailed than Matthew's. Jesus appears on the road to Emmaus and joins two followers, converses with them on the way, and reveals his identity to them at a meal that evening. The followers immediately returned to Jerusalem and reported the events to the eleven disciples. At that point, "Jesus himself stood among them," invited the disciples to handle his body, and ate a piece of broiled fish before them. After instructing the disciples, he admonished them, "You are witnesses of these things. And behold, I send the promise of my Father upon you; but stay in the city, until you are clothed with power from on high." Then Jesus "led them out as far as Bethany, and lifting up his hands he blessed them. While he blessed them, he parted from them."

---

[49] The supplementary endings found in several manuscripts did not form a part of the original text. Some scholars think that there was an original ending by Mark which was lost very early, at least before the writing of Matthew and Luke, since Matthew and Luke make no use of a common source after Mark 16:8. It is not necessary to assume that there was an ending which is now lost; Mark could have concluded his Gospel with the story of the empty tomb, but the concluding words do sound strange. See below, p. 462.

[50] Beare, *The Earliest Records of Jesus,* p. 243.

That such a unified and continuous passion narrative is followed by such disjointed accounts of the resurrection appearances may appear strange, but the needs of the Church in the earliest years may account for the differences. The passion narrative as a whole was needed to show how the Messiah came to be crucified by the Jews in accordance with God's will. "When at length the time came to co-ordinate the original facts in the Gospels, the evangelists could do no more than record the local traditions of the churches for which they wrote, traditions which vary in historical value and cannot in all points be reconciled." [51] Apparently the churches preserved various traditions about Jesus' post-resurrection appearances.

It must be emphasized that the resurrection narratives, although witnessing to the central fact from different viewpoints, are not the *primary* bases of the Christian belief in the resurrection of Jesus Christ. The narratives are later statements and indeed grow out of previous historical realities. Vincent Taylor says, "The resurrection narratives will always focus and quicken Christian belief, but they are not the primary basis of that belief." The historical arguments behind the narratives include "the immense change in the first disciples wrought by their knowledge of the risen Lord, the conversion and life of the apostle Paul, and the existence and continued life of the Christian Church. Coupled with these historical arguments is the living experience of the individual Christian believer of fellowship with the risen Christ." [52]

SUGGESTED READINGS

In addition to the appropriate books listed in Chapters 2 and 3 see:

JEREMIAS, JOACHIM, *The Eucharistic Words of Jesus* (Scribner's, 1966).
RAMSEY, A. M., *The Resurrection of Christ* (Allenson, 1956). A cautious and competent study of the resurrection.
WINTER, PAUL, *On the Trial of Jesus* (deGroyter, 1961). A detailed study of the trial of Jesus.

---

[51] Vincent Taylor, *The Life and Ministry of Jesus*, pp. 225–226. See C. H. Dodd, "The Appearances of the Risen Christ: An Essay in Form Criticism of the Gospels," *Studies in the Gospels: Essays in Memory of R. H. Lightfoot*, ed. D. E. Nineham, pp. 9–35, for a form critical study of the resurrection appearances.
[52] Taylor, *The Life and Ministry of Jesus*, p. 226.

PART II

Expansion of the Church to A.D. 60

6

The Setting for Expansion

Jesus' life, death, and resurrection understood together as the redemptive act of God was the event which made the Church. The Christian community, however, was not born complete and mature. At first it had only faith, hope, commitment, and courage. No doctrine or creed, no organization or plan of action, only the profound belief that in Jesus they had found the meaning of their own existence and the savior of the world identified the body of believers. In the decades following Jesus' death his followers accepted his call to discipleship and witness, and what began as an apparently insignificant movement in Judaism spread to the heart of the Roman empire and beyond. The Christian faith took form in the first century Mediterranean world where doctrine and ethics were hammered out in the context of expansion and growth and of trial and conflict.

THE MEDITERRANEAN WORLD

For New Testament writers the horizon of the Church lay in the west, the Mediterranean world of the Roman empire. A number of factors favored the westward expansion of the new religion. Jews were widely dispersed throughout the empire. In fact, in the first century more Jews lived outside of Palestine than in their traditional homeland. They were particularly numerous in Egypt, Syria, Asia Minor, Africa, and Italy. Christianity had obvious traditional affinities with Judaism and found in the Jews of the dispersion a proper audience for the proclamation of the gospel. In addition even before the advent of Christianity, there was in Judaism an affinity for Hellenistic culture and thought. Some Jews resisted this, but others were open to it. The latter group was notably represented in the early Church. Also of great importance was the widespread use of the Greek language which freed the communication of the new faith from normal language limitations. Finally, the stability and unity of the Roman empire greatly facilitated communication and travel.[1] Christian communities must have been established in the east and south, particularly in the Mesopotamian Parthian empire and among the Nabateans. Evidence, however, to that effect is lacking. Rather than conjecture about possible extensions of the gospel into such areas, or about the reliability of late traditions which describe one or more of the apostles as active in them, it is better to follow Acts and focus upon Paul's work in the Roman world.

The Roman Empire

By the time of the Christian movement Rome had extended its authority to a series of provinces, protectorates, and allied states which surrounded the Mediterranean making it virtually a Roman Sea, which the Romans fondly called *Mare Nostrum* ("Our Sea"). Rome had moved toward imperial rule under Julius Caesar, but Octavian (Augustus, 31 B.C.–A.D. 14) was actually first to exercise the power of emperor. Augustus was a capable ruler who kept control over the empire by careful organization of the provinces. Their administration depended upon their classification.[2] Stable provinces were under the senate, which sent out a governor each year. The other provinces, known as imperial, were under the emperor's direct control, but were usually delegated to legates or procurators for several years at a time. New territories and border areas were sometimes kept under indirect rule with a native ruler loyal to Rome and acceptable to the native population.

The power and authority of Rome depended upon its army which was used to control uprisings and to protect the frontiers. In the first century A.D. more than twenty-five legions were under arms, each at full strength composed of six thousand officers and men. Skillful and judicious use of the army preserved the stability of the empire and kept peace throughout the Mediterranean world during most of the first century. Syria-Palestine, Asia Minor, and Greece all enjoyed the benefits of imperial peace and security. Long linked together by

---

[1] This summary is taken in essence from George E. Wright and Floyd V. Filson, eds., *The Westminster Historical Atlas to the Bible*, pp. 101–102.

[2] Provinces were divided into two classes in A.D. 27 by the Act of Settlement, which ostensibly restored the republic and returned rule to the senate.

Hellenistic culture and the Greek language, they now formed part of the same noble state offering centralized control and security. Such unity created favorable circumstances for the spread of the community of Christ throughout the world.

However, the solidarity of the empire was not maintained by brute force. Roman law was highly developed and protected the state, the citizen, and private and public property. Equity was of increasing concern and the status of women and slaves had begun to improve. All peoples and areas in the empire benefited from Roman law which did not, however, supersede local law when the latter was just. Penalties for breaking the law were sometimes vindictive and harsh, especially for public offenses, but for the most part Roman law made significant contribution to the integrity and stability of the Roman state.

When Augustus died in A.D. 14 and was succeeded by a line of emperors called the Julio-Claudians (A.D. 14–68), the general shape of a new form of Roman government began to emerge. Augustus had believed that the Roman state should be under the single rule of some first citizen. This idea lived after him, supported by Rome's "gratitude for the benefits of his government and by his position after death as a god." [3] The "nature and manner of the ruler" became "the directive force of Rome" [4] and his policies affected every walk of life. The Julio-Claudian emperors were Tiberius (14–37), Gaius Caligula (37–41), Claudius (41–54), and Nero (54–68).

Palestine in the Empire

Under the Julio-Claudians Palestine was administered much as under Augustus. When Herod Philip, ruler of northern Transjordan, died in A.D. 37, his territory was assigned to Herod Agrippa, grandson of Herod the Great and protégé and intimate of Caligula. Two years later Antipas, ruler of Galilee and Perea, was banished to Lyons in France and his territory was also granted to Agrippa. Agrippa chanced to be in Rome when Caligula was murdered and was helpful in Claudius' ascent to the throne. As reward, Judea and Samaria, formerly under procurators, were added to his territories and he was appointed king. Thus he ruled over essentially the same area as had Herod the Great. To win favor with the Jews Agrippa persecuted the Church, killing James the son of Zebedee and arresting Peter (Acts 12:1–23). His reign, however, was ended by his sudden death in A.D. 44. Since

[3] Frank C. Bourne, *A History of the Romans,* p. 379.
[4] *Ibid.,* p. 379.

his only son, also named Agrippa, was still a minor, the kingdom temporarily became a province.

Most of Palestine remained a province through the period of our immediate concern. Galilee, Perea, and part of the old territory of Philip were given to Agrippa II when he came of age and he ruled them from A.D. 61 through the Jewish revolt of A.D. 66–73 and after. He moved to Rome around A.D. 75 and little else is known about him. Acts relates that he participated in the consultations which resulted in Paul's being sent to Rome for trial by Caesar.

Asia Minor and Greece, the principal areas of Paul's missionary activity, were variously administered by Rome throughout the New Testament period. Details pertinent to the present study will be given in the chapters to follow. Of particular importance is the fact that these various areas were well integrated into the empire and for the period covered by the book of Acts enjoyed uninterrupted peace and general stability.

SOURCES FOR UNDERSTANDING EXPANSION

Reconstruction in detail of the life of the early Church as it developed in the three or four decades after the crucifixion and resurrection of Jesus is virtually impossible. In spite of rather ample information about life and thought in the first century Roman world, specific literary references to the amorphous Christian movement are scanty and archaeological evidence for the Church of the mid-first century is entirely lacking. Fleeting references appear in the writing of Roman historians, but provide no new information which would contribute substantially to an understanding of early Christian history. The Jewish historian Josephus reflects controversy between Jews and Jewish Christians, but nothing more. The Apostle Paul, the most important character in the early Church, is unmentioned in any extant ancient non-biblical source. Although he was the foremost missionary and articulator of early Christian beliefs about Jesus, he evidently attracted more acclaim and recognition within the Church than outside it.[5]

Archaeology is of little help. An inscription discovered at Delphi has enabled archaeologists to fix the date of Gallio's rule in Corinth and so helped to approximate Pauline chronology.[6] Important excava-

[5] The apocryphal *Acts of Paul* aims to supplement the information about Paul in the canonical Acts. However, it is a late second century romance and, as such, is unreliable as an historical source.

[6] See Adolf Deissmann, *Paul,* pp. 261–286.

tions at some of the cities visited by Paul on his missionary tours (such as those conducted by the American School of Classical Studies at Corinth) have illuminated life as it was in these metropolitan centers.[7] However, discoveries directly related to the first century Christian community have not yet been made. Church buildings that have been excavated date no earlier than the mid-third century and most of these are from the period of Constantine or later.[8]

Thus, the discovery of the Church of the middle third of the first century is almost exclusively dependent upon biblical sources. In one sense these sources include the entire New Testament. The decades immediately following the historical Jesus were the very period in which the traditions, interpretations, etc., were taking shape in the early Church. A scholarly determination of the factors influencing the formation of the New Testament is, therefore, in essence a study of the Church as much as it is a study of the scriptures. Particularly, the Gospels took their shape according to the role given to Jesus by the early Church, so that they become sources for determining the thought of the early Christian community. Although the writing of the Gospels occurred largely in the last third of the first century, the traditions about Jesus which became their basis were being shaped in the earliest period of the Church's infancy. A careful study of their content may therefore reflect a great deal about the beliefs and commitments of this developing community in addition to events in the life and mission of Jesus (see below, pp. 451–496). For example, the dominant role of the crucifixion and resurrection narratives in the Synoptics or the passion speeches in John tell us certainly that the Church gave a major place to these events in their interpretations of Jesus. In this way they become source material for any thorough understanding of the early Church.

More specifically, however, two New Testament sources, the Pauline letters and the book of Acts, illuminate the period of our concern. The letters of Paul come directly from the life of the emerging Church and are especially helpful in reconstructing the mid-first century Christian community. The book of Acts is a particular type of early history writing which discusses episodes and characters from this period of

---

[7] Helful summaries may be found in *The Biblical Archaeologist* in such articles as Bruce M. Metzger, "Antioch on-the-Orontes," XI (1948), 70–88; Sherman E. Johnson, "Laodicea and its Neighbors," XIII (1950), 1–18; W. A. McDonald, "Archaeology and St. Paul's Journeys in Greek Lands," III (1940), 18–24; IV (1941), 1–10, V (1942), 37–48; Merrill M. Parvis, "Archaeology and St. Paul's Journeys in Greek Lands," VIII (1945), 62–80.

[8] See George E. Wright, *Biblical Archaeology*, pp. 245–247.

the Church's history. Neither Acts nor any of Paul's epistles, however, were written as technical histories. Many later questions about dating or sequence of events or even clarity of detail were not even anticipated in these early writings. Any attempt to study the history of the early Church using these materials as sources must be continually modified by a thorough understanding of their distinctively "non-historical" character.

The Pauline Corpus

The phrase "The Apostle Paul" appears in the titles of thirteen of the twenty-seven New Testament books. Almost certainly all of these writings do not come from the great Apostle to the Gentiles. It is unlikely that Paul wrote I and II Timothy and Titus. Considerable uncertainty exists about Ephesians and it is possible that this letter came from another's pen. But even omitting these, an amazingly large portion of the New Testament may still be attributed to Paul with reasonable certainty: Romans, I and II Corinthians, Galatians, Philippians, Colossians, I and II Thessalonians, and Philemon.

In form Paul's letters resemble the technical epistle, which in the ancient Greek and Roman world was a favorite form of literary expression. The letter *form* was often adopted as a means of general communication of an idea or thesis. The typical first century epistle included four distinctive parts. A salutation, including the name of the writer, the addressee, and a greeting, opened the letter. Next came a section expressing thanks and personal appreciation. The major body of the letter dealt with the issue or question up for discussion. And finally the letter closed with whatever personal remarks the writer wished to make and a formal farewell or benediction. If the letter had been dictated, the sender might write the last part himself.

These features are observable throughout the Pauline correspondence, leading some students of the letters to regard them as rigid, formal epistles, ". . . as treatises, as pamphlets in the form of letters, . . . as the theological works of the primitive Christian dogmatic theologian." [9] But to read Paul in this way is to misunderstand him. The letters must not be rooted out of the living situation to which they were addressed. The Apostle was not a literary man writing formal treatises for publication and preservation. Rather he was a separated missionary trying to replace conversation and sermon with the written word. He intended that the addressee, whether an individual or a

[9] Deissmann, *Paul,* p. 8.

group, open and read a message that was individual and personal. Thus the contents of Paul's letters are

. . . as varied as life itself . . . trifling, commonplace, passionate, kindly, trivial, wearisome, and . . . may reflect human fate or family tragedy, moving the souls of writer and recipient to mountain heights or to abysmal depths.[10]

In this sense then the Pauline epistles are important sources for understanding the Church of the mid-first century. Since they are largely responses to specific situations, they illuminate the life of the Christian community in the Roman world. Some of the conflicts implicit in a pluriform religious society become increasingly clear. Problems of those recently turned from paganism permeate Paul's candid discussions. The struggles of a people amorphous in organization and doctrine to give logical and organic expression to a deep commitment to Christ are painfully evident. Sometimes the issues stand out boldly (as in Paul's advice regarding marriage in I Corinthians 7); on other occasions they are known only by inference and implication (as the heresy reflected in Colossians 1–2). In either case, if one assumes that the letters are self-conscious attempts by the Apostle to address himself to definite problems and issues, the writings become primary documents from living history.

The Acts of the Apostles

The Acts of the Apostles, a second biblical source for studying the early Church, is almost universally accepted as the second part of a two volume work, the first volume of which is the Gospel of Luke. Although the title had already been attached to the book by the end of the second century,[11] it was not a part of the original work and does not convey the contents of the writing. The author does not aim to chronicle "the acts of the apostles." Most of the Twelve drop from the story after the first chapter. The title probably was attached to the work in connection with the formation of the canon because of the intense interest of the early Church in Peter and Paul as the two chief apostles.

Acts as History.   Acts, like Luke, is dedicated to Theophilus, and purports to continue the narrative of the Gospel by tracing the develop-

---

[10] *Ibid.,* p. 9.
[11] The title was included in the Muratorian Canon, was known to Tertullian and Clement around A.D. 200, and appears in Codex Vaticanus in the fourth century A.D.

ment of the early Church during the several decades immediately following the resurrection of Jesus. It is the only narrative of this particular period available to us and so constitutes a most important source.

The author of Luke–Acts is not known. Traditionally he is identified with Luke, a missionary companion of Paul. The classical arguments for this identification can be traced to Irenaeus,[12] about A.D. 180, and rest primarily upon the assumption that frequent passages in the second half of the book written in the first person plural (16:10–17; 20:5–15; 21:1–18; 27:1–28:16) reflect the author's presence. However, in a number of instances Acts seems unfamiliar with details of Paul's experience and thought.[13] Such unfamiliarity is difficult to explain if the author of Acts had been Paul's companion. The issue though is inconclusive and for convenience "Luke" may be used to designate the individual who wrote both the Gospel and Acts. Whoever composed Acts used a variety of written and oral sources [14] from which he selected episodes preserved from the period of the early Church and wove them together with materials of his own composition into a connected account consistent with his purposes in writing.

Thus Acts represents far more than the collection, assortment, and arrangement of traditional materials preserved by the Church. Whatever the materials that came to Luke from the Church tradition, Acts is the author's own creation. Luke was certainly no professional historian in the modern sense of the word, concerned to utilize primary documents to prepare a technically accurate history of early Christianity. The author, like the apostles of whom he writes,[15] understands himself as a preacher. He is motivated and his writing is molded by specific theological concerns growing out of the ecclesiastical environment of which he is a part. Luke wanted to pass on authentic Church tradition "only insofar as it was edifying, that is, as far as it inspired and strengthened faith." [16]

This milieu of the Acts narration is especially evident in the summary accounts and speeches which are a significant component of the book. Three summary accounts appear in connection with the primi-

---

[12] *Against Heresies*, III, xiii, 3.

[13] Cf. FBK, pp. 127–131.

[14] Cf. FBK, pp. 123–132. The only one which can be identified with certainty is "the travel account" in 13–28.

[15] C. K. Barrett, *Luke the Historian in Recent Study*, p. 51.

[16] Ernst Haenchen, "The Book of Acts as Source Material for the History of Early Christianity," *Studies in Luke–Acts*, eds. Leander E. Keck and J. Louis Martyn, p. 258.

tive Church community (2:43–47; 4:32–37; 5:12–16).[17] These passages are the author's composition. They do not carry forward the narration, but rather state an idealized view of the primitive Christian community. They express an interpretation prevalent in the time of the writing of Acts that the initial fellowship was ideally unified in prayer, table fellowship, and sharing of property and esteemed for the sake of its miraculous deeds.[18]

Even more, the speeches in Acts reflect an interpretative reporting of history. These speeches comprise approximately one third of the book and are attributed to nearly all its chief characters (Stephen: Acts 7:2–53; Peter: 2:14–36; 3:12–26; 4:8–12; 5:30–32; 10:34–43; Paul: 13:16–41; 14:15–17; 17:22–31; 20:18–35; 22:1–21; 26:2–23; 28:25–29). They regularly occur at strategic turning points in the narrative as literary devices for interpreting the meaning of events.[19] Whether or not Luke had reliable sources from which he could construct the speeches, we cannot tell. The sermons probably reflect a variety of sermonic forms that were current in the early Church and include those emphases that typical preachers of the period would have stressed. They certainly are not verbatim reports, but rather are molded, perhaps even invented, by Luke to proclaim God's work in history as he understood it. As one distinguished scholar summarizes:

He has found a new method of presenting material which has not yet been dealt with in literature; in doing so he has made new use of the traditional art of composing speeches, an art which had already been employed in many different ways. He used this device not only to illuminate the situation but also to make clear the ways of God; he did not desire to testify to the capabilities either of the speaker or of the author, but to proclaim the gospel.[20]

Only in this context, then, may Luke be understood as an historian and Acts read as history. That Acts is history as it actually happened, that it puts the right people in the right places at the right time, that proper sequence of events is maintained, or even that accurate motives and intentions are assigned to its characters cannot be assumed. Further, it must be accepted that the usual concerns of writing history are missing. Precision of detail, complete description, chronological

---

[17] Some also describe 9:31 and 16:5 as summary accounts, but these are general connecting statements and serve a function different from the summary accounts.

[18] FBK, p. 117.

[19] Cf. H. J. Cadbury, "The Speeches in Acts," *Beginnings of Christianity*, I, 5, 402f., and Martin Dibelius, "The Speeches in Acts and Ancient Historiography," *Studies in the Acts of the Apostles*, pp. 138ff.

[20] Dibelius, *Studies in the Acts of the Apostles*, p. 183, as cited in FBK, p. 119.

concern, and biographical accuracy are not to be forced upon Acts. Rather, the author writes history with the sensitive eye of one caught up in the spirit of the Church that is becoming a part of history. "Even though Luke is of all New Testament writers the most self-conscious author, we must recognize that in writing he has moved in the main by motives of which he was himself (in all probability) imperfectly aware."[21] His depiction of the Church of the first few decades may or may not be *accurate*, simply because it is *his* picture. This is not to Luke's discredit, but it is to recognize the meaningful frame within which Acts may be studied.

But if Luke may not be described as a dispassionately objective historian, neither is his writing to be understood as devoid of relationship to history. In fact, the need for the Church to come to grips with history may have been a primary factor which led to the writing of Acts. As the mid-century waned into the final decades of the first century, expectations of an imminent end of history began to give way to a realistic confrontation of ongoing time. Acts undoubtedly is an important part of this process. Luke aims to interpret history in the light of his theological purposes, but it is real history that is being interpreted. A Church and its apostolic leaders in real time and space are being discussed, although with the biases of proclamation and instruction. In this sense, Luke is a genuine literary pioneer. "He had no predecessor, nor any real successor."[22] His writing may be read meaningfully only when one discovers both the concepts which condition his work and the general patterns of history that are suggested by the narrative.

Acts and the Pauline Letters.   Such an approach to Acts raises at least two major questions which must be faced in any serious effort to understand the book. What were the specific purposes, insofar as they can be determined, which influenced the way Luke relates the history of the early Church? And how do Pauline epistles and the Acts compare with each other?

With regards to the latter question, several features become evident from even a cursory study. Judging from internal evidence, the two bodies of literature appear quite independent of each other. Nothing in Acts suggests an awareness of the Pauline correspondence[23] and

[21] Barrett, *Luke the Historian in Recent Study,* pp. 52–53. Cf. pp. 49–53.

[22] Haenchen, "The Book of Acts as Source Material for the History of Early Christianity," *Studies in Luke–Acts,* p. 258. The later apocryphal works on the "acts of the apostles" are almost completely legend and fiction.

[23] Morton S. Enslin, " 'Luke' and Paul," *Journal of American Oriental Society,* LVIII (1938), 81–91, makes a poor case for Luke's use of Paul.

nothing in Paul's letters indicates familiarity with Acts. If Acts were written during the last part of the first century, the latter is understandable. Acts had not been written before Paul's death. It is hardly conceivable, however, that Luke would have written a book in which the chief character is Paul without being aware of his extensive writings, even if they had not yet been collected.[24] Luke then must have known about Paul's letters, but "quite consciously and deliberately made little or no use of them." [25] Since use of the Pauline correspondence did not contribute significantly to his purposes,[26] Luke did not use the Pauline letters as source materials.

More than simply being independent of each other, Acts and the epistles often seem to be in conflict. A detailed comparison of the two reveal points of disagreement which are difficult, if not impossible, to reconcile.[27] For example, Acts depicts Paul as having been in Jerusalem twice before the conference on Gentile admission into the Church, whereas Paul in Galatians 2 places strategic importance on his claim to have been there only once previously. Luke also indicates that the conference issued a sort of apostolic decree to effect unity between Jews and Gentiles, but Paul seems to have been unaware of any such resolution (Galatians 2:6; I Corinthians 8–10). Further, Paul in the Corinthian correspondence (II Corinthians 11:23–25) refers to "far more imprisonments, with countless beatings" and three occasions when he had been shipwrecked. These are difficult to place in the Acts framework, where only the Philippian imprisonment and no shipwrecks are mentioned before the writing of Corinthians. In addition to these and other historical inconsistencies, there also seem to be many interpretative differences. Luke, in contrast to Paul, reserves the use of the term *apostle* for the Twelve, sometimes clearly placing Paul to one side (Acts 1:26; 15:2, 6, 22–29; 16:4). Also, although Pauline theology in his letters centers upon salvation wrought by God through Christ's death,[28] the Pauline speeches in Acts barely mention the death of Jesus

[24] Edgar J. Goodspeed, *An Introduction to the New Testament,* pp. 191–221, makes an interesting case for the publication of Acts as the occasion for the collection of Paul's letters.

[25] John Knox, "Acts and the Pauline Corpus," *Studies in Luke–Acts,* eds. Keck and Martyn, p. 284.

[26] Knox, *ibid.,* suggests further that the letters were originally associated with schismatic groups in the early Church and so were somewhat opposed to Luke's concern to emphasize the idealized unity and order of the early Church.

[27] A careful discussion of these problems appears in Ernst Haenchen's essay, "The Book of Acts as Source Material for the History of Early Christianity," in *Studies in Luke–Acts,* pp. 258–278. Cf. also FBK, pp. 127–130.

[28] Cf. Romans 3:24–26; 5:6–21; I Corinthians 1:18–25; Galatians 3:13.

(13:27–29; 20:28) and even then attach little redemptive importance to it.

These variations underscore the need to understand the distinctive character of Acts.[29] Its author was an edifier, a proclaimer, a preacher, who selected, reported, and composed materials according to his own intent. As Haenchen summarizes,

> The question of the historical reliability of the book of Acts does not touch the central concern of the book. By telling the history of apostolic times through many individual stories, the book primarily intends to edify churches and thereby contribute its part in spreading the word of God farther and farther, even to the ends of the earth.[30]

Structure and Controlling Themes. The theological character of Acts makes it imperative that another question be raised. What are the specific themes or ideas which motivate the author, control his use of data, and which he wishes to impart to his readers? The answer to this question, of course, rests largely on a study of general form and themes and therefore may be open to subjective conclusions.[31] Some salient points become immediately obvious as determinative for the author of Acts.

Acts is generally organized along geographical lines. The author describes the expansion of Christianity as moving from its beginning in Jerusalem to its final goal in Rome. An outline of the book reflects this geographical orientation:

Introduction. 1:1–11
    A. Link with Luke's Gospel. 1:1–5
    B. Ascension and charge to the Church. 1:6–11

  I. The Gospel in Jerusalem. 1:12–8:1a
    A. Restoration of the Twelve. 1:12–26
    B. The Jerusalem Pentecost. 2:1–47
    C. Conflict with Jerusalem authorities. 3:1–4:31
    D. Communal living. 4:32–5:11
    E. Further conflict with authorities. 5:12–42
    F. Stephen: Hellenists vs. Hebrews. 6:1–8:1a

[29] However, Ramsay's point that Luke is strikingly accurate must still be taken seriously, although with modification. See his *The Bearing of Recent Discovery on the Trustworthiness of the New Testament*. See also, H. J. Cadbury, *The Book of Acts in History*.

[30] Haenchen, "The Book of Acts as Source Material for the History of Early Christianity," in *Studies in Luke–Acts*, p. 278.

[31] The most significant and recent book on this problem is Hans Conzelmann, *The Theology of St. Luke*, a 1960 translation of an original German work which appeared in 1953 under the title *Die Mitte Der Zeit*. See also J. C. O'Neill, *The Theology of Acts*.

II. The Gospel Moves to Antioch. 8:1b–12:25
   A. Persecution. 8:1b–3
   B. Philip: The Samaritan Mission. 8:4–40
   C. Conversion of Saul of Tarsus. 9:1–31
   D. Peter: Early Gentile mission. 9:32–12:25

III. Paul's Galatian Mission. 13:1–15:35
   A. Paul's commission. 13:1–3
   B. Conduct of the mission. 13:4–14:28
   C. The Jerusalem conference. 15:1–35

IV. Paul's Aegean Mission. 15:36–20:38
   A. Return through Galatia. 15:36–16:5
   B. In Macedonia. 16:6–17:15
   C. In Achaia. 17:16–18:21
   D. In Asia. 18:22–20:38

V. Movement to Rome. 21:1–28:31
   A. Journey to Jerusalem and arrest. 21:1–23:11
   B. Imprisonment and defense in Caesarea. 23:12–26:32
   C. Voyage to Rome and shipwreck. 27:1–28:10
   D. Arrival in Rome. 28:11–31

In successive stages the book describes Church expansion to include first Samaria and the coastal areas of Palestine, then Antioch and the territory of Syria, subsequently Asia Minor and Greece, and finally the very seat of imperial authority and power, Rome itself.[32]

Undoubtedly early Christianity moved into other areas of the ancient Near East; scattered evidence suggests its spread southward into Nabatea and Egypt and eastward into Parthia and Armenia (see pp. 382–390). Early expansion into Galilee is virtually omitted from the Acts account.[33] The major thrust, however, seems to have been westward into the Mediterranean world. Acts demonstrates how the early Church fulfilled the commission of Jesus,

. . . you shall be my witnesses in Jerusalem and in all Judea and Samaria and to the end of the earth. (1:8b)

Luke is not concerned just to preserve the sequence of early Church growth. Rather the geographical design is a means through which Luke says something about the Church and the gospel which it possesses. Rome is not just a geographical goal; it represents the seat of empire, the heart of the Greco-Roman world into which the gospel now is extended.

[32] Actually Christianity reached Rome before the final chapters of Acts. Cf. Acts 18. Paul did not introduce the movement to Rome, although Acts by centering on the Apostle may leave the impression that he did.
[33] See L. E. Elliott-Binns, *Galilean Christianity*, pp. 43–53.

One interpreter of the book sees its testimony epitomized in the adverb *unhindered,* the word with which the book closes.[34] Accordingly the author's concern is the liberation of the gospel. The theme of both the Gospel of Luke and Acts is the freedom of the Christian gospel from the narrow confines of Palestinian Judaism and its extension to all men. This universal scope was implicit in the claims of Jesus as presented in Luke's Gospel and captivated the mission of the Church as demonstrated in the book of Acts. Christianity, according to Luke, has been liberated from its Jewish moorings and subsequently, unhindered by national and racial barriers, reaches for all men. Dramatic episodes from the lives of Stephen and Philip illustrate the crumbling of provincial barriers in the early Jerusalem church. Simon Peter is characteristic of traditionalists of whom reorientation is demanded. But primarily Paul champions the phenomenal inclusion of Gentiles from across the Mediterranean world.[35] The proclamation of the kind of gospel which so captivates the world motivates the author.

The book of Acts is also concerned to assist the Church to confront its own history. During the apostolic period (the mid-third of the first century), the Church had been motivated by the expectancy of the imminent *eschaton* or end. With the passage of time the delay of the *parousia* became obvious and raised serious questions about the continuing relevance of the gospel. If deliverance was not at hand, was the cause hopeless and therefore to be abandoned? Primitive Christianity which had taken great hope in the expectancy of imminent victory in the *parousia* had to reformulate its understanding in the light of passing time.

Acts contributes to the resolution of this problem by pushing the *parousia* into the indefinite future. At the outset of Acts Jesus informs the Church, "It is not for you to know times or seasons which the Father has fixed by his own authority." Rather they are to look forward to the coming end only in consciousness of their responsibilities to witness. The Church to which Acts is addressed at the close of the century is participant in an additional phase of redemptive history. Hans Conzelmann, *The Theology of St. Luke,* believes that Luke saw Christian history as three major epochs (the period of Jesus, the period of the apostolic Church, and the period of the Church after the apostles) and that this understanding of history dominates the structure

---

[34] Frank Stagg, *The Book of Acts,* p. 1.

[35] The argument of Edward Zeller in his *The Acts of the Apostles* that Acts is consciously written to reconcile the two great figures of the early Church is not convincing. See B. H. Streeter, *The Four Gospels,* pp. 542ff.

of Luke–Acts. God's plan is for the gospel to reach out from Jerusalem to the ends of the earth. The Church is enabled to share this redemptive plan because it is empowered by the Spirit.[36]

Another motivating idea, apologetic in character, is related to the Church's confrontation of history. When the end was expected immediately, the Church did not need to concern itself with long-range relationships. However, if history were to be seen from a wider perspective, these relationships were of paramount importance. Acts deals particularly with the relationships of the Church to Judaism and to the empire. Luke lays "as the foundation of his defence of the Church a comprehensive consideration of its general position in the world; he fixed its position in respect of redemptive history and deduces from this the rules for its attitude to the world." [37] Within redemptive history, the Church continues God's intentioned purposes for Israel and the breach between Christianity and Judaism comes only because the latter rejects the gospel. Acts emphasizes how Israel has rejected the gospel and thereby given way for Christianity to inherit the covenant role to continue God's goals in history. Further, Christianity as the continuity of Judaism, is a legitimate religion of the state, deserving maximum legal protection from the emperor. The author of Acts goes to great lengths to witness to the support of Christianity from official Rome. The emphatic, apologetic statement of these twin concepts permeates Acts' interpretation of the relationship of the Church to history.

When these real and legitimate purposes of Acts are remembered, the book may be used helpfully to discuss the historical development of the early Church. Although details and sequence ought not be pressed and appeal for historical validity ought to be made with considerable tentativeness, there is no reason to assume that at least broad patterns of Church expansion are not reflected in the book.

RELIGIOUS CLIMATE: FIRST CENTURY ROMAN WORLD

The thought of the Roman world into which the Christian faith expanded in the latter two thirds of the first century was characterized by variety and tolerance. The Church matured in a context influenced, besides Judaism, by Greek and oriental mystery religions and fertility cults, the official Roman cult, incipient Gnostic thought, and the sophistications of Greek philosophy.

[36] Conzelmann, *The Theology of St. Luke*, pp. 207–234.
[37] *Ibid.*, p. 137.

Greek and Oriental Mysteries and Fertility Cults

Cults celebrating the joys and intimacies of life were popular throughout the Mediterranean world. They provided "salvation or escape from fate and sometimes from death." [38] Some, like the Ephesian cult of Artemis (Diana), can be traced back to Near Eastern worship of a mother goddess and had much in common with earlier Semitic fertility cults. [39] Artemis was goddess of fertility in man and beast and vegetation. Her cult centered in Ephesus (see below, p. 302), but she was worshipped in nearly all the cities of Asia and throughout the Mediterranean world.

The Egyptian cult of Isis and Osiris was also popular. Although it had been repressed in Rome, it gradually spread throughout the empire gaining attraction by its impressive cultic rites. The myth of Osiris, a divine king who had been killed and dismembered by his enemies, was the basis of the cult. Isis wandered the earth searching for his body. By chance Osiris became god of the underworld and ruled over the dead. This cult was originally associated with the annual flooding of the Nile, but had become symbolic of the cycle of man's life, death, and promise of resurrection. Those who joined the cult reenacted Osiris' suffering and death and thus gained assurance of life beyond death. Asia Minor had a similar cult centering in Cybele, the earth-mother, and her lover Attis, the spirit of vegetation who died each autumn and rose from the dead in the spring. The Cybele rituals were frenzied and orgiastic in the extreme.

Typical of Greek cults were the Eleusinian and Dionysian mysteries. The rituals of the Eleusinian cult were based on the cycle of the seasons celebrated in a drama in which Demeter, spirit of fertility, struggled with Pluto, god of the dead. Thousands attended the drama at Eleusis [40] each year. Dionysian mysteries were celebrated at Athens in a theater at the base of the Acropolis. Dionysius was god of wine. His myth was similar to those of the other mysteries, involving brutal death and miraculous resurrection. Union with Dionysius was desired by many, especially women. By eating the raw flesh of animals sacrificed in the rites and by drinking new wine and engaging in ecstatic

[38] Robert M. Grant, "Roman Empire," *IDB*, IV, p. 106.

[39] The Ephesian Artemis or Diana bears the same name as the Greek and Roman virgin huntress, moon goddess, and patroness of maidens of marriageable age. There is little resemblance, however, apart from the name.

[40] A city on the coast of southern Attica about twelve miles from Athens.

dances they were filled with his spirit and thereby shared his divine life.

These mysteries and others like them, those of Apollo and Arclepius in Greece and of Mithra in Rome, had wide appeal among all classes. The initiates of each cult shared the fortunes of one another in a common brotherhood and each cult in its own way offered eternal salvation and security. It is unlikely that such cults had significant influence upon the life and thought of the early Church. They were foreign to Christian thought. The mysteries, however, were a real part of the cultural context in which the Church developed and expanded.

Roman State Religion and the Emperor Cult

By the time of Augustus old Roman polytheistic religion had lost much of its appeal. Its Greek parallel had been challenged and disenchanted by philosophy which answered ultimate questions without appeal to gods. When Rome adopted Greek culture, it essentially dethroned the classic deities. In addition the mystery cults with their international and universal characteristics were attractive in a way that the older autocratic system had never been.

Augustus and his successors were concerned about the decline of the state religion, believing it indicated lack of patriotism. Augustus apparently believed "that a religious restoration must be at the core of moral regeneration and that he must lead the way back to the old gods, back to their compact with the Romans, back to a restoration of ancient piety." [41] Besides restoration of temples and cultic offices he instituted the imperial cult by elevating Julius Caesar to divine status and decreeing that the genius of the emperor should be worshipped. Precedent for this was found in the common practice among the Hellenistic people of lavishing divine honors upon their rulers. What Augustus decreed for Julius and assumed for himself had been practically accorded them in the eastern half of the empire. In theory the emperor himself was not divine, only the genius of emperorship. In fact, however, the genius could not be separated from the living emperor and Augustus' successors considered the worship of the genius of the living emperor as a test of patriotism. Some like Nero and Domitian, especially the latter, thought themselves to be divine and demanded worship of themselves, not only their genius. Such attitudes were to have serious consequences for the Church.

[41] Bourne, *A History of the Romans,* p. 368.

Gnosticism

Gnosticism was a system of religious thought which emphasized knowledge (*gnosis*) as "the means for the attainment of salvation; or even as the form of salvation itself." [42] It is best known from its major second century Christian forms (the systems of Marcion, Valentinus, and Basilides), but may have originated earlier. The Church fathers knew Gnosticism as a Christian heresy and concentrated upon those groups which developed out of Christianity, adopting the idea of Christ to their thought, or upon those thought to be in competition with the Christian gospel. [43] Many modern scholars, however, argue the existence of a "*pre-Christian Jewish* and a *Hellenistic pagan* Gnosticism," [44] and in varying degrees assume Gnostic thought as the source of some Christian beliefs. [45]

Gnosticism was not, however, a single system of thought. Gnostics "displayed pronounced intellectual individualism, and the mythological imagination of the whole movement was incessantly fertile." [46] Irenaeus, a Church father of the second century, observed, ". . . everyone of them generates something new day by day, according to his ability; for no one is deemed 'perfect' who does not develop among them some mighty fictions." [47] If one includes as Gnostic the many pre-Christian groups which had some ideas in common with the later systems, the variety and creativity of the Gnostic mind is impressive indeed. Nevertheless, all the fully developed Gnostic systems shared a *basic myth*. [48]

Gnostic Beliefs. Certain beliefs were characteristic of most Gnostic systems, although it goes beyond the evidence to conclude that the various systems were identical or even related to one another. The Gnostic's "knowledge" was of God and included everything that belonged to the divine realm of being. It was also of himself for the Gnostics knew the nature of man's origin, his fall, his redemption, and his destiny. *Gnosis* comes through revelation, not reason. It is re-

[42] Hans Jonas, *The Gnostic Religion,* p. 32.
[43] *Ibid.*
[44] *Ibid.,* p. 33.
[45] Rudolf Bultmann is the notable example.
[46] Jonas, *The Gnostic Religion,* p. 42.
[47] *Against Heresies,* I, xviii, 1.
[48] Bultmann and Jonas and others find traces of this myth in supposedly pre-Christian systems, especially that of the Mandaeans. The Mandaeans were a Jewish sect east of Jordan who were Gnostic by the second century A.D. They still exist as a practicing Gnostic sect in Iraq. Whether they held any beliefs similar to Gnosticism before the Christian era is quite uncertain.

ceived "through sacred and secret lore or through inner illumination" and "transforms the knower himself by making him a partaker in the divine existence." [49] *Gnosis*, therefore, is not just theoretical or practical knowledge about certain things; it is the means of attaining salvation or is even salvation itself.

Essential to the Gnostic myth is radical dualism. Deity is absolutely transmundane, alien to the created order. The true God neither made nor governs the universe. He dwells in a divine realm of light over against which the created order stands as a realm of darkness. The world was created by lesser powers who may be mediatively descended from the true God but who do not share his nature or possess knowledge of him. Indeed they prevent him from being known in the world which they made and govern. The true God, therefore, cannot be known except by revelation and illumination, or, in other words, through the imparting of *gnosis*.

Man lives in the darkness of the universe, a prisoner in a dungeon. His world is separated from the realm of the true God by a series of extraterrestrial worlds ruled over by the lesser powers. Most frequently these were reckoned as the seven spheres of the planets plus that of the fixed stars, but there was a frequent tendency to expand them, once at least to a total of three hundred and sixty-five heavens. Man was created by the lesser powers, to possess and keep captive a spirit or "spark" of the divine substance from beyond which had fallen into the world. This spiritual self seeks deliverance from the bonds of darkness to return to its native realm of light. Deliverance, however, comes only through the discovery of "who we were, and what we become; where we were, whereinto we have been thrown; whereto we speed; where from we are redeemed; what birth is, and what rebirth." [50] Man is forbidden this knowledge by his created existence which binds him in ignorance. Redemption comes from the heavenly world, from the world of light. To save him from ignorance a messenger, or bearer of revelation, was sent to man even before the beginning of the world. He awakens the spirits of light and reminds them who they are and whence they came. In most systems this redeemer is identified with Jesus, who appeared to be human, but really was not, since he came from the realm of light into the created realm of darkness. Equipped with the knowledge brought by the divine messenger, man's soul or spirit escapes the realm of darkness and returns to the realm of light where its divine spark is reunited with God, re-

[49] Jonas, *The Gnostic Religion*, p. 35.
[50] *Excerpts from Theodotus* as quoted in Jonas, *The Gnostic Religion*, p. 45.

storing man's wholeness and achieving his salvation. Therefore, to know one's heavenly origins and the world's alienness is to know oneself as the "spiritual man," superior to men of the flesh. The Gnostic then demonstrates the freedom of the spirit over the flesh, either by asceticism or libertinism. The flesh is no longer important and can be either denied or indulged, because the "enlightened" man already enjoys the world of light which he will enter at death.

Gnosticism and the Church. There are many relations between this system of thought and the ideas of the early Church. Some scholars find extensive dependence upon Gnostic ideas in the New Testament literature. However, the only Gnostic groups known definitely are deviations from the Christian tradition. Caution, therefore, requires that the similarities be accounted for in other ways. Christian literature, for example, may well have drawn upon the same Jewish and Hellenistic wellsprings of ideas as the Gnostics and certainly addressed itself against Gnostic misinterpretations of the Christian tradition.

New Testament passages related to Gnosticism are of two kinds. The Church remaining true to the tradition of the Old Testament and Judaism and to the earliest Christian faith sought to counter certain ideas of the Gnostic "heresy" (see pp. 501–509). Bultmann lists the areas of thought in which Christian and Gnostic ideas stand in direct contrast: [51] (1) For Christians the creator God is the one true redeeming God. (2) Man is in his entirety the creation of the true God and no preexistent and eternal spark of heavenly stuff can be distinguished from his psychosomatic wholeness. (3) The redeemer is identified with Jesus, who was really and fully man and thus of this world. The argument with Gnosticism was sometimes no more than general warnings against false teachings.[52] Often, though, it involved direct refutation of Gnostic ideas as in the case of the Church's defense of the true humanity of Christ.[53]

The Church also utilized Gnosticism's thought, myth, and terminology (or at least, the sources from which these came) in the positive development of her own theology. For example, the oft repeated contrasts between light and darkness, life and death, heaven and earth

---

[51] *Theology of the New Testament*, I, p. 168. In addition to the three mentioned here he includes the difference between the Christian idea of reception of the righteous into heaven and the Gnostic heavenly journey of the self made possible by *gnosis*.

[52] Cf. I Tim. 1:4; 2:23; 6:4; II Tim. 2:23; 4:4; Titus 1:14; 3:9.

[53] Cf. John 1:14; I John 2:22; 4:2, 15; 5:1, 5–8; II John 7.

(Romans 13:12; I Thessalonians 5:4f.; II Corinthians 6:14; Colossians 1:12; Ephesians 5:8ff.; 6:12; I Peter 2:9) bear striking similarities to Gnostic dualism. Pauline references to "weak and beggarly elemental spirits" (Galatians 4:9) parallel the Gnostic *archons* or lesser powers, and the Ephesian reference to the descent and ascent of the redeemer (4:8–10) [54] is reminiscent of the Gnostic redeemer myth as are certain aspects of the Fourth Gospel's picture of Jesus (1:1–14; 4:14; 8:14; 9:29). Whether in cases like these Christianity is borrower or lender remains in doubt.[55] However, recently discovered Gnostic documents from Egypt all employ Jewish-Christian vocabulary, suggesting a Judaeo-Christian origin of the Gnostic movement, as do all other Gnostic documents we possess.

Whatever its origin Gnosticism provided Christian apologists an attractive format and vocabulary for presenting their faith to sophisticated pagans. Eventually, however, the Church had to repudiate Gnosticism and openly attack its ideas because their subtlety and sophisticated appeal coupled with their similarity to genuine Christian ideas began seriously to threaten the integrity of Christian faith.

Greek Philosophy

By New Testament times the golden age of Greek philosophy was past. Nevertheless, the ideas of Plato and his successors in the Academy were still influential, not only in Greece, but throughout the Roman world. The philosophers had generally discredited older polytheistic and anthropomorphic cults. They had advanced ideas of reality which left little room for *many* gods. In a way, therefore, philosophy, even when only partially understood, prepared for the wide diffusion of Christian and Gnostic thought.

Plato (428–348 B.C.) of course had been most eminent of the philosophers, and his view of reality as consisting of *ideas* had an important influence upon Christian thought. For every specific tangible object (such as house, man, tree) there exists in the metaphysical realm an *idea* or universal pattern. Reality, in fact, is a predicate more of the realm of *ideas* than of specific objects. The *idea* of *man* exists independent of any particular man. *Ideas* exist externally and independent of specific conceptualization. The invisible world, therefore, is

---

[54] Cf. also Col. 2:15.
[55] Other parallels in thought and vocabulary may be found in Bultmann, *Theology*, I, pp. 164–183, and Robert M. Grant, *Gnosticism and Early Christianity*, pp. 149–180.

the real world out of which the world of sense experience is perceived. Mankind's utmost desire should be to know by reason the perfect *ideas* that are reality.

Stoic thought had widespread appeal in the Roman world among all classes and, like Platonic ideas, was influential upon early Christianity. Zeno, the first Stoic (336–264 B.C.), taught in the *stoas* or colonnades of the Athenian public market, hence the name Stoics. Stoics advocated moral integrity and serene acceptance of all that life offered. Their behavior tended to be ascetic. Stoics believed that the universe was activated by a universal soul and in a similar way man was a body energized by a soul. Reality is the result of such energized bodies interacting upon one another. The world-soul is Reason, which moves history toward the appointed destiny of the universal brotherhood of man climaxed by the absorption of everything by God, who is ultimate and all and all.

Epicurean thought tried to free man from superstition and belief in gods by claiming that the material atom is the ultimate reality. Man's life is life in the world and is to be enjoyed as an end in itself. Gods, angels, spirits, demons, worship—in short, all of religion—had no part in the system of Epicurus (341–270 B.C.). Religion, in fact, was "the great enemy, the begetter of monstrous deeds and the bearer of needless terrors." [56] Gods do exist, but they are of no consequence for man. Human realization is to be achieved in this life and is self attained. The end of life is happiness achieved through balance and self control.

Naturally, these philosophical ideas were modified as time passed and as they were filtered through the minds of lesser thinkers in the broader world of Greek culture. Later philosophers chose from the variety of ideas they provided and developed systems—part Platonic, part Stoic, part Epicurean, and part new. One of the more interesting of these *eclectic* philosophers was Philo, a Jew of Alexandria. Philo was contemporary with Jesus. His extensive writings seek to interpret and defend the life and thought of Judaism. By forced and fanciful interpretations of Old Testament narratives he sought to show that the writers of Israel's scriptures had been concerned with and had found similar solutions of the same issues which had concerned the philosophers. Although his concern that the religious experience of God be rationally defensible did not gain wide acceptance among the Gentiles, it is indicative of the intense desire of Jews, and

---

[56] F. W. Beare, "Epicureans," *IDB*, II, p. 122.

Christians also, to represent their faith as intellectually and universally respectable.

Christianity could not enter the Roman world of the first century without encountering this multiform ideational context. The struggle to develop its own distinctive expression occurred in contact with systems which sometimes gave it a vocabulary for discussing reality and at other times occasion for heretical development.

SUGGESTED READINGS

Background

BARRETT, C. K., ed., *The New Testament Background: Selected Documents* (Harper, 1961). Gives relevant Roman, Greek, and Jewish sources in English translation.

BULTMANN, RUDOLF, *Primitive Christianity in its Contemporary Setting* (World, 1956). Gives the Old Testament, Jewish, Greek, and Hellenistic setting of early Christianity.

BAIRD, GEORGE B., *The Apostolic Age* (Duckworth, 1955). Gives an orientation to field of New Testament history and theology.

GRANT, FREDERICK C., *Roman Hellenism and the New Testament* (Scribner's, 1962).

GRANT, ROBERT M., *Gnosticism and Early Christianity* (Columbia University Press, 1959). Treatment by authority on Gnosticism.

MURRAY, GILBERT, *Five Stages of Greek Religion* (Doubleday, 1955). First published as *Four Stages of Greek Religion* in 1912. Chapter IV, "The Failure of Nerve," particularly helpful for understanding of early Christianity.

Sources

BARRETT, C. K., *Luke the Historian in Recent Study* (Epworth, 1961). Gives brief survey of research on Luke–Acts.

CADBURY, HENRY J., *The Making of Luke–Acts* (S.P.C.K., 2nd edition, 1958). Helpful work on the literary and historical background of the early Church.

DODD, C. H., *The Apostolic Preaching and its Development* (Harper, 1936). Treats the basic apostolic preaching and the eschatology of New Testament authors.

KNOX, JOHN, *Chapters in a Life of Paul* (Abingdon, 1950). Important for its approach to the chronology of early Christianity and the life of Paul.

LIETZMANN, HANS, *The Beginnings of the Christian Church* (Scribner's, 1937). Gives a general survey of the historical development of the New Testament Church.

7

The Gospel in Palestine
and Syria (Acts 1-12)

The basic source for studying the early Christian Church is the New Testament book, The Acts of the Apostles. The opening chapters of the book picture the Christian movement immediately following the resurrection of Jesus. The work is tied to its Gospel predecessor, Luke, by a subsidiary preface with a common dedication to Theophilus; and the materials in Acts are conditioned by the author's theological concerns. The religious purposes of Acts and the unfortunate lack of other source materials make impossible detailed reconstruction of the history of the early Church. Nevertheless, some vivid impressions about the apostolic Christian community emerge from the opening chapters of Acts and, since the initial state of any movement is influential on its later development, are important to an understanding of Church development.

THE JERUSALEM CHURCH

The early Christian community at its outset was largely confined to a small group of Jesus' followers in Jerusalem. Acts says that "the company of persons was in all about a hundred and twenty" (1:15). These faithful ones had been rallied by the resurrection of Jesus and gathered on the basis of their common commitment to him as Lord. This was the nucleus out of which the Church developed.

Rigid and uniform patterns of church organization and worship were absent at this stage and any specific labels for this early amorphous community are somewhat anachronistic. Believers were simply those who walked in "the way of the Lord" (18:25, 26) or "the Way" (9:2; 19:9, 23; 24:22). They were "disciples" or "saints" who were committed to "the Way" and who proclaimed "the Word" of their Lord. The name "Christian," introduced twice in Acts (11:26; 26:28), seems to have been a descriptive name applied by those outside the community to indicate that these were followers of Christ's way. Very early in their history, however, believers began to think of themselves as a distinctive group and borrowed from daily vocabulary a word to indicate the distinction. The Greek term *ekklesia*, translated "church," was commonly used in the Greek state to designate an assembly of citizens.[1] Even before the New Testament period this term had been adopted into religious usage. The Septuagint had used *ekklesia* to translate the Hebrew word *kahal*, designating Israel as Yahweh's "called out" or "gathered" community. In this tradition early Christians designated themselves as *ekklesia*. They were those who were "called out" in common commitment to Jesus, "gathered" to worship and proclaim him as Christ and Lord. They were the Church, not so much as an organization, as an event that was happening. In this primary and active sense the word *church* is appropriately descriptive of the Jerusalem company of believers.[2]

Continuity with Israel

The early Jerusalem church did not begin as a separate religious movement. The religious heritage of Judaism provided the context within which the Christian interpreted his relationship to Christ. Those who followed Jesus did so in full confidence that he was Israel's Messiah, bringing Torah and Prophets to their expected fulfillment. Later in the first century when the Church began to assume something of its own special character, factional conflicts became more and more evident and Christianity began to become a movement separate from Judaism. Initially, however, the two groups were one; the first believers continued to identify themselves with Judaism, thinking of themselves as loyal Jews who had now found in Jesus the fulfillment of their long-awaited hopes.

Settlement in Jerusalem. Illustrative of the intimate ties between early Christianity and Judaism is the settlement of the Church in Jerusalem. After the crucifixion, a number of factors must have

---

[1] The general use of the term is found three times in Acts 19:32, 39, 41.
[2] The word "church" to describe the early Christian believers must be used with some caution because of the various modern connotations of the word.

tempted the Apostles to return to Galilee. Their families and their work were there. With Jesus they had known a much more "successful" mission in Galilee than in Judea. There the followers of Jesus supposedly could have worked unmolested by Jerusalem authorities. Although the Apostles may have retreated to Galilee for a brief period following the arrest of Jesus,[3] they did not remain there long. Clearly, the early Church did not develop as an isolated Galilean sect. Jesus was accepted as the completion of an unfinished Jewish drama; hence Jerusalem as the hub of the faith of ancient Israel was the logical center for the life of the followers of Jesus, the new Israel of the last days.[4] Early believers, therefore, settled in the holy city and from there began the proclamation of their faith about Jesus.

Participation in Jewish Ritual. Those who confessed Jesus as Messiah continued to participate in the usual rituals of Judaism in Jerusalem. The priesthood, the sacrificial system, and temple and synagogue services, all remained valid for the primitive Church.[5] This relationship to Judaism is adequately attested in the early chapters of Acts. The usual places of prayer, the temple and the synagogue, continued to be frequented[6] and Pentecost was observed (Acts 2:1f.). When the Apostles were accused of being drunk, Peter's defense appealed to a Jewish eating regulation (Acts 2:12). The Jewish custom of providing funds for the relief of widows was quickly copied by the Church (Acts 6:1).

Even though many Jewish forms of worship were reinterpreted by the Church in the light of their confessions about Jesus, early Christians naturally developed their liturgical life within the milieu of their Jewish heritage. The summary in Acts 2:46 probably remained descriptive for several years.

And day by day, attending the temple together and breaking bread in their homes, they partook of food with glad and generous hearts, . . .

Evidently the early Church participated in a distinctive communal meal, but most of its "public" worship was associated with the ritual of the Jewish temple.[7]

[3] Cf. Mark 16:7; Matt. 18:7, 16. So Eduard Schweizer, *Church Order in the New Testament*, pp. 36–37. A contrary position may be found in Hans Conzelmann, "Auferstehung Christi," *Die Religion in Geschichte und Gegenwart*, I, p. 699. The Gospel tradition, however, is not entirely clear on this point. See Luke 24:13–26.

[4] Schweizer, *Church Order in the New Testament*, p. 38.

[5] *Ibid.*, pp. 34f.

[6] Cf. Acts 1:14; 2:42, 46; 3:1; 5:42.

[7] See C. C. Richardson, "Worship in New Testament Times, Christian," *IDB*, IV, pp. 883–894.

Replacement of Judas. A third illustration of the continuity between the early Church and Judaism is the preservation of the symbolism of the number of the Twelve. The first act of the new community was to select a replacement for the traitor Judas Iscariot. The Twelve had been chosen to correspond to the twelve tribes of Israel and the disciples wished to continue this symbolism by keeping the number intact. The appointment of Matthias probably had little to do with the organization of the early Church. There is no indication that the Twelve extended any kind of "official" leadership over the community by virtue of an office held. Matthias was selected, presumably to function like the rest of the Twelve, to witness to the life, death, and resurrection of Jesus.[8] Acts does not emphasize the role of the Twelve. Only Peter, James, and John are mentioned beyond chapter one and Matthias, the person chosen by lot as the successor to Judas, is not mentioned at all after his selection. Evidently the main concern in reporting the event is to indicate that the early Christian community considered itself the fulfillment of the destiny of the twelve tribes. It was indeed the new Israel.

The Central Place of the Resurrection

The continuity which existed between the early Church and the Jewish religious community seems to have been initially satisfactory to both groups. Since the Christians understood Jesus as the fulfillment of the messianic hopes of Judaism, they found the life and ritual to which they were already accustomed quite acceptable. Also, Judaism itself was extremely tolerant,[9] willing to include in its folds a variety of viewpoints. Messianic statements about Jesus would not necessarily have excluded early Christians from the Jewish religious community. If believers in Jesus had been content merely to affirm Jesus as Messiah, Judaism could probably have made a place for them. Christological confessions, however, were far more inclusive and led to an early cleavage with Judaism.

The Resurrection. The key to the early Christian understanding of Jesus, and to their divergence from Judaism, was the resurrection. Jesus was not merely "messiah" understood in a traditional Jewish sense. When the early Christians spoke of "Christ," they used a title redefined in the light of the life and ministry of Jesus. To the Jerusalem Church the resurrection was a unique event vindicating Jesus as the Christ, the Son of God, and introducing the new age of the

[8] Cf. Acts 1:22.
[9] See Schweizer, *Church Order in the New Testament*, p. 40.

Kingdom of God. God's messianic act was complete and the reign of Messiah had now begun. God, who had been at work in the history of the covenant people of Israel, had now fulfilled that work. For the followers of Jesus the resurrection initiated a new age in which the Church replaced Judaism as the redemptive instrument in history.

Although the early chapters of Acts are colored by Luke's purpose to demonstrate Judaism's rejection of Jesus, they realistically reflect a situation where Christianity became dramatically incompatible with traditional Judaism. The Acts account of the healing of a lame man in chapters 3 and 4 illustrates both the intensity of the conflict and how the differences centered in the resurrection. When Peter and John were brought to trial before the Jewish Sanhedrin after they had healed the man, the Apostles' defense was the radical demand of the resurrected Jesus:

This is the stone which was rejected by you builders, but which has become the head of the corner. And there is salvation in no one else, for there is no other name under heaven among men by which we must be saved.[10]

Clearly the issue is not that the Apostles healed a lame man, but that they proclaimed "Jesus Christ of Nazareth, whom you crucified, whom God raised from the dead . . ." (4:10).

For the early Church, however, the resurrection was not merely that which distinguished it from Judaism. It provided for the Church both its essential character and its primary mission. The resurrection gave birth to the Church by creating a bond of relationship with Christ and by authenticating its witness to Christ.[11] To affirm the resurrected Jesus meant at least these two distinctive things to early Christians. First, it meant that the Church was born and nurtured in repentance. To believe in Christ meant to share the responsibility for his crucifixion and to stand under the judgment of the resurrected Christ. Jewish leaders and Roman officials had expressed their rejection rather forcefully—Jesus had been crucified. But to the early Church these leaders were not alone in their guilt. Intimate disciples had also failed in the time of crisis. Yet, rejection by both Jew and Gentile had not negated the purposes of God in the Christ event. In the resurrection God's

---

[10] Acts 4:11–12.

[11] The resurrection was not just an event giving the believer hope for personal survival after death. "Nowhere in the New Testament is the resurrection hope deduced from the resurrection of Christ, as if his survival of death were the supreme instance that proved or guaranteed eternal life for others." J. A. T. Robinson, "Resurrection in the New Testament," *IDB*, IV, p. 43. The noun *anastasis*, "resurrection," is used in the New Testament only in reference to Jesus' resurrection.

mighty act had both vindicated his Son and brought judgment on all who had rejected him. Those who shared the life of the believing community could do so only in consciousness that they had rejected Jesus and, therefore, stood under the judgment of God. Thus being a Christian was necessarily an experience of repentance. Baptism into the Church involved recognition and acceptance of guilt for the crucifixion in the confidence that the mission of Jesus had been authenticated in the resurrection.[12] The resurrection then made repentance possible and brought the Church into being.

Second, the resurrection provided the Church with impetus for its mission. The words of Peter and John before the Sanhedrin expressed the compelling force permeating the community: ". . . we cannot but speak of what we have seen and heard" (Acts 4:20). The resurrection brought a fresh and invigorating enthusiasm to followers who earlier had been dispirited by the crucifixion. It said to them that their witness was a part of the eternal purpose of God and consequently they could passionately give themselves to the enterprise.

The Commission to the Church. The beginning of the mission of the Church is marked in the book of Acts by the ascension of Jesus. The event is strategic to the Acts story of Church expansion, for it is intimately tied to Jesus' commission:

But you shall receive power when the Holy Spirit has come upon you; and you shall be my witnesses in Jerusalem and in all Judea and Samaria and to the end of the earth.[13]

Immediately after the commission, Jesus' ascent is described:

And when he had said this, as they were looking on, he was lifted up, and a cloud took him out of their sight.[14]

The description is lacking in details because they were secondary to the theological import of the ascension for believers. In Luke the event is reported quietly "as if it were a matter of saying good-by with a view to meeting again the next day." [15] In Acts, however, an air of drama surrounds the report. Here Jesus' ascent brought to a close the story of Jesus and marked the beginning of the work of the Church.

---

[12] Søren Kierkegaard, *Purity of Heart*, pp. 38–52, develops this theme of repentance as more an attitude than an act.

[13] Acts 1:8. The statement seems to be as much a program for Acts as a commission from Jesus.

[14] Acts 1:9.

[15] Johannes Munck, *The Acts of the Apostles*, p. 7.

A new age of God's work in history began.[16] But the new age could not be separated from what had already been accomplished. The Church looked backward to confess the risen Christ now enthroned as Lord. She also looked forward with a commission to bear witness to the enthroned Lord.

The ascension may actually have been interpreted as a polemic against a Gnostic understanding of the event.[17] As the Gnostics understood themselves to be unified in baptism with Christ and therefore delivered of their finitude, they identified themselves with the risen Christ in the ascension and assumed that they had moved beyond human existence and therefore were above suffering and service. In contrast Acts understands the ascension to confirm the Church's commission to be witness to the end of the earth. Following the ascension the Church was to enter the world to accomplish the purposes of God in history.

The Concept of the Holy Spirit

The early Christians believed that they were empowered by the Holy Spirit to continue the work of the risen Christ. The coming of God's kingdom, closely identified with the Church in Acts, was not to be the restoration of a national theocracy in Palestine anticipated in typical Jewish messianism.[18] Rather the goal to be reached was life dominated by the presence of the Spirit. By virtue of this presence the early Church was empowered to carry on its mission of proclaiming Jesus "in Jerusalem and in all Judea and Samaria and to the end of the earth."

Pentecost. According to Acts, the gift of the Spirit occurred on Pentecost, the Hellenistic name for the Jewish Feast of Weeks, some weeks after the resurrection.[19] One hundred and twenty Christians were together on Pentecost and had an experience in which they "became conscious of a new inward power which completely transformed their whole outlook . . . they became conscious of the Spirit as *power* . . . wherein they might go forth to their work of witness-bearing." [20]

[16] Hans Conzelmann, *The Theology of St. Luke,* sees the periodization of history as the organizing principle of Luke–Acts.

[17] A thorough discussion of Luke–Acts and Gnosticism appears in Charles H. Talbert, *Luke and the Gnostics.*

[18] Acts 1:6.

[19] Note the tradition preserved in John 20:22 in which the Spirit is bestowed by Jesus himself on the day of the resurrection.

[20] G. H. C. Macgregor, "The Acts of The Apostles," *IB,* IX, p. 36.

The idea of "the Spirit of God" has an established and cherished biblical history.[21] In the Old Testament the phrase is repeatedly used to indicate Yahweh's active, creative, and energizing relationship to the world. By his Spirit Yahweh brought life to the formless chaos (Genesis 1:2) and sustained the life which he had created (Psalm 104:27–30). The Spirit of God filled the prophet with power (Micah 3:8) and upheld the believer in moral renewal (Psalm 51:10–12). Thus in the Old Testament "the Spirit of God" was God's activity in creation and history. Spirit was not an attribute or a characteristic of God so much as it was God at work in the world.

With the use of the idea of the Spirit of God the Gospels affirm that God is at work in the person of Jesus.[22] Jesus' birth, baptism and temptation, and his mission were accompanied by manifestations of the Spirit. In this way the Gospels declare that God, who had worked through the covenant community Israel, had also been present in the historical Jesus. In Acts the early Church is strikingly impressed with an immediate consciousness of being under the power and direction of the Spirit.[23] The presence of the Spirit at Pentecost is understood as both fulfillment of Jesus' promise (Acts 1:5) and authority for the future mission of the community (Acts 1:8). As the prophets were compelled by the Spirit to speak God's word, so the Church was filled with the power of the Spirit's presence in order to witness throughout the known world.

The association of the major visitation of the Holy Spirit with Pentecost is probably not accidental. Late Jewish tradition related this festival to the covenant tradition in the Old Testament.[24] What had originally been an agricultural festival was given historical meaning. Pentecost, then, was a moment of cultic importance and excitement when new action of God could be anticipated.[25] The coming of the Holy Spirit on Pentecost suggests that now the Church understands the

[21] An excellent summary of this may be found in William Barclay, *The Promise of The Spirit.* See also Maurice Barnett, *The Living Flame;* and G. W. H. Lampe, "The Holy Spirit," *IDB,* II, pp. 361–369; and S. V. McCasland, "Spirit," *IDB,* IV, pp. 432–434.

[22] The Synoptics emphasize the role of the Spirit in the birth, baptism, and temptations of Jesus. Cf. Mark 1:9–12; Matt. 1:18–25; 3:11–17; 4:1–2; Luke 1:16–38; 2:25–35; 3:21–22; 4:1–2, 16–30. John associates the Spirit with Jesus' passion and probably reflects the later developed understanding of the Church that it was empowered by the Spirit after the death of Jesus. Cf. John 14:16–20, 25–26; 15:26.

[23] See Barnett, *The Living Flame,* p. 57.

[24] Jubilees 6.

[25] In the second century A.D. the rabbis accepted this feast as commemorating the day on which the law was given on Sinai.

covenant of Torah to be replaced by the covenant of Spirit. As Torah was understood by the Jewish community to provide both impetus and direction to its religious life, so the early Church understood its course to be set by the presence of the Spirit.

Speaking in Tongues. The coming of the Holy Spirit is directly associated in the book of Acts with the gift of tongues. The Church first experienced the phenomenon at Pentecost. The language describing the experience is both dramatic and symbolic.

And suddenly a sound came from heaven like the rush of a mighty wind and it filled all the house where they were sitting. And there appeared to them tongues as of fire, distributed and resting on each of them. And they were all filled with the Holy Spirit and began to speak in other tongues, as the Spirit gave them utterance.[26]

The drama of the event is heightened by the fact that the multitude who heard the tongues was bewildered because each of them, although they came from all parts of the Mediterranean world, heard the disciples speaking in his own language.

Several approaches to interpreting this manifestation of the Spirit have been offered. It has been suggested that the description of Acts 2 is simply a dramatic way of saying that the disciples were empowered to speak the message of the gospel so straightforwardly that men of all backgrounds understood. This approach, however, seems far too simple. Later references to speaking in tongues are to unintelligible speech, not to straightforward presentation.

Second, many interpreters suggest that speaking in tongues refers to the ability to use a foreign language. Either the disciples were able to speak, or the hearers were able to understand, languages that were unknown to them.[27] This approach is particularly attractive because it seems clear that Luke intends to associate the gift of tongues with foreign languages. Several items, however, bring this interpretation into question. Later, converts at Caesarea and Ephesus are said to have spoken in tongues also when they received the Spirit,[28] but in neither case is there an association with foreign languages. Further Peter compared the experience at Caesarea with his earlier experience at Pentecost. Also later experiences of tongue speaking, a phenomenon that occurred many times in the early Church,[29] certainly were not

[26] Acts 2:2–4.
[27] Many of the early Church fathers held this view.
[28] Cf. Acts 10:46; 19:6.
[29] See I Cor. 14:1–33.

linguistic miracles. Moreover, in all their later evangelistic missions the disciples did not utilize the gift of a foreign language. In fact, since Greek was practically the universal language of the Mediterranean world, there was no need for such a gift. Evidence, then, seems to indicate that Luke for some reason reworked the Pentecost story to associate tongues with foreign languages.

What seems to be the most feasible approach to interpreting the gift of tongues is to identify the experience with ecstatic speech, articulated words but conforming to no set language patterns. In the ecstasy of a high religious moment the Spirit so possessed persons that the complete organism was under his control. Impressive speech, unintelligible as language, poured forth. Those who shared the experience were in such close rapport that the thoughts and feelings, particularly the latter, were caught as much as understood.[30] Such a subjective type of experience is, of course, fraught with dangers of individual misuse and exploitation. This happened later in the Church. Probably in the light of later distortions Luke aims in the Acts account to reinterpret the original Pentecost event in order to reduce the prestige of this unusual accompaniment of the Spirit's presence.

One thing, however, is clear in the entire episode. Early Christianity thrived in strong consciousness of being under the power and direction of the Spirit. The Church believed thoroughly that their community had been invaded by the gift of the power of God himself, the Holy Spirit. From the somewhat abnormal, unusual accompaniments they reasoned back to the cause and realized that they were filled with the Spirit, who had invaded and filled their lives.[31] In time the ecstatic speech would disappear, but at its best it was the evidence of the Spirit's work in establishing the Church and giving to it a missionary imperative. The consciousness of the Spirit motivating the Church would be kept even after the unusual manifestations had passed.

The Proclamation

The gift of the Holy Spirit brought, not only hope and affirmation to the apostolic believers, but also motivation and impetus to carry the good news "to the end of the earth." Central to the understanding of its mission was the commitment of the early Church to the proclama-

---

[30] A helpful summary of the problems associated with this event appears as an appendix written by C. S. Mann to Johannes Munch, *The Acts of the Apostles*, pp. 271–275.

[31] See Barnett, *The Living Flame*, p. 59.

tion of the meaning of Jesus for life and faith. The content of the preaching of the early Church is usually referred to as the *kerygma*, the transliteration of a Greek term popularized by Professor C. H. Dodd.[32] Dodd tries to describe with precision the actual form and content of the early *kerygma*. The term, however, is used more often to refer to the preaching of the early Church without concern to reconstruct an actual form.

Kerygmatic materials form a major portion of the book of Acts. Acts 2:14–40 reports a sermon by Peter on the day of Pentecost.[33] After a brief defense that the disciples were not drunk with new wine, the sermon proceeds immediately to the main issue of proclaiming Jesus. This sermon, like others in Acts,[34] is not to be understood, of course, as a verbatim report of what Peter preached on a specific occasion. The speech and others in the book in their present form are compositions of the author of Acts and must be read in the context of his intended theological purposes. They throw light upon the author's beliefs and literary aims, at least as much as they illumine the life and beliefs of the primitive Church. This is most obvious in the case of the longer speeches. Nevertheless, the speeches are related to the traditional gospel. The speeches in Acts, specially the short, relatively undeveloped speeches of Peter and Paul, summarize the traditional gospel of the early Church and may even represent a variety of sermonic forms used in early Church preaching.[35] They are a summary of the witness of the early apostles about the significance of Jesus for the life of the believing community and the rightful claim that he could make upon all men.

Several characteristics of the *kerygma* stand out in the Acts materials. Most striking is its startling simplicity. During the initial decades of church life, the witness probably was simply that Jesus, who had been unjustly crucified by the Jews, had been raised up by God and thereby established as Lord. The Church was commissioned to testify to this reality. The early believers were content, then, to proclaim the messiahship of Jesus; they were not yet asking what that

---

[32] See *The Apostolic Preaching and Its Development,* 1936.

[33] Other sermonic materials attributed to Peter occur in Acts 3:12–26; 4:8–12; 5:29–32; and 10:34–43.

[34] Cf. 3:12–26; 4:8–12; 5:29–32; 7:2–53; 10:34–43; 13:14b–41; 15:7–11; 15:13–21; 17:22–34; 20:17–35; 22:30–23:10; 21:37–22:21; 24:1–21; 25:13–26:32.

[35] C. H. Dodd, *The Apostolic Preaching and Its Development,* pp. 29ff.; Dibelius, "The Speeches in Acts and Ancient Historiography," *Studies in the Acts of the Apostles,* pp. 138ff. But see C. F. Evans, "The Kerygma," *JTS,* VIII (1956), 25ff.

messiahship entailed beyond an initial commitment to Jesus. As time passed and their original messianic expectations were altered, the full implications of their claims for Jesus would need to be worked out. But for the moment their emphasis was upon bearing witness to the enduring and authentic character of Jesus' life and mission.

In the Acts speeches the primary point made in demonstrating Jesus' messiahship was his resurrection. Little theological note is taken of the crucifixion. Paul attached purpose to the cross by saying, "Christ died for our sins in accordance with the scriptures," [36] but in the Acts *kerygma* the cross only betokened the unjustifiable action of "the hands of lawless men." [37] For Luke the cross illustrated the point that the Jews had rejected Jesus and thereby excluded themselves from the gospel.[38] But this is not the central point of the *kerygma* as Luke presents it. The main concern of the *kerygma* is whether or not Jesus will be recognized and confessed as God's anointed. The resurrection, not the cross, was the maximum argument for Jesus' messiahship. The crucified had been vindicated because God had raised him from the dead and exalted him to a place of highest honor.

The kerygmatic materials in Acts also stress the relationship of Jesus to the Old Testament. The development of the argument about Jesus' messiahship in Peter's Pentecost sermon proceeds in the context of Scripture. Since common messianic expectations did not include the idea of resurrection, the sermon seeks to demonstrate that the resurrection had been foretold in the Old Testament. Jesus had been loosed from the pangs of death in accordance with what "David says concerning him."

> I saw the Lord always before me,
> for he is at my right hand that I may not be shaken;
> therefore my heart was glad, and my tongue rejoiced;
> moreover my flesh will dwell in hope.
> For thou wilt not abandon my soul to Hades,
> nor let thy Holy One see corruption.[39]

The resurrection of Jesus fulfilled the Psalmist's hope of escaping the fear of death.[40] The same emphasis upon the resurrection as the ful-

---

[36] I Cor. 15:3.

[37] Acts 2:23.

[38] This in no way justifies antisemitism. The whole tradition of the early Church affirmed not only that Israel had rejected Jesus, but also that the band of disciples had both misunderstood and failed him.

[39] Acts 2:25–28 from Psalm 16:8–10.

[40] Acts 2:29–31.

fillment of Old Testament scriptures recurs in the kerygmatic materials of chapters 3 and 10.[41]

This argument would have been appealing to a Jewish audience. Interpretation of an event as fulfillment of a prophecy in the Old Testament would have been sufficient reason for believing its truth and divine significance. If Jesus' resurrection could be demonstrated to have been prophesied, then it was both credible and also convincing proof that he was the Messiah.[42]

The proclamation of the resurrected Jesus also stressed the introduction of the final and decisive stage in God's work in history. Israel's anticipation, based on the promises of God and prophesied in the Old Testament, was now made real in the resurrected Jesus. The expected response to God's redemptive activity was repentance and subsequent forgiveness of sins. The new age had started, the hour of salvation was at hand; to this the Church was compelled to bear witness. The brief kerygmatic statement attached to Peter's responses to the Sanhedrin summarized the essential points made by the Church.

The God of our fathers raised Jesus whom you killed by hanging him on a tree. God exalted him at his right hand as Leader and Savior, to give repentance to Israel and forgiveness of sins. And we are witnesses to these things, and so is the Holy Spirit whom God has given to those who obey him.[43]

Communal Life

The meaningful life of the Jerusalem church came from its identification with Christ in the continuing presence of the Holy Spirit and its sense of responsibility to proclaim the resurrected Christ. Individual members of the Church felt themselves bound together because of their common relationship to Christ. Essentially they understood the Church to be a charismatic reality whose relationships were sustained by the Holy Spirit.[44] At the deepest level possible all members were called to participation together in worship and witness. Each participant shared not only the confession of Christ as Lord and the responsibility to proclaim his intention in history, but also a distinctive relationship to other members of the community.

Two parallel passages in Acts 2:42–47 and 4:32–5:10 describe the

41 Cf. Acts 3:13, 18, 21–25; 10:43.
42 Macgregor, "The Acts of The Apostles," *IB*, IX, pp. 42–43.
43 Acts 5:30–32.
44 P. S. Minear, "Idea of Church," *IDB*, I, p. 616.

corporate character of the Jerusalem church, portraying what life within the primitive community was like. The following verses are illustrative.

Now the company of those who believed were of one heart and soul, and no one said that any of the things which he possessed was his own, but they had everything in common. And with great power the apostles gave their testimony to the resurrection of the Lord Jesus, and great grace was upon them all. There was not a needy person among them, for as many as were possessors of lands or houses sold them, and brought the proceeds of what was sold and laid it at the apostles' feet; and distribution was made to each as any had need.[45]

The striking emphasis upon the unity of believers is reminiscent of the covenant concepts of community so important in the Old Testament.[46] The apostolic Church, like ancient Israel, was the people of God in which each individual knew his worth primarily as a part of the total community. Personal needs were to be subjugated to the welfare of the whole. The community was essentially a *koinonia*, that is, a fellowship sharing a common life.[47] This unity was regularly expressed in "breaking of bread in their homes" (Acts 2:46). In addition to participation in the usual practices of temple worship, the early Christians gathered in their homes for a common religious meal and distinctly Christian fellowship and worship. Probably from a very early time the observance of the Lord's Supper was associated with this fellowship meal.

Additionally, the unity of the Jerusalem church was expressed in the practice of sharing possessions. This does not mean that members of the community sold all that they had and pooled the assets, as was the practice of the Essenes at Qumran. Entrance into the Qumran community was voluntary, but the surrender of the initiates' property and earnings was obligatory.[48] Christian communal ownership, however, was voluntary. As need arose property was sold and private possessions were distributed to care for less fortunate believers. The more prosperous members expressed their concern for and identity with the total community. No absolute rule was necessary; the practice was "an ideal motivated by simplicity, detachment, and charitable

---

[45] Acts 4:32–35.

[46] See Aubry Johnson, *The Vitality of the Individual in Ancient Israel.*

[47] The Aramaic equivalent of the word *koinonia* seems to refer to those who shared in the celebration of a common Passover meal.

[48] J. A. Fitzmyer, "Jewish Christianity in Acts in Light of the Qumran Scrolls," *Studies in Luke–Acts,* eds. Keck and Martyn, pp. 242–243.

sharing which springs from their corporate identity as the Jewish community." [49]

Two illustrations of the practice are given in the early chapters of Acts. In one Barnabas is introduced as an example of the generous individual who sold a field which belonged to him and brought the money to the common treasury. This is the Barnabas who became a leader in the early Jerusalem church and later was involved in the enlistment of Saul of Tarsus as a missionary. The other illustration presents Ananias and Sapphira as examples of abuse of the practice. They were condemned, not because they did not bring all the income from the sale of the property, but because they pretended to be more generous than they really were. Thus, they had violated the essential life of the new covenant community.[50] Since the Holy Spirit was the bond of community, their sin was basically a "lie to the Holy Spirit."

The practice of sharing possessions was not "communism" in the sense of usual associations of various political and economic structures with that word. Certainly no specific organization or patterning of life of the early Church was intended in the practice. It provided an immediate method for assisting the more needy members of the fellowship. The practice was undergirded by the belief that Jesus would return in the immediate future. Economic stress may have become crucial because some, perhaps many, members of the early Church had stopped work because they expected an early return of Jesus. When it became obvious that this anticipation would not be fulfilled, the community quickly adjusted its way of life and the practice of sharing possessions rapidly disappeared.[51] Nevertheless, for a brief period in the life of the Jerusalem community it was a dramatic illustration of the sense of unity involving mutual responsibility that was characteristic of the early fellowship.

These then are the major characteristics of the apostolic Church as preserved in the traditions and remembered by Luke toward the end of the first century. Although it was largely without organizational form, it was a vibrant organism, inspired by its commitment to a risen Lord and unified by responsible sensitivity of each member to the other. Luke saw in such a community the ideal for the Church of his

[49] *Ibid.* Note that Acts does not interpret the practice as fulfillment of the injunctions of Jesus in Mark 10:21; Matt. 19:21; and Luke 18:22.

[50] The motif and some of the wording resembles the Old Testament story of Achan where the preservation of the unity of the community is also the issue. Cf. Josh. 7:1ff.

[51] Cf. II Thess. 3:6–12.

day and attributed to them a proclamation which became the basis for the expansion of the Christian movement from Jerusalem to Rome.

PREFACE TO EXPANSION

After depicting the general character of life in the early Church, Acts moves rapidly into a stylized account of Christian expansion over the Mediterranean world. The story is told, however, with little concern for completeness. The author's purpose in writing controlled his selection of material and the use he made of it. We shall see later that Acts' preoccupation with Paul virtually eliminates from its narrative all areas outside those of the Pauline mission. Further, individual episodes are included and even repeated because they best suit the author's missionary purpose, not necessarily because they are essential to the full story of expansion.[52] Data irrelevant to his purpose are omitted.

Cleavage In Jerusalem: Hellenist Vs. Hebrew

The most important persons in Luke's description of the Church's expansion are Peter and Paul, particularly the latter. Early stages of expansion are discussed, however, around Stephen and Philip, two persons whose vision of the universal character of the faith disrupts narrow provincialism and prepares the way for the more dramatic accomplishments of Peter and Paul. Although Luke was concerned to emphasize that expansion was implicit in the nature of the Christian faith, the historical reality of cleavage in the early Church could not be written out of the story. Episodes about Stephen and Philip beginning in Acts 6 show that the apostolic Church was split into two independent groups, the "Hellenists" and "Hebrews." The latter were Aramaic-speaking Jewish Christians who tended to be traditional in their understanding of the gospel. They desired to preserve the cherished institutions of Torah and temple while maintaining their commitment to God in Christ. Their faith was intimately tied to a nationalistic spirit, and for them Christianity did not exclude maintaining a wall of separation between themselves and the Gentile world.

The Hellenists, on the other hand, were less conservative than the Hebrews. Although they were probably Jews identified by their use

---

[52] Kümmel in *FBK*, pp. 116–117, states that the literary form of Acts has no real prototype in either the Christian and pagan world.

Figure 7–1. This Greek inscription, once in a Hellenistic Jerusalem synagogue, relates that Theodotus, a priest, built a synagogue and hostel for foreigners in the city. (Source: Department of Archaeology, Hebrew University, Jerusalem.)

of the Greek language,[53] they were probably more obviously distinguished from their fellow Jewish Christians by a willingness to adapt to Greek ways. Contact with the world around them had broken down their particularism, enabling them to see the universal implications of the gospel. For them the new faith was not necessarily tied to traditional Jewish institutions.

Faction in the early Church had antecedents in long-standing Jewish problems. The tension certainly may be traced to the peak of Macedonian influence in Palestine during the fourth century B.C. when efforts to Hellenize the Jews had produced dual reactions.[54] The extremes of ardent Jewish exclusivism on the one hand and a type of universalism on the other had been woven into the fabric of postexilic Judaism.[55] In first century Christianity the same kind of tension reappeared.

[53] The argument of Cadbury, *Beginnings of Christianity*, V, pp. 55ff., that the Hellenists were not Jews, but Gentiles, is quite unlikely. See Ernst Haenchen, "The Book of Acts As Source Material for the History of Early Christianity," *Studies in Luke–Acts*, p. 263.

[54] For a brief summary, see Flanders, Crapps, and Smith, *People of the Covenant*, pp. 403–414.

[55] This is clearly illustrated in the contrasting religious attitudes depicted in the books of Esther and Jonah.

Selection of the Seven

Acts reports the conflict between the Hellenists and the Hebrews through a rather trivial incident (Acts 6:1–6), but one involving deep, underlying feelings. The Hellenists murmured that widows of their group were being repeatedly neglected in the daily distribution of food which had become an assistance plan of the Church. Evidently the distributors were Hebrews who performed their duties according to their sympathies. At least the more liberal Hellenists believed that their widows were being discriminated against by the conservative faction. The Twelve, whose sympathy was with the Hebrews, refused to "give up preaching the word of God to serve tables" (Acts 6:2). Subsequently, seven reputable men were selected and authorized to oversee the duty of the daily distribution.

The procedure for appointing the Seven is not clear. Whether only the Twelve or the entire congregation "prayed and laid their hands on them" (Acts 6:6) cannot be determined. The particular rite of laying on of hands seems to have been carried over from the Old Testament where the act conveyed some power or responsibility.[56] Luke certainly implies that the Seven were more than just servers of tables. They had authority and responsibility probably comparable to that of the Twelve. The Seven "were to be for the Hellenists exactly what the twelve were for the Hebrews."[57] The title "the Seven" thus parallels the title "the Twelve." All bear Greek names, suggesting strong alignment with the Hellenistic point of view.[58] Their appointment must have lent considerable authority to their ideas, and so was a strategic event in the pattern of early Church movement out of Palestine.

Some see in the selection of the Seven the beginning of the office of deacon. Although Luke repeatedly uses cognates of the word for "deacon" to describe the function of the Seven, they are not actually called deacons and Luke's description of Stephen and Philip is of independent missionaries. By the time that Acts came to be written, the deacon had become recognized in the Church as an important officer associated with the bishop.[59] Luke may aim to soften the in-

---

[56] Cf. Num. 27:15–33.

[57] Macgregor, "The Acts of The Apostles," *IB*, IX, p. 91. Cf. Maurice Goguel, *The Birth of Christianity*, pp. 167–169.

[58] Frank Stagg, *The Book of Acts*, p. 91, points out that two of the Twelve (Philip and Andrew) had Greek names but were not Hellenists.

[59] Cf. Philippians 1:1; I Tim. 3.

tensity of earlier controversy between Hellenists and Hebrews by associating with these events the establishment of an office that by his day was becoming increasingly important.[60] Although those selected are not directly called deacons, their work is that of deacons. In this way Luke plays down the controversy and gives status to characters who are important to his story.

Luke's major purpose in Chapter 5 is not to describe the factions in the apostolic Church, but to introduce Stephen and Philip. The remaining five, Prochorus, Nicanor, Timon, Parmenes, Nicolaus, are inconsequential to the purposes of Acts and are subsequently lost to obscurity.[61] The obscurity of the others simply points up Luke's interest in Stephen and Philip, not as successful and efficient administrators of relief funds for Hellenistic widows, but as key evangelizers whose work represents the initial stages of Christian expansion.

Stephen

The story of Stephen is one of the most crucial in Acts. In a brief and pointed way the universal nature of the gospel is laid out. Luke makes his point here (6:1b–8:3) by combining two narratives, Stephen's conviction by the Sanhedrin and his stoning by a rioting crowd, with an extended speech attributed to Stephen.

Throughout, the account focuses on Stephen's insight that Christianity breaks down barriers and makes all men brothers. The Jewish temple and Mosaic law are shown to be secondary. Luke indicates that these insights are typical of a person "full of faith and of the Holy Spirit" (Acts 6:5), "full of grace and power" (Acts 6:8), and "full of the Holy Spirit" (Acts 7:55). "Great wonders" and "signs" authenticated Stephen's work and "the wisdom and the Spirit with which he spoke" (Acts 6:10) could not be successfully countered.

The preaching of Stephen and the subsequent controversy that developed around him centered in the Hellenistic synagogues.[62] Ste-

---

[60] Paul uses the term "deacon" in a rather general way to describe his and his associates' work with various churches. This use is translated in the RSV as "servant." Cf. I Thess. 3:2; Col. 1:7; I Cor. 3:4; II Cor. 6:4; 11:15.

[61] Nicolaus is described as "a proselyte of Antioch" reflecting Luke's special interest in that city. A persistent tradition in the early Church favored Antioch as Luke's place of residence. Cf. Jerome, *Lives of Illustrious Men,* VII. The "Nicolaitans" mentioned in the Revelation of John (2:6; 15) have been traditionally traced to this man, but we cannot be sure whether they were derived from this or another Nicolaus.

[62] The description in Acts 6:9 does not make it absolutely clear whether one synagogue with diverse membership or several synagogues were involved.

phen's preaching was so radical that some Jewish Christians may have been aroused against him, but the real problem was with the non-Christian Jews. Although Jews may have been willing to retain in their fellowship Christians who maintained appreciation for Jewish tradition, Stephen was completely unacceptable. Their accusation, supported by false witnesses, was that,

> This man never ceases to speak words against this holy place and the law; for we have heard him say that this Jesus of Nazareth will destroy this place, and will change the customs which Moses delivered to us.[63]

Stephen's Speech. Acts reports Stephen's defense against the charges in a lengthy speech covering most of chapter seven. This passage is one of the more difficult problems in the book of Acts. For one thing, if the speech is omitted, a beautiful and well-connected description of the death of Stephen remains.[64] The insertion of the speech detracts from the impressive character of the description of Stephen's death. Further, the speech contains items inconsistent with the Old Testament which raise questions about the source of its content. Not only are materials foreign to the Old Testament included, but also differences in specific details occur.[65]

More important, however, is the apparent inappropriateness of the defense. It does not reply directly to the charges brought against Stephen. It recounts how God has graciously manifested himself in Israel's history and illustrates how Israel has continually rejected his goodness. It rebuffs Stephen's accusers as "stiff-necked people, uncircumcised in heart and ears," who resist the Holy Spirit (Acts 7:51), but does not really defend him. Although the speech condemns the temple because "the Most High does not dwell in houses made with hands" (Acts 7:48), it does not explain how Christ makes the temple (and Jewish law in general) irrelevant. There is no affirmation of the Christian faith; the name of Jesus Christ is not mentioned.

Can, then, the speech of Stephen be dismissed simply as irrelevant to the occasion and an unnecessary interruption in the narrative? If the speech is read to reconstruct an actual defense at a real trial, it is inappropriate and irrelevant. If, however, it is approached in the

---

[63] Acts 6:13–14.

[64] The sequence would be Acts 6:8–15; 7:55–60. See F. J. Foakes-Jackson, *The Acts of the Apostles*, pp. 57–58.

[65] Cf. as examples: Acts 7:2–4 with Gen. 11:26–32; Acts 7:6 with Gen. 15:13 and Ex. 12:40; Acts 7:14 with Gen. 46:26 and Ex. 1:5. A full treatment of these may be found in Lake and Cadbury, *Beginnings of Christianity*, I, pp. 71–83; Rackham, *The Acts of the Apostles*, pp. 99–102.

context of Luke's intention, the speech is not only relevant, but also strategically important. For Luke the primary issue at stake was the universal claim of the gospel. In this context Stephen's speech makes sense. It contains a radical insight; all barriers, even those of religious law and cult, are broken. In the light of this faith, the temple and its worship, as the entire Mosaic system, is "incidental and temporary." [66] Stephen's speech was composed to communicate this. "Luke cleverly combined a synagogue sermon about the destiny of Israel with compassionate complaints against Israel" [67] to say that God was working toward the redemption of all men and thus prepared the way for the story of Christian expansion.

The non-provincial character of God was emphasized to reply to the charge that Stephen had discredited the "holy place," "the law," and "the customs" delivered by Moses (Acts 6:13–14). The defense was that God himself had not chosen to work exclusively in a special land with special items of religion. "The Most High does not dwell in houses made with hands" (Acts 7:48). The cherished traditions of Israel were replete with notices of God's work outside Palestine. Mesopotamia, Egypt, Shechem (in Samaria), Midian, and Arabia were "holy places" where God had manifested himself to Israel's great patriarchs. [68] The main point of the speech, however, "is that the real violators of God's law are not the Christians but their accusers and the unconverted Jews in general. . . . Mere external worship is not enough if the hearts of the worshippers are turned away to other gods." [69]

The insight of Stephen that Christian faith broke the bonds of nationalism and particularism could not be tolerated by even the more open-minded Jews, who were too tied to Jewish religious life to see the implications of the gospel. The assertion that they were a "stiff-necked people" who resisted the Holy Spirit (Acts 7:51) only intensified their irritation.

In Jesus, the religion of the Spirit had met the religion of the letter, of ritual, of narrow nationalism and particularism. In Stephen, the message of Jesus was again being proclaimed. [70]

[66] Rackham, *The Acts of the Apostles,* p. 87.

[67] Haenchen, "The Book of Acts As Source Material for the History of Early Christianity," *Studies in Luke–Acts,* p. 264.

[68] In Israel's religious interpretations, possession of the "Holy Land" was an intimate part of covenant understanding. The argument of Stephen's speech may be directed toward a particularistic interpretation of this idea. See Lake and Cadbury, *Beginnings of Christianity,* I, p. 72.

[69] Macgregor, "The Acts of The Apostles," *IB,* IX, p. 93. Cf. Acts 7:51–53.

[70] Stagg, *The Book of Acts,* p. 99.

Figure 7–2. St. Stephen's Gate in Jerusalem's east wall, named for the first Christian martyr. (Source: Jordan Tourist Department.)

Jewish response was to purge the community of the one who combined such a radical message with what amounted to an accusation of idolatry.

The Martyrdom of Stephen. The circumstances of Stephen's execution are not precisely described in Acts. Luke suggests that Stephen was charged before the Sanhedrin and given a hearing with witnesses. It is questionable whether, under the Roman dominion in Jerusalem, the Sanhedrin could have carried through the trial and execution.[71] Probably Stephen came to his death by mob violence. Incensed by his challenge to their religious traditions and further enraged by the directness of Stephen's approach, the mob erupted in uncontrolled violence. Stephen was stoned—the first of many martyrs to the Christian faith.

The report of Stephen's execution intentionally parallels the crucifixion of Jesus. Both Jesus and Stephen were falsely accused of dishonoring the temple. Both prayed for their executioners. The Son of man[72] at God's right hand is present in both accounts. Stephen

---

[71] Macgregor, "The Acts of The Apostles," *IB*, IX, p. 93.

[72] This is the only New Testament use of the title other than as a self-designation of Jesus.

prayed, "Lord Jesus, receive my spirit." [73] Jesus cried, "Father, into thy hands I commit my spirit!" [74] In both cases the Jews were demonstrating their refusal to accept the purposes of God in Christ.

The Saul Persecution. The martyrdom of Stephen initiated intense persecution of Christians in Jerusalem (8:1–3). A leader in the persecution was Saul of Tarsus, a devout Pharisee, who gave approval to Stephen's death. Religious enthusiasts, aroused by an interpretation of the faith which challenged national and racial pride, attacked the Church under the guise of religious orthodoxy. Perhaps other believers who agreed with Stephen's views followed him in Christian martyrdom. The Twelve, probably because they were more conservative in their views, were untouched by the persecution and were able to remain in Jerusalem. However, those who were in sympathy with the ideas of Stephen were scattered by the persecution, preaching the gospel as they fled. Thus, both the preaching of Stephen and the persecution which followed prepared the way for the spread of the early Church. And, although Luke in the interest of the unity of the Church does not emphasize the point, the Hellenists pioneered the mission.

THE SAMARITAN MISSION

First Mission Field

Among those who fled the persecution in Jerusalem was Philip, one of the Seven appointed to serve tables but primarily known in Acts as an evangelist. This apostle "went down to a city of Samaria, and proclaimed to them the Christ" (Acts 8:5). Thus, Luke begins the account of the first stage in the expansion of the Christian movement outside Jerusalem. Undoubtedly individual believers had earlier migrated from Jerusalem, taking their faith with them. Now in some consistent fashion the gospel with its inherent claims upon all men began to spread over the eastern world. According to Luke, persecution rather than the purposeful intention of Jerusalem believers, was the primary factor in the expansion.

The first stage of expansion was to the Samaritans, a people who shared many Jewish religious traditions but who had been distinctly separated from the Jewish community. They had arisen out of the upheaval which followed the fall of Israel to Assyria in 722/21 B.C.

[73] Acts 7:59.
[74] Luke 23:46.

By the Assyrian policy of transcolonization, Israelite life had been amalgamated with foreign cultures. Gradually schism developed between the Samaritans and the Jews of the south, who had escaped Assyrian domination. By about 200 B.C. the separation had become complete, and over the years the religious differences between Samaria and Jerusalem became more and more pronounced. Although Samaritans continued their religious affinities with Judaism, they developed their own distinctive forms.[75] They worshipped Yahweh, kept the Sabbath, and practiced circumcision. But their scripture was the Pentateuch alone and they did not accept the Jerusalem temple; their worship centered in a temple on Mt. Gerizim.[76] By the first century A.D. relationships between Samaria and Judea were hostile and antagonistic. Jews considered Samaritans the epitome of social and religious compromise, more to be avoided than sinners. They might be nearer the household of God than the Gentiles, but they certainly were not full-fledged members.

The Gospel of Luke reveals a particular interest in Jesus' contact with Samaritans and prepares us for the Acts account of the expansion of Christianity among them. Luke omits Matthew's report of Jesus' instruction that his disciples "go nowhere among the Gentiles, and enter no town of the Samaritans" (Matthew 10:5). Further, in Luke's gospel the Samaritans repeatedly have a place in the mission of Jesus. In Luke, Jesus intends to visit Samaria on his final trip to Jerusalem and rebukes James and John when they want to call down fire from heaven because Samaritans refuse to offer hospitality (9:51–56). The parable of the good Samaritan with its implicit condemnation of racial prejudice is preserved only in Luke's Gospel (10:29–37). In Luke a Samaritan alone among ten healed lepers falls at Jesus' feet to give thanks (17:11–19). In giving the Samaritans a significant and favorable role in his Gospel Luke both prepares the way for the story of expansion and illustrates that the work of the apostolic Church grows naturally out of the intention of Jesus.[77]

Thus, the reader has been prepared in the Gospel for that which occurs in the Acts. Persecution may be the external force, but for Luke the expansion is consistent with Jesus' mission and implicit in

---

[75] See T. H. Gaster, "Samaritans," *IDB*, IV, pp. 190–197.

[76] See John 4:20. Would Stephen's preaching, which challenged the Jerusalem temple, have had a sympathetic ear among the Samaritans?

[77] The continuity that exists between the mission of the early Church and the work of Jesus is emphasized in regards to worship in Oscar Cullmann's, *Early Christian Worship*, 1953.

the universal gospel which Jesus proclaimed in word and person. Although the primary focus of Luke is on the spread of the gospel to the Gentile world and its liberation from narrow Jewish confines, Samaria represents "the actual beginnings of the Christian mission." [78] For the first time the gospel moves into an area which does not belong to the traditional Jewish community.

Philip

The story of the Samaritan mission illustrates the sketchiness of the information available to Luke about this period. The mission is epitomized in a single incident (Acts 8:9–13) relating the conversion of a certain Simon, a magician called "that power of God which is called Great." The identity of Simon and his role in the Samaritan community cannot be recovered. Later legend weaves around his name an elaborate and complicated scheme of heresy. Justin [79] associates him with early Gnostic heresy. Both Eusebius [80] and Irenaeus [81] add to the descriptions of Justin, associating Simon and his mistress with elaborate systems of worship and interpretation. This legendary material may reflect historical data, but more likely grew out of the condemnation in Acts of Simon's misinterpretation of the Holy Spirit. On this basis later distortions of the Christian faith were attached to Simon. [82]

The legendary confusion about Simon, however, should not cloud the meaning of the story in the book of Acts. Before his contact with Philip, Simon represents a magical religion of astrology, necromancy, and exorcisms. Exchange with Philip leads to his belief and baptism. Simon's misunderstanding (The term "simony" to designate the practice of buying church office is derived from this event.) and Peter's stinging denunciation, are no reasons for disregarding the change in Simon. In Acts this is used to typify the dramatic type of thing which happened in the Samaritan phase of expansion.

Apostolic Approval. Following the conversion of Simon the Jerusalem Christians sent Peter and John to "investigate" the mission in Samaria. As the Church expanded, the "home" church at Jerusalem was given status as the source of the Christian movement. No admin-

---

[78] Oscar Cullmann, *The Early Church*, p. 186.
[79] *Apology*, I, 26.
[80] *Ecclesiastical History*, II, xiii, 1–8.
[81] *Against Heresies*, I, xxiii, 1–5; xxvii, 1–4.
[82] See S. V. McCasland, "Simon Magus," *IDB*, IV, p. 360.

istrative authority over the new community was structured, but a kind of charismatic leadership and authority was accepted. The status given to the Jerusalem church was probably related to the fact that the Twelve were there. They had been with Jesus and so had an authentic first hand witness to his work and message. This is surely the understanding of the role of the apostle when Peter and John are sent to examine the work of Philip, who himself was not one of The Twelve. These materials may reflect a later ecclesiasticism when the Church had become more conscious of specific patterns of authority.

Luke's concern goes beyond either Jerusalem or apostolic confirmation of the new phase of Christian growth. The point made is that the extension is consistent with what God is seeking to accomplish through the Church. The coming of the Holy Spirit affirms the Samaritan mission as God's work. Additional outpourings of the Holy Spirit are reported in Acts when Cornelius became a believer at Caesarea and when believers at Ephesus were baptized in the name of Jesus. At these significant stages in Church expansion the Holy Spirit affirmed that the growth was of God.

The Ethiopian Eunuch. The conversion of an Ethiopian eunuch represents a slightly different emphasis upon the outreach of the Christian Church. Again Philip is the evangelist whose interest and attention contribute to the conversion of an outsider. The eunuch, a Nubian from south of Egypt, had come to Jerusalem to worship.[83] Philip readily interpreted Isaiah as pointing to the good news of Jesus and welcomed the eunuch to Christian baptism. Noteworthy in Philip's interpretation is the use of the suffering servant passage of Isaiah 53 with reference to Jesus. Early in the life of the Church the Old Testament was reinterpreted from the perspective of faith in Jesus, and the servant poems of Deutero–Isaiah were important in this interpretation. If the eunuch were excluded from full participation in Jewish worship, his request for baptism may point up an important feature of the episode: one ceremonially unacceptable to Judaism is accepted as a believer in Jesus. Luke sees this event as illustrating the kind of situation in which the growth of the Church could occur. "The conversion of the Ethiopian is significant, not as introducing a new principle, but as an illustration of how far afield the gospel was already spreading." [84]

[83] Of course, as a eunuch he would have been excluded from ordinary Jewish worship if the law were carried out. Cf. Lev. 21:20; Deut. 23:1.

[84] Macgregor, "The Acts of The Apostles," *IB*, IX, p. 113.

Philip was strategic in the expansion of the Church. His work illustrates the movement of the gospel into Samaria. In this movement the Hellenists, who had been persecuted because they rejected temple worship, played the major role. The apostles (such as Peter and John) had only to reap in Samaria where others, the largely anonymous Hellenists, had sown.[85]

INAUGURATION OF THE GENTILE MISSION

In the thinking of Luke the Samaritan mission was only prelude to the purpose of the Church in history. The most significant phase was to be the Gentile mission. In it the Christian faith would become more and more separated from its Jewish moorings and definitely established in its own right. The accomplishment of this objective was largely the work of the Apostle Paul. Consequently, following the narration of the Samaritan mission, Acts reports the dramatic conversion of the Apostle, an event considered so important that it is described three times (Acts 9:1-22; 22:4-16; 26:9-18). However, before coming to the actual work of the Apostle, Luke recounts the growing comprehension of Peter that the Gentile mission is the task of the Church.

Peter and Cornelius

The event around which Luke narrates the beginning of the Gentile mission is the conversion of Cornelius, a Roman centurion. Since no Roman soldiers were stationed in this territory during the reign of Herod Agrippa I, we cannot be sure of the historical character of Cornelius.[86] Perhaps Luke's description of Cornelius is modeled on the centurion whose servant was healed by Jesus (Luke 7:1-10), whose conversion typifies God's intention to redeem all Gentiles. Unknown to each other Cornelius and Peter were brought together by two concurrent visions. Also the first narration of the event (10:1-16) is repeated (10:30-33; 11:4-14) in the reports of both Cornelius and Peter. By this double miracle and double telling the supreme importance of the inauguration of the Gentile mission is stressed. Peter is the prime character in the inauguration of the mission, but later Paul

---

[85] The early activity of the Hellenists in Samaria makes sense of John 4:38. Here in the evangelist's epilogue to the story of Jesus' interview with the Samaritan woman Jesus indicates that others preceded the apostles into Samaria. Cf. Cullmann, *The Early Church*, pp. 188–192.

[86] Robert M. Grant, *A Historical Introduction to the New Testament*, p. 145.

will become *the* missionary to the Gentiles. Is Luke in this fashion trying to reconcile Petrine and Pauline factions which have developed in the early Church?

Cornelius' Conversion. Cornelius is introduced as friendly to Jewish faith. He was a "devout man who feared God with all his household, gave alms liberally to the people, and prayed constantly to God" (Acts 10:2). Although he worshipped the God of Judaism, he had not been circumcised into the covenant community. He was an outsider, but nonetheless in sympathy with Jewish religion. As such Luke sees him as an ideal candidate to bridge the gap between Jewish and Gentile Christianity.

The events which brought Peter and Cornelius together are narrated with drama appropriate to their importance to Luke. In divine vision "an angel of God" informed Cornelius that Simon was in Joppa at the home of a tanner and commanded that he be summoned. Even as the emissaries were on the way, Peter was also visited by a heavenly vision which compelled him to consider Gentiles as appropriate subjects for the Christian gospel. In the vision Peter was commanded to eat animals which Jews considered ceremonially unclean. Peter's protest, "No, Lord; for I have never eaten anything that is common or unclean" (10:14), was summarily answered, "What God has cleansed, you must not call common" (10:15). Evidently Jesus' instructions regarding the superficiality of food laws (cf. Mark 7:14–23) had not gotten through to Peter.

Peter's insight into the meaning of the vision developed with painful slowness. "For all the opportunity he had encountered as a follower of Jesus, and for all the pioneering of men like Stephen and Philip, he yielded to the light only after the greatest pressure was brought to bear upon him." [87] Although the vision was repeated three times, its impact was not felt by Peter until after his contact with Cornelius. Even then, Luke makes the reluctance of Peter perfectly clear. Cornelius responded to the vision eagerly; Peter was much more guarded. Somewhat defensively, the Apostle justified his presence at the home of Cornelius as coming only from a direct command from God.[88] If it is true that Peter inaugurated the Gentile mission, it is more true that "the Gentiles opened a door to a larger world for Peter!" [89]

---

[87] Stagg, *The Book of Acts,* p. 117.
[88] Cf. Acts 10:28–29.
[89] Stagg, *The Book of Acts,* p. 119.

In spite of Peter's reluctance and reservation, however, Acts emphasizes that this expansion is consistent with the purpose of God for the Church. The paragraph summarizing the Gentile reaction to the gospel is worth repeating:

While Peter was still saying this, the Holy Spirit fell on all who heard the word. And the believers from among the circumcised who came with Peter were amazed, because the gift of the Holy Spirit had been poured out *even on the Gentiles*. For they heard them speaking in tongues and extolling God. Then Peter declared, "Can any one forbid water for baptizing these people who have received the Holy Spirit *just as we have?*" And he commanded them to be baptized in the name of Jesus Christ.[90]

This is the third report in Acts of a visitation of the Holy Spirit. Previously at Pentecost and at the conversion of Samaritans the Holy Spirit had come as a manifestation of both the presence and approval of God himself. Now at the conversion of Cornelius and other "God-fearing" [91] Gentiles the Holy Spirit and the associated tongue-speaking was proof enough that Cornelius' conversion had God's approval. Peter himself was willing to concede this point, even though he protected himself by taking along witnesses. In spite of this concession, however, his subsequent work was largely with "those of the circumcision." Yet Luke's point is clearly made. The expansion of the Church into the Gentile world was grounded in God's call and achieved by the presence of God himself.

Peter's Speech. The purpose of Luke in narrating the conversion of Cornelius is made even more pointedly clear in the speech delivered by Peter to Cornelius and his associates (Acts 10:34–43). The sermon is one of the best examples of the *kerygma*. Included are those elements and emphases which were commonly a part of the proclamation of the early Church: the intent of God had been made clear in the ministry of John the Baptist; Jesus of Nazareth, who went about doing good and healing the oppressed, was anointed by God; God's chosen one had been crucified but vindicated by the resurrection; this had been authenticated by eyewitness testimony; forgiveness comes to those who receive him.[92] The sermon also bears a character distinctively its own and directly related to the intention of Luke.

---

[90] Acts 10:44–48. Italics added.

[91] This term is often used to describe those Gentiles who accepted the tenets of Judaism without becoming full members of the Jewish community. Cf. Acts 10:16, 26.

[92] See C. H. Dodd, *The Apostolic Preaching and Its Development,* for a full description of this content.

The material is skillfully adapted to a Gentile audience.[93] At the Jewish Pentecost Jesus had been proclaimed the Jewish "Lord and Christ" (2:36); now at the Gentile "Pentecost" he is "Lord of all" (10:36). "God shows no partiality, but in every nation anyone who fears him and does what is right is acceptable to him" (10:34). Purely nationalistic messianic interpretations must give way, in the thinking of Luke, to the catholic understanding that Jesus is "ordained by God to be judge of the living and dead" (10:42). If no other point in the Cornelius narrative is clear, this one certainly is. Luke intends to state without equivocation that the gospel is universal. To this character of the gospel the conversion of Cornelius is witness and the arrival of the Holy Spirit is affirmation.

The Gentile Problem. Although Luke carefully indicates that the nature of the gospel in Christ demands the inclusion of non-Jews in the Church, the idea was accepted in the apostolic Church only with great difficulty. The early community was thoroughly permeated with a strong nationalistic spirit which had become a part of traditional Judaism over several centuries. Many Jews had come to think of God as a sort of tribal God and their nation as his private possession. Not only were they *a* people of God, they were the *only* people of God. They believed that God had chosen them, blessed them in a special way, and thus given them distinctive status over other peoples of the world. National pride boasting of privileged position had replaced a sense of responsibility to be a blessing to other peoples.

Undoubtedly, this understanding of God's work in history and the spirit of exclusivism accompanying it carried over into the life of the early Church. Those who gave a primary and exclusive role to Israel in God's plan were concerned to apply their premise to life in the new Israel. Thus, they concluded that it was necessary for those who desired to become Christians to become first of all Jews by ceremonially entering the covenant community. This "circumcision party," as they are called in Acts (11:2), early became a sizeable and troublesome group. A part of the problem created by their ultra-conservative viewpoint was social in character. Since social exchange with non-Jews was frowned upon, there was serious question as to whether there could be "table fellowship." Ought the Christian eat with those who were non-Jewish in their background?

The cleavage that this caused in the early Church is noted in the incident that opens Acts 11. When word came to Jerusalem that Gen-

---

[93] Macgregor, "The Acts of The Apostles," *IB,* IX, p. 139.

tiles were receiving the gospel, members of the circumcision party criticized Peter, not only for eating with those who were outside Judaism, but also for going to them in the first place. The defense presented by Luke is that the way to the Gentiles has been opened and approved by God. The result of the argument, Luke reports, was that the opposition was silenced:

When they heard this they were silenced. And they glorified God, saying, "Then to the Gentiles also God has granted repentance unto life." [94]

The statement leaves the impression that the issue was settled, but such was not the case. The ugly problem of division between "circumcision party" and "uncircumcision party" repeatedly raised its head in the life of the apostolic Church. As greater numbers of Gentiles were included following Paul's successful work, the problem became more intense and took on theological character. The issue came to center not on social contact with Gentiles and table fellowship, but upon how the Gentiles could become Christians. The Judaizers demanded that all non-Jews actually enter Judaism by way of circumcision. The resolution of this problem is one of the major issues in the early work of Paul. Luke prepares the way for his account of Paul's mission to the Gentiles by asserting that they are included by the act of God, and that Peter, the leader of the Twelve, accepted the Gentiles. Paul, however, suggests that Peter was more compromising in his position.[95] In his concern for the universal appeal of the gospel Luke makes Peter and Paul more similar in viewpoint than they probably were.

Arrival in Antioch

Following the assertion in the Peter–Cornelius story of the availability of the gospel for the Gentiles, Luke returns to the story of expansion. The material about Philip and Peter as evangelists clarified the character of the gospel and its outreach from Jerusalem. Now Acts is prepared to commence the major chapter in the story of the expansion of the Church. At Antioch an extensive Gentile mission was undertaken.

Acts 11:19–21 is one of the significant turning points of Acts:

Now those who were scattered because of the persecution that arose over Stephen traveled as far as Phoenicia and Cyprus and Antioch, speaking the word to none except Jews. But there were some of them, men of Cyprus and

94 Acts 11:18.
95 Cf. Gal. 2.

Cyrene, who on coming to Antioch spoke to the Greeks also, preaching the Lord Jesus. And the hand of the Lord was with them, and a great number that believed turned to the Lord.

These verses suggest an early pre-Pauline mission to the Gentiles. Undoubtedly the great Apostle, whose story occupies most of the remainder of Acts, was already at work; but other, perhaps numerous, individuals were also involved in bringing Christianity to the non-Jewish and non-Palestinian world. Perhaps most were concerned to speak "the word to none except Jews," but "some of them . . . spoke to the Greeks also." [96]

Who were these men of Cyprus and Cyrene who came as missionaries to Antioch? Unfortunately it is impossible to say. Their conversion and work in spreading the gospel was a part of what must have been an extensive activity of early Church expansion peripheral to the purpose of Acts. Perhaps Barnabas was one of these early anonymous pioneers. Certainly the fact that he was sent to investigate what was going on in Antioch suggests some appreciation and sympathy with the cause. However, Barnabas was definitely identified with the Jerusalem community, although he himself was a native of Cyprus. All that can be concluded is that here is evidence of unacclaimed pioneering work which was an integral part of the growth of the Christian Church.

The focus of the new stage in Church expansion was Antioch in Syria (to be distinguished from Pisidian Antioch in Asia Minor), a most important city in the Roman world of the first century. Josephus [97] ranked it the third most important city of the empire, surpassed only by Rome and Alexandria. Located in northwestern Syria on the Orontes River, Antioch was an important hub in the Roman world. Its seaport, Seleucia, was a principal harbor on the eastern Mediterranean and land trade between Syria, Palestine, and Egypt to the south and Asia Minor, Greece, and Italy to the north and west moved though the city. Antioch's prominence as a commercial city added to its significance as a center of early Christian missions. Antioch was also the seat of the imperial legate of the Roman province of Syria and Cilicia. The city had been enlarged and beautified by a

[96] Manuscript evidence is not entirely clear as to whether the reference is to Hellenistic Jews or to Greeks unrelated to Judaism. Certainly "the Greeks" in verse 21 are contrasted to the "Jews" in verse 20 and thus, contextually the identification of Greeks here as non-Jews is to be favored. So Macgregor, "The Acts of The Apostles," *IB,* IX, p. 146. A contrary interpretation is found in Rackham, *The Acts of The Apostles,* p. 166.

[97] *Wars,* II, 4.

succession of emperors. Julius Caesar, Augustus, and Tiberius had contributed to the improvement of the road system, harbor, and architecture of the city. Thus political prestige was added to strategic location and commercial activity to keep Antioch closely in touch with both Rome and other important eastern cities.

Also, an energetic and eclectic intellectual spirit and an interest in religious inquiry characterized Antioch. Travelers brought Greek and oriental philosophies into the city along with their commercial goods. The mystery cults made popular their doctrines of salvation, death and regeneration, and the afterlife. In Greek-speaking synagogues an established Jewish colony contributed monotheistic and ethical ideas which attracted many Gentiles. Such a cosmopolitan environment made Antioch, like perhaps no other city outside Palestine, a likely place for the Church's mission to the Gentiles to take root. ". . . the whole history of the city . . . had given it a unique character as a place in which the followers of the Way could begin their expansion." [98]

"In Antioch the disciples were for the first time called Christians" (Acts 11:26). This designation is so rarely used in the New Testament [99] that both its origin and its meaning are difficult to determine.[100] Its infrequent use in the biblical materials suggests that the word was first used outside the Church itself. Believers preferred other terms, such as "disciples," "saints," "brothers," or simply followers of "the Way." Rather quickly, however, they saw the appropriateness of the word to indicate an intimate association with Christ and came to accept and use the word as a self-designation and by the beginning of the second century the Church had adopted the name "Christian."

Relation of the Antioch and Jerusalem Churches. The response of the church in Jerusalem to the movement of the gospel into Antioch was similar to its reaction to the work of Philip in the Samaritan expansion. They sent one of their honored members, Barnabas, to re-

---

[98] G. Downey, "Antioch (Syrian)," *IDB*, I, p. 147.

[99] Only two other times in Acts 26:28 and I Peter 4:16.

[100] For a discussion of the problem see H. B. Mattingly, "The Origin of the Name Christian," *JTS*, IX (1958), 26–37, and F. V. Filson, "Christian," *The Twentieth Century Encyclopedia of Religious Knowledge*, I, p. 239. It may have been a nickname used by Gentiles as a derision of the believers, or it may have been coined by Christians themselves to confess their faith in Jesus Christ and their aspirations to be like him. So E. J. Bickerman, "The Name of Christian," *Harvard Theological Review*, XLII (1949), 108–124. The term may have even originated with the Roman authorities as the designation of a new sect becoming increasingly distinct from Judaism.

view the work in this new city. Evidently the Jerusalem church claimed some oversight of the church in Antioch as it had the church in Samaria, but the relationship was more fraternal than administrative. Antioch believers revered the original community as the "first church" and consequently respected apostolic leadership and the authority associated with that role. Barnabas seems to rank as an apostle, although he was not one of the Twelve. At least his mission to Antioch is identical in purpose to that undertaken previously in Samaria by Peter and John, who were members of the Twelve.

The Antioch church demonstrated its regard for the Jerusalem church by sending relief when the latter was suffering from famine.[101] Although we cannot determine when this famine occurred,[102] Luke mentions it to point to a relationship in which Antioch Christians identify themselves with Jerusalem believers.

. . . The disciples determined, every one according to his ability, to send relief to the *brethren* who lived in Judea; and they did so, sending it to the elders by the hand of Barnabas and Saul.[103]

Barnabas.   In the description of relationships between these two groups of believers Barnabas receives less attention than he is probably due. One of the most attractive characters in the New Testament, he appears first in Luke's account of communal living in the Jerusalem church as a man of both means and generosity.[104]   He was a native of Cyprus and was thus among Hellenists converted to the faith. Subsequently he had moved to Jerusalem and, as indicated by his appointment to the mission to Antioch, risen to a place of prominence in the Jerusalem church, evidently having the confidence of the Apostles. After his arrival in Antioch, Barnabas became a leader in the church there. He supervised work among the Gentiles in Antioch and enlisted Saul of Tarsus in the Gentile mission. "Barnabas and Saul" carried the relief funds to famine-stricken Jerusalem and for a period Barnabas dominated the missionary enterprise sponsored by the Antioch church. The Acts description regularly mentions him first when discussing the first mission tour. When Paul emerged as the pre-eminent figure in the Gentile mission, Barnabas passed into the background seemingly without pride or jealousy. The role of

---

[101] Acts 11:27–30.
[102] For a discussion of this problem see Macgregor, "The Acts of The Apostles," *IB*, IX, pp. 150–156.
[103] Acts 11:29–30.   Italics added.
[104] Cf. Acts 4:36–37.

Barnabas as a genuine pioneer in establishing the Antioch base must not be overlooked.[105]

With the arrival of the gospel in Antioch Luke is ready to begin the description of another major episode in the expansion of the Church. The Antioch community under the leadership of Barnabas brought Paul from Tarsus to Antioch and commissioned both of them for a mission to the Gentiles. At this point the focus of Acts moves from Jerusalem to Antioch. Jerusalem had been the center from which the gospel moved out into Samaria and Syria. Henceforth the real center of the Christian mission will be Antioch. The church there commissioned the missionaries and heard reports when they returned. The major figure in the achievement of this expansion is the Apostle Paul, whose story is continued in the last half of the book of Acts, and whose achievement is largely the success of the outreach of the universal gospel.

SUGGESTED READINGS

Commentaries on Acts

BRUCE, F. F., *The Acts of the Apostles* (Eerdmans, 1952). Conservative and critical commentary.

FOAKES-JACKSON, F. J., and KIRSOPP LAKE, eds., *The Beginnings of Christianity, Part I: The Acts of the Apostles,* 5 vols. (Macmillan, 1920–33). Volume IV, *English Translation and Commentary,* is the best commentary on Acts in English.

STAGG, FRANK, *The Book of Acts: The Early Struggle for an Unhindered Gospel* (Broadman, 1955).

WILLIAMS, C. S. C., *A Commentary on the Acts of the Apostles* (Harper, 1957).

---

[105] The early Church gave importance to Barnabas by assigning him significant authorships. The New Testament book *Hebrews* and the apocryphal *Epistle of Barnabas* were both associated with Barnabas. On the authorship of Hebrews, see below, pp. 428–429. The Epistle was not written by Barnabas. Such associations with early Church writings, however, do indicate that the early Church thought of this individual as an important person.

8

The Gospel in Asia Minor
(Acts 13-15)

We have seen how Acts begins the story of the Christian movement from within Judaism and records its progress into a universal faith. Initially Christian believers interpreted Jesus in traditional Jewish terms and did not see any necessity to separate themselves from their historical religious background. Rather rapidly, however, the exclusively Jewish character of the Christian movement broke down because of the universal implications of the gospel itself. Hellenistic Jews, like Stephen and Philip, challenged traditional Jewish expressions of religion and extended the gospel even to Samaritans. Further, the work of Peter, Barnabas, and a host of anonymous pioneers carried the gospel to God-fearing Greeks and ultimately to pagans. In this process of early expansion the center of early Church life moved away from Jerusalem. Although the Jerusalem church continued to enjoy prestige as the place of Christian beginnings, real leadership in Church expansion came from other quarters. After the conversion of Cornelius and Barnabas' transfer to Antioch, the hub of Church life was in Syria instead of Palestine. Antioch, and not Jerusalem, fostered the primary mission to the Gentiles.

The story of the expansion of the Christian movement from Antioch eastward over the Roman world is told in the last part of the book of Acts (chapters 13–28). The theme is the same as that in the first part of Acts, namely, the gospel by its very nature reaches out to all men. Henceforth, some Jews will be won to the movement, but the most significant gains will be among the pagans.[1] The realization of a

[1] Frank Stagg, *The Book of Acts*, pp. 133–134.

vision of a kingdom including Gentiles as well as Jews is largely the story of the Apostle to the Gentiles, "Saul, who is also called Paul." [2] Paul was enlisted by Barnabas to assist with the work among Gentiles in Antioch and worked under his supervision for some months. Early, however, Paul came to the foreground in the movement of the gospel throughout the empire. An interpretation of this particular phase of Christian expansion necessitates an understanding of the dynamic and enigmatic native of Tarsus who almost single-handedly carried the gospel to the Roman world.

Sources. In spite of the Acts account of Paul's work and the Pauline letters themselves, many details of Paul's life cannot be recovered.[3] Acts 13–28 focus on the missionary achievements of the early Church in which Paul is the chief character, but these materials are dominated by the purposes of Acts, which do not include the preservation of a biography of the Apostle. Luke, in contrast to his attempts to date Jesus and John the Baptist,[4] does little to establish a chronology for the life of Paul. Jesus' age when he began his public ministry is given in Luke's Gospel, but Paul's age is not even hinted at in Acts. Extra-biblical information helps us to date certain items in the Book of Acts. For example, the Delphi inscription provides a close date for the proconsulship of Gallio mentioned in Acts (18:12–17). In a few places, moreover, Luke supplies definite chronological information,[5] but more often his temporal references are vague and indefinite.[6] Further, Acts ends the account of Paul with a general reference to his house arrest in Rome and gives no report of the close of his life.[7] In fact, the entire work selects only those events from Paul's life which develop the theme of the Church's expansion. The discovery of Paul through Acts must always take account of the controlling purpose of the Acts materials.

A second source of information about the Apostle is the Pauline let-

[2] Acts 13:9. *Saul* was his Jewish name, probably derived from the Benjamite hero Saul, the first king of Israel. *Paul* was the Apostle's Roman name. It is invariably used in his letters, signifying his pride in Roman citizenship. For a brief discussion of the names *Saul* and *Paul,* see Selby, *Toward the Understanding of St. Paul,* pp. 133–135.

[3] In spite of the many difficulties, several excellent studies of Paul's life have been made. See the references in the bibliography at the end of this chapter.

[4] Cf. Luke 2:1–2, 3:1–2.

[5] See Acts 18:11; 19:8, 10.

[6] Cf. 9:23; 14:28; 24:27.

[7] The abrupt ending of Acts has led some scholars to suppose Luke planned a third volume to complete the story. See W. L. Knox, *The Acts of The Apostles,* p. 59n.

ters which incorporate important biographical data. Sometimes these biographical passages are extensive; [8] more often they appear as short incidental or parenthetical remarks.[9] But as in Acts the biographical materials in the epistles are not biographical in purpose. Paul wrote to young churches not primarily to tell them of himself but to advise them on practical Church concerns or to answer particular theological problems. Personal references do occur in the discussion of these other matters (as when Paul aims to authenticate his apostleship to the Galatians), but they are secondary to his basic purposes in writing. Although the material is colored by the purposes, the biographical references do assist in the reconstruction of Paul's life, even though the two sources cannot be reconciled in some specific details. With the aid of Acts and the epistles, neither of which is primarily biographical, a fairly clear picture of the life and work of the Apostle can be structured. Although many problems of detail and sequence remain, the overall framework is dependable.

PAUL'S EARLY LIFE

By the time Barnabas arrived in Antioch as an emissary from the Jerusalem church, Paul was probably already at work as a Christian witness in his native Tarsus. When conflict over Jewish-Gentile relationships arose in the Antioch church, Paul was brought to Antioch at the suggestion of Barnabas to work specifically with the Gentile problem. For some time [10] Barnabas and Paul, along with certain Hellenists, sought to reconcile conflicts in the Antioch church so that Jew and Gentile could work together in mutual respect and fellowship. The success of their efforts is seen when ultimately the church accepted responsibility for spreading the faith to Gentiles beyond its immediate borders and selected representatives for that work. Barnabas and Paul were two of these representatives and before too many years Paul became the dominant figure in the enterprise. Before Paul was summoned to Antioch, however, much had already happened to prepare him for the tasks which he was to assume.

Man in Whom Jew and Gentile Meet

Native of Tarsus. Paul was born in Tarsus of Cilicia, a Roman province on the southeast coast of Asia Minor. The city of Tarsus had

[8] Cf. Gal. 1–2.
[9] Cf. I Cor. 7:7.
[10] See Acts 11:26.

Figure 8–1. Looking southward through the Cilician Gates, a pass through the Taurus Mountains bringing traffic to Tarsus. (Source: Foreign Mission Board, SBC.)

a long and distinguished history.[11] With the coming of Roman authority Tarsus had become the capital of Cilicia. Augustus made it a free city and increasingly Tarsus developed into a center of intellectual and commercial vigor. Its location just south of the renowned Cilician Gates through the Taurus Mountains caused traffic between the eastern and western parts of the empire to converge on Tarsus, bringing to the city a diversity of ideas and cultures. As a center of intellectual activity Tarsus competed successfully with Athens and Alexandria. Natives who were "fond of learning" patronized their own school rather than go away to Athens or Alexandria.[12] Athenodorus, a tutor of Augustus

[11] For a brief summary of this, see the resumé article by M. J. Mellink, "Tarsus," *IDB*, IV, pp. 518–519. A more detailed discussion occurs in W. M. Ramsay, *The Cities of St. Paul*, pp. 85–244.

[12] So Strabo, *Geography*, 14, 5, 13.

and a Stoic philosopher, was probably only one of several eminent thinkers associated with Tarsus.

Such was Paul's city, a cosmopolitan crossroads of culture and discussion. A justifiable pride can be detected in Paul's claim to be from "Tarsus in Cilicia, a citizen of no mean city." [13]   Although as a Pharisee he certainly would not have attended the university, he could not have escaped the indirect influence of debate and discussion present in Tarsus. As one writer has summarized, the influence of Tarsus was felt

. . . by a young Jewish lad in whom, as in Tarsus, the East and West met and in whom, with far-reaching results, the philosopher met the Pharisee. In the judgment of the succeeding centuries it is to this Jewish lad rather than the philosophers that Tarsus owes its place in history.[14]

Born a Jew.   The background of Paul's family, how they had come to be in Tarsus, and their standing in the cosmopolitan city are points concerning which we could hope for more detailed information. One tradition says that Paul first lived with his parents in Palestine and came to Tarsus after an unidentified capture of his home town by the Romans. Jerome [15] recounts the tradition that Paul was born in a certain Giscalis in Judea and many scholars see in this "a genuine reminiscence that Paul's family had migrated to Tarsus from Galilee." [16]   However, Palestinian history does not include Roman military action which fits Jerome's chronology nor can such a migration be validated from biblical data. On these and other grounds Ramsay concludes that the entire tradition must be rejected. He believes that Paul's ancestors settled in Tarsus about 171 B.C. as a part of Jewish migrations under Antiochus IV Epiphanes.[17]

Whenever or however Paul's family came to be in Tarsus, they were part of the city's Jewish colony. The father was a Pharisee (Acts 23:6) and the son followed in his footsteps. The strict regimen of this religious orientation was his daily meat. Israel's history, religious festivals, the law, eschatological expectations, all had become an intimate part of his self-consciousness by the time he reached maturity. His father would have taught him a trade (Acts 18:3) and reminded him regularly that he was a son of Abraham. Paul was not divorced from

---

[13] Acts 21:39. Citizenship was a carefully guarded privilege and Luke here may be using the designation loosely simply to indicate nativity or residence, rather than legal status. See A. D. Nock, *St. Paul*, p. 22n.

[14] Selby, *Toward the Understanding of St. Paul*, p. 126.

[15] *Lives of Illustrious Men*, V.

[16] Selby, *Toward the Understanding of St. Paul*, p. 218.

[17] Ramsay, *The Cities of St. Paul*, pp. 169–186.

this heritage, even after he became a Christian. Paul, however, did not simply reiterate traditional Jewish thought in new garments of Christian faith. At important points his Christian presuppositions are quite different from those of Judaism.[18]

The Pauline letters stress with pride the thoroughly Jewish character of the Apostle's background, and this emphasis is not absent from Acts. Luke states that Paul was educated after "the strict manner of the law" at the feet of Gamaliel, a Jewish rabbi of Jerusalem (Acts 22:3). Specific information about Gamaliel is meager and traditions that we do have often confuse him with his grandfather, who was also a revered rabbi. Gamaliel supported the rabbinic tradition established by his grandfather (called the school of Hillel) and himself became famous as a preserver of the religious traditions of his forefathers. Acts 5:34–39 suggests that Gamaliel discouraged violence and was held in honor by all the people, supporting the tradition that he was one of Judaism's most distinguished rabbis. Luke suggests that Paul, probably as a young man 15 or 16 years old, studied under Judaism's illustrious teacher and from him learned to recite Torah, to quote traditional interpretations of the Hebrew scriptures, and to argue according to established patterns of rabbinical debate.[19]

Paul never completely forsook his Pharisaic orientation. Two quotations from his writings dramatically reflect the passion with which he affirmed his Jewish background. In a defense against Corinthian Jewish accusers he boasted,

Are they Hebrews? So am I. Are they Israelites? So am I. Are they descendants of Abraham? So am I.[20]

When writing to the Philippians, he metaphorically identified Christians as those of the "true circumcision," but the description of himself that occurs in the discussion is intended to be taken literally:

. . . circumcised on the eighth day, of the people of Israel, of the tribe of Benjamin, a Hebrew born of Hebrews: as to the law a Pharisee, as to zeal a persecutor of the church, as to righteousness under the law blameless.[21]

---

[18] See Samuel Sandmel, *A Jewish Understanding of The New Testament,* pp. 37–38. See also his, *The Genius of Paul,* pp. 61–119.

[19] It is not at all certain that Luke's statement may be taken as literally historical. Paul's writings do not mention Gamaliel and his early persecution of the Church seems inconsistent with the attitude of the famous teacher. Luke may simply mean to suggest the thoroughness of Paul's Jewish background and training.

[20] II Cor. 11:22.

[21] Philippians 3:5–6.

Paul boasted in his Hebrew heritage. From his Christian perspective he felt that Judaism had been a tutor bringing him to Christ. In this he had surpassed his classroom companions. As a Christian he came to understand Christ as the fulfillment of all that he had learned. This interpretation produced for him both a justifiable pride in having discovered the real goal of his faith and a plaguing grief over fellow Jews who had rejected Jesus as the fulfillment of their tradition. The fiery confessions of Romans 9–11 reveal the anguish of a soul grieved for his kinsmen. Paul says,

For I could wish that I myself were accursed and cut off from Christ for the sake of my brethren, my kinsmen by race. They are Israelites, and to them belong the sonship, the glory, the covenants, the giving of the law, the worship, and the promises; to them belong the patriarchs, and of their race, according to the flesh, is the Christ.[22]

From Paul's Christian viewpoint the rejection of Jesus as Messiah was the denial of the whole Hebrew tradition. Paul could not discuss this matter dispassionately as a mere matter for theological debate. He remained identified with people whom he understood to have violated their best religious tradition when they turned away from Jesus the Messiah.[23] That he felt so deeply reflects the intensity with which he remained a Jew.

Roman Citizen. Paul was also a citizen of Rome.[24] In early days this had meant the right to popular vote. However, with the expansion of the Roman empire and the disappearance of popular elections, the meaning of Roman citizenship had taken other turns. Legal, social, and economic privileges came to one who could claim Roman citizenship. Cicero, for example, states:

To bind a Roman citizen is a crime, to flay him is an abomination, to slay him is almost an act of murder: to crucify him is—what? There is no fitting word that can possibly describe so horrible a deed.[25]

The Roman citizen was assured the right of trial and appeal to the emperor. He belonged to the ruling class and enjoyed the financial advantages of privileged aristocracy.

Since it did carry special civil rights, Roman citizenship was often granted by the emperor to gain favor or to give reward for outstanding

---

[22] Rom. 9:3–5a. For a fuller discussion of this entire section, see below, pp. 330–332.

[23] So Adolf Deissmann, *Paul: A Study in Social and Religious History*, p. 98.

[24] For fuller discussion see Ramsay, *The Cities of St. Paul*, pp. 205–214.

[25] Cicero, *The Verrine Orations*, II, 66, para. 170.

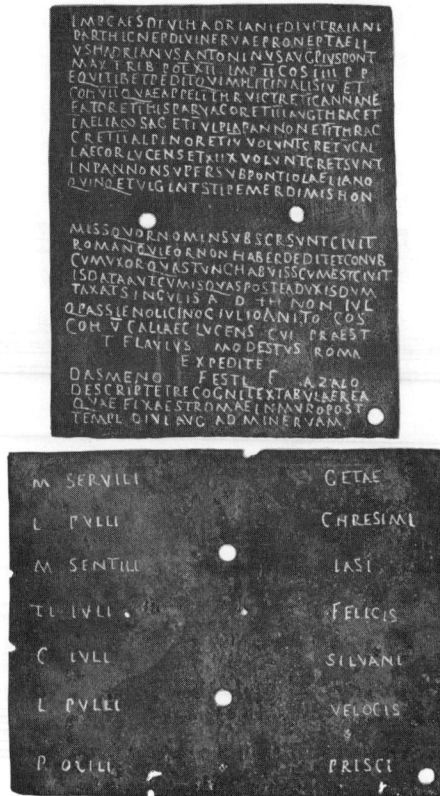

Figure 8–2. Two bronze plates from a military diploma, dating to the second century A.D. and granting citizenship to honorably discharged Roman soldiers and their wives. (Source: The Metropolitan Museum of Art, Rogers Fund, 1923.)

service. Under Mark Antony, Augustus, and Claudius citizenship was widely extended, often being granted to groups, as well as individuals. Paul, however, was "born a citizen" (Acts 22:28). Probably his father had been among pro-Roman provincials who had been officially declared citizens and the son had inherited the status, a fact of no little consequence for the life of the Apostle. Roman citizenship would deliver him from public embarrassment (Acts 16:39), save him from examination by scourging (Acts 22:24–29), and open the door for appeal to Caesar and trial at Rome (Acts 25:10–12). But more importantly, Roman citizenship enhanced Paul's ability to see beyond his local province with a sense of identification with the whole empire.

Paul, then, came to his new work in Tarsus with a cosmopolitan orientation. He belonged to the cherished heritage of Judaism, retaining with passionate zeal national and religious communion with his people.[26] But he also breathed the cosmopolitan air of an open city. He knew Gentile ideas and Gentiles first hand. Further, as a citizen of the empire his vision extended beyond the narrow confines of his local province. It is entirely fitting that one who was Roman, Hellenist, and Jew came onto the scene to participate in the outreach of the Church to the Gentile world.

A Jewish–Christian

Paul first appears in the New Testament record as a persecutor of those of The Way.[27] The men who stoned Stephen laid their garments at the feet of the young man Saul, reflecting his approval of Stephen's execution. The degree to which he participated in the persecution of the Church following Stephen's death we can only surmise because details are lacking in the sources. Acts indicates a predominant role, and Paul himself looked back upon his participation in the persecution with profound remorse.[28] To Paul, this persecution of Christians illustrated a zealous concern with the legalism of Hebrew religion from which he had been delivered in his relationship to Christ. For the Apostle (and for Acts) the crucial event which turned Paul the persecutor into Paul the missionary was an experience on the road from Jerusalem to Damascus.

The Damascus Road Conversion. The dramatic character of Paul's experience is seen more clearly when it is recognized that Acts 9:1 continues the story left off at Acts 8:3. Luke inserts materials about Philip to illustrate the movement of early Christianity into Samaria, but the sequence of his story is maintained even if these materials are omitted. In fact, the radical change brought about by Paul's conversion is more obvious when the reader moves directly from 8:3 to 9:1. The opening paragraph of chapter 8 describes a persecutor who "laid waste the church, and entering house after house, he dragged off men and women and committed them to prison" (8:3). Chapter 9 further intensifies the picture of Paul as the foremost persecutor of the Church:

But Saul, still breathing threats and murder against the disciples of the Lord, went to the high priest and asked him for letters to the synagogues at

[26] Deissmann, *Paul: A Study in Social and Religious History,* p. 97.
[27] See Acts 7:58; 8:1–3.
[28] See I Cor. 15:9.

Damascus, so that if he found any belonging to the Way, men or women, he might bring them bound to Jerusalem.[29]

That the high priest and Sanhedrin did not have jurisdiction to supervise the persecution of Christians in Damascus does not seem to bother Luke. Perhaps Paul lived in Damascus and persecuted the Christians there at the disposal of the local synagogue.[30] Luke obviously does not have full information about Paul's activities at this time, but he uses the limited reports that he has to emphasize both Paul's zealous concern for Hebrew religion and the transformation of "the fiercest enemy of the faith into its foremost apostle." [31]

Three accounts of Paul's experience appear in the Book of Acts. In Chapter 9 the description is part of the narrative and in chapters 22 and 26 speeches of Paul retell the story. Additionally a personal account of what happened to the Apostle occurs in Galatians 1:11–17. Although these reports differ considerably in details and, particularly the Acts reports, must be interpreted within the context of the author's own assumptions, two emphases permeate all descriptions of Paul's experience. First, the conversion is understood to come from God.[32] We might conjecture an intense psychological situation to account for the Apostle's conversion.

Unable to forget Stephen, Saul transferred his guilt into hostility against all the disciples of the Lord and tried to silence his conscience by feverish activity . . . The journey of several days gave Paul time to think, and he was inwardly in turmoil as he neared Damascus.[33]

The total complex of circumstances which produced so dramatic a change in Paul undoubtedly include such psychologically dynamic factors and make for both interesting and helpful surmise. But neither Acts nor Galatians aims to unravel Paul's transformation psychologically. Both sources understand the experience as an unanticipated interruption whose source is God in Christ. Looking back on the event Paul explained that God himself had set him apart before birth, called him through grace, and revealed to him the Son.[34] Luke clearly understands the encounter to be with Jesus, whom Paul in the Christians had

---

[29] Acts 9:1–2.

[30] So Ernst Haenchen, "The Book of Acts as Source Material for the History of Early Christianity," *Studies in Luke–Acts*, eds. Keck and Martyn, pp. 264–265.

[31] G. H. C. Macgregor, "The Acts of The Apostles," *IB*, IX, p. 119.

[32] See Karl H. Rengstorf, "Apostolos," *Theological Dictionary of the New Testament*, ed. Gerhard Kittel, I, pp. 407–447.

[33] A. C. Winn, *Acts of The Apostles*, pp. 66–67.

[34] Gal. 1:16.

been persecuting,[35] to be explained only as the mystical "act of God, penetrating, indeed to the innermost core of his being, but inexplicable, humanly speaking, and to be ascribed to the unmerited favor, the grace of God." [36]

Second, the accounts agree that the Damascus road experience summoned Paul to preach among the Gentiles.

But the Lord said to him, "Go, for he is a chosen instrument of mine to carry my name before the Gentiles and kings and the sons of Israel." [37]

.   .   .

The God of our fathers appointed you to know his will, . . . for you will be a witness for him to all men of what you have seen and heard.[38]

The Apostle himself states that God set him apart and called him as disciple ". . . in order that I might preach him among the Gentiles." [39] To this "heavenly vision" he could not be disobedient.[40] He had been appointed to a Gentile mission from which he could not turn back.

The word "conversion" should be used with great care to describe the Apostle's experience. Neither Acts nor Paul called the event a "conversion." Certainly Paul did not think of himself as converted from irreligion to religion or even from one kind of religion to another.[41] Rather, conversion meant the completion of a work already begun in the optimistic hopes of Judaism. Newer convictions did not so much turn him away from Judaism as enable him to comprehend the essence of true Judaism. Christ, who had taken possession of him and set him apart to apostleship and mission, came to be seen, not as a nullification of Judaism or the Old Testament, but as their fulfillment.[42] Thus one "untimely born" and "unfit to be called an apostle" because of his persecution of the Church, by the grace of God had been made both apostle and witness.

The conversion experience remained vivid in Paul's memory and molded the pattern of his daily commitment. Its intensity as an ever-present reality shines through the Apostle's own description:

. . . whatever gain I had, I counted as loss for the sake of Christ. Indeed I count everything as loss because of the surpassing worth of knowing Christ

[35] Acts 9:5; 22:7–8; 26:15.
[36] A. C. Purdy, "Paul the Apostle," *IDB*, III, p. 685.
[37] Acts 9:15.
[38] Acts 22:14a, 15.
[39] Gal. 1:16.
[40] Cf. Acts 26:19–20.
[41] Helpful discussions of this point occur in Selby, *Toward the Understanding of St. Paul*, pp. 161ff., and Purdy, "Paul the Apostle," *IDB*, III, pp. 684–685.
[42] Sandmel, *A Jewish Understanding of The New Testament*, p. 57.

Jesus my Lord. For his sake I have suffered the loss of all things, and count them as refuse, in order that I may gain Christ and be found in him, not having a righteousness of my own, based on law, but that which is through faith in Christ, the righteousness from God that depends on faith; that I might know him and the power of his resurrection, and may share his sufferings, becoming like him in his death, that if possible I may attain the resurrection from the dead.[43]

In this one great event the Apostle became committed to pursuit of "the prize of the upward call of God in Christ Jesus." [44] The remainder of his life is a pilgrimage toward this goal.

In Damascus and Jerusalem. The period between Paul's conversion and the first major mission tour from Antioch is illumined only slightly by the sources. Acts (9:18–20; 22:16–21; 26:19–20) omits details and compresses the time sequence.[45] When Paul in Galatians (1: 11–24) defends his apostolic authority as independent of any human authority, he refers to this period but reports only facts relevant to his argument. Acts states that after his conversion Paul went to Damascus where he was baptized and instructed. Following an initial ministry in and around Damascus, he then returned to Jerusalem for a brief visit with the church there. According to Galatians (1:18) Paul was in Damascus at least three years and the visit to Jerusalem was for fifteen days. However, the point from which the three years is intended to be calculated cannot be determined and even if it could, the reader must remember that the chief concern is not precise chronology.

According to the Acts sequence, Paul, after his call, went to Damascus where he was commissioned and baptized by Ananias. Subsequently, he began a long process of reevaluating the meaning of his religion in the light of his experience and his new relationship to the Christian faith. This reassessment occurred in the context of the Jewish faith in association with the Jewish synagogue in Damascus; and it involved the question how this Jesus, who had been seen on the road to Damascus, was to be interpreted as the fulfillment of Judaism. Out of intense wrestling with his own experience came initial attempts to be the missionary which he had been called to be. Luke suggests an excursion into Nabatea, the Arab kingdom whose borders extended to the very gates of Damascus during this period.[46]

---

43 Philippians 3:7–11.

44 Philippians 3:14.

45 Note the phrases "for several days" and "when many days had passed" in Acts 9:19 and 23.

46 The Nabatean kingdom, with its famous capital at Petra, reached its greatest extremity under Aretas IV in the first half of the Christian century.

During this early period, Paul began to proclaim Jesus as the Son of God in Damascus where his preaching aroused mixed reaction. Some were amazed that one who had wrought such havoc among believers was now promoting the cause. Others did not accept Paul's interpretation of Jesus and so opposed him. Acts reports that a Jewish plot to kill the Apostle led to his escape from Damascus by being lowered over the city wall in a basket.[47]

From Damascus Paul went to Jerusalem for a brief visit before returning to his home town, Tarsus in Cilicia. In Galatians Paul says that his purpose was to see Peter (1:18), but precisely why he wanted to see Peter is not known. It is unlikely that it had to do with Paul's mission to the Gentiles, for the Jerusalem apostles would not have been overly impressed with a claim that Paul was the apostle to the Gentiles, especially if he had little success in Damascus and Nabatea. Further, Paul did not need Peter's approval to authenticate his ministry. He makes it lucidly clear that his apostleship is from God and independent of human approval. His commission was not from men because his gospel was not from men. Paul states categorically:

When he . . . was pleased to reveal his Son to me, . . . I did not confer with flesh and blood, nor did I go up to Jerusalem to those who were apostles before me . . .[48]

On this point Paul was unwilling to equivocate. He was an apostle of Christ and "not from men or through men" (1:1). Thus his call demanded no validating witness from any of the Twelve.

Probably Paul was primarily concerned to convince Peter and James, the brother of Jesus who was already becoming influential in the Jerusalem church, that the Lord had really appeared to him. Early in the Church's history apostolic authority hinged upon being a witness to the resurrection of Jesus,[49] and Paul wanted to make clear that his apostleship had been authenticated by the risen Lord, who appeared to him on the road to Damascus. The Acts accounts emphasize the exchange, "Who are you, Lord?" and "I am Jesus, whom you are persecuting."[50] To Luke Paul had *seen* Jesus just as really as had Peter or any other of the apostles.[51] Since he had formerly persecuted

---

[47] Cf. Acts 9:23. The reference in 26:21 may be a confusion of the same tradition.

[48] Gal. 1:15–17.

[49] Cf. Acts 1:22.

[50] Cf. Acts 9:5; 22:8; 26:15.

[51] The vocabulary here corresponds closely with words used to describe Christophanies to the other Apostles. The words were already technical words for a divine epiphany in the Septuagint. See Deissmann, *Paul: A Study in Social and Religious History*, p. 129.

the Church, Paul also wanted to assure the Jerusalem leaders that he had genuinely changed. "Presumably the result of these discussions was that Paul was acknowledged as a Christian and a missionary who was now going or being sent to try to work in his home province of Cilicia." [52]

Throughout his ministry Paul valued both the friendship and the theological judgment of the Jerusalem leaders. Although at a major conference in Jerusalem he contended vigorously with the disciples over the admission of Gentiles into the Church, Paul gives us no reason to suppose that he considered the Jerusalem church as anything other than the "mother" church of the Christian movement or the Twelve as other than leaders to be revered. His brief visit introduced him to those leaders and undoubtedly diminished suspicion and hostility toward the former persecutor. Paul, however, left Jerusalem still largely unknown by the Judean church and relatively uninvolved in the mission which would preserve his name and to which he would bring vigorous dedication.

The Silent Years.   Following the brief visit to Jerusalem Paul, according to his own report, retired to the "regions of Syria and Cilicia" [53] where he stayed for "fourteen years." [54]   This chronology is exceedingly difficult to correlate with the sequences of Acts 9–13. From Luke's account one gets the impression that the interval between the Jerusalem visit and the beginning of the so-called first mission tour is much shorter.[55] Further, the discussion in Galatians is not clear as to whether the fourteen years includes the three years spent in and around Damascus following his conversion. The possibility that "fourteen" is a primitive scribal error for "four" further complicates the problem.[56] Again we are reminded that the primary purpose of neither Galatians nor Acts is chronological and consequently it is impossible to press the time details into any neat package.

Whatever their duration these must have been crucially important years in the life of the Apostle. Although we know absolutely nothing

---

[52] Haenchen, "The Book of Acts as Source Material for the History of Early Christianity," *Studies in Luke–Acts*, p. 269.

[53] Gal. 1:21.

[54] Gal. 2:1.

[55] John Knox, *Chapters in a Life of Paul*, pp. 47–88, suggests that the "fourteen years" includes the greater part of Paul's early missionary activities and thereby virtually eliminates the "silent years." Cf. Thomas S. Kepler, *Contemporary Thinking About Paul*, pp. 161–169.

[56] See Macgregor, "The Acts of The Apostles," *IB*, IX, pp. 148, 152.

about this period,[57] we can surmise that Paul spent the years in and around his native Tarsus engaged in proclaiming Jesus Christ. Possibly the Apostle engaged in preaching throughout Cilicia and perhaps into southeastern Asia Minor, possibly as far as Galatia.[58] It may be that some of the perils and hardships noted in II Corinthians 11:23–29 belong to this period.

Further, these must have been years in which Paul grew as a Christian and as a theologian. The process set in motion by his conversion and call had time to move toward maturity. The years gave opportunity for extensive reflection on the gospel's meaning and for trial-and-error experimentation in mission work. Exposure to Gentiles gave the Apostle new perspectives on the task to which he felt called. Thus the Paul summoned by Barnabas and the Antioch church was no mere novice in the faith. He was a comparatively mature adherent who possibly had already demonstrated in his native Tarsus both a willingness and an ability to interpret the gospel for Gentiles. Paul came to Antioch as one fitly prepared to bring out of the treasury of his life both the old and the new.

MISSION TO GALATIA

The expansion of the Church from Antioch to Rome is described in Acts 13–19 in a carefully worked out design. Activities of the Apostle Paul are arranged in three mission tours each reaching toward the imperial seat. The tours are broken each time by visits to Antioch and Jerusalem.[59] After the completion of the third tour, Luke records in detail the events leading to Paul's arrest and the subsequent events which bring him to Rome. Then the story ends abruptly with the Apostle imprisoned in Rome but continuing a faithful mission of preaching to his associates there. The following outline indicates the structure of the last half of Acts and reflects the ordered arrangement of materials relating to Paul.

1. Acts 13:4–15:35. The first mission tour: to Cyprus and Galatia. The Jerusalem Conference.
2. Acts 15:36–18:22. The second mission tour: revisiting Galatia; expansion to Macedonia and Achaia.

[57] Johannes Weiss, *The History of Primitive Christianity*, I, p. 205, argues that the silence of Acts on this period is testimony to its dependability as an historical document. He believes that an author fabricating an historical treatise would not have left such a major gap untouched by his imagination.

[58] See map, Fig. 8–3.

[59] See Acts 15:4; 18:22; 21:15.

3. Acts 18:23–21:16.　The third mission tour: to Ephesus; revisiting Macedonia and Achaia.
4. Acts 21:17–28:31.　Arrest, trials, and finally imprisonment in Rome.

The pattern of Luke's report more accurately reflects a literary arrangement of past events than any careful missionary design in Paul's mind. The Apostle gives no evidence in his letters that he thinks of his work in terms of successive stages to be accomplished as steps toward the ultimate objective of Rome. Nowhere does he indicate that he considers either Jerusalem or Antioch a type of home base from which the Church must expand in ever-widening circles. Although Paul desires fellowship and harmony with the Jerusalem church, the concern with the orientation of the missionary enterprise around Jerusalem as the mother church belongs more to Luke than to the Apostle. Paul's "home was with his churches," [60] and no preconceived travel arrangements could detract from the needs of the moment. He willingly gave way to sudden inspiration, convinced that the gospel should not be hampered by rigid schedules.[61]

Although the missionary journeys were not pre-planned in careful detail, Paul's work was not without purposeful movement. His eye was fixed upon the West. He not only envisioned reaching Rome,[62] but also looked beyond to the farthest extent of the empire—even to Spain.[63] Consequently, all that Paul did pointed toward carrying the gospel to the entire Roman world, and the major lines of Paul's missionary activities to accomplish this purpose are comparatively clear. Initially the gospel was taken to Asia Minor, particularly the region of Galatia. Thence the Apostle proceeded to the area around the Aegean Sea, where a major portion of his ministry was conducted in the metropolitan areas of western Asia Minor, Macedonia, and Achaia. Significant missions are conducted in Philippi, Thessalonica, Corinth, and Ephesus. A third phase of Paul's work is associated with his movement to Rome. In this phase Paul established no new churches, but ministered to the church in Rome and corresponded with churches already established during the Aegean mission. Paul's contribution then to the expansion of the Church may be discussed around three foci: the Galatian mission, the Aegean mission, and the Roman mission.

[60] Selby, *Toward the Understanding of St. Paul*, p. 183.
[61] Cf. Acts 16:6–10; 17:15.
[62] Acts 19:21.
[63] Rom. 15:24.

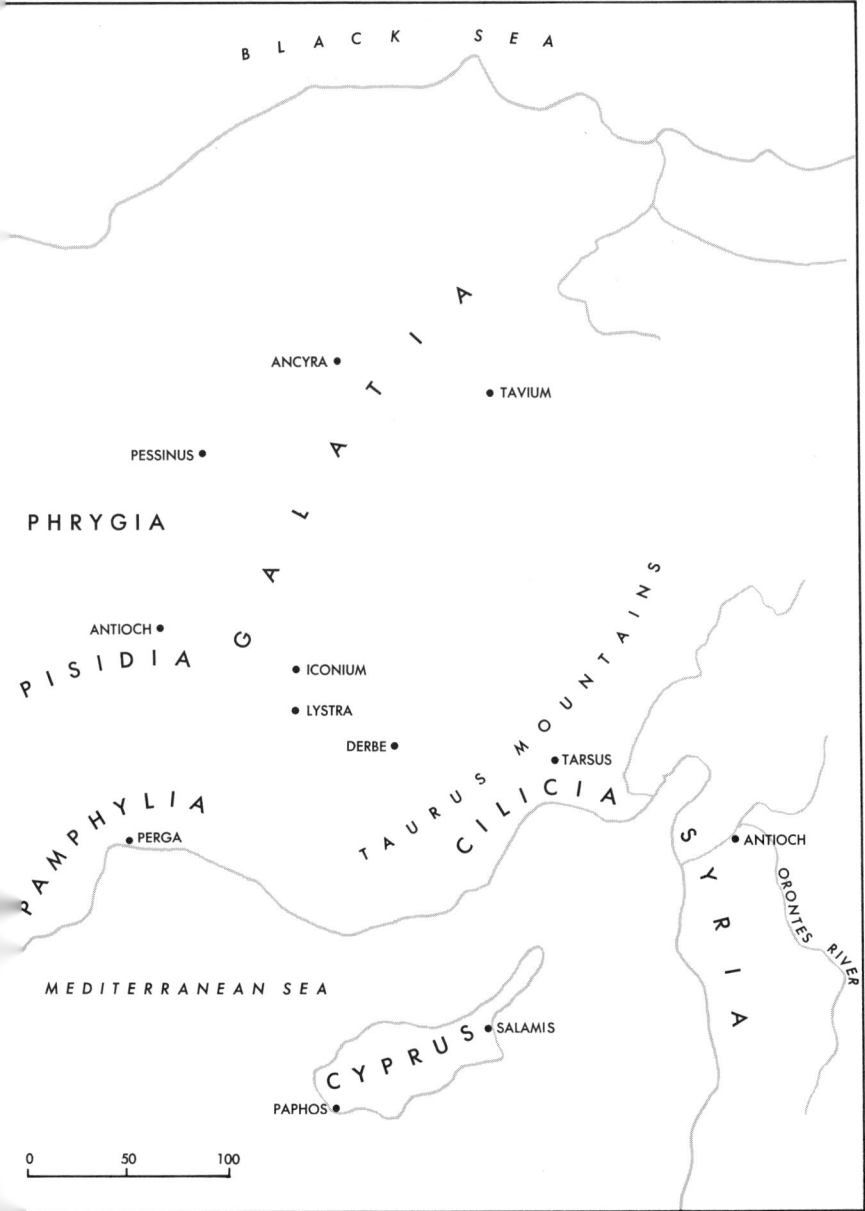

Figure 8–3. Paul's Galatian Mission.

Cyprus

For a year after Paul was brought from Tarsus, he and Barnabas labored in Antioch "while the seed of a daring new idea for the missionary enterprise grew in their minds." [64] The idea began to move toward fruition when these two were "set apart . . . for the work" (Acts 1:2) by the Antioch congregation, already established in its own right as an experiment in Gentile Christianity. Although this church served as a sort of base of operations for Paul and his missionary associates, Luke makes it clear that the enterprise belonged to the Holy Spirit. After fasting and prayer, the church "laid their hands on them," not to authenticate their mission, but to set them apart to a task that belonged to God. Thus Barnabas and Paul were designated to be formal representatives to extend into the Mediterranean world a work already begun in Antioch.

Luke's account of the initial Pauline mission is not too well documented. The earliest of Paul's journeys naturally was remembered least in the early Church and consequently Luke's sources provided few concrete details. The two pioneer missionaries left Seleucia, the seaport of Antioch, and sailed for Cyprus, the island home of Barnabas. John Mark, a cousin of Barnabas, accompanied the missionaries, but was separated from the mission after Cyprus. Barnabas seems to have dominated the initial phase of the first campaign; at least in the descriptions of the work on Cyprus, Luke consistently mentions his name first. It seems perfectly natural that Barnabas, who was an established leader in the Antioch church, should be the controlling figure in the mission to his homeland.

It should be remembered that Paul and Barnabas were not introducing Christianity to Cyprus. Men from Cyprus had been among those who had earlier brought the gospel to Antioch. This may account for the impression one gets from Paul's letters that his mission really began in Galatia. Perhaps Paul considered the visit to Cyprus nothing more than reestablishment and encouragement of the faithful already won to belief. There is no report of converts won or churches established during this phase of the mission.

Sergius Paulus. Two places are mentioned in connection with Cyprus: Salamis and Paphos. The company arrived at Salamis on the east end of the island where "they proclaimed the word of God in the

[64] Selby, *Toward the Understanding of St. Paul,* p. 185.

synagogues of the Jews" (Acts 13:5). The pattern of preaching in the synagogues is typical of Paul's approach throughout the Galatian mission. Until the doors of the synagogue were closed to his preaching, the Apostle aimed to reach both Jew and Gentile. His typical approach was through the established institution.

From Salamis Paul and his associates proceeded to Paphos, the capital of Cyprus lying at the western end of the island. Here the group encountered the proconsul Sergius Paulus and "a certain magician, a Jewish false prophet, named Bar-Jesus." [65] Sergius Paulus was a person of inquiring mind, but was diverted from hearing Paul by the efforts of Bar-Jesus [66] to discredit the Apostle. However, when Bar-Jesus was stricken with blindness, Sergius Paulus "believed, . . . for he was astonished at the teaching of the Lord" (Acts 13:12). That is, Sergius Paulus recognized in amazement that these were men of God and must be heard. We are not told how the incident concluded and no tradition in the early Church clarifies the event. Luke seemingly includes the story to emphasize favorable hearing secured by Paul and his party, as if to say that this is a preview of things to come.

Galatia

After Cyprus, the scene of Paul's work shifts to Galatia. Leaving the island, the missionaries landed at Perga on the southern coast of Asia Minor. For some undetermined reason John Mark left the group. Possibly as a Jerusalem Jew he had more reservations about the Gentile mission than did his colleagues. Or perhaps a rift was already beginning to develop between Paul and Barnabas and, as a kinsman of Barnabas, John Mark was unwilling to identify with a cause increasingly under Paul's influence and direction. Or he may have been homesick. For whatever reason, John Mark left. Although he and Paul later were personally reconciled,[67] the young cousin of Barnabas did not again accompany the Apostle on a mission tour. After John Mark's departure Paul and Barnabas proceeded to the Galatian centers of Pisidian Antioch, Iconium, Lystra, and Derbe.

Galatia: North and South. The term "Galatia" was used to designate two areas. The older use of the term refers to an area occupied

---

[65] Acts 13:6. Some see in this event a doublet of Peter's encounter with Simon Magus introduced to reconcile the careers of Peter and Paul. Details of the stories are different, however.

[66] Also called "Elymas" in the passage. The relationship between the names is not clear.

[67] Cf. Col. 4:10.

after the third century B.C. by a Gallic group who settled in the northern part of the central plateau of Asia Minor (North Galatia). Its chief towns were Ancyra, Pessinus, and Tavium.[68] However, in the first century B.C. by an act of Augustus the territory of the Gallic king was enlarged to include a substantial area to the south. The annexed area (South Galatia) included parts of Phrygia, Pisidia, Pamphylia, and Cilicia. Thus, the Roman province of Galatia during the first century A.D. encompassed both North and South Galatia. Paul usually uses the common Roman provincial designations and so for him "Galatia" would include the areas annexed under the authority of Augustus. The churches which Acts reports to have been founded on the first mission tour were confined to South Galatia. These included Pisidian Antioch (that is, the Antioch near Pisidia as distinguished from the Antioch in Syria), Iconium, Lystra, and Derbe.[69]

Paul's ministry to South Galatian churches seems to illustrate how spur-of-the-moment decisions often influenced the course of his mission. Had he originally planned to go to Pisidian Antioch, he undoubtedly would have gone from Syrian Antioch through Cilicia and Lycaonia. The route would have been more direct and also avoided the difficult and dangerous mountain terrain of the Taurus range which lay between Perga and Pisidian Antioch. Instead Paul had gone to Cyprus and, perhaps inspired by his encounter with Sergius Paulus, made an on-the-spot decision to take the gospel to the Roman colony of Antioch.[70] There he would not only be in contact with a major Roman center, but also strike the main road leading east to Ephesus and on to Rome.

In Pisidian Antioch. Pisidian Antioch was Paul's first stop in Galatia. It was a city which had formerly been under the control of the Seleucids but was now a free city by an act of Rome. In Paul's day it was the seat of Roman administration for South Galatia and consequently probably had a sizeable Roman population. Like most cities with a Seleucid history, Antioch had a long-established colony of Jews. Thus, in keeping with his method throughout the first mission tour, Paul was able to begin work in the local Jewish synagogue.[71] Gentile

---

[68] See map, Fig. 8–3.

[69] An extensive study of the cities visited by Paul is Ramsay's, *The Cities of St. Paul.* See pp. 247–419 for a discussion of the Galatian churches.

[70] So Macgregor, "The Acts of The Apostles," *IB*, IX, p. 175. W. M. Ramsay, *The Church in The Roman Empire*, pp. 61f., conjectures that an illness struck Paul in Perga and forced him to seek the healthier climate of Antioch. However, a sick man would hardly have attempted the perilous trip.

[71] Acts 13:43–49.

converts to Judaism were already a part of the synagogue and so Paul's message was directed at both Jew and Gentile. The events resulting from his preaching at Pisidian Antioch set a pattern which Paul encountered repeatedly in his work through the synagogues. The more conservative Jews opposed him, but many Gentiles believed. However, Luke's picture of Jewish opposition and Gentile support may be overstated in the interest of pointing out both Paul's success with Gentiles and the rejection of the gospel by the Jews. In fact, some of the leading Gentiles found Paul's preaching unacceptable and were instrumental in having the Apostle expelled from the city.

Luke includes in his description of the Pisidian Antioch mission one of the several sermons which appear in Acts. Paul's address to the synagogue,[72] like other Acts sermons, is not to be taken as a stenographic transcript of the Apostle's words. It does, however, indicate the kind of message which Paul, and other Christian preachers of the day, would address to a Jewish-Gentile congregation.[73] The sermon emphasizes that God, who had been redemptively engaged with Israel, had brought salvation in Jesus as the promised descendant of David. But "those who live in Jerusalem and their rulers" failed to accept Jesus as the fulfillment of prophetic utterances and killed him. Yet this Jesus had been raised by God and vindicated. The climax of the sermon comes in a final word of appeal:

Let it be known to you therefore, brethren, that through this man forgiveness of sins is proclaimed to you, and by him every one that believes is freed from everything from which you could not be freed by the law of Moses.[74]

In Iconium, Lystra, and Derbe. Hostility generated by Paul's message forced him and his companions to leave Antioch. The group turned east and south to the cities of Iconium, Lystra, and Derbe. In spite of the opposition aroused in Antioch, the missionaries apparently followed the same plan in the new cities. They entered the synagogues and proclaimed the gospel to both Jew and Gentile.[75] The response was the same; some believed and some opposed. Seemingly most of Paul's difficulty came from Jews who not only refused to accept his message, but also organized opposition to the Apostle. At Iconium "unbelieving Jews stirred up the Gentiles and poisoned their minds

---

[72] Acts 13:16–41.

[73] A more direct report on what Paul said to the Galatians is perhaps found in his own statements in Gal. 3:1–6:10.

[74] Acts 13:38–39.

[75] Acts 14:1. Luke does not provide details with regards to Lystra and Derbe, but apparently the pattern was the same.

Figure 8–4. The mound of ancient Lystra, looking south, with a typical well in the foreground. (Source: Foreign Mission Board, SBC.)

against the brethren" (Acts 14:2). And at Lystra factions who came from Antioch and Iconium "persuaded the people" (Acts 14:19) with the result that Paul was stoned, dragged from the city, and left for dead.

But before reporting the Jewish attempt to execute Paul, Luke tells the most impressive story associated with the Galatian mission. At Lystra Barnabas and Paul healed a cripple and were praised as Zeus and Hermes incarnate. The event follows the motif of a popular legend that told how Zeus and Hermes had visited earth. Supposedly a poor couple, Baucis and Philemon, welcomed the gods and were rewarded by concurrent deaths so that neither would mourn the other.[76] Perhaps familiarity with the legend prompted local residents to their declaration about Paul and Barnabas.

[76] Ovid, *Metamorphoses*, VIII, 631f.

Paul responded to the occasion with a speech directing praise to the real source of the man's healing. The one God, who is the maker and sustainer of all, has accomplished the mighty work and deserves their praise.[77] Paul, here speaking to a pagan audience, "voices the typical Jewish opposition to pagan idolatry and calls on the hearers to turn to the one living God."[78] Although Luke does not indicate a sweeping acceptance of Paul's message, some believers must have been won. Timothy, an intimate associate during the latter Aegean mission, was from Lystra and may have been in the audience when Paul preached his sermon.

After the miracle in Lystra and Paul's brush with death there, Luke in the briefest sort of way describes Paul's trip to Derbe and his return through South Galatia revisiting the churches of Lystra, Iconium, and Pisidian Antioch. From Antioch Paul returned to Perga and thence sailed to Antioch in Syria for a report on the beginnings of his mission activity. Later a second summary sketches Paul's return to South Galatia, this time directly from Syria through Cilicia. The second visit concludes Paul's ministry in Galatia.

THE JERUSALEM CONFERENCE

The success of the initial Galatian mission brought the Christian community to a genuine crisis. Many Gentiles had been brought into the Church by the campaign, and the presence of increasing numbers of non-Jewish Christians focused attention on the problem of their relationship to Judaism. Some of the new converts had been only indirectly related to the synagogue and others stood entirely outside the Hebrew tradition. If Paul's interpretation of Jesus as the fulfillment of Jewish hopes were taken seriously, what should be the Church's attitude toward converts who were not from within the community that had looked forward to the Messiah's coming? Was it necessary for them to enter the traditional Jewish covenant community before they could become Christians? The question had been implicit in the Antioch church where some individuals not in the Jewish tradition had responded to the gospel and had been included in the fellowship. Now the wider outreach of the Church made the question more acute. The problem focused in two issues: (1) Should circumcision, the Jewish initiation ritual, be required of Gentiles when they became Christians?

[77] Acts 14:15–17.
[78] Selby, *Toward the Understanding of St. Paul*, p. 191.

and (2) What should be the personal relationships between Jewish and Gentile Christians?

This was the general nature of the problem that faced Paul and Barnabas when they returned to Antioch from Galatia. Some men came down from Judea with the teaching,

Unless you are circumcised according to the custom of Moses, you cannot be saved.[79]

Paul and Barnabas vigorously disagreed with this position and, according to Luke's reconstruction of events, consequent dissension and debate led to a major conference with the leaders of ⌐ae Jerusalem church to try to settle the issue. "There is nothing to suggest that the church at Antioch was under necessity to appeal to the church at Jerusalem, and there is nothing to suggest that the church at Jerusalem considered itself in position to give a directive." [80]

The reconstruction of the Jerusalem conference, its arguments and conclusions, is an exceedingly difficult problem. The complexity grows out of the impossibility of reconciling the Acts 15 account of the apostolic council in Jerusalem with Paul's description of a meeting with the "pillars" in Jerusalem in Galatians 2.[81] The problem arises because in 9:26; 11:30; and 12:25 Acts mentions three journeys of Paul to Jerusalem up to and including the journey in Acts 15, but Galatians tells of only two trips (in 1:18; 2:1). Usually the visit reported in Galatians 2 is identified with that of Acts 15, but the atmosphere of the two accounts is significantly different. Acts 15 stresses harmony and agreement, but Galatians 2 leaves the impression of intense controversy, if not open hostility. Further, Paul in Galatians does not seem to be aware of regulations imposed on Gentiles which in Acts are important to the council's action. This has led many scholars to conclude that such divergent accounts as Galatians 2 and Acts 15 could not refer to the same conference. Thus, they see Galatians 2 to correspond to the visit mentioned in Acts 11:30 and 12:25.[82] Others interpret Acts 15 as a doublet resulting from a contaminated report of the visit mentioned

---

[79] Acts 15:1.

[80] Stagg, *The Book of Acts,* p. 158.

[81] A helpful summary of the nature of this problem and various resolutions that have been offered appear in Selby, *Toward the Understanding of St. Paul,* pp. 196–204.

[82] This position is forcefully argued in George S. Duncan, *The Epistle of Paul to the Galatians,* pp. xxi–xxxiv. A summary of Duncan's argument occurs in Stagg, *The Book of Acts,* pp. 267–273. See also *IB,* IX, pp. 198–200.

in 11:30 and 12:25.[83] Probably, however, Acts 15 and Galatians 2 refer to the same conference [84] with differences accounted for by the specific purposes of each author. Luke undoubtedly elaborates upon the story to credit the Jerusalem church with responsibility for the Gentile mission and to emphasize, perhaps more than the facts warrant, the unity of the Church. In Galatians, however, Paul angrily defends the unqualified authority of his apostleship. He completely disregards the apostolic decrees because they do not represent for him stipulations upon his missionary activity. There is no real reason to doubt the historical reality of a conference in Jerusalem,[85] convened to wrestle with the most crucial issue confronted by the apostolic Church.

Both Acts and Galatians indicate that the central issue is the circumstances under which Gentiles are to be admitted into the Church. Should Gentiles be required to be circumcised to become Christians? And should fellowship, particularly table fellowship, exist between Gentiles and Jews in the Church? According to both Galatians 2 and Acts 15, these are the items studied and debated in the Jerusalem conference. Some type of resolution was necessary if the Church was to proceed in any unified way with its outreach to the Roman world. The conference is described by Luke to emphasize the spirit of unity and advice; but the obvious antagonism between Peter and Paul certainly testifies that unanimity did not exist and, as reflected in Galatians, the debate must have been vigorous and often heated. The Judaizers insisted upon absolute allegiance to Judaism as prerequisite to membership, demanding that Gentiles both be circumcised and charged to keep the law of Moses (Acts 15:5). The Jerusalem apostles were not so rigid in their demands, but were probably unwilling to cast aside Jewish law. Both Peter and James seem to have had reservations about a completely open policy toward Gentiles. Contrariwise Paul, if the book of Galatians is taken seriously, must have insisted that the freedom implicit in Christianity as the universal faith delivered Gentiles from Jewish regulations. He was unwilling to attach any prerequisites to Gentiles becoming Christian.

Luke goes to some extent to emphasize that Peter, James, and Barnabas all agreed with Paul that Gentiles must be accepted without res-

---

[83] So Kirsopp Lake and Henry J. Cadbury, eds., *The Beginnings of Christianity,* V, pp. 195–212. See also Morton S. Enslin, *Christian Beginnings,* pp. 226–230.

[84] The discussion continues, as illustrated by Pierson Parker, "Once More, Acts and Galatians," *JBL,* LXXXVI (1967), 175–182.

[85] Haenchen, "The Book of Acts as Source Material for the History of Early Christianity," *Studies in Luke–Acts,* pp. 270–271, seems unduly suspicious that Luke has imaginatively constructed the conference.

ervation. Peter recounted his experience with Cornelius and pointed out that God had given the Holy Spirit to Gentile as to Jew, making "no distinction between us and them" (Acts 15:9). Thus, requiring circumcision would be making "trial of God by putting a yoke upon the neck of the disciples" (Acts 15:10). Such a requirement is not only ridiculous, but also irrelevant because cleansing of heart, whether Jew or Gentile, is by faith "through the grace of the Lord Jesus" (Acts 15:9, 11). Paul and Barnabas related signs and wonders done among the Gentiles by God (Acts 15:12). James pointed out that the extension of the gospel to Gentiles was consistent with the words of the prophet (Acts 15:15–18). Paul won the day. The Judaizers, although not silenced, certainly lost the debate on this occasion.

The Jerusalem conference also, according to Luke's report, gave attention to the second facet of the problem; that is, the relationship of Gentiles and Jews within the Church. James, the brother of Jesus, suggested that Gentiles be requested to make some concessions in the interest of not being unduly offensive to the more traditional Jewish elements of the Church. According to his viewpoint, those who remained loyal to the law of Moses deserved conscientious consideration from their more liberal brethren. Accordingly, Gentiles were enjoined to "abstain from what has been sacrificed to idols and from blood and from what is strangled and from unchastity." [86]

Because of the inclusion of the injunction against unchastity, some have seen these regulations as veiled moral instructions for the Gentiles. If "what is strangled" is omitted,[87] there remain prohibitions against three typical sins—idolatry, murder, and unchastity. It seems unlikely, however, that the conference would feel it necessary to impress the Gentiles to refrain from common sin or to make the maintenance of fellowship the ground for avoiding sin. Probably all of these injunctions relate to Jewish scruples about food practices. Eating food which had been offered to idols or which contained blood (perhaps because the animal had been strangled) would be offensive to many Christians still sympathetic with their Jewish tradition. The reference to unchastity was probably added because former pagans were prone to this sin.[88] It may have been suggested by the mention of idol worship where licensed prostitution was sometimes practiced in heathen cults.

---

[86] Acts 15:29. Cf. Acts 15:20.
[87] Some early manuscripts do not contain the phrase.
[88] Macgregor, "The Acts of The Apostles," *IB*, IX, p. 204.

Thus, the Jerusalem conference represents a type of compromise in the early Church. Gentiles were emancipated from strict Jewish legal requirements, but to foster harmonious living with Jewish elements in the Church, they were to refrain from offensive practices. Since principle was not involved, Paul could agree to the concessions and the unity of the Church could be maintained without the gospel being jeopardized. The decision was summarized in a letter sent to the Christians in Syria and Antioch (Acts 15:23–29). Paul himself would carry a report of the conference to the Galatian churches.

THE GALATIAN LETTER

Against the background of the issue confronted in the Jerusalem conference Paul wrote one of his most influential letters. The letter was addressed to the Galatian churches and discusses the specific situation and problems which they faced, but its message is timeless because it deals with salvation by faith, the foundation of Christian theology. The short letter has always ranked with the longer Roman and Corinthian epistles in importance. "It has figured prominently in every struggle of the church to maintain freedom of the Spirit against legalism of any kind." [89]

Author, Date, and Audience. There is no serious question that Paul wrote Galatians. The letter itself makes this claim and nothing contained in the letter is inconsistent with the claim. The Church has regularly ascribed the epistle to Paul from the very earliest tradition.

Although the authorship of Galatians is established, the date of its writing and its audience are far more uncertain. The crucial datum here is again Galatians 1–2 and its relationship to Acts 15. According to Galatians 1–2 Paul had made only two visits to Jerusalem prior to writing the letter. If this chronology is taken rigidly and forced to correspond with the Apostle's first two visits mentioned in Acts, then the letter would have been written before the Jerusalem council. It has already become clear, however, that Luke in Acts does not simply chronicle events in sequence and that chronological reconciliation between Acts and the Pauline epistles is not the major interpretative problem. If the visits of Galatians 2 and Acts 15 are different reports of the same event, as they probably are, then Galatians would have been written after the Jerusalem conference. The question then becomes, "How long after?" Some have answered that the epistle was

[89] John Knox, "Letter to the Galatians," *IDB*, II, p. 338.

written from Antioch immediately after the debate in Jerusalem before Paul set out on his second mission tour and therefore is the earliest of Paul's extant writings.[90]

On the other hand, Galatians itself seems to indicate that a second visit to the churches had already occurred before the book was written. Paul says to the churches, "You know it was because of a bodily ailment that I preached to you at first" (4:13). The words "at first" would ordinarily, though not necessarily,[91] indicate two previous visits. The first mission tour would qualify as the first visit and the revisit to South Galatia would count as the second occasion. According to this view, Galatians comes sometime after the Jerusalem meeting and would probably originate in either Corinth or Ephesus. Marked similarities of idea between Galatians and the Romans and Corinthian correspondence tend to support the later date for the writing of the book [92] and therefore suggest Ephesus as the place of origin.[93] At present the arguments for an Antioch origin seem to be less attractive. Probably the book comes from either the extended stay at Corinth toward the end of Paul's ministry there or the still later stay at Ephesus. Any conclusion, however, must be hedged with considerable uncertainty.[94]

The problem of the audience of Galatians is no more clear than that of its date. The question is essentially whether the letter is addressed to churches in North or South Galatia.[95] Those who hold to the North Galatia alternative presuppose a ministry of Paul in this territory during the silent years before his summons to Antioch and the first mission tour.[96] The book of Galatians, according to this view, was written following a second visit to the area reported in Acts 18:23.

[90] See Kirsopp Lake, *The Earlier Epistles of St. Paul,* pp. 265–266, 301–302; also Bernard Orchard, "A New Solution to the Galatian Problem," *Bulletin of John Rylands Library,* XXVIII (1944), 154f.

[91] The Greek phrase usually means "the first of two or more," but its Hellenistic usage was also in the sense of "the only earlier." See Ernest D. Burton, *A Critical and Exegetical Commentary on the Epistle to the Galatians,* pp. 239–241.

[92] Cf. J. N. Sanders, "Peter and Paul in The Acts," *NTS,* II (1955–56), 140f. Also C. H. Buck, "The Date of Galatians," *JBL,* LXX (1951), 113f.

[93] Extensive argument for this position appears in FBK, pp. 195–197. See also Knox, *Chapters In a Life of Paul,* pp. 85, 88. Ramsay, *St. Paul the Traveler,* pp. 189–192, argues for Antioch after the second mission tour as the place from which Galatians was written.

[94] A helpful summary of the entire problem, although it must be supplemented by more recent studies, appears in Burton, *A Critical and Exegetical Commentary on the Epistle to the Galatians,* pp. xliv–liii.

[95] An able summary of the possibilities and problems in these alternatives appears in Burton, pp. xxi–xliv.

[96] The classical statement of this viewpoint is J. B. Lightfoot, *St. Paul's Epistle to the Galatians,* pp. 18–35. Numerous scholars have defended his position.

Thus, Paul uses the term "Galatia" in its original sense to refer to the northern region inhabited by Gauls in the third century B.C.

The more popular view, however, holds that the epistle is addressed to South Galatia, specifically those churches visited on the first mission tour. Paul accordingly uses "Galatia" after his usual pattern. He employs the official Roman provincial designations. Thus, "Galatia" included the towns of Pisidian Antioch, Iconium, Lystra, and Derbe where churches had been established. Although the argument cannot be conclusive, the South Galatia view is the better working hypothesis and may be held tentatively pending additional evidence.[97]

The Occasion and Purpose. Whatever the conclusions about the date and audience, the situation to which Galatians is addressed is fairly clear. The letter was written to Gentile Christians who had been converted from paganism, primarily under the influence of Paul's preaching.[98] The Apostle had either come to Galatia or remained there because of an illness (4:13). He had proclaimed to them the crucified Christ, who gave life and freedom through faith apart from the law (3:1–2). He imposed no ritual obligations upon the converts, but declared to them a faith apart from the law (4:8–11; 5:1–6). The Gentiles had accepted the gospel with enthusiasm, been baptized, and received the gift of the Holy Spirit.

Since Paul's visit, however, a serious attempt had been made to unsettle his converts through an appeal to a strict, legalistic faith. It has often been assumed that Paul's opponents were Judaizers who had come from the church in Jerusalem to counteract the influence of the Jerusalem conference on the Galatian churches. The book of Galatians, however, contains no evidence that the troublemakers had come from Jerusalem and it is strange indeed that Paul would speak kindly of the churches in Judea, as he does in Galatians 1:22–24, had they been trying to undermine his mission to the Gentiles.[99] Whether from Jerusalem or Galatia, Paul's opponents were causing major difficulties among the Galatians. Some were insisting upon rigid observance of the Mosaic law, including circumcision. These may have even cited Paul's circumcision of Timothy to support their legalistic contentions. Although Paul himself may have intended this act merely as appease-

[97] See Raymond T. Stamm, "The Epistle to the Galatians," *IB*, X, pp. 435–437.
[98] Gal. 1:8–9; 4:14.
[99] Possibly the Galatian opponents were not even Jews, but Gentiles who misinterpreted Paul's gospel. So Charles Talbert, "Again: Paul's Visits to Jerusalem," *Novum Testamentum*, IX (1967), 27–29.

ment of Jewish associates involving no real religious principle, his opponents saw it as preaching circumcision. Additionally, they attacked Paul's authority as an apostle, claiming that he was abandoning the genuine gospel in the interest of pleasing men (1:6–10). Perhaps agitated by his recent report of the action of the Jerusalem council, they accused him of yielding to human authority, namely, that of the Jerusalem leaders. The confusion was compounded by others who saw a new form of legalism in Paul's demand that the believer produce the fruit of the Spirit (2:17–20). Still other Galatians moved toward libertinism. They took the concept of possession of the Spirit to mean no moral restraints (5:10–6:10). Their freedom in Christ was understood "as an opportunity for the flesh." [100]

To such a confused situation Paul addressed this "Magna Carta of the Christian faith." [101] In Galatians Paul aimed to chart the meaning of Christian freedom. Repudiating the authority of persons, laws and institutions, Paul insisted upon direct accessibility between every believer and God in Christ. His own apostleship and the Christian life of the Gentile believer were declared independent of men and dependent upon Christ. In a sense the authority of Paul's apostleship is at stake, but the more important issue is the nature of the gospel which he proclaims. Thus, the letter is a pointed polemic, abrupt and incisive, set within a controversy that threatened to divide the early fellowship. On the one hand, the narrow conception of the Judaizers aimed to keep Christianity subservient to the forms of Judaism. On the other hand, Paul championed an interpretation of the faith which would enable Christianity to become the universal gospel.[102]

Mandate for Christian Freedom

Paul in Galatians applied his understanding of Christian freedom to his own apostleship, to the Gentiles' relationship to Mosaic tradition,

[100] 5:13. It is exceedingly difficult to put a descriptive label on Paul's opponents. Enslin, *Christian Beginnings*, pp. 219–21, identifies two groups; Talbert, p. 29, one, which he calls, Galatian Syncretists. Galatians itself certainly reflects these "opposing ideas" whether or not they were advocated by an identifiable group.

[101] Stamm, "The Epistle to the Galatians," *IB*, X, p. 429.

[102] David Bronson, "Paul, Galatians, and Jerusalem," *Journal of The American Academy of Religion*, XXXV (1967), 119–128, argues that unacknowledged political and social issues lie in the background of the theological discussion in Galatians. Paul and Jews of the Diaspora aim to merge with Roman life while maintaining Jewish loyalty, but James and the Jerusalem leaders become increasingly nationalistic, an attitude which ultimately led to their destruction.

and to practical ethics. This development is evident in a brief outline of the epistle:

Introduction. 1:1–10
    A. Salutation. 1:1–5
    B. Occasion of letter. 1:6–10

  I. A Gospel by Revelation: Paul's Apostolic Authority From God Through Christ. 1:11–2:21
    A. Paul's commission as an apostle dependent upon Christ. 1:11–17
    B. Paul's role recognized by Jerusalem leaders. 1:18–2:10
    C. Paul's message affirmed in conflict with Peter. 2:11–21

  II. The Righteous Live by Faith: Defense of the Gospel of Christian Freedom. 3:1–4:31
    A. Experience of Galatians demonstrates Christian freedom. 3:1–5
    B. Abraham's faith illustrates freedom from law. 3:6–18
    C. Interim function of law. 3:19–25
    D. Status of free men. 3:26–4:11
    E. Appeal to personal relationships. 4:12–20
    F. Allegory of Christian freedom. 4:21–31

  III. For Freedom Set Free: Application of the Gospel of Christian Freedom. 5:1–6:10
    A. Preserve Christian freedom. 5:1–12
    B. Walk by the Spirit. 5:13–26
    C. Bear one another's burdens. 6:1–6
    D. Cultivate life in the Spirit. 6:7–10

Concluding appeal and benediction. 6:11–18

The abruptness with which Galatians begins is noteworthy among the Pauline epistles. In most Pauline letters the salutation is followed by a generous section expressing gratitude for the faithfulness of the believers, but in Galatians the argument is introduced even before the salutation is finished. The argument actually intrudes upon the salutation. The Galatians evidently were on the verge of abandoning the gospel which they had come to know through Paul. Some opponents of Paul's message had attacked his authority as an apostle in an effort to discredit his interpretation. In a spirit of urgency bordering on hostility Paul defended his commission as an apostle from the opening sentence:

Paul an apostle—not from men nor through man, but through Jesus Christ and God the Father, who raised him from the dead—and all the brethren who are with me, to the churches of Galatia. . . .[103]

[103] 1:1–2.

Friendly greeting and thanksgiving give way to surprise and indignation. The apostle is astonished that the Galatians have so quickly
turned away from the gospel which had been preached to them and
outraged at those who wished to pervert that gospel. After his vigorous opening statement Paul proceeded to defend the gospel which he
had preached to the Galatians along three lines corresponding to the
major divisions of the letter.

A Gospel by Revelation (1:11–2:21). The first part of the argument centers in Paul's understanding of his apostleship. Galatian opponents aimed to undermine Paul's interpretation of the gospel by
disclaiming his authority as a preacher. This may have taken either
one of two directions. Circumcision may have been justified on the
part of the opponents by associating Paul with the Jerusalem authorities who supported circumcision, or Paul's opposition to circumcision
may have been counteracted by claiming that he did not have the
approval of the Jerusalem leaders.[104] In any event, Paul vigorously
attacked his opponents not only to justify or defend his own role as
an apostle, but also to vindicate the gospel by separating it from any
external authority. The real point is that the authority of the gospel
as preached by Paul is independent of any human authority. Even if
Paul himself or "an angel from heaven" preached a different gospel,
the message could not be authenticated by the person doing the preaching (1:8–9). This is so because the gospel preached by Paul was not
man's gospel. Emphatically the apostle declares,

For I did not receive it from man, nor was I taught it, but it came through a
revelation of Jesus Christ. (1:12)

The defense of the concept of a gospel by revelation is then given
in one of the more extensive autobiographical sections in Paul's writing. It covers most of the first two chapters of the epistle and refers
to three important items. First, Paul recalls his participation in the
persecution of the Church. It is just as inconceivable to assume that
his gospel came from the Twelve as to assume that the persecution
was the result of consultation with them. "Just as he had no contact
with the pillars of the church in Jerusalem before his conversion, so
he sought no conference with them immediately afterward." [105] Sec-

---

[104] The entire attitude of Galatians demonstrates that the account of apostolic
harmony in Acts is overdrawn. Paul's assertion of independence illustrates conflicts which existed among the highest leaders of the Church. Cf. Sandmel, *A
Jewish Understanding of The New Testament*, pp. 89–90.

[105] Stamm, "The Epistle to the Galatians," *IB*, X, p. 456.

ond, when he did confer with the Jerusalem authorities, it was not to be taught the gospel in scribal fashion. In fact, the apostles heard him and gave approval to the expression of the gospel that he had already formulated. Paul "had been entrusted with the gospel to the uncircumcised" (2:7) by the pillars who gave him "the right hand of fellowship" (2:9). He refused to surrender the principle of Christian freedom from bondage to the law in order that "the truth of the gospel might be preserved" (2:5).

Third, Paul illustrates independence from all human authority by underscoring his resistance to Peter at Antioch (2:11–14). Peter on some unspecified occasion came to Antioch and was impressed by the harmony of Jewish and Gentile Christians living together in a single community. He willingly shared the full implications of Gentile freedom, abandoning not only circumcision but also the restrictive eating codes which had been traditionally maintained to keep the Jews distinctive and separate from Gentiles. However, when certain men of the ultra-conservative group arrived in Antioch from Jerusalem, Peter conceded to their position and refused to eat with the Gentile Christians. Other Jewish Christians, and even Barnabas, joined Peter obviously out of deference to the conscience of their less liberal brethren.

Paul saw this behavior as unforgivable compromise, a surrender to outworn customs and betrayal of basic principles. In a stinging speech (2:15–21) the Apostle severely rebuked Peter and those who shared his position (including Barnabas). They were all hypocrites of insincerity, concealing their straightforward understanding of the gospel behind the masks of peace at any price! This was inexcusable. Not only Mosaic law, but also any form of legalism, is a violation of basic freedom in Christ. Thus, Paul negatively demonstrated his independence from Peter's sanction and positively introduced the key idea in the gospel of freedom.

I have been crucified with Christ; it is no longer I who live, but Christ who lives in me; . . . I do not nullify the grace of God; for if justification were through the law, then Christ died to no purpose. (2:20a, 21)

The Righteous Live By Faith (3:1–4:31). The account of Paul's speech to Peter introduces the second main theme in the argument of Galatians. Ideas tumble over each other as the Apostle's enthusiasm almost overcomes his logic, but the controlling idea remains clear: faith in Christ is the sole ground for man's salvation. Faith surpasses law; faith replaces law. "He who through faith is righteous shall live" (3:11), but "all who rely on works of the law are under a curse" (3:10).

In chapters three and four of the epistle Paul leaves the defense of his own apostolic commission and deals directly with the main issue. He is concerned to refute the Judaizers, but more he wants to affirm that everyone, Jew and Greek, slave and freedman, male and female (3:28), are acceptable to God through faith rather than through works of law. Of all people the foolish Galatians should know this! Had they not received the Spirit and witnessed miracles before they had kept the law? The irony of desiring to turn to the law which could not bring them salvation and the Holy Spirit!

As primary witness to the truth of the gospel Paul calls Abraham, the father of Jewish covenant and promise. Whence came Abraham's salvation? Paul finds his answer in Genesis 15:6. Abraham "believed God and it was reckoned to him as righteousness" (3:6). The law, given centuries later than the great patriarchal founder, certainly did not annul the covenant previously ratified by God (3:17). Abraham lived before there was a Mosaic law and therefore, according to Paul, gained salvation without it.[106] The Church as spiritual descendant of Abraham shares his freedom from law. "God, in granting his Spirit to Gentiles who believed the apostolic message, has acted according to his promise to Abraham." [107]

The freedom of the believer from law is made even more emphatic by the insufficiency of law. Law had been given as a temporary custodian until Christ came (3:24), but in no sense could it "make alive" (3:21). Depending upon the law to bring life is no more valid than their earlier trust in the "elemental spirits" of paganism. These elemental spirits may well have been the planetary spirits of apocalyptic Judaism as it bordered on Gnosticism. If so, Paul is engaging in a mild anti-Gnostic polemic by speaking of the spirits' impoverishment through the triumph of Christ. Both law and spirits bring slavery, not life. Paul stresses the insufficiency of law by citing the Old Testament scriptures. Since "everyone who does not abide by all things written in the book of the law" [108] is guilty, man the lawbreaker is under the curse of the law. Law cannot be kept entirely; therefore it cannot bring righteousness. The curse of law has been removed by one "who hangs on a tree" [109] and thereby takes the curse upon itself. Only "he who through faith is righteous shall live" (Habakkuk 2:4).

---

[106] Contrariwise, the rabbis would have argued that Abraham observed the law, even before it was given. See Sandmel, *A Jewish Understanding of The New Testament*, p. 89.

[107] Nils A. Dahl, "The Story of Abraham in Luke–Acts," *Studies in Luke–Acts*, eds. Keck and Martyn, p. 140.

[108] Cf. Deut. 27:26.

[109] Cf. Deut. 27:23.

Paul pressed for acceptance of his gospel by an appeal to personal affection which the Galatians had demonstrated toward him (4:12–20). At one time they would have even plucked out their eyes for him! Their relationship had always been cordial and Paul wanted it to remain so. Would he, their friend who had been received as an angel of God, deceive them with a false gospel and risk their scorn? The Apostle implies that, although their apostasy has done him no personal harm, he will consider continued flirtations with the Judaizers a personal affront. Worse, their adoption as sons of God will be forfeited and they will be in bondage to law. The point is driven home through an allegory on Abraham's two sons (4:20–31). Those who insist upon law follow the way of Ishmael, the natural son, and are destined for exclusion from covenant. Those who walk in faith, however, are descendants of Isaac, the son of promise. Through Christ they belong to Abraham's family and become heirs of the promise as free persons. They must remain free by relying on "faith working through love" (5:6).

For Freedom Set Free (5:1–6:10). In the final chapters of Galatians Paul admonishes the believers not to surrender the freedom which has come so generously through Christ Jesus. They are not slaves who have purchased their freedom with their own ransom money. Rather it is God's grace-gift through Christ. "For freedom Christ has set us free" (5:1). Therefore, the Christian must not submit again to a yoke of slavery; he must be fully committed to God's grace.

Freedom, however, cannot be taken "as an opportunity to the flesh" (5:13). Probably some Galatians interpreted their freedom from law as an occasion to indulgence. If they were free from the law, could they not live freely? Paul responds that those who "live by the Spirit" must also "walk by the Spirit" (5:25). Through Christ the slave has been delivered from bondage to the law, but he has also been introduced to a new kind of self-imposed slavery. He who belongs to Christ crucifies his own flesh with its passions and desires (5:24) in order to live responsibly with his fellow man. In this way Christian freedom is man's task as well as God's gift.[110] It has been established freely by divine action, but it is also maintained by willing intention to follow the desires of the Spirit. Those who propose to live by the Spirit will demonstrate the good life as surely as those who obey the law. Christians need no law to make them love their neighbor.

For Paul the key to walking by the Spirit is love. For the Christian, love is the moral equivalent for the rules of law and as such safeguards

[110] Stamm, "The Epistle to the Galatians," *IB*, X, p. 556.

Christian freedom. "Through love" believers become "slaves of one another" because the whole law is fulfilled in one word, "You shall love your neighbor as yourself." [111] Every man considers himself his brother's neighbor in a relationship defined by freedom in Christ. Each so esteems the other that neither seeks to take advantage of the other's voluntary self-enslavement.[112] Both desire to invest their own gifts for the advantage of the other. In this way each person "bears one another's burdens" (6:2) at the same time that he bears "his own load" (6:5). The cultivation of these reciprocal relations in Christian freedom is part of the "sowing to the Spirit" which produces the harvest of eternal life (6:7–9). Paul concludes,

So then, as we have opportunity, let us do good to all men, and especially to those who are of the household of faith. (6:10)

Paul ends the letter to the Galatians in his own handwriting (6:11) with an emphatic warning against the Judaizers and a final appeal to reject every form of legalistic gospel. "For neither circumcision counts for anything, nor uncircumcision, but a new creation" (6:15). God's benediction is invoked upon all whose lives conforms to the essentially spiritual character of faith. Thus, the Galatian epistle becomes for the early believers a mandate for Christian freedom, denouncing any physical, material, or human sanction for faith and affirming the fundamental importance of God's work in Christ.

The letter catches the spirit of the Jerusalem conference and realistically confronts the early Christian community with its fundamental nature at the strategically important time of its movement into the non-Jewish world. It affirms the independence of the gospel from legalistic forms, either Judaistic or Christian. Although the issue of circumcision may sound strange to modern ears, the gospel of Christian freedom is enduringly relevant. "Paul's doctrines of freedom in the Spirit, the morality of love rather than law, and salvation by faith set forth here remain at the center of the Christian faith." [113]

SUGGESTED READINGS

In addition to the commentaries on Acts listed in Chapter Seven see:

DAVIES, W. D., *Paul and Rabbinic Judaism* (Seabury, 1955). Emphasizes Paul's inheritance from rabbinic Judaism.

[111] 5:13–14. Paul develops the theme of the "super-excellent way" in I Cor. 13. See below, pp. 317–318.
[112] Stamm, "The Epistle to the Galatians," *IB*, X, p. 556.
[113] Selby, *Toward the Understandting of St. Paul*, p. 250.

DEISSMANN, ADOLF, *Paul: A Study in Social and Religious History* (Harper, 1957). A classic on Paul published originally in 1910 and emphasizes "Christ mysticism" as a central concept of Paul's theology.

DIBELIUS, MARTIN, and WERNER G. KÜMMEL, *Paul* (Westminster, 1953). A helpful summary of Paul and his theology.

DUNCAN, GEORGE S., *The Epistle of Paul to the Galatians* (Harper, 1934).

HUNTER, A. M., *Interpreting Paul's Gospel* (SCM Press, 1954). A simple book on Paul's thought.

————, *Paul and His Predecessors* (Westminster, 1961). A helpful introduction to Paul's theology.

KNOX, JOHN, *Chapters in a Life of Paul* (Abingdon, 1950).

RAMSAY, WILLIAM M., *The Cities of St. Paul: Their Influence on His Life and Thought* (Baker, 1960). First published in 1907, but still a helpful volume.

————, *St. Paul the Traveller and Roman Citizen* (Baker, 1960). A classic which is still useful today.

SELBY, DONALD J., *Toward the Understanding of St. Paul* (Prentice-Hall, 1962).

STAMM, RAYMOND T., "Galatians: Introduction and Exegesis," *IB*, Vol. X.

STEWART, JAMES S., *A Man In Christ: The Vital Elements of St. Paul's Religion* (Harper, 1935). An examination of Paul's theology in light of his religious experience.

9

The Gospel in Macedonia
and Achaia (Acts 16-20)

Paul's Galatian mission and the liberalized attitude expressed in the Jerusalem conference set the door to the Roman world ajar for Christian expansion. The Church now undertook a more ambitious missionary venture which is described in Acts as a major mission of Paul into the regions around the Aegean Sea. The Apostle's work in this territory encompassed most of what has been commonly called his second and third missionary journeys. The mission began with a return visit to the churches of South Galatia and perhaps a trip into North Galatia. To Luke, however, the real enterprise was launched at Troas by a vision which summoned Paul into Macedonia and Achaia. Subsequently, the Apostle endeavored to evangelize the chief cities of the Aegean region until the mission was concluded with an extended stay in Ephesus, the most important city in southwestern Asia Minor. The period is probably the most significant epoch in Paul's life and certainly the most productive.

Paul's companions on this mission were Silas, Timothy, and Luke. Sometime after the Jerusalem conference, a breach between Paul and Barnabas developed. Acts suggests that the two missionaries could not agree over John Mark, who had prematurely left the Galatian mission. Barnabas, according to Acts (15:36–40), wanted to take Mark on the new mission, but Paul was unwilling to risk another defection. The controversy may have involved an even more basic issue. According to Paul,[1] Barnabas had yielded to Jewish Christian pressure to give up

[1] Gal. 2:13.

282

communion fellowship with Gentiles in Antioch. His conservative attitude must have been disappointing to Paul and perhaps was a more significant factor in their separation than the disagreement over John Mark. Paul would have seen Barnabas' attitude as too great a hindrance in a campaign that even more than the Galatian mission would move the Christian movement from traditional Judaism. Consequently, Barnabas took Mark and sailed to Cyprus while Paul chose Silas as an associate for the Aegean mission.

Very little is known about Silas.[2] Although he is mentioned frequently, he is never assigned the status accorded to Barnabas in the earlier Galatian mission. Silas had been one of the leading men in the Jerusalem church chosen to carry the findings of the Jerusalem conference to Antioch. From this and from the fact that Paul chose him to replace Barnabas we may conjecture that he was more Hellenistic than Barnabas. He is mentioned in I Peter and, after completing his work with Paul, may have been associated with Peter in a mission to northern Asia Minor.[3] Silas remained with Paul during most of the Aegean mission, but, like most of Paul's associates, Silas was overshadowed by the dominant and aggressive Apostle.

Timothy is more strategic in Luke's report of the Aegean mission. He first appeared as a disciple at Lystra (Acts 16:1f.), probably one of Paul's converts on the earlier Galatian tour. His mother was a Jewish Christian and his father a Gentile, presumably a pagan. When Paul revisited Galatia after the Jerusalem conference, he circumcised young Timothy [4] and enlisted him as a fellow minister. Timothy remained with him during the entire Aegean ministry and evidently became a trusted and faithful associate. Paul looked back upon their relationship with favor, mentioning Timothy with esteem and devotion. On at least two occasions Timothy was sent as Paul's representative to established churches to encourage them in the faith.[5] He is regularly included in the Pauline letters as a fellow correspondent.[6] An isolated reference in I Corinthians (16:10–11) hints that Paul's

[2] Also referred to by the Latinized form of his name, "Silvanus." Cf. I Thess. 1:1.

[3] Some suggest that he was the author or at least had a major hand in the composition of I Peter, but on this see below, pp. 418–421.

[4] Ernst Haenchen, "The Book of Acts as Source Material for the History of Early Christianity," *Studies in Luke–Acts,* eds. Keck and Martyn, p. 271, treats this simply as "one of those slanderous rumors which were spread abroad about Paul."

[5] Cf. I Thess. 3:2; I Cor. 4:17.

[6] Rom. 16:21; I Thess. 1:1; II Thess. 1:1; II Cor. 1:1; Philippians 1:1; Col. 1:1; Philemon 1:1.

young colleague may have lacked self-confidence, but Paul obviously accepted Timothy as worthy and assigned him major responsibilities in the Aegean mission.

Luke, usually identified as the author of Acts and the Third Gospel, was also a helper on this tour. The place of Luke's origin is uncertain, but it is entirely possible that he was a Macedonian, possibly from Philippi. The "we" passages [7] begin with the Acts narration of the Macedonian call (16:10–17). If it can be assumed that Luke wrote these firsthand accounts, then it follows that he joined Paul at Troas and remained with the missionary party as it moved into Macedonia. Professor Ramsay offers the attractive suggestion that the Macedonian in Paul's visionary experience was actually Luke, who through a series of contacts challenged Paul to carry the gospel into Greece by crossing the channel from Troas to Philippi.[8] Whether or not Luke wrote the "we" passages or was a native of Philippi, he was a Gentile well-fitted for assistance in the Gentile mission. He was also a "beloved physician" [9] and doubtlessly served Paul in medical ways.[10] Luke remained deeply loyal to the Apostle and earned both his gratitude and his admiration.[11]

THE AEGEAN MISSION

Paul's work around the Aegean Sea probably extended over the better part of the years A.D. 51 to 57. For convenience of discussion the Acts description of the Apostle's Aegean mission may be divided into three phases: the Macedonian, the Achaian, and the Asian. First, he spent some time in Macedonia preaching in the most important cities along the Via Egnatia, the main Roman road across northern Greece. Churches were established at Philippi, Thessalonica, and Berea. Then the Apostle moved into Achaia. After a brief and relatively unsuccessful ministry in Athens, Paul went to Corinth where he spent about eighteen months building one of the most important

[7] See above, p. 194.

[8] W. M. Ramsay, St. Paul the Traveller and the Roman Citizen, pp. 202–203. The fact that the first person form is dropped when Paul leaves Philippi suggests that the author of the "we" passages may have been a native of that city.

[9] Col. 4:14.

[10] W. K. Hobart, The Medical Language of St. Luke, on the basis of an extensive study of the language of Luke–Acts concluded that the medical terminology of the writings demonstrate conclusively that they were written by a doctor. This hypothesis has been shown to be untenable, however, by the careful study by H. J. Cadbury, The Style and Literary Method of Luke, pp. 39–72.

[11] II Tim. 4:11; Philemon 24.

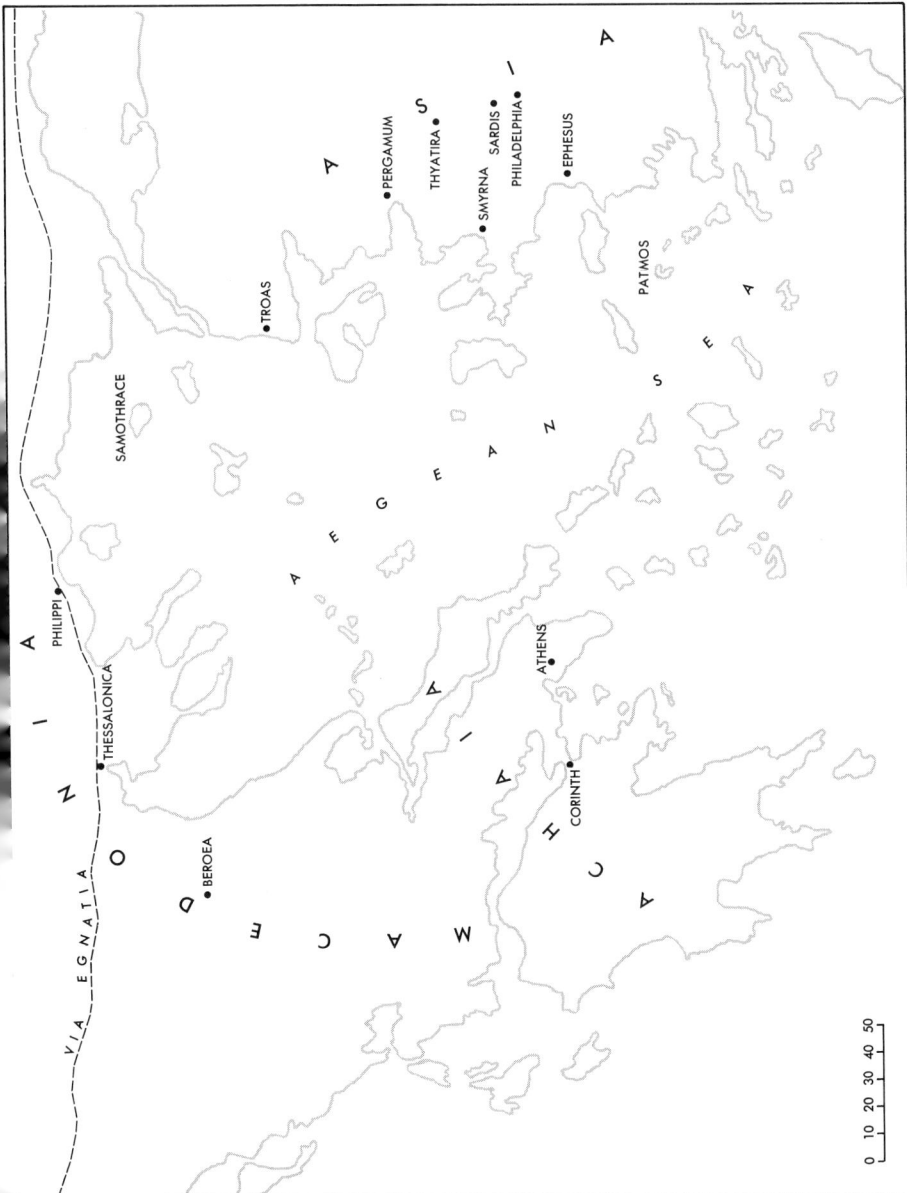

Figure 9–1. Paul's Aegean Mission.

churches of his entire career. After the stay in Corinth, Paul traveled to Jerusalem and Antioch and then returned to Ephesus for a mission of more than two years. During this period, an outstanding church was established in the city and preaching was done either by Paul or under his sponsorship throughout the surrounding area. While at Ephesus the Apostle renewed his contact with the Corinthian church and wrote several letters to them. During this second campaign, the Apostle was able to establish a strong foothold in Greece and western Asia Minor and thereby advance the cause of the faith farther into the Gentile world.

Macedonia

The Macedonian Call. After the Jerusalem conference and the subsequent visit to Antioch, Paul and Silas set out upon a major enterprise. They traveled northward from Antioch through Asia Minor to revisit Galatia. At Lystra Timothy joined the group and they proceeded to Troas on the western coast of Asia Minor. The book of Acts carefully notes that the course which brought the missionaries to Troas was determined by the Holy Spirit. The group did not linger in Galatia and was "forbidden by the Holy Spirit to speak the word in Asia" (Acts 16:6). Although they entertained the idea of a mission to Bithynia where there was a heavy Jewish population, "the Spirit of Jesus did not allow them" (Acts 16:7) to do so. Luke's point is perfectly clear: the missionaries were directed by the hand of God to a destiny at Troas, the door opening into Greece. To Luke, Troas marked the threshold of the West. Troas was the regular port of call for vessels journeying between Asia Minor and Macedonia and at this city the Apostle's most strategic work was to begin.

The book of Acts sees Paul's public mission largely in terms of the Aegean region. The Galatian mission was primarily prelude to work in this realm and the Acts story after the Aegean mission deals mainly with the circumstances which brought Paul to Rome. Most of Luke's missionary descriptions center in Paul's work around the Aegean Sea. The Pauline letters are also predominantly oriented around the Aegean region. Thus when the Apostle responded to the Macedonian call vision and crossed to Greece, he began a very significant part of his mission. Although the Apostle's eye was fixed on Rome, the Aegean mission represented the series of events by which the gospel genuinely passed to the Gentile world. For both Luke and Paul Aegea was the gateway to the imperial capital.

Acts emphasizes the importance of the Aegean period, not only by reporting the story in great detail, but also by emphasizing two companion themes in the story. First, Luke stresses the Jewish rejection of Christianity over against the Church's concern to interpret her faith as the fulfillment of Judaism.[12] Paul and his companions entered the synagogues, but encountered hostility and open rejection from the Jews. Correspondingly, Luke indicates that Paul increasingly turned to the Gentiles. After Troas the Apostle's work was concentrated in the influential Greco-Roman cultural centers, and in growing numbers pagans were converted to Christianity apart from any earlier connections with Judaism. The Lucan Paul is proud of being a Roman citizen and Christianity can spread without official resistance.[13]

Luke also stresses the importance of the Aegean mission with a dramatic report of the Macedonian call. The revelation of God's purpose through the visionary experience is reminiscent of an Old Testament motif which associates the revelation of God's will with an unavoidable and attention-claiming interruption. At Troas a Macedonian appeared to Paul and pleaded, "Come over to Macedonia and help us" (Acts 16:9). The Macedonian may have been Luke himself, who may have come to Troas and in several conversations convinced Paul that a mission to Macedonia would be worthwhile.[14] For Acts, however, the Aegean mission came about, not merely as the result of a conversation among concerned men, but through God's intervention to establish the direction of Paul's mission.

In Philippi. When Paul and his companions crossed the northern Aegean, a new day of possibility and promise lay before them. A two-day trip carried them by the island landmark Samothrace, landed them at Neopolis, and brought them to Philippi. Luke describes Philippi as "the leading city of the district of Macedonia" (Acts 16:12), although Thessalonica was the provincial capital and Amphipolis a more important center. Nevertheless Philippi, laying about ten miles inland, was a strategic city of no little import in Macedonia. Originally called Krenides because of nearby "springs," the city had been enlarged and renamed by Philip of Macedon. Nearby, more than a century prior

---

12 See Frank Stagg, *The Book of Acts,* p. 166.

13 Hans Conzelmann, "Luke's Place in the Development of Early Christianity," *Studies in Luke–Acts,* eds. Keck and Martyn, p. 301.

14 William Barclay, *The Acts of The Apostles,* p. 131, believes that Luke, whom he assumes to be the author of Acts, joined the group here because Paul needed his professional services. He conjectures that ill health had prevented Paul's proposed travel into northern Asia Minor provinces and thus Luke, the physician, became his personal doctor at Troas.

Figure 9–2. Ruins at Philippi; entrance to a prison traditionally associated with the Acts account of the Philippian jailer. (Source: Foreign Mission Board, SBC.)

to Paul's arrival, Anthony and Octavian defeated Brutus and Cassius in a struggle for control of the Roman empire. Subsequently, the city became a military outpost [15] and continually grew in size and influence. Through the city ran the famous Via Egnatia, the chief overland route through Macedonia carrying trade and traffic between Asia and Rome.[16]

The Lucan emphasis upon the separateness of Christianity from Judaism becomes evident in the description of Paul's work in Philippi.

[15] Cf. Acts 16:12.

[16] Important excavations at Philippi were conducted by École Francaise d'Athenes from 1914 to 1938. Reports of these may be found in *Bulletin de correspondance hellénique* for these years; for examples: Jacques Couprey at Michel Feyel, "Inscriptiones de Philippes," LX (1936), 37–58; Paul Lemerle, "Palestre Romaine a Philippes," LXI (1937), 86–102; Paul Collart, "Inscriptiones de Philippes," LXII (1938), 409–432.

The city may have been without a significant Jewish population. Paul found only a small band of Jews, mostly women, meeting on the Sabbath "outside the gate" at "a place of prayer" (Acts 16:13). A synagogue does not seem to have been available and the presence of ten adult Jewish men would have demanded one.[17] Jack Finegan offers the suggestion that the small group was meeting at the Roman arch over the Via Egnatia near the Gangites River about a mile from Philippi.[18] But whatever the situation, the point is important to Luke. An informal gathering, and not the official synagogue, was the focus of Paul's work at the outset of the Aegean mission. He preached to "the women who had come together" and from this group came Paul's first Macedonian convert, Lydia of Thyatira, apparently a Jewish proselyte and a woman of some wealth. Lydia offered the missionaries the hospitality of her home and probably the church itself assembled there.

Luke's account of Paul's preaching in Philippi also stresses the vindication of the Apostle's message before Roman authorities. In the story of Philippian imprisonment developed along the motif of reversal-of-fortune, Luke demonstrates the success of the gospel in the non-Jewish community. According to Acts 16:16–24, a deranged slave girl was being exploited for gain by owners who claimed that a "spirit of Python" spoke through her. According to popular belief, "Python" was a snake at Delphi embodying a God. The presence of the "spirit of Python" supposedly produced inspired speech.[19] When Paul exorcised the spirit, he was taken before the magistrates by the girl's enraged masters and charged with advocating unlawful practices. The charges were not theological, but financial; by healing the girl the missionaries caused her owners to lose their income and through their illegal proselytism disturbed the city.[20] Paul and Silas were beaten and imprisoned, providing the occasion for one of the key passages in the book of Acts.

An earthquake in the night freed the imprisoned missionaries and led to the conversion of the Philippian jailer. In this event, entirely apart from any previous Jewish connections and separate from any Judaistic context, a pagan became a Christian simply because he confessed belief in Jesus (Acts 16:31, 34).

---

[17] See The Babylonian Talmud, Seder Mo'ed, IV, Magillah.

[18] See his article, "Philippi," *IDB*, III, pp. 786–787.

[19] This is sometimes taken to refer to ventriloquism. Cf. F. J. Foakes-Jackson and Kirsopp Lake, eds., *The Beginnings of Christianity*, IV, p. 192.

[20] Kirsopp Lake and H. J. Cadbury, eds., *The Beginnings of Christianity*, V, p. 195.

The Samaritans were Israelites and cherished the Torah; the proselyte converts had fully embraced Judaism; the Ethiopian eunuch and Cornelius were God-fearers who had been students of Judaism, as were many others won to Christianity through the synagogues. But here is a pagan whose salvation is through faith in the Lord Jesus and without the influence of circumcision or synagogue. The last group has now been reached.[21]

Luke underscores the Gentile acceptance of the gospel by playing down as much as possible the discord between Paul and Silas and the leaders of the Roman colony.[22] Paul appealed to his Roman citizenship which exempted him from all degrading forms of punishment. Beating and imprisonment were unjust and demanded public apology. Yet vindictiveness is absent from the story. Although public apology is demanded, Paul's struggle is not essentially with Roman authority. He is concerned that even the jailer "believe in the Lord Jesus" and be saved. The real point is that the disturbance has not come from the conflict of Christianity with Roman order. Paul is a Roman proclaiming a gospel which is appropriate to Romans. Paul and Silas were officially released by the city magistrates and an apology completely exonerated the apostles and freed them to leave Philippi.

Although the Acts narrative suggests that Paul's stay in Philippi was comparatively brief, the Apostle's later correspondence indicates that he was in the city long enough to establish a strong church. His Philippian letter exudes affection and reflects that the church "remained unwaveringly loyal to its founder." [23] Paul's gratitude for their enduring faithfulness shines through his opening words to the Philippians:

I thank my God in all my remembrance of you, always in every prayer of mine for you all making my prayer with joy, thankful for your partnership in the gospel from the first day until now. (1:3–5)

In Thessalonica and Beroea. From Philippi, Paul and his companions traveled along the Via Egnatia, obviously hoping to plant the gospel firmly along this important thoroughfare. They came to Thessalonica, which with Philippi shared the prosperity associated with East-West commerce. The city had been founded by Cassander, who named it after his wife, a sister of Alexander the Great. When Macedonia was made a Roman province in 148 B.C., Thessalonica became

---

[21] Stagg, *The Book of Acts*, p. 172.

[22] Haenchen, "The Book of Acts as Source Material for the History of Early Christianity," *Studies in Luke–Acts*, p. 273.

[23] G. H. C. Macgregor, "The Acts of The Apostles," *IB*, IX, p. 217. Cf. Philippians 1:3–11; 4:14–20.

Figure 9–3. Roadbed of the famed Via Egnatia over which the Apostle Paul traveled around Philippi and Thessalonica. (Source: Foreign Mission Board, SBC.)

the seat of Roman administration and developed into the chief city of the province.

In Thessalonica the pattern of Paul's earlier work in Galatia reappeared. He entered the Jewish synagogue in the city and on three successive sabbaths discussed the Scriptures like a typical Jewish rabbi, demonstrating Jesus to be the Messiah (Acts 17:3). But, although Paul worked through the synagogue, the Thessalonian church was basically Gentile. This is confirmed by the Apostle's later comment that these believers had "turned to God from idols" (I Thessalonians 1:9).

The Jews in Thessalonica were incensed because the many God-fearing Gentiles turned to Paul's mesage. They incited a riot against Jason at whose house the missionaries were staying and Jason was hailed before the local authorities.[24] Accused of supporting a seditious movement against Caesar by proclaiming Jesus as rival king, he was required to post a bond to preserve the peace. Meanwhile Paul and Silas were hurried away by night.

Luke's account of Paul's work at Thessalonica is apparently telescoped. The three weeks' discussion in the synagogue probably represents only preliminary phases of the work. Since he engaged in his tentmaking trade in order not to be a burden to the local church, he must have spent some time at Thessalonica.[25] He may even have carried on a wider preaching mission around Thessalonica, but his primary concern was to build firmly a strategic church in the principal city of Macedonia. That he was successful before he was forced to leave is seen in his later letter to Thessalonica: "For not only has the word of the Lord sounded forth from you in Macedonia and Achaia, but your faith in God has gone forth everywhere . . ." (I Thessalonians 1:8).

From Thessalonica, Paul moved to Beroea, a city of some prominence slightly south of the Via Egnatia and about forty-five miles from Thessalonica. Luke tells us little about the mission and, since no extant Pauline epistle is addressed to Beroea, the history of Paul's work there is obscure. Acts indicates that the Jews were freer from prejudice and thus more open to Paul's arguments about Jesus than the bigoted Thessalonians.[26] These liberal Jews "received the word with all eagerness, examining the scriptures daily to see if these things were so" (17:11b). That Silas remained in Beroea,[27] and that one of Paul's later companions was a certain "Sopater of Beroea" (Acts 20:3) suggest that a church was established here, including both Gentile and Jewish believers (Acts 17:12).

---

[24] Luke properly identifies these local officials as "politarchs" as confirmed by an inscription taken from a first century A.D. arch in Thessalonica. A discussion of the term appears in E. D. Burton, "The Politarchs," *American Journal of Theology,* II (1898), 598–632.

[25] See I Thess. 2:9; II Thess. 3:7–12.

[26] 17:11. Following here an interpretation of "more noble" which appears in F. J. Foakes-Jackson, *The Acts of The Apostles,* pp. 161–162.

[27] Acts states that Timothy also remained, but Paul corrects this. I Thess. 3:1–6 reports that Timothy did go to Athens with Paul and was later sent back to Thessalonica when Paul became anxious about the young church there. Various attempts to reconcile the Thessalonians passage with Acts 17:13–16 remain tentative. See Haenchen, "The Book of Acts as Source Material for the History of Early Christianity," *Studies in Luke–Acts,* p. 273.

Figure 9–4. The awesome Acropolis dominating modern Athens as it did the ancient city. (Source: Foreign Mission Board, SBC.)

Achaia

In Athens. Troublesome Jews came from Thessalonica, incited opposition, and forced Paul's departure from Beroea. Thence he moved by way of the sea southward to the province of Achaia. His first stop was at Athens, a city of little political or commercial consequence, but the cradle of classical culture. Although her greatest creative age had passed, Athens remained the seat of great learning and was still "the world's intellectual mecca."[28] Her citizenry tolerated discourse and debate in the agora,[29] even if their interest sometimes was no more than academic. Paul was undoubtedly accepted without opposition as a disputant who could catch the fancy of garrulous and inquisitive Athenians. But their air was condescension. To them Paul was no more than a "seed-picker"[30] who like a common sparrow picked at the scraps in the market-place. His ideas on Jesus and the resurrection

---

[28] Macgregor, "The Acts of The Apostles," *IB*, IX, p. 231.
[29] The "marketplace" of Acts 17:17.
[30] The literal translation of the word rendered "babbler" in the RSV.

Figure 9–5. The Areopagus from which Paul addressed his Athenian audience. (Source: American School of Classical Studies, Athens.)

(*anastasis* in Greek, perhaps thought to be a new goddess by the Athenians) were novel and therefore worthy of hearing (Acts 17:21), but certainly not to be taken seriously. Such an attitude of patronizing curiosity undoubtedly irritated the Apostle and explains, at least to some extent, the vigor with which he denounced Athenian idolatry.

The Lucan presentation of Paul's work in Athens centers in an address on the Areopagus. The synagogue is mentioned, but no report that Paul preached there on the sabbath is given. Although Luke leaves the impression of a confident Apostle who successfully debates with the Athenians, neither Acts nor Paul's letters report the founding of a church in Athens. In fact, Paul states that he arrived in Corinth "in much fear and trembling" (I Corinthians 2:3), suggesting perhaps that he was despondent over what had happened in Athens.

The speech which Luke attributes to Paul in Athens undoubtedly represents an early Christian apology before Greek culture. The sermon is quite atypical of Paul, who says of his preaching,

. . . my speech and my message were not in plausible words of wisdom, but in demonstration of the Spirit and power, that your faith might not rest in the wisdom of men but in the power of God.[31]

---

[31] I Cor. 2:4, 5.

In contrast, the sermon in Athens, restated or perhaps composed by Luke, aims to fit the demands of the occasion.[32] As an apology for the faith, it is a "most momentous Christian document from the beginnings of that extraordinary confrontation between Christianity and philosophy which was destined to continue through the following centuries . . ."[33] It shows us how Christians living when Acts was written confronted the pagan world with their faith.

The setting for the sermon is the Areopagus, the well-known Mars Hill at the foot of the Acropolis.[34] Paul's text was a supposed altar inscription to an "unknown god." No evidence of an inscription to a single deity, "the unknown god," exists, but several inscriptions to "unknown gods" adorned Athenian altars.[35] The speech gave these polytheistic labels a monotheistic interpretation and proceeded to declare a God who "does not live in shrines made by man." In the shadow of the Acropolis, which with the Parthenon and full statue of Athena dominated Athens, a "new" religion represented by a babbling Jew confronted the "old" religion in faded glory. This is the central issue at stake in Luke's narration of the event and report of the address.

Cleverly, the speech opens with words of flattery and compatibility. The Athenians are ironically described as very devout.[36] Quotations from Greek poetry are cited to illustrate the argument.[37] Athenian philosophers would have found in the sermon much with which they would have agreed. Epicureans would have accepted the idea that God needed nothing from human hands and that consequently worship through shrine or sacrifice was meaningless. The fundamental unity of all men was pivotal in the thinking of the Stoics and thus they would have joined in the affirmation that "he made from one every nation of men to live on all the face of the earth" (Acts 17:26a).

Several emphases in the sermon, however, ran counter to the thinking of the Athenian philosophers. The Epicureans believed in a God

[32] Martin Dibelius, *Studies in The Acts of The Apostles*, p. 71, believes that a speech so obviously adapted to Greek philosophy could not possibly be traced to Paul. For an opposite view see N. B. Stonehouse, *The Areopagus Address*, pp. 5–9.

[33] Hans Conzelmann, "The Address of Paul on the Areopagus," *Studies in Luke–Acts*, p. 217.

[34] There is little reason to conclude, as do some commentators, that Areopagus refers to the ruling council of Athens charged with the supervision of religious and educational affairs.

[35] See Adolf Deissmann, *Paul*, pp. 287–291.

[36] Acts 17:22. The KJV rendering "too superstitious" is quite misleading.

[37] Acts 17:28. The first quotation is sometimes attributed to Epimenides; the second comes from Aratus' *Phaenomena*.

Figure 9–6. The bema, or platform, in the Corinthian agora from which public speeches were delivered. (Source: American School of Classical Studies, Athens.)

completely removed from the world and indifferent to human affairs. A God who made the world and "commands all men everywhere to repent" (Acts 17:30) would have been scandalous to them. Stoics would have much preferred to talk about the World-soul than the Creator God. Both Epicureans and Stoics would have found a discussion of resurrection as the key to life's meaning too strange to be seriously considered by reasonable men. Nevertheless, some were willing to talk further and a few, including Dionysius the Aeropagite, believed; but evidently the mission in Athens was not successful enough for a church to be established.

In Corinth. From Athens Paul made his way to Corinth, the chief city of the Peloponnesian area of Achaia. The Corinth of Paul's day lay about two miles inland and nestled at the foot of Acrocorinth, a rocky hill almost two thousand feet high. In 146 B.C. the city had been captured and burned by the Roman Mummius, but in 44 B.C. it had been refounded by decree of Julius Caesar. As a Roman colony strategically located on the isthmus connecting the Peloponnesus with northern Achaia, Corinth had taken advantage of trade. Sea travelers between Rome and the East preferred to portage their goods, and

Figure 9–7. Ruins of the ancient temple of Apollo standing in the shadow of Acrocorinth in background. (Source: Greek National Tourist Office.)

often the ship itself, across the narrow, three and a half mile isthmus rather than risk the stormy sea route around the southern tip of Greece. Corinth controlled the movement of wares across the isthmus and so reaped a profit on East-West trade.

Commerce increased the cosmopolitan character of Corinth, already open to a great mixture of peoples as the seat of Roman provincial government. Among these was the typical colony of Jews, whose population had recently been swelled by an expulsion of Jews from Rome by Claudius because of disturbance centering in one "Chrestus," probably a Roman misspelling of "Christ." [38] Aquila and his wife Priscilla, devout Jews who were probably Christians when they left Rome, came to Corinth as part of the Claudius expulsion and shared with Paul both the vocation of tentmaker and his intense concern for the gospel. The couple became fast friends of Paul and after a time entertained him in their home.

Paul's extensive correspondence with this church supplements the Acts report so that the Corinthian community is better known than any other church established by the Apostle. Luke's concern in Acts, however, is with only two points. He first demonstrates the separation of

[38] Suetonius, *Life of Claudius*, XXV, 4.

the church from the synagogue.[39]   Initially Paul followed his usual pattern of working through the synagogue, concerned both to keep Christianity's legal status intact and to gain access to pagans who had already been attracted to the synagogue. But opposition forced him to set up headquarters in the house of Titius Justus adjacent to the synagogue. Ironically, even the ruler of the synagogue, Crispus, became a convert. Acts drives home the point of the Jewish rejection of the gospel with a telling quote attributed to Paul,

Your blood be upon your heads! I am innocent. From now on I will go to the Gentiles. (18:6b)

Second, Luke reports a Jewish protest before the Roman proconsul Gallio. The basis of the charge was that Paul had been "persuading men to worship God contrary to the law" (Acts 18:13). Thus, the Jews aimed to enlist the Roman official to declare Christianity illegal, that is, unrecognized and unprotected by Rome. In what for Luke must have been an ideal response of a state official, Gallio refused to enter what he considered a totally private matter. "The State can declare that it has no interest in the controversy between Jews and Christians, for its Law is not affected by it." [40] Undoubtedly Luke sees in Gallio's non-action more than the proconsul intends, namely, that Christianity has the status of a recognized religion.

Paul remained in Corinth for a year and a half during A.D. 50–51, but beyond these two events Acts does not elaborate upon his activities. Judging from the later Corinthian correspondence, the church was predominantly Gentile and constantly plagued by moral problems arising from the inability of converted pagans to separate themselves from their former ways. The congregation was continually in turmoil because of divisions of loyalty to Paul, Peter, and Apollos. Further, I Corinthians 1:26–29 suggests that many members of the Corinthian church were from the lower economic and social classes:

. . . not many of you were wise according to worldly standards, not many were powerful, not many were of noble birth; but God chose what is foolish in the world to shame the wise, God chose what is weak in the world to shame the strong, God chose what is low and despised in the world, even things that are not, to bring to nothing things that are, so that no human being might boast in the presence of God.

---

[39] An inscription found on a stone from the ruins of ancient Corinth is believed to read, "Synagogue of the Hebrews." The inscription probably dates later than the time of Paul.

[40] Hans Conzelmann, *The Theology of St. Luke*, p. 142.

In contrast to the "dependable, warmhearted Philippians" the Corinthians were "fickle, childish, quarrelsome, selfish, and lacking in moral sense," [41] perhaps because of their varied and poor backgrounds. Yet Luke indicates that the Corinthian church grew considerably (Acts 18:10) and Paul's extreme concern when the church was threatened with internal division suggests a community of great significance.

Asia

Acts indicates that Paul left Corinth soon after the arrival of Gallio, whose proconsulship may be dated in A.D. 50–51 because of an inscription discovered at Delphi.[42] Although exonerated by the Roman proconsul, Paul probably felt increasing pressure from Jewish opposition and departed for Antioch and Jerusalem, taking Priscilla and Aquila with him as far as Ephesus. At Ephesus Paul's co-workers met Apollos, an eloquent, young Alexandrian who had already come under the influence of some Christian teacher. Priscilla and Aquila took him in their charge and "expounded to him the way of God more accurately" (Acts 18:26), that is, they instructed him in the meaning and implications of facts about Jesus which Apollos already knew. Undoubtedly Priscilla and Aquila delivered instructions according to what they had learned from Paul, but judging from Acts the paths of the Apostle and Apollos never crossed. While Apollos was in Ephesus, Paul was making his way to Caesarea, presumably to Jerusalem, and back to Antioch in Syria.[43] By the time Paul returned to Ephesus through Galatia, Apollos had crossed the Aegean to Corinth where he evidently enjoyed a successful ministry built upon the earlier work of the Apostle.[44]

In Ephesus. In Ephesus Paul began a new phase of work.[45] Here he revisited mission points earlier established and remained directly in contact, primarily through correspondence, with the Corinthian church. For approximately three years, however, his activity centered in Ephesus and Asia, the Roman province of which Ephesus was capital.

[41] So Donald J. Selby, *Toward the Understanding of St. Paul*, p. 214.

[42] See Deissmann, *Paul*, pp. 261–286, for a full discussion of the significance of the inscription.

[43] Acts summarizes these events in 18:18–28. John Knox, *Chapters in A Life of Paul*, pp. 47–48, believes that the Jerusalem conference occurred on this visit to Jerusalem.

[44] Cf. I Cor. 3:3–10.

[45] This is commonly referred to as his third missionary journey.

Figure 9–8. Panoramic view of the ruins of Ephesus, where Paul conducted one of his most extensive missions. (Source: Foreign Mission Board, SBC.)

Like the other cities in which Paul preached during the Aegean mission, Ephesus was an outstanding center of the area. Officially the city was thoroughly Roman. Earlier Ephesus had gained importance as a city of Alexander the Great and his Hellenistic successors. However, by 64 B.C. when Roman control was established over the western Mediterranean by the viceroys of Pompey, Ephesus was already the chief city of Asia Minor. By mid-first century A.D. she was flourishing under Roman patronage. As the seat of the proconsul she headed a confederation of Asian cities known as the Asiarchate. The imperial spirit was fostered by emperor worship, and civic benefactors of Rome called Asiarchs (Acts 19:31) promoted loyalty to imperial authority.

Culturally, however, Ephesus was cosmopolitan, in Paul's day a busy

Figure 9–9. The multi-breasted Artemis, a productive mother-goddess worshipped in Ephesus. (Source: Foreign Mission Board, SBC.)

seaport, the western terminus of overland trade routes from the East. Commercial activity undoubtedly brought to Ephesus people from all over the East. Some Ephesians, influenced by eastern attitudes, attributed reality to demonic powers and consequently gave high place to their control through magic.[46] Evidently, magic enjoyed considerable status among the Ephesians, because Luke goes to great extremes to demonstrate the superiority of Pauline exorcism over its Ephesian rivals.[47] He reports that Paul's mastery of itinerant Jewish exorcists led to the burning of magical books valued at "fifty thousand pieces of silver."

The outstanding illustration of the broad base of Ephesian culture confronted by the Apostle was the worship of Artemis.[48] This goddess was worshipped in the Greek world more widely than any other female deity.[49] Her temple, one of the wonders of the ancient world, was situated in Ephesus, but her worship was practiced widely in the cities of Asia and throughout much of the Roman empire. There is little exaggeration in the statement that Artemis was worshipped in "all Asia and the world" (Acts 19:27).

Artemis was a goddess of diverse characteristics. In classical mythology she was the virgin huntress, the protector of chastity, patron of marriageable women, and helper of women in childbirth. Popular religion through the years attached to these tender functions cruel and almost savage traits. Artemis became raw nature, wild and destructive, symbolized by such animals as the wild boar, the wolf, or the stag. The Ephesian Artemis, however, more resembled the Asian mother-goddess Cybele. She was the productive mother, protector of fertility in the whole creation, usually represented "as a female figure with multiple breasts, with lions, bulls, and rams worked in relief upon her shoulders and legs, with a bee just above her feet, and her head surmounted by a turret-crown." [50] The goddess with these general fertility associations achieved wide popularity in Ephesus.

Luke's account,[51] however, is not primarily concerned with theological assessment of the Artemis cult. Conflict developed because Paul's preaching threatened the vested interests of those who made and sold shrines to interested pilgrims. Demetrius, a silversmith, was

---

[46] A description of Ephesian magic appears in Bruce M. Metzger, "St. Paul and the Magicians," *Princeton Seminary Bulletin*, XXXVIII (1944), 27–30.

[47] Acts 19:11–20.

[48] KJV uses *Diana*, the Latin form of the name.

[49] So F. W. Beare, "Artemis," *IDB*, I, pp. 241–242.

[50] *Ibid.*, p. 242.

[51] Acts 19:23–41.

probably one among many who became concerned that Paul's preaching interfered with their income. So aroused were those whose business was threatened that a riot ensued, endangering the life of Paul's associates. Major trouble was averted only when the "town clerk" quieted the crowd with a reminder that disturbance of the peace might bring Roman intervention. In telling the story Luke probably aims to demonstrate both that Christianity is superior to the most outstanding of Ephesian cults and that it has the official protection of Rome's representative in the city.

During Paul's extended stay and ministry at Ephesus, his influence was felt throughout the province of Asia. The New Testament refers to nine churches in the area,[52] all presumably founded under the influence of Paul and his co-workers.[53] In addition to Ephesus, Pauline correspondence refers specifically to Colossae, Hierapolis, and Laodicea, all in the Lycus River valley and all on the trade route between Ephesus and the Euphrates. As centers of wealth and religious interest these cities attracted the attention and labor of the Apostle.

Imprisonment in Ephesus? Several references to Ephesus in the Corinthian correspondence suggest difficulties beyond that of the Demetrius riot. On one occasion Paul speaks of "many adversaries" (I Corinthians 16:9) in the city and on another asks, "What do I gain if, humanly speaking, I fought with the wild beasts at Ephesus?" (I Corinthians 15:32) Still another reference to "the affliction we experienced in Asia" when "we felt we had experienced the sentence of death" (II Corinthians 1:8, 9) may reflect serious trouble. Paul mentions "far more imprisonments" (II Corinthians 11:23) when up until this point Acts has reported only the Philippian experience. These references have led many scholars to conclude that, although Acts does not report the event, Paul was imprisoned in Ephesus.[54] Since Acts does not aim to include all events in Paul's life, its silence cannot be made the decisive argument. Yet it does seem strange that so momentous an event would not have been mentioned in a source which does give considerable attention to Paul's Ephesian ministry. The most that can be said is that Paul faced a major crisis in Ephesus which brought him close to death. Whether or not this included imprisonment is not certain.

[52] Cf. Rev. 1:11 where Ephesus, Smyrna, Pergamum, Thyatira, Sardis, Philadelphia, and Laodicea are mentioned.

[53] See Ramsay, St. *Paul the Traveller and the Roman Citizen*, p. 274.

[54] So A. H. McNeile, *An Introduction to The New Testament*, pp. 182–185. The fullest defense of this hypothesis is G. S. Duncan, St. *Paul's Ephesian Ministry*, pp. 59–161.

The possibility of an Ephesian imprisonment is important to the study of the Pauline correspondence. Several of Paul's letters, namely, Ephesians, Colossians, Philippians, and Philemon, were certainly written from prison. These have usually been consigned to the imprisonment in Rome reported at the end of Acts. If Paul had also been in prison in Ephesus, another possible origin of at least part of the prison correspondence must be considered. Decisions rest on detailed argument, however, and had best be left to careful study of each of these letters.

Luke's account of Paul's movement immediately after he left Ephesus is summary and sketchy.[55] Seemingly, the Apostle traveled through familiar territory around the Aegean to encourage and strengthen young churches which he had established. Also, he collected funds to be used for relief in Jerusalem.[56] Titus, who had been sent to Corinth, rejoined Paul in Macedonia and the two moved to Achaia for a three-month visit. They then retraced their steps through Macedonia and Asia, met the Ephesian elders for a final greeting, and set sail for Jerusalem, concluding the Apostle's work around the Aegean Sea.

THE AEGEAN CORRESPONDENCE

The Aegean mission was the most important period in Paul's missionary work. It was a major advance into the Gentile world. Churches were established in strategic commercial and political centers from which the gospel might easily spread. Extensive ministries at both Corinth and Ephesus firmly set the Christian faith in the two most influential cities of the Aegean area. During this period the Church reaped the harvest of Paul's vigorous investments of time and energy. The Lucan Paul of Aegea, unthwarted by Jewish opposition and consumed by an intention to turn to the Gentiles, almost single-handedly carried the gospel to the Greek world.[57]

Paul also emerged during this period as a Christian writer of real prominence. Over the span of seven or eight years the Apostle wrote the majority of the letters which can with reasonable certainty be attributed to him. The Epistle to Galatians came from this time. From Corinth Paul wrote two letters to Thessalonica and his letter to Romans. From Ephesus he addressed at least three letters to Corinth and, shortly after leaving Ephesus, he wrote the Corinthians a fourth letter from

[55] Acts 20:1–36.
[56] Cf. I Cor. 16:1–9; II Cor. 9:1–5; Rom. 15:25–29.
[57] Johannes Munck, *Paul and The Salvation of Mankind*, pp. 36–68.

Macedonia. If we properly assume that he wrote numerous epistles no longer extant, the number of Pauline letters from this phase of his ministry reaches impressive proportions, even if none of his prison correspondence were written from Ephesus.

The Aegean correspondence is exceedingly varied in character. Romans, which regularly stands at the head of the Pauline corpus in the New Testament, is formal and doctrinal; I Corinthians is instructive and practical. Galatians is bathed in a spirit of indignation; II Corinthians is at one time plaintive and at another effusive in gratitude. I Thessalonians is affectionately personal; II Thessalonians, coolly official. Paul's letters reveal an intensely creative human being responding to the needs of other human beings. Specific persons and churches confronting live problems in a real world became for him occasions for interpreting the gospel. To read his letters is to enter a turbulent world where Paul aims for Christianity to be taken seriously.

I and II Thessalonians

The Pauline corpus contains three letters addressed to churches in Macedonia. Of these, two were written to Thessalonica and, unless Galatians was written from Antioch after the first mission tour, represent the earliest of Paul's extant epistles. The Thessalonian letters were born out of the Apostle's concern for the young Christian community he had recently established and which were probably threatened by the same persecution that had caused Paul to leave Thessalonica. The crucial issue in the two letters is the expectation of the coming of Jesus in glory, usually referred to as the *parousia*, meaning "presence." In Hellenistic times *parousia* had become a technical word designating a state visit of a high official. Paul applied the term to the anticipated coming or return of Jesus.[58] The coming *parousia* is the central theme in both Thessalonian letters. Around this issue other ideas are woven to encourage the new Christians to continue their Christian growth.

Authenticity and Relationship of the Letters. Scholars generally agree that I Thessalonians is Pauline. Its vocabulary, style, and ideas leave no serious doubt about the origin of the letter. However, questions have been raised about II Thessalonians. The main difficulty centers in two points.[59] First, seemingly different interpretations of the *parousia* appear in the two letters. Whereas I Thessalonians stresses the nearness of "the day of the Lord," an event to be expected at any

---

[58] See H. K. McArthur, "Parousia," *IDB*, III, pp. 658–661.
[59] See John W. Bailey's introduction in *IB*, XI, pp. 249–250.

moment, II Thessalonians pushes the *parousia* into the indefinite and more distant future, giving more specific concern to details which precede the event. Second, the language and frame of thought of the two letters are nearly alike. Some scholars conclude that a person would not so imitate himself in writing to the same people in the same situation and, therefore, both letters could not come from Paul.

Efforts to resolve these difficulties are numerous. Some believe that a later writer produced II Thessalonians, probably in the early second century,[60] and followed a practice common in the Greco-Roman world by writing in a pseudonym. Accordingly, II Thessalonians purposely aims to imitate I Thessalonians, but also desires to explain the delay in the *parousia*. Others accept Pauline authorship of both letters but reverse their order.[61] According to this approach, placing II Thessalonians before I Thessalonians puts the ideas of the two letters in better sequence. Since the present arrangement in the New Testament was determined by the length of the letters and not the order of their writing, there is no reason why II Thessalonians may not have been written first. Still others explain differences in the letters by supposing that I Thessalonians was addressed to Gentile elements in the church and II Thessalonians to the Jewish segment.[62] All of these views, however, create their own problems and cannot be accepted as conclusive. The seemingly opposite views of the coming day of the Lord are not as contradictory as they first appear, and the stylistic similarities may just as easily be attributed to nearness of the time of writing as to deliberate imitation of the first epistle in the second. The weight of scholarly opinion seems to favor Pauline authorship of both letters and to accept the traditional order.

Occasion and Content of I Thessalonians. Paul had been forced to leave Thessalonica under the pressure of pagan hostility. Even after his departure, attacks upon the gospel and Paul's integrity had continued (2:3–6). The persecution had been extended to members of the fledgling church (3:3–4). The Apostle's affection for the church only increased his desire that they not be dismayed by the current persecution and that they hold to their hope until he could come to encourage them in person (2:17–18). By the time Paul reached Athens he could wait no longer to contact the church. Timothy, who had

[60] So Morton S. Enslin, *The Literature of The Christian Movement,* pp. 239–244.

[61] This view is illustrated by Johannes Weiss, *The History of Primitive Christianity,* I, pp. 289–291.

[62] See Kirsopp Lake, *The Earlier Epistles of St. Paul,* pp. 83–86.

shared Paul's mission in Thessalonica, was sent both to exhort the believers and to bring Paul news of their reaction to persecution (3:2–5). Paul proceeded to Corinth, where Timothy later rejoined him and reported the faithfulness and affection of the Thessalonians. The Apostle responded to Timothy's report with a letter expressing joy at their perseverance and answering some specific questions about the coming day of the Lord. The two main divisions of the epistle are reflected in its outline.

Greeting. 1:1

I. Thanksgiving. 1:2–3:13
   A. Remembering their perseverance. 1:2–10
   B. Remembering his work at Thessalonica. 2:1–3:13
      1. Reviews his labors. 2:1–12
      2. Recalls their response. 2:13–16
      3. Anticipates a visit. 2:17–20
      4. Timothy's visit. 3:1–10
      5. Intercession for the church. 3:11–13

II. Warnings and Instructions. 4:1–5:22
   A. Exhortation to purity. 4:1–13
   B. Concerning "those who have fallen asleep." 4:14–5:11
   C. Practical exhortations. 5:12–22

Prayer and Benediction. 5:23–28

After a word of greeting (the briefest in any of Paul's known letters) the Apostle extends thanksgiving for the "word of faith and labor of love and steadfastness of hope" (1:3) among Thessalonian believers. The church had become "an example to all the believers in Macedonia and Achaia" (1:7) so that work at Thessalonica had not been in vain (2:1). Paul's reminiscence about his labor among the Thessalonians serves both as a defense against opponents who have accused him of heresy, immorality, trickery, and greed (2:3–8),[63] and as encouragement to those who suffered persecution (2:13–16). Paul's gratitude for the church is epitomized in the sentence, "For you are our glory and joy" (2:20).

The second part of the letter (chapters 4–5) shifts to instruction and exhortation, probably in response to specific questions brought from Thessalonica by Timothy.[64] Apparently Paul had taught the Thessa-

[63] James E. Frame, *A Critical and Exegetical Commentary on the Epistles of St. Paul to the Thessalonians*, pp. 12–14, holds that the apologetic note runs throughout the letter, especially the first three chapters.

[64] C. E. Faw, "On the Writing of First Thessalonians," *JBL*, LXXI (1952), 217ff., believes that these chapters respond to a letter that had come from Thessalonica.

lonians that Christ's return was near at hand. Since the period when the Apostle had preached in Thessalonica, some believers had died. The church now wondered about those who had "fallen asleep" since Paul's visit. Would they be deprived of blessings associated with the second advent of the Lord? In his letter Paul assured them that the dead will even precede the living in the coming kingdom. "The dead in Christ will rise first; then we who are alive, who are left, shall be caught up together with them in the clouds to meet the Lord in the air . . ." (4:16b–17). Further, Paul stressed that the Thessalonians should be more concerned about the certainty of the *parousia* than its time (5:1). They knew, presumably because Paul had taught them, "that the day of the Lord will come as a thief in the night" or suddenly and unexpectedly as labor upon an expectant woman (5:2–4). They, therefore, were not to busy themselves attempting to calculate "the times and the seasons." Rather, as those upon whom the light of Jesus had shined, they were to await his coming with expectancy and hope, encouraging each other as Timothy had reported they were doing (5:5–11).

Occasion and Content of II Thessalonians. Soon after his first letter had been written, Paul received another report from Thessalonica. The source of the report and whether or not the church had received the first letter are not known. But clearly, misunderstanding of the *parousia* had arisen because of persistent rumors that the day of the Lord had already come. The rumors were even supported with a letter purporting to be from Paul (2:1–2). Anticipating full participation in the rewards prepared for the righteous, some were becoming idlers, giving up their jobs. "Why worry about such mundane things in the brief time remaining?" they reasoned. Paul, probably only a matter of days or weeks after having sent I Thessalonians, dispatched this second letter addressed to these two issues. The letter is essentially in three parts.

Salutation. 1:1–2

   I. Thanksgiving and Intercession. 1:3–12
  II. The Man of Lawlessness. 2:1–3:5
 III. Instructions for the Idle. 3:6–15

Prayer and Benediction. 3:16–18

The distinctiveness of II Thessalonians centers in the mysterious "man of lawlessness." After reviewing his gratitude for the faithfulness of the Thessalonians and reassuring them that their present affliction would be vindicated in the *parousia* (1:3–12), Paul proceeded to the main issue. The day of the Lord had not and would not come "unless the rebellion come first, and the man of lawlessness is revealed, the son of perdition who opposes and exalts himself against every God or object of worship, . . . proclaiming himself to be God" (2:3–4). The man of lawlessness, now restrained by some power mysterious to us but known to the Thessalonians (2:6), will eventually come with his own *parousia,* deceiving those who refuse to love the truth and be saved (2:10). The Thessalonians, however, are not to be deceived, but live in the confidence that the lawless one will be destroyed by the Lord's *parousia* (2:8) and that they have been chosen from the beginning to share God's victory and glory (2:13–15).

Precisely what Paul meant by "the man of lawlessness" cannot be determined with certainty. The Apostle had previously instructed the Thessalonians about this matter (2:5) and consequently omits many details undoubtedly familiar to the original readers. Possibly Paul had in mind the popular Jewish apocalyptic idea that widespread apostasy would be a sign of the coming end. The idea is used here to illustrate that the *parousia* had not come.

Finally Paul turned to those who were "living in idleness, mere busybodies, not doing any work" (3:11). The Apostle's advice was brief and to the point. "If anyone will not work, let him not eat" (3:10b). Members of the congregation were to follow Paul's example by each man doing his work in quietness and earning his own living (3:12). The coolly abrupt letter breaks off with an admonition to heed the content and a greeting in Paul's own handwriting.

The Thessalonian correspondence provides a vivid picture of the intense relationship of the Apostle to a church that remained unwavering in loyalty and love. Further, the letters illustrate some of the struggles typical in a "congregation newly come from paganism" [65] as it attempted to formalize its understanding of the gospel.

I and II Corinthians

A second group of Pauline letters coming from the Aegean mission is addressed to Corinth. The major portion of these is preserved in I and II Corinthians, among the "most illuminating documents in all Christian literature." [66] Through these letters Paul's relationship to the Corinthian church is more fully known than his work with any

[65] Selby, *Toward the Understanding of St. Paul,* p. 254.
[65] S. M. Gilmour, "First Corinthians," *IDB,* I, p. 684.

other church. Although Acts relates only the circumstances associated with the founding of the church,[67] I and II Corinthians cast valuable light on the course of events at Corinth after Paul left. The letters show the kinds of problems which arose in a church intimately in touch with pagan society. They are more pastoral than doctrinal and, therefore, illuminate the problem of making the Christian faith relevant in a Gentile situation where it is novel. Paul answered questions that were arising for the first time in an enthusiastic but undisciplined Gentile church which existed in a climate vigorously antagonistic to the Christian ethic. First Corinthians is particularly important to an interpretation of the life of the early Church because it contains the earliest account of the Church's celebration of the Lord's Supper (11:23–26), a magnificent hymn on Christian love (chapter 13), and an extensive treatise on resurrection faith (chapter 15).

Numerous Letters.   Most of Paul's letters to Corinth were sent from Ephesus. During his three-year Ephesian ministry, Paul remained in contact with the Corinthian church. Travel across the Aegean was regular and consequently over the period Paul must have frequently communicated with those in Corinth whom he knew so well. At least four formal letters were written to Corinth during this period; there may have been others.[68]

Paul's initial letter to Corinth has been lost to us. In I Corinthians Paul refers to an earlier letter advising the Corinthians to avoid association with "immoral men" (5:9). A fragment of this first letter may be preserved in II Corinthians 6:14–7:1,[69] but we cannot be sure. The first letter had been misunderstood. Paul meant to advise the church to keep itself pure by ostracizing members who continued certain immoral practices after they became Christians, but the congregation had interpreted the Apostle to forbid all contact with immoral men outside the church. Word had come to Paul that the Corinthians were confused as to how his instructions were to be interpreted and that additional complex problems had arisen in the church. "Chloe's people" (I Corinthians 1:11) had brought a first hand report on circumstances in Corinth. Also the church had written to secure the Apostle's advice on issues that threatened to debilitate their fellowship (I Corinthians 7:1). Paul responded with his second letter, largely a pas-

---

[67] Acts 18:1–17.

[68] See T. W. Manson, "St. Paul in Ephesus; (3) The Corinthian Correspondence," *Bulletin of John Rylands Library*, XXVI (1941–42), 101–120.

[69] A helpful résumé of the problem of the unity of II Corinthians appears in Floyd V. Filson, "The Second Epistle to the Corinthians," *IB*, X, pp. 269–271.

toral letter designed to clear up misunderstanding and to offer specific instructions and guidance in resolving the problems about which the church had inquired. This second letter is essentially our I Corinthians.

Evidently Paul felt that the situation was crucial because he attempted to buttress his correspondence with a personal trip to Corinth (II Corinthians 12:14; 13:1). The visit proved both futile and embarrassing. Opposition in Corinth was able to discredit Paul's work (II Corinthians 3:1; 11:4–6) and the Apostle returned to Ephesus rebuffed. He responded with an angry third letter, probably preserved in part in II Corinthians 10–13, strongly denouncing his Corinthian opposition. Titus carried the letter to Corinth while Paul left Ephesus for an excursion through Macedonia by way of Troas. Somewhere in Macedonia Titus met Paul with news that a reconciliation had been achieved and that the leader of the opposition had been punished (II Corinthians 2:5–7). Paul's fourth letter, essentially II Corinthians, was written to express gratitude that peace had been restored. The letter was reinforced by yet another visit to Corinth from which the Apostle retraced his steps around the Aegean (Acts 20:3–38) and began his final trip to Jerusalem.

I Corinthians: A Letter in Practical Christianity. Since the Corinthian letters grew out of Paul's almost constant interchange with the Corinthian church, their content is essentially the Apostle's various responses to the sundry problems and questions which arose in a church which was seeking self-identity in an unfriendly pagan world. The correspondence is a clinical study of the emerging Gentile Christian community. The letters paint a vivid picture of the pulsating life of an early church which "more nearly resembled the contemporary rural, enthusiastic churches than our sedate and decorous city churches." [70] Practical problems are isolated and discussed with more direct concern for their forthright resolution than their theological import. Consequently, the correspondence is somewhat fragmented, moving from item to item without concern to develop a central theme. An outline of I Corinthians reflects this composite character.

Introductory Salutation and Thanksgiving. 1:1–9

I. Problems in the Corinthian church. 1:10–6:20
    A. Divisions within the church. 1:10–4:21
    B. Immorality. 5:1–6:20
       1. Incest. 5:1–17

[70] Samuel Sandmel, *A Jewish Understanding of The New Testament*, p. 85.

The epistle opens with a typical Pauline greeting and thanksgiving (1:1–9) and then moves directly to the many practical issues which have been disturbing the Corinthian Christians. In almost disjointed style Paul responds to problem after problem, referring obliquely to doctrinal and ethical issues entailed in each situation and directly suggesting his resolution. The Apostle is unconcerned to develop a single motif or connect his various discussions into a unified whole. However, the book may be conveniently divided into two parts: 1:10–6:20 discusses those problems which had been reported to Paul by visitors from Corinth (1:11); chapters 7–14 answer specific questions raised in a letter which the church had written to the Apostle (7:1).

The first issue taken up by Paul was the matter of *factions* which had developed in the church. The Corinthians were not only divided in their loyalty to various leaders, but also quarreled about the comparative merit of those to whom they were devoted. One group supported Apollos, the Alexandrian Jew who had been taught by Priscilla and Aquila in Ephesus. He had later crossed the Aegean and preached in Corinth. Some believers had become admirers of Apollos, perhaps because they had become converts under his preaching and had been baptized by him, and proudly claimed, "I belong to Apollos" (1:12). Others confessed allegiance to Cephas (Simon Peter), who likely had paid a visit to Corinth. Still others remained adamantly faithful to Paul, boasting of their baptism at his hand (1:13–17). Possibly a fourth group claimed some type of esoteric relationship to Christ and thus identified themselves as the Christ party (1:12).[71] The divisions seem to have developed over personalities and not over doctrine. Factions were aligned according to personal

---

[71] Since this group is not mentioned in 3:22 or in I Clement 47:3, some interpreters consider "I belong to Christ" to be a later scribal gloss.

loyalties to one of the preachers rather than debate over theological matters. The antagonism between the Apollos and Paul parties seems to have been particularly acute. Converts of Apollos had been enamored by the "eloquent wisdom" (1:17) of the Hellenistic preacher. Paul's supporters may have countered that he did not preach in sophisticated philosophical language, but with a simplicity that made his gospel more effective. Divisions over such petty issues threatened to destroy the unity of the Corinthian church and stirred the Apostle to vigorous reaction.

Paul responded to the divided situation with a sweeping appeal to the basic unity of the Christian community. All believers, whoever their preacher, are united through the cross of Christ, the power and wisdom of God. No special wisdom,[72] particular powers, or family connections should be a source of private boasting (1:26–31). All alike were redeemed by the wisdom of God, namely Christ Jesus. How foolish, then, to debate the virtues of particular leaders! Christ alone must be the end of Christian allegiance and the subject of any boasting. Paul, Apollos, and Cephas were all servants of Christ and stewards of the mysteries of God (4:1), each to plant or water in God's field according to their assignment (3:5–6). The teachers themselves are answerable only to God and his gospel. If they cannot boast in their private accomplishments, neither can the parties. To do so with jealousy and strife is to behave like ordinary men (3:3) and not like stewards entrusted with the gospel (4:2). If this admonition is not enough, Paul warns as he concludes this section of the letter, he will come to punish those who replace commitment to God with arrogant talk.

Abruptly the letter turns to denunciation of *immorality* in the church. The situation within which the Corinthians lived was notorious for its vice. The openness of Corinth had brought to her wealth, magnificence, and an easy moral attitude. Taverns marked the agora.[73] The nearby Acrocorinth was topped by a temple of Aphrodite where according to Strabo,[74] a thousand temple prostitutes served the goddess. Although Strabo's descriptions of almost a century earlier cannot be applied to Paul's day, they do indicate an orientation long established in the Peloponnesian city.[75] The lax, easy life of Corinth made it difficult for new Christians to separate themselves

---

[72] Cf. 1:21–25. There may be here a veiled derision of those who took pride in Apollos' eloquent preaching.

[73] See Jack Finegan, "Corinth," *IDB*, I, p. 683.

[74] *Geography*, 8, 6, 20.

[75] Strabo visited Corinth about 44 B.C. and again about 35 B.C.

from its atmosphere. So Paul wrote about their moral responsibility. Undoubtedly he was even sharper with them because an earlier letter on the problem of association with immoral men had been misunderstood (5:9). He had advised them not to associate with a church member who practiced immorality and they had interpreted him to mean that Christians were not to associate with non-Christians. In order not to be misunderstood again, the Apostle referred directly to a Christian who was living with his father's wife (5:1). "Let him who has done this be removed from among you" (5:2b). Further, anyone who participated in the loose sexual Corinthian mores thereby separated himself from Christ (6:16–17). Immorality could not be condoned. The body is a temple of the Holy Spirit (6:19) and consequently the Corinthians must, Paul advised, "glorify God in your body" (6:20). Although Christians could not isolate themselves from the culture in which they had been nurtured, they could establish standards of purity and control which recognized that they were God's possession. Paul carried his idea of separation so far that even litigation in secular courts was forbidden (6:1–11).

When Paul concluded his instructions on those matters which had been reported to him, he turned in chapters 7–14 to questions raised in a letter from the Christians in Corinth. Some of these questions were about *marriage*. Should the believer get married? And what were the responsibilities of a person who had married before he became a Christian or whose mate was still an unbeliever? Paul's attitude toward marriage, and consequently his advice to the Corinthians, was highly conditioned by his ideas of the *parousia*. He expected that the end of the age was about to arrive; therefore marriage had no real point for him (7:26–31). The immediacy of the coming new age of the kingdom meant that every believer must be industriously concerned to prepare for the *parousia*. Since marriage might interfere with a person's complete dedication to God (7:32–35), the ideal state is for "a man not to touch a woman" (7:1), that is, to refrain from that which might divert his loyalty. The unmarried should remain single and widows should not remarry.

Paul's evidently negative attitude toward marriage, however, ought not be made the general rule for a sexual ethic. He did not in fact believe that sex itself was inherently evil. His advice to the Corinthians includes the admonition that husband and wife must grant each other their conjugal rights (7:3–5). Christians already married must not seek to be free (7:10, 27). Even if one's mate is an unbeliever, divorce is not to be sought (7:12–15). Those who cannot control their passions are free to marry (7:2). All of this is to say that sex itself is not evil, but in the present situation marriage is less important than the coming kingdom. Therefore, no one is to seek marriage (7:27). "The end of the age is so near and the urgency of spreading the gospel in preparation for it is so great that the normal pursuits of life must give place to the work of the Church." [76]

The Corinthians also inquired of Paul about *meat that had been offered to idols*. Much of the meat sold in the regular markets had come from animals sacrificed in pagan ritual. Ought a Christian to buy and eat such meat? Some Christians recognized that the idols had no existence and so felt free to use the sacrificed meats. They considered themselves so liberated from the idea of idols that they even attended banquets in the pagan temples (8:10). Further, many of these took pride in this special "knowledge," feeling that it made them superior to those who were offended by the practice of eating sacrificed meat. Thus the problem became one not only of eatir ₃ meat, but also of preserving meaningful fellowship within the church.

Paul's advice on this issue centered in the principle that the Corinthians ought to guide their behavior more by love for their fellow Christians than by any superior knowledge of the idol's unreality (8:1–3). The idol had no real existence, to be sure, but to participate in pagan cults would suggest to the weaker Christian (8:10b) that one still believed in the idols. He would be offended into a false conclusion about the nature of the Christian God. The Christian certainly could not avoid every act which might offend someone, else his ethics would become entirely relative to his surroundings. With the Corinthians, however, the Apostle was concerned with practices which, in a community of new believers accustomed to idols, endangered their confession about God. On this point he demanded careful self-restraint in the interest of the gospel's being unhindered (9:15–18). Each must shun the worship of idols (10:14) and seek the good of his neighbor (10:24). His guidelines for the Corinthians to assure that the weaker would not be offended were threefold: (1) sharing in the pagan sacrifice meal was strictly forbidden (8:10–13), (2) buying the meat in the market-place was permissible (10:25–26), and (3) eating in a pagan household was permitted unless the guest was informed that the meat had been offered to idols (10:27–30). The Apostle summarized his own attitude in the statement, ". . . if food is a cause of my brother's falling, I will never eat meat, lest I cause my brother to fall" (8:13). He obviously hoped that the Corinthians

[76] Selby, *Toward the Understanding of St. Paul*, p. 266.

would practice the same restraint. Although Paul's instructions have been given an overtone of undue legalism, they demonstrate the extent to which he was willing to go in order that his liberty would not become a stumbling-block to a weaker brother. In a religious community so recently separated from pagan culture, the adoption of such an attitude was undoubtedly necessary to preserve its integrity and witness.

A third area in which the Corinthians sought Paul's guidance was *worship.* Questions had arisen about the behavior of women in public worship, the observance of the fellowship meal, and the use of "spiritual gifts" in worship.[77] Respectable Jewish women customarily wore veils outside their homes and kept their hair long.[78] Evidently Christian women in Corinth were disregarding this custom when they came to worship or at least the church raised with Paul the question of whether or not Christian freedom liberated them from usual social expectations, especially in matters that seemed so trivial. Paul's response to their question rests on the unconvincing argument that man has a superior status over women as God's representative on earth (11:7).[79] The Apostle himself may have been aware of the less-than-Christian character of his point of view, because he parenthetically included the more insightful interpretation against his position:

Nevertheless, in the Lord woman is not independent of man nor man of woman; for as woman was made from man, so man is now born of woman. And all things are from God. (11:11–12)

In spite of this insight, however, Paul insisted that the women keep their hair long and wear veils in public worship to acknowledge due respect for man as "the image and glory of God" (11:7), illustrating that even the great Apostle was a child of his times and could not completely escape the limitations of his own culture and personality. However, the discussion relevantly teaches that public worship must be conducted in order and dignity. Anything which detracts should not be permitted.

Another problem associated with the *fellowship meal and the observance of the Lord's Supper* had arisen. In Corinth, as in other early

[77] I Cor. 11:2 begins a new section of the book. It is not entirely clear whether Paul continues to respond to questions raised by the Corinthians or returns to reports about the church.

[78] Cf. W. M. Ramsay, *The Cities of St. Paul,* pp. 202–205.

[79] Nothing in the passage suggests that Paul believes unveiled heads is indecent or immoral. In fact, usually a Jewish woman was permitted to remove her head covering in private houses and this is where the church would have been meeting.

Christian communities, the whole church came together for a common meal, presumably in the home of one of the members. Usually a simple liturgical act commemorating the crucifixion of Jesus accompanied the fellowship meal. In Corinth some members of the congregation were taking advantage of the love feast, becoming gluttonous and drunken. Others were going hungry (11:20). Paul regarded this as a perversion of the true character of the fellowship meal and Lord's Supper (11:22). An event intended to be a solemn occasion celebrating the unity of the fellowship and commemorating the Lord's death was being desecrated in personal indulgence.[80] Paul's remedy was simple: "So then, my brethren, when you come together to eat, wait for another—if any one is hungry, let him eat at home—lest you come together to be condemned" (11:33–34). Probably distortions such as these at Corinth led to the later detachment of Lord's Supper observance from the fellowship meal so that the liturgical act could clearly proclaim the Lord's death (11:26).[81]

Paul's correspondence with Corinth next takes up problems growing out of the *use of "spiritual gifts."* Corinthians came to worship with "a hymn, a lesson, a revelation, a tongue, or an interpretation" (14:26). Each individual boasted that his was the best gift, thereby threatening the fellowship. Paul's judgment was that, although various gifts had an appropriate place in worship, all must be tested by the dual criteria of whether or not they came from the Spirit (12:4–11) and contributed to the edification of the whole church, the body of Christ (12:12–31). Testing the gift of speaking in tongues, that is, ecstatic speech, by these standards is particularly important. Tongue speaking must be carefully controlled (14:27) and should never be an end in itself. If the tongues cannot be used in orderly worship or if they cannot be understood (14:5, 27–28), then they should be silenced. Even if they are properly used, preaching is more important (14:1–5).

To Paul, however, both tongues and prophecy were inferior to "a still more excellent way" (12:31). The greatest gift of the spirit is love. "This *love* is not love in an ordinary or general sense, but the

---

[80] Two varying interpretations of the meal, one emphasizing joyous festivity and the other stressing solemn commemoration, may be the issue at stake here. So Hans Lietzmann, *Messe und Herrenmahl,* according to Clarence T. Craig, "The First Epistle to the Corinthians," *IB,* X, p. 131.

[81] This passage includes the earliest and most illuminating account of the Lord's Supper celebration in the apostolic Church. A comparison of I Cor. 11: 23–32 with Matt. 26:26–29; Mark 14:22–25; Luke 22:14–20 is helpful. The Corinthians account most resembles the Mark materials.

love which is known within the church, the very love of God poured out in Christ." [82] Without love as known in the Church through Christ, tongues are no more than clanging cymbals (13:1). Even prophecy, faith, and Christian martyrdom fade into nothingness before Christian love. In a magnificent hymn recorded in I Corinthians 13 and rarely rivaled in any literature, the Apostle sings the praise of this "more excellent way" and advises the Corinthians to make love their aim (14:1).

The final subject to which Paul addresses himself in the body of I Corinthians is *the resurrection*. The precise character of the problem which provokes the discussion is not clear. We cannot tell whether Corinthian Christians were rejecting the idea of resurrection, unduly identifying resurrection with baptism, or misinterpreting the Christian resurrection in the light of typical Greek thought by conceiving life after death as the release of an immortal spirit from its fleshly prison. Paul's emphasis upon the resurrection body suggests the last. For the Greek, life after death was defined without the restraint of a body. Man's eternal spirit is released from a confining body into its *naturally* full life. On the other extreme, some Christians may have crudely hoped for the restoration of the actual physical body. In between these extremes Paul affirms that the raised body will not be simply flesh and blood which cannot inherit the kingdom (15:50), but will be a "spiritual body" fit for the glory of the new age (15:35–50). Concern for resurrection of the body must be understood as affirmation of both the meaningfulness of historical existence and of the Church's realization that only a recreative act of God can assure man's participation in eternity.[83]

For Paul, however, the most important point to be made was not about the resurrection body, but about the general belief in the resurrection. This to him was no trivial or peripheral matter; belief in the resurrection was at the heart of the gospel. There could be no denial of the general belief in the resurrection of the dead which did not involve a rejection of the particular belief in the resurrection of Jesus.[84] Jesus' resurrection was the keystone of faith and the basis of all Christian hope as attested by apostolic witness (15:3–11). God has shown his power [85] in raising Jesus, an act which vindicated the Son and

---

[82] *Oxford Annotated Bible,* p. 1390.

[83] Cf. Reinhold Niebuhr, *The Nature and Destiny of Man,* II, pp. 294–301.

[84] Craig, "The First Epistle to the Corinthians," *IB,* X, pp. 222–223.

[85] Regularly in verses 12–23 the perfect tense of the verb *raised* is used to emphasize that Jesus' resurrection is the finished mighty act of God.

assured the believer. The resurrection was the "assurance that the eschatological victory of Christ had begun and that his reign must continue 'until he has put all his enemies under his feet' and destroyed death." [86] For Paul this was reason enough to "be steadfast, immovable, always abounding in the work of the Lord" (15:58). Having arrived at this high point, Paul closes his epistle by instructing the Corinthians to share in the offering for Jerusalem Christians, informs them of his travel plans, includes some miscellaneous personal notes, and concludes with a greeting in his own handwriting.

II Corinthians: A Treatise in Reconciliation. As already noted, I Corinthians was not well received in Corinth. The letter was followed by a "painful visit," [87] but neither the letter nor the visit was able to quell the opposition to Paul which had swelled in the church. Another letter, candid and stern and included partially or totally in II Corinthians 10–13, was addressed to the conflict. In these chapters Paul vigorously defended himself against those inside or outside the church who were berating his apostleship. Although he thought himself indulging somewhat in foolish boasting, he nonetheless forthrightly claimed, "I am not in the least inferior to these superlative apostles" (11:5; 12:11). Modesty did not preclude defense of his apostleship because the gospel and the life of the Corinthian church were at stake.

The stern letter was sent with Titus to Corinth. Paul, restlessly awaiting word of their reaction (2:12–13), left Ephesus and moved northward around the Aegean into Macedonia, hoping to fulfill his desire for another visit to Corinth (12:14; 13:1–2). When Titus returned to report that the attitude of Corinthian opposition had softened, Paul responded with another letter, II Corinthians (with the exception of 10–13 and possibly 6:14–7:1).[88] The letter is in two parts each somewhat unconnected with the other.

Introduction and Thanksgiving. 1:1–11

    I. Paul's relationship to the Corinthian church. 1:12–7:16

        A. Explanation of changed travel plans. 1:12–2:13

        B. An apology for his apostleship. 2:14–6:13

        C. An excursus on relations with unbelievers. 6:14–7:1

        D. The Apostle's joy at reconciliation. 7:2–16

---

[86] James L. Price, *Interpreting the New Testament*, p. 381.

[87] II Cor. 2:3–9. Cf. II Cor. 7:8–12.

[88] Some scholars deny Pauline authorship of 6:14–7:1. J. A. Fitzmeyer, "Qumran and the Interpolated Paragraph in II Cor. 6:14–7:1," *Catholic Biblical Quarterly*, XXIII (1961), 271ff., emphasizes its close affinities with Qumran thought.

II. The offering for Jerusalem Christians. 8:1–9:15

Conclusion and Benedicton. 13:11–14

The tone of these chapters is much more conciliatory than that of chapters 10–13. The crisis with the Corinthian church had passed and the Apostle wanted to clear away all misunderstanding. He countered the charge that he had been fickle and vacillating (1:17–18) with an explanation of his change in travel plans. He had refrained from another visit, not as wanton disregard of his promise, but to spare the congregation the embarrassment of "another painful visit" (2:1–2). Now that the crisis was over, past differences should be put aside "to keep Satan from gaining the advantage . . ." (2:11). Even the ringleader of opposition, since he had been duly punished, must now be forgiven and comforted (2:6–7).

Paul then passed to an extended defense of his apostleship which was authenticated, not by letters of recommendation (3:1–2), but by divine commission (3:5–6). Because God had sustained his ministry, affliction, perplexity, persecution, and opposition could not blunt his confidence (4:8–9). Like an earthen vessel holding priceless treasure, the frail and suffering Apostle carried the gospel to show that God is the source of its transcendent power (4:7). The true apostle (and by implication all believers as well) understands crises, like that between Paul and the Corinthian church, as "slight momentary afflictions" which prepare for "an eternal weight of glory beyond all comparison" (4:17). On this ground Paul reiterated his appeal that the Corinthians remove any barrier which might still stand between them.

Open your hearts to us; we have wronged no one, we have corrupted no one, we have taken advantage of no one. . . . You are in our hearts, to die together and to live together. I have great confidence in you; I have great pride in you; I am filled with comfort. With all our affliction, I am overjoyed. (7:2–4)

In chapters 8 and 9 [89] Paul appealed for the church to return to gathering the offering for the saints in Jerusalem. The Apostle had been interested in this offering throughout the Aegean mission. Some specific hardship or calamity may have made the collection a real necessity, but Paul saw in the project an opportunity to bind Jewish and Gentile Christians together in Christian brotherhood. Collections had begun earlier in Corinth, but had been interrupted by the quar-

---

[89] Since chapter 9 repeats some matters discussed in chapter 8, some regard it as part of a separate letter. However, chapter 9 is incomplete when considered by itself and more probably represents an emphasis which Paul wanted to give to the collection. See FBK, pp. 213–214.

rel. Now it was important to resume the collection, both to bring a worthy project to completion and to demonstrate that the debate about Paul was over.[90] Therefore, Paul bragged on the generosity of the Macedonians and appealed to the Corinthians to demonstrate the same liberality. Titus and two other delegates sent with him were to oversee the offering to avoid any suspicion that the funds would be misappropriated (8:16–24). The Apostle wanted the collection to deepen the Corinthians' Christian life and widen their horizons in the Church. On this high note of aspiration he brought this letter to Corinth to a close.

II Corinthians adds little to an understanding of Pauline theology, but it is one of the most valuable sources for interpreting Paul's self-understanding. In the letter Paul pours out himself, and through the self-expurgation the temperament and character of Paul the man come through.

Romans: Salvation Through Faith

Because of its almost incomparable influence on the history of the Christian Church,[91] Paul's epistle to the Romans is usually considered the most important letter coming from his Aegean ministry and certainly one of the more important writings in the entire New Testament. It is Paul's longest and weightiest letter, systematically presenting the essence of the Apostle's interpretation of the gospel. Unlike I and II Corinthians, this letter is formal and carefully organized. Although it retains the basic form of a true letter warmly addressed to particular readers, more than any other of Paul's writings Romans is a formal theological treatise presenting a comprehensive account of Paul's "understanding of the gospel of Christ as the effectual divine remedy for the plight of man, the universal sinfulness which no human effort can remove." [92] This is not to say that Romans aims to be a comprehensive summary of Pauline doctrine. Christology and eschatology do not receive full attention and the Lord's Supper and Church polity are not even mentioned. Romans does, however, give what Paul believes to be the essence of Christianity, the core of the gospel which he as an apostle proclaims.[93]

---

[90] Filson, "The Second Epistle to the Corinthians," *IB*, X, p. 363.

[91] A summary of the early literary history of Romans appears in William Sanday and Arthur Headlam, *A Critical and Exegetical Commentary on the Epistle to the Romans*, pp. lxxiv–lxxxv.

[92] F. W. Beare, "Letter to the Romans," *IDB*, IV, p. 112.

[93] FBK, pp. 220–221.

Occasion and Purpose. Paul's authorship of Romans is one of the least contested facts in New Testament studies. The style of the letter is typically Pauline and none of his favorite words are missing.[94] Romans was known around the turn of the first century by Clement of Rome and Ignatius of Antioch, and all known listings of Pauline letters include it.

Romans was written during Paul's last stay in Corinth and so should be dated sometime between A.D. 56 and 58.[95] Soon after his reconciliation with the Corinthian church and the writing of II Corinthians 1–9, Paul came to Corinth for a three-month visit prior to taking the collection to Jerusalem (Acts 20:1–3). The visit marks a turning point in Paul's missionary career. His eye had been on the West, looking forward to a mission as far as Spain (Romans 15:24, 28), but the insistent demands of the Aegean mission [96] had absorbed his time. Now, however, with churches in the Aegean area firmly established, the Corinthian problem largely resolved, and the collection completed, the Apostle turned his attention to new mission fields, hoping to make Rome the focus of work in the western part of the empire. Romans was written to prepare the way for an intended visit. Paul was immediately concerned to introduce himself to the Roman Christians and invite their support for an envisioned western, Rome-oriented mission. The introduction is in the form of a "theological self-confession" [97] in which the Apostle stated the substance of the gospel which he hoped to carry to the West.

Although the reason Paul wrote to Rome is quite clear, why he included the contents he did in this particular letter is somewhat vague. The letter's considerable concern with the general problem of the relationship between Christianity and Judaism, particularly at the point of the legalistic emphasis of Judaism, suggests that Jewish-Gentile relationships may have been a genuine problem in the Roman church. Not enough is known, however, about the founding and early life of the church to be certain. The Roman church was composed largely of Gentiles (Romans 1:13b) and it is entirely possible that internal church struggles had led to the Claudius edict expelling Jews from Rome. Whether or not open conflict between Jewish legalism and

[94] See Robert M. Grant, *Historical Introduction to the New Testament*, pp. 175, 186–187.

[95] The arguments of L. P. Pherigo, "Paul and the Corinthian Church," *JBL*, LXVIII (1949), 341–350, for Athens and T. M. Taylor, "The Place of Origin of Romans," *JBL*, LXVII (1948), 281–295, for Philippi are unconvincing.

[96] Cf. Rom. 1:11–13.

[97] FBK, p. 221.

Christian freedom particularly prevailed in Rome, the problem of the role of Judaism, law, and Old Testament pervaded the life of the early Church and would have been of interest even to a church without a major Jewish population. The Romans had not known Paul and consequently may not have known fully how he interpreted the relationship of the gospel to the Jewish covenant tradition. Therefore, as Paul faced a visit to Rome as part of a larger mission to Spain, he presented to the Romans the gospel of salvation in Christ in careful detail.

Certain passages in Romans suggest that Paul had in mind specific false interpretations of the gospel as he wrote the letter. For example, chapter six raises and answers the rhetorical question, "Are we to continue to sin that grace may abound?" Does this mean that libertine deductions were being drawn from the message of God's free grace? Does the admonition that the "strong" and the "weak" not pass judgment on each other mean that divisions had grown up within the church (14:1–15:6)? Does the statement, "For not all who are descended from Israel belong to Israel and not all are children of Abraham because they are his descendants" (9:6–7), hint that Jews were pridefully boasting in the sanctity of their tradition? The letter at times does have the air of a polemic against false views, but primarily it is not addressed to specific problems that had arisen in the local congregation. (A comparison of the content and style of Romans and Galatians and I Corinthians helpfully illustrates this point.) The major motif throughout is redemption through faith in Christ and how this relates to Jewish appreciations of law and community. The letter is "basically a dialogue of the Pauline gospel with Judaism"[98] sent to Gentile Christians[99] to point up the essential gospel proclaimed by the Apostle.

Chapter 16. Before turning to the contents of the Romans epistle some attention needs to be given to the major critical problem associated with the book. Several features encourage the conclusion that the final chapter does not belong to the original letter. The list of personal greetings (16:3–16) suggests an unduly large number of acquaintances in a congregation that Paul had not visited. Aquila and Priscilla, who are included in the greetings, seem to have settled in Ephesus; it seems unlikely that they would have returned to Rome. Also, the authoritative tone of the material (16:17–20) is unlike the more guarded atmosphere of the remainder of the book. These char-

[98] *Ibid.*, p. 218.
[99] 1:13; 11:13. Cf. 9:3f.; 10:1f.

acteristics, combined with the fact that oldest manuscript of Romans (the Chester Beatty papyrus dating to the early third century A.D.) places the doxology of 16:25–27 at the end of chapter 15, make an imposing argument for considering Romans to end with chapter 15.[100] Probably chapter 16 was part of a letter addressed to Ephesus for the purpose of recommending Phoebe, a deaconess from Cenchreae, to the Ephesian Christians.[101]

Outline and Interpretation. The theological character of Romans is reflected in the outline of the book:

Introduction. 1:1–17
    A. Salutation. 1:1–7
    B. Thanksgiving. 1:8–15
    C. Statement of the main theme. 1:16–17

  I. The Human Predicament. 1:18–3:20
    A. Gentiles are guilty. 1:18–32
    B. Jews are guilty. 2:1–3:8
    C. Universal nature of sin and guilt. 3:9–20

 II. God's Saving Act in Christ. 3:21–4:25
    A. True righteousness comes through faith in Christ. 3:21–31
    B. Abraham illustrates righteousness through faith. 4:1–25

III. The New Life in Christ. 5:1–8:29
    A. The certainty of salvation. 5:1–11
    B. Christ and Adam compared. 5:12–21
    C. Union with Christ. 6:1–14
    D. Slavery to a new master. 6:15–23
    E. Marriage to a new partner. 7:1–6
    F. Ineffectual law. 7:7–25
    G. Life according to the Spirit. 8:1–39

IV. Israel's Rejection of the Gospel. 9:1–11:36
    A. Israel's unbelief. 9:1–5
    B. God is free to reject Israel. 9:6–29
    C. Israel's rejection results from her guilt. 9:30–10:21
    D. Israel's rejection is not final. 11:1–36

[100] According to Origen, *Commentaria in epistolam ad Romanos,* as cited in FBK, p. 222, Marcion cut off both chapters 15 and 16 as foreign to Romans. However, the doxology of 16:23 does not logically connect with 14:23.
[101] So John Knox, "The Epistle to the Romans," *IB,* IX, pp. 364–368; T. W. Manson, "St. Paul's Letter to the Romans—And Others," *Bulletin of John Rylands Library,* XXXI (1948), 224ff.; and others. Manson believes that chapter 16 was attached to a copy of Romans 1–15 and sent to Ephesus. For the position that 16 belongs integrally to Romans, see C. H. Dodd, *The Epistle of Paul to the Romans,* pp. 234ff., and FBK, pp. 224–226.

V. Practical Instructions in Christian Responsibility. 12:1–15:13
  A. The dedicated life. 12:1–2
  B. The duty of love. 12:3–21
  C. Responsibility to civil authority. 13:1–7
  D. The urgency of Christian conduct. 13:8–14
  E. The strong and the weak. 14:1–15:6
  F. The example of Christ. 15:7–13
Conclusion: Personal Matters and Benediction. 15:14–33

INTRODUCTION (1:1–17). The opening of the Romans letter is interesting because of both the elaborate salutation and the overt statement of the theme of the letter. At the very outset of the letter Paul makes crystal clear his apostolic credentials. His proposed visit (1:13) is not merely a matter of personal desire; it is also the fulfillment of an apostolic commission which comes from Christ. Christ had called Paul to be an apostle, made him a slave to a new master, and set him apart for the gospel (1:1) which he now proposed to represent in Rome. The essential character of the gospel is briefly set forth in words generally regarded as the statement of the letter's theme:

For I am not ashamed of the gospel: it is the power of God for salvation to everyone who has faith, to the Jew first and also to the Greek. For in it the righteousness of God is revealed through faith for faith; as it is written, "He who through faith is righteous shall live." (1:16–17)

All the necessary elements of salvation to be discussed in the letter are introduced here. Salvation is a mighty work [102] of God. It is available to all, both Jew and Greek. Faith is the avenue by which it is received. The righteousness of God reaches out and embraces the man of faith who thereby finds forgiveness and life.

I. THE HUMAN PREDICAMENT (1:18–3:20). Paul begins the development of the theme with a diagnosis of the human situation. This section of the letter is somewhat disjointed. The argument is interrupted by digressions, and transitions from idea to idea are not always smooth. The central point, however, is perfectly clear. All men, both Gentile and Jew, stand guilty before God and are incapable of deliverance from their sin through the law. Gentiles know the power and deity of God through natural order (1:19–20), but demonstrate their sin by violating natural relationships in lustful and shameless acts (1:24–27). Jews, although possessing the advantage of the law, dishonor God by breaking the law (2:23). The law cannot redeem; it

---

[102] The word used here is *dunamis* from which *dynamite* and kindred words are derived.

succeeds only in making men aware of their condition (3:20). The
Jew cannot hide behind possession of the law and Gentile is not ex-
cused for lack of knowledge. Sin and guilt is a universal problem.
The Apostle's massive indictment is underscored with quotations from
the Old Testament (3:10–13a):

> "None is righteous, no, not one:
> No one understands, no one seeks for God.
> All have turned aside, together they have gone wrong;
> No one does good, not even one." [103]
> "Their throat is an open grave,
> they use their tongues to deceive." [104]

Paul took the plight of sinful man with deadly seriousness. Each
man by sin is estranged from God and stands under the judgment of
God. The Apostle described this judgment as the wrath of God "revealed from heaven against all ungodliness and wickedness of men"
(1:18). To Paul the wrath of God is associated with the will of God.
Anything which opposes God's will or violates his holiness is victimized by the wrath of God. God's wrath is to be sharply distinguished
from both personal anger and impersonal moral order. It is not simply
the anger of a despot peeved at man's wrongdoing. Rather it is God's
steadfast opposition to sin. The phrase describes, not an emotional
attitude of God toward man, but the destructive character of the
breach between God and man. According to C. H. Dodd, Paul meant
to say that man is victimized by an "inevitable process of cause and
effect in a moral universe." [105] The Apostle, however, was not describing just the irrational and inscrutable function of order in the
universe. Divine wrath rather was God's intentional opposition to
individual or collective efforts to thwart his purposes in history. In
the Old Testament the wrath of God opposes those who threatened to
destroy the covenant relationship with Israel, from either inside or outside the religious community.[106] In the prophetic tradition the inflic-
tion of God's wrath came to be associated with a great day of judgment, the Day of the Lord.[107] In that day all opposition to God
would be brought to its final judgment. The New Testament looks
forward with hope to that day when whatever opposes God ceases to

---

[103] Cf. Psa. 14:1–2; 53:1–2.
[104] Cf. Psa. 5:9.
[105] Dodd, *The Epistle of Paul to the Romans*, p. 23.
[106] A brief and helpful summary of the biblical use of this phrase appears in
B. T. Dahlberg's article, "Wrath of God," *IDB*, IV, pp. 903–908.
[107] See Isa. 2:10–22; Jer. 30:7–8; Zeph. 3:8.

be, so that his wrath is stilled.[108] ·This eschatological understanding is typical of Paul's description.[109] The tragedy of the human predicament is that man by his hard and impenitent attitude toward sin alienates himself from God and his eternal purposes. The present wrath of God (1:18) is only a foretaste of the final woe (2:5).

Sin for Paul was not just an individual matter—a wrong committed by a single person against another person or a breach of a single law. Rather, he understood sin in the context of the biblical understanding of the individual's identity with the community. By birth man is more than an individual; he shares familial, national, and racial identity. Thus, individual or private acts of rebellion against God or violence against neighbor are merely witnesses to the basic disorder which is the human situation. To the Apostle the human predicament, then, is being human, belonging to a morally impotent race. Man particularly is incapable of keeping the law as a means of his own liberation.

II. GOD'S SAVING ACT IN CHRIST (3:21–4:25). Over against the seeming hopelessness of the human situation stands the new order which is man's only hope. Release from the bondage of the human predicament cannot come by any moral struggle on man's part. Simply by trying hard enough to keep the law man cannot bridge the chasm of his estrangement from God. Efforts to obey any law only remind him of his sin and do not produce righteousness. True righteousness, which cannot be gained by human effort, reaches out to embrace man. It comes as the free, gracious gift of God. In contrast to man's somber condition when he attempts to live apart from God, the gospel introduces him into a new state of righteousness. This righteousness is made possible by the death of Christ, an act whereby God both demonstrates the seriousness with which he regards sin and ransoms those formerly enslaved by sin (3:26). God is not only revealing himself as righteous in his own purpose, but also acting with power to make right triumphant over wrong.[110]

English usage of the term "righteousness" usually refers to guilt or innocence before the law. A righteous person is innocent of wrongdoing and the unrighteous is guilty. To Paul, however, "righteousness" is a covenant term whose meaning is discovered in the relationship between God and man.[111] "Those acts which preserve a covenant

---

[108] Rev. 20:14–21:4.
[109] Cf. I Thess. 5:9.
[110] Beare, "Letter to the Romans," *IDB*, IV, p. 116.
[111] Gottlob Schrenk, "Dikaiosune," *Theological Dictionary of The New Testament,* Gerhard Kittel, ed., II, pp. 192–210.

relationship . . . are righteous, while those acts which break this relationship are unrighteous." [112] Thus, when Paul talks about God justifying man, he does not mean to imply that God treats evil deeds as if they did not happen or man as if he were not a sinner. Rather God, who himself is righteous, acts to restore a covenant broken by man's unrighteous rebellion. God's righteousness recognizes sin as sin in order that covenant may be restored. To the Apostle the elemental gospel miracle was that "God shows his love for us in that while we were yet sinners Christ died for us" (5:8). God's righteousness is most clearly demonstrated in Christ's death by which he upholds the covenant relationship with sinful man.

Paul insisted that the saving act is wholly God's doing, independent of any works of law (3:21, 28). The only appropriate act for enslaved man is to respond with faith that God can accomplish that which man cannot do for himself. Faith as confidence in the faithfulness of God in performing his promises surpasses any effort to remove guilt by keeping the law. Faith's primacy over law is illustrated in Abraham. He was declared righteous by the free act of God in response to his faith, even before his obedience to the law (4:10–13). All who have faith, whether Gentile or Jew, are Abraham's descendants, sharing in the promise that rests on God's grace (4:16–25).

III. THE NEW LIFE IN CHRIST (5:1–8:39). In chapters 5–8 Paul turns his attention to the life of the believer. His understanding of the objective reality of sin, the corporate nature of human responsibility, and the mystical identification of the believer with Christ permeates the discussion.[113] The sin from which man is set free is not simply the transgression of known legal commands. It is an objective condition of disharmony with God. The whole human race, symbolized in Adam (5:12–14), share this disruption and "fall short of the glory of God" (3:23). This is the breach which is reconciled in Christ's death (5:6–11). The believer is identified with Christ, restoring his "peace with God" (5:1), that is, harmony with God and his purposes. Logically the next question is, "How does the reconciled believer live his daily life?" If the law is ineffectual to achieve redemption, is it also irrelevant to practice?

Some of the Romans may have responded to Paul's antilegalistic

---

[112] P. J. Achtemeier, "Righteousness in the New Testament," *IDB*, IV, p. 91.

[113] A full discussion of these concepts may be found in the commentaries on the epistle. Three standard ones are Knox, "The Epistle to the Romans," *IB*, IX; Dodd, *The Epistle to the Romans;* and Sanday and Headlam, *A Critical and Exegetical Commentary on the Epistle to the Romans.*

interpretation of the gospel with antinomianism, holding that because of God's gracious forgiveness the Christian is morally unobligated. Paul's reaction is that one who is in harmony with God cannot take his new life in Christ as an opportunity for sinful indulgence (6:1–2). Restoration creates motivation to live as a new creature. The believer is no longer a slave to his old master (6:15–23). He has died to sin in his identification with Christ and is no more bound to sin than a woman to a deceased husband (7:1–6). The Christian is dead to sin, but alive to God (6:11). He is God's slave entirely devoted to his owner. This means that the believer is under deep moral obligation, not to the law, but to God.

Likewise, my brethren, you have died to the law through the body of Christ, so that you may belong to another, to him who has been raised from the dead in order that we may bear fruit for God. (7:4)

Paul describes the new relationship of the believer to Christ by the formula, "in Christ." The tyranny of sin has been dislodged from the human heart by the spirit of Christ. To be "in Christ" is to be in communion with Christ in such a way that normal living is motivated by his presence.[114] Paul believed "that Jesus Christ is not merely a posthumous influence but a personal presence," [115] so that being "in Christ" was to be directed by Christ.

To Paul the secret of the believer's victory over sin and the law is the Spirit of God. "For the law of the Spirit of life in Christ Jesus has set me free from the law of sin and death" (8:2). Men of faith live in a new order which moves toward eschatological fulfillment in which Christians become finally and completely "the sons of God" (8:19). But what of the interval between now and the coming fulfillment? This interim is the period of the Spirit's working. New life in Christ, therefore, consists of submission to the Spirit, God's real and vital presence in human life.[116] The Spirit sustains human weakness (8: 26), gives meaning in the midst of suffering (8:18), and assures the Christian of his relationship to God.

When we cry, "Abba! Father!" it is the Spirit himself bearing witness with our spirit that we are children of God, and if children, then heirs, heirs of God and fellow heirs with Christ. . . . (8:15b–17a)

---

[114] The description of Paul's idea as mysticism is more confusing than illuminating, as Bultmann, *Theology of The New Testament*, I, p. 311, points out. Paul's idea is more akin to Buber's I-Thou model, although Buber aims to describe interpersonal relations. See his *I and Thou*, p. 11.

[115] A. M. Hunter, *Interpreting Paul's Gospel*, p. 97.

[116] A helpful popular survey of the biblical idea of Spirit is William Barclay, *The Promise of The Spirit*.

Paul dramatizes the importance of life "in the Spirit" through an extended comparison with life "in the flesh" (8:3–13). Traditionally these two phrases have been interpreted in terms of Greek dualism, so that "flesh" is equated with man's baser nature and "spirit" with his higher nature. Body and its appetites are considered essentially evil, whereas good derives from non-material dimensions of man.[117] But Paul does not mean to imply such a dichotomy. "Flesh" and "spirit" are not two parts of a person, but two relationships.[118] "Flesh" denotes man's bondage to the powers of evil; "spirit," his life in faith.[119] Men who have not responded in faith to God's gracious act in Christ are absorbed in humanness, that is, in the interests of the flesh. They are dominated by thoughts and motives that are temporal and therefore fleeting. In a real sense such men are already dead because they belong to an old age soon to pass away. In distinction, the believer lives "in the Spirit." He still may belong to the temporal order, but his motives are set toward the new age which is promised.[120] Even the sufferings of "this present time" cannot divert the true Christian from his sure hope.

An atmosphere of exhilaration surrounds Paul's closing affirmation that all things are powerless before God's mighty act in man's behalf. In tribulation, persecution, famine, or any other suffering the Christian is more than conqueror. Paul asserts,

I am sure that neither death, nor life, nor angels, nor principalities, nor things present, nor things to come, nor powers, nor height, nor depth, nor anything else in all creation, will be able to separate us from the love of God in Christ Jesus our Lord. (8:38–39)

IV. ISRAEL'S REJECTION OF THE GOSPEL (9:1–11:36). Chapters 9–11 in Romans constitute a type of excursus in which Paul applies his general interpretation of the gospel to the specific status of the Jews in God's redemptive plan. The section is relatively self-contained so that one may skip from the end of chapter 8 to the opening of chapter 12 without any feeling of omission. The excursus, however, bears no mark of a separate letter and most certainly is an intimate part of Romans. Here Paul relates his discussion of law and Spirit to a reli-

---

[117] This approach to Pauline anthropology has been classically expressed by F. C. Baur, *Paul, His Life and Work*, p. 139.

[118] See Bultmann, *Theology of The New Testament*, I, pp. 191–210.

[119] Reginald H. Fuller, *The New Testament in Current Study*, p. 69.

[120] An extensive treatment of Pauline anthropology and its relationship to Jewish and Greek concepts may be found in W. David Stacey, *The Pauline View of Man*. For his treatment of Paul's understanding of the natural and spiritual man, see pp. 146–153.

gious community which to his thinking had been so zealous to keep the law that the work of the Spirit had been thwarted.

It plagued Paul that Israel, the covenant community through which God had sought to make himself known and the proud possessors of the law, had failed to be responsible to its privileged position. By religious tradition, sonship, covenant, law, promise, and the patriarchs belonged to Israel (9:4–5), but she who pursued righteousness based on law did not succeed in fulfilling that law (9:31). They had not moved beyond the law to faith in Christ and so had rejected their own destiny as the people of God. "The Jew cannot claim salvation, for it is God who has the sovereignty over salvation and perdition." [121] Israel's misguided zeal for the law had blinded them to righteousness through Christ, the end of the law (10:1–4). The Jews had not received salvation because they would not take God's way to it. Ironically Gentiles outside the history of God's covenant work were gaining through faith what Israel might have discovered more opportunely.

Israel's unbelief brought Paul intense grief. The Jews were his kinsmen (10:11) and he was even willing to sacrifice himself for his people's good (9:3). However, Israel's refusal to accept the gospel had its positive side—because of Jewish unbelief, the gospel was now being preached to the Gentiles (11:11). Paul understood his own apostleship to the Gentiles within this context. Jewish apocalyptic hopes envisioned the salvation of Israel first, after which Gentiles would be admitted to the kingdom. Apparently Jerusalem Christians adopted this hope and consequently focused upon a mission to Israel. Paul, however, conceived his mission to represent a reversal of this order. As apostle to the Gentiles he plays a decisive role in bringing Gentiles into the kingdom preceding the Jews.[122] This did not mean that the Jewish plight was God's plan or intention (11:1), although sovereignty gave him that freedom (9:14–29). Rather Israel's refusal to accept Christ through faith (9:30–33) has ended in rejection. However, Paul hoped that ultimately Israel would be provoked to jealousy (11:14) when they realized that Gentiles were attaining what had been promised to Jews. In the end Israel's central place in salvation history will be clearly shown. Her current rejection leads to salvation of the Gentiles, but more her later repentance will mark a decisive

[121] Munck, *Paul and The Salvation of Mankind*, p. 42.
[122] *Ibid.*, 11:68, develops extensively Paul's eschatological understanding of his apostolic role, suggesting that the only serious theological difference between Paul and the Jerusalem church was on the interpretation of the *parousia*. The Jerusalem church believed Israel would precede the Gentiles, but Paul reversed the order.

turning-point in her own redemption. For Paul, Israel remains the main branch upon which has been grafted the Gentile olive shoot (11:17–23). Israel's rejection is not final. At present Gentiles are being converted, but ultimately "all Israel will be saved" (11:26).

V. PRACTICAL INSTRUCTIONS IN CHRISTIAN RESPONSIBILITY (12:1–15:13). In a final major section of his letter Paul describes the behavior required of those who live in the Spirit. Having established that God in Christ justified men of faith and set them in a new order in which the Spirit prevails, the Apostle turns to ethical instructions for the Romans. This instruction is set in a frame of the Christian's responsibility to consecrate his total self to the life for which he has been set apart. Paul summarizes this responsibility in 12:1–2:

> I appeal to you therefore, brethren, by the mercies of God, to present your bodies as a living sacrifice, holy and acceptable to God, which is your spiritual worship. Do not be conformed to this world but be transformed by the renewal of your mind, that you may prove what is the will of God, what is good and acceptable and perfect.

Believers belong to an order which is not of this present world and therefore must transform their lives accordingly. The imminence of the arrival of the new age makes it urgent that Christians conform to a morality which prepares for Christ's coming.

Paul's exhortations stress two features. First, the Christian best grows in moral integrity within the Church where relationships are characterized by love (12:1–21). The individual member is no "practitioner of a private virtue," but as a vital part of the body of Christ lives "in a nexus of mutual responsibilities and benefits." [123] Each member performs his separate spiritual gift for the harmonious function of the whole (12:3–8). In Romans as in Corinthians, Paul saw love as the dominating principle creating and sustaining the corporate life of the community (12:9–10; 13:8–10). Love typifies relationships with enemies who thereby may become friends (12:20–21); love also resolves rivalries within the community so that "the weak" and "the strong" live harmoniously, neither injuring or exploiting the other (14:1–15:6). No one lives to himself or dies to himself, but each is bound to the other by what Christ has done. Christ is the Christian's example in living by the law of love's generosity (15:7–13). The imminence of his coming makes it all the more imperative that the believer conduct himself becomingly, subjecting his own desires to identification with Christ (13:11–14).

---

[123] Beare, "Letter to the Romans," *IDB*, IV, p. 121.

In this section Paul also gives instruction in a matter that must have been a live issue for the early Church; namely, the responsibility of the Church to civil authority (13:1–7). Intense persecution of the Church by Rome still was in the future (although not-too-distant), but those with Jewish background undoubtedly brought into the Christian faith their strong anti-Roman feelings and many Gentiles may have believed that their loyalty to Christ released them from responsibility to Rome. On this matter Paul spoke rather decisively. Civil rule is a part of divine order and ought to be obeyed (13:2–3).[124]

Paul's confidence in the beneficence of Rome must have been enhanced by his personal experience. Roman authority had protected him from violent hands, and the unity of the empire facilitated the spread of the gospel over open roads and sea lanes. Prevalent religious tolerance made possible open adherence to a legally recognized faith. If Paul had written during the Roman persecution of the Church,[125] his instructions might have included the possibility of resistance to the tyranny of civil authority. During Paul's lifetime, however, Rome appeared to be more friend than enemy.[126] Yet the Apostle's instructions here are not merely kind words for a patronizing political rule. Rather government is seen as the extension of God's authority and rulers are the servants of God (13:1, 4). This is the foundation for the Christian's civil responsibility as a religious duty.

CONCLUDING PERSONAL MATTERS (15:14–33). The epistle to the Romans concludes, assuming that chapter 16 is not an integral part of the original letter, with an explanation for writing such a long letter to a church which he did not know personally and a review of his plans to come to Rome after taking the offering to Jerusalem.

With Face Toward Rome

The Roman epistle marked a watershed in the experience of Paul. It is the ripened fruit of accumulated personal struggles. Deeply imbedded in the consciousness of its author is the revolutionary personal encounter in which the Apostle himself has been made aware of a new power coming into the world through Christianity. The planting of the gospel in the major eastern cities, Antioch, Corinth, and Ephesus, had convinced him of the universal relevance of the gospel which

---

124 See below, Chapter 12, for a discussion of attitudes toward the empire.
125 See below, pp. 410–416.
126 Knox, "The Epistle to the Romans," *IB*, IX, p. 600.

he had come to know personally. Now his enthusiasm turned westward in eager anticipation of a fruitful ministry in Rome, ultimately reaching toward Spain.

SUGGESTED READINGS

In addition to the commentaries on Acts and the books on Paul see:

BAILEY, JOHN W., "The First and Second Epistles to the Thessalonians: Introduction and Exegesis," *IB*, Vol. XI.

BARRETT, C. K., *A Commentary on the Epistle to the Romans* (Harper, 1957).

CRAIG, CLARENCE T., "The First Epistle to the Corinthians: Introduction and Exegesis," *IB*, Vol. X.

DODD, C. H., *The Epistle of Paul to the Romans* (Harper, 1932).

FILSON, FLOYD V., "The Second Epistle to the Corinthians: Introduction and Exegesis," *IB*, Vol. X.

KNOX, JOHN, "The Epistle to the Romans: Introduction and Exegesis," *IB*, Vol. IX.

MOFFATT, JAMES, *The First Epistle of Paul to the Corinthians* (Harper, 1938).

NEIL, WILLIAM, *The Epistles of Paul to the Thessalonians* (Harper, 1950).

STRACHAN, R. H., *The Second Epistle of Paul to the Corinthians* (Harper, 1935).

10

Paul, the Prisoner

For all practical purposes Acts concludes the description of Paul's public ministry with the Aegean mission. In chapters 21 through 28, comprising a quarter of the book, no new churches are founded by Paul and nothing about the growth of previously established churches or of the Apostle's relationship to them appears. Nevertheless, these chapters develop two themes essential to the purposes of Acts.[1] First, Luke demonstrates the increasing self-exclusion of Jerusalem Jews who not only reject the gospel preached faithfully by Paul, but also instigate the process which leads to the arrest and imprisonment of the Apostle. Then Luke presents the theme of the inclusion of the Gentiles and transforms Paul's seemingly hopeless plight into victory. The trial of Paul brings the Apostle to Gentiles in Rome itself, the final episode in Luke's drama of Christian expansion. Masterfully Luke delivers Paul from a situation which is on the verge of destroying him and turns the circumstances to positive use in bringing the gospel to Rome.[2]

In this final quarter of Acts Paul's faithfulness to Judaism is also stressed. The Apostle defends himself in successive scenes before the Roman tribune in Jerusalem, the Sanhedrin, the provincial governors in Caesarea, and King Agrippa. Finally on appeal he is transported to Rome with the intimation that he will appear before Caesar himself. Throughout the discourses the apologetic note sounds clearly.

Again and again Paul speaks . . . of his past; he never tires of demonstrating how faithful to the law he is as a Jew, and how irreproachably he has

---

[1] See Frank Stagg, *The Book of Acts,* p. 1. Also Jacques Dupont, "Le Salut des Gentiles et la Signification du Livre des Actes," *NTS,* VI (1959–60), 139–155.
[2] Ernst Haenchen, "The Book of Acts as Source Material for the History of Early Christianity," *Studies in Luke–Acts,* eds. Keck and Martyn, pp. 275–276.

lived. But such apologies are not a retreat into memories of happy days now past. Rather, they step up the dramatic action to higher and higher levels.[3]

Interestingly Acts makes little, if anything, of the offering for the poor Christians in Jerusalem. The Pauline letters, however, give a major role to this, suggesting that Paul's primary purpose in going to Jerusalem was to take the offering, probably to cement Gentile and Jewish relationships. Although Acts regards the visit as strategically important, the fulfillment of a vow, and not an offering, seems to be the motive (18:18; 21:23–26). The one reference, "I came to bring my nation alms and offering" (24:17), could refer to a temple offering as easily as to aid for the church. Possibly Luke felt the hostility between Gentile and Jew had already been resolved and so did not regard the collection as strategic,[4] but more probably he subordinated this event as detracting from his theme of Jewish self-exclusion.

ARREST AND IMPRISONMENT

Last Journey to Jerusalem

Transition: The Ephesian Speech. The transition between the Aegean mission and the final phase of Paul's life is marked by a major Pauline speech. The leaders of the Ephesian church were called to the seacoast town Miletus for a final farewell visit with the Apostle. In a strongly personal and moving address (20:18–35) he eloquently confessed his thorough commitment to the Christian ministry and admonished the elders to accept their privileged responsibility: "Take heed to yourselves and to all the flock, in which the Holy Spirit has made you guardians, to feed the church of the Lord which he obtained with his own blood" (Acts 20:28). Tenderly the Apostle's speech encourages faithfulness to an uncontaminated gospel. The speech is one of the non-kerygmatic speeches in Acts, aiming to present Paul as an ideal missionary and to reflect the concern of the Church with increasing false teaching.[5]

This speech is also important because of what it has to say about early Church leadership. Luke refers to the Ephesian leaders as "presbyters" (20:17); the speech of Paul calls them "bishops" (20:28). The two designations are used for the same "officers," illustrating that at

---

[3] *Ibid.*, p. 275.

[4] So A. C. Purdy, "Paul, The Apostle," *IDB*, III, p. 687.

[5] G. H. C. Macgregor, "The Acts of The Apostles," *IB*, IX, p. 270, argues for Pauline composition of this speech. Cf. also F. J. Foakes-Jackson and Kirsopp Lake, eds., *Beginnings of Christianity*, V, pp. 412–413.

the time Acts was written, toward the end of the first century, no clearly defined order of church officers had developed.[6] Terms such as "presbyter" and "bishop" were used interchangeably to designate those who by personal and religious prestige naturally exercised leadership without any official election or appointment.

Incidentally, the speech also contains one of the infrequent sayings of Jesus not found in the Gospels: "It is more blessed to give than to receive" (20:35).

Journey to Jerusalem. The story of Paul's journey from Miletus to Jerusalem (21:1–16) is told with the dramatic flair of a literary artist. With a participant's enthusiasm [7] the sea voyage is recounted in detail. The sailing party traveled on a small coasting boat along the southwestern shore of Asia Minor, landing successively at Rhodes and Patara. Then they boarded a larger ship for the open sea voyage south of the island Cyprus directly to Tyre. While the ship unloaded its cargo, Paul spent a week with the church in Tyre. From Tyre they sailed south along the Palestinian coast [8] to Ptolemais. After a day's visit with the church there, Paul moved on to Caesarea, where he spent several days before going up to Jerusalem.

The mood of the narrative is urgency. Paul was hastening to Jerusalem to be present for the observance of Pentecost (20:16). Luke indicates that nothing could deter the Apostle from the final trip to Jerusalem. At Tyre he was advised to change his plans (21:4) and at Caesarea a prophet-like figure, Agabus, came down from Judea and in acted parable warned Paul of the danger that awaited him in Jerusalem (21:10–11). But the Apostle could not be turned back. His determination to continue the enterprise is reflected in words that seem to settle the issue: "For I am ready not only to be imprisoned but even to die at Jerusalem for the name of the Lord Jesus" (21:13). Here again is illustrated how Luke uses his materials to communicate his message. Even as he recounts a sea voyage, he intertwines those items which increase the reader's anticipation of the Apostle's arrival in Jerusalem. The story of Paul's last journey to the holy city gradually builds to the climax when the Apostle arrives in Jerusalem and antagonism breaks into open violence.

---

[6] B. H. Streeter, *Primitive Christianity*, p. 114, indicates that no passage in the New Testament demands that "bishop" and "presbyter" be names for different offices.

[7] The voyage is part of the "we" section 20:5–16 and 21:1–18.

[8] It is possible that the trip from Tyre to Caesarea was made by land, but probably the ship was moving down the coast loading and unloading cargo.

Riot in Jerusalem. Luke's report of what happens in Jerusalem emphasizes that Paul is blameless. He immediately went to the elders, including James, the leader of the church, to report the success of his Gentile mission. The report was received with mixed feeling. The elders glorified God for the success, but feared the reaction of their more conservative peers who felt that Paul was leading Jews too far from Mosaic tradition. James suggested that Paul placate these by assisting four Jerusalem Christians in the fulfillment of a religious vow.[9] Although Paul recognized the act as an expedient compromise, he agreed to it in the interest of decreasing antagonism. He still had enough sympathy for his Jewish heritage to participate in the ritual act. Paul was not an iconoclast, seeking to break old forms simply because they were old. He even expressed a willingness to become a Jew to the Jews in order to win them to the gospel.[10]

But granting the Apostle this concession, was his behavior a denial of the gospel he had preached? Did his proclamation of the inability of Jewish law to reconcile man to God make participation in a cultic act hypocritical? The Jerusalem charges that Paul was leading men away from Jewish legalism were true, even if they may have been exaggerated. The Apostle's correspondence makes this lucidly clear. Paul may have agreed to the act as a means for improving relationships between Jewish and Gentile Christians, but he surely made no concession about the gospel of salvation apart from the law.

Luke. uses the incident to place responsibility for rejection of the gospel where he feels that it belongs, namely, on the Jews themselves. The Lucan Paul was still loyal to Judaism, seeing no particular sacrifice of principle in taking part in a Jewish religious ritual.[11] According to Luke, conflict arises, not because Paul rejects Judaism, but because the Jews reject the Christian gospel. Responsibility for the rift rests solely upon Paul's opponents.

Unfortunately Paul's compromise did not achieve the desired results. If he had hoped to reconcile Jewish and non-Jewish elements in the church, trouble came from other quarters. "Asian Jews" slanderously charged that a Gentile from Ephesus, Trophimus, had been taken into the temple, an act punishable by death. The entrance to the temple carried an inscription warning non-Jews that trespassing the sacred area would bring their death. Whether the charge was really believed by the Jews or merely utilized to achieve their purpose, the result was

[9] Probably a Nazarite vow. Cf. Num. 6:1f.
[10] Cf. I Cor. 9:20.
[11] Cf. C. W. Emmet, *Beginnings of Christianity,* II, p. 294.

Figure 10–1. This Greek inscription from Herod's temple reads: "Let no foreigner enter inside the barrier and the fence around the sanctuary. Whosoever is caught will be the cause of death following as a penalty." (Source: Department of Archaeology, Hebrew University, Jerusalem.)

the same. A riot threatening the Apostle's life was incited. Only the intervention of the Roman tribune (a point of no little consequence to Luke) saved Paul from almost certain death.

The Defense Speeches. In this last section of Acts four major defense speeches are attributed to Paul (22:3–21; 23:1–6; 24:10–21; 26:2–23). Three of these are before Roman officials and the other one before the Sanhedrin. The first speech is reported in connection with the Jerusalem riot (22:3–21).

It may be questioned whether rioting Jews would have calmed enough for Paul to deliver a major address. Luke's concern here, however, is to say more about the nature of the Christian faith and Paul's ministry and their relationship to Roman authority than to report precisely on events that may have transpired. As the story goes in Acts, the Jews heard Paul speaking Hebrew and quieted enough for the Apostle to recount his conversion and early Jewish associations. The speech stresses that Ananias, the man who commissioned Paul, was no renegade Jew, but "a devout man according to the law, well spoken of by all the Jews" (22:12). The crowd listened patiently while Paul reviewed his conversion, but when he mentioned his commission to go to the Gentiles, the riot flared again.

Events which followed led to Paul's imprisonment in Caesarea. The tribune proposed to determine the cause of the riot through "examination by scourging" hoping to discover what about Paul aroused such antagonism, but before he could carry out his intention Paul appealed to his Roman citizenship and escaped the lash. Subsequently the tribune brought Paul before the Sanhedrin still searching for the real reason for Jewish opposition to the Apostle. Paul's defense before the Jewish court is reported in only enough detail to communicate a caricature of the Sanhedrin. Paul introduced a discussion of the resurrection, a subject upon which Pharisaic and Sadducean elements in the Sanhedrin violently disagreed. Such dissension arose that again the Roman tribune was forced to intervene. Avoiding a Jewish plot to kill Paul, the official delivered the Apostle to the custody of the governor, who resided in Caesarea. But Luke indicates clearly where the complex series of events leads:

The following night the Lord stood by him and said, "Take courage, for as you have testified about me at Jerusalem, so you must bear witness also at Rome." (23:11)

The letter which accompanied the prisoner to Caesarea completely vindicates Paul before Roman authorities:

Claudius Lysias to his Excellency the governor Felix, greeting. This man was seized by the Jews, and was about to be killed by them, when I came upon them with the soldiers and rescued him, having learned that he was a Roman citizen. And desiring to know the charge on which they accused him, I brought him down to their council. I found that he was accused about questions of their law, but charged with nothing deserving death or imprisonment. And when it was disclosed to me that there would be a plot against the man, I sent him to you at once, ordering his accusers also to state before you what they have against him. (23:26–30)

Paul had done nothing worthy of imprisonment or death! This is precisely the point that Luke is making. "Wherever in Acts Christianity is brought to the cognizance of Roman authorities, its innocent character is vindicated to their entire satisfaction." [12] Whereas orthodox Judaism is consistently hostile to Paul and his gospel, the verdict of Roman officialdom is always favorable. Thus Luke demonstrates that Christianity, even as Judaism, is *religio licita*, recognized if not promoted, by Roman authority. The same theme will be emphasized in additional encounters with official Rome.

From Caesarea to Rome

Before Felix. Paul's removal to Caesarea by Lysiás, the tribune who discovered the plot to assassinate Paul, brought the Apostle before Felix, the Roman procurator stationed in Caesarea. The trial reported

[12] Macgregor, "The Acts of The Apostles," *IB*, IX, p. 285.

Figure 10–2. Roman amphitheatre at Caesarea. (Source: Foreign Mission Board, SBC.)

in Acts 26 must have been typical of exchanges between Felix and Paul over a considerable period.[13] Although "there is nothing in Luke's narrative that is either improbable or inconsistent," [14] we cannot be certain that Acts preserves an historically reliable description. Certainly, in telling the story Luke continues to demonstrate the vindication of the gospel before Rome in spite of Jewish opposition. Also, he is interested to clarify the circumstances whereby Paul appeals to Caesar and thereby goes to Rome with the gospel.

Paul's trial before Felix continues the encounter between the Apostle and the Jews. Ananias, the high priest, and Tertullus, a spokesman for the Jews, came to Caesarea to present their case against Paul before Felix (24:1–6). Paul was accused not only of profaning the temple and agitating "all the Jews throughout the world," but more seriously of being ringleader of a Nazarene sect (24:5). If the Jews could con-

---

[13] Cf. 24:27. The "two years" here could mean two years after Paul's arrest or two years after Felix began his term of office.

[14] Macgregor, "The Acts of The Apostles," *IB*, IX, p. 307.

vince Felix that the latter charge involved seditious revolt against Rome, their case would be made and their objective easily achieved.

In the third non-kerygmatic speech in this section of Acts, Paul defended himself against these charges (24:10–21). He was in the temple for worship, not desecration. He had brought gifts to Jerusalem, proving that he had not broken connections with Jewish traditions. And, more importantly, he worshipped the God of the Jews and believed in the law and the prophets. The clear implication is that, since Judaism is a sanctioned religion, his practice of the Way still considered a sect of Judaism, should not be interpreted as seditious. Even the Sanhedrin had found no wrongdoing at this point.

Felix was convinced of Paul's innocence, but was unwilling to make any decision which might antagonize the Jews (24:22–23, 27). Therefore, on the pretext of awaiting additional information, he reserved decision on the matter. Paul was kept in custody, but granted considerable freedom (24:23). Discussion between Paul and Felix continued, probably on the basis of the procurator's fancied interest in Jewish matters because of his marriage to the Jewess Druscilla.[15] Debate and delay continued throughout Felix's tenure as procurator. When he was recalled to Rome in A.D. 60 and replaced by Porcius Festus,[16] Paul's case had still not been decided. Why the situation was carried over to Festus, rather than dismissed as was provided by Roman law, is uncertain. Some have supposed that this, along with the beginning of trial under Festus as if nothing had previously been done, prove that Luke invented the Felix trial. It is not too incredible to suppose, however, that one whose rule was so characterized by maladministration would have left Paul's case unresolved.[17]

Before Festus. Paul's trial under Festus was essentially a repeat of what had transpired under Felix. The new procurator heard the Jewish authorities first in Jerusalem and later in Caesarea. Unconvinced by their charges, Festus sought some peaceful means to do justice for Paul and at the same time satisfy the Jews. The determining factor was his official concern to placate the Jews and avoid disturbing the always tenuous *pax Romana*. When Festus proposed to take Paul back

---

[15] 24:24. Druscilla was the daughter of Herod Agrippa I and sister of Agrippa II and Bernice. Cf. 25:23f.

[16] Josephus, *Antiquities*, XX, viii, 5–6, credits Felix with the kind of cruelty and oppression which produced the Jewish war against Rome in A.D. 66.

[17] For an interesting and informative discussion of the legal aspects, see, H. J. Cadbury, "Roman Law and The Trial of Paul," *The Beginnings of Christianity*, eds. Foakes-Jackson and Lake, V, pp. 297–338.

to Jerusalem for trial, the Apostle exercised his right as a Roman citizen to appeal to Caesar. Paul apparently interpreted the procurator's attitude to be moving in the direction of an unfavorable verdict and did not want to risk the return of his case to Jewish jurisdiction. Certainly Luke sees in Paul's appeal the hand of providence guiding the Apostle to the imperial capital. When Festus had conferred with his advisors, he stated, "You have appealed to Caesar; and to Caesar you shall go" (25:12).

For all practical purposes the appeal concluded the jurisdiction of Festus and transferred the trial to Rome. However, Luke includes a dramatic appearance before Herod Agrippa II and his sister Bernice (25:13–26:32). In this way he introduces a third account of Paul's conversion and further demonstrates the Apostle's innocence. The details are colored by the apologetic character of the narrative, but there is no real reason for doubting the essential historicity of the event.[18] Agrippa II, whose father had been king of Judea until his death in A.D. 44, was ruler of the old tetrarchy of Philip northwest of the Sea of Galilee. He was thoroughly Roman in upbringing and loyalty and his constant companionship with his sister Bernice created a scandal among the Jews.[19] When Festus succeeded Felix as procurator of Judea, Agrippa, accompanied by Bernice, came to Caesarea to salute him. According to Luke (25:13) this was the occasion when Paul appeared before him.

Paul's appearance before Festus, Agrippa, and Bernice was more a hearing than a trial. Acts suggests that Festus was enlisting the aid of Agrippa in formulating charges to be forwarded with Paul to Caesar (25:26–27), but Luke was more interested in introducing another Pauline speech. The address attributed to Paul stands as a model defense of Christianity. A third summary of Paul's conversion is included and the continuity between Judaism and Christianity is stressed. Paul declared his obedience to "the heavenly vision" which had summoned him to proclaim light to all peoples (26:23). Festus thought the speech was illustration enough that Paul was mad[20] and Agrippa became impatient with his consistent proclamation of Christ, but Luke emphasizes that both officials judged, "This man is doing nothing to deserve death or imprisonment" (26:31). Indeed Paul might have been set free had he not appealed to Caesar.

[18] Macgregor, "The Acts of The Apostles," *IB*, IX, pp. 318–319.

[19] *Antiquities*, XX, vii, 3.

[20] 26:24, not "inspired," as F. J. Foakes-Jackson, *The Acts of The Apostles,* p. 226, contends, but "irrational."

Voyage to Rome. Acts 27:1–28:16 is one of the classic accounts of sea voyage in ancient literature [21] and throws considerable light on ancient nautical methods. The passage is the final of the "we" sections of Acts, and we may appropriately assume that the vivid and dramatic story is a trustworthy picture of Paul's voyage as a Roman prisoner.[22] The description catches the tension and violence of the dangerous winter voyage which ended in shipwreck. One can almost sense the personal anxiety written into the account:

And when the south wind blew gently, supposing that they had obtained their purpose, they weighed anchor and sailed along Crete, close inshore. But soon a tempestuous wind, called the northeaster, struck down from the land; and when the ship was caught and could not face the wind, we gave way to it and were driven. And running under the lee of a small island called Cauda, we managed with difficulty to secure the boat; after hoisting it up, they took measures to undergird the ship; then fearing that they should run on the Syrtis, they lowered the gear and so were driven. As we were violently storm-tossed, they began next day to throw the cargo overboard; and the third day they cast out with their own hands the tackle of the ship. And when neither sun nor stars appeared for many a day, and no small tempest lay on us, all hope of our being saved was at last abandoned.[23]

The vivid description, however, does not veil Luke's purpose in telling the story. Primarily, he aims to glorify Paul. Throughout the narrative the Apostle, although a prisoner, is the dominant character. He openly advises against sailing so late in the fall because of the danger of contrary winds and storm (27:9–10). When hope had been lost in the storm, Paul encouraged the sailors to take heart, assuring them that God would protect all life (27:21–25). The Apostle persuaded the centurion to allow no soldiers to leave the ship (27:31) and urged the passengers and crew to eat to keep up their strength (27:33–36). After the shipwreck on Malta, Paul befriended the chief official of the island and was honored with many gifts. To Luke, Paul's spiritual perception (27:10) was superior to those better endowed with worldly wisdom. Clearly the writer is particularly concerned to dem-

---

[21] An old but still classic study of this passage is James Smith, *The Voyage and Shipwreck of St. Paul.* A shorter study appears in W. M. Ramsay, *St. Paul the Traveller and the Roman Citizen,* pp. 314–346.

[22] Some have supposed that the passage represents the secular account of a shipwreck to which have been added Pauline references. So Martin Dibelius, *Studies in The Acts of The Apostles,* pp. 134, 204–206; Hans Conzelmann, "Geschichte, Geschichtsbild und Geschichtsdarstellung bei Lukas," *Theologische Literaturzeitung,* LXXIX (1960), 242–248; and others. A contrary view, however, is expressed by Ernst Haenchen, "Das 'Wir' in der Apostelgeschichte und das Itinerar," *Zeitschrift für Theologie und Kirche,* LVIII (1961), 358f.

[23] Acts 27:13–20.

Figure 10–3. The old Via Appia leading into Rome. (Source: Foreign Mission Board, SBC.)

onstrate that nothing, including storm and shipwreck, could deter the Apostle's arrival in Rome.

After waiting out most of the winter in Malta, the company boarded another ship and sailed for the Italian mainland. Luke traces the ports of call through Puteoli where Paul met fellow Christians and was "invited to stay with them for seven days." [24] Afterwards Christians came to the Forum of Appius and Three Taverns to meet Paul and escort him up the Via Appia to Rome. "The warmth of their greeting may

[24] 28:14. This may represent an insertion to allow the Roman Christians time to hear of Paul's arrival and come to meet him.

Figure 10–4. The Roman Forum, center of the city's social, political, and commercial life. (Source: Foreign Mission Board, SBC.)

be taken as an indication of the effect of Paul's letter written from Corinth to them." [25]

In Rome. In the imperial capital Paul remained a Roman prisoner, but regrettably Acts does not tell the story of how the Apostle's case was resolved. The author simply relates that Paul was allowed to stay in his own quarters with a soldier as personal guard (28:16). He lived in these circumstances for two years (28:30), permitted to welcome all who came to him and to preach the gospel of Christ freely.

Luke concludes his narrative of the spread of the gospel from Jerusalem to Rome emphatically. The central purpose of Acts is brought to climax in a single episode. Paul called together the local leaders of the Jews who presumably would press the charges brought against the Apostle by the Jerusalem leaders. They, however, had had no letters from Judea and knew of no brethren coming from Jerusalem to accuse him before Caesar (28:21). Surprisingly Luke practically brushes this

[25] Donald J. Selby, *Toward the Understanding of St. Paul*, p. 229.

issue aside in the interest of demonstrating once again the Jewish rejection of the gospel already observed in other contexts. In spite of intensive effort Paul had been no more than modestly successful in converting the Jews, so the Apostle is made to apply Isaiah 6:9–10 to the Jews, describing them as a people whose heart had grown dull and whose ears were hard of hearing. Consequently, ". . . this salvation of God has been sent to the Gentiles, they will listen." [26] Luke obviously considers the Jews to have been rejected. In Rome to the Gentiles Paul continued "preaching the kingdom of God and teaching about the Lord Jesus Christ quite openly and unhindered" (28:31). With this, Luke brings his work to an abrupt, but nonetheless artistic and intended ending.[27] The Jews had rejected the gospel and it had been brought to Rome. Now that gospel, universal in design, stood on the threshold of unimagined possibilities—unhindered.[28]

Luke finished Acts without so much as a hint at the final outcome of Paul's appeal to Caesar and no other extant source provides any data about Paul between his arrival in Rome and his death. Early noncanonical references consistently indicate a martyrdom in Rome, but the source of this tradition cannot be traced with accuracy.[29] The theory that Paul was released from prison and conducted a mission to Spain, perhaps followed by a return to the Aegean region, before his rearrest and execution has been attractive to some scholars. Lake suggested a statute of limitation of two years so that, when neither the Jerusalem leaders nor their representatives carried through on their charges, Paul was released.[30] Some see a visit to Spain implied in the statement in I Clement that Paul came "to the boundary of the West" (5:7). Further the idea that Paul was released is attractive to those who consider the Pastoral Epistles wholly or predominantly Pauline.[31] First Timothy and Titus might then be placed in the interval of release and II Timothy in the second imprisonment. Thus it is supposed that the reference in II Timothy to rescue "from the lion's mouth" (II

---

[26] 28:28. Cf. 13:46; 18:6.

[27] Other possible explanations for the abrupt ending of Acts are summarized by Macgregor, "The Acts of The Apostles," *IB*, IX, p. 351–352. See also Lake and Cadbury, eds., *The Beginnings of Christianity*, IV, pp. 349f. The suggestion that Luke planned a third volume seems improbable, although possible.

[28] Cf. Stagg, *The Book of Acts*, p. 1.

[29] I Clement 5:7; the Muratorian Fragment; Tertullian, *Scorpiace*, 15; Eusebius, *EH*, II, xxv, 5–8; Jerome, *Lives of Illustrious Men*, V; all refer to martyrdom in Rome. A summary of these ancient traditions appears in W. J. Conybeare and J. S. Howson, *The Life and Epistles of St. Paul, II*, pp. 488–490.

[30] Foakes-Jackson and Lake, *The Beginnings of Christianity*, V, pp. 325–336.

[31] See below, p. 511.

Timothy 4:17), referred to Paul's deliverance from the first imprisonment.[32]

However, the evidence supporting a release from prison is not at all clear and had Paul been exonerated, it is highly improbable that Luke, who was continually concerned with the Apostle's good standing before Roman authority, would have neglected to tell us so. Additionally it would undoubtedly have become a major topic of discussion in the early Church. The absence of any such record "alone almost compels us to pronounce Paul's alleged acquittal to be a fiction, and to conclude that his two years' captivity ended with conviction and death." [33]

PRISON CORRESPONDENCE

Four letters in the traditional Pauline corpus which were written from prison are usually referred to as the "prison correspondence" and treated as a group. In Philippians Paul is imprisoned and awaiting trial, a fact which "has really served to advance the gospel" (1:12). Both Colossians and Philemon, dispatched concurrently by a certain Tychicus, refer to the author's imprisonment.[34] Ephesians also, although more complex problems are associated with its date and authorship, was written from prison. (Second Timothy also is written from prison, but it is treated along with I Timothy and Titus as a Pastoral Epistle.)

However, to recognize these as prison letters does not resolve the problem of their origin. Assuming that the epistles are from Paul, from which of his imprisonments were they written? Clearly, Caesarea and Rome are two alternatives. At these places the Apostle was confined for considerable time,[35] but with sufficient liberty to engage in both writing and preaching. Traditionally the prison correspondence has been traced to Rome, primarily because of references in Philippians to the praetorian guard (1:13), to "those of Caesar's household" (4:22), and to Paul's freedom to preach the gospel from prison. These references fit most naturally into the Roman situation.[36] But the assump-

---

[32] The reference may be to persecution in the early Church.

[33] Macgregor, "The Acts of The Apostles," *IB*, IX, p. 350.

[34] Col. 4:3, 10, 18; Philemon 1, 9, 10, 13, 23.

[35] Cf. Acts 24:27; 28:30.

[36] C. H. Dodd, *New Testament Studies*, pp. 85–108, argues vigorously for Rome in a detailed critique of G. S. Duncan's statement of the Ephesian hypothesis in his *St. Paul's Ephesian Ministry*. See also P. N. Harrison, "The Pastoral Epistles and Duncan's Ephesian Theory," *NTS*, II (1955–56), 250–261; and Rahtjen, "The Three Letters of Paul to the Philippians," *NTS*, VI (1959–60), 167–173.

tion that the prison correspondence comes from Rome is not without numerous difficulties in the individual letters. Consequently, scholarship has turned its attention to other possibilities for the origin of one or more of these letters. Considerable study has been given to Caesarea and Ephesus, especially the latter.

It has become increasingly popular to conjecture an imprisonment in Ephesus from which one or more of the prison letters could have been written.[37] Arguments rest largely on Paul's reference to "far more imprisonments" in II Corinthians (11:23) and the silence of Acts. The Corinthians reference suggests more than the imprisonment at Philippi (the only one preceding the writing of the Corinthian letter of which we are certain). Further, Paul reports that he had "fought with beasts at Ephesus" (I Corinthians 15:32), metaphorically hinting at extraordinary difficulties. Since he was in Ephesus for some time, it is highly possible that one of Paul's many imprisonments was in Ephesus. The silence of Acts on such an experience is not considered too significant because of the selective method with which Luke regularly deals with his materials. Evidence is simply too scarce for certainty.

Even if an Ephesian imprisonment is conjectured, the question of whether the letters were written from Ephesus remains. Here it is easier to argue against Rome than for Ephesus. One key point is that in none of the so-called prison letters is there a single identifying reference to Paul's difficulties in Jerusalem, his imprisonment in Caesarea, his harrowing ordeal of the sea voyage and shipwreck, or his arrival in Rome. Why would letters written from Rome to fellow Christians intimately interested in the Apostle not contain at least passing mention of the dramatic events associated with Jerusalem, Caesarea, and Rome? Would not these letters then have been written before these momentous events? Certainly the question is serious enough that the Rome hypothesis cannot be accepted uncritically.

All of this simply indicates the complexity of the problem of the origin of the prison correspondence. Until more positive evidence becomes available, the question is not likely to be settled, and then answers are more likely to come concerning the individual letters than about the whole "collection." Generalizations about the four letters at this point in biblical studies cannot go beyond the observation that they all were written from prison. Continuing study and discussion must entertain Rome, Ephesus, Caesarea, or some as yet undesignated place as possibilities.

[37] See above, pp. 303–304.

Philippians: Epistle of Christian Gratitude

The origin of Philippians during the Roman imprisonment is supported by references to the praetorian guard and Caesar's household (1:13; 4:22). Ordinarily these references point to Rome. Recent inscriptional materials indicate, however, that the praetorian guard existed in many imperial cities and groups of Roman citizens anywhere in the empire might have been referred to as those of Caesar's household. Thus, although evidence of Roman origin is strong, it is not conclusive.[38] Some understand the letter itself to presuppose quick communication and exchange of reports between Paul and the church. Before the letter was written, the distance between Philippi and the place of Paul's imprisonment had been traversed at least four times. Since four journeys between Rome and Philippi would have demanded several months, it seems unlikely that the Apostle would have been so far away. Would Paul have waited so long to thank the Philippians for their gift? Further, why does the Apostle propose a trip to Philippi, as he does in the letter (2:24), if he has his eye set on Spain as a mission field? On the basis of these and other arguments [39] some scholars lean strongly toward Ephesus as the place most nearly fitting the requirements for Philippians.[40] Arguments for Ephesus are not conclusive however. Is Ephesus that much nearer Philippi than Rome? Without new sources the question of where Philippians was written cannot be answered with certainty, and Rome creates as few problems as either Ephesus or Caesarea.

Occasion and Purpose. Philippians was addressed to the first congregation established by Paul during his Aegean mission. The immediate occasion which prompted the letter was the return of Epaphroditus, who earlier had brought a gift to Paul from the church.[41] Seemingly, the intent had been for Epaphroditus to remain with Paul as a helper, but he had become ill. Now he was sufficiently recovered to be sent back to Philippi. Paul wrote the letter to accompany Epa-

[38] T. W. Manson, "The Date of the Epistle to the Philippians," *Studies in the Gospels and the Epistles,* ed. M. Black, pp. 149–167, argues for the origin of Philippians in Ephesus when Paul was not in prison. E. Lohmeyer, *Der Brief an die Philipper,* pp. 3–4, argues for the origin of Philippians from Caesarea.

[39] A summary of these may be found in FBK, pp. 229–235.

[40] See, for example, G. S. Duncan, "Paul's Ministry in Asia—The Lost Phase," *NTS,* III (1956–57), 218.

[41] See C. D. Buchanan, "Epaphroditus' Sickness and the Letter to the Philippians," *Evangelical Quarterly,* XXXVI (1964), 157ff.

phroditus to assure the church that he was returning because of illness and not inefficiency. Additionally, Paul repeated the gratitude which had earlier been expressed for their gift, reported on his status in prison, and included exhortation and instructions for the church. He hoped that the written word would be implemented by the personal testimony of Epaphroditus.

These purposes are achieved in a letter reflecting Paul's close and satisfying relationship with the Philippians. The letter is intensely personal, a "most unlabored, spontaneous expression of the Christian way . . . by one who had lived it out, fought it out, and thought it out under the severest pressure to the bitter end." [42] Personal radiance overflowing the confidence of a full life "in Christ" undergirds the epistle. The word *joy* and its equivalents appear in Philippians more often than in all other Pauline writings combined. The Apostle's attitude in writing is adequately expressed in the forceful saying in the letter's introduction: "For me to live is Christ, and to die is gain" (1:21).

Outline and Interpretation. The thought of Philippians does not easily yield to a logical outline. Ideas tend to tumble over each other as the Apostle pours out his personal reflections to a church with which his relations have been continually cordial.[43] Their recent gift even heightens the emotion with which he writes. Thus, as much as any other of Paul's writings, Philippians bears the marks of personal correspondence. A brief outline suggests the major items that appear in the book.

Introduction. 1:1–11
    A. Salutation. 1:1–2
    B. Thanksgiving. 1:3–11

  I. Paul's Response to his Present Situation. 1:12–26

 II. Living the Worthy Life. 1:27–2:18
    A. Exhortation to stand firm. 1:27–30
    B. Pursuit of Christ's example. 2:1–18

III. Recommendation of Epaphroditus. 2:19–30
    A. Plans for Timothy. 2:19–24
    B. Epaphroditus' illness. 2:25–30

[42] Ernest F. Scott, "The Epistle to the Philippians," *IB*, XI, p. 14.

[43] Some account for the character of the epistle by assuming that the present letter represents several letters or fragments of letters woven together. So Rahtjen, "The Three Letters of Paul to the Philippians," *NTS*, VI (1959–60), 167–173. See also Edgar J. Goodspeed, *An Introduction to the New Testament*, pp. 90–92. B. S. Mackay, "Further Thoughts on Philippians," *NTS*, VII (1960–61), 161–170, argues against the three-letter hypothesis.

I. Paul's Response to his Present Situation (1:12–26). After opening his letter with the warmest gratitude for their partnership in the gospel, Paul reports to the Philippians his reaction to imprisonment. The church may have heard many, and perhaps conflicting, stories about how Paul was faring in prison and what the outcome was likely to be. The Apostle himself at times seems to think that his deliverance is imminent (1:19), but then again seems to see death close at hand (1:19–26). He wants the Philippians to know that he faces whatever outcome with confidence in Christ. He indicates his purpose to come to Philippi (1:25–26), but also seeks to reassure them in event he is not delivered from prison.

The most important point, however, which he makes about his imprisonment is that the proclamation of the gospel was unhindered. His associates had been encouraged to more boldness because of the Apostle's imprisonment and even some who were dissociating themselves from him were still proclaiming the name of Christ. This progress of the gospel, and not his own troubles, was Paul's concern. He could pass over his own situation in the confidence that what was happening "really served to advance the gospel" (1:12).

II. Living the Worthy Life (1:27–2:18). From his response to his own situation Paul turned to admonish the Philippians to cultivate the worthy life. They too must be willing to suffer for the faith, standing firm in a manner of life worthy of the gospel of Christ (1:27–30). The character of this life is above all else unselfish and loving participation in the unified body of Christ (2:1–5), and the single criterion by which the good life is measured is the example of Christ. The Philippians are encouraged to have among themselves the same controlling idea demonstrated in Christ, who "emptied himself, taking the form of a servant, being born in the likeness of men. And being found in human form he humbled himself and became obedient unto death, even death on a cross" (2:7–8). Such self-forgetting renunciation must become the Christian's guide for working out his salvation without grumbling or questioning (2:12–14). Emphasis is laid on obedience grounded in the will of God which has been clearly demonstrated in the utter self-giving and subsequent exaltation of Christ.

The passage which defines the mind of Christ, 2:6–11, is "the chief glory of the Epistle to the Philippians." [44] Stylistically these verses are very different from the remainder of the letter. The general character of the letter is informal. This passage, however, is carefully and poetically structured, and may represent an early Christian hymn or poem inserted here by Paul for illustrative purposes.[45] Whatever their origin, the verses represent a height of eloquence rarely achieved in the Pauline epistles and one of the finest Christological statements known from the early Church.

III. RECOMMENDATION OF EPAPHRODITUS (2:19–30). Paul now comes to the immediate purpose for writing the letter, the commendation of Epaphroditus, who is returning to Philippi after recuperating from an illness. An apologetic air surrounds these paragraphs. Paul would like to come himself, but cannot; he would like to send Timothy, but now needs his most valued assistant (2:19, 22–23). Perhaps Timothy will be able to come when the uncertainty of the trial has passed, and Paul himself hopes to be free shortly for a visit. In the meantime Epaphroditus is being sent, primarily because his recent illness makes it practical for him to return to the Philippians. Paul undoubtedly wanted to make sure that his return was interpreted, neither as an affront to their generosity in sending him, nor as a rejection of the ministry of Epaphroditus. Thus he admonished the Philippians to receive him with all joy and honor (2:29).

IV. VARIOUS REFLECTIONS AND ADMONITIONS (3:1–4:20). The final section of Philippians is most disjointed. The first sentence in chapter three seems to prepare for an epistolary conclusion, but then an abrupt transition introduces a miscellaneous series of warnings, exhortations, and reflections. The abruptness of this change of direction and the altered tone of the materials has led some to conclude that this section represents either one or two additional letters written by Paul to Philippi. Generally the assumption is that the materials thanking the Philippians for the gift (4:10–20) is the initial letter, the major description of the Christian life and recommendation of Epaphroditus

---

[44] E. F. Scott, *The Literature of The New Testament*, p. 46.
[45] See FBK, p. 237.

(1:1–3:1) a second letter, and the warnings and instructions (3:2–4:9) a third letter.[46] The arguments are not convincing, however, and there is no sufficient reason to doubt the original unity of the epistle.[47] In a letter as personal and informal as Philippians one would hardly expect a carefully worked out order. The only real difficulty is the abrupt transition in 3:1. The remainder of the chapter, although dealing with various subjects, has some logical consistency.

The opening verses of this section (3:2–3) are an impassioned invective against Jewish legalists. The Apostle violently denounces these leaders as "the dogs, . . . the evil workers, . . . who mutilate the flesh." But immediately the violent language gives way to an important autobiographical passage [48] in which Paul enjoins the Philippians to follow his example (3:17), rather than that of the Jewish legalists. In striking personal confession he recounts his credentials as "a Hebrew born of Hebrews," all of which have been "counted as loss . . . because of the surpassing worth of knowing Christ Jesus" (3:14). He has discarded his Jewish privileges to "press on toward the goal for the prize of the upward call of God in Christ Jesus" (3:14). Paul's objective was to ". . . know him and the power of his resurrection, and . . . share his sufferings, becoming like him in his death . . ." (3:10). Although the Apostle had not attained perfection, he had begun the spiritual pilgrimage toward Christlikeness and entreated the Philippians to join him as those who belonged to the same commonwealth (3:20).

To this longer warning and invitation Paul adds a series of short and specific admonitions, stressing the need for unity and forbearance (4:1–9). Finally, he comes to the gift that had been sent by the Philippians. He has already alluded to their graciousness (1:7; 2:25), but now he thanks them specifically for the gift. He does so with a cordiality mixed with an independence typical of Paul.[49] To the Apostle the gift betokened both the distinctive generosity of the Philippians and the steady faithfulness of God's providence. The concluding words, followed by greetings and benediction, summarize the Apostle's attitude toward the gift and his imprisonment: "And my God

---

[46] In slightly varying forms such a division of the book appears in the writing of various scholars. For examples, see Walter Schmithals, "Die Irrlehrer des Philipperbriefes," *Zeitschrift für Theologie und Kirche*, LIV (1957), 297–341; Rahtjen, "The Three Letters of Paul to the Philippians, *NTS*, VI (1959–60), 167–173; F. W. Beare, *The Epistle to the Philippians*, pp. 24–29.

[47] See FBK, pp. 235–237, for a good summary of the arguments.

[48] Other such passages appear in Gal. 1:13–2:21 and II Cor. 11:22–12:10.

[49] Cf. 4:11, 17.

will supply every need of yours according to his riches in glory in Christ Jesus" (4:19).

Colossians: Treatise on Christ's Fullness

The letter to Colossians was addressed to Christians in Colossae, located near Hierapolis and Laodicea in the Lycus valley, not far from Ephesus. Colossae was the earliest of the three Lycus towns to achieve city status and in pre-Hellenistic times was the most prominent city in the valley. But by the New Testament period Hierapolis and Laodicea were more economically vigorous and had overtaken their neighbor in importance. Christian congregations with close connections to each other (4:13, 15) existed in all three towns. Paul did not found the Colossian church nor had he visited it (2:1), but there is no reason to suppose that during his long Ephesian ministry, he had not been indirectly in contact with the congregation.[50] Paul certainly considered the church a part of his mission in Asia and probably had commissioned Epaphras to establish and minister to the congregation (1:7–8).

The Pauline origin of Colossians has been widely accepted, although not without question.[51] Objections to Pauline authorship have usually been built upon obvious vocabulary and stylistic peculiarities in Colossians and its close similarity with Ephesians, which is assumed to have been written by someone other than Paul. Certainly in language, style, and theology the letter has much that is peculiar and its relationship to Ephesians is undeniable.[52] Neither of these facts, however, necessarily preclude Pauline authorship. The matter of who wrote Ephesians is far from settled and the differences in content and style between Colossians and recognized Pauline epistles may easily be understood in terms of the particular problems dealt with in this letter.[53] Besides this, the appearance of distinctive Pauline formulae, such as "in Christ," in the letter along with several points of correspondence with Philemon strengthens the argument for the Pauline origin of Colossians.[54]

---

[50] Cf. 1:4.

[51] Rudolf Bultmann, *Theology of The New Testament*, II, pp. 175–180, believes that Pauline tradition is preserved in Colossians and Ephesians, although the Apostle did not write the letters. See Ernst Percy, *Die Probleme der Kolosser- und Epheserbriefe*, for a defense of Pauline authorship.

[52] John Coutts, "The Relationship of Ephesians and Colossians," *NTS*, IV (1957–58), 201–207, represents an effort to compare the styles of the two letters.

[53] So FBK, pp. 241–243. Also H. Chadwick, "All Things to All Men," *NTS*, I (1954–55), 261–275.

[54] FBK, pp. 243–244.

Occasion. The immediate purpose of Colossians was to counteract a strange philosophy which had distorted Colossian Christianity. False teachers had appeared with teachings similar to ideas of later second century Gnosticism. Although the epistle does not present a systematic description of beliefs held by the false teachers, the reader may reconstruct some of their basic tenets from allusions in the epistle. The heresy seems to have been a syncretistic cult drawn from pagan and Jewish sources,[55] and closely akin to the Gnostic rejection of the world as evil. A doctrine of "the elemental spirits of the universe" (2:8), angelic beings which may have been associated with unusual natural phenomena of the area, was fundamental in their thought. These spirits were being preached to the Colossians as the essence of ultimate reality and superior to Jesus. Since the fulness of God was discovered in the elemental spirits, the heretics reasoned, believing in Jesus was considered at best only an incomplete or immature form of religion.[56] The historical Jesus tied to human flesh was no more than a veiled and insufficient expression of the ultimate mystery which could be better known through visionary relevations. According to the false teachers, true and mature worship ought to get beyond the mundane by being initiated into something greater (2:18, 19). The way to do this was to keep certain liturgical and ascetic practices akin to Pharisaic legalism. The teachers demanded rigid observance of festivals, new moon, and sabbath, and strict dietary regulations were imposed (2:16). Taboos were clearly stated (2:21) and devotional ritual prescribed (2:23). Seemingly, the aim of the cult was to gain access to the esoteric domain of wisdom by way of rigorously defined patterns of self-abasement, suggesting that the heretics rejected associations with the mundane as evil.

Precise identification of the Colossian cult is impossible. The heresy probably "represented a form of Jewish Gnosticism combined with Christianity."[57] Paul aims to combat some type of interpretation which confines man to astrological control and to discredit Gnostic-type cults which propose to control the astral spirits, that is, the "elemental spirits of the universe."[58] Certainly, the heresy is not synony-

---

[55] G. Johnston, "Colossians," *IDB,* I, p. 660.

[56] Cf. 1:28. See A. H. McNeile, *An Introduction to the Study of the New Testament,* p. 160.

[57] FBK, p. 240. Some scholars see a relationship with a piety sect of the Qumran community. So W. D. Davies, *The Scrolls and The New Testament,* pp. 166–169.

[58] F. W. Beare, "Colossians," *IB,* XI, pp. 191–193.

mous with the fully developed cults of second century Gnosticism, but the seed of that which would become full grown later had already been planted. In Colossians Christianity meets the idea world into which it had been born. Since angelology combined with legalistic practices was typical of some pre-Christian Jewish groups,[59] the struggle of Jewish Christianity with kindred ideas in embryonic Gnosticism is not surprising. By his Colossian letter Paul hoped to introduce a certain orthodoxy of thought about Jesus into this amorphous and fluid situation. He first defended Jesus against those who would depreciate him as revelation of God and redeemer by proclaiming Christ's supremacy. Then he addressed himself to practical problems faced by Colossian Christians. Paul's two edged attack is evident in an outline of the letter.

Introduction. 1:1–14
   A. Salutation. 1:1–2
   B. Thanksgiving and intercession. 1:3–14

 I. The Doctrinal Polemic. 1:15–3:4
   A. The supremacy of Christ. 1:15–2:7
     1. A Christ hymn. 1:15–20
     2. The source of the Colossians' salvation. 1:21–23
     3. The sustaining mystery of Christ. 1:24–2:7
   B. The problem faced by the Colossians. 2:8–3:4

II. Practical Instruction. 3:5–4:6
   A. Immorality. 3:5–11
   B. Church fellowship. 3:12–17
   C. Family relations. 3:18–21
   D. Masters and slaves. 3:22–4:1
   E. Prayer. 4:2–4
   F. Outsiders. 4:5–6

Epilogue. 4:7–18
   A. Tychicus and Onesimus. 4:7–9
   B. Greeting. 4:10–17
   C. Benediction. 4:18

The Cosmic Christ (1:15–3:4). The pivotal idea of Colossians is the absolute preeminence of Christ over all things. Against the false teachers who were depreciating the earthly Jesus, Paul unequivocally affirmed that "in him all the fulness of God was pleased to dwell"

---

[59] Johnston, "Colossians," *IDB*, I, p. 659.

(1:19).[60] In what was probably an early Christian hymn [61] Paul asserted Christ's cosmic supremacy:

He is the image of the invisible God, the first-born of all creation; for in him all things were created, in heaven and on earth, visible and invisible, whether thrones or dominions or principalities or authorities—all things were created through him and for him. He is before all things, and in him all things hold together. He is the head of the body, the church; he is the beginning, the first-born from the dead, that in everything he might be preeminent. For in him all the fulness of God was pleased to dwell, and through him to reconcile to himself all things, whether on earth or in heaven, making peace by the blood of his cross. (1:15–20)

Contrary to the Gnostic idea that material existence represents the weakness of Jesus, the Apostle declares that this is his strength, for deity chose to dwell fully in the concrete reality of his body (2:9). Moreover, he is Lord over angels, good and bad, ruling in triumph and authority (1:16; 2:10, 15). Because of Christ's supremacy over all things, past and present, mundane and ethereal, the Colossians need not be deluded by the beguiling speech (2:4) of purported philosophy which is nothing more than "empty deceit" (2:8).

Additionally, the preeminent Christ is the head of his body, the Church, mediating full reconciliation with God (1:18–22). Identification with Christ is not merely a preparation for some esoteric higher or deeper faith. Rather, in Christ ultimate reconciliation is achieved —the bond of sin is canceled (2:14), principalities and powers are disarmed (2:15). Those who once were estranged and hostile, Christ has now reconciled and presented holy, blameless, and irreproachable before God (1:22). The Colossians, then, are to forsake worship of the elemental spirits (2:8, 18, 20) in order to respond to Christ with stable and steadfast faith (1:23). Once they have received him as Lord, the preeminent Christ will become the vital center of their entire life.

Practical Instruction (3:5–4:6). Paul continues his polemic against the false teachers by explaining the ethical responsibility of those who "have been raised with Christ" (3:1). They are to forsake the ritualistic and legalistic requirements of the local cults and "seek the things

---

[60] The word *pleroma*, translated here "fulness," was undoubtedly a technical term borrowed from the Colossian heresy being attacked.

[61] See James M. Robinson, "A Formal Analysis of Colossians 1:15–20," *JBL*, LXXVI (1957), 270–287. Ernst Käsemann, *Essays on New Testament Themes*, pp. 149–168, believes the hymn was a primitive Christian baptismal liturgy. See also Eduard Schweizer, "Die Kirche als Leib Christi in den paulinischen Antilegomena," *Theologische Literaturzeitung*, LXXX (1961), 242–255.

that are above" (3:1). Ethics is spelled out, not so much as impersonal rigor of devotion and self-abasement, but as personal compassion,
tenderness, charity in human relationships (3:12–17). Sketchily Paul
illustrates this principle with teachings about relationships between
husbands and wives, children and parents, and masters and slaves. Although the Apostle's instructions are summarily stated, the point is
nonetheless clear: The Christian who focuses all his thought and desires on the exalted Christ is unconcerned to "win his faith" through
earthly discipline. He rather aims "to give effect in all earthly relationships to the heavenly nature which he shares with Christ." [62] This too
may be aimed at Gnostic ideas that salvation is won by the achievement of some esoteric redemptive knowledge.

The final verses of the letter are given over to various personal
matters. Tychicus, the bearer of the letter, is introduced, as is Onesimus, the subject of the Philemon epistle. Greetings are sent to the
church at Laodicea along with instructions to share the letter with
them and read "the letter from Laodicea" (4:16), an epistle which cannot be further identified.[63] The letter closes with a subscription in
Paul's own hand and a plea, "Remember my fetters" (4:18).

Philemon: Note on Human Brotherhood

The leaflet letter to Philemon is intimately associated with the Colossian epistle. The addressee Philemon [64] was a resident of Colossae [65]
and the letter deals with the status of his slave Onesimus. Many of
the same persons, including Onesimus (Colossians 4:9), are mentioned
in the two letters and both were carried by Tychicus to Colossae at
the same time.

Of all Pauline writings Philemon comes closest to being a private
letter. The occasion for its writing was a personal situation which had

---

[62] Beare, "The Epistle to the Colossians," *IB*, XI, p. 209.

[63] Marcion identified Ephesians as "the letter from Laodicea." John Knox,
Philemon Among the Letters of Paul, pp. 45–55, suggests that the letter is Philemon. Probably, however, the letter was lost before the Pauline corpus was gathered. The reference here led to the fabrication of an apocryphal "Epistle of Paul
to the Laodiceans," an English translation of which may be found in M. R. James,
The Apocryphal New Testament, pp. 478–479.

[64] The letter is also addressed to Apphia and Archippus (1:2), but the content
makes it clear that Philemon is intended to be the primary recipient.

[65] Goodspeed, *An Introduction to the New Testament*, pp. 119–120, says that
Philemon was from Laodicea and that the exchange of letters suggested in Col.
4:16 was to bring pressure from the Colossian church upon Laodicea to reinforce
Paul's request for the services of Onesimus. Without evidence such a reconstruction cannot be accepted as more than a theory.

arisen between Paul and Philemon. Onesimus had run away from his master Philemon,[66] and perhaps had stolen some of his master's funds. He had come in contact with Paul and been converted. Now he was being sent back, accompanied by a brief but pointed appeal by Paul that Onesimus be received "as a beloved brother" (18). But beyond this, the Apostle hoped that Philemon would send Onesimus back to continue to assist him. Selby [67] believes the real burden of the letter is recorded in verses 13–14, "one of the broadest hints in history":

I would have been glad to keep him with me, in order that he might serve on your behalf during my imprisonment for the gospel; but I preferred to do nothing without your consent in order that your goodness might not be my compulsion but of your own free will.

Did Philemon comply with Paul's request? We cannot say with certainty. Knox believes that he did and the memory of this generous act was a major reason for the inclusion of the letter in the New Testament canon. He further identifies the liberated slave as the same Onesimus mentioned by Ignatius as bishop of Ephesus around the beginning of the second century A.D.[68] Goodspeed builds upon this idea, suggesting that Onesimus was responsible for a collection of Paul's letters appearing around the turn of the century.[69] Although these theories cannot be demonstrated, they are plausible and attractive, and may help to explain why a personal letter came to be included in the New Testament.

In Philemon Paul does not deal directly with the issue of slavery and, in this sense, the letter is not doctrinal. Personal relations between Christian brothers, and not the institution of slavery, is the focus of Paul's attention. The book, however, is a primary document in understanding the Apostle's ethical viewpoint. It is a practical illustration of the position stated in I Corinthians 7:20–24 and Colossians 3:22–4:1. Paul did not propose to reorder social and legal structures. Slavery as an institution was accepted and the believer enjoined to

---

[66] Knox conjectures that Onesimus had not run away, but had been sent to Paul by Philemon. See his *Philemon Among the Letters of Paul*, pp. 17–18.

[67] *Toward the Understanding of St. Paul*, p. 276. Cf. Knox, "The Epistle to Philemon," *IB*, XI, p. 557.

[68] Ignatius, *Ephesians*, I, 3; II, 1; VI, 1. For a full discussion of the problem see Knox, *Philemon Among the Letters of Paul*, pp. 71–108. A shorter summary statement appears in his introductory article on Philemon in *IB*, XI, pp. 556–560. See also P. N. Harrison, "Onesimus and Philemon," *Anglican Theological Review*, XXXII (1950), 268–294.

[69] See *An Introduction to the New Testament*, pp. 121–124.

faithfulness in whatever state he was called, slave or freeman.[70] Evidently Paul felt that the end of the age was so fast approaching that it was not expedient to attack established social structures. However, both the Corinthians and the Colossians passages and the Philemon appeal rest upon principles which, if carefully applied, would ultimately lead to the banishment of slavery. Paul hoped that Onesimus would be taken back, "no longer as a slave, but more than a slave, as a beloved brother" (16). In this way the Apostle affirmed that Christian faith transcends class barriers to bind men together in brotherhood. His understanding of the worth of every person required the runaway slave to return to his master and the master to receive him in forgiveness. Paul was confident that Philemon would do even more than take Onesimus back as a Christian brother (21), perhaps hinting that he should be granted freedom. This may explain to a large extent why the letter was to be read by the entire congregation as well as by Philemon (1:2).

Ephesians: The Universal Church

The Epistle to the Ephesians has been traditionally considered a part of Paul's prison correspondence. It bears a striking similarity to Colossians and purportedly was carried to Ephesus by Tychicus at the same time that Colossians and Philemon were taken to Colossae. The letter has been acclaimed as a monumental document on the establishment of God's community of believers among whom no barriers exist. In sonorous and moving style God's eternal purpose in bringing the Church to its full privilege and destiny is affirmed. "Its lofty description of the significance of Christ and its inspiring theme of oneness in Christ make this letter one of the important and influential books of the New Testament." [71]

Authorship and Destination.   Yet Ephesians, as much as any other writing in the New Testament, has created critical problems which virtually defy resolution. Intense controversy among biblical scholars has developed around two intertwined issues: (1) the general character and content of the letter raise serious questions regarding the possibility of Pauline authorship, and (2) manuscript and internal evidence strongly suggest that the epistle was not addressed to Ephesus. The extended debate over these issues has brought little certainty as to the identity of either the author or the recipients of the letter.

[70] See I Cor. 7:24.
[71] Selby, *Toward the Understanding of St. Paul,* p. 278.

Pauline authorship is supported and denied by numerous reputable New Testament scholars.[72] A strong case may be made for the view that the letter is authentically Pauline. The epistle itself claims Paul as author (1:1; 3:1) and seems to have been known as Pauline from the early second century A.D. Ephesians is included in the earliest collections of Paul's letters and is accepted as Pauline by Marcion, Irenaeus, and Clement of Alexandria. Further, Paul's situation is much the same as in Colossians and Philemon [73] and many Ephesian passages are similar to other materials generally accepted as Pauline. The lofty character of 1:3–14, for example, is reminiscent of the magnificent poem in I Corinthians 13. Such evidence leads many to conclude that Paul wrote Ephesians as a fervent manifesto on the meaning of Christ and his Church. The aging Apostle, without any particular controversy in mind, is understood to bring to fruition extended thinking on God's eternal purposes and to set forth a profound statement echoing all that he had been saying throughout his Christian life and mission.

Several features of Ephesians, however, have led many scholars to raise serious question about Pauline authorship of the epistle. For one thing, the letter omits details relating to any concrete church situation. The writer has heard of the faith of those to whom he writes (1:15), but gives no indication that he is personally acquainted with the church or individuals within it. He discusses no specific problems of the congregation and omits all personal greetings. Since Paul worked for more than two years in Ephesus, a letter so impersonal would hardly have been written to that congregation. This line of argument, however, is more relevant to the question of the epistle's destination than to the question of authorship. More serious arguments against Pauline authorship have been found in language and style peculiarities of the epistle. The use of long, meandering sentences; [74] an unusual number of relatives, participles, and infinitives; and distinctive kinds of grammatical structure seem to be atypical of Paul.[75] Also, some take the relationship between Ephesians and other Pauline epistles to argue

---

[72] Able defenses of Pauline authorship appear in F. J. A. Hort, *Prolegomena to St. Paul's Epistles to the Romans and the Ephesians,* and E. Percy, *Die Probleme der Kolosser- und Epheserbriefe.* Extensive statements against Pauline authorship may be found in E. J. Goodspeed, *The Meaning of Ephesians,* and C. L. Mitton, *The Epistle to the Ephesians.* For a summary of the issues and an extensive listing of scholars on both sides of the debate, see FBK, pp. 248–256.

[73] Cf. 6:21–22 with Col. 4:7–8 and Philemon 1, 10, 23–24.

[74] Cf. 1:15–23; 3:1–7; 4:11–16.

[75] See James Moffatt, *An Introduction to the Literature of the New Testament,* pp. 385–389. For a contrary opinion, see Percy, *Die Probleme der Kolosser- und Epheserbriefe.*

against Paul's authorship.[76] Parallels between Ephesians and these other writings, particularly Colossians, suggest that a different author wrote Ephesians with the Pauline epistles before him.[77] A final argument stresses that Ephesians contains distinctive ideas and word meanings that could not come from Paul. For example, the apostles and prophets, rather than Christ, are described as the foundation of the Church.[78] In Ephesians the word *church* itself means exclusively the universal Church whereas in accepted Pauline writings *church* refers to both the local congregation and the total body of believers. Other words, such as *mystery*, seem to be used in Ephesians with different meaning than is customarily found in the writings of the Apostle. These and other features of Ephesians lead many to conclude that "we cannot seriously doubt that Ephesians does not derive from Paul and is, therefore, a pseudonymous writing." [79]

These observations, however, are highly subjective and do not necessarily preclude Pauline authorship. The degree of difference between Ephesians and the other Pauline writings in vocabulary and style carries little weight with a person so versatile as Paul. Shades of meanings, even for the same words, might be expected for one who was not writing a systematic theological statement for scholarly scrutiny. Some differences in style may be accounted for by differences in subject matter, and parallel passages could indicate the same writer as easily as a different one. Therefore, other scholars have been more cautious in discarding Pauline authorship, feeling that the question should at least be left undecided pending additional information.[80]

Problems of the epistle are further compounded by the fact that we cannot be sure that it was written to Ephesus. According to the best manuscript evidence, the words "in Ephesus" did not appear in the address (1:1) of the original letter.[81] Marcion, around A.D. 140, considered the letter to have been written to Laodicea,[82] but generally the letter was closely associated with Ephesus. Scribes as early as the second century included "To the Ephesians" in their title. Probably

[76] G. Johnston, "Ephesians," *IDB*, II, pp. 109–111.

[77] For an example of parallels between Colossians and Ephesians, compare Col. 3:6–8 with Eph. 5:6–8.

[78] Cf. 2:20–22 with Col. 2:6–7.

[79] FBK, p. 255.

[80] So H. J. Cadbury, "The Dilemma of Ephesians," *NTS*, V (1958–59), 91–102.

[81] Note that the RSV assigns these words to a footnote. The phrase is absent from the second century P[46] and originally appeared in neither Codex Sinaiticus or Codex Vaticanus, both dating to the fourth century A.D.

[82] See Tertullian, *Against Marcion*, V, 17.

from the scribal title the words "in Ephesus" were incorporated into the text itself. Textual evidence indicates, however, that this did not occur until towards the end of the fourth century.[83] Lacking both internal and textual evidence, it is therefore risky to assume that the letter was written specifically for the church at Ephesus.

The confusion about the authorship and destination of Ephesians has produced many interesting and suggestive hypotheses about the writing. Some have supposed that Ephesians was a circular letter with a blank in the address to be filled in by the recipient church.[84] This practice, however, cannot be illustrated from antiquity and it seems unlikely that the writer would have invented such a procedure. More likely we are dealing with a general letter which was not sent to any specific church, but rather grew out of the concern of the writer with the idea of the Church.

The general character of Ephesians, along with its striking dependence upon accepted Pauline letters, has influenced E. J. Goodspeed to hypothesize that it was written to serve as an introduction to an early collection of Paul's letters.[85] Someone, probably Onesimus, who had become bishop of Ephesus, was stimulated by the publication of Acts to collect and publish known Pauline letters. Ephesians was then composed to stand at the head of the corpus, summarizing Paul's gospel and commending it to all readers. But Goodspeed's theory, although it is attractive and certainly plausible, rests largely on conjecture and does not answer the criticism that Ephesians is not really a summary of Paul's message.[86] This reconstruction may be taken as no more than a reasonable possibility.

For the moment the problems of Ephesians remain unresolved. Pending further evidence, the Epistle may be understood as a general letter written by the Apostle. The traditional view of authorship creates as few problems as trying to discover another author. Even those who categorically deny Pauline authorship admit that the character of the writing "leads us very close to Paul, who here found a worthy disciple."[87] Yet the letter is as valuable without as with Pauline author-

[83] FBK, p. 249.

[84] See T. Henshaw, *New Testament Literature in the Light of Modern Research,* pp. 298–299, as representative of this point of view.

[85] This thesis is stated in many of Goodspeed's works and developed in *The Key to Ephesians.* His basic idea is accepted by Mitton, *The Epistle to the Ephesians,* although the latter does not identify the author of the Epistle.

[86] A critique of Goodspeed may be found in F. W. Beare, "Ephesians," *IB,* X, p. 603.

[87] Ernst Käsemann, "Ephesians and Acts," *Studies in Luke–Acts,* eds. Keck and Martyn, p. 288.

ship. Its enduring merit is not determined by who wrote it, but by its capacity to become an authentic vehicle for communicating truth. As a document witnessing to the redemptive work of the Church in history and appealing for the ecumenical character of the believing community, Ephesians justifies its own honored place in Scripture.

The Contents of Ephesians. The enigmatic problems associated with Ephesians make it no less valuable as a document enduringly relevant to the Church. Its sublime proclamation of God's eternal purposes in establishing a community of kindred believers and its articulate statements of the ethical life which typifies the Church in the world make Ephesians peculiarly significant for a Church which in any age wrestles with its own ethical and ecumenical character. The sublimity of its themes makes precise analysis of the epistle difficult. However, a brief sketch of the epistle reveals its two basic parts:

The Address. 1:1–2

I. Doctrinal: God's Perfect Workmanship. 1:3–3:21
   A. Thanksgiving for salvation accomplished by God. 1:3–14
   B. Intercession for reader's enlightenment. 1:15–23
   C. God's redemptive achievement. 2:1–22
      1. Has its source in God's gracious gift in Christ. 2:1–10
      2. Issues in unity among believers. 2:11–22
   D. Paul's missionary responsibility to God's purpose. 3:1–13
   E. A prayer for the recipients. 3:14–21

II. Practical: The Worthy Life. 4:1–6:20
   A. Maintain the unity of the faith. 4:1–16
   B. Renounce pagan ways; be imitators of God. 4:17–5:20
   C. Be subject to one another. 5:21–6:9
   D. Put on the whole armor of God. 6:10–20

The Closing. 6:21–23

I. God's Perfect Workmanship (1:3–3:21). Following a brief address, Ephesians moves into an expression of thanksgiving for blessings that come to the believer from God in Christ (1:3–14). Unlike the typical Pauline thanksgiving, this section has no personal orientation. The letter neither reminisces of former relationships with a church nor dwells on hopes for good health and prosperity. Rather the thanksgiving is intertwined with a majestic proclamation of doctrinal themes. The perfect work of God in Christ [88] by which matchless salvation is wrought among men of faith is the basis of Christian

---

[88] Cf. Marcus Barth, *The Broken Wall*, pp. 33–68.

gratitude. Paul [89] thanks God, not for *a* church and its faithfulness, but for the salvation brought into the world in Christ, an act bringing *the* Church into being.

In Ephesians God's work in the Church is an expression of his eternal purposes. God "has blessed us in Christ with every spiritual blessing in the heavenly places, even as he chose us in him before the foundation of the world . . ." (1:3–4). Among New Testament writings the phrase "in the heavenly places" is distinctive to Ephesians, but it is used five times in this letter, emphasizing that what God has done in Christ and the Church belongs to the realm of the eternal and divine. The phrase was possibly borrowed from the vocabulary of some semi-Gnostic astrological doctrine of redemption and consequently its use in Ephesians may have been somewhat polemical.[90] Yet the major intent is a positive affirmation of the grandeur of God's universal and eternal act of reconciliation. God's redemptive work has relevance, not only for human existence and history, but also for the ultimate achievement of his cosmic purpose. God's gift of Christ came as no historical accident or afterthought. Nor is the Church which has been created in Christ's coming merely a temporal institution. Rather both Christ and the Church had been contemplated in the mind of God from the very beginning and are eternal in influence and effect.[91] Further, God's great act is its own motivation, an expression of his purpose and will (1:5, 9, 11). No factors outside God himself have motivated his course of action. It has been God's good pleasure to lavish his glorious grace upon those whom he has chosen to love (1:4–8).

From the lofty proclamation of what God has done, the author moves to intercession with his readers (1:15–23). But even here his petition is that they may understand the mighty work of God. He prays for their enlightenment about God's mystery, that is, God's age-old purpose to redeem both Jews and Gentiles, a purpose which has now been made known in Christ. To know the mystery of God is the highest form of wisdom and comes from God (1:17). Here the epistle intends to describe knowing God's mystery within the context of the usual biblical understanding of knowledge. Typical Western definitions of knowledge emphasize rational and scientific analysis and understanding. "To know" usually indicates acquaintance with a sum of data about persons, things, or events. Knowledge thus is a rather

---

[89] The subsequent references to Pauline authorship must be understood in light of the reservations noted above.

[90] Beare, "The Epistle to the Ephesians," *IB*, X, p. 614.

[91] 1:4. See E. F. Scott, *The Epistle of Paul to the Colossians, to Philemon, and to the Ephesians*, p. 139.

objective and impersonal collection of observable, related facts. In biblical usage, however, knowledge is more a word of relationship. This is clearly illustrated in the use of "to know" for sexual intimacy between husband and wife.[92] The union of persons expressed in the sexual act is understood as knowledge that unites man and woman. Similarly, knowing God is not collecting facts about God, but accepting the intimacy of relationship to him.[93] In Ephesians God himself is both the one who is known in redemption and the one who by revealing himself in Christ makes knowledge possible. The writer prays that,

. . . the God of our Lord Jesus Christ, the Father of glory, may give you a spirit of wisdom and of revelation in the knowledge of him. . . . (1:17)

Noticeably the letter is "little concerned with the self as subject matter of understanding."[94] Knowing God is not so much recognizing one's needs and how God in Christ meets those needs as it is an inward renewal of the total person by God. The figure used here to describe the renewal wrought by God is an interesting one: "having the eyes of your heart enlightened" (1:18). Here biblical and mystery or Gnostic religious imagery are combined. In the Bible *heart* regularly denotes the seat of the self and includes both rational understanding and purposeful decision. In mystery religions current in the first century enlightenment referred to an initiation ritual in which the candidate was declared illuminated in his new way of life. But to the author of Ephesians a true enlightenment may come only when God himself fills the heart of a person with new light, that is, when a person's reason and will, in fact his total self, operates consistent with God's eternal purpose to redeem all men. Thus, the enlightened believer, that is, the person who genuinely knows God, is the beneficiary of an act of the living God.[95] This act occurs only because God "is rich in mercy, out of the great love with which he loved us" (2:4).

Thanksgiving for the salvation accomplished by God and petition that his readers may know "the immeasurable greatness" (1:19) of what God has done leads the author to the central affirmation of the epistle, namely, that God's redemptive achievement has brought forth the ecumenical and unified Church (2:1–22). The Church is not some external and institutional structure, but the community of those who acknowledge God as the creator of a new way of life (2:8–10). Those formerly "dead through trespasses and sins" have now been "made

[92] See Gen. 4:1, 17, 25; Matt. 1:25; *passim.*
[93] This emphasis is clear in numerous passages throughout the New Testament. For examples, see Matt. 11:27; John 17:25–26; I Cor. 8:1–3; Gal. 4:8–9.
[94] Barth, *The Broken Wall,* p. 71.
[95] *Ibid.,* pp. 72–73. See also Rom. 1:19; Philippians 3:10; I Cor. 2:12.

alive" (2:1) by the same power which raised Christ from the dead (2:5–6). The Church is God's Church and its members those who belong to the "household of God" (2:19). Both Gentile and Jew belong to this created community. In Christ the "dividing wall of hostility" has been broken down and restraining "commandments and ordinances" abolished, so that "one new man in place of the two" might be created to live in unity and peace (2:14–18). "The ultimate divine purpose to bring the whole created universe into an all-embracing unity is foreshadowed, and indeed is actually begun, in the Church, where a divided humanity is brought together as Jew and Gentile are united in a single worshiping community." [96] This is the gospel to which the Apostle has been called as a minister (3:1–13) and for which he prays that his readers may be strengthened (3:14–21).

II. THE WORTHY LIFE (4:1–6:20). The first three chapters in Ephesians, then, focus upon the perfect work of God in bringing the Church into being. Although the style and atmosphere is devotional, the objective is doctrinal. The author aims to show that the believer has been made alive in Christ and therefore introduced into a fellowship that knows no barriers in sharing God's eternal purposes. Following this doctrinal affirmation, the letter moves into a second part (4:1–6:20), primarily hortatory in character. Practical ethical demands are seen as implicit in the perfect work of God. Certain ethical responsibilities are corollary to participation in God's work in the world. Because of what God has done, believers are "to lead a life worthy of the calling" (4:1).

First, participants in an undivided community are to "maintain the unity of the Spirit in the bond of peace" (4:2). Although God has bestowed upon individual members a variety of gifts (4:11), the Church is not fragmented. The Church resembles a human body, whose multiple parts function to help and supplement each other. Each individual should contribute to the maturity of the common life (4:13). Unity of the Church consists, not in an artificial uniformity in which all differences are suppressed, but in the subjection of diverse members to Christ, the gift of God and the head of the body. The epistle affirms the inherent unity of the Church with a sevenfold formula:

There is one body and one Spirit, just as you were called to the one hope that belongs to your call, one Lord, one faith, one baptism, one God and Father of us all, who is above all and through all and in all. (4:4–6)

The unity of God to whom the Church gives allegiance and worship is the foundation for its corporate life. To be the Church is to share

[96] Beare, "The Epistle to the Ephesians," *IB*, X, pp. 648–649.

God's oneness. Where this unity does not manifest itself, the Church does not exist.

The first admonition is deeply grounded in the doctrinal concern of the epistle. True believers really have no alternative to maintaining the unity of the body. This is what it means to be *Church!* The remaining admonitions, however, are more practical and derivative. Believers are admonished to renounce pagan ways (4:17–24). Incorporation into the body of Christ entails putting off "your old nature which belongs to your former manner of life" (4:22) and putting on "the new nature, created after the likeness of God in true righteousness and holiness" (4:24). Christians are to "be imitators of God" (5:1), walking in love as beloved children and shunning all forms of immorality, impurity, and covetousness (5:3–5).

From the contrast between Christian and pagan morality, Ephesians turns to an admonition about domestic relationships. The principle which is stated as a guideline takes account of both the cultural patterns of the day and the mutual responsibilities of fellow believers: "Be subject to one another out of reverence for Christ" (5:21). Wives and husbands, children and parents, slaves and masters are all to be reciprocally responsible to each other in the context of prevalent and accepted social patterns. Special emphasis is given to husband-wife responsibilities (5:22–33) because the author sees in that relationship a symbolic reflection of Christ's relation to the Church.[97]

For the husband is head of the wife as Christ is head of the church, . . . As the church is subject to Christ, so let wives be subject in everything to their husbands. (5:23–24)

From a social situation which accepted the subservient role of the woman, Paul drew an analogy of the Church's subjection to Christ. The Genesis injunction (2:24) that a man leave his father and mother to be united with his wife is quoted to illustrate the spiritual union of Christ with his Church. Thus in this passage the Apostle affirms both the high estate of marriage and Christ's sovereignty over the Church.

The final appeal of Ephesians is made through an extended metaphor (6:10–20). Christians are advised to "put on the whole armor of God" (6:11, 13). The armor which God supplies for the Christian is described in detail, but the central issue in the passage is not discovered

---

[97] Some say that the same person who wrote I Cor. 7 could not possibly have written this passage—that the two are incompatible. This, therefore, is used as an argument against Pauline authorship of Ephesians. The passages, however, arise out of quite different situations and may not therefore be incompatible. Yet the eschatological urgency behind I Cor. 7, an attitude more compatible with the Pauline Church, seems to be absent from the Ephesians passage.

in the various parts of the armor. The writer's main concern is to clarify that the believer is involved in the eternal struggle for the preservation of God's purpose over "the spiritual hosts of wickedness in the heavenly places" (6:12). If, as many hold, these spiritual beings are planetary angels, then the thought here is close to that of incipient Gnosticism. As member of the Church the Christian is charged as a good soldier to do his part with valor and fidelity (6:10, 13, 14). In order to do so, he must be equipped with the armor which God wears and which he supplies for the believer. As the panoply of a Roman soldier protects him from the arrows of the enemy and enables him to wage aggressive battle, so God's armor prepares the Christian to participate in the eternal struggle which will end in the complete victory of God's Church. After this dramatic and climactic analogy, the Ephesian epistle closes with a brief appeal for prayer, a personal note commending Tychicus, and a benediction.

In Ephesians Paul offers an embracing doctrine of the Church. The realistic recognition that his present world is neither friendly nor sympathetic does not dim his vision of God's eternal purpose which has brought forth the Christian community. God's gracious love has been fully expressed in the gift of Christ revealing the eternal, divine intention. The Church, inspired by the Spirit, is charged with continuing Christ's work until all men are incorporated in the design. In this community no walls partition one part of the body from another or, for that matter, separate the whole body from its responsible evangelistic task to the entire world. God himself in Christ has done away with all dividing walls and enmities.

SUGGESTED READINGS

In addition to commentaries on Acts and books on Paul see:

BEARE, FRANCIS W., *The Epistle to the Philippians* (Harper, 1959).

———, "The Epistle to the Colossians: Introduction and Exegesis," *IB*, Vol. XI.

———, "The Epistle to the Ephesians: Introduction and Exegesis," *IB*, Vol. X.

KNOX, JOHN, "The Epistle to Philemon: Introduction and Exegesis," *IB*, Vol. XI.

MICHAEL, J. H., *The Epistle of Paul to the Philippians* (Harper, 1957).

MOULE, C. F. D., *The Epistles to the Colossians and to Philemon* (Cambridge, 1957).

SCOTT, ERNEST F., "The Epistle to the Philippians: Introduction and Exegesis," *IB*, Vol. XI.

———, *The Epistles of Paul to the Colossians, to Philemon, and to the Ephesians* (Hodder and Stoughton, 1930).

PART III

Conflict and Consolidation:
A.D. 60-150

11

A Century of Consolidation: to A.D. 150

Christian development centering in the work of the Apostle Paul represents no more than the initial thrust of the Church extending itself into the world of its day. During the apostolic period (A.D. 30–65), less well-known, if not less significant, phases of expansion must have transpired. Further, in the post-apostolic age down to the mid-second century A.D. the Christian community was engaged in a life-and-death struggle with a world often hostile to its goals. In this context the Church endeavored to define its own reason for being and gradually developed structural forms which would enable it to survive.

A terminal date of A.D. 150 may be selected for this period of conflict and consolidation with reason. By this time the New Testament literature had been composed and was being circulated among the churches. Formal attempts to compile canons of Christian writings had begun; the time of oral tradition was past and appeal to the written word had dawned. Further, the center of Christian activity had shifted from Palestine and the Church had become primarily Gentile, defining its own distinctive character somewhat independently of Judaism.

An understanding of this period in the life of the early Church involves initially an attempt to sketch some of the areas into which the developing Church moved. Although a linear history of both extra-Pauline and post-Pauline expansion is impossible from our present sources, some attempt must be made to discover the Church's physical outreach. In the final analysis, however, geographical developments are less important than the Church's changing attitudes toward Judaism and Rome, its development of fluid patterns of organization, its creation of patterns of worship, and its structure of doctrine. To these matters, this and subsequent chapters now turn.

SOURCES FOR THE CHURCH'S HISTORY

Surviving traces of the spread of Christianity in the apostolic and post-apostolic periods are tantalizingly brief. The limitations of the book of Acts in this regard have already been noted. Acts does provide us with an outline of the Church's expansion toward Rome, but after the first few chapters, it is preoccupied with Paul and leaves much of the story untold. Absent from Acts is any information about the development, beyond simplest beginnings, of the Church in Palestine (Judea and Samaria) and of its expansion and consolidation in Syria, to say nothing of its spread eastward to Mesopotamia and south and west into North Africa. No other extant source adequately fills these gaps in the Church's history. Of the origin of many important Christian communities nothing is known. We need only be reminded of a Christian congregation in Rome to which Paul wrote before he visited the city on the Tiber. These areas were outside the purpose of the writer of Luke–Acts, and information about them is keenly missed by all who seek to reconstruct a full picture of the early Church. Further, the story in Acts ends in the sixties with Paul a prisoner in Rome. Of the post-apostolic expansion we know little.

Thus, whatever may be said about the developing Church must be pieced together from inferences in the religious literature of the period. The New Testament provides the primary source. Although the New Testament contains no narrative of Church expansion, except the suggestive material in Acts, much of it was written during the period A.D. 65–150. From this time came the Four Gospels, Acts, Hebrews, Revelation and the Johannine letters, I and II Peter, James and Jude and the Pastoral Epistles. These materials are of primary value for reconstructing the development of the early Church's organization and thought and, when supplemented by the non-canonical writings of leaders in the infant Church and by contemporaneous secular documents, give some insight into Christianity's expansion in the Hellenistic world.

We are largely, however, dependent upon non-biblical sources for information about the extra-Pauline and post-Pauline expansion of Christianity. One of the most important of these is the *Ecclesiastical*

History of Eusebius,[1] written around A.D. 305–324. Eusebius was bishop of Caesarea, friend and confidant of the emperor Constantine, and respected leader of the Church at the Council of Nicaea and the Synod of Jerusalem. He had access to the Christian libraries of Caesarea and Jerusalem and purposed to write an ordered account of early Church history. The *Ecclesiastical History* is not "history" in the modern scientific sense of the word, but overall the work is extremely useful. His sources are generally identified,[2] and to a considerable extent the history gives access to original documents which no longer exist. *Ecclesiastical History* is not, however, without severe limitations. Eusebius did accept uncritically some uncertain traditions and his methods of quotation are not always satisfactory. His treatment of the first century is sketchy at best and does not begin to tell us all we would wish to know about the early Christian movement. Nevertheless, without Eusebius a history of early Christianity could not be reconstructed at all and, judged by the standards of his age, Eusebius was a reasonably critical writer and is a fairly reliable source for our study.

Another valuable source is the writings of Epiphanius, a fourth century bishop of Constantia on Cyprus. The work of Epiphanius contains references to important second century documents, and therefore, like Eusebius' *Ecclesiastical History*, gives access to original materials which no longer exist. Unfortunately, he shows little historical sense and his sources are reproduced without identification.

Considerably valuable for understanding the development of the Church's organization and thought, and incidentally and inferentially for her expansion, are certain writings which by mid-second century had not yet been clearly eliminated from canonical consideration and consequently were still associated with the New Testament literature. The earliest of these works is the *Epistle of Clement* (commonly designated I Clement) written from the Roman church to Corinth around A.D. 96–97. The name Clement does not appear in the text, but is almost universally used in the earliest references to the writing. Apart from the work itself, nothing is known about Clement the man, but the epistle was held in great esteem by the Church. Eusebius relates:

There is one recognized epistle of Clement, long and wonderful, which he drew up for the church of the Corinthians in the name of the church of the Romans when there had been dissension in Corinth. We have ascertained

[1] All references to *Ecclesiastical History* are to the *Loeb Classical Library* edition (1926) trans. by Kirsopp Lake.
[2] In this he was forerunner of the modern historian.

that this letter was publicly read in the common assembly in many churches both in the days of old and in our own time.[3]

Apparently I Clement was read in numerous churches with a reverence almost equal to that given the canonical writings.

A similar source is the letters of Ignatius, bishop of Antioch around the turn of the first century. Early in the second century Ignatius was seized in a persecution and taken to Rome to be thrown to wild beasts in the arena. On the way to martyrdom in the imperial capital he wrote at least seven epistles. From Smyrna he wrote to the churches in Ephesus, Magnesia, Tralles, and Rome; from Troas he wrote to Smyrna and Philadelphia and to Polycarp, bishop of Smyrna. These epistles are the most important Christian documents of the period.

When Ignatius arrived at Philippi on the way to Rome, he asked the Philippian church to send an encouraging word to his church at Antioch. The Philippians wrote to Polycarp, bishop of Smyrna, and requested him to forward their letter to Antioch. They also asked him for copies of any of Ignatius' letters which he might possess. Polycarp forwarded the Ignatius corpus to the Philippians together with a letter of his own. This letter is another source of primary importance for understanding the early second century Church. So too are the so-called *Epistle of Barnabas* (A.D. 125), an apocalyptic document coming out of the fierce controversy with Judaism of the late twenties of the second century, and the *Didache* or *Teaching of the Twelve Apostles,* a catechetical text which may have originated as a supplement to the Gospel of Matthew sometime in the second quarter of the second century. All of these writings apparently had important circulation in the early Church and, for some at least, they appear to have attained a semi-canonical status.

The works of two other second century Christian writers by their own merit and because of the references they make to canonical and non-canonical sources provide us with exceedingly valuable information about the development of the Church's doctrine and its refutation of contrary ideas. These are the five books *Against Heresies* of Irenaeus, a disciple of Polycarp, and *Dialogue with Trypho* and *Apologies* of Justin Martyr, a converted Samaritan philosopher. Irenaeus and Justin Martyr were zealous to defend the faith, using both Scripture and Christian tradition to that end.

Finally, among non-canonical sources are materials from early Christian writers known to us only from quotations in later sources. These

[3] *EH,* III, xvi.

are, of course, fragmentary and not always clear, but they help supply light for a period in the Church's history which is all too dark to us.

A study of the Church during the period of its conflict and consolidation demands an examination of these materials, both canonical and non-canonical, in some detail. The literature must be related to the proper historical and ideological developments in the Church. Unfortunately we cannot be absolutely certain about our arrangement of much of this literature, since its historical allusions are subject to a variety of interpretations. Careful analysis, however, of the appropriate New Testament and extra-canonical documents make possible at least a sketch of the story of the Church's expansion and the development of its thought and organization. However, since the context for this growth was a world dominated by Rome, an examination of certain relevant developments in the empire between Nero (A.D. 54–68) and the reign of Antoninus Pius (A.D. 138–161) is appropriate.

ROME: NERO TO ANTONINUS PIUS

Nero's reign which had been scarred by the great fire in A.D. 64 was toward its end marked by Jewish revolt in Palestine.[4] Antagonism against the Judean procurators, pent up for a long time, burst in A.D. 66 into open rebellion. When the procurator Florus allowed a Gentile onslaught upon the Jewish residents in Caesarea to take its course, a retaliatory uprising in Jerusalem followed. Sacrifices offered in the temple on behalf of the emperor ceased and the small Roman garrison was put under siege and massacred after a capitulation on terms. Roman attempts to put down this rebellion were mismanaged and the rebellion swept throughout Judea and spread into Galilee and parts of Transjordan.

Nero then appointed T. Flavius Vespasianus, who, though not in favor at court, had a good military record, to head a large army to crush the rebellion. With a force of 50,000 men Vespasian systematically reduced Galilee in A.D. 67 and the Transjordan lands in A.D. 68. About this time Nero was deposed and executed. Vespasian, doubtless aware that he stood an excellent chance in the struggle for succession to the emperor's seat, terminated his effort to subdue the Jewish rebels and entered the competition for control of the empire. The year A.D. 68–69 was the "year of the four emperors" as four aspirants came forward to claim the throne, each supported by a portion of the

[4] For a brief sketch of Nero's relation to early Christianity, see Robert M. Grant, "Nero," *IDB*, III, pp. 537–539.

Figure 11–1. Coin of Vespasian (A.D. 69–79), struck in the year A.D. 71 to commemorate the conquest of Judea. Judea is depicted on the reverse as a mourning Jewess seated under a palm tree guarded by a Roman soldier. (Source: American Numismatic Society.)

army. Vespasian won. Soon the Jewish war was resumed with Titus, son of Vespasian, in command of Roman forces. In spite of the opportunity given them in the interval to regroup, the Jews could not long withstand Titus' attack on Jerusalem. In A.D. 70, after sheer hard fighting and torn by internal strife, the city fell. Defenders had contested every position inch by inch "and when Titus carried the last two strongholds, the plateau of the Temple and the citadel, he occupied little else but a field of ruins." [5] The revolt continued outside of Jerusalem and hostilities did not end until the siege of Masada in A.D. 73.[6] The surviving population of Jerusalem was partially reduced to slavery, the Sanhedrin was abolished, the temple was not rebuilt, and a Roman legion was permanently stationed in Jerusalem. Henceforth, the holy city ceased to be a hub for either Christianity or Judaism. Judaism reorganized in Jamnia (Jabneh) under the leadership of Johanan ben Zakkai, a rabbi and a Pharisee.[7] Whatever remnants of the Christian community escaped the city's siege and destruction either fled the city to become parts of Christian settlements elsewhere or remained in the environs as an inconsequential and uninfluential part of the total Church.

Vespasian remained emperor until A.D. 79 when he was succeeded by his son Titus (A.D. 79–81). These years were relatively calm for the Church. The next crisis came in the reign of Domitian

[5] Max Cary, A History of Rome, p. 614.
[6] Cf. Yigael Yadin, Masada.
[7] For details about the war, see Josephus, Wars. His account is of course here, as elsewhere, not to be accepted uncritically.

Figure 11–2. The Arch of Titus erected in the Roman Forum by the Senate about A.D. 100 to commemorate the war with the Jews which Titus brought to a climax with the fall of Jerusalem in A.D. 70. A bas-relief under the arch shows Roman soldiers crowned with victory wreaths, bearing objects from the Jerusalem temple. (Source: David A. Smith.)

(A.D. 81–96), who "paraded absolutism, giving to the imperial position the airs of divinity and the pomp of a despot." [8] In the second half of his reign Domitian styled himself *dominus et deus*, "master and god," moving along a path that Nero had already trod.[9] Since Augustus' time, men had been accustomed to revere the "genius" or general prin-

[8] M. P. Charlesworth, "The Flavian Dynasty," *The Cambridge History*, XI, p. 43.
[9] Cf. Suetonius, *Domitian*, XIII, 2.

ciple of the emperor. In Domitian's reign this reverence was for the first time directed toward a living emperor. Some wishing to flatter him made sacrifices to his "genius." Domitian not only accepted the acclaim, but also turned it into a test of loyalty. Neither Jews nor Christians could, of course, acknowledge his divinity and so were set at odds with the emperor. Apparently, antagonism rapidly turned into open hostility and persecution. Both Jewish and Christian tradition branded Domitian as a persecutor who sought out the kindred of Jesus Christ and punished adherents of the new religion.[10]

For a number of years Jews and Christians, as well as Romans, had much to fear from an emperor who could demand worship of himself as proof of loyalty. Even close and trusted friends fell victim to his ego. T. Flavius Clemens, the emperor's cousin, and his wife Flavia Domitilla, parents of sons Domitian had chosen to be his successors (Domitian had no son of his own), were accused of atheism. Clemens was executed and Domitilla was exiled. It is possible that both were Christians.[11] Perhaps the "sudden and successive calamitous events" mentioned in Clement's *Epistle to the Corinthians* (1:2) refer to Domitian's persecution.

Domitian was murdered in a palace conspiracy and imperial power was transferred to a senior senator, M. Cocceius Nerva (A.D. 96–98). Nerva adopted Trajan, an army commander in upper Germany, and made him co-regent and successor. Trajan was first and foremost a military man and his reign (A.D. 98–117) was marked by an eastward extension of the empire. Arabia, Armenia, and Mesopotamia became Roman provinces. Over several years these eastern areas were quite unstable and problems arising out of the need to control them often strained Trajan's personal courtesy and tolerance. Since disturbances could not be ignored, the emperor's effort to be patient was sometimes conditioned by the necessity of firm control. In this light we understand Trajan's correspondence with Pliny the Younger, his governor in Bithynia (see pp. 391, 415f). Around A.D. 112 Pliny as a new provincial governor wrote Trajan to inquire about proper measures against

---

[10] Eusebius, *EH*, III, xix, 1, says, "The same Domitian gave orders for the execution of those of the family of David, and an ancient story goes that some heretics accused the grandsons of Judas (who is said to have been the brother, according to the flesh, of the Saviour) saying that they were of the family of David, and related to Christ himself." In *EH*, III, xx, 7, he quotes Tertullian as follows, "Domitian also once tried to do the same as he, for he was a Nero in cruelty, but, I believe, inasmuch as he had some sense, he stopped at once and recalled those whom he had banished."

[11] An early Christian cemetery in Rome was the gift of a Flavia Domitilla.

Christians who refused the prescribed allegiance to Rome. The emperor's reply shows some restrained tolerance, but at the same time reflects the necessity to keep order and uphold the law. The correspondence throws light on the situation of the Church in Bithynia and on the empire's attitude toward Christians. While it does not reflect any real persecution of the Church, it does clearly indicate that it was illegal to be Christian. In A.D. 115–117 Trajan had serious trouble with a savagely ferocious Jewish uprising in Cyrene, Egypt, and Cyprus, an omen of what was to come.

Hadrian (A.D. 117–138), successor to Trajan, had to take drastic and relentless measures against the Jews. On a journey through Jewish territory in the summer of A.D. 130 he ordered the building of a new town on the site of Jerusalem, destroyed half a century earlier by Titus. The town, to be called *Aelia Capitolina,* was to be a Roman colony with Greek settlers. Hadrian also ordered the construction of a temple to Jupiter Capitolinus, in which he himself would be honored, on the site of the old temple to Yahweh. Thus new life was to rise from the ruins, and the site of old Jerusalem would become a center of flourishing Greco-Roman culture. The Jews greatly resented this and everywhere among them revolt was talked. The opposition remained veiled until Hadrian left the east, but then "there began a guerrilla war of caverns, ravines, mountain fastnesses." [12] This ferocious opposition was led by Bar Cochba, hailed by Jews as the expected Jewish Messiah. Bar Cochba, "the Son of the Star," was the messianic designation of a strong Jewish military leader, Simeon son of Chosiba. The Jews rallied behind him and revolt was on. It had to be taken seriously. Aelia Capitolina was taken by storm and Rome's capable leaders and troops had great difficulty coping with the superior numbers of the Jews. The frenzy grew until finally in the summer of A.D. 134 Hadrian traveled from Rome to the scene of the war. Hundreds of villages and cities were taken; thousands of Jews died. The report that 50 mountain fortresses, 985 villages, and 585,000 men fell before Rome—to say nothing of the people who perished by famine and pestilence—seems near the facts. This second Jewish War was little else than a manhunt in which the Romans exterminated a large part of the population of Palestine.[13]

The reign of Antoninus (A.D. 138–161) was without major incident affecting the Church or Judaism and need not concern us.

---

[12] Wilhelm Weber, "Hadrian," *The Cambridge Ancient History,* XI, p. 314.
[13] Cary, *A History of Rome,* p. 649.

THE EXPANSION OF THE CHURCH

As we have already noted, Acts focuses upon the spread of the Church to certain cities of Palestine and Syria and particularly its spread, through the work of Paul, among the Gentiles of Asia Minor and Greece until it reaches Rome. The Acts narrative does not, however, tell the whole story. The Church was also extended into areas which Acts does not mention. Harnack's *The Expansion of Christianity in the First Three Centuries* lists over eighty places or locales where Christian communities can be traced before A.D. 180. Of these, only twenty-eight are mentioned in Acts and only thirteen more elsewhere in the New Testament. Some of the places mentioned in the New Testament were evangelized by Paul or some other apostolic missionary. Many of them, however, are known only by name, and nothing is known of the establishment of Christianity in such important places as Damascus or Rome. Christian communities remained relatively small and obscure, for to the casual observer Christianity was one of many cults which were springing up regularly among the cosmopolitan populations of the cities of the empire. Therefore, few references to Christianity appear in contemporary non-Christian books and letters. Records are, however, adequate to show that by A.D. 150 Christians were in all provinces of the empire and in Mesopotamia, and that the main outlines of the Church's organization and doctrine were appearing.[14]

Within a generation after the death of Jesus, Christianity had claimed a place in the urban life of the Hellenistic world. It was quickly and enthusiastically carried beyond Jerusalem to Jews of the far-flung dispersion where it early outgrew its Jewish "swaddling-clothes." [15] Whether the impulse to venture into the Gentile world came from Jesus himself [16] or Paul,[17] the new religion bore within it-

[14] The substance of the last few sentences is from Kenneth Scott Latourette, *A History of the Expansion of Christianity: the First Five Centuries*, p. 85. He sets A.D. 180, the end of the reign of Marcus Aurelius, as the terminus for the immediate post-apostolic expansion. It is reasonable to believe, however, that the Church had reached throughout the empire as early as A.D. 150. See also Adolf Harnack, *The Expansion of Christianity in the First Three Centuries*, II.

[15] Latourette, *A History of the Expansion of Christianity: the First Five Centuries*, p. 72.

[16] This is the implication of Matt. 28:19. Even if this saying is a construct of the Church, it reflects the belief that the missionary commission was true to the wishes and purposes of Jesus.

[17] Cf. Acts 13–15. Unquestionably Paul was both guiding genius and driving power behind the Church's missionary expansion.

self inherent qualities of universalism and caught the attention of those who were seeking for a different expression of religious values. Some had already turned to Judaism. To them Christianity offered the ethical and spiritual values of Judaism apart from its narrow nationalistic and racial confines. It also offered "the extraordinary attraction of Jesus." [18] Through such converts the Church entered the stream of urban Hellenistic life, which in turn facilitated the spread of Christianity. The Hellenistic culture which unified the Roman world centered in the cities so that "a faith with its stronghold in them would tend to penetrate to the connecting towns and countryside." [19]

At first the new faith had some success among Jewish populations and Gentile-proselytes to Judaism in the Hellenistic cities (cf. the discussion of Paul's missions on pp. 259–271, 282–304). The majority of Jews, however, resented Christianity as a dangerous threat to their ancestral faith and angrily rejected and opposed the Christians. Consequently, before A.D. 150 the Church had become predominantly non-Jewish in membership and after some initial sharp clashes the two traditions practically ignored one another. Early Christian apologists for the most part wrote against rivals other than Judaism, while Jewish leaders for their part gave little heed to Christianity. The Church by the end of the period of our concern was predominantly Hellenistic and Gentile.

The Church in Palestine to A.D. 150

Acts implies that the Church expanded from Jerusalem to Judea and Samaria and thence to the end of the earth (1:8). The formula suggests that the first steps of diffusion were throughout Palestine with the hub in Jerusalem. In spite of the fact that Galilee had been the scene of most of Jesus' public ministry, the Christian mission seemingly did not flourish there.[20] Jerusalem, not the towns of Galilee, formed the center of Christendom in Palestine and, therefore, most discussion must focus primarily upon Judean strongholds of the Church.

Jerusalem and the Jewish Christian Church. The Jerusalem church was, of course, a Jewish Christian congregation. It appears even to have contained two different strata of Jewish Christianity. On one

[18] Latourette, *A History of the Expansion of Christianity: the First Five Centuries*, p. 73.
[19] *Ibid.*
[20] Cf. L. E. Elliott-Binns, *Galilean Christianity,* and Ernst Lohmeyer, *Galiläa und Jerusalem.*

hand were the extremely conservative opponents of the Pauline mission to the Gentiles, some of whom may even have actively sought to obstruct or counteract his work. On the other hand was a more moderate group represented by men like the Apostles, Barnabas, and James the brother of Jesus. In fact, James was head of the church, a role he assumed when, after Stephen's unhappy encounter with Jewish authority, the Apostles had fled Jerusalem and perhaps subsequently had come to see that their vocation meant the mission enterprise of Christianity.[21] The choice of James was doubtless a compromise attempt to hold the two factions together, since he was a man of deep Jewish piety and adequate Christian insight. Under his leadership the Jerusalem church apparently did not adhere to the extreme claims of the radical Jewish Christians, nor was it willing to forsake completely the Jewish heritage of the Church. It approved the Gentile mission of Paul, but, if Acts 15 correctly reports the Jerusalem conference, aimed to preserve a relationship with those within the Church with more conservative Jewish leanings.

Any harmony which was achieved, however, was too fragile and superficial to survive the trying times that led up to the fall of Jerusalem in A.D. 70. In A.D. 62, during a lapse in direct Roman control in Judea, James was martyred at the instigation of the high priest, Annas.[22] His death was a severe loss to the Jewish church and perhaps led to its disintegration in the hectic years that followed. Symeon, a cousin of Jesus, was chosen as successor to James and, according to Eusebius, continued as head of the Jerusalem congregation until his martyrdom during the reign of Trajan.[23] So far as we can ascertain, and our evidence is quite meager, the Jewish Christians of Jerusalem and to some degree in the rest of Palestine became embroiled in the internal conflicts that tore Judaism during the revolt of A.D. 66–73. The extremely conservative element found its nationalistic ties too strong to break and participated in the bitter and tragic fighting against Rome.[24] They apparently perished with their Jewish companions by sword and famine in Titus' long and horrible siege of Jerusalem and their stream

---

[21] See Harnack, *The Expansion of Christianity in the First Three Centuries,* II, p. 247.

[22] This occurred between the death of the procurator Porcius Festus and the arrival in Jerusalem of his successor, Albinus.

[23] *EH,* III, xi, 1 and III, xxxii. Eusebius says that Symeon was chosen by the apostles, disciples, and the family of Jesus. Whom he means by apostles we do not know. They cannot have been the Twelve.

[24] So S. G. F. Brandon, *The Fall of Jerusalem and the Christian Church,* pp. 179–180.

of Jewish Christianity dried up. Another group, unable or unwilling to support the cause of Jewish nationalism, fled Jerusalem sometime before or during the siege. Warned, Eusebius says,[25] by a divine revelation, they fled to Pella, a Decapolis city in Transjordan. A saying which appears in the apocalyptic section of Mark (and its Synoptic parallels, Matthew 24:15 and Luke 21:20) fits this occasion:

> But when you see the desolating sacrilege set up where it ought not to be (let the reader understand), then let those who are in Judea flee to the mountains. (Mark 13:14)[26]

This passage may well have been the basis of the Eusebius reference to the warning from Jesus. Remembering it, some Christians interpreted the impending disaster as "the desolating sacrilege," left the city and fled to Pella in Transjordan. Jews, on the other hand, rushed into Jerusalem where by the thousands they died of slaughter and starvation.[27] Other Jews abandoned the city and settled in Jamnia (Jabneh) where they became the founders of a new Judaism. According to Mishnaic traditions, their leader, Johanan ben Zakkai, escaped by being carried out of the city in a coffin.

The tradition of the Christian flight to Pella is fraught with difficulties and is doubted by many.[28] It is difficult to understand how the Christians were able to flee a city either threatened by or actually under siege and then cross miles of hostile territory when Jews would have regarded them traitors and Romans would have considered them Jews and enemies. Pella too would conceivably have been unfriendly to a Jewish group, even if Christian, because early in the revolt Jewish nationalists attacked Pella and mistreated its Gentile population. Nevertheless, the tradition has some basis and probably it is best to assume that a small community of Jewish Christians left Jerusalem during the revolt and settled in Pella. That they were able to do so is one of the unresolved mysteries of history.

Neither the New Testament nor other extant writings from the subapostolic age describe the fortunes of Palestinian Christians amid the convulsion and overthrow of their nation's life. Up to approximately A.D. 70 the Jerusalem church was looked to as the mother community

---

[25] *EH*, III, v, 3.

[26] The Marcan and Matthean forms of the saying seems to anticipate the event, whereas the Lucan form presupposes it.

[27] Cf. *Wars*, V, VI.

[28] See especially Brandon, *The Fall of Jerusalem and the Christian Church*, pp. 167–184. Brandon believes that there is some validity to the tradition of a Christian flight to Pella but not from Jerusalem.

with impressive authority and prestige, but after that date the community so disintegrated that it played no effective part in the life of the movement it had generated. Jewish Christianity had for the most part been unable to separate itself from its Jewishness. It ignored the universalist dimensions of the Christian faith by clinging tenaciously to Jewish exclusiveness. Those who fought with Judaism against Rome were annihilated. Those who fled Jerusalem and other Palestinian Christian centers largely lost their Christian distinctiveness and existed apart from the main-stream of the Church.

Writers in the second and fourth centuries tell of various sects living east of the Jordan who may have been descendants of Jewish Christianity.[29] One of these groups, called the Ebionites ("the poor"), may have been directly related to the Jerusalem community which was also called "the poor" (Galatians 2:10, Romans 15:26). The Ebionites based their practice upon the Jewish law and tradition. They denied the virgin birth of Jesus, used only Matthew's Gospel, and rejected the mission and writings of Paul. They prayed with faces toward Jerusalem, as if God dwelt there. A similar group called "Nazorenes" or "Nazarenes" is mentioned by later writers.[30] Related to this sort of Christianity was the second century prophetic community led by Elxai (*Alexis* in Greek), for whom Christ was the Son of God, but who also insisted upon observance of a modified Jewish ritual. Elxai had envisioned Christ as a giant figure as tall as a mountain 96 miles high. Beside Christ stood his equally impressive sister, Rucha, the Holy Spirit.[31] None of these Jewish Christian sects was ever large or influential.

If Jewish Christianity lived on at all in the mainstream of Christian tradition, it was among some of the Pella group who may have returned to Jerusalem sometime after the end of the Jewish revolt. We do not know for certain that there was such a return, but the tradition of Symeon's leadership of the Jerusalem church until his martyrdom during the reign of Trajan could be so interpreted. Also the tradition [32] of thirteen Jewish bishops (and presbyters?) of Jerusalem between the reign of Trajan and the eighteenth year of Hadrian lends some credi-

[29] Cf. Justin Martyr, *Dialogue with Trypho*, XLVII; Irenaeus, *Against Heresies*, I, xxvi, 2; Origen, *Against Celsus*, V, xli; Epiphanius, *Heresies*, XXIX, vii, 4; ix, 4.

[30] Epiphanius, *Heresies*, XXIX, vii, 4; ix, 4; Jerome, *Lives of Illustrious Men*, II, III; *Dialogue against the Pelagians*, III, 2.

[31] On Elxai see the brief analysis in Hans Lietzmann, *The Beginnings of the Christian Church*, pp. 185–189. The ancient references are Hippolytus, IX, and Epiphanius, *Heresies*, XIX.

[32] Cited by Harnack, *The Expansion of Christianity in the First Three Centuries*, II, p. 247.

bility to the existence of a Christian church in the city. This community would have been short-lived, since two generations later Jerusalem had become *Aelia Capitolina* and Jews were forbidden to enter upon punishment of death. Never during the period of our concern did the city of *Aelia* or the Gentile church there attain any real importance.

The Church in Greater Palestine. Elsewhere in Palestine Jewish Christianity was eventually superseded by the more orthodox movement of the Gentile Church, even east of the Jordan, and for the most part "the conquering, universal form of Christianity . . . took no notice of the decease of her elder sister." [33] Galilean Christianity is known to us only by inference. Eusebius [34] quoting Hegesippus tells that two grandsons of Jude, the brother of Jesus, were arrested during the reign of Domitian and charged with teaching that Jesus as Messiah would be an earthly ruler and overthrow Roman rule. [35] The grandsons were probably Galilean. In addition, rabbinical references to disputes between rabbis and Jewish Christians may have a late first century Galilean setting since Jamnia (Jabneh) became a center of rabbinic activity after A.D. 70. The absence of Galilee from the evangelistic charge of Acts 1:8 leaves open at least the possibility that it was already Christian by the time of the writing of Acts. The idea that early preachers from Galilee founded the church in nearby Damascus is both credible and attractive. [36] Conclusions drawn from silence, however, are at best suggestive and should be considered as likely possibilities rather than demonstrated fact.

More certain data about Samaritan Christianity are available. The Gentile mission of the Church was preceded and prepared for by a mission in Samaria. Samaria saw "the actual beginnings of the Christian mission," since there for the first time the gospel entered an area which did not belong to the Jewish community. [37] The area was evangelized by the Hellenists who had been driven from Jerusalem because of their opposition to the temple. These Hellenists found refuge among the Samaritans, whose hostility to the Jerusalem temple was longstanding (cf. John 4:20–21). This transitional expansion of the Church, which was supported by the apostolic authority of Peter and

---

[33] Lietzmann, *The Beginnings of the Christian Church*, p. 90.
[34] *EH*, III, xix–xx.
[35] Another tradition places this under Vespasian.
[36] Cf. Lohmeyer, *Galiläa und Jerusalem*, p. 52. Whether the Galilean church was independent of Jerusalem and influential as he also maintains is a matter of serious question.
[37] Oscar Cullmann, "Samaria and the Origins of the Christian Mission," *The Early Church*, pp. 185–192.

John, was not destined for complete success. Samaritan Christianity was regarded by the Church fathers as the peculiar spawning ground of the Gnostic heresy. Justin Martyr, himself a Samaritan, believed Simon Magus, with whom Peter had an encounter (Acts 8:9–24), to be the father of Gnosticism.[38] Simon is reported to have traveled as a prophet, miracle worker, and magician. He was worshipped as the First God, and Helen, a former prostitute who accompanied him, as the First Thought which he brought into existence.[39] According to various Christian traditions, Simon met a tragic end while attempting to fly over Rome when Peter by a prayer caused him to fall.[40] There is uncertainty about the degree of historicity in these traditions, particularly the identification of the Simon of Christian tradition with Simon Magus of Acts. Nevertheless, they reveal opinion in the early Church that Gnosticism, one of the most dangerous ideological threats to Christianity, had early connections with Samaria. Samaritan Christianity, then, as known to us from tradition had less than the best reputation. It cannot have been all bad, however, since Justin Martyr, a noble leader of the Church in the second century, was himself from Samaria.

The most enduring Christian center in Palestine was Caesarea (see pp. 234, 337). This coastal city was the scene of extended apostolic activity. At Caesarea Philip, one of the Seven, ministered for many years (Acts 8:40; 21:8), Peter preached to Cornelius (Acts 10 and 11), and Paul was imprisoned for two years (Acts 23:33–26:32). The church at Caesarea became a center of independent Hellenistic Christianity and consequently endured the fall of Jerusalem. Origen, the great exegete and theologian, worked there in the third century, and Eusebius, the Church historian, was bishop of the Caesarean church in the fourth century.

Early Christianity: Syria and the East

Outside Palestine Christianity first took deep root in Syria. Almost from the beginning Christians could be found in Damascus (Acts 9:1–25), Tyre (Acts 21:4), Ptolemais (Acts 21:7), and Sidon (Acts 27:3), all centers of Greek population and culture. The major center of Christian activity in Syria, however, was Antioch (see pp. 240–

---

[38] *Apology,* I, xxvi, lvi; *Dialogue with Trypho,* CXX.

[39] Justin Martyr, *Apology,* I, xxvi.

[40] For details about Simon Magus and the Samaritan Gnosis, see Hans Jonas, *The Gnostic Religion,* pp. 103–111, and Robert M. Grant, *Gnosticism and Early Christianity,* pp. 70–96.

244). Jesus may have first been called Lord *(Kurios)* in Antioch.[41] The church in Antioch was the first truly Gentile-Christian community. While respecting the traditions of the Jerusalem church and acknowledging a certain responsibility to it, Antioch sponsored the first ecumenical mission outreach and defended it when the conservatives in Jerusalem opposed such an extension of the gospel (cf. Acts 13–15). The Antioch church was something of a middle ground between Palestinian Jewish Christianity and the Pauline missionary Church. From the beginning Antioch was regarded as a sort of colony of Jerusalem and the mother church exercised a certain control over it which continued for decades. To the credit of Jerusalem Christianity, however, Antioch was relatively free to develop a theology of Christian mission that surpassed the conservative limitations of the mind of Jewish Christianity. This, of course, was not achieved without opposition and an able assist from the Apostle Paul. That it was achieved at all was due to the strength of Antioch's conviction about the Gentile mission and the ability of sane and moderate minds to prevail in Jerusalem.

Information about the Antioch church beyond its relationship to the Gentile mission is quite meager. While Antioch may have been the origin of the Gospel of Matthew and perhaps the letter of James, we know nothing about the church there in the last quarter of the first century. In the first decade of the second century, however, its bishop, Ignatius, who took office around A.D. 69,[42] was seized in a persecution and taken to Rome. On his way to martyrdom he wrote seven letters which are important sources for the life and thought of the early Church.

This, then, is the little that we know of the Church's beginnings on its home soil and immediate environs. Jewish Christianity vanished and that of Samaria apparently took disappointing and dangerous form. Caesarea and Antioch, therefore, stand out as the enduringly important centers of Christian faith. From them the Church expanded "into all the world."

The Church in Egypt and North Africa

A grievous blank in knowledge of the early Church is the ignorance of its history in Alexandria and Egypt before A.D. 180. The evangeliza-

[41] See Johannes Weiss, *The History of Primitive Christianity*, II, pp. 741–742, who sees the title as taken from Hellenism. On the use of this title in the New Testament, see Rudolf Bultmann, *Theology*, I, pp. 121–133, and Werner-Foerster and Gottfried Quell, "Kurios," *Theological Dictionary of the New Testament*, Gerhard Kittel, ed., III, pp. 1039–1098.

[42] *EH*, III, xxxvi, 2.

tion of North Africa is not mentioned in the New Testament. A hearsay report that Mark was the first to be sent to Egypt as a Christian must be treated cautiously. This tradition lacks early support and is questionable.[43] Apollos, who was a Christian missionary when he succeeded Paul at Corinth, was an Alexandrian Jew, but we do not know that he acquired his Christian faith in Alexandria. If he did, it was a different form of Christianity from that of Paul (cf. Acts 18:24–26). At the end of the second century, when for the first time it appears in the daylight of history, the Alexandrian church was stately and strong, with an attached school of higher learning which would diffuse its influence and bear its fame far and wide. Christian writings were circulated in Egypt before A.D. 150. A papyrus fragment of the Gospel of John from Egypt may date as early as A.D. 130, perhaps earlier,[44] and the so-called Fragments of an Unknown Gospel, which dates from about A.D. 150, is dependent upon the canonical Gospels. Other Christian literature, strongly Gnostic in character, was recently discovered near modern Nag Hammadi. These materials are Coptic translations and revisions of Gnostic Greek texts which may go back as early as A.D. 150. By mid-second century, then, there existed in Egypt a strong Christian tradition with several forms, some of which were decidedly heretical by usual standards.

Since decades of Christian activity must have stood behind the developed Church tradition of Alexandria and the extensive literary activity just described, the foundation of the Church in Egypt must go back into the first century. Eusebius' statement that by A.D. 202 Christians were dragged to Alexandria "from Egypt and the whole Thebias" indicates that there must have been Christians in all parts of the country.[45] Such a wide spread of the Church would have taken considerable time, but just how or when the gospel was first taken to Egypt is unknown. Perhaps some of the Christians fleeing Jerusalem during the revolt of A.D. 66 migrated to Alexandria,[46] but they could hardly have founded the Alexandrian church if Apollos learned his Christianity there. The origin of Egyptian Christianity remains a tantalizing mystery.

---

[43] *EH*, II, xvii.

[44] This is the John Rylands Fragment. Cf. C. H. Roberts, *An Unpublished Fragment of the Fourth Gospel in the John Rylands Library.*

[45] *EH*, VI, i, 1.

[46] Brandon, *The Fall of Jerusalem and the Christian Church*, pp. 217–243. Brandon's argument for an Alexandrian origin of the Gospel of Matthew is not convincing nor is his contention that Paul did not include Egypt in the wide field of his missionary endeavor because of the strongly Jewish character of Christianity there.

About the early spread of Christianity into other parts of Africa there is even less information. The isolated tradition of the conversion of the eunuch from Ethiopia hints at the early spread of the gospel to that country (Acts 8:26–39), but the initial stages of Christian expansion along the North African coast can only be assumed, not verified. By the third century, however, the area in and around Carthage, along with Asia Minor, comprised the two greatest numerical strongholds of the faith. The Christian faith may have had its beginnings among the large Jewish population of Carthage as early as the first half of the second century. Whenever and however it was established in the region, North African Christianity moved out most markedly from the borders of Hellenism and became at home in the Latin speaking world. The North African church produced in the third and fourth centuries the first important Latin Christian literature. (See particularly the works of Tertullian and Cyprian.) But beyond these general descriptions the evidence does not permit us to go.

Consolidation in Asia Minor

The status of Christianity in Asia Minor is a little more certain, although major gaps remain in the available information. Except for our incomplete knowledge of Paul's missionary activity in the region, we have no information about the means by which Christianity won its way in Asia Minor or of the missionaries who propagated it. Paul's work was doubtless more extensive than described in Acts and throughout the region his associates probably established numerous house churches, small groups meeting in homes for worship and common meals.[47] The movement spread rapidly so that Asia Minor became the foremost Christian area during the pre-Constantine era. There Hellenism had assumed a form which rendered it peculiarly susceptible to a universal religion like Christianity, thanks to numerous Jews who, even though hostile to Christianity, had made preparations for it in the minds and feelings of the Hellenistic population. Many of the Jews themselves took their hereditary faith lightly and were, therefore, open-minded to Christian preaching. Christianity penetrated different parts of Asia Minor with varying degrees of rapidity. Ephesus in Asia, for example, was early one of Christianity's chief centers. Pliny's letter to the emperor Trajan around A.D. 112 reports strong Christian activities in his territory. He described Christianity as hav-

[47] Cf. Floyd V. Filson, "The Significance of the Early House Churches," *JBL,* LVIII (1939), 105–112.

Figure 11–3. Excavation of a church building in Laodicea in Asia, an important Christian center around the end of the first century and included in the book of Revelation as one of the seven churches in Asia. (Source: Foreign Mission Board, SBC.)

ing spread widely in the towns and also in the countryside.[48] Thus the spreading faith seems to have been strongest on the west coast, in the province of Asia, and in Phrygia and Bithynia. In North Galatia, however, the Church made little progress and into the fourth century paganism was still the dominant religion of the area.

Asia Minor was a center of Christian literary activity. The Gospel of John and the three Johannine letters originated there toward the end of the first century, and the books of Revelation and I Peter are addressed to churches of the region which faced persecution because of their religion. By the end of the century the churches of Asia Minor had begun to collect the letters of Paul, some of which had earlier been written to them. The letters of Ignatius apparently circulated among these churches as did the writings of Polycarp and Papias, both bishops of the area.

The Christians of Asia Minor were concerned to maintain sound doctrine and strong leadership in the face of persecution and the rise of false teaching. As early as the time of Paul's letter to Colossae

[48] Cf. Pliny's Letter to Trajan in *The New Eusebius*, pp. 13–14.

Gnostic ideas were a threat to the Church and continued to be so in the docetic denial that Jesus Christ came in the flesh.[49] A more overt threat to the Church's integrity came from the notable Marcion of Pontus, who came to Rome from Asia Minor in A.D. 142 with a well-formed religious position. He rejected the Old Testament, in which he found a God of wrath and judgment who could not be, in his opinion, the Father of Jesus. He formed a canon consisting of the Gospel of Luke and ten Pauline letters (excluding the Pastorals). From these he excised all passages which tended in any way to relate the Old Testament God to Jesus and the Church. The Christian literature, both canonical and non-canonical, from Asia Minor reflects these ideological threats to the thought of the Church.

The Elders. To counter the spread of false teaching, among other reasons, schools of prophecy, evangelism, and theology which were influential into the third century were established at Ephesus and Smyrna. The founders of these schools were Christian Jews from Palestine, some of whom may have been followers of Jesus. Like the masters in the rabbinic teaching tradition, they were called by the honorific title, "the elders." These men were prominent leaders with authority over a considerable area. A good deal about them and their work has been preserved, but its meaning is by no means certain. Much of the evidence comes from Papias, who in the introduction to his early second century book, *Exposition of the Oracles of the Lord*, told how, when he was a young man, men who could repeat the words of the "elders" were still visiting the churches. Papias' book has not survived, but Eusebius gives an interesting extract from it.

. . . If ever anyone came who had followed the presbyters, I inquired into the words of the presbyters, what Andrew or Peter or Philip, or Thomas, or James, or John, or Matthew or any other of the Lord's disciples had said, and what Aristion and the presbyter John, the Lord's disciples were saying.[50]

Whether any of the Apostles had been active in the church of Asia Minor is uncertain. Rather, Papias probably is reporting what the "elders" had preserved from the named Apostles. This seems clear when we read on in Eusebius:

It is here worth noting that he twice counts the name of John, and reckons the first John with Peter and James and Matthew and the other Apostles, . . . but by changing his statement places the second with the others outside

[49] Cf. John 1:14; I John 4:2; II John 1:7, and especially the letters of Ignatius to the churches of Asia Minor.
[50] *EH*, III, xxxix, 4.

the number of the Apostles, putting Aristion before him and clearly calling him a presbyter.[51]

Also a bit further on:

The Papias whom we are now treating confesses that he had received the words of the Apostles from their followers, but says that he had actually heard Aristion and the presbyter John.[52]

The tradition of the elders is respected and venerable. Their association with the Apostles doubtless added to their prestige and the value of their teachings. Some among them were exceptionally influential, especially the elders John and Philip.

Papias lists John among the Apostles whose teachings had been passed on by the elders at Ephesus. He also says that he himself had heard John the elder. Apparently Papias had in mind two men named John, one the Apostle, the other the elder. The latter was active in Asia Minor, a key figure in the strong apostolic tradition which had been established among the churches of Asia Minor by the middle of the second century. He may have been a student of the Apostle John. Irenaeus, on the basis of his memory of something he had once heard from Polycarp bishop of Smyrna, identified the elder John with the Apostle,[53] a tradition which has tenaciously persisted. Irenaeus, however, seems to have misinterpreted Polycarp. He was very young when he heard Polycarp and apparently thought that Polycarp claimed to be a disciple of John the Apostle. This is not likely. Polycarp probably referred to John the Ephesian elder. The fact that there are some similarities between the elder and the Apostle doubtless contributed to the tendency to identify the two. John of Ephesus, the elder, seems to have been a follower of Jesus during his lifetime; he was held in special esteem as "a disciple of the Lord." His Palestinian background is borne out by the tradition that he had been a priest. He became a distinguished leader of the church at Ephesus and a teacher in its school. To identify him as the Apostle John, however, goes beyond the limits of the meager evidence, so that the two should be distinguished from each other.

The relationship between the elder John and the Apostle has a direct bearing on the problems of authorship of the various Johannine writings (the Gospel of John; I, II, and III John; and Revelation). The author of the Gospel of John may have utilized the traditions of

[51] *EH*, III, xxxix, 5.
[52] *EH*, III, xxxix, 7.
[53] *Against Heresies*, III, iii, 4; V, xxxiii, 4.

Figure 11–4. Ephesus showing the ruins of the library of Celsus and the agora. Ephesus was the center of Asian Christianity. (Source: Foreign Mission Board, SBC.)

the elders in interpreting Jesus in light of the intellectual crises arising from the Church's confrontation with extensive Hellenistic thought. Revelation, written by a certain John, is addressed to seven churches in the province of Asia, encouraging them to remain faithful in the face of persecution. The author of the Johannine letters actually calls himself "the elder" and writes to churches with open affection and concern for their welfare. These obvious connections must be remembered in any serious attempt to discover the identity of the author of the various writings, although clearly the traditional association of Johannine literature with John of Ephesus does not necessarily connect it with John the Apostle.

Another person associated with the "elders tradition" in Asia Minor was Philip. The earliest traditions identified him with the Apostle Philip,[54] but a more likely identification is with Philip of the Hellenistic Seven.[55] He settled in Hierapolis in western Phrygia, an important city in the neighborhood of Colossae and Laodicea, both of which are mentioned in connection with Paul. Philip had daughters who were prophetesses, whose activities may be related to later prophetic emphases in the Montanist movement of the middle of the second century.[56]

Both Papias and Irenaeus record opinions of the elders which seem to have been handed down orally. They concern the interpretation of parables and prophecy, the age of Jesus when he began teaching, and the length of Jesus' ministry. Other concerns of their tradition are unknown to us.

These scanty data about the Church in Asia Minor are insufficient for any complete description of apostolic and post-apostolic Christianity in the region, but are sufficient enough, even apart from information coming from the Pauline corpus, to designate Asia Minor as a strategic stronghold of early Christian growth and consolidation.

The Church in Greece and Crete

The progress of Christianity in Greece and the Balkan peninsula is only faintly known before the time of Constantine. Of course, from biblical sources come glimpses of groups of Christians in some of the chief cities during the time of Paul, and non-biblical references testify to the continued existence of the Church in Corinth, Athens, and Thessalonica. The larger part of the peninsula, however, cannot have had more than a scanty Christian population before Constantine.[57] No outstanding figures emerge and the spread of Christianity was not

---

[54] Cf. Papias as understood by Eusebius, *EH*, III, xix, 7–10.

[55] This identification was first made c. 200 by the Montanist leader Proclus, who is said by his opponent Gaius to have identified this Philip with the evangelist of the same name.

[56] Montanism was a movement which gave particular emphasis to the role of the Holy Spirit. About A.D. 156 Montanus proclaimed himself the passive instrument through whom the Holy Spirit spoke. Two prophetesses were associated with him. Together they affirmed that the end of the world was at hand and the heavenly Jerusalem was about to be established in Phrygia, to which believers should gather. In preparation for the approaching end of this age the most strenuous asceticism was practiced. In its ascetic demands Montanism represented a wide-spread tendency and prepared the foundation for later monasticism.

[57] Harnack, *The Expansion of Christianity in the First Three Centuries*, II, pp. 371–376.

uniform. The information about the churches of Athens and Corinth after the time of Paul is meager, but interesting. Certain evidence of Athenian Christianity is found in two apologetic works. The first of these is Quadratus' defense of Christianity written from Athens to the emperor Hadrian about A.D. 125.[58] The other Athenian apologist was Aristides who addressed himself to Antoninus Pius between A.D. 138 and 147.[59] The Athenian church remained small, "for in this city of philosophers Christianity could find little room," [60] but certainly not inconsequential. In the third century Origen, who spent some time in Athens, wrote, "For the Church of God, which is at Athens, is a meek and stable body, as being one which desires to please God, who is over all things; whereas the assembly of the Athenians is given to sedition, and is not at all to be compared to the Church of God in that city." [61] According to early tradition, Dionysius the Areopagite was the first bishop of Athens, suggesting a community of some import.[62] The stature of the Athenian church is further verified by a decree sent by Antoninus Pius (A.D. 138–161) to Thessalonica, Athens, Larissa, and "the Greeks," forbidding these cities to rise against the Christians. The strength of the Church in these cities should not be underrated.

A glimpse into the life of Corinthian Christianity is provided by I Clement. The troubled and explosive ways so well attested by the Corinthian letters of Paul had obviously continued. The church deposed certain elders and the Roman church intervened on behalf of the deposed, blaming the trouble upon some leaders who did not have the good of the church at heart. Apparently this intervention was successful, for the letter was read regularly in the liturgical assemblies of Corinth. In spite of its erratic character the Corinthian church apparently extended its influence into the countryside. Churches existed there as early as A.D. 170, evidence of missionary activity from Corinth. About the church in Thessalonica we know only what is implied by the decree of Antoninus Pius.

There is some uncertain evidence of the early presence of Christianity on the Aegean islands, but none that is unquestionable before the third century. We know, however, from the Epistle of Titus that

---

[58] *EH*, IV, iii.

[59] *Ibid.*

[60] Harnack, *The Expansion of Christianity in the First Three Centuries*, II, p. 373.

[61] *Against Celsus*, III, xxx.

[62] Cf. Dionysius of Corinth as referred to by Eusebius, *EH*, IV xxiii, 3.

Christianity had reached Crete before the end of the apostolic age (Titus 1:5). Of its extent and character nothing is known.

Early Roman Christianity

The church of Rome was founded by unknown missionaries at the beginning of the apostolic age. Rome was the imperial capital to which many ideas and cults naturally gravitated. Inevitably, the Christian faith made its way there early. Perhaps Christianity first reached Rome when witnesses to the Pentecost events in Jerusalem were converted and returned or traveled to Rome. Or it may have been that Christians from Pauline churches migrated to Rome and established the church.[63] The Roman church was already considerably important when Paul wrote to it from Corinth (c. A.D. 58). Several small congregations composed the larger body, whose faith was known throughout Christendom (Romans 1:8). By the time Paul reached Rome there were Christians in Caesar's household (Philippians 4:22).[64] If venerable and tenacious tradition is correct, Peter came late in his life to Rome.[65] Since neither the book of Acts nor Paul's writings to and from Rome mention Peter's presence in Rome, he must not have been there before the end of Paul's known missionary activity. He does seem to have been there before the Neronic persecution fell upon the Church. By that time many Christians were in the imperial city.[66] Paul and Peter were struck down by this persecution but the Church soon recovered. Its survival through this and subsequent moments of trial and terror is evidence of strong and stable faith.

The Epistle of Clement pictures the Roman church around A.D. 96 as consolidated, strong, and conscious of its obligation to care for the whole Church. Already it thought of itself as the church of the world's capital. Just after the turn of the century Roman Christianity was extolled by Ignatius as "worthy of God, worthy of the highest happiness, worthy of praise, worthy of obtaining here every desire,

[63] Sometimes Romans 16 is cited in support of this suggestion. This chapter, however, was probably addressed to Ephesian Christians.

[64] If Philippians were written from Rome. There were members of Caesar's household in Ephesus too.

[65] I Clement, VI; Ignatius, *Epistle to the Romans,* IV; Papias as quoted by Eusebius, *EH,* II, xv, 2. Cf. Oscar Cullmann, *Peter: Disciple, Apostle, Martyr,* for a thoroughly documented discussion of Peter's relationship to the early Roman church.

[66] Tacitus, *Annals,* XV, lxiv, 5, has "a great multitude"; I Clement, VI, 1, reads *polu plethos eklekton,* "a great multitude of the chosen."

worthy of being deemed holy, and which presides over love." [67] In fact, he even requested the Roman church not to intervene in his martyrdom. Was it influential enough to have done so? Ignatius probably overestimated the power of the Roman congregation, but that it was becoming increasingly influential is evident in the *Shepherd of Hermas*, which allows us to see into the state of the church in Hadrian's reign. Many Christians resided in Rome then and some of them were wealthy. Apparently the church's position in the city grew stronger daily as large numbers of Christians from all the provinces flocked to Rome and local Christianity continued to increase. By the middle of the second century Justin Martyr had established himself at Rome as a lay "teacher" of Christianity and brought the church there into the mainstream of theological development. As an active apologist he debated with both Jew and Gnostic, but of his many works only two remain, an *Apology* addressed to Antoninus and a long apology against Judaism called *Dialogue with Trypho.*

It can be assumed that churches were established in other Italian cities before A.D. 150, but there is no certain evidence for this except at Puteoli, the port of Rome (Acts 28:13f.). The presence in A.D. 250 of sixty Italian bishops at a synod held in Rome is persuasive evidence for early and rapid spread of Christianity throughout the Italian peninsula.

No further attempt will be made to describe the expansion of Christianity, although by the end of the New Testament period the Church was probably present throughout the empire, in areas as far as Spain and Gaul to the west and Mesopotamia to the east. Evidence is inadequate to trace in detail the spread of Christianity, but testimony to the evangelical and missionary zeal of the early movement is present in the literature of both saint and Caesar.

FACTORS IN THE SPREAD OF CHRISTIANITY

The spread of the Christian faith was true to its character. Early Christians were conscious of being the people of God, of possessing the true religion, and intimately aware of the missionary implications of their faith. Their attitude was not to take exclusive and provincial pride in their possession, but to broadcast its claims. Christianity was a religion to be shared; the blessings of redemption were for men of all classes and status. The faith spread initially in the cities and was

---

[67] *The Epistle to the Romans,* Introduction.

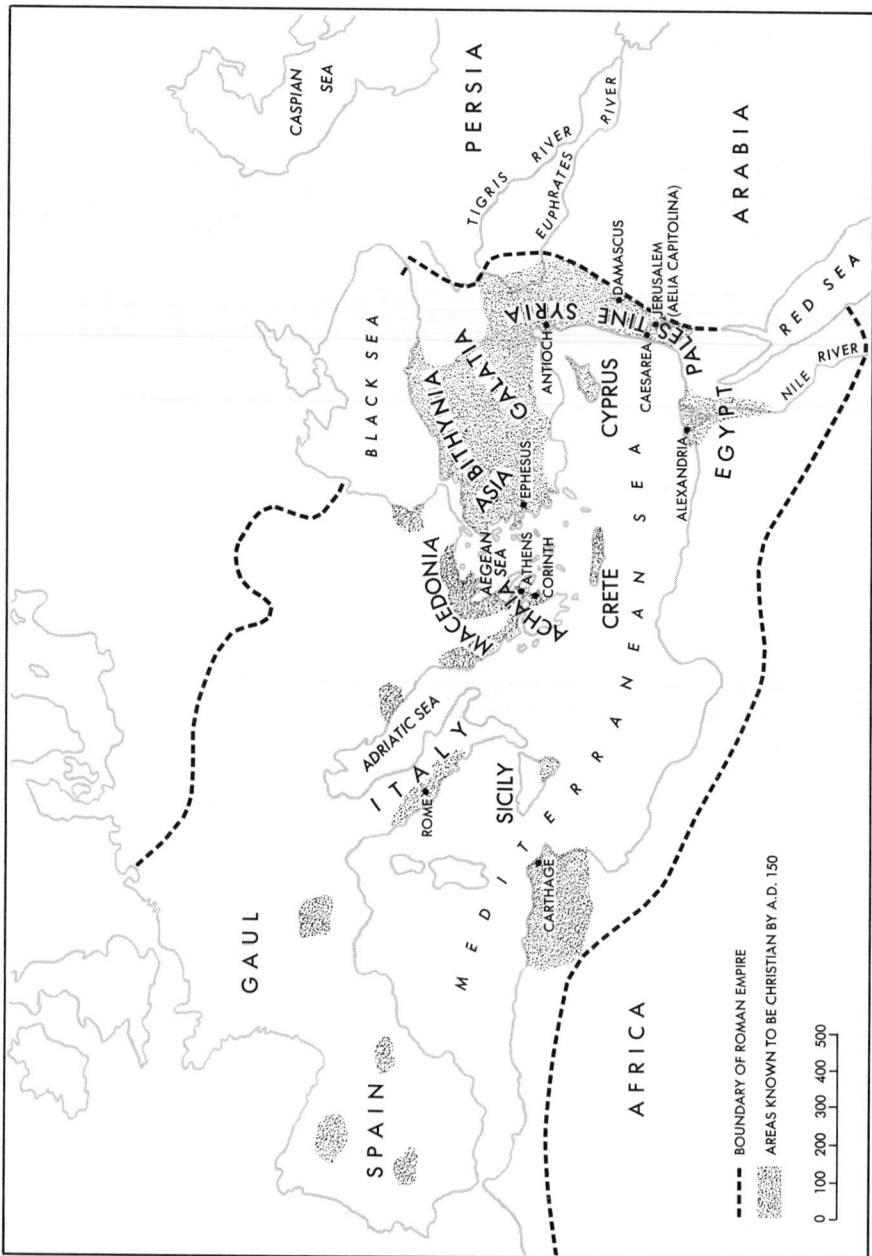

Figure 11–5. The expansion of the Church down to A.D. 150.

thus predominantly urban. At first it was confined for the most part to the Jewish populations but soon spread among those of Greek speech and Hellenistic culture. In the west it eventually entered the circles of the Latin speaking, while in Mesopotamia its home was among those of Syriac speech. Within these linguistic and cultural groups persons from all social classes were responsive to the gospel. Christianity appears to have spread widely among the working classes and small tradesmen of the empire, even among the slaves, common laborers, and people without recognized social standing.[68] From the beginning, however, a number of men and women of wealth, education, and social consequence entered the Church.[69] Even among those of the imperial court Christianity made some converts.[70] On the other hand, few Christians could be found in the army, since the life of the soldier seemed incompatible with the Christian ideal and because those few soldiers who were Christian were ferreted out and forced to leave the army.[71] It is fairly certain that the early Church contained more women than men, at least from the higher classes,[72] and that these women played an important role in the community. They participated in the local assemblies of the church and prayed and prophesied in public.[73]

Thus the movement that began as a small sect within Judaism and which won only a small minority of fellow Jews moved on into the stream of Hellenistic culture and Roman life. There it survived the competition from the many cults and philosophies which fought for men's minds and hearts and by the third century represented an important minority in Antioch, Alexandria, the important centers of Asia Minor, and even in the capital of the empire. In a few of these places Christians may already have formed a majority.

Surprisingly, with the exception of Peter the apostles did not play a major part in the spread of early Christianity. The "commission" given the Church (whether by Jesus or as a result of the Church's concretizing its understanding of its role) was taken up instead by men who functioned as peripatetic missionaries. They traveled from place to place proclaiming the gospel and seem to have been chosen for

---

[68] Shirley Jackson Case, *The Social Triumph of the Ancient Church*, pp. 61–64.
[69] Cf. Acts 4:32–37, II Cor. 8:1–3; also Harnack, *The Expansion of Christianity in the First Three Centuries*, II, 183–192.
[70] Cf. Harnack, II, pp. 192–204.
[71] C. J. Cadoux, *The Early Church and the World*, pp. 116–122, 183–190, 269–280, 402–442; Harnack, II, pp. 204–217.
[72] Harnack, II, pp. 217–239.
[73] Cf. I Cor. 11:5f., Rom. 16:1f., 16.3f., II Tim. 4:19, Col. 4:15, etc.

Figure 11–6. Early Christian cemetery at Salona in Yugoslavia. (Source: Philip Gendreau.)

such calling by the Spirit of God through a local congregation of Christians. Paul, Barnabas, John Mark, Silas, and Apollos are New Testament examples of this kind of charismatic ministry.[74] In the beginning of the third century Origen refers to those "who make it their business to itinerate not only through cities, but even villages and country houses that they might make converts to God." [75] Prophets also traveled from place to place and spoke to Christians and non-Christians alike. By their travels they, with the peripatetic Christian missionaries, not only gained converts for the new religion but also strengthened the local congregations of the Church by binding them together.[76] Teachers formed a third group whose profession was the propagation of Christianity. These early Christian teachers were catechists who instructed catechumens and had a large part in the extension and unification of the Christian faith.

The chief agents, however, in the expansion of Christianity were

[74] Cf. *Didache*, XI:3, 4.
[75] *Against Celsus*, III, 9.
[76] Cf. *Didache*, XI, 7–12; XIII.

laymen, men and women who earned their living in some secular manner and spoke of their faith in the process of everyday affairs.[77] The Christian faith made many converts through the commerce and travel of Christian merchants and tradesmen. This was not the result of any fanatical missionary zeal or any sense of lay evangelism. The rank and file of the Church did not consider it their duty to communicate their faith to others in any prescribed or professional way. They did talk about it in incidental conversation with the persons they encountered in the round of daily activity. By the end of the second century such informal witness, complemented by the ordered work of missionaries, prophets, and teachers, had carried Christianity into all the Roman provinces and even beyond the limits of the Roman empire.

TRENDS IN THE DEVELOPING CHURCH

The new faith which got off to such a handsomely good start was not only an expanding community, but also a body seeking self identity in the world. The century preceding A.D. 150 was a strategic epoch in which the Church sought to resolve problems they faced, state somewhat systematically the faith believers shared, develop an organization which would preserve their identity, and structure meaningful creeds and worship forms. Although each of these items will need to be discussed in considerable detail, a brief summary may be helpful at this point.

The Church early found itself in conflict with hostile elements in its environment. The initial, if not the most serious, of these was Judaism. Interpreting itself as the New Israel of God, the Church rapidly became alienated from Judaism. Christianity claimed to interpret correctly the faith of Old Israel. Gradually, therefore, it aroused the enmity of the race and tradition within which it began. In some sense in acting as judge and conscience of the established Jewish cult and practice the Church separated itself from the religious community which it proposed to serve as redeemer. Christianity's first martyrs were victims of Jewish opposition. Judaism, however, had neither the inclination nor the opportunity after A.D. 70 to harass the Church seriously. Instead Rome confronted the Church with more serious persecution. Nero, Domitian, and Trajan all took harsh measures against Christians in one or more parts of the empire. Perse-

---

[77] Cf. Celsus' remark as quoted by Origen, *Against Celsus*, III, 55, about children who learned Christianity from workers in wool or leather and other uneducated persons.

cution weakened the Christian convictions of some individuals and churches but for the most part called to the fore the best that was in the Christian tradition. Some of the New Testament's most interesting documents relate to persecution, and the Church shared the strength and found reason for pride in the courage of her martyrs.

Another facet of early Church life in the apostolic and post-apostolic period was the development of systematic statements of faith. The Church gave written form to their faith in four interrelated but independent religious statements which appear in the New Testament as Four Gospels: Matthew, Mark, Luke, and John. The Church is not yet agreed about the precise nature of this development, but its significance is beyond question. The writers of the New Testament Gospels were creative theologians in their own right, each offering a distinctive interpretation of the tradition with which he worked. They were not each saying the same thing with slight variation, but each evangelist was making a serious theological statement with an integrity of its own. Nor were they merely individualists simply expressing a message with creative genius. Rather they wrote out of a religious tradition, giving theological form to that which belonged to them only because it belonged to the Church. In this sense the Gospels represent four statements of the Church's faith in Jesus, a faith which took shape during the late apostolic and early post-apostolic periods.

The Church was also giving statement to her faith in credal and confessional words which, like the word of the Gospels, were related to life and worship. In fact, creed, worship, and Gospels grew up together as early Christians sought to express and involve themselves meaningfully in what they considered to be the redemptive activity of God. Heresy or false teachings in various forms served as the "touchstone of truth" testing and trying the genuineness of the Church's faith.[78] With intense sensitivity to their heritage from Israel, deeply conscious of the Christ event, and in reaction to notions of subtle and monstrous kinds, the Church developed canon, creed, and theology. Alongside Gospel, creed, and doctrine developed also ethical teachings. The problem of Christian living was present in the Church from the beginning. The Church understood itself as an eschatological entity which belonged to the new age, but which also had to live its life in the present age. It had to struggle, therefore, with the ethical

[78] Cf. J. F. Bethune-Baker, *An Introduction to the Early History of Christian Doctrine*, p. 7; also 2–5.

dimensions of the dialectic of law and grace [79] in order to define in some consistent way the responsibility of the Church to the world.

Another trend which appeared early in the developing Church was institutional structure in at least rudimentary forms. During the formative years between the death of Paul and the middle of the second century, the Church was developing some fluid but stabilizing patterns of organization. The idea of Church as organization was secondary to the idea of Church as community of faith. Nevertheless, organization and structure were necessary and inevitable. Authority was being assumed by some and delegated to others. Certain influential Christian centers may already have begun to exercise influence over churches in their area. All of these issues, persecution, gospel literature, organization, creeds and worship, must now be given detailed consideration.

SUGGESTED READINGS

GOGUEL, MAURICE, *The Primitive Church* (Macmillan, 1964).

HARNACK, ADOLF, *The Mission and Expansion of Christianity in the First Three Centuries* (Harper, 1961). A thorough study of the development of the Church in relation to its environment.

LIETZMANN, HANS, *The Beginnings of the Christian Church* (Scribner's, 1937).

STAUFFER, ETHELBURT, *Christ and the Caesars* (Westminster, 1955). Essays on various Roman emperors to the fourth century.

STEVENSON, J., ed., *A New Eusebius: Documents Illustrative of the History of the Church to A.D. 337* (Seabury, 1957).

WEISS, JOHANNES, *Earliest Christianity: A History of the Period A.D. 30–150.* 2 vols. (Harper, 1959). First published in German in 1917 and in English in 1937. Books IV and V of Volume II deal with "the Missionary Congregation and the Beginnings of the Church" and "The Separate Areas."

[79] Rudolf Bultmann, *Theology of the New Testament,* II, p. 203.

12

The Church and Persecution

Almost from the beginning the Church was opposed and often persecuted. It is, of course, difficult to determine at what point the former became the latter. The change was not just sequential. What at one time in one place was only opposition was at the same time in another place persecution. The early chapters of Acts record conflicts with Judaism resulting in the martyrdom of some of the Church's apostolic leadership and other of its stalwarts. Later parts of Acts and several New Testament epistles reflect the continuation of this opposition and increasing and more serious conflicts with Rome. In spite of the obstacle of opposition and the losses she suffered by martyrdom, the Church was strengthened in her faith and under conflict and persecution achieved a vitality and courage not to be gained in better times and circumstances.

CONFLICT WITH JUDAISM

A clash of the Church and Judaism was inevitable. Sharing a common heritage, each nevertheless followed distinctly different paths and held tenaciously to different beliefs. At first the common heritage overshadowed the differences and, in spite of the hard feelings ensuing from the crucifixion of Jesus, the Church and Judaism got along well together. Jewish Christians, and there were in the beginning few if any Christians who were not Jewish, continued to participate in the temple cult and to attend the synagogue. Nascent Christianity, closely bound up with Judaism, entertained no thought of repudiating its heritage and Judaism looked upon the Church with some tolerance and perhaps even favor. It was not long, however, before the close juxtaposition of the two, centered as they were in Jerusalem, magnified their differences, and their radically different interpretations of their common heritage led to conflict.

Although the Christians did not consider themselves as hostile toward Judaism, they did understand their faith to go beyond Judaism as the only fulfillment of the Old Testament prophetic expectation. They were convinced that Christianity was the religion which could bring salvation to the Jews. They saw themselves, believers in Christ, as the true spiritual Israel of God to be distinguished from the racial and cultic Israel of Judaism. Only in Christ, not in obedience to the Torah and observance of temple ritual, could Israel be redeemed. This position was presented with great passion and with little sympathy for Judaism's feelings about its heritage. The Church could not, of course, thus reinterpret the traditional faith and attack prevailing practice without arousing animosity from within Judaism. One such impassioned proclamation of the gospel and attack on Judaism, the preaching of Stephen, precipitated the first sustained persecution. Among other things he accused the Jews of rejecting Moses and the prophets, murdering those who announced the coming of Messiah, and finally betraying and murdering Jesus, who was the Messiah (Acts 7). Perhaps even more inflammatory were his claims, or the Jewish misunderstanding of his claims, "that this Jesus of Nazareth will destroy this place (the temple), and will change the customs which Moses delivered to us" (Acts 6:14, parenthesis added). Judaism could not ignore this proclamation.

In spite of the radical claims of the infant Church, Judaism's early attitude was one of toleration and restraint. Two factors contributed to her moderation. First, Judaism itself was not a monolithic structure. Within the general framework of orthodox sentiment a wide variety of ideas and beliefs were tolerated. In the first half of the first century A.D. she abounded in contrasts, which failed, for the most part, to cause trouble. In fact these contrasts were largely ignored by a system which had always allowed for some divergence of thought and practice. The existence of the Pharisees, Sadducees, Essenes, Zealots, and Herodians illustrates the variety of patterns which could be considered as Judaism. The differences between apocalyptic and prophetic eschatology, as well as the assortment of messianic ideas current in the first centuries B.C. and A.D., could also be cited. Such freedom was limited, however, at the points of the absolute value and divine origin of the law of which the Pharisees were champions, and the place of the temple cultus within the system of the law of particular importance to the Sadducees.[1]

Judaism was also restrained from too violent action against the Christians by Rome. The Sanhedrin at Jerusalem and the local governing bodies apparently did not often impose capital punishment without the permission of the Roman governor.[2] Further restrictions, unknown to us, may also have been imposed. Under any circumstances, local authorities tried to avoid actions which would cause Rome to intervene. This led to a certain measure of discretion and reserve in their treatment of the Church.[3]

The understandably limited persecution of the Church at the hands of Judaism began with harassment. The Jerusalem Sanhedrin attempted to prohibit public preaching by the apostles, flogging those who persisted in defiance of their injunctions.[4] There are indications that at this point the apostles were popular with the common folk and were considered by the Sanhedrin to be dangerous, not because of their doctrine, but because they endangered the *status quo* in Jerusalem. Too much enthusiasm about the man Jesus of Nazareth might still stir up emotions to a pitch which Rome would not tolerate. On the other hand, too harsh treatment of the Church might also attract Rome's attention, and the Sanhedrin wanted to avoid this.

Drastic action, however, could not be avoided in the case of Stephen, whose sermons threatened Judaism at the very points where she was not tolerant. This Hellenist-Jewish-Christian preacher went beyond the Galilean leaders in his views about the transience of the temple and the law. He was stoned, either by decision of the Sanhedrin or by mob action, and a general persecution led by Saul of Tarsus followed (see pp. 231–232). It centered in Jerusalem and Damascus, perhaps the only other center of important Christian activity. Christians were thrown in prison and many, particularly the Hellenists, were forced to flee from Jerusalem. Their flight contributed to wide expansion of the Christian mission. The gospel was taken to Samaria and to Antioch of Syria. Persecution thus helped launch the world mission of the Church.

Upon two other occasions even more drastic action was taken

---

[1] The substance of this paragraph is taken from Maurice Goguel, *The Birth of Christianity*, pp. 451–452.

[2] There is the possibility that the Jews could try capital cases, although it is often argued that they could not.

[3] Could this have been one of the reasons for Gamaliel's reluctance for the Sanhedrin to take punitive action against the apostles? Cf. Acts 5:34ff.

[4] Acts 4 and 5. See above, p. 214.

against the Church. Both occurred when Roman rule in Jerusalem was indirect or indefinite and might well indicate what the Church would have had to face had it not been for the strong arm of Roman authority. When Herod Agrippa I was king in Jerusalem (A.D. 41–44), he "laid violent hands upon some who belonged to the church," executed James, son of Zebedee,[5] and had Peter imprisoned. This was apparently an attempt to win added favor with the Jews with whom he was already popular because of his support of Pharisaism. That he took this action to gain popularity with the Jews and that his action "pleased the Jews" (Acts 12:3) indicates that the public generally had become hostile to the Church in contrast to the more favorable attitude of earlier days. With the death of Agrippa the Church was able to resume its work with more enthusiasm than before (Acts 12:20–24) because Roman authority in the hands of the procurators, who again ruled Palestine, kept the smoldering hostility of Judaism in check.

The animosity of the Jews found opportunity for expression again in A.D. 62 when, during temporary vacancy in the procuratorship, Roman authority was at best indirect and indecisive. James, the brother of Jesus and head of the Jerusalem church, was killed by a fanatical mob perhaps angered because some in the church refused to take part in the opposition against Rome which climaxed in the rebellion of A.D. 66–73.

In spite of these incidents many Jewish Christians continued to participate in the practices of both temple and synagogue when permitted to do so by the Jews. However, the destruction of Jerusalem in A.D. 70 ended the temple cultus and at some point official decision was made to expel the Christians from the synagogues (John 9:22; 16:2).

Outside Palestine the Jews of the Diaspora tried to stem the tide of the Church's advance by countering Christian propaganda, especially seeking to hinder the missionary work of Paul. Paul's first opponent was Elymas Bar-Jesus, a Jew of Cyprus, who tried to dissuade the

---

[5] Eusebius, *EH*, II, ix, 3, relates that, according to the *Hypotyposes* of Clement of Alexandria, the man who brought James before the council was moved by James' confession of faith to declare himself Christian and so was beheaded with the apostle. There is an early Christian tradition that the Apostle John was martyred with his brother. A Papias fragment reads, "Papias reports in his second book that John the divine and James, his brother, were killed by the Jews." Cf. C. de Boor, *Neue Fragmente des Papias, Hegesippus und Pierius ases der Kirchengeschichte des Philippus Sidetes*, p. 170. This tradition seems to spring from the reference in Mark 10:39 where Jesus said to James and John, "The cup that I drink you will drink; and with the baptism with which I am baptized, you will be baptized."

Roman proconsul from becoming a Christian. His main opposition in Galatia came from Jews, some perhaps even sent from Jerusalem. The same was true at Thessalonica and Corinth (Acts 17 and 18). Finally Paul's arrest was inspired by Jewish opposition and only his appeal to Rome saved him from immediate death (Acts 21–28; see above, pp. 265–267, 291–293, 338–343).[6]

After A.D. 70 Judaism became almost exclusively Pharisaic and intensely jealous of its beliefs. The relative tolerance of earlier times succumbed to an intense desire for survival and was replaced by a hostile attitude toward any movement which did not conform with Pharisaic Judaism's belief and practice. Since it had been uprooted from Jerusalem, however, Judaism no longer had a base from which to press attacks on the Church.

CONFLICT WITH ROME

In the beginning there was virtually no conflict between the Church and Rome, and throughout the first century persecution by the empire was more a matter of the personal whims of certain emperors than official imperial position. While there was a law restricting the establishment of new religions, this was not at first applied to the Christians, who were regarded as members of a Jewish sect. Whatever persecution of Christians occurred was not on the charge of being Christian, but on charge of disturbing the peace, sedition, or some such threat to Roman order. Christianity became illegal, as far as our information goes, only after the turn of the century during the reign of Trajan (A.D. 98–117). Then Christians were arrested and persecuted because of the name, *i.e.*, because they were Christians.[7] But during the first generation of the Church Rome was its protector, not its persecutor. Christians had to face hostility from Judaism and occasionally from other elements of the populace. As a rule Roman administrators protected them from mob violence and, as was indicated above, kept Jewish opposition in check.

The evidence from Acts and the Pauline letters reflects generally

---

[6] It should be noted here that the author of Acts wants to make a point about God's rejection of the Jews. Therefore, he presses the issue of Jewish opposition to the gospel. This does not, however, alter the point about Jewish opposition to Paul.

[7] On the subject of Roman persecutions of the Church, see E. Stauffer, *Christ and the Caesars;* Robert M. Grant, *The Sword and the Cross;* Goguel, *The Birth of Christianity,* pp. 502–544; and particularly W. H. C. Frend, *Martyrdom and Persecution in the Early Church,* pp. 151–235.

favorable attitudes on the part of the Church and Rome towards one another. Paul even calls Roman authorities "servants of God" who are to be obeyed because "rulers are not a terror to good conduct but to bad" (Romans 13:1–3). He had good reason to have such respect for Roman government. He mentions three beatings with rods (II Corinthians 11:25), a Roman punishment, in contrast with five beatings with lashes "at the hands of the Jews" (II Corinthians 11:24). On the only occasion of Roman punishment mentioned in Acts, the magistrates apologized profusely when they discovered Paul to be a Roman citizen (Acts 16:22–33, 35–40) and, when the Jews in Corinth complained against Paul, the proconsul of Achaia refused to take action against him (Acts 18:12–17). Paul was again protected by Roman authority at Ephesus where he was befriended by Roman officials (Asiarchs), and where the town clerk pacified a hostile crowd by threatening them with Roman sanctions (Acts 19:30–41). In Jerusalem Roman troops saved Paul from a mob (Acts 21:27–36) and, when an accusation was brought against him by the Jews, he appealed to Caesar, preferring Roman justice to Jewish.

The first direct persecution of Christians by Roman authority was the infamous incident which followed the burning of Rome in A.D. 64. It was rumored, probably without foundation, that Nero the emperor, wanting to beautify Rome by enlarging his palace complex and gardens, was responsible for the fire.[8] Nero apparently attempted to shift the blame upon the Roman Christians. The emperor may have been influenced by a wife, a Jewess, to put the blame on Christians. Clement of Rome, a Christian leader writing about A.D. 96, referred to "a great multitude of the elect" who, because of Nero's policy, "suffered terrible and impious indignities and thereby safely completed the race of faith and, though weak in body, received a noble reward of honour." [9] Later the Roman historian Tacitus (c. A.D. 112) described the situation in detail:

Consequently, to get rid of the report, Nero fastened the guilt and inflicted the most exquisite tortures on a class hated for their abominations, called Christians by the populace. Christus, from whom the name had its origin, suffered the extreme penalty during the reign of Tiberius at the hands of one of our procurators, Pontius Pilatus, and a deadly superstition, thus checked for the moment, again broke out not only in Judaea, the first source of the evil, but also in the City, where all things hideous and shameful from every part of the world meet and become popular. Accordingly, an arrest

[8] For a thorough analysis of Nero's role, see Goguel, *The Birth of Christianity*, pp. 510ff. Cf. also Robert M. Grant, "Nero," *IDB*, III, pp. 537–539.
[9] *First Epistle to the Corinthians*, VI, 1, 2 as quoted in *A New Eusebius*, p. 4.

was first made of all who confessed; then upon their information, an immense multitude was convicted, not so much of the crime of arson, as of hatred of the human race. Mockery of every sort was added to their deaths. Covered with the skins of beasts, they were torn by dogs and perished, or were nailed to crosses, or were doomed to the flames. These served to illuminate the night when daylight failed. Nero had thrown open his gardens for the spectacle, and was exhibiting a show in the circus, while he mingled with the people in the dress of a charioteer or drove about in a chariot. Hence, even for criminals who deserved extreme and exemplary punishment, there arose a feeling of compassion; for it was not, as it seemed, for the public good, but to glut one man's cruelty, that they were being destroyed.[10]

The exact circumstances of these events now escape us, but the general situation can be reconstructed. When Nero felt the pressure of blame for the tragic fire which damaged ten of the fourteen districts of Rome (three were destroyed, and of seven only ruins remained),[11] he diverted attention by a purge of Christians who may also have been blamed for the fire. Some who were arrested confessed, perhaps to arson, and implicated others. A large number were victims of severest measures in what amounted to little less than a massacre of brutal proportions. Even the Romans disapproved. Both Paul and Peter were probably victims of this persecution, although the evidence is not conclusive.[12]

The legal basis of this persecution is not clear. Some think there was special legislation, an *institutum Neronianum,* against the Christians which would have taken the form of *non licit esse Christianos* ("it is illegal to be Christian").[13] But there is no evidence of a widespread or continuing purge of the Church at this time. More likely the action was an arbitrary exercise of police powers.[14] Such action would neither have changed the legal position of Christianity nor had effect elsewhere in the empire. Even if there had been a decree from Nero, its validity would have ended with his death, for the Senate condemned his memory and nullified all his decrees. The Neronic persecution, therefore, was severe and very cruel, but limited in time and place. After it, as before, the Christians were merely again subject to public harassment. Their position in the eyes of the empire had not changed. However, as Goguel argues, with the Neronic persecution a clear distinction may well have been made between Chris-

---

10 Tacitus, *Annals,* XV, xliv, 3–8.

11 *Ibid.,* XVI, xxxviii–xliv.

12 On this question see Clement of Rome, *First Epistle to the Corinthians,* V, 1–7; Eusebius, *EH,* II, xxv, 5–9; Cullmann, *Peter: Apostle and Martyr,* pp. 89ff.

13 This was the opinion of Tertullian, *Against the Nations,* I, 7.

14 Cf. Goguel, *The Birth of Christianity,* pp. 506ff.

Figure 12-1. Coins of Nero (A.D. 54-68) and Domitian (A.D. 81-96), both emperors who fiercely persecuted Christians. Nero's coin at the top has a portrait of the emperor and on the reverse the temple of Janus, closed to indicate universal peace. The Domitian coin has his portrait and a scene commemorating ceremonies connected with Saecular Games of A.D. 88. (Source: American Numismatic Society.)

tians and Jews; the latter were in no way implicated in the entire event. "Perhaps also the fire of Rome gave the latent hostility of public opinion against the Christians the chance to crystallize and appear in the open." [15] At least a precedent had been set for later anti-Christian activities, and the name of Christians had been darkened in official memory.[16]

For some time after Nero Christians were exposed to increasing harassment; their position grew considerably worse during Domitian's reign (A.D. 81-96).[17] Christian tradition makes Domitian the next

[15] *Ibid.*, p. 523.
[16] Grant, *The Sword and the Cross*, p. 52.
[17] Cf. Robert M. Grant, "Domitian," *IDB*, I, pp. 863-864.

emperor after Nero to persecute the Church.[18] Under Domitian state persecution on religious grounds took place for the first time. Domitian had come to think of himself as divine and sought, therefore, to defend and restore the Roman national religion which was threatened by oriental cults. In A.D. 89 he issued an edict banishing astrologers and philosophers from the city of Rome and republished the edict in A.D. 93. Both groups presumably had been critical of his regime, perhaps specifically of the revival of the emperor cult. Christians and Jews obviously suffered under such circumstances. In the years following 93 when courtiers and court poets were flattering the emperor by addressing him as "Master and God," Domitian accused the consul Falvius Clemens of godlessness and executed him with many others and exiled his wife Flavia Domitilla.[19] The consul and his wife may have been Christian converts, but more likely only leaned toward Christianity.[20] The Domitian purge does not seem to have been directed primarily against Christians as such, but Christians nevertheless inevitably became involved. The book of Revelation, which comes from this time,[21] is dominated by the idea of a struggle to the death between Rome and Christianity and, writing to Corinth in A.D. 96–97, Clement of Rome mentions troubles afflicting the Church.[22] It is not known whether the trouble extended into the provinces, although Revelation leads us to assume "that in the province of Asia an enthusiastic proconsul had taken upon himself to enforce Domitian's edict with some vigor." [23] Under Domitian Ephesus received a new temple to the emperor.

After Domitian's murder, brought on by measures which had made him hated, Christians may have fared better, although we lack sufficient information to be certain. At least further persecution cannot be documented until the reign of Trajan (A.D. 98–117). By the end of the first century Rome had established a tradition of suppressing foreign religions. The Druids had been abolished and the Jews and Christians had been frequent objects of official action. In the beginning of the second century some specific anti-Christian legislation

---

[18] Dio Cassius, *Roman History,* LXVII, 14; *The Apology of Melito of Sardis* as quoted by Eusebius, *EH,* IV, xxvi, 5–11; Tertullian, *The Apology,* V; Lactantius, *On the Manner in Which the Persecutors Died,* III; *EH,* III, xvii–xx; Clement of Rome, *Epistle to the Corinthians,* I, 1.

[19] Their sons, whom Domitian intended to succeed him as emperor (Suetonius, *Domitian,* XV), disappeared from history after the death of their father.

[20] Cf. Dio Cassius, *Roman History,* LXVII, 14.

[21] Irenaeus says "towards the end of Domitian's reign." See pp. 441–442.

[22] *First Epistle to the Corinthians,* I, 1; LIX, 4.

[23] Grant, *The Sword and the Cross,* p. 56.

Figure 12–2. Coin of Trajan (A.D. 98–117). By his time Christianity had become illegal. The coin shows the emperor and his commemorative column at Rome. (Source: American Numismatic Society.)

came from either the Senate or the emperor Trajan. Christianity for the first time became an illegal religion. Our best indication of this is the Pliny–Trajan correspondence. Pliny was imperial legate in Bithynia and Pontus. Sometime in the year 112 or 113 he investigated Christian activity in his region, but was reluctant to take final action without writing to the emperor for advice.[24] His letter opens:

It is my custom, lord emperor, to refer to you all questions whereof I am in doubt. Who can better guide me when I am at a stand, or enlighten me if I am in ignorance? In investigations of Christians I have never taken part; hence I do not know what is the crime usually punished or investigated, or what allowances are made. So I have had no little uncertainty whether there is any distinction of age, or whether pardon is given to those who repent, or whether a man who has once been a Christian gains nothing by having ceased to be such; whether punishment attaches to the mere name apart from secret crimes, or to the secret crimes connected with the name.[25]

He then goes on to describe the procedure he had followed and what had been its results. Pliny clearly thought Christianity was a dangerous superstition, but at the same time he did not believe Christians were evil persons. The letter makes it clear that some official charge was active against Christians. It is not clear, however, whether the

[24] Pliny was accustomed to refer problems to the emperor, for whom he was personal representative and with whom he enjoyed friendship. We possess more than a hundred letters exchanged by Pliny and Trajan.

[25] *Pliny's Letter to Trajan* in *A New Eusebius,* p. 13.

crime was the mere fact of being a Christian, or whether Christians as Christians were involved in certain criminal actions, or whether the crime was refusal to worship the emperor. Pliny had decided to judge them on the third ground, interpreting their refusal to worship Trajan as indicating disloyalty to the empire.

The emperor's reply is brief:

You have adopted the proper course, my dear Secundus, in your examination of the cases of those who were accused to you as Christians, for indeed nothing can be laid down as a general ruling involving something like a set form of procedure. They are not to be sought out; but if they are accused and convicted, they must be punished—yet on this condition, that whoso denies himself to be a Christian, and makes the fact plain by his action, that is, by worshipping our gods, shall obtain pardon on his repentance, however suspicious his past conduct may be. Papers, however, which are presented unsigned ought not to be admitted in any charge, for they are a very bad example and unworthy of our time.[26]

This correspondence presupposes a definite law against Christianity, but for whose enforcement legal precedent had not yet been established and which had not been widely applied and enforced.

Other evidence of persecution during Trajan's reign is preserved in a Roman Christian tradition from the middle of the second century. According to the tradition, an earlier bishop of Jerusalem was accused by "the sects," probably Jews and other non-Christians, and brought before a Roman official who tortured and finally crucified him. This occurred early in the second century, either in A.D. 101 or 107.[27]

Ignatius, bishop of Antioch, was also martyred at some time during Trajan's reign.[28] While on his way to Rome to face execution, Ignatius wrote to the Roman church. He was in the custody of ten soldiers and expected to be devoured by wild beasts. He was determined to die for his faith and, if, as he had heard, the beasts refused to touch their prey, he would force them to grind him with their teeth as the "wheat of God" so that he might become "the pure bread of Christ." [29] Other martyrdoms during this period must have occurred, although we do not know about them. The evidence we have certainly indicates that Trajan persecuted the Church upon the basis of Christianity's illegality.

[26] *Trajan's Reply to Pliny* in *A New Eusebius*, p. 16.
[27] Eusebius dates the martyrdom in 101 in his *History*, while in his *Chronicle* he puts it in 107.
[28] Eusebius, Jerome, and Origen all date the martyrdom of Ignatius in Trajan's reign. Eusebius places it in the tenth year, but only on the basis of tradition.
[29] Ignatius, *Epistle to the Romans*, IV.

THE LITERATURE OF PERSECUTION

The conflicts with Judaism and Rome are reflected widely in the literature of the early Christian movement. The stories of Jesus' controversies with the Pharisees and other Jewish groups were included in the Gospels partially because they paralleled the Church's difficulties with the Jews. Paul's references to his persecutions and his admonitions about loyalty to the state as an instrument of God (cf. II Corinthians 11:25; Romans 13:1ff.) are part of the Church's attempts to establish itself and adjust to an environment which was at least partially hostile. Luke and Acts at least secondarily aimed to demonstrate that Christianity was the fulfillment of Judaism and, therefore, a legal religion whose attitude toward the state was not intentionally hostile.

In addition to these indirect allusions to the influence of persecution upon early Church literature, three New Testament documents seem to have been primarily occasioned by persecution. They are I Peter, Hebrews, and Revelation. Unfortunately, limited knowledge of the situations faced by the Church in its earliest years and the uncertain references to persecution which these three letters contain make it impossible to relate any of them with absolute certainty to a specific period of persecution.

I Peter

First Peter is an open letter of comfort and exhortation (5:12) to Christians living in five provinces of Asia Minor. It challenges them in the face of "persecution, hate, suffering, and humiliating defamation"[30] to remain steadfast in their Christian faith. It lacks the elements of personal reminiscence and of direct address to particular local issues and problems which are characteristic of Paul's letters to specific churches. The author does not seem to have been directly related to the churches he addresses, although they may have known him and surely knew about him.

The author of the letter freely used liturgical and catechetical forms typical of the early Christian mission to recall to his readers the resources of the gospel and to rally their courage and hope. It is "a microcosm of Christian faith and duty, the model of a pastoral charge."[31]

[30] FBK, p. 294.
[31] Edward Selwyn, *The First Epistle of St. Peter,* p. 1.

The Authorship of the Letter. First Peter was composed in the name of "Peter, an apostle of Jesus Christ" (1:1) with the aid of Silvanus, called by the author "a faithful brother" (5:12). On the basis of evidence in the letter, many interpreters challenge this claim of Petrine authorship and argue that the epistle was pseudonymous.[32] Their case is impressive. First of all, I Peter is written in fluent and idiomatic Greek with a natural and unforced style indicating that it belongs to one who not only wrote, but also thought, in Greek.[33] The letter "exhibits a felicity of phrase, a suppleness of expression, and a wealth of vocabulary which betoken a mind nourished in the best Greek tradition."[34] In addition quotations from the Old Testament are from the Septuagint, not the Hebrew. Is such intimate knowledge and skill in Greek conceivable for Aramaic speaking Peter, the Galilean?

In the second place, I Peter presupposes Pauline theology,[35] apparently depending upon some of the collected letters of the Apostle to the Gentiles, especially Romans and Ephesians.[36] Evidence for basic disagreement between the two men is found in Galatians 2:11–21 where Peter is able to follow only with reluctance and uncertainty the Pauline idea of Gentile-Christian freedom from the Law.[37] Presupposing a real difference between Peter and Paul over basic issues, it would not be likely that Peter would have directly used specific Pauline materials and ideas.

A third objection to Petrine authorship is based upon the absence in the letter of the personal quality one would expect if written by a disciple of Jesus. Kümmel states, "I Peter contains no kind of hint of an acquaintance with the earthly Jesus, his life, teaching, and death, but refers only generally to the 'suffering' of Christ."[38] Finally it is

---

[32] The authenticity of I Peter has been impugned since F. C. Baur. Cf. FBK, pp. 296–298, and for a more extensive analysis, F. W. Beare, *The First Epistle of Peter*, pp. 14–31.

[33] Selwyn, *The First Epistle of St. Peter*, p. 15.

[34] *Ibid.*, p. 25.

[35] FBK list the following: (1) a similar attitude toward the law, (2) a similar attitude toward Christians suffering with Christ, (3) a similar demand that civil rulers be obeyed, (4) use of the formula *en Kristo.*

[36] On the question of Pauline authorship of Ephesians, see above, pp. 361–365.

[37] E. F. Scott, *The Literature of the New Testament*, p. 217, even goes so far as to state: "From all that we can gather, it may be surmised that Peter was the victim of a moral tragedy, such as has befallen not a few of the great leaders in history. After a period of noble service in the cause of freedom and progress, he took a false step and allowed himself to be captured by the forces of reaction. Henceforth there was no place for him." Surely this is an overstatement.

[38] FBK, p. 298.

objected that the situation of persecution implied by several statements in I Peter, particularly the following, "If you are reproached for the name of Christ," and "if one suffers as a Christian, let him not be ashamed, but under that name let him glorify God" (4:14, 16), can only refer to persecution under Domitian or the beginnings of civil persecution under Trajan. We do not know of any widespread persecution before Domitian or that the confession of the name Christian constituted a crime against the state until the time of Trajan.[39] Therefore, it is argued, the letter must be dated late and Petrine authorship denied.

The evidence against Petrine authorship of the letter, however, is not conclusive. If Silvanus helped in the composition of the letter (a possibility admitted by the phrase in 5:12 "by Silvanus . . . I have written briefly to you."), the objection about its superior Greek is removed. This is particularly true if, as Hunter suggests, "Silvanus acted as a trusted secretary who was given considerable scope in interpreting his master's mind." [40] There is no reason for questioning the traditional identification of the Silvanus in Peter with the Silvanus who is named in I Thessalonians 1:1 and II Thessalonians 1:1 as joint author with Paul and Timothy of these two epistles. This Silvanus is surely the Silas mentioned in Acts as a "leading man among the brethren" in the Jerusalem church (Acts 15:22). With Judas Barsabbas he drafted the circular letter to the Christians of Antioch, Syria, and Cilicia, stating the conclusions reached by the Jerusalem council on the question of Gentile inclusion in the Church and accompanied Paul and Barnabas in delivering the letter to Antioch. Silvanus or Silas then was chosen by Paul to accompany him to Asia and Macedonia in place of Barnabas.[41]

If Silvanus helped write the letter of I Peter, the objection concerning Pauline influence is also removed. One who long and intimately had been associated with Paul would naturally reflect the great Apostle's ideas if given freedom to do so. Moreover, the dependence upon Paul might be no more than a knowledge of his Epistle to the

---

[39] Cf. above, pp. 412–416, and also Pliny's letter to the emperor in *A New Eusebius*, p. 13.

[40] *IB*, XII, p. 78. Kümmel objects that it cannot be demonstrated "that γράφω διά τινος can mean to have a piece of writing composed by another." See FBK, p. 298. Beare claims that "the mention of Silvanus in the closing greeting is merely part of the apparatus of pseudonymity." See F. W. Beare, *The First Epistle of Peter*, p. 29; cf. also, pp. 182–183.

[41] For a more complete discussion of the Silvanus/Silas tradition, see M. J. Shroyer, "Silas," *IDB*, IV, pp. 351–352, and Selwyn, *The First Epistle of St. Peter*, pp. 9–17.

Romans, already a treasured possession of the Roman church at the time of the writing of I Peter. Also, may it not be assumed that the Apostle to the Gentiles had some influence even upon Peter? Must we conclude from Galatians 2:11–21 that Peter and Paul came to a final parting of ways?

Whether the letter has a personal quality one would expect from an apostle is a matter of opinion. Defenders of the tradition of Petrine authorship find many allusions to Jesus' teachings and to events from his life and argue that they are evidence confirming that Peter stands behind the letter.[42] It is not now possible, however, to determine whether these are apostolic memories of intimate acquaintance with Jesus or come from the traditions of the Church concerning him. Neither defenders nor challengers of the Petrine tradition gain from this argument.

The objection about the nature of persecution is vulnerable at two points. First, most of the references to "sufferings" in the letter reflect no more than the public hatreds and abuses which Christians commonly faced from the beginning. They do not have to be interpreted as references to state persecution. Even if this is their reference, the Roman attitude toward the Church prior to A.D. 112 is largely unknown. Even Pliny's letter reflects his ignorance about earlier precedents for persecution "for the name." The persecution argument then gains its only strength from silence and is therefore tenuous. The persecution background of the letter may well be around the year A.D. 64. We have no evidence that the Neronic persecution extended beyond Rome itself, but it is conceivable that Peter "may well have supposed that it would do so."[43] The Neronic persecution in any case provides a believable setting for a letter like I Peter.

All things considered, there seem to be no conclusive reasons for denying that Peter wrote I Peter with the aid of Silvanus. The letter lacks certain prime qualities of pseudonymity. A pseudonymous letter would surely have made much of its claimed author's relation to Christ and would rigorously have avoided any Paulinisms. Arguments brought against Petrine authorship of I Peter weigh just as heavily against pseudonymous authorship. Since none of the arguments for pseudonymous authorship is decisive, it seems best to conclude that the letter's claim to have apostolic origins is genuine.

If this is true, it is an easy matter to determine I Peter's date and

---

[42] They cite 1:8; 2:21–24; 5:1, 2, 5. Cf. Hunter, *IB*, XII, p. 79, and Selwyn, *The First Epistle of St. Peter*, pp. 23–24.

[43] Robert M. Grant, *A Historical Introduction to the New Testament*, p. 226.

Figure 12–3. The Roman Forum, the heart of the secular and cultic life of ancient Rome. Christians' unwillingness to participate fully in Roman secular life opened them to accusations of "hatred of the human race." Their theological rejection of the emperor cult brought upon them the wrath of certain emperors. (Source: Lufthansa Airlines.)

place of origin. It must have been written during the lifetime of Peter, who, according to a tradition there is no reason to doubt, was martyred by Nero. Sometime in the sixties, then, meets the requirement of Petrine authorship and explains the references to persecution. The letter was written either in anticipation of the Neronic persecution or during that ordeal for the Church.

Literary Form and Interpretation. First Peter has been explained as the expansion of a baptismal sermon, or, as some even suggest, the transcript of a baptismal service in progress.[44] Accordingly the epistle would be a copy of a baptismal address and liturgy with added exhortations sent to a community facing persecution. Admittedly a number of allusions to baptism (1:3, 12, 23; 2:2, 10, 25; 3:21) do appear in the letter, but these are not necessarily proof even of a bap-

[44] Cf. the bibliographical data on this point in FBK, p. 295.

tismal setting, to say nothing of a baptismal sermon or liturgy. In fact, the letter actually contains a variety of liturgical and hymnic materials (2:6–8; 2:21–25; 3:18–22). Among them there may well be baptismal materials which along with others the author felt appropriate for his purpose. Primarily he intended to reassure believers who faced persecution. Thus the letter is better understood as an epistle of exhortation which utilizes baptismal materials, rather than as baptismal liturgy to which is appended exhortation.

> Salutation. 1:1–2
> I. Praise of God. 1:3–12
> II. Exhortation to Holy Living. 1:13–2:3
> III. The Nature of the Church. 2:4–10
> IV. Exhortation Dealing with the Christian's Relationship to the World. 2:11–4:11
> V. Exhortation in Face of Persecution. 4:12–5:11
> Conclusion. 5:12–14

With what great joy the opening words of I Peter must have been received by those persecuted Christians of Asia Minor who first heard them:

> Peter, an apostle of Jesus Christ,
> To the exiles . . . chosen and destined by God the Father and
> sanctified by the Spirit for obedience to Jesus Christ and
> for sprinkling with his blood;
> May grace and peace be multiplied to you. (1:1–2) [45]

The apostle "reminds them of their election, consecration and forgiveness and prays for them increase of grace and peace." [46]

I. Praise of God (1:3–12). After the salutation the epistle passes into doxology, into praise of God.[47] Its audience's hope comes from the resurrection of Jesus from the dead (1:3). For them the words of the prophets have been fulfilled (1:10–12). By the inconceivable mercy of God they have been born anew to hope in present and future salvation. This is certain in spite of persecution and suffering which is only a test of their faith. In fact, trial and tribulation may be a source of joy because it is necessary prelude to the dawning of eschatological age.[48]

[45] Note the mention together of Father, Spirit, and Son, "the trinity of experience" which was the basis for the later rational dogma.

[46] Hunter, *IB*, XII, p. 86.

[47] Cf. II Cor. 1:3ff.; Eph. 1:3ff.

[48] 1:7. W. Nauck, "Freude im Leiden," *Zeitschrift für die neutestamentliche Wissenschaft*, XLVI (1955), 68ff., has shown that this idea of "joy in suffering" originated in a primitive Jewish Christian persecution tradition in which the suffering was interpreted as the eschatologically necessary and expected suffering.

II. Exhortation to Holy Living (1:13–2:3). Having entered into the new life with its hope and promise of ultimate fulfillment, the readers must meet its strenuous moral demands. Since, as Hunter points out, truth for the apostolic writers "is always 'truth in order to goodness'," it is not surprising that here as in Paul the doxology is followed by exhortation. "Pull yourselves together,"[49] Peter writes, "You are no longer what you once were but have been born anew" (1:23). Live, therefore, holy lives, because God is holy and because you have been redeemed by "the precious blood of Christ" (1:18–19). The basis of the exhortation, then, was their redemption and the nature of God. Christian ethics and faithfulness, even in face of persecution, have their foundation in God's character as holy redeemer.

III. The Nature of the Church (2:4–10). Using a powerful mixed metaphor, Peter challenges his readers to become the Church, here conceived as a spiritual house and a holy priesthood offering spiritual sacrifices. In coming to Christ they have become temple and priesthood. The Church has a mission to the world and is undergirded in that mission by her union with Christ, who is cornerstone.[50] This point is supported by quotations from the Old Testament, which probably had widespread liturgical and evangelical use in the Church.[51]

Behold, I am laying in Zion a stone, a cornerstone chosen and precious, and he who believes in him will not be put to shame.[52]

. . .

The very stone which the builders rejected has become the head of the corner,[53]

. . .

A stone that will make men stumble,
a rock that will make them fall.[54]

So to those who believe, Christ is the cornerstone of faith, but, the author adds as a parenthetical aside, to those who do not believe and obey he is a stone of stumbling. There is a "scandal" to the Cross; that redemption comes through divine suffering is hard to accept. "Those

[49] Selwyn, *The First Epistle of Peter*, p. 139, suggests this as expressing the meaning of *anazosamenoi tas osphus tes diavoias humon*, "gird up the loins of your minds."

[50] See I Cor. 3:11 where Christ is foundation stone. The apostles and prophets are foundation stone in Eph. 2:20.

[51] Rendel Harris has shown that the bringing together of much Old Testament quotations formed *testimonia*, anthologies of messianic proof texts. They may also have been brought together as an early Christian hymn. Cf. Selwyn, *The First Epistle of Peter*, p. 163.

[52] 2:6. An adaptation of the LXX of Isa. 28:16.

[53] 2:7 = Psalm 118:22.

[54] 2:8. A free rendering of the LXX of Isa. 8:14.

who have stumbled" must refer to the Jewish rejection of Jesus. To those who refuse to believe, Jesus "is a constant anomaly, meeting them in unexpected places and challenging their indifference." [55] Since the author has related the Church as holy building, *i.e.*, temple, to Christ as chief cornerstone, one wonders why he did not go on to draw the analogy between the Church as priesthood offering spiritual sacrifices and Christ as perfect and complete sacrifice.[56]

What follows is a magnificent statement of the nature and function of the Church, wherein all the faithful, in living union with their Lord and with one another, serve God and proclaim His glories." [57] Titles which the Old Testament uses of Israel are here used perceptively to describe the true nature and vocation of the Church. Although it was made up of many different nations, the Church is called with "considerable boldness" a chosen race and a holy nation.[58] Racial and national ties had been replaced by the bond of union with Christ which made them "God's own people," chosen and set apart (the meaning of "holy") for the service of God. The Church is to be a "royal priesthood" offering themselves to God in complete and continual dedication. Her priesthood is a mediation of the divine blessing and power to all mankind. "God's own people" find the end of their existence in their possession by God, who has called them into being from darkness into light, here as elsewhere symbolic of conversion from paganism to Christianity.[59] Clearly the writer of I Peter sees the Church as the New Israel with a mission to declare God's "wonderful deeds." [60]

IV. EXHORTATIONS DEALING WITH THE CHRISTIAN'S RELATIONSHIP WITH THE WORLD (2:11–4:11). From the nature of the Church I Peter turns to an extended exhortation, making at least three important points regarding the Christian's relationship with the world. First is the question of the Christian's relationship to the state, particularly in time of persecution. Believers are called aliens and exiles against whom war is waged (2:11). Yet their persecution is not to be taken as occasion for rebellion. The state has a positive claim on man's moral allegiance and the emperor and his subordinate officials in the provinces are the

[55] Selwyn, *The First Epistle of Peter*, p. 164.
[56] See the discussion of Hebrews which follows.
[57] Beare, *The First Epistle of Peter*, p. 93.
[58] Cf. Ex. 19:5–6 and Isa. 43:20–21.
[59] Cf. Acts 26:18; II Cor. 4:6; and Eph. 5:1–14.
[60] This material may be drawn from a collection of *testimonia*. See note 51 above in this chapter. Selwyn, however, finds here a liturgical piece or hymn. Cf. his *The First Epistle of St. Peter*, pp. 277–298, for a detailed analysis of the entire passage.

assurance of law and order (2:13–17). This is said in spite of Nero's persecution of the Church. Peter here thinks of the emperor, not as an individual, but "as performing a certain indispensable function in human society."[61] The startling parallelism with which the author expresses himself indicates the intensity of his feelings: "Honor all men. Love the brotherhood. Fear God. Honor the emperor" (2:17). Against persecution the best defense is an upright life, since the Christian's good behavior in Christ shames his persecutors (3:16). And, after all, it is better to suffer for doing right than for doing wrong (3:17).

Second, obedient submission to suffering is after the example of Christ, who to redeem mankind took the role of suffering servant (2:18–25). Here the author relates the "Suffering Servant" of Isaiah 53 to the atonement Christ made for sin.[62] The example of Christ, however, is not just his meekness and suffering, but also his courage and strength. Christ is not only suffering servant, he is also victor (3:18–22). The death of Christ can bring encouragement to those who suffer for righteousness because (1) it embodied in history the principle of the transformation of suffering and death, (2) it had redemptive and sacrificial significance, and (3) it revealed the victory of good.[63] The author does not imply that the sufferings of Christians have the same redemptive significance, only that recollection of the meaning of Christ's sufferings should encourage them.

What follows is exceedingly difficult to understand:

. . . he went and preached to the spirits in prison, who formerly did not obey, when God's patience waited in the days of Noah . . . (3:19–20a)

The passage is one of the more obscure in the New Testament. Interpreters have differed about the interpretation of every word.[64] The simplest meaning is that Christ descended between his passion and

---

[61] Selwyn, p. 86.

[62] Cf. Hunter, "I Peter," *IB*, XII, p. 178, for a parallel showing the dependence of this section of I Peter on Isa. 53. See Selwyn, pp. 90–101, for an analysis of the theology of atonement in I Peter.

[63] Selwyn, pp. 195–196.

[64] Rendell Harris, followed by Goodspeed and Moffat, suggests that the passage is based upon the apocryphal story of Enoch 6:4ff. of Enoch's preaching doom to imprisoned angels. He conjectures that by textual error the word Enoch has fallen out of the verse. No textual evidence supports this conjecture. Selwyn, pp. 198–199, interprets the spirits in prison as fallen angels. For a comprehensive survey of the interpretations of verse 19, see Bo Reicke, *The Disobedient Spirits and Christian Baptism, Acta Seminarii Neotestamentici Upsaliensis*, XIII, pp. 7–51; Reicke, p. 91, identifies the "disobedient spirits" as beings who form the principles behind the heathen.

resurrection to preach to the spirits in Hades. Such a tradition probably arose in speculation about what happened to Jesus between
his death and resurrection and about the fate of those who had died
before his coming. Christ, says Peter, descended into Hades to offer
salvation to sinners who had died without hearing the gospel.[65] The
tradition may be an application to Jesus of the redemption mythology
of Oriental religions with their concept of the descent to the underworld of various agricultural deities, especially Ishtar.[66] Whatever its
origin, the tradition of Christ's descent into Hades and of the "harrowing of hell" became a part of the Church's theology as expressed in the
Apostle's Creed.[67] It probably had antecedents in the kerygmatic and
credal materials of the early Church.[68] Its appearance here may be
intended as an encouragement to Christians to bear witness to un-
believers, as Christ preached to the disobedient spirits.[69] It may, however, only be intended to express the extent of Christ's redemptive
work.[70]

The extended exhortation rests first on the necessity of orderly and
righteous attitudes toward the state, even under persecution, then upon
Christ's death as an example and source of encouragement. Finally,
the concern is with calm good behavior in face of the end of all things.
Like nearly all early Christians, Peter believed that the world's end was
near and that this time of crisis demanded faithfulness, love, and caring
(4:7–11).

V. Exhortations in Face of Persecution (4:12–5:11). The final
exhortations honestly recognize the difficulties faced by the recipients
of the epistle, but find in them an opportunity to encourage those who
are persecuted.[71] Here the author deals with "the distress and terror

---

[65] Hunter, "I Peter," *IB*, XII, p. 133.

[66] Beare, *The First Epistle of Peter*, p. 145.

[67] Cf. the apocryphal *Gospel According to St. Peter* where in the story of the
crucifixion Christ is asked, "Hast thou preached to those who have fallen asleep?"
The answer is, "Yes."

[68] Cf. Bo Reicke, *The Disobedient Spirits and Christian Baptism, Acta Seminarii
Neotestamentici Upsaliensis*, p. 126. I Tim. 3:16 contains a similar reference,
"seen by angels," in credal or hymnic context.

[69] This is the conclusion of Reicke.

[70] Cf. 4:6 and Hunter, "I Peter," *IB*, XII, p. 133, and S. E. Johnson, "Preaching
to the Dead," *JBL*, LXXIX (1960), 48–51.

[71] Some scholars see a difference between 1:3–4:11 and 4:12ff. In the first part
they find only the possibility of suffering, whereas in 4:12ff. suffering is described
as a present condition. 1:3–4:11 has no real epistolary character and closes with
a doxology, while 4:12ff. has a concrete setting and definite epistolary characteristics. Cf. FBK, pp. 290–295, for a survey of the question.

occasioned by an actual persecution," described as a fiery ordeal under which Christians suffer "for the name," *i.e.*, for being Christians (4:16). They had been accused of mysterious withdrawal from the pleasures of ordinary life (4:3) and with civil crimes like murder, theft, "wrongdoing" and "mischief making" (4:15). Apparently some had suffered[72] harshly under cruel punishment without opportunity for defense or appeal. Their only recourse was to show innocence by correct behavior (3:15; 4:15) and avoidance of provocative action. By blameless conduct they could clarify the issue as religious, not civil, and prove that Christians were good citizens. Christians must beware, however, in this grave situation lest they become apostate since the "adversary, the Devil, prowls around like a roaring lion seeking someone to devour" (5:8). Courage could be found in the knowledge that they did not suffer alone, but were joined by their Christian brethren around the world.

Suffering was also to be accepted as an opportunity to share Christ's sufferings in anticipation of sharing his glory.

If you are reproached for the name of Christ, you are blessed, because the spirit of glory and of God rests upon you. (4:14)

. . .

And after you have suffered a little while, the God of all grace, who has called you to his eternal glory in Christ, will himself restore, establish, and strengthen you. (5:10)

Christians, then, were to rejoice in suffering.[73] The final exhortation is followed by a brief conclusion (5:12–14), verses probably from the hand of Peter himself as Paul ends II Thessalonians and Galatians with an autograph message.

Hebrews

The book of Hebrews is a "work of exhortation" to a Christian community faced with persecution, or perhaps one which had already experienced persecution, and in danger of rejecting the Christian faith. It heralds Jesus Christ as God's finest word to man and bids the faltering congregation to hold fast to him as their heavenly high priest and the pioneer and perfecter of their faith.

---

[72] Suffering in II Peter surely means more than just bearing the hostilities of one's surroundings, as W. C. Van Unnik suggests in "Christianity According to First Peter," *Epository Times,* LXVIII (1956), 79–83; and "Peter, First Letter of," *IDB,* III, p. 762.

[73] Cf. Nauck, "Freude im Leiden," *Zeitschrift für die neutestamentliche Wissenschaft,* XLVI (1955).

General Character, Origin, and Audience. In many ways Hebrews is unlike any other book in the New Testament. It is written in unique literary form with a stylistic flavor which reveals its author's knowledge of Greek rhetorical style. Its Greek is perhaps the best in the New Testament. Some have described Hebrews as an epistle, either a real letter like those of Paul or a literary epistle, i.e., a literary piece of art meant for general reading rather than a particular congregation.[74] It does have an epistolary conclusion but lacks other characteristics of an epistle. In fact, Hebrews more resembles a theological treatise than an epistle. Instead of treating a number of related matters and dealing with specific problems facing a definite congregation, it develops a single theme, the High Priesthood of Jesus Christ. It is not, however, merely a theological treatise explaining a theological idea in abstract fashion. It is at the same time an exhortation to the readers "to hold loyally to the profession of Jesus as the one Mediator of salvation."[75] Hebrews, then, is a sermon sent with an epistolary conclusion to a particular community.[76]

In another way Hebrews more or less stands alone. Its thought is quite unlike that found elsewhere in the New Testament. The author has a religious philosophy of his own, with a fundamentally Platonic view of the world and God. Like Philo[77] he interprets history on the theory that the phenomenal is an imperfect shadowy copy of what is eternal and real. The idea that the apparent world of sense impressions is "a poor provisional replica of the unseen and real order of things" pervades Hebrews.[78] By using this contrast between the real and the unreal the writer declares "that Christianity is eternal, just as it shall be everlasting, and that all else is only this, that the true heavenly things of which it consists thrust themselves forward onto this bank and shoal of time, and took cosmical embodiment, in order to suggest their coming everlasting manifestation."[79] The Priesthood of

[74] So E. Dinkler, "Hebrews, Letter to the," *IDB*, II, p. 572. If it is a literary epistle, the personal conclusion has to be considered a later addition or deliberate fiction. There is nothing to support the former and, if the latter is the case, we would expect a similar fictitious introductory greeting.

[75] Alfred Wikenhauser, *New Testament Introduction*, p. 460.

[76] So FBK; Wikenhauser, McNeile-Williams, *An Introduction to the Study of the New Testament*.

[77] Philo was an Alexandrian Jew contemporary with Jesus. As a Jew living outside of Palestine whose extensive philosophical writings survive, he is a most important source for estimating the impact of Hellenism upon Judiasm.

[78] James Moffatt, *A Critical and Exegetical Commentary on the Epistle to the Hebrews*, p. xxxi.

[79] A. B. Davidson, *Biblical and Literary Essays*, p. 317, as quoted in Moffatt, p. xxxi.

Jesus Christ mediates between the phenomenal world and the real world. Through his sacrifice the eternal enters history, or by it the historical is caught up into the eternal. Ideas like this are without real parallel in the New Testament.

Hebrews is, nevertheless, reminiscent of some Pauline themes. Christ the Son, the preexistent agent in creation; Christ's death for sins as the means of salvation; the idea of God's new order; and the decisive significance of faith are all present in Hebrews and indicate Pauline influence upon its conceptual world. Possibly its author was acquainted with some of Paul's writings; however, claims that he was a disciple of Paul [80] or that he was influenced directly by the collected letters of Paul [81] go beyond the evidence. Such claims may be unduly influenced by the traditional ascription of Hebrews to Paul's pen. This is an early Christian tradition, and it may well be that Hebrews was accepted into the canon as one of the Pauline writings. Some apostolic association would have been necessary.[82] However, the book varies so decisively from Paul, both literarily and theologically, that it is impossible to imagine him as its author. Although diverse suggestions have been made,[83] neither internal nor external evidence makes the author's identity ascertainable. From the character of Hebrews we can only conclude that its author was a Christian thinker deeply learned in the Old Testament and Platonic/Philonic philosophy. He was probably a Hellenistic Jewish Christian, who would have been at home in a Gentile Christian congregation. His knowledge of Greek rhetoric and philosophical writings seems to indicate that he had been educated in Alexandria.

When Hebrews was written is as difficult to determine as the identity of its author. It appears to have been sometime within the decade A.D. 80–90. Considerable time had passed since the beginnings of the Christian movement (cf. 10:32; 2:1ff.). The Church was no longer in its infancy and the problems it faced were those of the post-apostolic age, when the Church-come-of-age encountered strong opposition from outside and was threatened by internal weakness and uncertain faith

[80] Some have suggested Barnabas, but their arguments are not convincing.

[81] Edgar J. Goodspeed, An Introduction to the New Testament, pp. 256ff., and "The Problem of Hebrews," JBR, XXII (1954), 122.

[82] Cf. above, pp. 10–15.

[83] Clement of Alexandria suggested that Luke translated into Greek an epistle first written by Paul in Hebrew, and Origen knew a tradition that identified Clement of Rome as its author. Martin Luther, followed by Bleek, T. W. Manson, and others, favored Apollos. Finally, Tertullian knew a tradition which ascribed Hebrews to Barnabas.

and beliefs. A time early in the post-apostolic age seems preferable, for Timothy, who as a young man was a helper of Paul, was still alive (13:23). Further, Hebrews was already known to the author of I Clement, who wrote around A.D. 96. Perhaps, then, Hebrews was written during the time of Domitian (A.D. 91–96) to a church which had suffered under or feared Roman persecution.[84]

Hebrews probably was addressed to a community of Christians in Rome. The earliest non-canonical reference to the book is in I Clement which was written in Rome, and Hebrews itself perhaps betrays its Roman destination when it states, "Those who come from Italy send you greetings" (13:24), a statement most naturally understood by assuming that the writer is outside of Italy and that Italians among his associates send greetings to their fellow countrymen. References to the church's past faithfulness when "exposed to abuse and affliction" and to the eminence of its former leaders also fit Rome. It has even been suggested that the author was an esteemed elder in that church who wrote home while he was away.[85]

Was the audience the entire Roman church or its Jewish members? The superscription "To the Hebrews" is not original,[86] but was merely hypothesized from the contents of the book. However, it is early, stemming from the primitive collection of Christian writings, and reflects the opinion that Hebrews was written to Jewish Christians.[87] That the readers were Jewish Christians who were in imminent danger of abandoning Christianity has been widely accepted.[88] The author assumes that his audience is well acquainted with the Old Testament and particularly the Old Testament cultus (9:2–5, 12–13, 25; 10:11); and the theological antitheses of Christ and Moses, Christ and Melchizedek, Christ's High Priesthood and the Levitical priesthood could well have been designed for former Jews.

The audience, however, may not have been Jewish at all, but rather a Christian community well acquainted with the Old Testament and Judaism.[89] Almost from the beginning the Gentile Christians were re-

---

[84] William Manson, *The Epistle to the Hebrews,* pp. 162–167, thinks Hebrews was written before the fall of Jerusalem in A.D. 70.

[85] James L. Price, *Interpreting the New Testament,* p. 495.

[86] Dinkler, "Hebrews, Letter to the," *IDB,* II, p. 572, suggests that the original title would have been outside the papyrus scroll and was probably never copied.

[87] The earliest (P[46]) already has the superscription which is first attested by Pantaenus in Eusebius, *EH,* VI, xiv, 4, then by Clement of Alexandria and Tertullian.

[88] Some suggest that the danger was reversion to Judaism, or an overemphasis on certain aspects of the Church's Jewish inheritance.

[89] Romans and Galatians were not written to Jewish Christians but do presuppose a detailed knowledge of the Old Testament.

garded as the heirs of the blessings and promises of the Old Testament people of God.[90] The Old Testament was scripture to the new Christians and for them it was an incontestable authority and a conclusive source of information about the actions of God which were fulfilled in the Christ event. Nowhere in Hebrews is any distinction made between Jews and Gentiles within the Church and no warnings against circumcision, food laws, or other typically Jewish ordinances appear in the book. Surely some distinctions would have been intimated had the work been intended for one segment of the community. Probably then the readers of Hebrews were merely Christians who enjoyed a thorough Jewish heritage.

Content and Interpretation. Whether Jewish or Gentile the addressees were in danger of "falling away from the living God" (3:12).[91] In spite of an admirable Christian past characterized by work and love "in serving the saints" (6:10), they were now cowed by some external threat or weakened by inner loss of faith and stamina and were marked by lassitude of faith, fear of suffering, and lack of congregational integrity.[92] The letter in ordered exposition regularly interrupted by exhortations (indicated by italics in the outline below) aims to encourage its recipients to faithfulness and hope by virtue of Jesus Christ.

    I. Hear the Word of God in the Son Jesus Christ, who is superior to the angels and Moses. 1:1–4:13
        A. The Son is superior to the prophets and angels as bearer of the Word of God. 1:1–14
        Therefore, Christians must pay close attention to his word. 2:1–4
        B. The Son is representative man (Incarnation, Passion, and Death) in order to be the pioneer of salvation for all men. 2:5–18
        C. Jesus is exalted above Moses as Son and Lord. 3:1–6
        Therefore, Christians must take care lest they lose the promised rest of God by unbelief and disobedience. They must strive to win their share of the promise which is theirs as the people of God. 3:7–4:13

   II. Hold fast to Jesus who as representative man is the true High Priest. 4:14–10:18
        Since Jesus is the great High Priest, Christians should turn to him with confidence. 4:14–16
        A. Christ as representative man possesses the requirements of a genuine High Priest. 5:1–10
           1. He shares human weakness. 5:2–3
           2. He was called by God. 5:4–6

[90] Cf. Gal. 6:16; I Cor. 10:11; I Peter 1:12.
[91] This may better fit a Gentile audience than a Jewish one.
[92] Cf. 5:11f.; 10:25 and 35; 12:3f. and 13:17.

3. He was obedient in suffering. 5:7–10
Christians should hold to their hope and in spite of temporary weakness should attend to the fundamentals of their faith. 5:11–6:20

    (a) *They must overcome their spiritual dullness.* 5:11–6:8
    (b) *They must hold loyally to their hope and attend to the fundamentals of their faith which are developed in the author's presentation of his main theme which follows.* 6:9–20

  B. Christ is a perfect and eternal High Priest after the order of Melchizedek. 7:1–28
  C. Christ is the heavenly High Priest who mediates the new covenant of promise. 8:1–13
  D. The sacrificial work of Christ, as perfect and eternal, is superior to the Old Testament sacrificial system. 9:1–10:18
    1. Christ's sacrifice secured an eternal redemption. 9:1–14
    2. The sacrifice of Christ establishes the New Covenant. 9:15–28
    3. The once-for-all sacrifice of Christ provides the perfect forgiveness of sin. 10:1–18

 III. *Hold Fast to Jesus Christ, the Pioneer and Perfector of Faith.* 10:19–12:29
  A. *Hold fast to the hope of eternal salvation.* 10:19–39
    1. *Avail yourselves of "the new and living way."* 10:19–25
    2. *Apostasy has fearful consequences.* 10:26–31
    3. *Recollecting the past, face the present with confidence and faith.* 10:32–39
  B. *There is abundant witness to the power of faith.* 11:1–40
  C. *In suffering look back to faith's witnesses and to Christ lest you fall into apostasy.* 12:1–29

 IV. *Closing exhortations.* 13:1–17

  V. Epistolary Conclusion: personal message, blessing and greeting. 13:18–25

Hebrews is a carefully reasoned exposition of the theme, "Jesus Christ is representative man and High Priest." The author, however, is not content merely to expound his theme. Its truth calls for strong exhortation addressed to readers who are on the point of abandoning the one true faith. To a congregation whose faithfulness and hope had been blunted by persecution the Christian religion is extolled as superior to all other religions, including Judaism, the highest revelation of the true God previously known to the Church. Christianity's superiority lay in the unique action of God in their living Lord, who though man like themselves had been God's climactic word, their High Priest and sacrifice for sin.

The following key quotations reveal the meaning of Hebrews.

In many and various ways God spoke of old to our fathers by the prophets; but in these last days he has spoken to us by a Son, whom he appointed the heir of all things, through whom also he created the world. He reflects the glory of God and bears the very stamp of his nature, upholding the universe by his word of power. When he had made justification for sins, he sat down at the right hand of the Majesty on high, having become as much superior to angels as the name he has obtained is more excellent than theirs. (1:1–4)

. . .

But we see Jesus, who for a little while was made lower than the angels, crowned with glory and honor because of the suffering of death, so that by the grace of God he might taste death for everyone.

For it was fitting that he, for whom and by whom all things exist, in bringing many sons to glory, should make the pioneer of their faith perfect through suffering. For he who sanctifies and those who are sanctified have all one origin. (2:9–11)

. . .

Since therefore the children share in flesh and blood, he himself likewise partook of the same nature, that through death he might destroy him who has the power of death, that is, the devil, and deliver all those who through fear of death were subject to lifelong bondage. (2:14–15)

. . .

Therefore he had to be made like his brethren in every respect, so that he might become a merciful and faithful high priest in the service of God, to make expiation for the sins of the people. For because he himself has suffered and been tempted, he is able to help those who are tempted.

Therefore, holy brethren who share in a heavenly call, consider Jesus the apostle and high priest of our confession. (2:17; 3:1).

. . .

Now the point in what we are saying is this: we have such a high priest, one who is seated at the right hand of the throne of the Majesty in heaven, a minister in the sanctuary and the true tent which is set up not by man but by the Lord. (8:1–2)

Jesus was God's finest word to man, spoken not through prophets but through the Son, who was uniquely related to God and to man. As representative man he suffered and died for man's redemption, and, sharing the infirmities and sufferings of humanity, he was appointed by God to serve as mankind's High Priest opening to man the realm of God. Since there is nothing in religion comparable to this, Christians make a tragic mistake to abandon their faith or even to falter in it. To the writer of Hebrews revelation climaxed in the earthly ministry of Jesus. What had gone before was merely a shadowy prefigurement of ultimate reality. Using a two-story view of reality like that of Plato and Philo, Hebrews assumes two realms of existence, the heavenly and the earthly. Man lives in the earthly and less than satisfactory realm of history. What he needs is access to the superior and eternal realm. In Christ God has acted in shadowy and transcient history to rescue man for the realm of ultimate reality. Christ, who participated in both realms as perfect High Priest and perfect sacrifice, has opened the way into the heavenly realm for all who would follow him in faith. His priesthood is perfected through the unique relationship he has to humanity as representative man.

I. CHRIST IS GOD'S FINEST WORD TO MAN (1:1–4:13). The author begins to develop his argument with the idea that Christ is the perfect revelation of God, superior to the prophetic word (1:1–2), to angels (1:3–14; 2:1–18), and to Moses (3:1–19). The revelation through law, prophets, and angels is not to be compared to the word spoken through Jesus Christ. This is so because Jesus, the Son of God and citizen of the eternal realm, is also man who shares the reality of human existence. His incarnation is the final and effective redeeming word of God. Like the writer of the Fourth Gospel, the author of Hebrews sees the eternal present in history in the Word who "became flesh and dwelt among us." Sharing at the same time the life of God and the life of man, Jesus Christ is representative man summing up in himself the whole human race, bearing humanity's lot and facing its temptations, yet unswervingly obedient to God. In his humanity all men and all history were recapitulated.[93] Becoming "for a little while lower than the angels," he tasted death for everyone and by suffering became the perfect pioneer of humanity's salvation. Man's divinely appointed destiny to be "crowned with glory and honor" with "everything in subjection under his feet" is realized only by the representative man, Jesus Christ, who through death "destroyed him who has the power of death, that is, the devil." Christ's death, moreover, is a representative act in which all men may participate by faith. For it was fitting that God's "purpose of redemption—His act of bringing 'many sons' to the glory of the World to Come—should plumb the whole depth of human anguish and death." [94] Christ in his own person exhibited perfect obedience to God and perfect identification of himself with man. The author's primary emphasis in this passage is on

[93] This idea of atonement was given classic expression by Irenaeus. It takes seriously the question about both the person and the work of Christ. By the incarnation Christ summed up in himself the whole human race, becoming its representative. He concentrated humanity in himself and the triumph over evil which he won is shared by all men. His relationship to men can be described as *recapitulatis* and renewal and restoration of the race, effected because Christ overcame Satan at the level where Satan had won his victory, in humanity.

[94] Manson, *The Epistle to the Hebrews*, p. 101.

the suffering by which in his identification with man Christ was prepared for his role as our High Priest.[95]

Thus by introduction of the idea of atonement the author leads to
his central concern, the High Priesthood of Jesus Christ. Before turning to it, however, he pauses to exhort his readers to renewed faithfulness in their Christian commitment (3:7–4:13). Using Psalm 95 as a
text the author reminds his readers that "we share in Christ, if only
we hold our first confidence firm to the end." That is to say, one shares
in the representative act of Christ only if he is faithful (3:12–14).
Confidence in Christ and faithfulness assures the Christian a place
in the household of God in which Christ is the Son and a share of
the "rest" promised long before to Moses and the people of Israel but
still to be realized and enjoyed (4:1–13).

II. JESUS CHRIST IS THE TRUE HIGH PRIEST (4:14–10:18). Now the
author begins to develop his main point, the High Priesthood of Christ.
Jesus, the Son of God and man's High Priest, has the two qualifications
of true priesthood, divine appointment and ability to sympathize with
and share human weaknesses. Here too, the writer is concerned with
Jesus' role as representative man. He sympathizes with man's weaknesses, not as an onlooker in whom they arouse pity and compassion,
but as one, who, through common experience, has a kinship with those
who suffer. The true priest, exemplified by the High Priest in Israel,
was appointed by God to represent man before deity. He had the
capacity to take the sins and frailties of man on himself. Jesus' call was
to be Son of God (Psalm 2:7) and priest forever after the order of
Melchizedek (Psalm 110:4).[96] His unique relationship to God bestowed upon him a unique High Priesthood which was made perfect
by his unique representative relationship to man (4:14–5:6). "He
learned obedience through what he suffered" and "offered up prayers
and supplications, with loud cries and tears," as part of the sacrificial
offering by which he became the perfect High Priest, leading man into
the eternal realm (5:7–10). Hoping that his readers are devoted to
Christ (surely they have not actually abandoned the faith), the author
encourages them to attend to the fundamentals of their faith and to
advance toward Christian maturity (5:11–6:20).

After the interruption to exhort his readers, the author returns to the

[95] Cf. E. F. Scott, *The Epistle to the Hebrews*, pp. 98f. As Manson, p. 100,
points out, "everything is subordinated to the cultus and, in particular, to the
priesthood."

[96] Manson, *The Epistle to the Hebrews*, p. 108, suggests that the latter commission, like the former, was part of the primitive tradition.

main line of argument to make three further points about Christ as High Priest. The first is a labored, rabbinic type argument that the High Priesthood of Christ is eternal like that of Melchizedek (cf. Genesis 14:17–20) and is therefore superior to the Levitical priesthood of Israel (7:1–28). The Levitical priesthood which belonged to the shadowy realm of this world was provisional and temporary. Christ's priesthood is eternal and superior to that of the Levitical priesthood in providing the perfect once-for-all sacrifice, i.e., the sacrifice of Christ himself. Since the priesthood of Christ is superior to the Levitical priesthood, it follows, so the author argues, that the law establishing Levitical priesthood has been superseded (7:12, 18). Like Paul, the author of Hebrews believed that with the coming of Christ the law had been set aside. There are differences, however, in the ways the two men understood law and its fulfillment in Christ. To Paul the law represented an unrealizable ethical demand which left man condemned and damned. The coming of Christ broke the power of the law, for man is justified by faith not by obedience of the law. To the author of Hebrews law means cultus, priesthood, and sacrifice which cannot redeem. Christ, to the contrary, represents the true priesthood and the perfect sacrifice made for man's redemption since "he always likes to make intercession for them" (7:25) and is holy and blameless, unfettered by sin.

Next, the argument turns to Christ as the heavenly High Priest who mediates the new covenant of promise (8:1–13) anticipated by the prophet Jeremiah (31:31–34). The author of Hebrews is not the only person in the New Testament who saw in the work of Christ the fulfillment of Jeremiah's hope. The Pauline account of Jesus' words of institution of the Last Supper (I Corinthians 11:25) and the longer version of the Lucan account (Luke 22:20) [97] suggest that Jesus himself viewed his own death as inaugurating the new covenant. In interpreting Christ's work as fulfilling Jeremiah's hope, the author of Hebrews uses the contrast between the temporal and the eternal realm to clarify Christ's superior priesthood. It is exercised in the true sanctuary in the heavens of which the Levitical sanctuary is an inadequate copy or shadow. Christ's "ministry of sacrifice is a transcendent one." [98] It belongs to the heavenly and eternal realm and,

[97] Although most manuscripts and versions contain vs. 19b–20 of Luke 20, some see them as an importation from I Cor. 11:24–25. Aland, Black, Metzger, and Wikgren, The Greek New Testament, regard 19b–20 as a later addition to the text, but retain them because of their evident antiquity and importance in the textual tradition.

[98] Manson, The Epistle to the Hebrews, p. 126.

therefore, brings together God and man [99] in a way that Moses and the Levitical priesthood could never do. Thus a superior relationship between God and man is established by the word of Christ. The new covenant promises more because it "has the nature of eternity" in it.[100] In it the eternal world has been mediated to man. The section concludes with the idea that the old age has ended and a new age has dawned in Christ.

The argument for the priestly superiority of Christ then describes the sacrificial work of Christ as perfect and eternal (9:1–10:18). His sacrifice secured an eternal redemption (9:1–14). "He entered once for all into the Holy Place, taking not the blood of goats and calves but his own blood, thus securing an eternal redemption" (9:12). If the ritual sacrifices of the Levitical cultus cleansed the worshipers for access to God in matters of external cultic purity, how much more would the blood of Christ achieve. It will purify even "the conscience from dead works to serve the living God" (9:14). Manson lists five points which the writer here drives home upon his readers.[101] First, "the offering is the *blood of the Messiah*" (italics added). Second, the death of Jesus "expresses the very nature of the eternal Mind and Word." Third, "the *fullness* of all sacrifice is in that utter, completely moral and personal, self devotion of Jesus to death" for the forgiveness of sin. Fourth, the application of the atoning virtue and redemption which are in Jesus' death cannot be limited to ritual guilt but extends as far as the moral consciousness extends. Fifth, the death of Christ brings man to the living God. Having underscored that Christ's death mediates the new covenant (9:15–18) and provides the perfect forgiveness of sins (10:18), "by a single offering perfecting for all time those who are sanctified" (10:14), the author has completed his analysis of the High Priestly role and is prepared to move to exhortation derived from the theme.

III. Exhortation (10:19–12:29). The author now challenges his readers to hold fast to the "new and living way." Reminding his readers of other men who under trying circumstances were found faithful, he encourages them to heed their example. So much more should they be faithful since they have received the promise in Christ for which faith's former heroes could only hope. Not only are his readers surrounded by this host of witnesses to faith but they can look to Jesus,

---

[99] This is the sense of the words *mediate* and *mediator*.
[100] Manson, *The Epistle to the Hebrews*, p. 126.
[101] *Ibid.*, pp. 134–136.

the pioneer and perfecter of faith. Suffering can be borne for discipline for they have in Christ received "a kingdom that cannot be shaken" (12:28).

IV. CLOSING EXHORTATIONS (13:1–17). Something still remains to be said, and here the author of Hebrews is specific. He certainly has some knowledge of the congregation he addresses and in a Pauline manner confronts a series of specific issues that he feels need his attention. He then closes with an appeal that his exhortations be heeded and with greetings.

Although it might appear that the many and extensive exhortations interrupt the development of the author's theological theme, this is not really the case. They are in fact his primary purpose in writing. The theological theme is actually the heart of exhortations which seek to encourage a frustrated and wavering congregation and to call them to renewed dedication to Christ. The theme of the infinite superiority of Christ becomes the inspiration of the exhortation. If at times the argument is belabored and wordy, it is because the author desired to press his point so that it would not be missed. We can only speculate as to whether he was successful in rescuing his readers from a fate which he surely considered worse than death itself (6:1–8).

Revelation

Sometime during the reign of Domitian a patriarch of the Church in Asia Minor took up pen to protest that emperor's cruel persecutions of Christians. He scathingly condemned Rome as the seat of evil and described the emperor as the eschatological beast whose rampages were prelude to the dawning of the age of righteousness. To the persecuted Church he offered participation in the righteous age as reward for their sufferings. In the end, he claimed, God and the Church would triumph over all forms of tyranny and evil. This seer put his ideas into dramatic and exciting form using both the thought and literary form of apocalypticism.

Apocalypticism and Apocalypses.[102] Apocalypticism originated in the ancient Near East in those religions which at one time in their development were preoccupied with eschatological concerns, that is,

[102] On apocalyptic literature see R. H. Charles, *The Apocrypha and Pseudepigrapha of the Old Testament,* II (for the text of Jewish apocalypses); H. H. Rowley, *The Relevance of Apocalyptic;* M. Rist, "Apocalypticism," *IDB,* I, 157–161; and D. S. Russell, *The Method and Message of Jewish Apocalyptic.*

with the problems of the end of the world and the close of history.[103] It developed profusely in post-exilic Judaism and in early Christianity as a by-product of their similar concerns. Between the Maccabean wars and the end of the second century A.D. many apocalyptic works were produced in Judaism. Among them were the Books of Enoch, the Testaments of the Twelve Patriarchs, the Jewish Sibyllines, the Assumption of Moses, II Esdras, the "War Scroll" from Qumran, and the canonical book of Daniel. The book of Revelation is the only fully apocalyptic work in the New Testament, but the Church also produced noncanonical works like Shepherd of Hermas and the Apocalypse of Peter. All of these books, biblical and extra-biblical, are dominated by an eschatological atmosphere.

Apocalypticism is controlled by an historical and ethical dualism. Its thought may be defined as "the dualistic, cosmic, and eschatological belief in two opposing cosmic powers, God and Satan (or his equivalent); and in two distinct ages—the present, temporal, and irretrievably evil age under Satan, who now oppresses the righteous but whose power God will soon act to overthrow; and the future, perfect and eternal age under God's own rule, when the righteous will be blessed forever." [104]

The literature of Judaeo-Christian apocalypticism is generally pseudonymous, the true identity of the author being veiled behind the assumed authority of some ancient figure of importance.[105] Visions are the typical literary form of apocalyptic literature, and in them parable, symbol, and allegory abound. Persons are represented by animals and historical events by natural phenomena. Colors and numbers have secret meanings. All such imagery and its meaning undoubtedly emerged from the mythological, cosmological, and astrological traditions of the ancient Near East. To understand apocalyptic literature, therefore, one would need to know the background out of which it came. The modern interpreter, however, is unable to discover the proper precedents for many apocalyptic figures and thus a full explanation of many details in apocalyptic writings is often closed to him.[106] Ignorance of the background or refusal even to consider it

[103] Apocalypticism apparently originated in Iranian religion, but is prevalent in the Hellenistic and ancient Germanic religions.

[104] Rist, "Apocalypticism," *IDB*, I, p. 157.

[105] Pseudonyms used in the apocalyptic literature of Judaism and Christianity are Enoch, Noah, Abraham, the Twelve Patriarchs, Moses, Elijah, Daniel, Baruch, and Ezra.

[106] This accounts, of course, for the wide disagreement among scholars about the meaning of certain apocalyptic passages.

leaves this literature an open field for fanciful speculation and has led to gross misinterpretation.[107]

The name apocalyptic comes from Revelation 1:1, "The revelation (*apokalypsis*) of Jesus Christ, which God gave him . . ." Here for the first time a book is called an "Apocalypse" or a "Revelation."

Introduction to the Book of Revelation.   The New Testament book of Revelation, the classic example of apocalyptic literature, comes to us from an author about whom we know little.   The visions which provide the basis of his apocalyptic interpretation of events were experienced in exile on the Isle of Patmos, which lies off the coast of Asia Minor by Miletus (see the map on p. 285).   His book was directed as a circular letter to the seven churches in the Roman province of Asia (Ephesus, Smyrna, Pergamum, Thyatira, Sardis, Philadelphia, and Laodicea). He knew a great deal about the life of these churches and addressed them with a matter-of-fact authority.   He must have been well known to them and before his exile a man of great stature among them, but at the same time their brother.   He was on Patmos "on account of the word of God and the testimony of Jesus" (1:9).   If this refers to banishment, and it usually has been so interpreted since Tertullian,[108] he doubtless was a prominent preacher of the gospel.[109]   His refusal to deny Christ and worship the image of the emperor [110] would have won him their respect.

Four times the author of Revelation calls himself "John" (1:1, 4, 9; 22:8), and as early as the second century he was identified with the apostle John, the son of Zebedee.[111]   This opinion, however, was contested even in the early Church [112] and is rejected by the majority of modern scholars.   The identification with John the apostle contradicts an impressive array of evidence.   When the New Testament canon was being formed in the second and third centuries, there was a hesitancy

[107] All attempts to find in apocalyptic books like Daniel and Revelation specific predictions of modern events are more the product of imagination than understanding.

[108] Tertullian, *On Prescription Against Heretics*, XXXVI; see also Clement of Alexandria, *Who is the Rich Man That Shall be Saved*, XLII.

[109] FBK, p. 329.

[110] This can be inferred from the usual demands made upon Christians in time of persecution.

[111] Justin Martyr, *Dialogue with Trypho*, LXXI; Clement of Alexandria, *Who is the Rich Man That Shall be Saved*, XII.

[112] Anti-Montanist opponents of the Gospel of John and the Roman anti-Montanist, Gaius, traced Revelation to the Gnostic, Cerinthus.   In the third century Dionysius of Alexandria denied Revelation to the apostle John, claiming its author to have been another man named John.

to accept Revelation.[113] Obviously there was disagreement about its apostolic origin. Had the author been known definitely to be the apostle John, Revelation would have been unchallenged. Nothing in the book supports apostolic authorship; the author never claims apostolic authority and, in fact, twice refers to the apostles in a way to distinguish himself from them.[114] Moreover, nowhere in Revelation is there any indication that its author was an eyewitness to the life of Jesus. Furthermore, if the dating of Revelation near the end of the first century is correct, it is doubtful that it could have been written by John the son of Zebedee.[115]

It would appear, then, that John the apostle was not the author of Revelation. The book, however, is not pseudonymous. There are in it scarcely any characteristics of pseudepigraphy. Had the author been writing in the name of the apostle, he would have made it clear. The author's name, therefore, was John and this raises an important question. Was the John of Patmos the author of the Fourth Gospel and the Epistles of John? [116] Probably not, because the style and perspective of the Apocalypse is radically different from that of the Fourth Gospel and the Johannine letters. The ancient tradition that associates them may be understood to trace them to a common circle of Christian teaching in Asia, but not to the same author.[117]

As to when Revelation was written, we can be more certain. According to the earliest tradition, John "saw the apocalyptic vision . . .

[113] Revelation was not completely accepted in the Eastern Church until the tenth century. Chrysostom and Theodoret were against its acceptance as were the three great Cappadocians. A scriptural catalogue of the ninth century did not list Revelation among the books of the New Testament. Through the late Byzantine period few manuscripts of the Greek New Testament contained Revelation and most of the Greek manuscripts of the book had its text as part of a commentary or with non-biblical writings.

[114] In 18:20 and 21:14 he seems to imply that the apostolic age is past and that he himself was not one of the Twelve.

[115] There is even the possibility that John had been martyred with his brother James before A.D. 70, while the temple was still standing. If so, the apostle could not be the author of Revelation. There is, however, another tradition that John lived in Ephesus to a ripe old age. According to Apollonius (Eusebius, *EH*, V, xviii, 14), he raised a dead man at Ephesus. Clement of Alexandria tells how he reclaimed a robber for Christ (*What Rich Man Can Be Saved*, XLII). Irenaeus tells of his opposition to Cerinthus, the heretic (*Against Heresies*, III, iii, 4). Jerome says that in his old age he was carried about to greet the Christian brethren, "Little Children, love one another" (*Commentary on Galatians*, 6:10). It is not, however, absolutely certain that these references are to John the Apostle.

[116] See below, pp. 487–490, for the discussion of the authorship of the Gospel and p. 501, for the Epistles.

[117] See for details FBK, pp. 329–331 and the works there cited.

towards the end of Domitian's reign." [118] Internal evidence supports this. The book was written to the severely oppressed churches of Asia. Persecution by the authorities was imminent (2:10). The blood of martyrs had already been shed (2:13; 6:9), and all Christendom was faced with the frightful danger of a general persecution (3:10). John depicts Rome as Babylon, a harlot drunk from the blood of the saints who are witnesses of Jesus (17:6; cf. 18:24; 19:2; 16:6; 6:20). Christianity was in life-and-death conflict with the state and the state religion of emperor worship. In defense of the faith the Apocalypse "raised vehement opposition against Rome and the emperor cult" [119] and promised to the martyrs who refused to worship the emperor participation in the thousand year kingdom of Christ (20:4).[120] Conflict between Christianity and the state religion began in the reign of Domitian, who claimed to be divine and commanded that he be worshipped as emperor during his lifetime. No time in primitive Christianity seems a more appropriate background for the Apocalypse than his reign.[121]

Literary Heritage. The Apocalypse drew upon a varied literary heritage. Numerous doublets and contradictions are evidence that the author incorporated various traditional materials into his apocalyptic vision of the end of time.[122] The apocalypticist fitted together originally independent materials with little or no concern about their duplications or contradictions. Further, he writes in the language of scripture. The book contains over five hundred allusions to the Old Testament, but not a single verbatim quotation.[123] The author has rephrased or restated much of the imagery of the Old Testament in

[118] Irenaeus, *Against Heresies,* V, xxx; *EH,* III, xviii, 1.

[119] FBK, p. 327.

[120] Cf. 13:4, 12a; 14:9, 11; 16:2; 19:20.

[121] Admittedly, we cannot be certain about the extent of Domitian's anti-Christian policies. Enslin, *The Beginnings of Christianity,* pp. 364f., suggests that the picture in the Apocalypse might arise, not from actual knowledge of a persecution, but from the seer's fear and hatred of Rome and from his prophetic insight. Nevertheless, all things considered, a date in Domitian's reign seems best for the Apocalypse of John.

[122] Critics have long tried to explain these numerous contradictions with literary-critical conjectures. Some suggest that various Jewish or Christian written sources have been woven together. Others suggest a thorough revision of a "basic document" by redactors. In recent scholarship the view that Revelation as we know it was put together out of two writings composed at different times by the same author has been popular.

[123] These allusions are sometimes parallel to the LXX and later versions of the O.T. but in the majority of cases reflect a good knowledge of the Hebrew and Aramaic primitive texts. Cf. Charles, *The Apocrypha and Pseudepigrapha of the Old Testament,* I, lxvff.

describing his visions. Many scholars claim that he also drew heavily upon several Jewish apocalypses which were in circulation during his time. To what extent this is true is difficult to determine because the parallels are rarely verbatim, and the borrowed symbols are not always employed in the same sense in which they were used in the original apocalypses. What John has borrowed from the Jewish apocalypses is more literary form than specific meaning.[124]

The author of Revelation, then, has freely used both scriptural and apocalyptical imagery for his own distinctive purpose. The Apocalypse is, therefore, more than a crude editing of various traditional materials, and its author more than a skillful borrower. The Apocalypse contains both traditional and original materials, all woven together according to the author's apocalyptic purpose. Notable among the original compositions are several majestic hymns expressing his apocalyptic hope.[125]

> Holy, holy, holy is the Lord God Almighty,
> who was and is and is to come! (4:8)
>
> .   .   .
>
> Worthy art Thou, our Lord and God,
> to receive glory and honor and power,
> for thou didst create all things,
> and by thy will they existed and were
> created. (4:11)
>
> .   .   .
>
> Hallelujah! Salvation and glory and power
>   belong to our God,
> for his judgments are true and just;
> he has judged the great harlot who corrupted
>   the earth with her fornication,
> and he has avenged on her the blood of his
>   servants. (19:1–2) [126]

Even the author's Greek style, which is highly unorthodox, ungrammatical, irregular, and abrupt, seems to be, not just poor Greek, but the invention of his purpose.[127] John's use of traditional materials in his own particular way and in combination with ideas and images of his own produced what can be called a Christian prophetic apocalypse.

[124] Philip Carrington, *The Meaning of Revelation*, p. x.

[125] Some trace these liturgical materials to the Christian liturgy of his time. Cf. Oscar Cullmann, *Early Christian Worship*, p. 7; S. Läuchli, "Eine Gottesdienstrucktur in der Johannesoffenbarung," *Theologische Zeitschrift*, XVI (1960), 359–378.

[126] In addition see 1:5f.; 5:9.; 12f.; 7:10, 12, 15–17; 11:15, 17f.; 12:10–12; 15:3f.; 19:5–8; 22–13.

[127] FBK, p. 326.

Apocalyptic and Prophetic Character. Revelation is, therefore, not just another Jewish apocalypse. It is thoroughly Christian. Its eschatological hope is based upon the saving act of God in Christ. The events of Jesus' life and death [128] were for John the eschatological turning point of history and the basis of his confidence in the historically powerful God. John of Patmos is a prophetic seer. Frequently he speaks of his apocalypse as prophecy (1:3; 19:10; 22:7, 10, 18–19), and describes his mission as that of prophesying. Moreover, he borrows freely from the imagery of the prophetic literature of Judaism. True to Israelite prophecy, however, he is no mere foreteller of events. In fact, he is most characteristically prophet at the point of the relevance of his predictions to the immediate situation of his readers. The goal of his prophetic-apocalyptic portrayal of the end-time was to comfort and assure the Church of his time. In the certainty that the course of history moves ever under the control of a sovereign God to an appointed destiny he wrote a book of comfort for the Church facing martyrdom. The Apocalypse is "a book of its time, written out of its time and for its time." [129]

Outline and Interpretation of Revelation. The seer of the Johannine Apocalypse feared that the life of the Church was in danger. The Christian community was not strong enough to face the crisis precipitated by Domitian's insistence that the emperor be worshipped. Faced with persecution, they might fail because already they had lost their early devotion (2:4) and were only "lukewarm" in matters of Christian faith and life (3:16). Fear for themselves and frustration because of the apparent futility of their Christian hope—how could the Church win against the power of Rome?—might well defeat them. John, however, saw the crisis of the present time, not just from the perspective of the moment, but with faith's grander and broader vision which interpreted current events in light of God's sovereign scheme for history. Admittedly, the present situation was grim. Rome's attacks on the Christians were representative of the final conflict between God and the powers of evil. This, however, meant that the Church, if it stood firm in its faith, fought with God in a struggle whose outcome was sure. The ultimate victory would be God's and a faithful Church would share in it. Suffering, even martyrdom, in such a struggle could only bring special reward.

---

[128] Cf. 12:5; 1:5; 7:14; 12:11; 3:21; 5:5; 17:14.
[129] FBK, p. 324. We are indebted to FBK, pp. 321–324, for the substance of this paragraph.

Since he wrote to a troubled area where any disloyalty to the emperor would be viewed with grave suspicion and even suppression,[130] John used involved and highly figurative language and elaborate symbolism to voice his call to resistance. The dramatic flare and apocalyptic imagery of the book of Revelation defy simple analysis, since "the book shows no clearly recognizable arrangement."[131] The course of eschatological events is interrupted by chronological retrospections and repetitions. The author looks ahead and then back as his thought roams the scope of the eternal purposes of God.[132]

Introduction. 1:1–20
    A. Preface. 1:1–3
    B. Epistolary introduction. 1:4–8
    C. John the seer's vison of Christ. 1:9–20
   I. Open Letters to the Seven Churches of Asia. 2:1–3:22
  II. Apocalyptic Visions. 4:1–22:5
    A. Audience in heaven. 4:1–5:14
    B. Vision of the seven seals. 6:1–8:1
    C. Vision of the seven trumpets. 8:2–11:19
    D. Vision of the dragon and the lamb. 12:1–14:20
    E. Vision of the seven bowls. 15:1–16:21
    F. Vision of the fate of Babylon (Rome). 17:1–19:10
    G. Vision of the coming of Christ and the time of the end. 19:11–22:5
Conclusion. 22:6–21
    A. Warnings and exhortations. 22:6–20
    B. Benediction. 22:21

Although the introduction gives the author's credentials, reasons for writing, and the identity of his audience, it is most impressive in its focus upon the seer's vision of Christ who, as "Alpha and Omega" encompasses all history in his being and activity (1:8, 17) and who is sovereign over life and death (1:18).

I. OPEN LETTERS TO THE SEVEN CHURCHES OF ASIA (2:1–3:22). In these letters John censures the churches of Asia and condemns their practices because they fall short of his ideal for the victorious Church. Each letter contains warnings and deprecations appropriate to the

---

[130] The Parthians, who lived on the eastern edge of Asia Minor, were a constant threat to the Roman control of that area.

[131] O. A. Piper as quoted in FBK, p. 324.

[132] This outline essentially follows E. Lohmeyer, *Handbuck zum Neu Testament.* For possible variations, see John Wick Bowman, "Revelation, The Book of," *IDB,* IV, pp. 64–67.

circumstances in the church to which it is addressed. Only the church at Smyrna escapes judgment. The purpose of these letters is more than criticism. They honestly face the troubles confronting the churches and promise to the faithful martyrs eternal rewards.

II. THE APOCALYPTIC VISIONS (4:1–22:5). The major section of Revelation consists of a series of visions, each patterned after the other, addressed to the churches of Asia. Among those who see Revelation as an unfolding of all future events, a plan of the ages, fancy has run wild in interpreting these materials. The visions are, however, related to the time of their readers by specific historical allusions which, although not clear to us, were understood by the original recipients of the Apocalypse. These visions of the end do not describe a series of events in strict chronological fashion. Eschatological events seem instead to be presented either in cyclical form where they are described several times in succession [133] or in dramatic presentation as overture, preparation, and final events.[134] In either case the general character and import of the vehicles are more significant than their chronology. The visions describe the life and death struggle between the Church and Rome as part of the eschatological conflict between God and the powers of evil. Those to whom the seer writes are caught in a conflict which encompasses the entire universe and whose ultimate meaning cannot be understood apart from the sovereign purpose of God.

The apocalyptic section opens with an audience in heaven, where John "in the spirit" has a vision of God, described, not directly, but in typically Jewish fashion in terms of his surroundings. The eschatological events can be understood only as God reveals them and as they are viewed from a heavenly perspective. The visions provide their own setting of cataclysmic upheavals and terrors. Seals opened on cosmic upheavals (6:12ff.) and on the four horses of the apocalypse, symbols of war (the white horse, 6:2),[135] civil dissension (the red horse, 6:4), famine (the black horse, 6:5–6), and plagues (the pale horse, 6:8). Here as elsewhere in biblical thought the destiny of the universe is tied to the destiny of man. Trumpets announced astronom-

---

[133] Cf. M. Rissi, *Zeit und Geschichte in der Offenbarung des Johannes,* in *Abhandlungen zur Theologie des Alten und Neuen Testaments,* XXII (1952).

[134] G. Bornkamm, "Die Komposition der apokalyptischen Visionen in der Offenbarung Johannes," *Zeitschrift für die Neutestamentliche Wissenschaft,* XXVI (1937), 132ff. See also Bowman's more elaborate but forced analysis along the lines of drama in "Revelation, The Book of," *IDB,* IV, pp. 58–71, and "The Revelation to John: Its Dramatic Structure and Message," *Interpretation,* IX (1955), 436ff.

[135] Some interpret the white horse as Christ to whom the ultimate victory belongs. Cf. the note on 6:2 in the *Oxford Annotated Bible,* p. 1497.

ical disturbances (8:7–12) and the release of the malevolent forces of heaven and hell. Such are the inevitable woes and judgments of the eschatological end of time.

Three figures dominate the visions: the evil powers (of which Rome is representative), the faithful witnesses or martyrs,[136] and the Christ.

A. Rome: The representative of the evil powers. Evil powers (symbolized as a star falling from heaven) were released on earth where as a great and vicious dragon they sought to destroy the Christ and the Church (chapter 12). These Satanic powers (12:9) gave supernatural strength to the Roman emperor symbolized as "the beast." Satan gave him his power, throne, and great authority (13:2). This emperor beast is represented by a second beast, the imperial priesthood which vigorously enforced the emperor cult in Asia (13:11–16), or, as Cullmann describes it, "the religio-ideological propaganda authority of the totalitarian state." [137] Together these beasts claimed the allegiance and devotion of all mankind, usurping that which man owed to God alone. The second beast deceived the inhabitants of the earth with miracles performed in the strength of the first beast (13:14) and ordered the inhabitants to worship an image of the first beast or be slain (13:15). Clearly the reference is to worship of the emperor. For the writer of the Apocalypse the satanic element in the Roman empire lay in the deification of the emperor.[138]

The identity of the emperor beast is revealed by a cryptic number, 666.

. . . let him who has understanding reckon the number of the beast, for it is a human number, its number is six hundred and sixty six. (13:18)

This obviously was a clear clue to John's original readers, but is somewhat obscure to us. It is apparently a cryptogram, since both Hebrew and Greek letters were used as numbers.[139] A later reference to the seven heads of the beast (17:3) obviously refers to seven emperors of the Roman empire, but helps little in identifying any of them since there is no certain way to determine with which emperor the series begins. The most likely solution of the cryptic 666 is Nero Caesar, but there are many other possibilities.[140] The specific identity escapes our certainty, but its general import is clear. The reference is to an em-

[136] The word *martyr* is a simple transliteration of *marturion,* the Greek word for "witness."

[137] Oscar Cullmann, *The State in the New Testament,* p. 76.

[138] *Ibid.,* pp. 79–80.

[139] *Aleph* and *alpha* were 1; *beth* and *beta* were 2; etc.

[140] Cf. Cullmann, *The State in the New Testament,* pp. 80–83, for a partial list of the suggested meanings of the number 666.

peror who claims to be divine, probably Domitian seen as the demonic figure of Nero *redivivus,* a Nero come alive again! [141]

Whoever is identified as the emperor beast, the book of Revelation clearly intends a gigantic indictment against the Roman state. Rome, the beast, is also Rome, the harlot city of Babylon, "who made all nations drink the wine of her impure passion" (14:8). As Babylon had been the persecutor of Israel, so Rome was persecutor of the Church, the true Israel of God. But, like the ancient city, the harlot Rome was condemned to the judgment of God. John's hatred of Rome is severe. To him the state has demanded what is God's, that is, *authority,* and has become a satanic power. The deified emperor makes a totalitarian demand which must be resisted even to blood. Even so, Christians must have courage to die like martyrs rather than as soldiers. Although as a Christian John was compelled to resist passionately ultimate claims made by a temporal and ephemeral state, he did not summons his fellow believers to wage war even against the satanic state.[142]

B. The faithful witnesses or martyrs. Caught in the conflict between the demonic powers and God were the faithful Christians of Asia. To them the Apocalypse had much to say. Amid the chaotic events of the end time they had assurance of triumph because they trusted in God. Although they appeared to be at the mercy of the emperor, it was only for the moment. Their suffering and even their martyrdom was their guarantee of ultimate victory. The faithful witnesses were special objects of God's concern. In the heavenly court they were gathered before the throne of God. Of them John could write:

> Therefore are they before the throne of God,
>   and serve him day and night within his
>   temple;
> and he who sits upon the throne will
>   shelter them with his presence.
> They shall hunger no more, neither thirst
>   anymore;
>   the sun shall not strike them, nor
>   any scorching heat.
> For the Lamb in the midst of the throne
>   shall be their shepherd,
>   and he will guide them to springs of
>   living water;
> and God will wipe away every tear from
>   their eyes. (7:15–17)

---

[141] During the reign of Domitian, Dio Chrysostom says that "most men believe that Nero is still alive." *Discourses,* XII, 10.

[142] Cf. Cullmann, *The State in the New Testament,* pp. 83–84.

Figure 12–4. The Colosseum, built by Vespasian and Titus as a public arena. In the later years of the empire many Christians died before the more than 50,000 spectators who could crowd into the arena. (Source: Foreign Mission Board, SBC.)

Much that he wrote them was of different character with awesome terror prevailing. These terrifying visions, however, were intended to comfort the persecuted, conveying to them a veiled message of the ultimate victory of God. In this victory they were to share. In fact they were, if faithful, to live and reign with Christ (2:4).

C. The Christ. The victory over the evil powers typified by Rome would be won by Christ. He dominates the Apocalypse; the book is his revelation. He is the slain Lamb to whom belong "power, and wealth, and wisdom, and might, and honor, and glory, and blessing" (5:12). Against him and his Church the satanic powers unloose their fury, but against their worst he stands defiant and undefeated. Their victories are only vaporous because the Christ wins the ultimate victory over the evils of life, even Roman persecution and death which the persecuted needlessly fear. Christ is "the Alpha and the Omega, the first and the last, the beginning and the end" (22:12). To the faithful he promises life and power in a restored and redeemed universe where the powers of Rome, even of Satan himself, will be no threat.

If John writes vehemently about Rome, he writes triumphantly about Christ. His bitterness against Rome is understandable, if not acceptable, and in the end the inspired scope of his hope in Christ overshadows his human hatred of Caesar.

CONCLUSION

Relations between the Church and Judaism and the Church and Rome were often strained and in both cases finally reached the breaking point. The Christian community had to oppose ideologically both Judaism and Caesarism as threats to the integrity of its own beliefs. This opposition was strong and often heated. Judaism was considered an inferior religion (cf. Hebrews) and characterized or caricatured as Pharisaic.[143] Rome was depicted as barbaric or beastly in invectives which are climaxed in the Apocalypse's cries against the harlot of Babylon. The primitive Church, however, met her opponents with ideas and character, with faith and life, not with violence. She was neither anti-semitic nor anti-Roman. It was not her nature to be so, and in the early years of her life she still remembered the dimensions of her nature.

SUGGESTED READINGS

BEARE, FRANCIS W., *The First Epistle of Peter* (Macmillan, 1958).

CULLMANN, OSCAR, *The State in the New Testament* (Westminster, 1956). Treats the relation of the Church and the Roman government.

GRANT, ROBERT M., *The Sword and the Cross* (Macmillan, 1955). Covers the relation of the Church and Roman government up to the beginning of the fourth century. Deals extensively with non-Christian sources.

HUNTER, A. M., "The First Epistle of Peter: Introduction and Exegesis," *IB*, Vol. XII.

KEPLER, THOMAS, *The Book of Revelation* (Oxford, 1957).

KIDDLE, MARTIN, *The Revelation of St. John* (Harper, 1940).

MANSON, WILLIAM, *The Epistle to the Hebrews* (Hodder and Stoughton, 1951).

NEIL, WILLIAM, *The Epistle to the Hebrews* (SCM, 1955). Short and nontechnical.

PURDY, ALEXANDER C., "The Epistle to the Hebrews," *IB*, Vol. XI.

RAMSAY, WILLIAM M., *The Letters to the Seven Churches* (Armstrong, 1905). The most complete survey of the historical setting of the Book of Revelation.

RIST, MARTIN, "The Revelation of St. John the Divine: Introduction and Exegesis," *IB*, Vol. XII.

---

[143] This largely accounts for the generally unfavorable impression of Pharisaism left by the Synoptic Gospels.

13

The Gospels: Statements of Faith in Jesus

The writers of the New Testament Gospels were creative theologians in their own right, each offering a distinctive interpretation of the tradition with which he worked. Each of their works represents the artistic use of available materials to communicate a characteristic understanding of Jesus. The Synoptic Gospels particularly, but also the Fourth Gospel, consist of four main strata: Jesus' *ipsissima verba* (the exact words of Jesus) and authentic memories of his deeds essentially and substantially uncolored by the resurrection faith of the early Church, the Church's reinterpretation of Jesus' words and deeds in the light of her Easter faith, the further reinterpretation which occurred in the arena of Jewish and Hellenistic Christian thought, and finally the editorial contribution of the evangelists themselves. In each Gospel materials from the first three strata are selected and woven together according to the fourth to present a unified interpretation of Jesus.

REDACTION CRITICISM

Source criticism and form criticism, which are discussed above in Chapter Two, are primarily concerned with the first three of these strata, ignoring the individual contributions of the evangelists. One of the youngest concerns of Gospel scholarship is the examination of the editorial or redactional work of each evangelist. Redaction criticism, as this study has come to be called, believes that the last strata, the editorial work of the evangelist, in each case gives distinction to the individual Gospels. The Gospels are not all saying the same thing with slight variations. Rather they are "documents expressing a definite, though in each case very different theology, which gives to each of them, without detriment to what they have in common, a more or less consistently and systematically developed theme, which makes it possible to recognize as their background, different communities with their particular problems and views." [1] That is to say, the Gospels are to be characterized as "Kerygma of a definite situation and task." [2] In this regard the Synoptic Gospels and the Fourth Gospel stand closer together than they might seem to at a casual reading. Both the synoptic writers and the author of John use oral and written traditions freely edited and arranged for specific kerygmatic purposes. The writers reveal "by their editing and construction, by their selection, inclusion and omission, and not least by a characteristic treatment of the traditional material, that they are by no means mere collectors and handers-on of the tradition, but are also interpreters of it." [3] If the Gospels are to be adequately understood, the efforts of redaction critics to examine the editorial characteristics of each Gospel must be considered. What was the rationale for the arrangement of the stories? By what editorial devices have they been joined together? How have sources been altered? Any complete analysis of the Gospels must take seriously these and kindred questions to understand the works as theological statements with individual independent integrities.

THE GOSPEL OF MARK

Mark is the earliest Gospel, the first narrative proclamation of Jesus as the Christ, crucified and risen. It does not, however, just transmit the original form of the Jesus tradition. Its picture of Jesus is shaped by theological concerns. The Gospel's purpose is betrayed by the arrangement of materials and by the editorial notes which the author used to combine the materials into a unified, interpretative account of Jesus. The lines along which Mark's author organized separately transmitted units of oral and written tradition [4] correspond to a kerygmatic interpretation of Jesus present in the early Church and recog-

---

[1] Günther Bornkamm, Gerhard Barth, and Heinz Joachim Held, *Tradition and Interpretation in Matthew*, p. 11.

[2] J. Schniewind, "Zur Synoptikerexegese," *Theologische Rundschau*, N. F. II (1930), p. 153, as quoted in Bornkamm, Barth, and Held, p. 12.

[3] *Ibid.*, p. 11.

[4] Some of these were quite short, containing only one story or saying. Others were already joined together because of common form or subject, *e.g.*, controversy discourses (2:9–3:25), parables (4:1–32), the passion narratives (14:1–16:8).

nizable in Acts.[5] In its preaching about Jesus the Church developed and transmitted a patterned sequence of Jesus' history. The outline of this sequence is traceable in certain summaries used in the Gospel of Mark:

> Now after John was arrested, Jesus came into Galilee, preaching the gospel of God, and saying, "The time is fulfilled, and the kingdom of God is at hand; repent, and believe in the gospel." (1:14–15)

· · ·

> And they went into Capernaum; and immediately on the sabbath he entered the synagogue and taught. And they were astonished at his teaching, for he taught them as one who had authority, and not as the scribes. (1:21–22)

· · ·

> And he went throughout all Galilee, preaching in their synagogues and casting out demons. (1:39)

· · ·

> He went out again beside the sea; and all the crowd gathered about him, and he taught them. (2:13)

· · ·

> Jesus withdrew with his disciples to the sea, and a great multitude from Galilee followed; also from Judea and Jerusalem and Idumea and from beyond the Jordan and from about Tyre and Sidon a great multitude, hearing all that he did, came to him. And he told his disciples to have a boat ready for him because of the crowd, lest they should crush him . . . (3:7–9)

· · ·

> With many such parables he spoke the word to them, as they were able to hear it; he did not speak to them without a parable, but privately to his own disciples he explained everything. (4:33–34)

· · ·

> And he called to him the twelve, and began to send them out two by two, and gave them authority over the unclean spirits. . . . So they went out and preached that men should repent. And they cast out many demons, and anointed with oil many that were sick and healed them. (6:7, 12–13)

· · ·

> The apostles returned to Jesus, and told him all that they had done and taught. (6:30)

Some scholars think they have found more extensive sources of Mark: a combination of three separate gospels, one of which goes back to Peter; a Petrine gospel expanded by sources from the Twelve; a short Mark plus three additional sources; an Aramaic Jewish Christian Gospel revised by Mark from a Gentile Christian perspective; a combination of individual papyrus pages organized into a connected book. For others and for full bibliographical information, see FBK, pp. 60–61, 63. The variety of these suggestions itself argues against its validity. No extensive sources underlie Mark. The evangelist combined small collections of separate traditions and single units of tradition into a somewhat connected narrative. So FBK, p. 63.

[5] Cf. Acts 10:37–41; 13:23–31. This is the thesis of C. H. Dodd, *New Testament Studies*, pp. 1–11.

Around this framework, which reflects the preaching of the early Christian community, Mark organized the units of material which came to him from oral and written tradition about Jesus. The discovery of this outline of Jesus' ministry does not, however, provide adequate basis for writing a life or biography of Jesus.[6] It does suggest that the early Christian community remembered or shaped some chronological framework for Jesus' life and that Mark in some sense expanded the early Church's proclamation about Jesus. Particularly, the Gospel's narratives are linked to the passion story and point forward to it. In the Marcan arrangement of materials each story about Jesus looks beyond itself to his death and resurrection which reveal its full meaning. At the same time each story is a commentary on the true character of him who was crucified, telling who he was and what he did.

Another factor creative of Mark's arrangement is the theological conception of the significance of Galilee as the place of Jesus' eschatological activity and the starting point of the Gentile mission. Even a casual examination of the Gospel reveals a geographical organization: Galilee; Galilee and surrounding areas; journey to Jerusalem; Jerusalem. This organization must be theological, as well as historical. Doubtless Jesus, whose home was in Galilee, worked there extensively. That he was never in Jerusalem before the time of his passion, however, is questionable. Mark's scheme is followed by Matthew and Luke, but the Fourth Gospel reports visits Jesus made to Jerusalem prior to the week of his passion. The Johannine position at this point seems more probable than that of the Synoptics. Apparently Mark emphasized the concentration of Jesus' ministry in and around Galilee for theological reasons. All his crucial statements about Jesus are linked with Galilee.[7] Jesus came from Galilee, he began his ministry there, won there his first disciples and followers, announced there his passion, and promised to return there as the risen one. Jerusalem, on the other

---

[6] Cf. D. E. Nineham, "The Order of Events in St. Mark's Gospel—An Examination of Dr. Dodd's Hypothesis," *Studies in the Gospels, Essays in Memory of R. H. Lightfoot,* pp. 223–239, for a critique of Dodd's thesis.

[7] Cf. W. Marxsen, *Der Evangelist Markus,* in *Forschungen zur Religion und Literature des Alten und Neuen Testaments,* LXVII (1956). Marxsen argues that Mark's Gospel is the product of Palestinian Christianity coming between A.D. 66–70 from the remnant of the Jerusalem church which had fled to Galilee and was waiting for the *parousia.* For a brief English summary of Marxsen's view, see Reginald H. Fuller, *The New Testament in Current Study,* pp. 78–79. E. Lohmeyer, *Galiläa und Jerusalem,* argues that for Mark Galilee was the land of Jesus, because Jesus continued to work there in the time of the evangelist in the preaching of Christian communities.

hand, appears as the place of Jesus' death and as the place where Jewish hardness of heart toward Jesus originated.

And the scribes who came down from Jerusalem said, "He is possessed by Beelzebub, and by the prince of demons he casts out demons." (3:22) [8]

Mark, and the other Synoptics with him, lays repeated stress upon Jewish unbelief and God's judgment upon it.[9] There is doubtless historical validity here, but the emphasis is theological. Jerusalem is the place of his rejection and death; Galilee, the place of his eschatological activity and starting point of the Gentile mission (7:24, 28, 37; 14:28). In the way he divides the story of Jesus between Galilee and Jerusalem Mark shows his belief that salvation had been rejected by nonbelieving Jews and was therefore being offered to Gentiles who would believe.[10]

Outline and Interpretation of Mark

Mark's theological expansion of the kerygma of the early Church is evident in an outline of the Gospel. The respective roles of Galilee and Jerusalem are clearly seen as Jesus dramatically moves from his mission in the north to his crucifixion at the hands of unbelieving Jews, only to be vindicated by the resurrection.

Introduction. Preaching of the Baptist, Jesus' Baptism and Temptation. 1:1–13

I. Jesus in Galilee. 1:14–6:6a
   A. The beginning of Jesus' ministry in Capernaum and the surrounding area. 1:14–45
   B. Controversy discourses. 2:1–3:35
   C. Parable discourses. 4:1–34
   D. Miracle stories. 4:35–5:43
   E. Conclusion of the Galilean ministry. 6:1–6a

II. Jesus Journeying Inside and Outside Galilee. 6:6b–9:50
   A. Sending out the Twelve. 6:7–13
   B. First journey of Jesus and his return to Galilee. 6:14–7:23
   C. Second journey and return. 7:24–8:12
   D. Third journey and return. 8:13–26
   E. Peter's confession at Caesarea Philippi and the first passion announcement. 8:27–9:1
   F. The transfiguration and related events. 9:2–29
   G. The second passion announcement. 9:30–32
   H. Discussions at Capernaum. 9:33–50

[8] See also 7:1ff.; 10:33; 11:18.
[9] 3:6; 7:6, 8; 8:31; 9:31; 10:33; 12:12.
[10] So FBK, p. 65.

III. Jesus' Journey to Jerusalem. 10:1–52
    A. Stories and events associated with the journey to Jerusalem.
       10:1–31
    B. Jesus walks ahead of fearful disciples; the third prediction of the
       passion. 10:32–34
    C. Jesus and the sons of Zebedee: misunderstanding of the passion
       announcements. 10:35–45
    D. Jesus heals the blind man of Jericho. 10:46–52

IV. Jesus in Jerusalem. 11:1–13:37
    A. The messianic entry. 11:1–11
    B. Acted parables: cursing of fig tree and cleansing of the temple.
       11:12–25
    C. Conflict stories in Jerusalem. 11:26–12:44
    D. Eschatological discourse. 12:1–37

V. Passion and Resurrection Narrative. 14:1–16:8
    A. The arrest and trial. 14:1–15:15
    B. Death, burial, and resurrection. 15:16–16:8

Clearly Mark was more than an editor; he was also a theologian and "one of the early Christian prophets with a 'word' for his church." [11] This is to say that Mark was concerned with the gospel, the good news of God's action in Jesus, and its meaning for the Church. God's deeds in Jesus Christ were for Mark the kernel of the gospel.[12]

The Authority of Jesus. God's action in the life of Jesus was seen in the "authority" of Jesus. He taught "as one who had *authority*, not as the scribes" (1:22, italics added). With authority he rejected much Jewish tradition and even challenged and reinterpreted the Torah (7:1–20; 10:7–12). He even added to the teachings of the Torah and implied that obedience to his teaching and following him surpassed allegiance to Torah in importance (10:17–22). Time, custom, and scripture-honored institutions like sabbath and temple fell under his authority (2:27–28; 11:15–18). Hence the whole cultus of Judaism was subject to reinterpretation by Jesus in whom the ultimate authority of God was present.

The Messianic Secret.[13] From its beginning the Gospel of Mark tells the true identity of the one who had such great authority. The

---

[11] Leander E. Keck, "The Introduction to Mark's Gospel," *NTS*, XII (1965–66), 369.

[12] Eduard Schweizer, "Mark's Contribution to the Quest of the Historical Jesus," *NTS*, X (1963–64), 421–422.

[13] William Wrede first used the term "messianic secret"; cf. *Der Messiasgeheimnis in den Evangelien.* For a summary in English, see A. E. J. Rawlinson, *The Gospel According to St. Mark,* pp. 258–262.

book is "the Gospel of Jesus Christ" (i.e., Jesus, the Messiah), maybe
also "the Son of God" (1:1).[14] Later at his baptism Jesus is again identified as "Son of God" (1:11). Yet many who witnessed his ministry
did not understand and even the few who believed were confused.
Jesus' real identity was known only through his death and resurrection.
Through suffering and exaltation he was revealed as Messiah. The
Gospel, therefore, must be read through to the end before the true
nature of Jesus and the significance of what he said and did can be understood. Only in and through the passion narrative is the true nature
of Jesus revealed. In it the reader perceives that beneath the tragic
story of Jesus runs an undercurrent of promise and hope. Jesus' true
identity is treated as a secret in the first half of Mark's Gospel. Up to
8:26 Jesus does not speak of the necessity of his passion and resurrection and the disciples do not comprehend who he is. The emphasis is
upon Jesus' conflict with demons and the religious and civil authorities of Galilee. The average people who gathered about Jesus were
astonished by what they saw, but could not understand the meaning
of what he said or did.[15] The Twelve also, to a large measure, did
not understand.

For Mark the turning point comes at Caesarea Philippi. In the
Great Confession the Twelve thrust upon Jesus the title of Messiah.
Of Jesus' response to the implication of that claim Mark says:

And he began to teach them that the Son of Man must suffer many things,
and be rejected by the elders and the chief priests and the scribes, and be
killed, and after three days rise again. (8:31)

The Apostles neither understand fully nor accept completely the suffering revealed to them, but Mark nonetheless, after presenting the incident at Caesarea Philippi, concentrates on answering the question about
the nature of Jesus. The second half of the Gospel is filled with Christological and soteriological material,[16] making clear the true nature of
Jesus' person and mission.

Some see all of this as the historical reality of Jesus' life.[17] They believe that Jesus, knowing the misunderstanding which would follow his
proclamation as Messiah, sought to keep it a secret from all save those

---

[14] Some ancient authorities omit the phrase "the Son of God."

[15] Cf. 1:44; 5:43; 8:12; 4:10–13.

[16] Cf. 8:27–31; 9:2ff., 12, 31, 41; 10:33–34; 11:1ff., 27ff.; 12:6ff., 35ff.;
13:26–27; and the entire passion narrative.

[17] Cf. Vincent Taylor, *The Gospel According to St. Mark*, pp. 122–124; C. E. B.
Cranfield, *The Gospel According to St. Mark*, pp. 78f., and his article in *IDB*, III,
267–277; W. D. Davies, *Invitation to the New Testament*, pp. 203–206; A. E. J.
Rawlinson, *The Gospel According to St. Mark*, pp. 258–262.

for whom he had opportunity to interpret it. He de-emphasized his miracles because he did not want to be known and followed as a wonder worker, and forbade the demons and disciples to make known his messiahship because it would activate false political hopes associated with Messiah. Jesus interpreted his mission in terms of suffering servant and did not wish to be known as Messiah before his suffering and death made its meaning clear.

Others see no historicity in the secrecy motif. They claim that it is found only in Marcan redactions (or editorial comments), not in the pre-Marcan traditions. They argue, therefore, that the secrecy motif is Mark's creation and deny that Jesus himself had any messianic consciousness.[18]

This debate continues without decisive results.[19] More important for our concern than the historicity of the messianic secret is the creative use made of it by the author of Mark.[20] The early Christian community believed and its kerygma proclaimed (Cf. Acts 2, Romans 1:4) that by virtue of his death and resurrection Jesus was Lord and Christ (Messiah). But he had always been what the resurrection had revealed him to be. This was discernible, however, only to those who have faith. Mark seeks to make this clear. Christ is known as Messiah, i.e., the true nature of his person and purpose is known only to the Church. The Church alone knows who Jesus is and they know this because they know the power of his death and resurrection.[21] What is clear to men of faith is a secret to those who do not believe.

This accounts for the major place given by Mark to the narrative of the passion and his dramatic, though brief, presentation of the resur-

---

[18] Cf. Wrede, *Der Messiasgeheimnis;* Rudolf Bultmann, *Theology of the New Testament,* I, 32.

[19] Cf. the works listed in the footnotes immediately above and recently, James M. Robinson, "The Recent Debate on the New Quest," *JBR,* XXX (1962), 198–208, and G. H. Boobiyer, "The Secrecy Motif in St. Mark's Gospel," *NTS,* VI (1959–60), 225–235.

[20] This is, of course, not unrelated to the question of its historicity. There is no common agreement about Mark's intention in his use of the messianic secret. See FBK, pp. 65–67, for a brief summary of alternative interpretations. Some of the more important ones are: (1) an attempt to reconcile the non-messianic character of Jesus with the messianic faith of the post-resurrection Church. The Gospel of Mark, however, knows nothing of a non-messianic Jesus. (2) The secret is linked with the concept of the hidden, pre-existent Son of man as portrayed in The Similitudes of Enoch and IV Ezra. (3) The secret is the inevitable consequence of combining the traditional material about Jesus with the passion-resurrection narrative. It presents a concept of revelation conceived in terms of paradox.

[21] Cf. Lewis S. Hay, "Mark's Use of the Messianic Secret," *Journal of the American Academy of Religion,* XXXV (1967), 26.

rection. In these events the true nature of Jesus is seen to faith. Indeed, when one reads about them, he recalls that Jesus had earlier spoken of himself as God's Servant Son who would suffer. In this sense he understood himself to be the Messiah. This was the nature of Jesus' messianic consciousness. When one, therefore, reads Mark through to the end, he sees what the Gospel is all about.

The Gospel of Mark as a Call to Discipleship. The Gospel of Mark begins with a summary of Jesus' ministry and the call of the first disciples (1:1–20). Those who followed Jesus did so because his call was stronger than they and overcame them.[22] The gospel is *euangelion,* "good news," because Jesus as Son of God calls men to follow him with complete and unrelenting loyalty (8:34–38). The disciples are called to share both Jesus' life and mission (1:17).

In Mark's Gospel Jesus is presented in a way that makes clear a call to share Jesus' suffering and death (Ch. 13).[23] The Pharisees accused the disciples as they accused Jesus (2:18, 24) and continued faithfulness is likely to involve disciples in the same fate as Jesus.

If any man would come after me, let him deny himself and take up his cross and follow me. For whoever would save his life will lose it; and whoever loses his life for my sake and the gospel's will save it. (8:34b–35)

The disciple cannot escape Jesus' suffering destiny revealed at Caesarea Philippi. In fact, three times in the second half of the Gospel the passion of the Son of man is predicted (8:31; 9:31; 10:32–34). Each time it is misunderstood by the disciples; yet each time Jesus calls them to follow him in his suffering. Eduard Schweizer has pointed out that the mention of Jesus and his followers going to Jerusalem, the place of his suffering (10:32), is followed by the account that a blind man whose eyes had been opened followed Jesus. In this way Mark aims to indicate metaphorically that God's work in Jesus is seen only if God opens the blind eyes of men. Only then could they follow Jesus in suffering.[24] Early in the Gospel men followed Jesus out of interest or curiosity, but in the last half, *i.e.,* after Caesarea Philippi, following involves the true disciples in suffering.[25] Merely going after Jesus is not real following. Only the disciple who follows with a devotion which

[22] Schweizer, "Mark's Contribution to the Quest of the Historical Jesus," *NTS,* X (1963–64), 424.

[23] The theme of this paragraph is drawn from Keck, "The Introduction to Mark's Gospel," *NTS,* XII (1965–66), 352–370.

[24] Schweizer, "Mark's Contribution to the Quest of the Historical Jesus," *NTS,* X (1963–64), 428.

[25] *Ibid.,* p. 429.

includes suffering understands who Jesus is and what he does. Only for such ones does the suffering and death of Jesus mean anything. Schweizer says, "This is what the so-called secret of the Messiah means. It is the hiddenness of God in Jesus, which despite all its mighty manifestations, is not seen by a blind world, is often totally misunderstood, and opens itself only to the follower who goes himself on the road of Jesus." [26] He adds, "It is Mark who depicts clearer than anyone else in the New Testament that faith always means discipleship, following Jesus." [27]

The call to follow is also a call to faithfulness. Mark apparently wrote for a martyred church (probably Rome at the time of Nero). He encouraged them to take confidence because with the teaching of Jesus the Kingdom of God had arrived. Sensitive to the conflicts facing an embattled church, Mark linked the sufferings of Jesus and the sufferings of those who followed him (2:18, 24). Perhaps the inclusion of the stories of Jesus' power over the storms (4:38–40; 6:48–50) and over the demons possessing the wild man (5:1ff.) was to offset the fears which beset the Christians at Rome persecuted by Nero. Mark 13 is particularly relevant to a persecuted church.

But take heed to yourselves; for they will deliver you up to councils; and you will be beaten in synagogues; and you will stand before governors and kings for my sake, to bear false testimony before them.

. . .

And brother will deliver up brother to death, and the father his child, and children will rise against parents and have them put to death; *and you will be hated by all for my name's sake. But he who endures to the end will be saved* (13:9, 12–13, italics added).

Mark wanted the Church to see that suffering is the inevitable corollary of following Jesus and to be faithful to the end (13:13, 37). The call in the Gospel was to share his life and death.

Authorship and Date of Mark

The Gospel of Mark nowhere reveals the identity of its author. The oldest tradition, first attested by Papias, mentions Mark, who wrote down the reports of Peter from memory, as author of the Gospel. Papias, as quoted in Eusebius, said:

Mark became Peter's interpreter and wrote accurately all that he remembered, not, indeed, in order, of the things said or done by the Lord. For he

---

[26] *Ibid.*, p. 431.
[27] *Ibid.*, p. 432.

had not heard the Lord, nor had he followed him, but later on, as I said, followed Peter, who used to give teaching as necessity demanded but not making, as it were, an arrangement of the Lord's oracles, so that Mark did nothing wrong in thus writing down single points as he remembered them. For to one thing he gave attention, to leave out nothing of what he had heard and to make no false statements on them.[28]

There is real reason to question the Gospel's direct dependence upon Peter. Since the organization and interpretation of the Jesus traditions in Mark are the product of the author's theological creativity, the book should not be interpreted as a mere recollection of facts about the life and ministry of Jesus. "Without the suggestion of Papias we would hardly have claimed Peter as authority for the material of the Markan report." [29] The association of the Gospel with Peter may be more an inference by Papias than the preservation of an established tradition.[30] Petrine background to the earliest Gospel is, therefore, questionable. On the other hand, the identification of the Gospel's author as Mark is probably correct. Some see in the Gospel some lack of familiarity with the Palestinian geography and customs and more particularly the polemic tendency to sharply reject unbelieving Jews and on these grounds question Marcan authorship. It is entirely possible, however, that a Jewish Christian living in a Gentile environment and writing for Gentile Christians was ignorant of details about Palestine and was capable of a negative attitude toward unbelieving Jews. There is, then, no convincing reason to reject the tradition of Marcan authorship.

The Mark to whom Papias refers is of course John Mark, who is mentioned often in the New Testament. The primitive Christian congregation met in the Jerusalem home of his mother. He accompanied Paul and Barnabas, his cousin, on the first missionary journey, but soon returned to Jerusalem. In dispute over this Barnabas and Paul separated. Later Mark returned to the circle of Paul, who named him as a fellow worker and commended him to the church at Colossae.[31]

Mark wrote the Gospel around A.D. 70 when the evangelical tradition was already well developed and when the Jewish war of A.D. 66–73 was imminent or in progress (cf. Mark 13). He wrote for the church at Rome with which he may have been associated, to encourage them in a time of crisis (the Neronic persecution and its aftermath) by con-

28 Eusebius, *EH*, III, xxxix, 14.
29 A. Jülicher and E. Fascher, *Einleitung in das Neuen Testament,* as quoted in FBK, p. 68.
30 F. C. Grant, "Mark," *IB*, VII, p. 630.
31 Acts 12:12, 25; 13:5, 13; 15:37ff.; Philemon 24; Col. 4:10.

fronting them with what he believed to be the meaning and implications of Jesus' life and death. This was indeed for him *the gospel*.

Postscript: the Ending of Mark. In the oldest manuscript tradition Mark did not include the report of the resurrection and ascension found in many manuscripts and versions (16:9–20).[32] The Gospel ended abruptly with the somewhat enigmatic statement:

And they went out and fled from the tomb; for trembling and astonishment had come upon them; and they said nothing to any one, for they were afraid. (16:8)

Early the feeling arose that such an abrupt and negative declaration could not have been the original ending. It was supposed that for some unexplained reason the author's conclusion had been lost and a number of attempts were made to bring the book to a proper conclusion. The most elaborate of these efforts produced the resurrection-ascension material printed in the KJV as 16:9–20. However, the manuscript evidence, as well as the content of this material, is persuasive against its genuineness. It seems preferable, therefore, to accept the abrupt ending of 16:8. The gospel Mark began proclaiming in 1:1 had reached its goal in the events of 16:7–8. For Mark fear and astonishment were appropriate reactions to the empty tomb's revelation of the true nature of Jesus.

THE GOSPEL OF LUKE

Introduction and Structure

The Gospel of Luke and Acts are both dedicated to Theophilus and belong together in language, style, and theological attitude. They are the work of one author[33] whose identity cannot be determined from data related to or in the Gospel. A late second century tradition claims that Luke the physician wrote Luke–Acts. Full confidence in this tradition is, however, impossible. Already by the end of the second century the Church presupposed that a canonical Gospel must have apostolic authority behind it. A Pauline apostolic authority for Luke was supplied by assuming that the "we" of Acts revealed its author as a companion of Paul. Probably on this basis it was inferred that Luke was the author of the Gospel. Such an analysis, however, is far too simple

---

[32] ℵ, B, k, cf. also the testimony of Eusebius and Jerome. The section on the resurrection and ascension originated in the second century, since Tatian and Irenaeus knew it. It was not attested in Greek manuscripts of the New Testament before the fifth century.

[33] The entire analysis presupposes common authorship.

and will not stand the scrutiny of critical inquiry. Even if it is assumed that Luke wrote the "we" passages in Acts, it does not necessarily follow that he was the author of either Acts or the Gospel.

The internal evidence of the Gospel is inadequate for identification of its author. The style and language establish nothing for or against a physician as author.[34] The Gospel's lack of familiarity with Pauline theology calls in question the tradition that its author was a close companion of Paul. The work seems unfamiliar with the geography of Palestine, avoids all Semitic words except *amen,* and omits traditions concerning Jesus' conflict with the Pharisaical understanding of the law. The Gospel does not have a Jewish interest. Thus, the only sure conclusion which may be drawn from the internal evidence is that the author of Luke was a Gentile Christian.

The Gospel was written between A.D. 70 and A.D. 90, after the fall of Jerusalem and before Acts, which was written around A.D. 90. No early tradition concerning the place of composition exists and for scholarly conjectures (Caesarea, Achaia, Decapolis, and Rome) no conclusive arguments can be adduced. The only certainty is that the Gospel of Luke was written outside of Palestine.

From whomever or wherever the Gospel came, Luke and its companion volume Acts represents a theology of Jesus and the early Church. The theological perspective may have been a part of early Christian tradition, but it is certainly given expression in the specific literary design of the author.[35] Luke in a real sense is the first volume in a *Heilsgeschichte* (salvation history) in which the Christ-event (his life, death, and resurrection) is seen as the act of redemption, with Acts continuing as the story of the redeemed community. The gospel events, therefore, stand in the "middle of time" [36] since they were preceded by the actions of God in and through the history of Israel and followed by God's work in the Church. The inspiration and genius of Luke's theological intent was the delay of the *parousia* and the lessening of immediate eschatological expectation. For Luke the eschatological kingdom of God had not come in the time of Jesus. The good news of the gospel was "not that the Kingdom of God has come, but

[34] Cf. H. J. Cadbury, *The Making of Luke–Acts,* pp. 219–220.

[35] Since Acts has already been examined as the framework for the study of the first generation of the Church's history and for the discussion of the Pauline epistles, attention here is largely confined to an analysis of the Gospel. Any division imposed upon Luke–Acts, however, is largely artificial. The analysis of Acts above, pp. 193–201, should be reviewed at this point.

[36] The phrase is from Hans Conzelmann, *Die Mitte der Zeit,* in English translation as *The Theology of St. Luke.*

that through the life of Jesus the hope of the coming kingdom has been established." [37] Therefore, Luke embarked upon an historical work which described both the Christ-event and the Church, its mission and its relation to the world. The Gospel, of course, is concerned with the first of these items. Its outline, since Luke draws upon Mark for his organization, does not show clearly the distinctive intention of Luke, but it does indicate the three-stage structure within which the author expresses his ideas.

Introduction. 1:1–2:52
    A. Prologue: plan and purpose of the Gospel. 1:1–4
    B. Preparation for the ministry of Jesus: the infancy and childhood narratives. 1:5–2:52

I. The Ministry in Galilee: The Call of Jesus and the Gathering of the Witnesses. 3:1–8:56
    A. The call of Jesus. 3:1–4:13
        1. The ministry of John. 3:1–20
        2. Jesus' baptism and temptation: response to call. 3:21–4:13
    B. Jesus' ministry at Nazareth and Capernaum: acceptance and rejection. 4:14–6:11
        1. Programatic sermon in Nazareth synagogue: inauguration and rejection. 4:14–30
        2. Healing ministry at Capernaum and call of first disciples. 4:31–5:16
        3. Conflict with the synagogue. 5:17–6:11
    C. Choice and training of the Twelve as witnesses. 6:12–8:56
        1. Choice of the Twelve. 6:12–16
        2. Training of the Twelve. 6:17–8:56
            a. Sermon on the Plain. 6:17–49
            b. Concern for the outcast and oppressed. 7:1–8:3
            c. Teaching in parables. 8:4–21
            d. Miracles. 8:22–56

II. End of the Galilean Ministry and the Journey to Jerusalem. 9:1–19:27
    A. End of the Galilean ministry. 9:1–17
    B. Peter's confession, the prediction of Jesus' passion, and related events. 9:18–50
    C. Journey to Jerusalem: emphasis upon the responsibility and cost of discipleship. 9:51–19:27. (This extensive section is quite miscellaneous in character and almost impossible to outline.)

III. Jesus in Jerusalem. 19:28–24:53
    A. Ministry in Jerusalem. 19:28–21:38
        1. Triumphal entry and cleansing of the temple; royal and cultic claims. 19:28–48

---

[37] Conzelmann, *The Theology of St. Luke*, p. 27.

      2. Public ministry of varied activity. 20:1–21:4
      3. Eschatological discourse. 21:5–38
   B. Passion narrative. 22:1–24:53
      1. Preparation for the Passion. 22:1–53
         a. Judas' act of betrayal. 22:1–6
         b. Preparation of disciples: The Last Supper and farewell discourse, an invitation to communion in suffering. 22:7–38
         c. Preparation of Jesus: Jesus on the Mount of Olives. 22:39–65
      2. Trial and crucifixion. 22:66–23:56
      3. Resurrection and appearances; preparation for the era of the Church. 24:1–53

Luke as an Historian

Luke is the only evangelist who prefaced his Gospel with a prologue stating his sources, methods, and purpose.[38]

Inasmuch as many have undertaken to compile a narrative of the things which have been accomplished among us, just as they were delivered to us by those who from the beginning were eyewitnesses and ministers of the word, it seemed good to me also, having followed all things closely for some time past, to write an orderly account for you, most excellent Theophilus, that you may know the truth concerning the things of which you have been informed. (1:1–4)

The prologue follows the literary conventions of the time and was intended to catch the serious attention of the literarily sophisticated. In it Luke reveals himself to be a member of the second generation of the Christian tradition. Upon the basis of first generation tradition he purposed to give a reliable representation of what had taken place, since a valid evaluation of Christianity depended upon a certain knowledge of "the things which have been accomplished among us" (1:1). His stated goal was to establish for his readers the reliability of the contents of Christian teaching by trustworthy reproduction of his sources. To accomplish this he investigated "from the beginning" and strove for complete and accurate information in order to "write an orderly account" (1:3). This does not mean, however, that in writing orderly Luke intended to give a precisely arranged biography of Jesus in the Gospel or an accurate chronicle of Church history in Acts. The nature of his sources and the way he used them precluded this. For Jesus no chronology or sequence of events was available except Mark's, which has already been shown to be largely interpretative. Since Luke presents the traditionally transmitted materials in essentially the same

---

[38] This prologue is preface to both the Gospel and the book of Acts.

sequence he found in his sources, his purpose in writing "an orderly account" could not have been to present the historical course of events more accurately than his predecessors. Luke was primarily a theologian and his work must be judged on the quality of its theological concern, not on its historical accuracy. In this sense traditional efforts to evaluate Luke as an historian [39] have been largely misdirected.

Nevertheless Luke was also historian. In contrast to Mark he calls his work about Jesus "narrative" (*diegesis*) not "gospel" (*euangelion*), and it comes closer than any of the other Gospels to being a life of Jesus.[40] Luke approached his task with a knowledge of the historical and literary methods of the Hellenistic age and a thorough familiarity with the language and content of the Greek Old Testament. His primary sources were Mark and Q, both of which were made up of independently circulating units of traditional material. To these sources he added a considerable amount of material which is unique to the third Gospel. Luke reproduced about seven-tenths of Mark's material in three great blocks and followed extensively the Marcan sequence except in the early history (Luke 1–2) and the passion narrative. Between and within the material taken from Mark he inserted traditions not derived from Mark.[41] The Lucan revision of Mark further involves the closer linking of accounts with one another, the replacement of vulgar words and expressions and the formation of better Greek sentences, the deletion of all foreign words except the Hebrew *amen*, and the removal of offences like the healing of "many" (Mark 1:34; 3:10) instead of "all" (Luke 4:40; 6:19) and the mention of emotional states of Jesus, and finally less emphasis upon the messianic secret.[42]

Luke clearly related the history of Jesus to the history of Jesus' time. The birth of Jesus in Bethlehem is connected with the reign of Herod (1:25) and the census command of Emperor Augustus under Quirinius (2:2).[43] The beginning of the Baptist's ministry is fixed on the basis of dates in both Roman and Jewish history (3:1f.). Luke says expressly, "This was not done in a corner" (Acts 26:26). Luke also seeks to demonstrate the political innocence of Jesus in the eyes of the Romans (Luke 23:4, 14, 20, 22, 47) and to show the Jews as unjust ac-

[39] Some have considered him a sound one; others, a poor one.

[40] Fuller, *The New Testament in Current Study*, p. 90.

[41] The best analysis with bibliography of this and related questions is FBK, pp. 91–102.

[42] Cf. FBK, pp. 97–98.

[43] This is not without problems since Herod died c. 4 B.C. and the Quirinian census was after A.D. 6. Attempts to clear up this apparent contradiction by postulating an earlier Roman census in Palestine have not been entirely successful.

cusers of Jesus as a political agitator (Luke 20:20, 26; 23:2, 5). Clearly the evangelist intended to relate the history of Jesus and the Church directly to the general history of their time. In this sense Luke tried to write "an orderly account."

Luke's Theological Purpose

The Gospel as Salvation History.[44] Behind Luke's particular interpretation of Christian history was a change in the understanding of the "last days." The Church had at first expected the imminent consummation of history. They believed that the eschatological kingdom of God had come with Jesus and, as a consequence, that life in the world was merely transitional. But the *parousia* of Christ and the end of history had been delayed, and eschatology as an imminent hope belonging to the present was beginning to fade. The idea that what is hoped for is near could not be reconciled with delay. History was manifestly continuing. Luke, therefore, interpreted Christian history with more emphasis upon the present (*i.e.*, the age of the Church) as the time of salvation than upon the imminent expectation of the end.

[44] The essential interpretation of Luke in terms of redaction criticism is Hans Conzelmann, *The Theology of St. Luke.* Our interpretation of the third Gospel is dependent upon Conzelmann's analysis to which the reader is referred for details. Conzelmann has perhaps overstated the case for the totally imminent nature of the Church's early eschatology and the degree of the Church's upset at the delay of the *parousia*. So FBK, pp. 100–101; Charles H. Talbert, *Luke and the Gnostics,* pp. 105–108. His analysis of Luke, however, does not turn upon the extremes of imminence or upset, but upon the significant presence of an imminent eschatology and the Church's concern about the delay of Jesus' return, which few would deny. Overall he has presented an interpretation of Luke that is both convincing and insightful. It is not, however, the only alternative. Talbert suggests that the purpose of Luke–Acts is anti-Gnostic (*Luke and the Gnostics*), F. F. Bruce that Luke–Acts is an apologetic for the intelligent Roman public (*The Acts of the Apostles*), J. C. O'Neill that Luke–Acts was written to evangelize an educated Roman public (*The Theology of Acts in its Historical Setting*), others think that the Lucan writings were intended as an apology directed to the Roman state (B. S. Easton, "The Purpose of Acts," *Early Christianity,* ed. F. C. Grant, pp. 33–118), finally John Knox interprets Luke–Acts in its present form as a product of the middle of the second century with an anti-Marcionite purpose (*Marcion and the New Testament*). Conzelmann's analysis, in our opinion, excludes only the last of these alternatives as possible concerns of the author of Luke–Acts. No author writing in the post-apostolic age could have been unaware of any of the other issues. Conzelmann is guilty of focusing almost exclusively upon the issue of changing eschatological expectations. It is an oversimplification to confine the Lucan purpose to any one of the above. This perhaps assumes a modern dissertational mentality for an ancient Christian evangelist which would have been alien to his person and culture. Luke was not writing *to prove a thesis.* He was writing as a Christian historian to place the life of Jesus and the Church in proper historical and theological perspective.

The *parousia* was no longer the urgent concern of the Church.[45] For Luke the history of Jesus, not the eschatological events, was the decisive time in the course of salvation history, and was followed by "the elongated time of the church." [46] The *parousia* was not imminent and did not decisively determine and control the present as it had for the earliest Church.

Luke dealt with the problem of the *parousia's* delay by presenting a "Christian perspective on the whole scope of history." [47] He conceived a divinely ordered salvation history in the middle of which stood the time of Jesus. For Luke there were three periods in this history:

1. The period of Israel which ended with the preaching of John the Baptist.
   "The law and the prophets were until John; since then the good news of the kingdom of God is preached, and everyone enters it violently." (Luke 16:16)
2. The period of Jesus' ministry, which Luke introduced as the fulfillment of promise.
   "And he began to say to them, 'Today this scripture has been fulfilled in your hearing.'" (Luke 4:21)
3. The period of the Church living in the tensions of the world by looking back to the time of Jesus and forward to the *parousia*.
   ". . . for we cannot but speak of what we have seen and heard" (Acts 4:20) [48]

These three epochs are preceded by the creation and will be followed and ended by the *parousia*. Salvation history was seen as co-extensive with all of history. World history and cosmic history were not distinguished from redemptive history.[49] The Christ-event occurred within and as part of secular history to which the entire Christian movement belonged and gave meaning.[50]

For Luke the Christ-event was climactic but not culminating, so the "narrative of the things which have been accomplished among us" had

---

[45] Conzelmann, *The Theology of St. Luke*, pp. 95–136, believes that Luke completely rejected the imminent expectation. Kümmel suggests, however, that the idea is not completely given up, but "has lost its urgent character." See FBK, p. 101.

[46] E. Grässer, *Das Problem der Parusieverzogerung in den synopt Evv. und in der Apg.*, Beih. ZNW, XXII (1957), 194, as quoted in FBK, p. 100.

[47] The phrase is from Kee, Young, Froehlich, *Understanding the New Testament*, p. 299.

[48] This third period is in two parts: the time of the Apostles and the time of the author.

[49] Conzelmann, *The Theology of St. Luke*, p. 17.

[50] Cf. Bultmann, *Theology*, II, p. 116.

to continue beyond the Gospel into the book of Acts. He molded his Gospel into a "history of Jesus" and in Acts he put this history "into the mouth of the apostles as the central content of their preaching of salvation." [51] Luke's decision to write Acts as a continuation of his Gospel was "a theological achievement of the first order," [52] for he saw that the period after Jesus' ascension had its own positive meaning as "the period in which ecumenical preaching showed the story of Jesus to be salvation for all mankind." [53] Salvation history found its meaning in the world mission of the Church, a universalizing demanded by the salvation offered in the "history of Jesus."

Luke's reworking of the traditional material in the light of the delay of the *parousia* was not independent of parallel developments in the thought of the Church. The concept of salvation history is not the single-handed creation of the delay of the *parousia*,[54] nor was Luke its only spokesman in the early Church. The gospel tradition which Luke received had already solved the problem of the delayed *parousia* by concentrating in Jesus and by affirming that his followers participate in salvation now, not merely anticipate it.[55]

Christology. Luke's concern for salvation history influenced his thought and expression about Christology. For Luke the life of Jesus is a fact of history, the center of salvation history, and his Gospel unfolds the ministry of Jesus in three stages each with a corresponding Christological emphasis.[56]

1. THE CALL OF JESUS AND THE GATHERING OF THE WITNESSES (3:1–9:50). This section opens with the baptismal proclamation of Jesus as the Son of God, who is "anointed" by the Spirit of God (3:22). The story of Jesus' preaching in the synagogue at Nazareth follows immediately. Luke gives prominence to the Nazareth preaching by shifting it from its obscure place in Mark and rewriting the event to present his interpretation of Jesus as one who brings salvation now, *i.e.*, in the time of Jesus' own life.[57] Jesus' work is seen as the work of God, pro-

51 Ulrich Wilckens, "Interpreting Luke–Acts in a Period of Existentialist Theology," *Studies in Luke–Acts*, eds. Keck and Martyn, p. 64.
52 *Ibid.*
53 *Ibid.*
54 See Grässer, p. 224, as quoted by Wilckens, p. 80, n. 40.
55 Wilckens, p. 67.
56 This framework has been incorporated into the outline of the Gospel given above.
57 In describing Jesus' preaching at Nazareth Luke has deliberately understood that the announcement of scriptures' fulfillment (4:18–19) belongs to the time of Jesus, not to the eschatological future, *i.e.*, it belongs to the past about which he writes. It continues in the present in the life and preaching of the Church.

claiming good news to the poor, deliverance for captives, sight for the blind, freedom for the oppressed. To sum it all up, it is the proclamation of the "acceptable year of the Lord," bringing fulfillment and salvation *today* (4:18–19). This emphasis upon Jesus as God's servant who does good is connected by Luke with Jesus' rejection by the Jewish leaders and prepares the readers for the later unjust suffering and martyrdom of the innocent Jesus.

In at least one place in his presentation of the Galilean ministry the evangelist foreshadows in the life of Jesus the later ministry of the Church.[58]

After he had ended all his sayings in the hearing of the people he entered Capernaum. Now a centurion had a slave who was dear to him, who was sick and at the point of death. When he heard of Jesus, he sent to him elders of the Jews, asking him to come and heal his slave. And when they came to Jesus, they besought him earnestly, saying, "He is worthy to have you do this for him, for he loves our nation, and he built us our synagogue." And Jesus went with them. When he was not far from the house, the centurion sent friends to him, saying to him, "Lord, do not trouble yourself, for I am not worthy to have you come under my roof; therefore I did not presume to come to you. But say the word, and let my servant be healed. For I am a man set under authority, with soldiers under me: and I say to one, 'Go,' and he goes; and to another, 'Come,' and he comes; and to my slave, 'Do this,' and he does it." When Jesus heard this he marveled at him, and turned and said to the multitude that followed him, "I tell you, not even in Israel have I found such faith." And when those who had been sent returned to the house, they found the slave well. (Luke 7:1–10)

Jesus' favorable attitude toward the centurion and his faith is like that of the later Church toward believing Gentiles. This story illustrates "the evangelists' concern to ground the ministry of Christians in the ministry of their Lord." [59]

The calling of disciples as witnesses to all that Jesus did in Galilee is also prominent in the Lucan account of the Galilean ministry. These men who followed Jesus and learned from him after his death became witnesses of his life and teaching. One of the speeches in Acts attributed to Paul says of them, "Those who came up with him from Galilee . . . are now his witnesses to the people" (Acts 13:31). Thus Luke tied the time of Jesus with the time of the Church, which is the continuity of Jesus' life and ministry under the Spirit and through the testimony of the witnesses.

[58] Cf. Charles H. Talbert, "The Lucan Presentation of Jesus' Ministry in Galilee," *Review and Expositor*, LXIV (1967), 491–492.
[59] *Ibid.*, p. 492.

2. THE JOURNEY TO JERUSALEM (9:51–19:27). Luke's second phase of Jesus' ministry is characterized by the complex of events formed by Peter's confession, the prediction of the passion, and the transfiguration followed by a journey to Jerusalem. It comprises almost one third of Luke's Gospel and includes much material found nowhere else. No progress, either geographically or chronologically, can be traced in this section. The journey is a framework created by the author to accommodate additional material from his tradition and to express his interpretation of Jesus' suffering. The journey is not so much a journey to Jerusalem as it is a journey toward Jesus' passion. He goes to suffer according to God's will. In the meantime he prepares his disciples for their mission of preaching after his death.[60] The account of the confession, the prediction of the passion, and the transfiguration are all intended to convey to the disciples the necessity of messianic suffering.[61] It also serves to impress upon them the cost of discipleship. One who desires to be Jesus' disciple is advised to consider the cost (9:57–62). Jesus himself was "homeless" in the world and likewise his followers will be separated from ordinary relationships. Even primary duties, like burial of father and claims of family (14:25–33), had to be subordinated to the claims of the kingdom. Jesus, with face set toward Jerusalem in commitment which would cost his life, required no less from those who followed him.

3. THE PASSION NARRATIVE (19:28–24:53). Luke's concern with Jesus' suffering is climaxed with his account of the passion. The time of the passion opens with the "triumphal entry," used by Luke to place Jesus' royal title in the foreground. Luke's Jesus is king, entering Jerusalem in triumph. However, lest his readers misinterpret the nature of Jesus' kingship, Luke in the account of the Supper and the crucifixion describes the sense in which Jesus is king. The goal of the ministry of Jesus is kingship, but "the way to glory leads on to the Passion." [61a] Jesus' kingship is that of a suffering servant who is radically obedient to the will of God. This section closes with the account of the resurrection, the great deed of God to transform suffering and death into exaltation.[62] Luke describes the resurrected Jesus as summoning

---

[60] FBK, p. 99. Kümmel gives a number of more specific interpretations of the "travel" narrative all of which he implies are too restrictive.

[61] Conzelmann, *The Theology of St. Luke,* pp. 197–198, argues that in Mark *messiahship* is misunderstood by the disciples while in Luke it is the misunderstanding of *the relation of suffering to messiahship.*

[61a] *Ibid.,* p. 199.

[62] Cf. James L. Blevins, "The Passion Narrative," *Review and Expositor,* LXIV (1967), 513–522.

disciples to follow in the way of suffering (24:44–49), thus preparing his readers for the story of the Church.[63]

Christian Salvation and Life: The Nature and Mission of the Church. Luke's theology of the Church is expressed more fully in Acts than in the Gospel, but in the Gospel some ideas to be developed more fully in Acts stand out clearly. Primary in Luke's ideas of the Church is the role of the Spirit. The Church, like its Lord, is a community commissioned and empowered by the Spirit. The same sense of the presence of God which Jesus had (Luke 3:22) is the possession of the Church (Acts 2:1–4), not as the eschatological gift at the end of history, but as her enabling strength for an indefinitely continuing life in the world.

Luke more than any other evangelist envisioned the universal nature of the Church. The community created and sustained by the Spirit *has a mission to the whole world.* Luke makes this point throughout the Gospel and it is, of course, fundamental to the structure of Acts. His universalist concern appears in the speech composed for Simeon, who recognized in the infant Jesus man's hope for redemption:

> Lord, now lettest thy servant depart in peace,
>   according to thy word;
> for mine eyes have seen thy salvation
>   which thou hast prepared in the presence of all peoples,
> a light for revelation to the Gentiles,
>   and for glory to thy people Israel. (2:29–32)

and in phrases like "and on earth peace among men" (2:14) from the angels' song and "all flesh shall see the salvation of God" (3:6) from the extended quotation of Isaiah 40 in the speech of John the Baptist. Further, Luke's emphasis upon Jesus' concern for outcasts and the poor illustrates that none are excluded from the Church's mission. In

---

[63] Luke recognized continuity of person between the "Jesus of history" described in the Gospel and the post-resurrection Christ of faith. He does not, however, interpret them in the same way. In the Gospel the title "Lord" (*kurios*) is with rare exceptions confined, as uttered by men, to passages in which the narrator alludes to Jesus. That is, they are redactional, not historical. It is otherwise in Acts. A similar, though not identical, distinction can be discerned in the use made in Luke and Acts of the concepts of Jesus as prophet, Son of man, Savior, and Son. This is to say that the consciousness of the resurrection marked a decisive vindication of Jesus and was the point of departure for a new interpretation. (On all of this see C. F. D. Moule, "The Christology of Acts," *Studies in Luke–Acts,* pp. 159–185.) Only after the resurrection was Jesus understood in the fullest sense as Lord, Savior, and Son of God.

Jesus the divine love for those rejected by men had actually become salvation in the present. Sinners, Samaritans, the poor, and all who are despised are seen by Luke to be objects of God's love expressed through Jesus.[64] Notice particularly the three parables: the Lost Sheep, the Lost Coin, and the Lost Son (15:1–32).

Luke is also concerned that the life of the Church be rooted in discipleship. His realization that the age of the Church is an extended time, not just the eschatological interim, created for him a unique sensitivity to the Church's life in the world. Neither the life of Jesus nor the life of the primitive Christian community are presented as ideals to be copied. Luke's Christian ethic is not an *imitatio Christi*. Jesus is, of course, an example, but to be followed by discipleship in a form appropriate to the particular time, not imitation.[65] Neither can the continuing community imitate the early community, since the structure and practice of the earliest community was uniquely related to that community's own ties with history. The continuity between the primitive community and the continuing community is found in the relation of both to the time of Jesus, and behind that the hope of Israel, and in the continuing community's responsibility to be witness in its day to the saving event of Jesus Christ. The continuity, then, is of discipleship not imitation.

Finally the Church in continuing history had to live in and with the empire. Luke wrote with the politically motivated apologetic purpose of recommending Christianity to the Romans. He sought to show that the Church was not a community in rebellion, but one in reasoned obedience. To Caesar it renders what is Caesar's, to God it renders what is God's (20:25). This political apologetic is more obvious in Acts, but is present in the Gospel, where Luke seeks to make it clear that Jesus' messianic program was non-political (4:18–19), that his entry into Jerusalem was not a claim for power (he entered the temple, not the city), and that Jesus was innocent of crimes against Rome.[66] Worthy of special notice are Pilate's repeated comments about Jesus' innocence and the centurion's protest, "Certainly this man was innocent" (23:47; cf. 23:13–15, 22). Luke at his moment in history saw no real conflict between God and Caesar.

---

[64] Cf. 5:1ff.; 7:36ff.; 15:1ff. for sinners; 10:39ff.; 17:11ff. for Samaritans; 7:12, 15; 10:38ff. for women; and 12:15ff.; 6:20ff. for the poor.

[65] Conzelmann, *The Theology of St. Luke*, p. 233.

[66] Cf. 23:8; 13:13–34, where Jesus' coming death is represented as that of a prophet and, therefore, non-political.

THE GOSPEL OF MATTHEW

"No other Gospel is so shaped by the thought of the church as Matthew, so constructed for use by the church." [67] The Gospel's importance in the esteem of the early Church explains its place at the head of the list of New Testament books, indefensible on basis of primacy of origin. Matthew's [68] Gospel is a masterful transformation and supplementation of Mark, using a collection of the sayings of Jesus (Q) and additional traditions, which he has arranged and presented to suit his own theological and polemical aims. He is interested to prove that Jesus is "the Christ, the Son of the Living God" (16:16), who will "save his people from their sins" (1:21) and to show that this salvation is obtained as a member of that assembly of people (*ekklesia*, church) which produces its fruits (21:43).[69]

Place and Time of Composition and Authorship

The Gospel of Matthew was written for Greek speaking Christians, most of whom were of Jewish origin. Most scholars think that Matthew was written in Antioch, or somewhere in Syria.[70] That the oldest witness for knowledge of the First Gospel is Ignatius, who was bishop of Antioch, supports this position. Since the Gospel is dependent upon Mark, it must have been written after A.D. 70. The reference to Jerusalem's destruction which is added to the parable of the marriage feast also points to an origin after 70: "The king was angry, and he sent his troops and destroyed those murderers and burned their city" (22:7). Clear evidence in Matthew of development in the ecclesiastical and theological situation rules out a date shortly after Mark and points toward the time between A.D. 80 and 100, perhaps between 85–90.

The Gospel makes no identification of its author. The oldest witness is the testimony of Papias: "Matthew collected the oracles in the Hebrew language, and each interpreted them as best he could." [71] Some have tenaciously argued for the reliability of this report. Since Matthew's dependence upon Mark excludes the apostle's authorship of the Gospel as such, the Papias report is interpreted to mean that the

---

[67] Günther Bornkamm, "End Expectation and Church in Matthew," *Tradition and Interpretation in Matthew*, p. 38.

[68] For convenience we use the traditional name for the author.

[69] FBK, p. 83.

[70] Cf. B. H. Streeter, *The Four Gospels*, pp. 500–523.

[71] As quoted in Eusebius, *EH*, III, xxxix, 16.

apostle wrote at least a chief source of the Gospel. T. W. Manson [72] suggests that Matthew the apostle was author of Q. However, there is no evidence of the existence of any significant portion of the Gospel in the Hebrew language or of its association in any way with the apostle. The most that can be said with certainty about the author of Matthew is that he was "a Greek-speaking Jewish Christian, who possibly had rabbinic knowledge." [73]

The Structure of the Gospel

Two things are clear about the structure of the Gospel of Matthew. The Marcan framework is the basis of its expanded presentation, and catechetical and liturgical features are more characteristic than historical or theological ones. While the Marcan materials were suitable for Matthew's purpose, they were enriched by adding massive blocks of didactic materials to achieve Matthew's distinctive contribution. Five distinct discourses are present in Matthew, each concluding with the formula, "and when Jesus finished" (7:28; 11:1; 13:53; 19:1; 26:1). Each discourse is immediately preceded by a narrative section (taken largely from Mark) reflecting the theme of the discourse with which it is climaxed. The following outline emphasizes this fivefold division of the Gospel.[74]

Prologue: The Infancy Narratives. Chapters 1–2.

Part I: The Conduct of the Church. 3:1–7:29
  A. Narrative material: the establishment of the Kingdom of Heaven. 3:1–4:25
    1. John's ministry in preparation for the Kingdom. 3:1–12
    2. The inauguration of Jesus' ministry: baptism and temptation. 3:13–4:11
    3. Jesus' ministry in Galilee. 4:12–25
  B. Discourse: The Sermon on the Mount. 5:1–7:29

Part II: The Mission of the Church. 8:1–11:1
  A. Narrative material: mighty works of the Kingdom. 8:1–9:34
    1. Three healings and a lesson on discipleship. 8:1–22
    2. Miracles of power and a lesson on discipleship. 8:23–9:17
    3. Other miracles. 9:18–34
  B. Discourse on mission and martyrdom. 9:35–11:1

---

[72] "The Gospel According to St. Matthew," *Studies in the Gospels and Epistles,* ed. Matthew Black, pp. 68–104.

[73] FBK, p. 85.

[74] This outline is based in part upon Stendahl, *The School of St. Matthew,* p. 25, and William E. Hull, "A Teaching Outline of the Gospel of Matthew," *Review and Expositor,* LIX (1962), 436–444.

Part III: Christ and the Kingdom of Heaven. 11:2–13:52
  A. Narrative and debate material. 11:2–12:50
    1. Responses to Jesus' ministry. 11:2–30
    2. Controversy debates. 12:1–50
  B. Discourse: parables of the Kingdom. 13:1–52
Part IV: The Community of the Church. 13:53–18:35
  A. Narrative and debate material: the founding of the Church. 13:53–17:21
    1. Rejections and retreats with the disciples. 13:53–16:12
    2. Revelation at Caesarea Philippi. 16:13–17:21
  B. Discourse on life in the Christian community. 17:22–18:35
Part V: Eschatology for the Church. 19:1–26:2
  A. Narrative and debate material: Jesus goes to Jerusalem. 19:1–23:39
    1. The journey to Jerusalem. 19:1–20:34
    2. Events in Jerusalem. 21:1–23:39
  B. Eschatological discourse. 24:1–26:2
Epilogue: The Passion Narratives. 26:3–28:20

Thus the book falls into five distinct narrative-discourse divisions preceded by a prologue (Chs. 1–2) and concluded with an epilogue (26:3–28:20).[75] This structure of the five parts in Matthew is an impressive example of the combination of *kerygma* and *didache* which are consistent features of the theology of the early Church.[76] It has been suggested that for catechetical and liturgical purposes the Matthean pairs correspond to the five books of the Torah to demonstrate that the Law of Christ fulfills the Law of Moses.[77]

But whether or not the evangelist intended the comparison of his work with Torah, he clearly addressed his Gospel to the needs of a specific congregation as a "churchbook." The *Sitz im Leben* (life situation) of the material has been shifted from the ministry of Jesus to

[75] The five-discourse approach to Matthew was first proposed by B. W. Bacon, *Studies in Matthew*, pp. xiv–xvii, 80–82, 265–335. This analysis is not without problems: (1) It leaves Ch. 23 out of consideration. Stendahl, *The School of St. Matthew*, pp. 25–26, suggests, however, that "the speech in Ch. 23 is rather an enlarged edition of debate material, considered as preparatory to the concluding discourse of the fifth part of the gospel." (2) It is not certain that chs. 1–2 are prologue and 26–28 epilogue. (3) There is no indication in the Gospel that the concluding formula is more than a standardized way of ending a speech. (4) The Gospel makes no suggestion that the narratives and discourses are supposed to be paired.

[76] Cf. C. H. Dodd, *Gospel and Law*, pp. 10–12.

[77] Bacon, *Studies in Matthew;* Edward P. Blair, *Jesus in the Gospel of Matthew*, pp. 124–136; and Howard M. Teeple, *The Mosaic Eschatological Prophet*, pp. 74–83, discuss the thesis that Matthew presented Jesus as a new Moses.

the life and work of the early Church.[78] Narratives about Jesus and his teachings are presented, not merely with a historian's interest in the past, but as instructive for the life and mission of the community of faith which continues Jesus' work in the generations following his death and resurrection. In this sense the Gospel of Matthew is a vivid portrayal of how the Church initially conceived its own mission as the continuity of God's work in Christ and its responsibility to instruct believers in that task.

Matthew as a Catechetical Book

It has been suggested that the Gospel of Matthew was written "to supply, from the treasure of the past, material for the homiletical and liturgical use of the Gospel in the future." [79] However, outside liturgical emphases present in the Sermon on the Mount,[80] Matthew is no more oriented toward worship than the other Gospels. A more convincing theory is that the First Gospel was written in and for a school for teachers and leaders as a manual of Church instruction and administration with the needs of a specific congregation in mind.[81] It is similar in a number of ways to the *Manual of Discipline* (the rules for order and instruction among the Essenes at Qumran) and to the *Didache*.[82] Yet only a part of the material in the Gospel fits easily into such a catechetical context and it may be that Matthew's exact *Sitz im Leben* has not yet been found.[83] Nevertheless, its systematic arrangement, adaptation of teaching to specific problems of a community, and concern for the position and responsibilities of leading disciples favor its didactic background. We must confess, however, that the exact purpose to which such a manual was put escapes us. Much in it is not suited for pre-baptismal instruction [84] and the entire book is more comprehensive in its concerns than a manual of discipline and Chris-

[78] Hence the headings in our outline deal with the Church rather than moments in Jesus' life.

[79] G. D. Kilpatrick, *The Origins of the Gospel According to St. Matthew,* p. 99.

[80] Compare the Lord's Prayer in Matthew to the Lucan version; also the Beatitudes.

[81] Stendahl, *The School of St. Matthew.*

[82] Stendahl, *ibid.,* p. 27, finds counterparts in the *Manual of Discipline* to parts one, three, and four of Matthew and in the *Didache* to parts one, four, and five.

[83] So W. Trilling, *Das wahre Israel: Studien zur Theologie des Matthäus,* p. 197, as cited in FBK, p. 83.

[84] It is uncertain that early Christian instruction was to any extent pre-baptismal. Cf. Stendahl, *The School of St. Matthew,* p. 22.

tian behavior.[85] Probably the Gospel was intended to be a handbook
of general Christian instruction for use in a variety of circumstances
which demanded that believers possess a thoroughgoing rationale for
their relationship to Christ and his Church.

The Theology of the Gospel

Two theological themes dominate the Gospel of Matthew. The first
is Christology and the second is ecclesiology and discipleship.[86] Each
theme is presented to show the relevance of its content to the catechetical, liturgical, and missionary needs of the Church. Matthew like
Luke has an interest in the Church as a continuing community of faith
and discipleship. What had been proclaimed expectantly and anxiously in the supposedly short interim before Jesus' return and the consummation of history was now interpreted and applied in light of an
extended Christian life in the world. This may not have been a completely conscious intention of the writer of Matthew. Probably he inevitably reflects the mood in an active second and third generation
Christian congregation living in an antagonistic world and culture.
He wrote about Jesus and the Church in a full confidence shared by
the congregation that the alienated world could be redeemed.

Christology.   Jesus is presented in Matthew as the "lowly king" of
Zechariah 9:9 (21:1–17) whose coming fulfilled all Israel's messianic
expectations. This "lowly king" suffers and dies, but by the exaltation
of his resurrection promises those who follow him eschatological fulfillment in the kingdom of heaven.[87] Matthew is particularly concerned
to show that the action of God in Jesus was the unfolding of a divine
plan clearly discernible in the Torah and the Prophets.

1. FULFILLMENT OF PROPHECY. More than the other evangelists
Matthew seeks to establish faith in Christ by the authority of the
Hebrew scriptures. From them he offers proof that Jesus was the
anticipated Messiah and King of Israel. He "authenticates" from scripture all the messianic titles given Jesus, even those which originated,

---

[85] Against E. von Dobschutz, "Matthäus als Rabbi und Katechet," ZNW, XXVII
(1928), 338–348.

[86] Bornkamm, "End-Expectation and Church in Matthew," *Tradition and Interpretation in Matthew*, pp. 15–51. Cf. Gerhard Barth, "Matthew's Understanding of the Law," and Heinz Joachim Held, "Matthew as Interpreter of the Miracle
Stories," in the same volume.

[87] Matthew's equivalent for the term "kingdom of God" as used in the other
Synoptics.

not in Jewish, but in Christian tradition. Jesus was the Son of David, the King of Israel, the fulfiller of the Immanuel-Bethlehem-Galilee prophecies (Isaiah 7:14; 9:1ff.; Micah 5:2). He was the Suffering Servant of Isaiah and the Psalms (Isaiah 53, Psalms 22, 40), the Lowly King (Zechariah 9:9), and the Son of man (Daniel 7:13; II Esdras 13). In proving the scriptural authenticity of these titles Matthew used the Hebrew scriptures with a freedom that seems strained. For example, he quotes Hosea 11:1 as a prediction of the return of the infant Jesus from temporary Egyptian exile, when in original context the phrase "Out of Egypt have I called my son" is an historical reference to the exodus from Egypt of the Israelite people. Nevertheless, his use of scripture must not have been too different from the accepted canons of his day [88] when it was assumed that the interpreters of scripture could see hidden even in obscure places clues to the actions and purposes of God in their own historical circumstances.

Matthew's extensive use of scriptural quotations [89] in relation to events in the life of Jesus drew upon an already established usage of Hebrew tradition. This tradition may have come from a Christian school using exegetical methods similar to those of the Dead Sea community, or from Jews or Christians who used collections of scriptural texts in messianic interpretation, or perhaps from the use of scriptural texts in the missionary activities of the early Church.[90] By applying the quotations to the life of Jesus Matthew sought to strengthen his congregation's understanding of Jesus as the Christ (Messiah) for controversy with and evangelization of contemporary Judaism (10:17).

However, in Matthew Jesus is not just the simple fulfillment of Jewish messianic expectations. He is also the Jesus who lives in history and who is the eschatological judge over history. In the Gospel there is tension between the humility of Jesus' earthly life and the exaltation of his eschatological return. The kingdom of God in which Jesus is "the world-judge of all nations (25:31) is in the future." [91] But the Jesus of history functions already as Messiah as the giver and interpreter of law.

---

[88] Cf. the methods of the Dead Sea community's Habakkuk commentary and early rabbinical forms of exegesis.

[89] Especially those which are introduced by the formula, "This was to fulfill what the Lord had spoken by the prophet." With variations, 1:23; 2:5, 15, 17, 23; 4:14; 8:17; 12:17; 13:34; 21:4; 27:9.

[90] Bertil Gärtner, "The Habakkuk Commentary (DSH) and the Gospel of Matthew," *Studia Theologica*, VIII (1954), 1–24.

[91] Bornkamm, "End-Expectation and Church in Matthew," *Tradition and Interpretation in Matthew*, p. 34.

2. FULFILLMENT OF LAW.   The model used by Matthew to describe Jesus' earthly function as Messiah is Moses.[92]   This typology dominates the infancy narratives, the mountain of the Sermon on the Mount may be intended as an analogy to Sinai, and the history and teaching of Jesus are presented as fulfilling of the law (5:17).   Jesus is a giver and interpreter of law.   In fact he is the true interpreter who gives law its full and complete meaning.   This is clearly the intent of Matthew's quotation of Jesus in 5:17–18:

Think not that I have come to abolish the law and the prophets; I have come not to abolish them but to fulfil them.   For truly, I say to you, till heaven and earth pass away, not an iota, not a dot, will pass from the law until all is accomplished.

Luke interprets this saying (16:17) as an ironical mocking of Pharisaic legalism.   In Matthew, however, it is not ironical, but expresses the notion that Israel's sin was their failure to obey the law and to expect its complete fulfillment in Jesus.   The saying which follows in Matthew is absent in Luke:

Whoever then relaxes one of the least of these commandments and teaches men so, shall be called least in the kingdom of heaven; but he who does them and teaches them shall be called great in the kingdom of heaven.   For I tell you, unless your righteousness exceeds that of the scribes and Pharisees, you will never enter the kingdom of heaven.   (5:19–20)

Clearly, Matthew emphasizes the centrality of the law and the imperative of obedience, radical obedience motivated by love.

Matthew, however, was not a legalist.   He believed in the validity of the law as newly and radically interpreted by the love-commandment:

You shall love the Lord your God with all your heart, and with all your soul, and with all your mind.   This is the first and great commandment.   And a second is like it, You shall love your neighbor as yourself.   On these two commandments depend all the law and the prophets.   (22:37–40)

The love-commandment is then the foundation for the entire religious and moral tradition of Judaism, perhaps for the cultic tradition as well. "The law and the prophets" must be interpreted according to the love principle.   Of course Matthew here is ruled by the sayings of Jesus and the tradition of the Church, but his editorial interpretation stresses the love-commandment.   Thus, Matthew sees Jesus as giving new dimension and meaning to the law.   Because Jesus has revealed God pri-

---

[92] See especially B. W. Bacon, *Studies in Matthew.*

marily to be merciful, gracious, and loving (9:13; 12:7), man's conduct under law is to be determined by the love-commandment. God's love expressed in Jesus must motivate the Christian to show love.[93]

The First Evangelist gives added stress to the radical obedience demanded by Jesus by the way he presents certain teachings of Jesus. Immediately following the passage on the permanence and importance of the law, he presents a series of teachings illustrating the comprehensive character of Jesus' interpretation of the law. Each illustration is introduced by the formula, "You have heard that it was said, . . . but I say to you." One example will suffice to demonstrate the character of these sayings:

You have heard that it was said to men of old, "You shall not kill; and whoever kills shall be liable to judgment." But I say to you that every one who is angry with his brother shall be liable to judgment; whoever insults his brother shall be liable to the council, and whoever says, "You fool!" shall be liable to the hell of fire. (5:21–22)

Matthew's point is not that Jesus aims to supplant one law with another one, but that the existing law has broader implication and more stringent demand than is immediately obvious. Anger, the lustful look, the "legal" divorce of wife, love of neighbor which leaves room for hatred of enemy are contrary to the will of God. These too are "illegal" even if not an explicit breach of the stated law. Thus Jesus' ethic demands that the believer "break through a law which has been perverted into formal legal statements under cover of which the disobedient heart fondly imagines that all is well, and at the same time to urge the original radical will of God with its call to perfection." [94]

Ecclesiology and Discipleship. The second theological theme which dominates Matthew is ecclesiology and discipleship. The Gospel is a churchbook. Here alone in the Gospels the Christian congregation is called "church" (ekklesia, 16:18; 18:17) and throughout there is concern for the ministry of discipleship. The major reference is in Jesus' reply to the messianic confession of Peter at Caesarea Philippi:

Blessed are you, Simon Bar-Jona! For flesh and blood has not revealed this to you, but my Father who is in heaven. And I tell you, you are Peter, and on this rock I will build my church, and the powers of death shall not prevail against it. I will give you the keys of the kingdom of heaven, and whatever

[93] Barth, "Matthew's Understanding of the Law," *Tradition and Interpretation in Matthew*, p. 85.

[94] Bornkamm, "End-Expectation and Church in Matthew," *Tradition and Interpretation in Matthew*, p. 25. Cf. Matt. 5:48.

you bind on earth shall be bound in heaven, and whatever you loose on earth shall be loosed in heaven. (16:17–20)

This saying, whether originating with Jesus or the Church, is used by Matthew to relate the mission of the Church to the sufferings of Jesus. Its context emphasizes Jesus' suffering at Jerusalem and includes the charge that believers follow him in suffering.

If any man would come after me, let him deny himself and take up his cross and follow me. (16:24)

Decisions made by the Church are placed under the standard of "imitation in suffering and life devotion." [95] The Church is derived from the suffering and risen Christ, who calls his disciples to come after him and die.

Particularly in this Gospel the suffering Church stands in continuity with the Old Testament people of God. Matthew's use of the word *ekklesia* reflects the Old Testament idea of the *kahal* or assembly of God's people, the congregation of those whom God has called. Jesus' ministry and the life and work of his followers are set within the context of Judaism. Jesus is the messianic king of Israel; he relates to his followers as teacher (*didaskalos*) to disciples (*mathetai*), a common relationship in Judaism; Jesus himself ministered to Jews, only at urgent request to Gentiles. On the other hand, Matthew makes it clear that he is not writing for an exclusively Jewish audience. Gentile magi journey from the East to adore the child king; Jesus' teacher-disciple relationship to his followers is unique, his disciples become witnesses to one who is no longer teacher but Lord (*kurios*). Indeed, Jesus' ministry and message themselves are understood by Matthew to be a reinterpretation or fulfillment of Judaism. Matthew's Church, therefore, is a Church of Jews and believing Gentiles with a mission to the world:

Go therefore and make disciples of all nations, baptizing them in the name of the Father and of the Son and of the Holy Spirit. (28:19)

For Matthew the Church is led by disciples who like Peter confess that Jesus is the Christ and who learn, as Peter did, to share Jesus' suffering. Jesus chose the Twelve and gave them special responsibility (10:2–4) for a mission during his ministry and for the future. They were given special knowledge of his teachings about the Kingdom of God (13:11). Peter is given special prominence among them. In all three Synoptic Gospels he is pictured as the most dynamic of the

[95] *Ibid.*, p. 48.

Twelve, but in Matthew he is reported to have been given a unique place in the life of the Church (Luke confirms this in 22:32). Peter's role in the crisis years of the early Church supports this report. It may even be its basis, although there is no real reason to doubt that Jesus singled him out for leadership. Peter, however, had no privileges not extended to all the disciples and was not the founder of a hierarchy.

In the Church the Kingdom of God is already present, even if not fulfilled. It began in the work of Jesus and in its initial stage is present in the community of Jesus' disciples. In time the rule of God over the lives of the suffering community would give way to his reign over all men. To this end the Church dedicated its mission. Its prayer was "Thy kingdom come" and its task was to evangelize and teach "in order to bring men to faith and train them in obedience to God's will . . . In that active work he (Matthew) took his place, and to further that work he wrote his Gospel." [96]

THE GOSPEL OF JOHN

The "Milieu" of the Fourth Gospel

The Gospel of John draws upon various materials and backgrounds to weave an interpretation of Jesus which calls for skilled and imaginative study. Clement of Alexandria called it a "spiritual gospel." The Fourth Gospel contains a depth of theological perspective which is unique in many ways and the Fourth Evangelist is one of the most exciting thinkers in the early Church. How may the unusual characteristics of his outlook and insight be explained?

Relation to the Synoptic Tradition. The thought of the Gospel of John is dissimilar to that of the Synoptic tradition. Clearly this Gospel reflects influences and concerns beyond those streams of tradition which flow together in the Synoptics. Although each of the Synoptic Gospels has distinctive purposes and ideas which give it an integrity of its own, Mark, Luke, and Matthew are more alike than they are different. Compared to them, the Fourth Gospel is in a category by itself. Its order and arrangement of material is quite different, and, most striking of all, the Johannine Jesus speaks in a completely different language from that of the Synoptics. This language is characterized by opposites: light and darkness, falsehood and truth, above and below,

[96] Floyd V. Filson, *A Commentary on the Gospel According to St. Matthew,* p. 44.

father and son. It includes the "I am" sayings of Jesus and concepts like water of life, bread of life, and light of the world, none of which appear in the other Gospels. Throughout John's presentation of Jesus "the majestic timelessness of divinity stands forth more clearly." [97]

Nevertheless, the Fourth Gospel, in spite of these obvious differences, is enough like the other canonical Gospels to cause some scholars to trace its dependence to one or another of them.[98] John's Gospel shares with the Synoptics information about John the Baptist (1:19, 23, 32), the cleansing of the temple (2:13–22), the healing of the royal official's son (4:46–54), the multiplication of the loaves (chapter 6), the anointing of Jesus (12:1–8), the entry into Jerusalem (12:12–15), the general framework of the Passion tradition, and many isolated sayings of Jesus. Some believe that the author of the Fourth Gospel knew Mark and Luke and used them from memory. Such dependence cannot be established, however.[99] The information which John has in common with the Synoptics may have come from an independent tradition about Jesus which was similar to the sources underlying the Synoptics. Any material known to him from the Synoptic sources is used with complete freedom, for John used his sources in a manner entirely different from the way the Synoptics used theirs. Yet John's distinctiveness cannot be explained on the basis of its use of a more primitive Jesus tradition, for here the Fourth Gospel is independent but similar.

Relationship to Hellenistic Thought. Three strains of Greek thought have been suggested as explanation of certain ideas in the Fourth Gospel. First, relationships to Greek philosophy are assumed. In John certain contrasts between what is above and the earth (3:31), spirit and flesh (3:6; 6:63), eternal life and life in the world (11:25–26), bread from heaven and natural bread (6:32), and water of life and natural water (4:14) are compared to popular Platonism's contrast between the real, invisible, and eternal world and the apparent world of time and space. Any parallels, however, probably came through Palestinian Judaism, which already contained a strain of Greek thought and which in its Old Testament tradition already knew contrasts between spirit and flesh (Isaiah 31:3) and between the bread of God and natural bread (Isaiah 55:1–2).

The term *logos* in the prologue to John is sometimes traced to the

---

[97] Brown, *The Gospel According to John, I–XII*, p. LII.

[98] C. K. Barrett, *The Gospel According to St. John*, pp. 34–35; and B. H. Streeter, *The Fourth Gospel*, pp. 395–426, argue for John's dependence upon Mark and Luke.

[99] See Brown, *The Gospel According to John*, pp. XLIV–XLVII, for details.

important use of that word in Stoic philosophy. But because the meaning of the term is not the same in the two cases and because the prologue seems to have an independent history in Johannine circles, there is no real reason to assume dependence in the Gospel upon Stoic thought. Indeed, "there is no real reason to suppose that the Gospel was influenced by any more Greek philosophy than what was already present in the general thought and speech of Palestine." [100]

C. H. Dodd and others have found in the Fourth Gospel interesting parallels to the ideas and vocabulary of the *Hermetica*, the Greek literature of a second and third century A.D. philosophical religion.[101] This religion was a syncretism of Platonic and Stoic philosophy with oriental mystic religion. The literature focuses on Hermes Trismegistus, a legendary and deified sage of ancient Egypt, and is cast in the form of dialogues between Hermes and his sons. It contains a high concept of God and ethics in which man is saved through the knowledge of God possessed and made known by the perfect man. None of the Hermetic writings is as early as the Fourth Gospel, but they may reflect an early combination of oriental speculation on Wisdom and Greek philosophical thought. If so, they possibly "represent a type of religious thought akin to one side of Johannine thought" [102] against which the distinctively Christian teaching of the Fourth Gospel is to be understood.

Influence of Incipient Gnosticism. Many of the distinctive emphases of the Fourth Gospel are reminiscent of the basic tenets of Christian Gnosticism. But since classic Gnosticism was not fully developed until the second century A.D., it could not have influenced the Gospel. There may, however, have been earlier pre-Christian forms of Gnosticism. The term itself is used somewhat comprehensively to include some of the components of Gnostic thought present when the Gospel traditions were taking normative form.[103] Rudolf Bultmann claims to find the major source of Johannine thought in such an incipient Gnosticism.[104] He presupposes that Gnosticism as a dualistic-mytho-

---

[100] *Ibid.*, p. LVII.

[101] *The Interpretation of the Fourth Gospel*, pp. 10–54. Hereafter referred to as Dodd, *Interpretation*.

[102] Dodd, *Interpretation*, p. 53.

[103] Johannes Munck, "The New Testament and Gnosticism," *Current Issues in New Testament Interpretation*, ed. Klassen and Snyder, p. 224, notes that Gnosticism is "a scientific term that has no generally accepted scientific definition."

[104] His definitive work is *Das Evangelium des Johannes*. For English summaries and critique, see Reginald H. Fuller, *The New Testament in Current Study*, pp. 119–125, and Brown, *The Gospel According to John*, pp. XXIX, XXXII, LIV–LVI. A more thorough analysis of Bultmann's literary theory appears in Dwight Smith, Jr., *The Composition and Order of the Fourth Gospel*.

logical religion of redemption through revelation was pre-Christian. In its "redeemer myth" he finds the background to the Johannine Jesus, who is redeemer and heavenly revealer. As known from later Gnostic documents this myth presupposes the existence of an Original Man, a figure of light and goodness, who was divided into small particles of light which were seeded (as human souls) in a world of darkness and evil where they forgot their heavenly origins. The God sends his Son in bodily form to waken these souls, liberate them, and lead them to their heavenly home, a deliverance accomplished by proclaiming the truth and giving them *gnosis* (true knowledge). Parallels are apparent, but to suppose with Bultmann that the Fourth Gospel is a veneered reworking of this tradition by an ex-Gnostic goes beyond the evidence. In fact it is not yet certain that a fully-developed Gnostic tradition and myth existed before Christianity. As Brown notes, "The figure of Christ seems to have been the catalyst that prompted the shaping of proto-Gnostic attitudes and elements into definable bodies of Gnostic thought." [105] At most Johannine and Gnostic thought draw upon a common body of ideas.

The Influence of Palestinian Judaism. Another possible source of Johannine thought is the many-faceted Palestinian Judaism of Jesus' time. The language of the Gospel contains strong Semitic elements; the author either thought in Aramaic and wrote in Greek or lived in a bilingual environment. Further the evangelist's familiarity with Jewish thought is illustrated by its dependence upon both the Old Testament and Pharisaic/rabbinic tradition.

The Fourth evangelist cites the Old Testament fewer times than the Synoptic writers, but his Gospel reflects more clearly than any other the great themes of the Old Testament.[106] Jesus is Messiah, King of Israel, Servant of Yahweh, and the Prophet. The entire Gospel draws upon both Torah and Prophets, and the Jewish Wisdom tradition influences the form and style of the Johannine discourses.[107] Also certain legalistic aspects of rabbinical Judaism were known to the author of John (cf. 7:22–23; 5:10; 9:14) and he was acquainted with rabbinical exegesis.[108] At such key points as the interpretation of

[105] Brown, *The Gospel According to John,* p. LV. The theory of a pre-Christian Gnostic redeemer myth rests entirely on sources within the New Testament itself or which are later than the New Testament.

[106] Cf. C. K. Barrett, "The Old Testament in the Fourth Gospel," *JTS*, XLVIII (1947), 155–169.

[107] Brown, *The Gospel According to John,* pp. CXXII–CXXVI.

[108] Rabbinic documents are later than the New Testament but preserve material going back to the first century A.D. and earlier.

Torah, Messiah, and name of God the Fourth Gospel is influenced by rabbinic thought and methods.[109]

John also shows evidence of the influence of ideas from Qumran. The literature of the Essene community depicts ethical struggle between opposing principles of truth/light and deceit/darkness. This dualism probably has its ultimate root in Zoroastrianism where two opposing principles independently and eternally coexist, but Qumran dualism is modified in that the opposing forces are created by and dependent upon God. In some ways the Fourth Gospel shares the Qumran perspective. Jesus has come into the world as light to overcome darkness (1:4–5, 9) and men must choose between light and darkness. Johannine terminology is also amazingly similar to that of Qumran, sharing such expressions as "the spirit of truth," "the sons of light," "the light of life," "to do the truth," "walking in darkness," and "the works of God." It is difficult to see how the Gospel could have been directly dependent upon Qumran, but the parallels are striking enough to suggest mutual dependence upon some facet of Palestinian Jewish thought. Johannine thought may be closer to Jewish apocalyptic sectarianism as represented at Qumran than to any supposed incipient Gnostic dualism.

The many and varied possibilities for the origin of Johannine ideas illustrate the fascinating complexity of this Gospel. At this point evidence is too circumstantial to lead to categorical conclusions about the possible influences of one or all of these intriguing streams of thought upon the Fourth Gospel. Certainly this evangelist, with a sweep of insight surpassing that of his Synoptic counterparts, has garnered from the profoundly complex patterns of first century thought an exciting panoply of material which he skillfully used to show who Jesus was and what he had done. It scarcely seems fair to his scholarship to confine him to one or even a few of the possible sources upon which he may have drawn or to imagine that none of his thought is original genius.

The Authorship of the Fourth Gospel

The question about the authorship of the Fourth Gospel is one of the most tantalizing in biblical studies. Tradition affirms that the Gospel was written by John, the son of Zebedee. In some respects the evidence in support of this tradition seems overwhelming; in others it is quite unsatisfactory.

[109] Dodd, *Interpretation*, pp. 74–96.

The Internal Evidence. Does the Gospel itself contain any evidence about its author's identity? In a way it does. Two passages identify a source of some of its tradition.

So the soldiers came and broke the legs of the first, and of the other who had been crucified with him; but when they came to Jesus and saw that he was already dead, they did not break his legs. But one of the soldiers pierced his side with a spear, and at once there came out blood and water. *He who saw it has borne witness—his testimony is true,* and he knows that he tells the truth—that you also may believe. (19:32–35. Italics added.)

This witness is not clearly identified, but earlier the passage mentions the presence at the crucifixion of the disciple whom Jesus loved (19: 26–27). The second passage says of the same disciple, "This is the disciple who is bearing witness to these things, and who has written these things; and we know that his testimony is true" (21:24).

Both of these passages, however, belong to a secondary stage in the development of the Gospel. The first (19:35) is an editorial parenthesis and chapter 21 is an editorial expansion, both apparently added by the same hand. Even so, they reflect an early judgment of the Johannine circles that the beloved disciple was the source of some of their Gospel's tradition. How much of the tradition came from him is uncertain, for the references may intend no more than the immediate events. They do not, however, exclude a broader interpretation

Figure 13–1. Papyrus dating from the first half of the second century A.D. containing parts of John 18:31–33, 37–38. (Source: The John Rylands Library, Manchester.)

and 21:24 could certainly imply that the beloved disciple was responsible for the writing of the whole Gospel to which chapter 21 is appended by an editor.

If the disciple whom Jesus loved was author of the Fourth Gospel, the question of his identity is crucial. Among those who have been suggested in addition to the son of Zebedee are Lazarus, Matthias, John Mark, and an ideal figure. Unfortunately none of these is entirely satisfactory. A more convincing case can be made for John, the son of Zebedee, but it is not without problems.[110] Internally, then, the Fourth Gospel is anonymous but does associate its tradition with the beloved disciple.

The External Evidence. From the closing decades of the second century the tradition is firm that John the son of Zebedee wrote the Fourth Gospel.[111] Theophilus of Antioch (c. A.D. 181) was the first writer to cite a passage from the work expressly as from John, but the more important reference comes from Irenaeus at about the same time.

Afterwards, John, the disciple of the Lord, who also had leaned upon His breast, did himself publish a Gospel during his residence at Ephesus in Asia.[112]

Irenaeus clearly believed the Fourth Gospel to be the work of the apostle John. He claims that in his boyhood he had listened to Polycarp, who had heard John.[113] If this implies a chain of tradition from John to Polycarp to Irenaeus, it gives special strength to the latter's testimony about the Fourth Gospel. The fact that Irenaeus was very young at the time he claims to have heard Polycarp speak of John weakens the chain. Confusion is at least a possibility.[114] Irenaeus' evidence is formidable but not conclusive.

At first glance the internal and external evidence combine into an almost unassailable circumstantial proof that the Gospel came from John, the son of Zebedee. Indeed, eyewitness authority for the Johannine tradition could be claimed with more assurance than for any of

[110] For good analyses of this entire question see FBK, p. 168, and Brown, *The Gospel According to John,* pp. XCII–XCVIII. Brown accepts the identification with John, the son of Zebedee, as a strong hypothesis.

[111] Cf. Barrett, *The Gospel According to St. John,* pp. 83–96, and Brown, *The Gospel According to John,* pp. LXXVIII–XCII, for detailed presentations of the evidence. Dodd, *Historical Tradition in the Fourth Gospel,* pp. 10–13, has a briefer account.

[112] *Heresies,* III, i, 1 = Eusebius, *EH,* V, viii, 4.

[113] Eusebius, *EH,* IV, xiv, 3–8.

[114] Polycarp perhaps referred to John, the Ephesian elder.

the Synoptics if it were not for several considerations. The Fourth Gospel did not find ready acceptance in the Church and already in the fourth century was attributed to Cerinthus, a Gnostic author. Further, the differences between the Johannine and Synoptic presentations of Jesus are difficult to account for if both have any eyewitness quality at all.[115] Finally the Gospel shows evidence of considerable editorial expansion. Differences of Greek style, breaks and inconsistencies in sequence, and repetition and dislocation of passages probably indicate stages in the development of the Gospel. Some parts of its tradition may be traced back to the apostle, but his material was elaborated by a group of his disciples. Apparently the Fourth Gospel grew up in a circle that traced its earliest elements back to "the beloved disciple" who was early identified with John, the son of Zebedee.[116]

Historical Supplement to Synoptic Tradition

There is increasing respect for some of the historical traditions in the Fourth Gospel. In an important book C. H. Dodd isolates an "ancient tradition independent of the other gospels, and meriting serious consideration as a contribution to our knowledge of the historical facts concerning Jesus Christ." [117] He believes this tradition contained the following salient points which supplement the Synoptic tradition.[118]

a. A fuller account of the ministry of John the Baptist with explicit references by the Baptist to the messianic status of Jesus.

b. An account of an early ministry of Jesus in southern Palestine paralleling that of John the Baptist, including the administration of baptism and indicating that disciples of the Baptist followed Jesus.

c. Some account of the work of Jesus as a healer, less than the Synoptics, but enough to indicate that it occurred both in Galilee and the south.

d. Topographical information, indicating certain steps in the itinerary of Jesus especially in southern Palestine and Transjordan, material virtually ignored in the Synoptics.

e. Information about the events in which Jesus' Galilean ministry ended,

---

[115] Some are now suggesting that the Johannine tradition is at certain points more reliable than the Synoptic one. Cf. A. M. Hunter, "Recent Trends in Johannine Studies," *Expository Times*, LXXI (1960), 164–67, 219–222.

[116] See Barrett, *The Gospel According to St. John*, pp. 113–114, for an attractive hypothesis about the origin of the Fourth Gospel in Johannine circles. Brown, *The Gospel According to John*, pp. XCVIII–CII, presents a more elaborate but similar analysis.

[117] Dodd, *Historical Tradition in the Fourth Gospel*, p. 423.

[118] These are summarized on pp. 429–430 of Dodd's book.

including an attempted messianic uprising followed by widespread desertion of followers.

f. A full account of the Passion which in some sense supplements the Synoptics or deviates from them.

g. A body of traditional sayings, parables, which are difficult to define because of the use made of them in dialogues which appear to be the creation of the evangelist.

A. M. Hunter adds to these the evidence for an extended Judean ministry during the last six months of Jesus' life, with an interval of retirement.[119] Some of these traditions appear more historically reliable than others, but none is impossible. Any serious attempt to reconstruct even the essentials of Jesus' public life must consider these materials from the Gospel of John.

Interpretation of the Fourth Gospel

Divergent motives have been suggested for the composition of the Fourth Gospel. Some suggest a missionary or apologetic purpose, but disagree about its audience, suggesting such diverse groups as the followers of John the Baptist, Jews, or various Gnostic groups. Others believe that John was written to confirm Christians in their faith. Neither motive necessarily excludes the other and both are implicitly present in the Gospel's own statement of purpose:

. . . these are written that you may believe that Jesus is the Christ, the son of God, and that believing you may have life in his name. (20:31)

John is certainly an interpretation of Jesus and intends "to make the believer see existentially what this Jesus in whom he believes means in terms of life." [120] The Gospel itself suggests that the purpose is achieved along the following lines:

    I. The Introduction. 1:1–51
        A. Prologue. 1:1–18
        B. The opening revelation of Jesus. 1:19–51

    II. The Book of Signs. 2:1–12:50
        A. The sign at Cana in Galilee. 2:1–12
        B. Cleansing of the temple. 2:13–25
        C. Discourse with Nicodemus. 3:1–21
        D. The Baptist's final testimony about Jesus and Jesus' response.
            3:22–36
        E. Discourse with the Samaritan woman. 4:1–45

[119] Hunter, "Recent Trends in Johannine Studies," *Expository Times*, LXXI (1960), p. 219.

[120] Brown, *The Gospel According to John*, p. LXXVIII.

F. The second sign in Cana. 4:46–54
G. The Sabbath. 5:1–47
H. Passover. 6:1–71
I. Tabernacles. 7:1–10:21
J. Dedication. 10:22–42
K. The raising of Lazarus, the victory of life over death. 11:1–54
L. Passover, death and life. 12:1–36
M. Conclusion of the Book of Signs. 12:37–50

III. The Book of Passion. 13:1–20:31

A. Farewell discourses. 13:1–17:26
B. The Passion: Death. 18:1–19:42
C. The Resurrection: Life. 20:1–31

Epilogue. 21:1–25

The Introduction (1:1–51). John's prologue represents "an early Christian hymn, probably stemming from Johannine circles, which has been adapted to serve as an overture to the Gospel narrative of the incarnate Word." [121] The Gospel begins with the *logos,* the Word of God, by which heaven and earth were framed, which came through the prophets to Israel, and which gave to those who accepted it the status of children of God. *Logos* is also the divine wisdom (the Hebrew parallel to the Platonic *Ideas* and the Stoic *logos*), the "thought of God which is the transcendent design of the universe and its imminent meaning." [122]

John's claim that "the Word became flesh" gives a clue to the meaning of the Gospel. It is "a record of a life which expresses the eternal thought of God, the meaning of the universe." [123] The eternal Word of God is apprehended in the life of Jesus, who gave to his disciples "words of eternal life." The meaning of the cosmos is found in Jesus, whose life is a *sign* of eternal reality. All that is real and meaningful is found in the life, death, and resurrection of Jesus Christ. For the Fourth Evangelist the *Word made flesh* is Messiah and is so attested by John the Baptist, the last of the prophets:

Behold, the Lamb of God, who takes away the sin of the world! (1:29)

The Baptist's testimony is confirmed by an impressive group of witnesses. Andrew says to Peter, "We have found the Messiah" (1:41); Philip to Nathanael, "We have found him of whom Moses in the law and also the prophets spoke" (1:45); and Nathanael to Jesus, "Rabbi, you are the Son of God! You are the King of Israel" (1:49)!

[121] *Ibid.,* p. CXXVIII.
[122] Dodd, *Interpretation,* p. 295.
[123] *Ibid.*

The Introduction ends with Jesus' statement to Nathanael, "You will see heaven opened, and the angels of God ascending and descending upon the Son of man" (1:51). C. H. Dodd interprets this as equivalent to the evangelist's proclamation that "the Word became flesh." [124] It is certainly a claim that the life of Jesus is a *sign* of the activity of God.

The Book of Signs (2:1–12:50). In a major section, designated the Book of Signs, the Fourth evangelist aims to authenticate Jesus as the *logos* of God. His method is to present a series of *signs* which tell who Jesus is and how God's glory is present in him. The intention of the materials in chapters 2–12 is indicated in a statement appearing toward the end of the section: "Though he had done many signs before them, yet they did not believe in him" (12:37).

The theme "a new beginning" unites the first two signs and the discourses with Nicodemus and the Samaritan woman (2:1–4:42).[125] At Cana water is changed to wine, a sign representing the difference between the religion of ceremonial law (the waterpots were there according to the cleansing laws of the Jews) and the religion of "grace and truth" (1:17) which came with Jesus. The old order of religion is replaced by a new order. John places the story of the cleansing of the temple here to make the same point, but includes a cryptic reference to Jesus' death and resurrection for which the reader may expect later explanation. The two signs are then clarified in two discourses. A dialogue with Nicodemus, a friendly and capable representative of the old order which is being superseded, passes into a monologue which focuses on a new birth, a forceful symbol of how the new replaces the old. Jesus dramatically asserts, ". . . unless one is born anew, he cannot see the kingdom of God" (3:3). Nicodemus is perplexed by this saying and so is the reader. The whole Gospel seeks to answer the question, "How can this be?" The dialogue with the Samaritan woman contrasts the water of Jacob (Israel) with "living water" and the ancient cults of the Jews and Samaritans with worship in "spirit and truth." When the woman told the Samaritans of her conversation with Jesus, they came out to hear him themselves and confessed, ". . . this is indeed the Savior of the world" (4:42). The first two signs with the accompanying dialogues thus constitute a "compact episode in the presentation of the ministry of Jesus Christ" [126] representing Jesus, God's *logos*, as the new religious beginning.

[124] *Ibid.*, p. 296.
[125] *Ibid.*, pp. 297–317.
[126] *Ibid.*, p. 316.

The next narrative tells of the healing of an official's son at Capernaum. This third sign both completes the theme of a new beginning and introduces a new thought.

> Jesus said to him, "Go; your son will live." The man believed the word that Jesus spoke to him and went his way. (4:50)

The word of Jesus gives life. A second narrative confirms this and introduces Jesus' challenge of institutional Judaism (5:1–16). The healing of Bethzatha occurred on the sabbath. The discourse which replies to the accusation about violation of the sabbath claims for Jesus the power to bestow life because he is the Son through whom the Father effectively works.

> For as the Father raises the dead and gives them life, so also the Son gives life to whom he will. . . . Truly, truly, I say to you, he who hears my word and believes him who sent me, has eternal life; he does not come into judgment, but has passed from death to life. (5:21, 24)

The evangelist relates this event to an unidentified feast which may have been Pentecost. If so, the Book of Signs includes a full religious calendar: Pentecost, Tabernacles, Dedication, and Passover. The supposition that the feast is Pentecost adds significance to the narrative. Pentecost had come to be understood as commemoration of the giving of the Torah. Perhaps the evangelist wanted to show that the revelation which Jesus gave was superior to the law given through Moses.[127]

Jesus is not only the water of life and one whose word gives life, but also "the bread of life." Using a story which also appears in the Synoptic tradition, the evangelist describes Jesus' multiplying bread and feeding the multitudes to say that he is more than a second Moses who in the messianic age would restore the gift of manna (6:1–71). Jesus himself is the bread of life and union with him is eternal life.

The Feast of Tabernacles is the setting of the next scene (7:1–8:59). Unlike the preceding scenes where discourses follow and interpret the signs, this one opens with Jesus' proclamation that he is the living water and the light of the world. This was done in the context of two rituals of the festival, pouring out the water libation and lighting the candelabra in the court of the women. When Jesus said, "If any one thirst, let him come to me and drink" and "I am the light of the world; he who follows me will not walk in darkness but will have the light of life," he directed attention from the rites of the festival to himself. The climax came with the healing of the man born blind, whose pro-

---

[127] Cf. T. C. Smith, "The Book of Signs," *Review and Expositor*, LXII (1965), 453.

gressive illumination stands in stark contrast to the spiritual blindness of the Pharisees.

The final sign is the raising of Lazarus (11:1–57) which "adds to the presentation of Christ as giver of life, which has already taken such varied forms of expression, this special new element: that the gift of life is here presented expressly as victory over death. Resurrection is the reversal of the order of mortality, in which life always hastens towards death." [128] The author prepares for the Lazarus story with a discourse at the feast of Dedication (10:22–40) which concludes with Jesus' claim of oneness with God (10:30). Whatever the historicity of Lazarus' restoration, the evangelist intends it to prepare the reader for the resurrection of Jesus, which eternally achieves for all men what is only promised in the temporal raising of Lazarus.

The Book of Signs concludes with Jesus' anointing at Bethany (12: 1–8), his entry into Jerusalem (12:12–19) and a discourse on his approaching Passion and its significance (12:23–36). The evangelist thus ends his account of Jesus' public ministry with hints and promises of what Jesus is and does, and adds a word about the failure of the Jews to believe (12:37–50). [129]

The Book of Passion (13:1–20:31). The Book of Passion is divided into two parts: the farewell discourses (13:1–17:26) and the Passion narrative (18:1–20:31). The farewell discourses, like the other Johannine discourses, have no parallel in the Synoptic Gospels. They draw on themes from the general kerygmatic tradition and also echo the themes of the Book of Signs. [130] They have the character of the esoteric teachings addressed to the disciples in the Synoptic Gospels. In these discourses Jesus teaches those who believed in the signs of his earlier ministry. He talked to his disciples about the meaning of his death and resurrection and about the nature of the new life these events will bring to them. In some way each narrative or discourse approaches both issues.

At the Last Supper (13:1–30) Jesus in an acted parable washed the disciples' feet, a service ordinarily provided for dinner guests. The event both teaches humility and proclaims Jesus' role as servant. In having their feet washed the disciples were forced to confront the servant role of Jesus. This humble service was not part of messianic expectation and Peter's embarrassment certainly reflects the Church's

---

[128] Dodd, *Interpretation*, p. 366.

[129] For an analysis of the Fourth Gospel's interpretation of Jesus, see T. C. Smith, *Jesus in the Gospel of John.*

[130] Dodd, *Interpretation*, p. 396.

problem with the offensiveness of the cross (I Corinthians 1:23–25). After the resurrection, the Church would see that the apparent shame and defeat of the cross was actually glory and triumph. Christ who is Servant is for that very reason Lord!

The Supper narrative is followed by a dialogue on Jesus' departure and return (13:31–14:31). It opens with a new commandment to "love one another; even as I have loved you" (13:34). Love is a key word in the farewell discourses, indeed in the whole Gospel. Man's salvation is achieved by the love of God for the world; God's love in action is expressed in the Son whom he loves (3:16). The Son's obedience is in love of the Father (3:35; 5:19–20). With the eternal love of God Jesus loves his disciples (13:1) and inspires them to love one another (13:34). The disciples "are to reproduce, in their mutual love, the love which the Father showed in sending the Son, the love which the Son showed in laying down his life." [131] In love Jesus promises the disciples the comfort of a continuing sense of God's presence which will enable them to love one another. The evangelist is also concerned here to give a promise for the present and the future. His eschatology allows for present realization as well as future consummation. Jesus' death did not end but enriched the communion with God which the disciples experienced in Jesus' presence.

The final discourse (15:1–16:33) deals with Christ and the Church. Jesus is the vine; the disciples, the branches who bear the fruit of love. In fact, the fruit of love is the love which they have for one another. The world, however, persecutes the Church and is judged by its failure to trust Christ.

A prayer (17:1–26) closes the farewell discourses. Jesus prays for himself and his servant mission. He prays that the disciples might be united and that the Church might be filled with love and thus lead the world to believe.

Like the Book of Signs, the Book of Passion contains narratives along with these interpretive discourses. The farewell discourses serve to interpret the Passion, as the earlier discourses interpret the signs. Jesus' Passion is interpreted as the work of God, a *word* of love and a redemptive sacrifice for all men. In complete control (Pilate and the rest are mere puppets in the story) Jesus performs the supreme *sign*. Dodd's summary states it succinctly:

. . . the motives of a whole series of σημεια are gathered up in this supreme σημειν: the sign of the wine of Cana, which we now perceive to be the blood

---

[131] *Ibid.*, p. 405.

of the true Vine; the sign of the temple (which is the Body of Christ) destroyed to be raised again; the signs of the life-giving word (at Cana and Bethesda), since the Word Himself is life and dies that men may be saved from death; the sign of the Bread, which is the flesh of Christ given for the life of the world; the sign of Siloam—the light of truth which both saves and judges; the sign of Lazarus—life victorious over death through the laying down of life; the sign of the anointing for burial; and the sign of the 'King of Israel' acclaimed on His entry to Jerusalem to die. . . . As everywhere, so most emphatically in the story of Christ's arrest, trial and crucifixion, what happens and is observed in the temporal and sensible sphere signifies eternal reality; the life eternal given to man through the eternal Word.

. . .

Thus the cross is a sign, but a sign which is also the thing signified. The preliminary signs set forth so amply in the gospel are not only temporal signs of an eternal reality; they are also signs of this Event, in its twofold character as word and as flesh. They are true—spiritually, eternally true—only upon the condition that this Event is true, both temporally (or historically) and spirtually or eternally.[132]

Therefore, there can be no conclusion to the Gospel other than the resurrection which confirms the authenticity and victory of the crucifixion.

Epilogue (21:1–25). This chapter is obviously a postscript. It was probably added by editors of the Gospel as a way of confirming its authenticity. Peter and the beloved disciple are represented as partners, neither taking precedence over the other. "Peter is head of the evangelistic and pastoral work of the Church, but the beloved disciple is the guarantor of its tradition regarding Jesus."[133]

SUGGESTED READINGS

BARRETT, C. K., *Luke the Historian in Recent Study* (Epworth, 1961). A brief survey of research on Luke–Acts.

BLAIR, EDWARD P., *Jesus in the Gospel of St. Matthew* (Abingdon, 1960).

BORNKAMM, GÜNTHER, G. BARTH, and H. J. HELD, *Tradition and Interpretation in Matthew* (Westminster, 1963).

CADBURY, HENRY J., *The Making of Luke–Acts* (S.P.C.K., 1958). First published in 1927.

COLWELL, E. C., and E. L. TITUS, *The Gospel of the Spirit* (Harper, 1953). A short book on the Gospel of John.

CONZELMANN, HANS, *The Theology of St. Luke* (Harper, 1960).

DIBELIUS, MARTIN, *Studies in the Acts of the Apostles* (SCM, 1956). Essays on Acts along form-critical lines.

[132] *Ibid.*, pp. 438–439.
[133] Barrett, *The Gospel According to St. John*, p. 480.

HOWARD, WILBERT F., *Christianity According to St. John* (Westminster, 1956).

——, "The Gospel According to St. John," *IB*, Vol. VIII.

JOHNSON, SHERMAN E., *The Gospel According to St. Mark* (Harper, 1960).

——, "The Gospel According to St. Matthew: Introduction and Exegesis," *IB*, Vol. VII.

LEANEY, A. R. C., *A Commentary on the Gospel According to St. Luke* (Harper, 1958).

LIGHTFOOT, R. H., *The Gospel Message of St. Mark* (Clarendon, 1950).

NINEHAM, D. E., *St. Mark* (Pelican, 1963).

RICHARDSON, ALAN, *The Gospel According to St. John* (Collier, 1962).

ROBINSON, JAMES M., *The Problem of History in Mark* (Allenson, 1957).

14

Struggle for Identity: Creed, Organization, Ethics

The Church's thought and organization matured as the Church found a stable place in a world not altogether willing to receive it. Over several decades during the post-apostolic period, the Christian community began the tenuous process of developing specific order and organization. In some sense the Church began to become an institution. Offices began to be assigned specific function and the temptations of an immoral and alien society demanded a definition of ethics by the Church. In a word, the fledgling community was "not of the world" but set in a world in which she had to discover and state who she was. Within a world which was often antagonistic to her existence, the Church struggled with her identity and began to mature in idea and organization. The organism began to carve a place for herself in the real world.

The New Testament does not describe this maturation directly, but does hint at the circumstances under which it occurred and gives some general impressions of the kind of thought, organization, and ethics which the Church developed. Christian doctrine, ecclesiastical organization, and even ethics took shape in the context of conflict with false ideas. Certainly doctrine and organization would have developed even without opposition, but the historical fact is that controversy encouraged and sharpened both doctrine and churchmanship. False teachings had to be repudiated categorically and Christian ideas had to be stated clearly and without compromise. Proper administration of the Church was also necessary to assure validity of both idea and practice.

CONFLICT WITH FALSE TEACHING

The primary ideological enemy of early Christianity was Gnosticism (see pp. 204–207). Marked similarities between Christianity and Gnosticism made it a formidable enemy. The two grew up together, both addressing themselves to humanity's dire sense of need for deliverance or salvation. Many men in the Roman world felt uprooted and estranged, subject to malevolent forces before whom they appeared to be powerless. Both Christianity and Gnosticism acknowledged the need for salvation, drawing from, among other sources, the Jewish tradition of "fallen" and sinful humanity. Both proclaimed the descent of a redeemer, who delivered man from the world of evil and darkness to the realm of God. Christ was for the Gnostics a classic example of the redeemer figure, one who comes from the true God to free man from worldly and bodily imprisonment by the lesser powers. Christ in some way also seemed to repudiate the Jewish doctrines of creation and law, both of which Gnosticism rejected. Before the lines of division between orthodoxy and heresy were well defined, these similarities between the two traditions made it easy for Gnostic teachers to invade the Church and attract individuals and even entire house-congregations to their way of thinking. In fact, "invasion" is not exactly the correct figure, for many early Gnostics may well have come out of the Church itself. Clearly the Gnostic threat was considered to be from within more than from without and almost before they knew it, Christians were in danger of fatally altering the nature of their faith and hope.

Although similarities existed between Christianity and Gnosticism, basic differences likewise were present. For Christians the creation was of God's doing and was good. The Church, therefore, rejected dualism and its radical separation of God from the creation. Further, history was the area of God's activity as he sought to sustain and redeem it. In particular, Christians championed the true humanity of Jesus and the real incarnation of God, neither of which Gnostics accepted. For the Gnostics there could be no real relation between the true God and the created order. History, therefore, had no meaning and human experience was dismal. When the true God sent a messenger to save man from the despair of his life, he may have *appeared* to be man but could not have *been* man. Incarnation of the true God, for the Gnostic, was a contradiction in terms. For them Christ only "seemed" to be flesh. This particular Gnostic heresy was called *do-*

cetism from the Greek verb *dokein*, "to seem." The Church rejected this Gnostic pessimism about history by affirming its meaning and ultimate fulfillment. God was really in Christ as a true human seeking to redeem fallen man.

A further corollary of Gnostic dualism was the separation between man's physical being and the true being that indwells him. Thus one's attitude toward either his own body or that of another person was irrelevant. The physical was relegated to the realm of evil. On one hand this led to either extreme asceticism or excessive libertinism in one's personal behavior, on the other hand it resulted in a kind of spiritual egotism which prevented genuine Christian love for neighbor. Against such ideas the Church had to take its stand and affirm its faith. This struggle dominates the Johannine letters, Jude, and II Peter, and in part the Pastorals (I and II Timothy and Titus).

The Johannine Letters

The three short Johannine writings are dominated by the conflict with false teaching. They belong together and almost certainly come from the same author who refers to himself in the third letter as the "elder." The striking resemblance in language, style, and thought between I John and the Fourth Gospel indicates that the Johannine letters came from the same milieu and probably from the same author as the Gospel.[1] Thus, the specific identification of the author of these letters is as impossible as determining who wrote the Gospel.

While the author remains anonymous, the origin of the letters is not without possible discovery. The literature is doubtless from the area around Ephesus in Asia Minor where Gnosticism was particularly strong. One early Gnostic, Cerinthus, is known to have been active in Asia toward the end of the first century. He taught that Jesus was a mere human into whom at baptism the "supreme power Christ" descended in the form of a dove. Jesus was thus able to proclaim the unknown father and perform miracles. Then, before Jesus suffered, Christ withdrew untouched by the passion, "being pure spirit."[2] Whether the heresy which the Johannine literature attacks was instigated by Cerinthus is not known, but it was positively of the same nature and order of seriousness.

The Johannine author describes the heresy and its advocates with considerable clarity. They claim knowledge of God (I John 2:4;

---

[1] For analysis of the question see FBK, pp. 310–312.
[2] Irenaeus, *Against Heresies*, I, xxvi, 1.

4:8), love of God (I John 4:20), and fellowship with God (I John 1:6; 2:6, 9). They boast of peculiar spiritual experiences (I John 4:1–3). They deny that Jesus is the Christ (I John 2:22–23) and explicitly deny the incarnation (II John 7; I John 4:2). Men who believe and teach such things had originally been members of the Christian community, but had gone out from it (I John 2:18–19). For the Johannine apologist, therefore, such men are "false prophets" (I John 4:1) and "antichrists" (I John 2:18). Their seductive teachings have been mightily resisted by true believers (I John 4:4), but their doctrine remains subtly dangerous.

With both passion and compassion the "elder" deals with this problem directly in three works which are of different styles. Second and III John are typical letters, which treat public, not private concerns, "matters of the faith and life of Christian congregations." [3] Since they are from a person of recognized ecclesiastical stature, they carry a note of authority. First John lacks the characteristics of an epistle, and scholars debate whether it was addressed to a particular audience or to all Christian believers. [4] The former is preferable. First John was probably addressed to a number of congregations in the province of Asia with whom the author had particular relationships. [5]

Since II and III John are more precise in address, they may be examined as background to the more generally directed I John. Second John is addressed to a church pictorially designated as "the elect lady" and to its congregation, designated "her children" (vs. 1). It warns against docetic ideas and admonishes the church against showing hospitality to false teachers who deny the coming of Christ in the flesh. Such ones know neither the Father nor the Son (vs. 9). Third John is addressed to Gaius, a friend of the author. A certain Diotrephes had opposed the "elder," rejecting his emissaries and prating against him with evil words (vs. 10). He had completely rejected the "elder's" authority, so he was to be condemned as an evil man who had not seen God (vs. 11). There is no evidence that Diotrephes was Gnostic, only that he opposed the "elder." Gaius, on the other hand, was faithful and could be relied upon to accept the missionaries and stand for the truth as taught by the "elder." Both II and III John reflect a period in the life of the Church when organization was loose and churches were bound together by letters from those in authority,

---

[3] FBK, p. 313.
[4] Cf. FBK, pp. 307–308, for details.
[5] Amos N. Wilder, "I, II, and III John," *IB,* XII, p. 211.

but still a time when lines of authority had not been firmly established and were open to challenge. Already in the Church certain lines of administration were developing. The "elder" assumed or held authority over some congregations; nevertheless, Diotrephes apparently championed local autonomy. The controversy then in III John is more administrative than doctrinal.

The issue, however, in I John is clearly drawn. This book warns against heretical teachers who have arisen in Christian churches. At the same time it presents a "profound meditation on the nature of the Christian faith." [6] As Kümmel points out, "the Epistle has no clearly recognizable plan, but presents frequent variations on two themes: right faith in Christ and the necessary connection between faith and proper conduct." [7] Rather than force an outline upon I John, it is better to follow Kümmel's suggestion that the book contains an "address" (1:1–4) followed by three courses of thought in which an ethical thesis and a theological thesis are presented with variations. These courses are found in 1:5–2:27, 2:28–4:6, and 4:7–5:13. Doctrine and ethics, theology and behavior are woven together throughout the letter. Indeed, one had to deal this way with the Gnostic problem which corrupted both faith and behavior. Ideas recur again and again: God is light, love, truth. To be a child of God is to walk in light, hold to truth, and love one's brother. In a way it is all summed up in a statement about the incarnation:

In this is love, not that we loved God but that he loved us and sent his Son to be the expiation for our sins. Beloved if God so loved us, we also ought to love one another. (4:10–11)

In the address to his readers the author states clearly the case against the Gnostics. Using language reminiscent of the prologue to the Fourth Gospel, he declares that the reality of life has been made known in the incarnated *logos:*

The life was made manifest, and we saw it, and testify to it, and proclaim to you the eternal life which was with the Father and was made manifest to us. (1:2)

This Christological issue was at the heart of the matter. God and salvation were made known in the man Jesus, who was the Christ (see especially 2:18–27). This coming in the flesh was the revelation of God's love. It was the means of reconciling man to himself (1:9; 2:2, 12; 3:5). To fail to believe this was to live in darkness, because dis-

[6] J. Christiaan Beker, *The Church Faces the World*, p. 65.
[7] FBK, p. 306.

belief was rejection of the essence of redemptive action. Men who deny the incarnation are antichrists, and their claims of ecstasy and possession by the spirit mean nothing (4:1–3). With such men there can be no compromise because their ideas could bring the death of the Church.

While some Gnostics were antinomian and libertine, the Johannine epistle does not directly accuse its opponents of such behavior. Their ethical sin was their failure to love. Arrogant spiritual self-assurance —"I know him" (2:4), "I am in the light" (1:6), "I have no sin" (1:8) —makes them look down upon others in the Church. Again and again the Johannine writer rejects them as liars who walk in darkness (1:5– 2:6). One cannot love God and hate his brother. Love is the essence of ethics, not as an idea but as the action of brotherly concern. If a man really knows God as the Gnostics claimed to know him, he will love his brother. Since the Gnostics do not love their fellows, they cannot claim to know God.

God is love, and he who abides in love abides in God, and God abides in him. (4:16)

The Christian should know the dimensions of love, for Jesus is his example. Denial of love, therefore, is denial of Christianity.

In such manner the Johannine disciple tried to deepen the spiritual life of the Church and to counteract the heretical views of Gnostic teachers. His is no textbook of theology and ethics; it is for life and faith. The matter was one of urgent importance:

Children, it is the last hour; and as you have heard that antichrist is coming, so now many antichrists have come; therefore we know that it is the last hour. (2:18)

It appeared to him to be the ultimate crisis of history. Without the incarnation and without love for brother there would be no Christian faith, no Church.

Jude

The Epistle of Jude is a pseudonymous writing in the name of "Jude . . . brother of James." It thus represents itself as coming from one of the brothers of Jesus. Frequent references, however, to late Jewish and primitive Christian prophecy and its pure Greek language seem to rule out Jude, brother of James and Jesus, as author. There was no reluctance in antiquity to use a pseudonym. Frequently it was a means of undergirding one's ideas by claiming for them the authority of some recognized and respected person. Pseudonymity was not meant to deceive, but to assure a hearing for an urgent message.

This short epistle fights against libertine Gnostic leaders, advocates of a Gnostic trend which contended that the real "spiritual" person is not affected by what the flesh does. They either denied Christ by licentiousness, or more likely they combined rejection of the incarnation with exciting voluptuous living. They had no regard for authority and like dumb animals followed their physical desires. Jude's condemnation is impassioned. Such men walk in the way of Cain, Balaam, and Korah, three Old Testament villains, and will suffer punishment like that meted out to Sodom and Gomorrah. Faithful Christians are admonished to build up their faith, pray in the Holy Spirit, live in the love of God and wait for the coming of Christ. Apart from this admonition the epistle contains no positive theological word and no proclamation of Christ. Moreover, for its author faith has become a fixed body of doctrine "once for all delivered to the saints." This is an unfortunate ossification of the vital idea of faith as living commitment to God through Christ. Fortunately for the Christian faith, its other defenders were less given to prating against false teachers and more to positive presentation of Christian ideas.

II Peter

The Second Epistle of Peter is an apologia for primitive Christian eschatology.[8] It is written in the form of a last testament of the apostle Peter in anticipation of his death (1:13–15). This claim of apostolic authorship is further emphasized by the author's allusion to Jesus' prediction of Peter's martyrdom and by his eyewitness reference to Jesus' transfiguration (1:16–18). He also places himself on the same level of apostolic authority as Paul (3:15–16). Peter, however, cannot have written this epistle for the following reasons: [9] (1) Second Peter is clearly dependent upon Jude, which is itself a late post-apostolic writing. (2) The conceptual world and the language of II Peter are too Hellenistic to be attributed to Peter. (3) The epistle's concern to oppose those who deny the Christian expectation of the *parousia* hardly fits the apostolic period. (4) The system of thought against which the epistle is addressed bears the essential character-

[8] Ernst Käsemann, "An Apologia for Primitive Christian Eschatology," *Essays on New Testament Themes*, p. 169.

[9] For details see FBK, pp. 303–305; Bo Reicke, *The Epistles of James, Peter, and Jude*, pp. 143–147.

istics of second century Gnosticism. (5) The appeal in 3:16 to a collection of Pauline letters and to other normative writings indicates the second century, as does the implication in 1:20–21 that the interpretation of scripture is reserved to those of ecclesiastical office. (6) In spite of the strong claims for Petrine composition (which by being overzealous create more doubt than confidence), II Peter is nowhere mentioned in the second century. This would be unusual for a letter written by the Apostle. Second Peter, therefore, is a middle second century pseudonymous work. The unknown author apparently believed he wrote in Peter's spirit and, since the Apostle represented original and authoritative Christianity, condemned heresy by his authority.

The writing of II Peter was occasioned by derisive Gnostic rejection of the primitive Christian eschatology (3:3–4). The delay of Christ's return had been a problem for the Church since apostolic times. The believing community which had expected the immediate establishment of the kingdom of God had learned to be content with the delay. Some among them, however, were ripe for the mocking challenges of those who asked: "Where is the promise of his coming? For ever since the fathers fell asleep, all things have continued as they were from the beginning of creation" (3:4). The stereotyped denunciation of heretics typical of II Peter obscures their identity. Presumably they were Gnostics whose radical dualism made it impossible for them to accept doctrines of the redemption of creation and the resurrection of the dead. Eschatology for them meant denial of the creation, not its perfection.[10] For them, therefore, eschatological hopes were present possessions of the spiritually illuminated. They had already experienced a spiritual resurrection and already fully were sharing in the Kingdom of God.

Second Peter's counter argument falls naturally into three parts sandwiched between brief introductory and concluding charges to faithfulness (1:1–11 and 3:14–18).

The Apostolic and Prophetic Guarantors of the Christian Hope (1:12–18). Here the author, writing in the spirit of and from the viewpoint of Peter, appeals to the tradition based upon the seeing and hearing of the apostles. Particularly important was their witness to the transfiguration of Jesus, which is an example of what awaits all Christians. Like Jesus they will participate in the divine nature. This appeal to the apostolic guarantee is supported by the witness

---

[10] Beker, *The Church Faces the World*, p. 71.

of Old Testament prophecy. In the apostolic experience a bit of prophecy had already been realized. This is all the more reason for heeding the prophetic word which will continue to be fulfilled. However, neither apostolic word nor prophetic word is open to free interpretation. Only those who possess the spirit can understand that which the spirit has inspired. Interpretation, therefore, must be left in the hands of the leaders of the Church. As Käsemann pointedly states it, "Faith is transformed unmistakably into *fides implicita:* I believe what the church believes." [11]

The Polemic against the Heretics (2:1–22). This section is a recasting of Jude and lacks the force of creativity. The author's refutation of heresy is not constructive theological statement but diatribe. Käsemann sums it up:

The enemy is disposed of in very primitive fashion, first by accusing him of moral depravity, then by showering him with well-chosen proverbs (as in v. 22) and, thirdly, by painting the punishment of the heretic in lurid colours. Our chapter is a classic example of these tactics, which obviously found ready hearers then as now. [12]

Rebuttal of Heresy by Restating Apocalyptic Eschatology (3:1–13). The third section of II Peter returns to an emphasis upon eschatology to counter the false teachings. Christ will come as God has promised, so the scoffing of heretics is to be ignored. Again the writer appeals to prophets and apostles against those who scoff at "the promise of his coming." The flood of Genesis is cited as proof that all things will not continue forever, and delay is dismissed by denying the identity of the divine and human schemes of time (3:8–9). The delay may seem long to man, but not to God.

Second Peter is not a particularly able defense of Christian eschatology. Its author, unlike Paul or the author of the Johannine literature, seems to have been incapable of creative theological statement. His thought is stalely repetitious and his understanding is shallow. When he appeals dogmatically to "holy" tradition, he all but confesses that he lacks that creative presence of the Spirit of God which the Church believed to be the inspiration of scripture. For him revelation is "a piece of property which is at the community's disposal," [13] and to believe is "to accept the tradition of the apostles." [14]

[11] Käsemann, "An Apologia for Primitive Christian Eschatology," *Essays on New Testament Themes*, p. 191.
[12] *Ibid.*
[13] *Ibid.*, p. 174.
[14] *Ibid.*, p. 187.

In addition, abuse overshadows logic in his argument to such a degree that one almost sympathizes with the heretics. He gives the impression that the heretics are the foulest and most lustful of men. This abuse was characteristic of second century Christian polemic when the Church in struggle for survival was driven to extreme means. Finally, and most disappointing of all, he offers no meaningful reinterpretation of eschatology. Eschatology means for him simply the triumphal entry of believers into an eternal kingdom and the destruction of the ungodly (1:11). There is no constructive interpretation of the "power and coming of our Lord Jesus Christ" (1:16). Rather a hope which was grand enough to include the fulfillment and redemption of all creation is reduced to the level of ambitious personal fulfillment.

There will be richly provided for you an entrance into the eternal kingdom of our Lord and Savior Jesus Christ. (1:11)

And, compounding the inadequacy, this defender of the faith claims for his defense ideas he ought to have repudiated because they belonged to the Gnostics or at least to the world of Hellenistic dualism. He promises those who await the eschaton escape from the world of evil and lust and entrance into the incorruptible world where they will partake of the nature of God. This is nothing less than denial of true humanity and acceptance of the Gnostic idea that in every man is imprisoned a bit of the divine substance.

In the Church II Peter may be sentimentally remembered for stating:

. . . no prophecy ever came by impulse of man, but men moved by the Holy Spirit spoke from God. (1:21)

This when taken in context is scarcely enough to save the epistle from mediocrity.

The best defense against heresy was the Church's faith in and commitment to Jesus as Lord and the transforming power of his redemption. Strategic also was the warmth of the Christian fellowship inspired by *agape* love. No community, however, can ignore challenges to its integrity. A voice of protest and rebuttal inevitably is raised by those who care. They do not always speak clearly and their defense is not always brilliant, but they mean well and their courage is admirable. Jude and II Peter do not compare favorably with I John or the Gospels or the Pauline letters, but as attempts to uphold truth against error they are important.

The Church's other defense against heresy was its organization and its doctrine, both of which were given rudimentary shape in the post-apostolic age.

THE CHURCH'S ORGANIZATION AND CREED

In the beginning the Church or churches had no single comprehensive organization. No commonly agreed upon and binding creedal statements existed apart from the confession, "Jesus Christ is Lord." Regional and local differences and "conflicts and divisions among the churches were not infrequent." [15] But the churches did share "a deeply unifying common memory and common life and a surprisingly wide and significant common faith" [16] out of which organization and creed developed as the Church faced the world and the threat of opposing ideas and interpretations of reality.

The evidence for emerging organization is confusing. Information is ample, but it is contradictory and/or ambiguous. No coherent overall picture emerges. But it is clear that without uniform plan there was definite development from loose organization to structured ecclesiastical order. At first there seemed to be little need for organization. The Church was born with eschatological expectation of the near end of the age. Communal life in Jerusalem is adequate proof of the Church's existential approach to structure, as are the Pauline challenges of Jerusalem and apostolic authorities and the fluid but firm Pauline "administration" of churches in Asia Minor and Greece.

Pauline guidance and supervision probably represents an early stage in development of ecclesiastical organization. Although the local congregations had their own leadership, Paul clearly stood over them and could offer advice and make demands. This was of course assumed—but undeniably influential—authority. Paul's claim to be an apostle is the base of his authority and indicates that the Church from the beginning recognized certain men as leaders. Inevitably, however, the close of the apostolic age and the postponement of history's consummation left the churches in a kind of organizational uncertainty at the very time that heresy was making its dangerous but attractive challenge. A Church with no authority might have lost integrity of faith and purpose. More specific organization, then, developed primarily in reaction to heresy. The ministry "became in the first place the guardian of tradition, legitimized by special ordination,

---

[15] John Knox, *The Early Church and the Coming Great Church*, p. 83.
[16] *Ibid.* See especially Chapters 3 and 4.

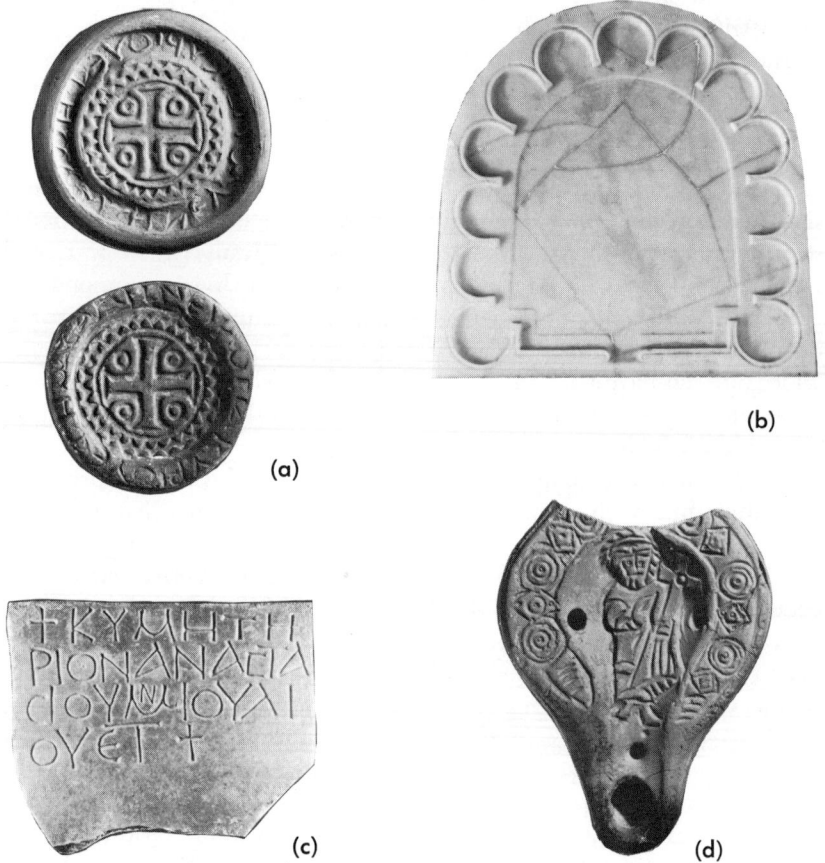

(a)

(b)

(c)

(d)

Figure 14–1. Objects representing the early Church's use of various Christian symbols: (a) Bread stamp from Athens. (b) Church offering table from Corinth. (c) Gravestone of a Corinthian Christian named Anastasios, who died on June 15. (d) Lamp with Christian saint (5th century A.D., from Athens). (Source: American School of Classical Studies, Athens.)

and thus at the same time a guarantee of the effectiveness of all salutary activity in the Church." [17] Early growth in Church organization is illustrated in the Pastoral Epistles.

[17] Kee, Young, Froelich, *Understanding the New Testament*, p. 403.

The Pastorals

The Pastoral Epistles, a label to designate the three letters I and II Timothy and Titus, illustrate how the Church tried to deal with the growing problem of faith and order. They were written to churches troubled by heresy from a leader who assumed for literary and religious purposes the identity and authority of Paul. He may have even incorporated a few genuine fragments of Pauline correspondence.[18] Tradition and some modern scholars even hold that the author was Paul himself. One cannot be certain; but this seems improbable, since the situation presupposed in these letters cannot readily be fitted into any known or conceived period of Paul's life. The situation faced by the Church which is the Pastoral's primary concern is quite unlike that to which any certain Pauline letter is addressed. In addition, their language and style are not typically Pauline and their theology lacks the sharpness and insight we would expect from Paul.[19] These letters were probably written just after the turn of the second century to churches near the author—most likely in Asia Minor. Their author wrote in the name of Paul to show church leaders "how to repulse the false teachers through correct order in the churches, through sound doctrine, and through a pious life according to the teachings of Paul." [20]

The "pastor" of these letters attacks heresy directly by denouncing antinomian teachers and gnostic-like ascetics who do not genuinely understand the Christian faith (I Timothy 4:3 and 6:3–20). He dismisses their speculative mythology as "godless and silly myths" (I Timothy 4:7) and false knowledge (I Timothy 6:20). This is little different from the similar emphasis in II Peter and Jude. The Pastorals go further, however, in the expansion of II Peter's concern that the interpretation of faith be in the hands of those in designated places of authority. This involved two things; a careful delineation of the roles and responsibilities of those who minister in the churches and a championing of *the apostolic faith* or *the tradition.*

The Ministry of the Church

Since leadership had to be strong in the struggle with heresy, the clergy was crucial to the developing Church. They were responsible

[18] Possibly I Timothy 1:3; Titus 1:5; 3:12; II Timothy 1:8, 15 and 4:9ff.
[19] More detailed analyses of the question of the authorship of the Pastorals can be found in FBK, pp. 261–271, and in the works cited there.
[20] FBK, p. 272.

for establishing and maintaining orthodoxy and for preaching the true faith with devotion. They selected the professional workers for the churches and supervised worship.[21] Three specific ecclesiastical offices are listed in the Pastorals: bishop, deacon, and presbyter or elder.[22] The author assumes that his readers know well the function and responsibilities of these offices. What he says about them, therefore, does not provide adequate information to determine the state of the Church's organization in his day.

We know that early in the second century "the church was formulating an apostolic tradition along with reliable interpreters of it." [23] From the time of Paul two types of ministry were active. One was charismatic or prophetic; the other regularly appointed. Paul had emphasized ministries under the guidance of the Spirit:

Now there are varieties of gifts, but the same Spirit; and there are varieties of service, but the same Lord: and there are varieties of working, but it is the same God who inspires them all in everyone. To each is given the manifestation of the Spirit for the common good. (I Corinthians 12:4–7)

Alongside these charismatic ministries of apostles, prophets, and teachers a more established and regular ministry was developing. It consisted of persons to whom specific tasks had been assigned.[24] Within this group lies the origin of the offices of bishop, deacon, and presbyter.

The Pastorals reflect a time when apostles and prophets still work side by side with bishops and presbyters (I Timothy 4:14), but when the latter are beginning to supersede the former. The Church was moving toward a stabilized organization. The fire and enthusiasm of the apostolic era was in process of taking on ecclesiastical form, a development that can be seen more clearly in the *Didache* and the letters of Ignatius.

What were the ministries which developed in the post-apostolic age? Uncertainty characterizes any evaluation, but some things seem clear. There were bishops. The title "bishop" comes from the Greek *episcopos* and means "overseer." These leaders were apparently administrators of local congregations. At first there were several bishops in a congregation, but later only one (monarchical bishop). Ignatius' letters provide a clear picture of the position and responsibility of a bishop in the Church. For his congregation he embodied the "power

[21] Fred D. Gealy, "I and II Timothy and Titus," *IB*, XI, pp. 348–350.
[22] Widows may perhaps be included as a fourth.
[23] Beker, *The Church Faces the World*, p. 32.
[24] Cf. I Thess. 5:12 and I Cor. 16:16.

of God the Father." [25]   The church could not gather for any purpose without his authorization. He was the chief pastor and administrator, aided in his work by elders and deacons. The bishop was spokesman for the church in all correspondence. He was also responsible for all preaching and teaching, although he might delegate this function to others. Even though the Pastorals may not reflect so advanced a stage, they anticipate it in their outline of the qualifications of character and ability for the office of bishop. The "office of bishop" is "a noble task" (I Timothy 3:1), since the bishop is responsible for caring for God's church, which he should manage as he does his own household (I Timothy 3:4–5). He is God's steward "to give instruction in sound doctrine" (Titus 1:9). Since the office carried prestige its occupant must avoid excessive pride and conceit (I Timothy 3:7). One need only glance at the list of a bishop's qualifications in I Timothy 3:1–7 to see that he was to be a man of character and ability.

The clear identity of presbyters is less certain. *Presbuteros* means "elder" and can simply be a designation for respected older members of a Christian community. In Jewish congregations such older ones were responsible for administration and occasionally the word seems to have this technical use.[26] By the time of Ignatius presbyters were clearly separate officers in the Church. Although their function is not clearly defined, they were subordinate to the bishop. In the Pastorals and elsewhere the issue is not so clearly defined. Some writings do not mention presbyters (for example, the *Didache*). Others, on the other hand, do not mention bishops (James, I Peter, Revelation). Apparently for a time the two titles were designations of the same office. The difference perhaps can be accounted for by geography, presbyter being the term used in one region, bishop in another. In the Pastorals, however, both terms are used, but not synonymously. Apparently bishops and presbyters have different functions, but we cannot be certain about the role of the latter.

Finally there are deacons, who already in Paul's time and in the Pastorals held specific office. The word is from the Greek *diakonos* and means "servant." This is its obvious reference in Acts 6 when the Seven were elected to supervise the care of the Hellenistic widows and orphans.[27] Paul often uses the word of anyone who serves Christ or brother in the Church, but in Philippians 1:1 he uses deacon to refer

---

[25] *Magnesians*, III, 1–3.

[26] Acts 15; 21:18; 11:30; 20:17.

[27] The noun is not used in Acts 6 or anywhere in Acts. The verb *diakoein* is used of the Seven.

to a specific office. Here and elsewhere the combination bishop and deacon (the combination is quite common) implies an hierarchial subordination. Deacons assist the bishops in their ministerial work. Like the bishops they are to be men of integrity, faith, and ability (I Timothy 3:8–13).

Again we must remember that the development of the Church's ecclesiastical structure was not uniform and that the data relevant to it can be variously interpreted. Nevertheless, it is apparent that leaders of local congregations carried tremendous responsibility after apostolic ministries were past. The Pastoral use of the Pauline pseudonym was an anachronistic appeal to apostolic authority. Charismatic prophetic ministries continued but were increasingly subject to abuse and were suspect. The leaders of the local congregations, therefore, were responsible for combating heresy by control of orthodoxy and ethics.

Tradition and Creed

The Pastorals also reflect protection against heresy by perpetuation of a tightly controlled tradition. "Faith" had become the *apostolic tradition* and the Church was reducing that vital eyewitness proclamation and search for the truth of Christ into creedal formulations of faith. The recipients of II Timothy are charged to "guard the truth that has been entrusted to you" and to "follow the pattern of sound words which you have heard from me" (II Timothy 1:13). Heretics had upset *"the faith"* (I Timothy 2:18) and had departed from *"the faith"* (I Timothy 4:1). Whereas Paul had inspired and challenged to faith, the pastor passes it on. Of course, a living vital Christian faith must be related to *the faith*, a body of Christian convictions. The Pastorals, however, like Jude and II Peter reflect an unfortunate misemphasis upon an unchangeable tradition.

It follows that the Church in the apostolic age possessed a creed only in the sense of a recognized body of teaching. But already by the beginning of the second century the faith was "beginning to harden into conventional summaries." [28] Here and there in the New Testament there are passages which by context, phrasing, and content have creedal character. This beginning of crystallization was in response to particular occasions or needs in the life of the churches. Candidates for baptism were required to make some confession of faith, some avowal of belief. The need for catechetical instruction was another factor conducive to the shaping of creedal summaries. Others were the

[28] J. N. D. Kelly, *Early Christian Creeds*, p. 13.

polemic against heresy and the development of liturgy, where expressions of faith in the form of hymns and prayers had appropriate place. Exorcism and healing and the formal correspondence of ministers with their churches were also occasions of creedal summary.[29] These various occasions each influenced the style that semi-creedal statements took, so that the fragments which have been preserved in scripture are quite diverse.

The earliest creedal statements were simple one-phrase Christologies. Some of them were quite to the point and brief. The most popular was "Jesus is Lord" used in confession of faith at baptism, in crises, or in liturgy. Another was the brief messianic claim "Jesus is the Christ" (I John 2:22; Mark 8:30). Still another was "Jesus is the Son of God" (Acts 8:36–38; I John 4:15 and 5:5). More elaborate Christological statements were built up by adding selected incidents in the redemptive story. An impressive example is the ancient Christian hymn quoted by Paul in Philippians 2:6–11:

Who though he was in the form of God, did not count equality with God a thing to be grasped, but emptied himself, taking the form of a servant, being born in the likeness of men. And being found in human form he humbled himself and became obedient unto death, even death on a cross. Therefore God has highly exalted him and bestowed upon him the name which is above every name, that at the name of Jesus every knee should bow, in heaven and on earth and under the earth, and every tongue confess that Jesus Christ is Lord, to the glory of God the Father.

Another hymn-like fragment in I Timothy 3:16 is similar:

> He was manifested in the flesh,
> vindicated in the Spirit,
>   seen by angels,
> preached among the nations,
> believed on in the world,
>   taken up in glory.

Christological statements similar to these are manifestly summaries drawn up for catechetical purposes:

For I delivered to you as of first importance what I also received, that Christ died for our sins in accordance with the scriptures, that he was buried, that he was raised on the third day in accordance with the scriptures, and that he appeared to Cephas, then to the twelve. Then he appeared to more than five hundred brethren at one time . . . Then he appeared to James, then to all the apostles. . . . (I Corinthians 15:3–7)

---

[29] This list of creedal occasions is based on that of Kelly, *ibid.*, pp. 13–14.

Similarly in Romans 1:3:

. . . the gospel concerning his Son, who was descended from David according to the flesh and designated Son of God in power according to the Spirit of holiness by his resurrection from the dead, Jesus Christ our Lord.

And briefer:

Remember Jesus Christ, risen from the dead, descended from David. . . . (II Timothy 2:8)

Obviously from the beginning the Church found various uses for confessional statements which centered in the redeeming work of Jesus Christ.

Some creedal statements went further and placed side by side confession of God the Father and Jesus Christ his Son. One of the most important of these is Paul's:

Yet for us there is one God, the Father, from whom are all things and for whom we exist, and one Lord, Jesus Christ, through whom are all things and through whom we exist. (I Corinthians 8:6)

Closely related are three passages from the Pastorals:

For there is one God, and there is one mediator between God and men, the man Christ Jesus, who gave himself as a ransom for all. . . . (I Timothy 2:5f.)

.   .   .

In the presence of God who gives life to all things, and of Christ Jesus who in his testimony before Pontius Pilate made the good confession, I charge you to keep the commandment unstained and free from reproach until the appearing of our Lord Jesus Christ. (I Timothy 6:13–14)

.   .   .

I charge you in the presence of God and of Christ Jesus who is to judge the living and the dead, and by his appearing and his kingdom (II Timothy 4:1).[30]

Trinitarian statements are also common, but not as full creedal statements. The best known are Paul's benediction at the end of II Corinthians:

The grace of the Lord Jesus Christ and the love of God and the fellowship of the Holy Spirit be with you all,

and the baptismal formula given in Matthew 28:19:

Go therefore and make disciples of all nations, baptizing them in the name of the Father and of the Son and of the Holy Spirit.

[30] Similar confessions are found in Romans 4:24 and 8:11; II Cor. 4:14; Gal. 1:1; I Peter 1:21; etc.

Formulae like these [31] provide the base from which later trinitarian creedal confessions developed.

These are only samples of the numerous semi-creedal statements which appear in the New Testament and which show some variety. The New Testament examples are not adequate, however, for tracing and analyzing creedal development. What is clear is that "the church's beliefs about Jesus only acquired significance in the setting of its belief in God the Father, whose Son He was and who had raised Him from the dead" [32] and that the Church's life was empty without the presence of the Spirit of both Father and Son. Thus while there are no complete creedal statements in the New Testament, there is "a common body of doctrine, definite in outline and regarded by everyone as the possession of no individual but of the Church as a whole." [33] At the time the Pastorals were written this corpus of teaching was beginning to take definite pattern and form.

WORSHIP: DEVELOPING LITURGICAL PATTERNS

Related to the formulation of creedal statements was a growing concern for worship. The Pastorals do not have much to say about this apart from a rule about the way worship should be conducted (I Timothy 2:1, 8, 9). Yet, when information is gleaned from various other early Christian sources, the essential features of the cultic life of the early Church begin to come clear.

At first Christians gathered daily for worship (Acts 2:46; 5:42) and presumably, in keeping with Jewish custom, they also kept the sabbath. But from earliest times the Church created for itself a specifically Christian day for religious services. In deliberate distinction from Judaism they chose the first day of the week, since on that day Jesus had been raised from the dead. They called this "the Lord's Day," that is, the day that peculiarly related to and belonged to Jesus Christ as Lord. [34] The Christian day of worship, therefore, was a festival day of joy in the living Christ. Tertullian later notes that this sense of joy was expressed in that one does not kneel at prayer or fast on the Lord's Day. [35] The place of Christian gathering from the beginning was kept

[31] See also I Cor. 6:11; 12:4–6; II Cor. 1:21–22; Gal. 3:11–14 and I Peter 1:2.
[32] Kelly, *Early Christian Creeds*, p. 27.
[33] *Ibid.*, p. 24.
[34] The name the Lord's Day first appears in Revelation 1:10; see also *Didache* 14:1. At first it was simply called "the first day of the week," I Cor. 16:2; Acts 20:7.
[35] *De Corona*, III.

distinct from associations with Jewish worship. They met in the home, forming what might be called "house churches" (I Corinthians 16:19; Romans 16:5; Philemon 2; Colossians 4:15). Christians may have continued to attend temple and synagogue as long as they were allowed, but their uniquely Christian meetings were held in homes. Later, church buildings were constructed, but none remain from the first or second century. Special importance was attached to the fact that the whole community came together at one place (I Corinthians 11:20–22); separate gatherings were thought improper. Ignatius of Antioch was particularly critical of separate and divisive gatherings.[36]

The elements of early Christian worship are fairly well known. Acts mentions instruction, preaching, and breaking of bread (2:42, 46; 20:7). These were the foundation of all the worship life of the Church. All of these except breaking of bread had antecedents in synagogue worship. Breaking of bread was a distinctively Christian innovation and was the climax of each service. Instruction included reading of scripture. Readings were primarily from the Jewish scriptures, but Christian writings like the Pauline letters and the Gospels were also used when and where available.[37] The early preaching was kerygmatic and like that found in the sermons in Acts. We can be certain that it centered in the work of God in Christ.

Prayers were also a regular part of early Christian worship. They were sometimes free as the *Didache* indicates: "The prophets are allowed to give thanks as they wish" (10:7). These free prayers probably reflected the situation and the needs of the congregation. Liturgical prayers were also used. The oldest liturgical prayer was *Maranatha*, Aramaic for "Come Lord Jesus." Cullmann relates this prayer to the resurrection and to the breaking of bread. It invited Christ to be with the worshipping congregation as they ate the eucharistic meal.[38] According to Cullmann, *Maranatha* "points at the same time backwards to Christ's appearance on the day of his resurrection, to his present appearance at the common meal of the community and forwards to his appearance at the end. . . ."[39] The Lord's Prayer was also used liturgically by the Church, as the addition of the doxology indicates. The doxology was probably an early congregational response. The *Didache* instructs Christians to pray the Lord's

---

[36] *Ephesians*, V, 2; *Trallians*, VII, 2; *Magnesians*, VII, 1; *Smyrnaeans*, VIII, 1; and IX, 1.

[37] Some scholars believe that a number of canonical writings grew out of liturgical use in the Church.

[38] Oscar Cullmann, *Early Christian Worship*, pp. 13–14.

[39] *Ibid.*, p. 14.

Prayer "three times a day" (8:3), indicating that the prayer Jesus taught his disciples to pray was used privately, as well as liturgically. Doxologies and benedictions, which abound in the New Testament, also had a common place in Christian worship.

Psalms and hymns were likewise important in worship (I Corinthians 14:26; Galatians 3:16). The psalms of the Jewish scriptures were used along with others and Christians composed hymns of their own. Some of these are preserved, at least in part, by New Testament writers who made use of local or regional liturgical traditions. Some of them are the hymns of Luke 1 and 2, *Magnificat* (1:46–55), *Benedictus* (1:68–79), and *Nunc dimittis* (2:29–32); the hymns in Revelation (4:8, 11; 19:1–2); and scattered fragments elsewhere (I Timothy 3:16; Ephesians 5:14; Philippians 2:5–11).

The "characteristic expression of early Christian worship" [40] was breaking of bread. The Church thus remembered the death of Christ and at the same time rejoiced in his living risen presence. This "joy of knowing the presence of Christ . . . was a foretaste of the final reunion in the Kingdom of God." [41] The Lord's Supper, as this sacral meal is now commonly called, was variously designated in the early Church. Besides "breaking of bread," are found *agape*, "love feast," and increasingly *eucharist*, "thanksgiving." Both terms reflect important dimensions of the meal's meaning. It was a meal of Christian fellowship and a meal of gratitude for the grace of God in Christ.

Formulae used in its celebration are traced back to Jesus himself:

And as they were eating, he took bread, and blessed, and broke it, and gave it to them, and said, "Take; this is my body." And he took a cup, and when he had given thanks he gave it to them, and they all drank of it. And he said to them, "This is my blood of the covenant, which is poured out for many" (Mark 14:22–24).[42]

Paul preserves a more elaborate form of the eucharistic invitation:

For I received from the Lord what I also delivered to you, that the Lord Jesus on the night when he was betrayed took bread, and when he had given thanks, he broke it, and said, "This is my body which is for you. Do this in remembrance of me." In the same way also the cup, after supper, saying, "This cup is the new covenant in my blood. Do this, as often as you drink it, in remembrance of me." (I Corinthians 11:23–25)

The earliest celebrations of the Supper took place in the setting of an actual meal, but it became a separate observance late in the first cen-

[40] *Ibid.*
[41] A. J. B. Higgins, *The Lord's Supper in the New Testament*, p. 89.
[42] Cf. Matt. 26:26–29 and Luke 22:15–20.

tury or early in the second. The *Didache* shows us further how the meal was liturgically observed. After a prayer of confession (*Didache* 14), words were said about the cup of wine:

We give thanks to thee, our Father, for the Holy Vine of David thy child, which thou didst make known to us through Jesus thy child; to thee be glory for ever. (9:2)

And then concerning the bread:

We give thanks our Father, for the life and knowledge which thou didst make known to us through Jesus thy child. To thee be glory for ever. As this broken bread was scattered upon the mountains, but was brought together and became one, so let thy Church be gathered together from the ends of the earth into thy kingdom, for thine is the glory and the power through Jesus Christ for ever. (9:3–4)

The other important rite of early Christian worship was baptism. Baptism was originally informally and spontaneously administered "in the name of Christ" (Acts 2:41; 8:36–37), but already the Gospel of Matthew preserves a trinitarian baptismal formulae, "in the name of the Father and of the Son and of the Holy Spirit" (28:19). Further indication of more formal administration of baptism is found in the common use of the verb *koluein*, "to hinder" (Acts 8:36; 10:47; 11:17; Matthew 3:14). This may be evidence of a liturgical question "put by a candidate for Baptism to the person administering Baptism." [43] "What hinders me from being baptized?" he would ask. The administrant then would answer, "If you believe with all your heart, you may." The candidate's answer would then be, "I believe that Jesus Christ is the Son of God." Both questions are from an ancient addition to the text of Acts 8:37 and almost certainly reflect an early baptismal liturgy.

The *Didache* describes a more structured procedure for baptism.

Concerning baptism, baptize thus: Having first rehearsed all these things, "baptize, in the Name of the Father and of the Son and of the Holy Spirit," in running water; but if thou hast no running water, baptize in other water, and if thou canst not in cold, then in warm. But if thou has neither, pour water three times on the head "in the Name of the Father, Son and Holy Spirit." And before the baptism let the baptizer and him who is to be baptized fast, and any others who are able. And thou shalt bid him who is to be baptized to fast one or two days before. (Ch. 7)

This alludes to pre-baptismal catechetical instruction. The phrase "having first rehearsed all these things" refers to the earlier chapters of the *Didache* which contrast the "Way of Life" with the "Way of Death."

---

[43] Cullmann, *Early Christian Worship*, p. 25.

How widely catechetical instruction like this was practiced and for how long is not known, but many of the didactic materials in the New Testament would have been suitable for pre-baptismal instruction.[44] Baptism as the symbol of entry into the Christian community was practiced from the day of Pentecost onward. It was linked with repentance and with the reception of the Holy Spirit. Although its purpose made its observance less frequent than the Lord's Supper, the occasions when it was celebrated were moments of sober and worshipful importance. Evidence of such moments and the more usual and regular experiences of worship make it clear that toward the end of the first century the Church was well on the way to developing a distinguished and meaningful liturgical tradition. Patterns of worship were still fluid and subject to local variations, but all forms aimed to express a faith and commitment which hallowed the liturgy.

FORMULATION OF A CHRISTIAN ETHIC: JAMES

The formulation of a Christian ethic, like the development of liturgical patterns, rested upon the basic character of the faith of early Christians. Although good behavior was not necessarily considered the essence of the Christian faith, believers understood that there could be no genuinely Christian life that is unconcerned with and unresponsive to ethical demands. Thus admonitions to good behavior are characteristic of many parts of the New Testament. Paul regularly challenged his readers to be better behaved than their non-Christian neighbors, not as a matter of law but in response to grace. The Christian religion early took seriously man's responsibility to God and his responsibility to his fellow man. Regularly, however, in the New Testament one is encouraged first to faith, then to morality. Faith and the new life are the basis of ethical action. The New Testament "does not present ethical principles but calls men to respond to the action of God." [45] The ethical teachings of the New Testament must be understood "as the description of the result of the proclamation of the redemptive act of God in the life, death, and resurrection of Jesus the Christ." [46]

---

[44] Discussions of the complex questions of the meaning of baptism, its method, and the qualifications of candidates may be found in Oscar Cullmann, *Baptism in the New Testament;* Joachim Jeremias, *Infant Baptism in the First Four Centuries;* Kurt Aland, *Did the Early Church Baptize Infants?;* Karl Barth, *The Teaching of the Church Concerning Baptism;* and W. F. Flemington, *The New Testament Doctrine of Baptism.*

[45] George W. Forell, *Christian Social Teachings,* p. 13.

[46] *Ibid.*

If the Pastorals are a reliable indicator of the Church's thought, Christian ethics were undergoing a subtle transformation when the letters were written. The dynamics of the Pauline antithesis between gospel and law was no longer characteristic of admonitions to good behavior. The basis of Christian behavior was no longer guidance by the Spirit of God through Christ, but a code of ethics. Thus the law entered again. This concern for an ethical code was partially called for by the disturbing behavior of Gnostic-like heretics who denied the world and their responsibility for decency. The Gnostic interpretation of the Christian faith did not inspire morality; world denial led to both asceticism and libertinism. The Church, therefore, sought an incentive to righteousness in codes of behavior. The author of the Pastorals appealed to "the sound word of our Lord Jesus Christ and the teaching which accords with godliness" (I Timothy 6:3). Christians were advised to avoid hatred and bickering and to manifest meekness, gentleness, obedience, and courtesy (Titus 3). The minister must insist on these things (Titus 3:8). Thus there was an ethic of law not of redemptive grace.

The epistle of James likewise emphasizes Christian deeds rather than Christian faith. The writing obviously presupposed that it was necessary to give concrete directions about the conduct of the Christian life. To some this is considered a serious weakness. The early Church did not readily include James in its canon and Luther characterized it as "a right strawy epistle" whose author "threw things together in a messy way." [47] Many modern interpreters concur and find in James an unfortunate legalizing of the Christian faith. Whether this is correct cannot be determined without examining the book.

We are immediately confronted with a problem of authorship and origin. The epistle clearly claims as its author "James, a servant of God and of the Lord Jesus Christ" (1:1). Only one James could be intended, he who was brother of Jesus and leader of Jerusalem Christianity.[48] This, however, is a pseudonym. The letter uses cultured Greek, makes no specific references to the life of Jesus or the content of his teaching, and reflects a period in the life of the Church after the death of James in A.D. 62. Further, had James the brother of Jesus really been the author, his work would surely have found ready and wide acceptance in the early Church, which it did not.

The epistle has a strong Jewish flavor that betrays the Jewish back-

[47] From his introduction to the New Testament of 1522.
[48] The Apostle James was martyred early and no other man by that name is probably author.

ground and interests of its author. Some scholars even consider it to be a Christian edition of some Jewish ethical codes. More probably it is an originally Christian writing whose author drew upon known ethical traditions some of which were Jewish, but others were Greek. His model was the literature and tradition of Hellenistic Judaism, but he wrote as a Christian for Christians.[49]

At first glance James appears to be a letter, but, in spite of its epistolary address, the book is not a letter. It is an essay of exhortation which joins together a series of aphorisms and brief discussions. No formal plan is recognizable, and no theme permeates the whole. This essay was apparently sent to as many churches as possible. It is addressed "to the twelve tribes of the dispersion" (1:1), that is, to the scattered Christian congregations, to be read to the gathered assemblies. Its author, who assumed the pseudonym James, was probably a Christian teacher, an ecclesiastical office recognized in the Pauline literature and the *Didache* as charismatic.

The teacher who wrote James, or who edited the ethical materials out of which the book is fashioned, was not a legalist. He writes of law and he gives rules and regulations, but he is ultimately concerned that faith have meaning for life and action:

Religion that is pure and undefiled before God and the Father is this: to visit orphans and widows in their affliction, and to keep oneself unstained from the world. (1:27)

The order here is proper and hardly that of a legalist, whose concern for the unstained life might well lead to neglect of the widows and orphans. This passage illustrates the two basic concerns of James. He sides with the poor against the rich (2:1–13) against his own advice about partiality (2:1). The rich are the object of his judgment, even his scorn, not because they are rich, but because they oppress the poor. He considers this almost inevitable. If two men arrive at the same time at the assembly, one rich and the other poor, everyone shows deference to the rich man. How unlike the attitude of God, who has chosen the poor to inherit his kingdom (2:5)! Unfortunately, for James "rich" seems to equal "wicked" and "poor" to equal "Christian."

The second emphasis is upon the works of faith. James was an activist who believed that "faith without works is dead" (2:17). He was struggling against Paulinists who drew upon slogans of Paul but did not live the life in Christ which the apostle championed. For them Paul's words, "For we hold that a man is justified by faith apart

[49] For detailed analysis of this problem see FBK, pp. 287–289.

from works of law" (Romans 3:28), made ethics irrelevant. This was not, of course, the intention of Paul for whom faith is active in love (Galatians 5:6). This misunderstanding needed correction. Admittedly James himself did not adequately understand the Pauline idea of faith. For James faith was intellectual belief in a statement of truth (2:19), dogmatic faith, not relational and creative faith. Thus it was imperative for him that belief not be shallow and empty. It had to result in Christian works. "You see that faith was active along with his works, and faith was completed by works" (2:22). "I by my works will show you my faith" (2:18). This emphasis was appropriate at a time when faith was increasingly identified with a body of correct doctrinal beliefs. Such faith without works of love was meaningless.

The emphasis of James "is indispensable to Christianity because he seeks to 'maintain the solidarity of the life of the community' over against the danger of a mere internalization of faith." [50] His emphasis, however, must be understood as a correction, not as a statement of the essence of Christianity. James serves the Church "only where Christians have previously heard the message of Jesus or Paul, and then let their eyes be sharpened for the exhortation to the work of faith which is already contained in this message, but not so exclusively formulated." [51]

It would really be incorrect to compare the theology of James with that of Paul. The teacher in James wanted to provide concrete ethical instruction. He developed no theology. He may give too much emphasis to works, even to the point of appearing to reject justification by faith. Whether he does or not is a moot question. By no means, however, does James develop a theology of salvation by works. Luther may have found the emphasis upon works distasteful and been correct in thinking the book was theologically barren. But he also recognized that the book "sternly declares the law of God." No false antithesis, therefore, should be created between Paul and James.

The ethical concern of James does presuppose the theology of the Gospels and Paul, as must any Christian ethic. Conditions faced by the Church now extended into a pagan and wicked Roman society presented a crisis. New converts from this society needed elementary instruction about the ethical way of the Christian life. But it should be remembered that instruction like that of James, and it is found everywhere in the New Testament, is given in the context of the whole

[50] FBK, p. 292.
[51] *Ibid.*

Christian faith. In the final analysis ethics rests upon the transforming grace of God. Jesus taught that a good tree brings forth good fruit and that no amount of external compulsion can make men really good. The Christian responds, not to imperatives, but to the leading of the Spirit. To say it another way, the ethical behavior of Christians grows out of the quality of their inner life.

The "mother" of all Christian virtues is faith in God. "Single-minded belief in the true God, . . . is the great inward virtue that marks off the Christian." [52] Closely related to this is *agape*, "love," a passionate unqualified, selfless concern for the well-being of neighbor. This love is the reflection of the love of God for man. All men are to be the objects of love, even the enemy. The early Christians were admittedly more charitable toward fellow Christians than to those outside the Church. If they were exclusive and narrow, it may have been necessary for survival, and their love for their brethren was exceptional and praiseworthy. A third moral quality of the Christian's life is humility. He is not proud. With faith in God, love for brother, and humble estimate of self he was to act in harmony with his fellow believers in response to the example of Christ. So too he was to act toward all men. The final ethical quality is personal purity. Christians had to avoid the temptations of licentious pagan life, lest they bring disgrace to Christ. This is the point at which James speaks its word. Purity of life, however, must relate to faith in God and love of neighbor. Beach and Niebuhr sum it up well:

Unless sustained by a constant inward moral mood of fidelity to God in Christ, these virtues are of no avail. When practiced out of obedience to God in Christ, they are the true fruits of the Spirit of God, who alone can redeem man's life from destruction. Thus the new life in Christ was presented as demand, as requirement, but also it was known as a gift of the Spirit, as a free and glad response to God for what he had done for men in Christ.[53]

In the New Testament ethics grows out of faith and the renewal of life in Christ. The man of faith is enabled to be ethical.[54]

The Church's attempts to structure its life and faith and to govern its behavior continued beyond the coverage of the New Testament.

---

[52] Waldo Beach and H. Richard Niebuhr, eds., *Christian Ethics*, p. 52. The paragraph which follows is based on the analysis of Beach and Niebuhr, pp. 52–56. For a more comprehensive and different analysis of the theological foundation of Christian ethics, see Rudolf Bultmann, *Theology of the New Testament*, II, pp. 203–231.

[53] Beach and Niebuhr, *Christian Ethics*, p. 56.

[54] That James stresses the latter is to his credit.

The writings of the Church Fathers reflect the sometimes bitter nature of the struggle. The Church was destined to dark and trying days when structural unity and dogmatic orthodoxy became tests of fidelity to Christ. However, in free creative understanding and faith the Church ever anew found vitality and courage to manage well its affairs and to make credible its repeated claim to be Christ's body in the world.

SUGGESTED READINGS

BARRETT, C. K., *The Pastoral Epistles in the New English Bible, With Introduction and Commentary* (Oxford, 1963).

BEASLEY-MURRAY, G. R., *Baptism in the New Testament* (St. Martin's, 1962).

BEKER, J. CHRISTIAAN, *The Church Faces the World: Late New Testament Writings* (Westminster, 1960).

DELLING, G., *Worship in the New Testament* (Westminster, 1962).

DODD, C. H., *The Johannine Epistles* (Harper, 1946).

EASTON, BURTON SCOTT, "The Epistle of James: Introduction and Exegesis," *IB*, Vol. XII.

HIGGINS, A. J. B., *The Lord's Supper in the New Testament* (SCM, 1960).

JEREMIAS, JOACHIM, *The Eucharistic Words of Jesus* (Macmillan, 1955).

KELLY, J. N. D., *The Pastoral Epistles* (Harper, 1963).

KNOX, JOHN, *The Early Church and the Coming Great Church* (Abingdon, 1955). Illuminates the development of organization in the early Church.

MOULE, C. F. D., *Worship in the New Testament* (John Knox, 1961).

REICKE, BO, *The Epistles of James, Peter, and Jude* (Doubleday, 1964).

SCHWEIZER, EDUARD, *Church Order in the New Testament* (SCM, 1961).

STREETER, BURNETT H., *The Primitive Church: Studied with Special Reference to the Origins of the Christian Ministry* (Macmillan, 1929).

WILDER, AMOS N., "The First, Second and Third Epistles of John: Introduction and Exegesis," *IB*, Vol. XII.

Appendix

CHRONOLOGY CHART FOR THE NEW TESTAMENT PERIOD

I. The Hellenistic Period

333–323 Control of East by Macedonian empire under Alexander. Following his death, Ptolemies controlled Egypt and Seleucids controlled Syria.

Egypt

Ptolemy I	323–285
Ptolemy II	285–246
Ptolemy III	246–221
Ptolemy IV	221–203
Ptolemy V	203–181
(Egypt controlled by Rome after 180 and became Roman province in 30 B.C.)	

Syria

Antiochus III	223–187
Seleucus IV	187–175
Antiochus IV Epiphanes	175–163
Antiochus V	163–162
Demetrius I	162–150
Alexander Balas	150–145
Demetrius II	145–139/8
Antiochus VI	145–142/1
Trypho, claimant of Syrian throne	142/1–138

Palestine

323–198	Judah under control of Ptolemies
198	Battle of Panium in which Seleucids gained control of Palestine
	(Took Palestine from Ptolemies in 198)
167	Maccabean Revolt
166–160	Judas the Maccabean leader
165	Religious emancipation of Jews
160–142	Jonathan, high priest
142–134	Simon, high priest
142	Beginning of Jewish political independence

II. Period of Jewish Political Independence, 142–63 B.C.

Simon, high priest	142–134
John Hyrcanus, high priest (and king?)	134–104
Aristobulus I, high priest and king	104–103
Alexander Janneus, high priest and king	103–76
Alexandra, queen	76–67
Hyrcanus II, high priest	76–67
Aristobulus II, king and high priest	67–63

67–43	Antipater the Idumean active in Palestinian affairs
63	Pompey captures Jerusalem

III. The Roman Period

63 B.C.	Pompey captures Jerusalem
48 B.C.	Julius Caesar defeats Pompey at Pharsalus
44 B.C.	Julius Caesar assassinated
42 B.C.	Octavian and Mark Antony defeat Brutus and Cassius at Philippi
31 B.C.	Battle of Actium, Octavian defeats Antony

63 B.C.	Hyrcanus appointed ethnarch and high priest under Roman control
c. 55–43	Antipater virtual ruler of Palestine under Roman grant
41 B.C.	Herod and Phasael, sons of Antipater, named tetrarchs
41–37	Parthian thrust into Palestine
40(37)–4 B.C.	Herod the Great, King of Palestine

Important Events

20–19 B.C.	Herod begins to rebuild the temple
c. 8–6 B.C.	Birth of Jesus
A.D. 27–28	Preaching of John the Baptist
A.D. 28	Baptism of Jesus by John
A.D. 30	Crucifixion
A.D. 33	Conversion of Paul

Roman Emperors

Augustus	31 B.C.–A.D. 14
Tiberius	A.D. 14–37
Caligula	A.D. 37–41
Claudius	A.D. 41–54

Rulers in Palestine

Herod the Great	37–4 B.C.

Sons of Herod

Archelaus, ethnarch of Judea, Samaria, and Idumea	4 B.C.–A.D. 6
Philip, tetrarch of Ituraea and Trachonitis	4 B.C.–A.D. 34
Herod Antipas, tetrarch of Galilee and Perea	4 B.C.–A.D. 39

Procurators of Judea

Coponius	A.D. 6–9
Ambibulus	A.D. 9–12
Annius Rufinus	A.D. 12–15
Valerius Gratus	A.D. 15–26
Pontius Pilate	A.D. 26–36
Marcellus	A.D. 36–37
Marullus	A.D. 37–41

Roman Emperor	Ruler of Palestine	Date	Event
	Herod Agrippa I — A.D. 41–44	A.D. 41–44	Peter imprisoned by Herod Agrippa I
		A.D. 44	Execution of James, son of Zebedee
	Procurators		
	Cuspius Fadus — A.D. 44–46		
	Tiberius Alexander — A.D. 46–48	A.D. 47–48	Paul in Galatia
	Ventidius Cumanus — A.D. 48–52	A.D. 49	Jews banished from Rome by Claudius
Nero — A.D. 54–68	Herod Agrippa II, king of parts of Palestine		
	M. Antonius Felix — A.D. 50–? / A.D. 52–60	A.D. 50–51	Paul in Corinth
		A.D. 53–56	Paul in Ephesus
		A.D. 58	Paul arrested in Jerusalem
	Porcius Festus — A.D. 60–62	A.D. 60	Paul in Rome
	Albinus — A.D. 62–64	A.D. 62	Death of James, brother of Jesus
	Gessius Florus — A.D. 64–66	A.D. 66–67	Flight of Christians from Jerusalem to Pella, virual end of Jerusalem Jewish church
Galba — A.D. 68		A.D. 66–73	War with Rome
Otho — A.D. 69			
Vitellius — A.D. 69			
Vespasian — A.D. 69–79		A.D. 70	Jerusalem and temple destroyed
Titus — A.D. 79–81			
Domitian — A.D. 81–96		A.D. 90	Council of Jamnia
Nerva — A.D. 96–98			
Trajan — A.D. 98–117		c. A.D. 107	Ignatius martyred in Rome; on the way to martyrdom wrote seven letters from Asia Minor
		A.D. 111–113	Pliny the Younger, governor of Bithynia
Hadrian — A.D. 117–138		A.D. 132–135	Jewish revolt under Bar-Cochba. Jerusalem made into a Gentile city, Aelia Capitolina
Antoninus Pius — A.D. 138–161			

BIBLIOGRAPHY

ABBOT, T. K., *The Epistles to the Ephesians and to the Colossians.* International Critical Commentary series (T. & T. Clark, 1897).

ALAND, KURT, *Did the Early Church Baptize Infants?* (Westminster Press, 1963).

————, MATTHEW BLACK, BRUCE METZGER, and ALLEN WIKGREN, *The Greek New Testament* (American Bible Society, 1966).

BACON, B. W., *Studies in Matthew* (Henry Holt & Co., 1930).

BARCLAY, WILLIAM, *The Acts of The Apostles.* The Daily Bible Study series (Saint Andrew Press, 1953).

————, *The Promise of the Spirit* (Epworth Press, 1960).

BARNETT, MAURICE, *The Living Flame* (Epworth Press, 1953).

BARRETT, C. K., *A Commentary On The Epistle To The Romans.* Harper's New Testament Commentaries series (Harper, 1957).

————, *The Gospel According to St. John* (S.P.C.K., 1955).

————, *Luke the Historian in Recent Study* (Epworth Press, 1961).

————, "The Old Testament in the Fourth Gospel," *Journal of Theological Studies,* XLVIII (1947), 155–169.

BARTH, KARL, *The Teaching of the Church Concerning Baptism* (S.C.M. Press, 1948).

BARTH, MARCUS, *The Broken Wall: A Study of the Epistle to the Ephesians* (Collins Press, 1960).

BATEY, RICHARD, "The Destination of Ephesians," *Journal of Biblical Literature,* LXXXII (1963), 101.

BAUER, W., "The Alleged Testimony of Josephus," *New Testament Apocrypha,* eds. Edgar Hennecke and Wilhelm Schneemelcher, tr. R. McL. Wilson (Westminster Press, 1963).

BAUR, F. C., *Paul, the Apostle of Jesus Christ, His Life and Work,* tr. Edward Zeller, rev. Alan Menzies (2nd ed., Williams and Norgate, 1876).

BEACH, WALDO, and H. RICHARD NIEBUHR, eds., *Christian Ethics* (Ronald Press, 1955).

BEARE, FRANCIS W., *The Earliest Records of Jesus* (Abingdon Press, 1962).

————, *The Epistle to the Philippians.* Black's New Testament Commentaries series (Adam and Charles Black, 1959).

BEASLEY-MURRAY, G. R., *A Commentary on Mark Thirteen* (Macmillan, 1957).

————, *Jesus and the Future* (Macmillan, 1954).

BEKER, J. CHRISTIAAN, *The Church Faces the World: Late New Testament Writings* (Westminster Press, 1960).

BETHUNE-BAKER, J. F., *An Introduction to the Early History of Christian Doctrine to the Time of the Council of Chalcedon* (4th ed., Methuen & Co., 1929).

BICKERMAN, E. J., "The Name of Christian," *Harvard Theological Review,* XLII (1949), 108–124.

BLACK, MATTHEW, "The Son of Man Problem in Recent Research and Debate," *Bulletin of the John Rylands Library,* XLV (March, 1963), 305–318.

————, ed., *Studies in the Gospels and the Epistles* (Westminster Press, 1962).

BLAIR, EDWARD P., *Jesus in the Gospel of St. Matthew* (Abingdon Press, 1960).

BLEVINS, JAMES L., "The Passion Narrative," *Review and Expositor*, LXIV (1967), 513–522.

BOOR, C. de, *Neue Fragmente des Papias, Hegesippus und Pierius. Die Abfassungszeit der Schriften Tertullianus*, von E. Noeldechen (J. C. Hinrichs'sche Buchhandlung, 1888).

BORNKAMM, GÜNTHER, *Jesus of Nazareth*, tr. Irene and Frazer McLuskey with James M. Robinson (Harper, 1960).

————, "Die Komposition der apokalyptischen Visionen in der Offenbarung Johannes," *Zeitschrift für die Neutestamentliche Wissenschaft*, XXVI (1937), 132–149.

————, GERHARD BARTH, and HEINZ J. HELD, *Tradition and Interpretation in Matthew* (Westminster Press, 1963).

BOSLOOPER, THOMAS, *The Virgin Birth* (Westminster Press, 1962).

BOURNE, FRANK C., *A History of the Romans* (D. C. Heath, 1966).

BRAATEN, CARL E., and ROY A. HARRISVILLE, trs. and eds., *The Historical Jesus and the Kerygmatic Christ: Essays on the New Quest of the Historical Jesus* (Abingdon Press, 1964).

BRANDON, S. G. F., *The Fall of Jerusalem and the Christian Church: A Study of the Effects of the Jewish Overthrow of* A.D. *70 on Christianity* (S.P.C.K., 1951).

BRONSON, DAVID B., "Paul, Galatians, and Jerusalem," *Journal of The American Academy of Religion*, XXXV (1967), 119–128.

BROWN, RAYMOND E., ed. and tr., *The Gospel According to John* (Doubleday, 1966).

BRUCE, F. F., *The Acts of the Apostles* (Eerdmans, 1952).

————, *Commentary On The Book of The Acts*. The New International Commentary on The New Testament series (Eerdmans, 1954).

————, *The English Bible: A History of Translations from the Earliest English Versions to the New English Bible* (Oxford University Press, 1961).

BUBER, MARTIN, *I and Thou*, tr. R. G. Smith (2nd ed., Charles Scribner's Sons, 1958).

BUCHANAN, C. O., "Epaphroditus' Sickness and the Letter to the Philippians," *Evangelical Quarterly*, XXXVI (1964), 157–166.

BUCK, C. H., "The Date of Galatians," *Journal of Biblical Literature*, LXX (1951), 113–122.

BULTMANN, RUDOLF, *Das Evangelium des Johannes* (15th ed., Vandenhoeck und Ruprecht, 1957).

————, *Exegetische Probleme des zweiten Korintherbriefes. Symbolae Biblicae Upsalienses* series, No. 9 (Wretmans Boktryckeri, 1947).

————, *The History of the Synoptic Tradition*, tr. John Marsh (Harper, 1963).

————, *Jesus and the Word* (Scribners, 1934).

————, *Theology of The New Testament*, tr. Kendrick Grobel (S.C.M. Press. Vol. I, 1952. Vol. II, 1955).

————, and KARL KUNDSIN, *Form Criticism: A New Method of New Testament Research*, tr. and ed. Frederick C. Grant (Willett, Clark, and Co., 1934).

BURKITT, F. CRAWFORD, *The Gospel History and Its Transmission* (2nd ed., T. & T. Clark, 1907).

BURTON, ERNEST D., *A Critical and Exegetical Commentary on the Epistle to the Galatians.* The International Critical Commentary series (T. & T. Clark, 1921).

————, "The Politarchs," *American Journal of Theology,* II (1898), 598–632.

CADBURY, HENRY J., *The Book of Acts in History* (Harper, 1955).

————, *The Making of Luke–Acts* (2nd ed., S.P.C.K., 1958).

————, *The Style and Literary Method of Luke* (Harvard Univ. Press, 1920).

————, "The Dilemma of Ephesians," *New Testament Studies,* V (1958–1959), 91–102.

CADOUX, C. J., *The Early Church and the World* (T. & T. Clark, 1925).

CAIRD, G. B., *The Apostolic Age* (Gerald Duckworth & Co., 1955).

The Cambridge Ancient History, eds. S. A. Cook, F. E. Adcock, M. P. Charlesworth. Vol. XI. (Cambridge Univ. Press, 1936).

CARLSTON, CARL E., "A Positive Criterion of Authenticity?" *Biblical Research,* VII (1962), 33–44.

CARRINGTON, PHILIP, *The Meaning of Revelation* (S.P.C.K., 1931).

CARY, MAX, *A History of Rome Down to the Reign of Constantine* (2nd ed., St. Martin's Press, 1954).

CASE, SHIRLEY J., *The Social Triumph of the Ancient Church* (Harper, 1933).

CHADWICK, HENRY, "All Things To All Men," *New Testament Studies,* I (1954–1955), 261–275.

————, ed., *The Library of Christian Classics.* Vols. I–V. (Westminster Press, 1954).

CHARLES, R. H., *The Apocrypha and Pseudepigrapha of The Old Testament.* Vol. II. (Clarendon Press, 1913).

CICERO, *The Verrine Orations,* tr. L. H. G. Greenwood. Loeb Classical Library series. Vols. I–II. (G. P. Putnam's Sons, 1928).

COLLART, PAUL, "Inscriptiones de Philippes," *Bulletin de correspondance hellénique,* LXII (1938), 409–432.

COLWELL, ERNEST C., *What Is the Best New Testament?* (Univ. of Chicago Press, 1952).

CONYBEARE, W. J., and J. S. HOWSON, *The Life and Epistles of St. Paul.* 2 Vols. (Scribner's, 1899).

CONZELMANN, HANS, *The Theology of St. Luke,* tr. Geoffrey Buswell (Harper, 1960).

————, "Auferstehung Christi," in *Die Religion in Geschichte und Gegenwart.* Vol. I (J. C. B. Mohr [Paul Siebeck], 1957).

————, "Geschichte, Geschichtesbild und Geschichtsdartellung bei Lukas," *Theologische Literaturzeitung,* LXXIX (1960), 242–248.

COUPREY, JACQUES, and MICHEL FEYEL, "Inscriptions de Philippes," *Bulletin de correspondance hellénique,* LX (1936), 37–58.

COUTTS, JOHN, "The Relationship of Ephesians and Colossians," *New Testament Studies,* IV (1957–1958), 201–207.

CRANFIELD, C. E. B., ed., *The Gospel According to St. Mark* (Cambridge Univ. Press, 1959).

CULLMANN, OSCAR, *Baptism in the New Testament* (S.C.M. Press, 1961).

——, *Early Christian Worship*. Studies in Biblical Theology series, No. 10 (S.C.M. Press, 1953).

——, *The Early Church*, ed. A. J. B. Higgins (S.C.M. Press, 1956).

——, *Peter: Disciple, Apostle, Martyr* (Rev. ed., Westminster Press, 1962).

——, *The State In The New Testament* (Westminster Press, 1956).

DAUBE, DAVID, *The New Testament and Rabbinic Judaism* (Athlone Press, 1956).

DAVIDSON, A. B., *Biblical and Literary Essays*, ed. J. A. Paterson (Hodder and Stoughton, 1902).

DAVIES, W. D., *Invitation to the New Testament* (Doubleday, 1966).

——, *The Setting of the Sermon on the Mount* (Cambridge Univ. Press, 1964).

DEISSMANN, ADOLF, *Light From the Ancient East*, tr. Lionel R. M. Strachan (Hodder and Stoughton, 1927).

——, *Paul: A Study In Social and Religious History*. Harper Torchbook series (Harper, 1957).

DIBELIUS, MARTIN, *From Tradition to Gospel*, tr. Bertram Lee Wolfe (Charles Scribner's Sons, 1935).

——, *Jesus*, tr. Charles B. Hedrick and Frederick C. Grant (Westminster Press, 1949).

——, *Studies In the Acts of the Apostles*, tr. Mary Ling (S.C.M. Press, 1956).

DIO CASSIUS, *History of Rome*, tr. Earnest Cary. Loeb Classical Library series. Vols. I–IX (Harvard Univ. Press, 1916).

DIO CHRYSOSTOM, *Discourses*, tr. J. W. Cohoon. Loeb Classical Library series. Vols. I–IX. (Harvard Univ. Press, 1916).

DODD, C. H., *The Apostolic Preaching and Its Developments* (Harper, 1936).

——, *The Epistle of Paul To The Romans*. The Moffatt New Testament Commentary series (Harper, 1932).

——, *Gospel and Law: The Relation of Faith and Ethics in Early Christianity* (Columbia Univ. Press, 1951).

——, *Historical Tradition in the Fourth Gospel* (Cambridge Univ. Press, 1963).

——, *The Interpretation of the Fourth Gospel* (Cambridge Univ. Press, 1953).

——, *New Testament Studies* (Charles Scribner's Sons, 1952).

——, *The Parables of the Kingdom* (Nisbet & Co., 1935).

——, "The Framework of the Gospel Narrative," *Expository Times*, XLIII (June, 1932), 396–400.

——, "The Life and Teaching of Jesus Christ," *A Companion to the Bible*, ed. T. W. Manson (T. & T. Clark, 1947).

DORESSE, J., *The Secret Books of the Egyptian Gnostics* (Viking Press, 1960).

DUNCAN, GEORGE S., *St. Paul's Ephesian Ministry* (Scribner's, 1930).

——, *The Epistle of Paul To The Galatians*. The Moffatt New Testament Commentary series (Harper, 1934).

————, "Paul's Ministry In Asia—The Last Phase," *New Testament Studies,* III (1956–1957), 211–218.

DUPONT, JACQUES, "Le Salut des Gentils et la Signification Theologique du Livre des Actes," *New Testament Studies,* VI (1959–1960), 132–155.

ELLIOTT-BINNS, L. E., *Galilean Christianity.* Studies In Biblical Theology series, No. 16 (S.C.M. Press, 1956).

ENSLIN, MORTON S., *The Literature of the Christian Movement.* Harper Torchlights series (Harper, 1956).

————, *Christian Beginnings.* Harper Torchlights series (Harper, 1956).

————, " 'Luke' and Paul," *Journal of American Oriental Society,* LVIII (1938), 81–91.

EPSTEIN, I., tr. and ed., *The Babylonian Talmud.* 17 Vols. (Soncino Press, 1961).

EUSEBIUS, *The Ecclesiastical History.* The Loeb Classical Library series (William Heinemann) Vol. I, tr. Kirsopp Lake (1926). Vol. II, tr. J. E. L. Oulton (1932).

EVANS, C F., "The Kerygma," *Journal of Theological Studies,* VIII (1956), 25–41.

FAW, CHALMER E., "On the Writing of First Thessalonians," *Journal of Biblical Literature,* LXXI (1952), 217–225.

FEINE, PAUL, JOHANNES BEHM, and WERNER G. KÜMMEL, *Introduction To The New Testament,* tr. A. J. Mattill, Jr. (14th rev. ed., Abingdon Press, 1966).

FILSON, FLOYD V., *A Commentary on the Gospel According to St. Matthew.* (Harper, 1960).

————, *A New Testament History: The Story of The Emerging Church.* (Westminster Press, 1964).

————, "Christian," *The Twentieth Century Encyclopedia of Religious Knowledge,* ed. L. A. Loetscher. Vol. I, 239 (Baker Book House, 1955).

————, "The Significance of the Early House Churches," *Journal of Biblical Literature,* LVIII (1939), 105–112.

FITZMEYER, J. A., "Qumran and the Interpolated Paragraph in II Cor. 6:14–7:1," *Catholic Biblical Quarterly,* XXIII (1961), 271–280.

FLANDERS, H. J., ROBERT CRAPPS, and DAVID SMITH, *People of The Covenant: An Introduction to the Old Testament* (Ronald Press, 1963).

FLEMINGTON, W. F., *The New Testament Doctrine of Baptism* (S.P.C.K., 1957).

FOAKES-JACKSON, F. J., *The Acts of The Apostles.* The Moffatt New Testament Commentary series (Harper, 1931).

————, and KIRSOPP LAKE, eds., *The Beginnings of Christianity.* Vols. I–V. (Macmillan, 1920–1933).

FORELL, GEORGE W., *Christian Social Teachings* (Anchor Books, 1966).

FRAME, JAMES E., *A Critical and Exegetical Commentary on the Epistles of St. Paul to the Thessalonians.* International Critical Commentary series (Scribner's, 1912).

FREND, W. H. C., *Martyrdom and Persecution in the Early Church: A Study of the Conflict From the Maccabees to Donatus* (Blackwell, 1965).

FULLER, REGINALD H., *Interpreting the Miracles* (Westminster Press, 1963).

————, *A Critical Introduction to the New Testament* (Duckworth, 1966).

————, *The Foundations of New Testament Christology* (Charles Scribner's Sons, 1965).

————, *The New Testament in Current Study* (Charles Scribner's Sons, 1962).

GARTNER, BERTIL, "The Habakkuk Commentary (DSH) and the Gospel of Matthew," *Studia Theologica*, VIII (1954), 1–24.

GLOVER, T. R., *The Jesus of History* (Association Press, 1917).

GOGUEL, MAURICE, *Introduction au Nouveau Testament* (Ernest Leroux, 1922).

————, *The Birth of Christianity*, tr. H. C. Snape (Allen and Unwin, 1953).

————, *The Life of Jesus*, tr. Olive Wyon (Macmillan, 1933).

GOODSPEED, EDGAR J., *An Introduction to the New Testament.* (Univ. of Chicago Press, 1937).

————, *The Key to Ephesians* (Univ. of Chicago Press, 1956).

————, *The Meaning of Ephesians* (Univ. of Chicago Press, 1933).

The Gospel According to Thomas, tr. A. Guillaumont, H. C. Puech, G. Quispel, W. Till, and Y. 'Abdal Masih (Harper, 1959).

GRAMBERG, K. P. C. A., "Leprosy and the Bible," *The Bible Translator*, XI (January, 1950), 10–23.

GRANT, F. C., *The Earliest Gospel* (Abingdon Press, 1943).

————, ed., *Early Christianity* (Seabury Press, 1954).

GRANT, ROBERT M., *Gnosticism and Early Christianity* (Columbia Univ. Press, 1959).

————, *A Historical Introduction to the New Testament* (Harper, 1963).

————, *The Sword and the Cross* (Macmillan, 1955).

GROBEL, K., ed. and tr., *The Gospel of Truth* (Abingdon, 1960).

HAENCHEN, ERNST, "Das 'Wir' in der Apostelgeschichte und das Itinerar," *Zeitschrift für Theologie und Kirche*, LVIII (1961), 329–366.

HARNACK, ADOLF, *The Mission and Expansion of Christianity in the First Three Centuries*, tr. and ed. James Moffatt. Vols. I–II (G. P. Putnam's Sons, 1904).

HARRISON, P. N., "The Pastoral Epistles and Duncan's Ephesian Theory," *New Testament Studies*, VII (1955–1956), 250–261.

————, "Onesimus and Philemon," *Anglican Theological Review*, XXXII (1950), 268–294.

HAY, LEWIS S., "Mark's Use of the Messianic Secret," *Journal of the American Academy of Religion*, XXXV (1967), 16–27.

HENNECKE, EDGAR, *New Testament Apocrypha*, ed. Wilhelm Schneemelcher, tr. R. McL. Wilson. Vol. I (Westminster Press, 1963).

HENSHAW, THOMAS, *New Testament Literature in the Light of Modern Research* (Rev. ed., Allen and Unwin, 1957).

HIGGINS, A. J. B., *The Lord's Supper in the New Testament* (S.C.M. Press, 1960).

————, ed., *New Testament Essays: Studies In Memory of Thomas Walter Manson* (Manchester Univ. Press, 1959).

HOBART, W. K., *The Medical Language of St. Luke* (Baker Book House, 1954). Reprint.

HORT, F. J. A., *Prolegomena to St. Paul's Epistles to the Romans and the Ephesians* (Macmillan, 1895).

HOSKYNS, E. C., *The Fourth Gospel* (Faber & Faber Ltd., 1947).

HULL, WILLIAM E., "A Teaching Outline of the Gospel of Matthew," *Review and Expositor*, LIX (1962), 436–444.

HUNTER, A. M., *Interpreting Paul's Gospel* (S.C.M. Press, 1954).

———, "Recent Trends in Johannine Studies," *Expository Times*, LXXI (1960), 164–167, 219–222.

HYATT, J. PHILIP, ed., *The Bible In Modern Scholarship* (Abingdon Press, 1965).

The Interpreter's Bible. Vols. VII–XII (Abingdon Press, 1953).

The Interpreter's Dictionary of The Bible. Vols. I–IV (Abingdon Press, 1962).

JAMES, M. R., *The Apocryphal New Testament* (Clarendon Press, 1924).

JEREMIAS, JOACHIM, "Isolated Sayings of the Lord," in Hennecke and Schneemelcher, eds., *New Testament Apocrypha*, I, tr. R. McL. Wilson (Westminster Press, 1963).

———, *The Central Message of the New Testament* (Charles Scribner's Sons, 1965).

———, *The Eucharistic Words of Jesus*, tr. Norman Perrin (Charles Scribner's Sons, 1966).

———, *Infant Baptism in the First Four Centuries* (S.C.M. Press, 1960).

———, *The Parables of Jesus*, tr. S. H. Hooke (6th ed., Charles Scribner's Sons, 1962).

———, *The Problem of the Historical Jesus* (Fortress Press, 1964).

JOHNSON, AUBREY, *The Vitality of the Individual in The Thought of Ancient Israel* (Univ. of Wales Press, 1949).

JOHNSON, SHERMAN E., "Laodicea and its Neighbors," *The Biblical Archaeologist*, XIII (1950), 1–18.

———, "The Preaching to the Dead," *Journal of Biblical Literature*, LXXIX (1960), 48–50.

JONAS, HANS, *The Gnostic Religion: The Message of the Alien God and the Beginnings of Christianity* (2nd ed., Beacon Press, 1963).

JOSEPHUS, FLAVIUS, *The Life and Works of Josephus*, tr. William Whiston (John C. Winston Co., n.d.).

KÄSEMANN, ERNST, *Essays on New Testament Themes*. Studies in Biblical Theology series, No. 41 (S.C.M. Press, 1964).

———, "Das Interpretationsproblem des Epheserbriefes," *Theologische Literaturzeitung*, LXXX (1961), 2–7.

KECK, LEANDER E., "The Introduction to Mark's Gospel," *New Testament Studies*, XII (1965–1966), 352–370.

———, and J. LOUIS MARTYN, eds., *Studies in Luke–Acts* (Abingdon Press, 1966).

KEE, HOWARD, FRANKLIN YOUNG, and KARLFRIED FROEHLICH, *Understanding the New Testament* (2nd ed., Prentice-Hall, 1965).

KELLY, J. N. D., *Early Christian Creeds* (Longmans, 1960).

KEPLER, THOMAS S., *Contemporary Thinking About Paul* (Abingdon Press, 1950).

KIERKEGAARD, SØREN, *Purity of Heart Is To Will One Thing*, tr. Douglas V. Steere. Harper Torchlight series (Harper, 1948).

KILPATRICK, G. D., *The Origins of the Gospel According to St. Matthew*. (Clarendon Press, 1949).

KITTEL, GERHARD, ed., *Theological Dictionary of the New Testament*, tr. Geoffrey W. Bromiley. Vols. I–IV (Eerdmans, 1964).

KLASSEN, WILLIAM, and GRAYDON F. SNYDER, eds., *Current Issues in New Testament Interpretation* (Harper, 1962).

KLAUSNER, JOSEPH, *Jesus of Nazareth: His Life, Times, and Teachings*, tr. Herbert Danby (Macmillan, 1925).

KNOX, JOHN, *Chapters in a Life of Paul* (Abingdon Press, 1950).

———, *The Early Church and the Coming Great Church* (Abingdon Press, 1955).

———, *Marcion and the New Testament* (Univ. of Chicago Press, 1942).

———, *Philemon Among the Letters of Paul* (Rev. ed., Univ. of Chicago Press, 1959).

KNOX, WILFRED A., *The Acts of The Apostles* (Cambridge Univ. Press, 1948).

KRAELING, CARL H., *John the Baptist* (Charles Scribner's Sons, 1951).

KÜMMEL, WERNER G., *Promise and Fulfillment: The Eschatological Message of Jesus*, tr. Dorothea M. Barton (3rd ed., Allenson, 1957).

LAKE, KIRSOPP, *The Earlier Epistles of St. Paul* (Rivingtons, 1911).

LATOURETTE, KENNETH S., *A History of The Expansion of Christianity: The First Five Centuries*. Vol. I (Harper, 1937).

LÄUCHLI, S., "Eine Gottesdienstrucktur in der Johannesaffenbarung," *Theologische Zeitschrift*, XVI (1960), 359–378.

LEMERLE, PAUL, "Palestre Romaine a Philippes," *Bulletin de correspondance hellénique*, LXI (1937), 86–102.

LIETZMANN, HANS, *The Beginnings of the Christian Church*, tr. Bertram Lee Woolf (Charles Scribner's Sons, 1937).

LIGHTFOOT, J. B., *St. Paul's Epistle To The Galatians* (Macmillan, 1880).

LIGHTFOOD, R. H., *The Gospel Message of St. Mark* (Clarendon Press, 1950).

LOCKWOOD, D. P., *A Survey of Classical Roman Literature, II* (Univ. of Chicago Press, 1962).

LOETSCHER, LEFFERTS A., ed., *Twentieth Century Encyclopedia of Religious Knowledge*. Vols. I–II (Baker Book House, 1955).

LOHMEYER, ERNST, *Galiläa und Jerusalem* (Vandenhoeck & Ruprecht, 1936).

———, *Der Brief an die Philipper*. Kritisch-exegetischer Kommentar über das Neu Testament, 13. Auflage (Vandenhoeck & Ruprecht, 1964).

MACHEN, J. GRESHAM, *The Virgin Birth of Christ* (Harper, 1930).

MACKAY, B. S., "Further Thoughts on Philippians," *New Testament Studies*, VII (1960–1961), 161–170.

MANSON, T. W., *The Sayings of Jesus* (S.C.M. Press, 1949).

———, *The Servant-Messiah: A Study of the Public Ministry of Jesus* (Cambridge Univ. Press, 1953).

———, *Studies in the Gospels and Epistles*, ed. Matthew Black (Westminster Press, 1962).

———, *The Teaching of Jesus* (2nd ed., Cambridge Univ. Press, 1948).

———, ed., *A Companion to the Bible* (T. & T. Clark, 1947).

————, "St. Paul in Ephesus; (3) The Corinthian Correspondence," *Bulletin of John Rylands Library*, XXVI (1941–1942), 101–120.

————, "St. Paul's Letter to the Romans—and Others," *Bulletin of John Rylands Library*, XXXI (1948), 224–240.

MANSON, WILLIAM, *The Epistle to the Hebrews* (Hodder and Stoughton, 1951).

MARXSEN, W., "Der Evangelist Markus," *Forschungen zur Religion und Literature des Alten und Neuen Testaments.* LXVII (1956).

MATTINGLY, H. B., "The Origin of the Name Christian," *Journal of Theological Studies*, IX (April, 1958), 26–37.

McARTHUR, HARVEY K., *Understanding the Sermon on the Mount* (Harper, 1960).

McCASLAND, S. VERNON, *By The Finger of God: Demon Possession and Exorcism in Early Christianity in the Light of Modern Views of Mental Illness* (Macmillan, 1951).

McDONALD, W. A., "Archaeology and St. Paul's Journeys in Greek Lands," *The Biblical Archaeologist*, III (1940), 18–24; IV (1941), 1–10; V (1942), 36–48.

McNEILE, A. H., *An Introduction To The Study of the New Testament* (2nd ed., Clarendon Press, 1953).

METZGER, BRUCE M., "Antioch-on-the-Orontes," *The Biblical Archaeologist*, XI (1948), 70–88.

————, "St. Paul and the Magicians," *Princeton Seminary Bulletin*, XXXVIII (1944), 27–30.

MILLER, DONALD G., *The Gospel According to Luke.* Layman's Bible Commentary, ed. Balmer H. Kelly (John Knox Press, 1959).

MITTON, CHARLES L., *The Epistle to the Ephesians: Its Authorship, Origin, and Purpose* (Clarendon Press, 1961).

MOFFATT, JAMES, *A Critical and Exegetical Commentary on the Epistle to the Hebrews.* International Critical Commentary series (T. & T. Clark, 1924).

————, *An Introduction to the Literature of the New Testament* (3rd ed., T. & T. Clark, 1918).

MOORE, GEORGE F., *Judaism.* Vols. I–II (Harvard Univ. Press, 1927).

MUNCK, JOHANNES, *The Acts of The Apostles.* The Anchor Bible series, Vol. XXXI (Doubleday, 1967).

————, *Paul and The Salvation of Mankind* (S.C.M. Press, 1959).

NAUCK, W., "Freude im Leiden," *Zeitschrift für die neutestamentliche Wissenschaft*, XLVI (1955), 66–80.

NEILL, STEPHEN, *The Interpretation of The New Testament, 1861–1961* (Oxford Univ. Press, 1964).

The New English Bible: New Testament (Oxford and Cambridge Univ. Presses, 1961).

NEWMAN, BARCLAY M., *The Meaning of the New Testament* (Broadman Press, 1966).

NIEBUHR, REINHOLD, *The Nature and Destiny of Man.* The Scribner Library edition. 2 Vols. (Charles Scribner's Sons, 1964).

NINEHAM, D. E., *Studies in the Gospels: Essays in Memory of R. H. Lightfoot* (Basil Blackwood, 1955).

O'Neill, J. C., *The Theology of Acts in Its Historical Setting* (S.P.C.K., 1961).

Orchard, Bernard, "A New Solution to the Galatian Problem," *Bulletin of John Rylands Library*, XXVIII (1944), 154–174.

Ovid, *Metamorphosis*, tr. Frank J. Miller. Loeb Classical Library series. Vols. I–II (G. P. Putnam's Sons, 1916).

Parker, Pierson, "Once More, Acts and Galatians," *Journal of Biblical Literature*, LXXXVI (1967), 175–182.

Parvis, Merrill M., "Archaeology and St. Paul's Journeys in Greek Lands," *The Biblical Archaeologist*, VIII (1945), 62–80.

Percy, Ernst, *Die Probleme der Kolosser– und Epheserbriefe* (C. W. K. Gleerup, 1946).

Perrin, Norman, *The Kingdom of God in the Teaching of Jesus* (Westminster Press, 1963).

———, *Rediscovering the Teaching of Jesus* (Harper, 1967).

Pherigo, L. P., "Paul and the Corinthian Church," *Journal of Biblical Literature*, LXVIII (1949), 341–350.

Price, James L., *Interpreting The New Testament* (Holt, Rinehart and Winston, 1961).

Rackham, Richard B., *The Acts of The Apostles*. Westminster Commentary series (Methuen & Co., 1901).

Rahtjen, B. D., "The Three Letters of Paul to the Philippians," *New Testament Studies*, VI (1959–1960), 167–173.

Ramsay, W. M., *The Bearing of Recent Discovery on the Trustworthiness of the New Testament* (Hodder and Stoughton, 1920).

———, *The Cities of St. Paul* (A. C. Armstrong & Son, 1908).

———, *St. Paul The Traveller and the Roman Citizen* (6th ed., Hodder and Stoughton, 1902).

Rawlinson, A. E. J., *The Gospel According to St. Mark* (5th ed., Methuen & Co., 1942).

Redlich, E. Basil, *Form Criticism: Its Value and Limitations* (Duckworth, 1939).

Reicke, Bo, "The Disobedient Spirits and Christian Baptism." *Acta Seminarii Neotestamentici Upsaliensis*, XIII (Munksgaard, 1946).

———, *The Epistles of James, Peter, and Jude* (Doubleday, 1964).

Rissi, M., "Zeit und Geschichte in der Offenbarung des Johannes," in *Abhandlungen zur Theologie des Alten und Neuen Testaments*, XXII (1952).

Roberts, Alexander, and James Donaldson, eds., *The Ante-Nicene Fathers*. Vols. I–IX (The Christian Literature Pub. Co., 1885).

Roberts, C. H., *An Unpublished Fragment of the Fourth Gospel in The John Rylands Library* (Manchester Univ. Press, 1935).

Robinson, James M., *A New Quest of the Historical Jesus* (Allenson, 1949).

———, "A Formal Analysis of Colossians 1:15–20," *Journal of Biblical Literature*, LXXVI (1957), 270–287.

———, "The Recent Debate on the New Quest," *Journal of Bible and Religion*, XXX (1962), 198–208.

Rowley, H. H., *The Relevance of Apocalyptic* (Lutterworth Press, 1944).

RUSSELL, D. S., *The Method and Message of Jewish Apocalyptic, 200 B.C.–A.D. 100* (Westminster Press, 1964).

SANDAY, WILLIAM, and ARTHUR HEADLAM, *A Critical and Exegetical Commentary on the Epistle to the Romans.* International Critical Commentary series. (5th ed., T. & T. Clark, 1902).

SANDERS, J. N., "Peter and Paul In The Acts," *New Testament Studies,* II (1955–1956), 133–143.

SANDMEL, SAMUEL, *The Genius of Paul: A Study In History* (Farrar, Straus & Cudahy, 1958).

———, *A Jewish Understanding of the New Testament* (Hebrew Union College Press, 1956).

SCHAFF, PHILIP, and HENRY WACE, eds., *A Select Library of the Nicene and Post-Nicene Fathers of the Christian Church* (Eerdmans, 1953). First series, 14 Vols.; second series, 14 Vols.

SCHMITHALS, WALTER, "Die Irrlehrer des Philipperbriefes," *Zeitschrift für Theologie und Kirche,* LIV (1957), 297–341.

SCHWEIZER, EDUARD, *Church Order in the New Testament.* Studies in Biblical Theology series, No. 32 (S.C.M. Press, 1961).

———, "Mark's Contribution to the Quest of the Historical Jesus," *New Testament Studies,* X (1963–1964), 421–432.

———, "Die Kirche als Leib Christi in den Paulinischen Antilegomena," *Theologische Literaturzeitung,* LXXX (1961), 242–255.

SCOTT, ERNEST F., *The Epistle To The Hebrews* (T. & T. Clark, 1922).

———, *The Epistle of Paul to the Colossians, to Philemon, and to the Ephesians.* Moffatt New Testament Commentary (Hodder and Stoughton, 1930).

———, *The Literature of The New Testament* (Columbia Univ. Press, 1932).

SELBY, DONALD J., *Toward The Understanding of St. Paul* (Prentice-Hall, 1962).

SELWYN, EDWARD, *The First Epistle of St. Peter* (Macmillan, 1955).

SMITH, DWIGHT M. J., *The Composition and Order of the Fourth Gospel* (Yale Univ. Press, 1965).

SMITH, JAMES, *The Voyage and Shipwreck of St. Paul* (4th ed., Longmans, Brown, Green, Longmans and Roberts, 1880).

SMITH, T. C., *Jesus in the Gospel of John* (Broadman Press, 1959).

———, "The Book of Signs," *Review and Expositor,* LXII (1965), 441–457.

STACEY, W. DAVID, *The Pauline View of Man* (Macmillan, 1956).

STAGG, FRANK, *The Book of Acts: The Early Struggle for an Unhindered Gospel* (Broadman Press, 1955).

STAUFFER, E., *Christ and the Caesars,* tr. K. and R. Gregor Smith (Westminster Press, 1955).

STENDAHL, KRISTER, *The School of St. Matthew and Its Use of the Old Testament* (C. W. K. Gleerup, 1954).

———, ed., *The Scrolls and the New Testament* (Harper, 1957).

STEVENSON, J., ed., *A New Eusebius: Documents Illustrative of the History of the Church to A.D. 337* (S.P.C.K., 1957).

STONEHOUSE, NED B., *The Aeropagus Address* (Tyndale Press, 1949).

STRABO, *The Geography of Strabo*, tr. Horace L. Jones (G. P. Putnam's Sons, 1917).

STREETER, B. H., *The Four Gospels: A Study of Origins* (Rev. ed., Macmillan, 1951).

———, *The Primitive Church Studied with Special Reference to the Origin of the Christian Ministry* (Macmillan, 1929).

SUETONIUS, GAIUS, *The Twelve Caesars*, tr. Robert Graves. Penguin Classics series (Penguin Books, 1957).

TALBERT, CHARLES H., *Luke and the Gnostics* (Abingdon Press, 1966).

———, "Again: Paul's Visits To Jerusalem," *Novum Testamentum,* IX (1967), 26–40.

———, "The Lucan Presentation of Jesus' Ministry in Galilee," *Review and Expositor,* LXIV (1967), 485–497.

TAYLOR, T. M., "The Place and Origin of Romans," *Journal of Biblical Literature,* LXVII (1948), 281–295.

TAYLOR, VINCENT, *The Formation of the Gospel Tradition* (Macmillan, 1933).

———, *The Gospel According to St. Mark* (Macmillan, 1952).

———, *The Historical Evidence for the Virgin Birth* (Clarendon Press, 1920).

———, *The Life and Ministry of Jesus* (Abingdon Press, 1955).

TEEPLE, HOWARD M., *The Mosaic Eschatological Prophet* (Society of Biblical Literature, 1957).

THROCKMORTON, B. H., JR., ed., *Gospel Parallels: A Synopsis of the First Three Gospels* (2nd ed., Thomas Nelson & Sons, 1957).

VAN UNNIK, W. C., *Newly Discovered Gnostic Writings* (S.C.M. Press, 1960).

———, "Christianity According to First Peter," *Expository Times,* LXVIII (1956), 79–83.

VIA, DAN O., JR., *The Parables: Their Literary and Existential Dimension* (Fortress Press, 1967).

VON DOBSCHÜTZ, E., "Matthäus als Rabbi und Katechet," *Zeitschrift für die neutestamentliche Wissenschaft,* XXVII (1928), 338–348.

WEISS, JOHANNES, *The History of Primitive Christianity,* ed. Frederick C. Grant. Vols. I–II (Macmillan, 1937).

WIKENHAUSER, ALFRED, *New Testament Introduction* (Herder & Herder, 1963).

WILLIAMS, C. S. C., *A Commentary on The Acts of the Apostles*. Harper's New Testament Commentaries (Harper, 1957).

WINN, A. C., *Acts of the Apostles*. Layman's Bible Commentary series (John Knox Press, 1960).

WREDE, WILLIAM, *Der Messiasgeheimnis in den Evangelien* (Vandenhoeck & Ruprecht, 1963).

WRIGHT, GEORGE E., *Biblical Archaeology* (Westminster Press, 1960).

———, and FLOYD FILSON, eds., *The Westminster Historial Atlas to the Bible* (Rev. ed., Westminster Press, 1956).

YADIN, YIGAEL, *Masada: Herod's Fortress and the Zealots' Last Stand,* tr. Moshe Pearlman (Random House, 1966).

ZELLER, EDUARD, *The Contents and Origin of the Acts of the Apostles,* tr. Joseph Dare (Williams & Norgate, 1875–1876).

GLOSSARY

Agrapha—The "unwritten things." A term used for sayings purported to be from Jesus but not in the canonical Gospels. So called because some of the sayings are survivals from the oral tradition of the early Church.

Apocalypse—Greek word meaning "revelation." Used of literature characterized by:
1. Conflict between good and evil.
2. Speculation about the end of the present evil age and the dawn of the age to come.
3. Encouragement to the faithful to endure to the end.

Apocalyptic—Type of literature common in Judaism in the late centuries B.C. and early centuries A.D. Characterized by symbolic language and elaborate imagery. Takes its name from the Greek word *apocalupsis,* "revelation." See *Apocalypse.*

Apocrypha—Greek word meaning "hidden things." Used in the early Church for books withheld from the public because of their strange character and because they were thought to contain unusual knowledge. Later it referred to certain Jewish writings which did not become part of the Old Testament Canon. For Protestants it applies specifically to books included in the Septuagint and Vulgate, but not in the Hebrew Bible.

Apocrypha, New Testament—Books of all kinds similar to the writings in the New Testament Canon. These writings are of different values and dates.

Apostle—A commissioned "messenger" or "ambassador." In Christian usage it designates:
1. Certain men of the first Christian generation, the Twelve plus Paul.
2. A missionary of the gospel.

Apostolic Fathers—Term commonly used to designate a group of writings by authors reputed to have been associated with the apostles or their immediate disciples.

Baptism—A water rite imposed upon converts from the beginning of the Christian Church. It identified the baptized as a member of the Christian community.

Bishop—From the Greek *episkopos,* "overseer." An official in the early church whose qualifications are stated in I Timothy 3:1–7. Bishops were to care for local congregations and were responsible for preaching, correspondence, administration, and soundness of doctrine.

Canon—A term which means "standard." Used as a technical term for an authoritative collection of religious literature.

Charismatic—Possessed by the spirit; led by the power of God. The word refers to certain leaders in the early Church whose authority came not from appointment but from personal gifts or talents understood as clear evidence of God's guidance.

Christ—See *Messiah.*

Church—See *Ekklesia.*

Church Fathers—The leaders and writers of the early Church. Their works
are the primary source for understanding the life and thought of the
Church in the early centuries of Christian history.

Circumcision—The act of cutting off the foreskin of the male genital. Among
the Israelites circumcision was a religious rite performed on the eighth
day after birth as a sign of the covenant between Yahweh and Israel.

Deacon—A title of one of the major orders of ministry in the Church. The
word means "servant" and in the New Testament applies to men who,
with bishops, were responsible for the life and order of specific congregations.

Dead Sea Scrolls—Biblical and non-biblical manuscripts and fragments found
since 1947 in caves along the Dead Sea; they came from the Essene
community of Qumran. These scrolls contain ideas which provide
background for certain New Testament concepts.

Didache—The Greek word for "teaching." Specifically used for the content
of the early Church's teaching. As a proper name, *Didache* refers to
the oldest known document of a class denoted as "Church Orders."
The document is fully titled *The Didache of the Twelve Apostles* and
contains instructions in doctrine, ministry, and worship.

Disciple—A "learner" or "pupil." In the New Testament it designates:
1. An adherent of almost any leader.
2. Believers in Christ.
3. One of the Twelve.

Dualism—Theory that reality is composed of two opposing forces.
1. Cosmic dualism: belief in two equal and opposing gods, one good
and the other evil.
2. Metaphysical dualism: belief that matter is imperfect or evil and
the world of the spirit or gods is good. Related to this is the idea that
the body and soul are essentially incompatible with one another.
Body is inferior to soul and serves as its prison; salvation is the
deliverance of the soul from the body.

Ekklesia—The Greek word for Church. Properly refers to "an assembly"
of citizens. In the LXX it refers to the congregation or community of
Israel. In the New Testament it is used especially of an assembly or
company of Christians, of local congregations, of house congregations,
and of the whole body of Christians.

Elders—See *Presbyters*.

Epistle—A letter, either personal or literary. The New Testament contains
many works in the form of letters. Some are genuine letters written
to specific congregations or persons (as I and II Corinthians, Galatians,
II and III John). Others use the literary form of epistle to make
a theological or ethical statement to a general audience (as James,
I John, II Peter).

Eschatology—A Greek word meaning "doctrine or teaching concerning the
end." It broadly refers to biblical views of God's bringing his purpose
on earth to completion at the end of the present historical epoch.

Essenes—Ascetic Jewish sect of late pre-Christian and early Christian period.
Lived in monastic establishments, the most famous of which was
at Qumran.

Eucharist—Greek for "thanksgiving." The name commonly used in the early Church for the rite of the Lord's Supper.

Evangelist—A title of early Christian missionaries and preachers of the gospel (*euangelion*). A more restrictive use designates the authors of the four canonical Gospels.

Exorcism—The expelling of evil spirits from persons or places by a variety of means, usually by incantations or cultic rites. In the New Testament Jesus and the Apostles exorcise unclean spirits without resorting to cultic practices or other aids.

Form Criticism—A method of studying and analyzing materials which for some time had been passed on orally. Based on the assumption that such material was passed on in small units and in a limited number of set formal types. In New Testament studies Form Criticism has been applied to the traditions about Jesus.

Fourth Gospel—A name used for the Gospel of John which because of its different character is studied apart from the first three or Synoptic Gospels.

Gentiles—Common translation for the Greek word *ethne*, "nations." Specifically the non-Jewish peoples in contrast to the Jews.

Gnosticism—A system of thought prominent in the second century A.D. but with earlier antecedents. Gnostics claimed to have superior knowledge (*gnosis*) of God and his purposes. Their elaborate mythology posed a serious threat to the integrity of the early Church.

God-fearer—A non-Jew who showed interest in the Jewish religion, who attended the synagogue and tried to learn the Jewish way, but was not a full convert to Judaism.

Hellenism—The spirit of Hellas, Greece. The civilization which spread over the Mediterranean world and the Near East as the result of the conquests of Alexander the Great.

Hellenists—Greek-speaking Jews contrasted to the "Hebrews," or Jews who spoke Hebrew or Aramaic. The Hellenists to varying degrees adopted Greek culture.

Infancy Narratives—Narratives in Matthew and Luke of the birth of Jesus and related events.

Internal Evidence—A term referring to a book's own testimony about its author, audience, occasion, and purpose.

Johannine Literature—The Gospel of John, sometimes called the Fourth Gospel; I, II, and III John; Revelation. Literature which in the tradition of the Church is associated with a certain John, sometimes identified as the Apostle.

Josephus—Jewish historian, born A.D. 37/38. His works are: *The Jewish Wars, Antiquities of the Jews,* the *Life,* and *Against Apion.* As a historian he is often uncritical, but he is the only source for much postexilic Jewish history.

Judaism—The belief and life of the Jews; the total life of the Jewish community. Technically speaking the religion of Israel developing after the time of Ezra (fifth century B.C.).

Judaizers—Jewish Christian conservatives who wanted to force all Christians to observe Jewish cultic and ritual laws.

Kerygma—The general Greek term for "preaching." Specifically used of the content of the early Church's proclamation about Jesus.

Kingdom of God—The idea of the kingly rule or sovereignty of God. The Kingdom of God was the central theme in the teachings of Jesus.

Kingdom of Heaven—Matthew's circumlocution for Kingdom of God. Used by Matthew to follow the Jewish custom of not using directly the divine name.

Koinonia—The "common" fellowship of the early Church. At first applied to the infant Jerusalem Church whose members held all things in "common." More generally applied to the "fellowship," within the Christian community.

L—Symbol used for the materials peculiar to the Gospel of Luke.

Logos—Greek word meaning "speaking," "statement," "word," "matter," "reason." Used by the author of the Fourth Gospel as a designation of Jesus. This use draws from both Old Testament and Hellenistic concepts of word, wisdom, and reason.

Lord—The English translation of *kurios,* a Greek word expressing the idea of one who commands respect and authority; it may mean "sir," or "master." The Septuagint used Lord (*kurios*) as a substitute for Yahweh, and this usage carried on into the New Testament with the result that Lord (*kurios*) is a title of confession of the divinity or diety of Jesus Christ.

M—Symbol used for the materials peculiar to the Gospel of Matthew.

Maccabees—The family of Mattathias, priest of Modin. Mattathias began, and his five sons continued, a Jewish revolt against the Seleucid Greeks in the second century B.C.

Messiah—Hebrew word meaning "the anointed one." Kings, priests, and others were anointed with oil and set apart for a particular office or function. *The Messiah* refers to an individual whom God will use to establish his authority over all the earth. In Israelite literature the coming one is a kingly figure, a priestly figure, or a prophetic figure. The kingly figure is more prominent. *Christ* is the Greek translation for *messiah.*

Miracle—An act or event in which is seen the power and presence of God. The miracle stories of the Gospels have the same form as Jewish and Hellenistic miracle stories: first a description of the situation which calls forth the miracle, then a description of the miraculous act itself, and finally an account of the consequences of the miracle.

Mystery Religion—Religious rites of esoteric character which were common in the Hellenistic world. The rites aimed to gain life, to strengthen its forces, and to prolong it after death. There were many different mysteries, but all contained the common elements:
1. Ritual enactment of the myth.
2. Participation in ritual renewal of the cycle of life.

New Quest for the Historical Jesus—The modern study of the life of the earthly Jesus, especially his teachings. The major impetus for this quest came from an address by Ernst Käsemann, a student of Rudolf Bultmann who disagreed with some of the presuppositions of his teacher. The new quest uses literary, form, and redaction criticism and differs from the old nineteenth century quest in that it disavows any hope of writing a biography of Jesus.

Parable—An extended metaphor or simile forming a brief narrative. Differs from an allegory in that a parable basically illustrates a single idea. The parable is the characteristic form of Jesus' teachings and the rediscovery of its nature and meaning has assisted greatly in the rediscovery of the message of Jesus.

Parousia—A transliteration of a Greek word meaning "presence" or "coming." Used as a technical term for the future eschatological coming of Christ. See *Eschatology*.

Passion Narrative—The account of Jesus' death and the events that immediately preceded. In all four canonical Gospels the passion accounts are very similar. This narrative was the first extended story about Jesus told by the early Church.

Passover—Jewish festival commemorating the Exodus deliverance of Israel from Egypt.

Pentecost—The Greek name for the Jewish Feast of Weeks, so called because it occurred on the fiftieth day after the ceremony of the barley sheaf during Passover. Christians reinterpreted Pentecost as the day when the Holy Spirit came upon the Church.

Pharisees—A post-Maccabean Jewish sect which was devoted to the law, written and oral. Pharisees were very influential in the synagogue.

Presbyters—Transliteration of the Greek word meaning "elder."
1. Sometimes refers only to the older, respected members of a Christian congregation.
2. Specifically refers to leaders of the church whose responsibilities were similar to those of bishops. Sometimes presbyters and bishops appear to hold identical office, but on other occasions are to be distinguished from one another.

Procurator—Financial and military official representing the Roman emperor in administration of certain provinces which were under the authority of the emperor rather than the Senate. Palestine was administered by procurators during most of the New Testament period.

Proselyte—A person associated with a religious community not his own. More specifically, a convert to Judaism.

Pseudonymous Authorship—The use of a fictitious or pen name. The adoption of the name of a prominent person was an ancient literary device for acknowledging indebtedness or for securing a hearing for an idea or ideas. Pseudonymous books in the New Testament are II Peter, James, Jude, and possibly the Pastoral Epistles.

Q—Short for *Quelle*, "source." Used to designate a hypothetical collection of Jesus' teachings made by the apostolic community of the early Church. The Q materials were used by the authors of Matthew and Luke.

Rabbi—Hebrew for "my master." As a title the term means "master" in the sense of teacher. Rabbis in New Testament times were men learned in the Torah as well as teachers of the law. They did not necessarily hold official appointment.

Rabbinic Tradition—The scriptural interpretation of the rabbis, especially of

Torah. The kind of material which was eventually incorporated into the Talmud.

Redaction Criticism—The study of the editorial or redactional elements in each of the four Gospels to determine each author's theological purposes and emphases.

Sadducees—A Jewish religious sect which originated during the late pre-Christian era. Conservative and aristocratic. Rejected the authority of oral tradition and theological belief in the resurrection. Held fast to the Torah. Controlled the temple and Sanhedrin in Jerusalem.

Seleucids—Rulers of the Hellenistic state in Syria from 305–64 B.C. Their kingdom was commonly called the Seleucid state.

Sermon on the Mount—A collection of Jesus' teachings on the subject of the true disciple. The Sermon is found in Matt. 5:3–7:27 and is one of five long discourses which are a characteristic of the First Gospel.

Son of David—The title for the Messiah used from the late second and early first centuries B.C. (Ps. of Sol. 17:28) and based on the idea of a Messiah descended from the family of David.

Source Criticism—A study of the literary sources and relationships of the first three Gospels (Synoptic Gospels). The basic conclusion of Source Criticism is that Mark was the earliest of the Synoptic Gospels, that Matthew and Luke both used Mark along with another source (See Q), and that Matthew and Luke also had independent sources (See L and M).

Suffering Servant—The ideal for Israel as envisaged by the author of Isaiah 40–55. The perfectly obedient, self-sacrificing servant of God. The Gospels interpret Jesus as Messiah in light of the idea of the Suffering Servant.

Synagogue—The local institution for Jewish religious instruction and worship. Synagogues became widespread in the fourth and third centuries B.C. They are not mentioned in the Old Testament, but reference in the New Testament is common.

Synoptic Gospels—The Gospels of Matthew, Mark, and Luke which share to a large degree a common framework and content.

Talmud—1. "Learning," but specifically Torah and its interpretation.
2. The literary combination of Mishnah (the codified "tradition of the elders") and Gemara (the explanation of Mishnah).
A Palestinian Talmud was completed about A.D. 275 and a Babylonian Talmud was completed about A.D. 500.

Temple—The primary center of the Jewish cultus. The temple was in Jerusalem. There were three successive temples on the same site: Solomon's, Zerubbabel's, and Herod's. Herod's temple was in use in Jesus' day.

Textual Criticism—Comparative study of ancient manuscripts of biblical literature to arrive at the best possible reading of all passages where there are textual variants.

Torah—Hebrew word meaning "instruction" or "law." Sometimes used to refer generally to the scriptures of Judaism, but specifically the first five books of the Old Testament, the "law of Moses."

Tradition—That which is passed down from one generation to another.

The term is used of the narratives and teachings of Jesus which passed down in oral form through the Palestinian, Jewish-Hellenistic, and Hellenistic stages of the development of the Church and which came to be written down in the Synoptic Gospels.

Travel Narrative—A section of the Gospel of Luke, 9:51–19:27 (sometimes 9:51–18:14). Used by Luke as a setting for a variety of material, much of it peculiar to his Gospel.

The Twelve—Jesus' closest associates, chosen to extend and continue his ministry. Referred to in the New Testament, with Paul, as Apostles.

"We" Passages—Sections of Acts which are written as a first person account. They occur in 16:10–17; 20:5–15; 21:1–18; 27:1–28:16. These passages probably represent a source used by the author of Luke–Acts.

Yahweh—The Israelite personal name for God. Rendered LORD (sometimes GOD) in the King James Version and the Revised Standard Version of the Bible.

Zealots—Palestinian Jews who strongly resented foreign rule, especially Roman. Zealots were eager to overthrow Rome and instigated periodic rebellions.

Index